Praise for
Inside Inside

"Every page brings forth revelations and experiences that could not possibly have happened in one single life. But in James Lipton's case, they certainly did. A joyful read." —Martin Landau, co–artistic director, Actors Studio West

"Theatrical truths emerge and amusing anecdotes abound since Lipton is a witty and engaging writer. The free-associative transitions from interviews to autobiography . . . make this exaltation of Lipton doubly enjoyable."
—*Publishers Weekly*

"The protean Lipton, exhibiting the dexterity with which he has combined his lifelong creative endeavors, seamlessly weaves all these artistic pursuits and more into his autobiography. An unqualified hit."   —*Library Journal*

"Great, colorful stories about every side of show business. James Lipton lets it all go; his openness about himself, and artists of all stripes, is refreshing."
—Paul Newman

"Once in a blue moon a person comes along whose genuine interest in craft excites an artist, and rekindles his own interest in his craft. In these pages you'll find out how James Lipton does it."   —John Travolta

"What could be more fun than to spend more time with the delightful James Lipton, the man who gets inside everybody's mind, heart, and method?"
—Sharon Stone

continued . . .

"Very few books take you this *far* inside. It's gloriously rich with fine artists putting into words what seems impossible to put into words."   —Alan Alda

"James Lipton is the most penetrating and compassionate interviewer I've ever known, but, more important, a terrific guy."   —Anthony Hopkins

"James Lipton's epic interview with the Simpsons taught me things I didn't know about the actors I've been working with for fifteen years."
—Matt Groening, creator, *The Simpsons*

"James creates such a warm environment that you feel as though you're among friends. I just loved this experience."   —Michelle Pfeiffer

"James Lipton knows an awful lot about acting, and all of it is in this wonderful book."   —Sidney Lumet

"This is a spectacular book that illuminates the creative process and the soul of the artist more than any book I've read in a very long time."
—Ellen Burstyn, copresident, Actors Studio

"James Lipton writes the way he talks, with fluency and passion. His own story is as startling and revealing as his interviews. We at the Actors Studio treasure him."   —Lee Grant, co–artistic director, Actors Studio

"In this rich memoir and scholarly treatise, James Lipton takes us on a Nantucket sleigh ride that will seize your emotions, challenge your intellect, and deepen your reflections on yourself and life."

—Jonathan Fanton, president, the MacArthur Foundation

"James Lipton brings to us a very considered intelligence and a discerning appreciation of our leading artists in theater and film."

—Gay Talese, author, *The Kingdom and the Power*

"With all due respect to the actors and actresses he has famously interviewed, James Lipton is as interesting a character as any of them. Happily, he has the wit, erudition, and storytelling skills to do justice to his own amazing story."

—Jay McInerney, author, *Bright Lights, Big City*

"I don't know anyone more qualified than James Lipton to write a book about actors and their work processes. I consider this book the most comprehensive look into the lives and thoughts of the gifted people that he has interviewed. It's wonderful."

—Martin Bregman, producer, *Serpico, Dog Day Afternoon, Scarface*

"James Lipton is our cultural insider for all seasons. As an actor, director, playwright, author, host, and friendly provocateur, he has seen it all and indeed lived it all!"

—Bruce Lundvall, president and CEO, Blue Note Label Group

James Lipton

Inside *Inside*

 NEW AMERICAN LIBRARY

NEW AMERICAN LIBRARY
Published by New American Library, a division of Penguin Group (USA) Inc., 375 Hudson Street, New York, New York 10014, USA • Penguin Group (Canada), 90 Eglinton Avenue East, Suite 700, Toronto, Ontario M4P 2Y3, Canada (a division of Pearson Penguin Canada Inc.) • Penguin Books Ltd., 80 Strand, London WC2R 0RL, England • Penguin Ireland, 25 St. Stephen's Green, Dublin 2, Ireland (a division of Penguin Books Ltd.) • Penguin Group (Australia), 250 Camberwell Road, Camberwell, Victoria 3124, Australia (a division of Pearson Australia Group Pty. Ltd.) • Penguin Books India Pvt. Ltd., 11 Community Centre, Panchsheel Park, New Delhi - 110 017, India • Penguin Group (NZ), 67 Apollo Drive, Rosedale, North Shore 0632, New Zealand (a division of Pearson New Zealand Ltd.) • Penguin Books (South Africa) (Pty.) Ltd., 24 Sturdee Avenue, Rosebank, Johannesburg 2196, South Africa

Penguin Books Ltd., Registered Offices: 80 Strand, London WC2R 0RL, England

Published by New American Library, a division of Penguin Group (USA) Inc. Previously published in a Dutton edition.

First New American Library Printing, October 2008
10 9 8 7 6 5 4 3 2 1

For author copyrights and permissions and photo credits see pages 495–96.

REGISTERED TRADEMARK—MARCA REGISTRADA

New American Library Trade Paperback ISBN: 978-0-451-22501-6

The Library of Congress has cataloged the hardcover edition of this title as follows:

Lipton, James
Inside *Inside*/By James Lipton.
   p.   cm.
ISBN 978-0-525-95035-6 (hardcover)
1. Inside the Actors Studio (Television program)   2. Lipton, James, 1926–   3. Actors Studio (New York, NY)
I. Title.
PN1992.77.I557L57 2007
792.0'2807117471   2007012790

Set in Celeste
Designed by Amy Hill

Printed in the United States of America

PUBLISHER'S NOTE
While the author has made every effort to provide accurate telephone numbers and Internet addresses at the time of publication, neither the publisher nor the author assumes any responsibility for errors, or for changes that occur after publication. Further, publisher does not have any control over and does not assume any responsibility for author or third-party Web sites or their content.

To Kedakai . . .
and all the other heroes
in these pages

Inside *Inside*

CHAPTER *One*

I made myself a promise that I would not begin this book with the first-person singular pronoun *I* . . . and I've already broken that promise four times—five if you count the pronoun *myself,* which the *Oxford American Dictionary* defines as "corresponding to *I* and *me.*" An unpromising sign.

I made the pledge because, if I realize my design, this book won't be about me as much as it will be about a vibrant troop of other people who have quickened the most exciting adventures of my life, which will, if fortune smiles, be the subject of these pages. That pretty much answers the question posed by Charles Dickens, in the person of the eponymous David, as *David Copperfield* begins: "Whether I shall turn out to be the hero of my own life, or whether that station will be held by anybody else, these pages must show."

The mask is off, mystery and suspense evaporate: Inside *Inside* will be about a considerable number of "anybody elses," as I intended that title to hint. As compensation for revealing the drama's end at the beginning, I offer, with appropriate diffidence, the prospect that the journey on which we're embarking together will be populated by the most intriguing souls I've ever encountered. I'm encouraged in this notion by the fact that *Inside the Actors Studio,* the television series that has presented more than two hundred of these "anybody elses," is seen in eighty-four million homes on the Bravo network in America, is on the air in 125 countries, and has received thirteen Emmy nominations, which leads me to suspect that I'm not alone in my estimation of the allure—and lure—of these heroes of my life, hence of this book, and of some other heroes I've met along the way to *Inside the Actors Studio.*

I confess that I am hugely fond of beginnings and, by logical inference, averse to endings. I don't know whether this makes me an optimist or a pessimist, but I've long since reconciled myself to the fact that it's there and it's never going to go away.

April may be the cruelest month to Eliot, but to me it's the kindest, with its portents of spring, which is crammed with beginnings. Of holidays, I enjoy Memorial Day because it officially begins the pleasant summer season, and dislike Labor Day because it ends it. Thanksgiving is welcome because it begins the Christmas season, of which I confess to being inordinately fond, and I'm resistant to the compulsory joy of New Year's Eve, because it ends it.

This affection for beginnings has had a predictable effect on my preferences. Though I should know better than to invite comparison with my betters as I begin my own literary effort, I confess to unbridled admiration for the blunt simplicity of "Call me Ishmael"; the instant dramatic engagement of "It was the best of times, it was the worst of times"; the authorial certainty of "Happy families are all alike; every unhappy family is unhappy in its own way"; the ringing challenge of Donne's "Go and catch a falling star/Get with child a mandrake root"; the quiet fury of Yeats's "Turning and turning in the widening gyre/The falcon cannot hear the falconer;/Things fall apart; the center cannot hold"; the stately opening chords of Tchaikovsky's Serenade for Strings, which greet us not with the C-major tonic but with a submediant A-minor chord, as if the boat had left the dock without us, and we had no choice but to jump in and swim after it; the ominous minor key (verbally and musically) of Irving Berlin's "There may be trouble ahead," before he shifts jubilantly to a major key for "Let's face the music and dance!"

The art of beginning a tale with compelling grace and economy has found a particularly congenial home in motion pictures from their inception, since the filmmaker, from Griffith, Dreyer, Renoir and Eisenstein to Truffaut, Bergman, Scorsese and Spielberg, differs from all his creative predecessors in possessing the godlike power of holding in his or her hands two of the essential elements of art—and life: time and space.

I believe that when cultural archaeologists look back from a distant time, they will see cinema montage—the art of film editing—as the preeminent artistic innovation of the twentieth century. Its juxtaposition of images and ideas, fracturing and rearranging the viewer's spatial and temporal assumptions; its willful, artful compression—or expansion—of time; its magisterial presumption and confident command of our perception have affected not only film but every other medium and art form—theater, television, music, fiction, nonfiction, fine art, design—and changed the public's way of looking at and listening to all of them.

When Martin Scorsese brought the rat-a-tat delivery of his formidable cinematic scholarship to *Inside the Actors Studio,* he reminded the students who comprise its live audience of the historic experiment conducted by the Russian director Lev Kuleshov for members of the cultural bureaucracy in the fledgling Soviet Union. The ostensible purpose of the experiment was to demonstrate to the politicians the informational and propaganda potential of the still infant art, but it's probably a safe assumption that, as a filmmaker, he was hopeful of steering government subsidies toward his industry—and perhaps his own films, which would ultimately bear such titles as *The Project of Engineer Prete, On the Red Front* and *The Extraordinary Adventures of Mr. West in the Land of the Bolsheviks.*

On the occasion of the experiment, he screened a short film he had shot and edited for the express purpose of demonstrating the way in which juxtaposing unrelated images could evoke new and unexpected emotions and meanings. He had begun the project by filming the prominent Russian actor Ivan Mozhukin, looking straight into the camera, with the instruction, in Scorsese's words, "to think of nothing, just look."

Kuleshov filmed separately, without the actor, four shots, a bowl of soup, a girl, a teddy bear and a child in a coffin, then, in the edit room, intercut the close-up of the actor after each of the other images. When the viewers of the finished footage were asked to describe what they had seen, they ascribed to the actor ("with great admiration," Scorsese chortled) a wide range of reactions and emotions, hunger, tenderness, amusement, sadness, despite the fact that the actor had never seen what the viewer saw and, most important, that each cutaway to the actor was exactly the same shot, frame-for-frame, with no change of expression from one appearance to the next. The "change" was in the viewers.

Kuleshov—and Scorsese—were teaching the fundamental lesson of cinema montage: that the juxtaposition of any two images creates, according to Scorsese on our *Inside the Actors Studio* stage, a nonexistent image, "another thought that comes into your mind"—an entirely new reality that has been created (literally) by the filmmaker. In sum, *your* thoughts have been edited by the editor, and that, as Kuleshov knew, and directors with Scorsese's skill have demonstrated countless times, means that your movie ticket is a pact between you and the film, delivering you into the director's hands until the lights come up and the ushers rush down the aisle to sweep up the popcorn before the next signatories arrive.

Consider what Steven Spielberg did to you in *Jaws* by intercutting (what may in fact have been stock footage of) a shark gliding (innocently) through its rightful habitat in search of a finny morsel, with a swimmer paddling happily on the sparkling surface of the sea, accompanied by the shark's leit-motif, the brooding, throbbing "fate" theme of John Williams's score—an additional element added in the edit.

When Spielberg was a guest on *Inside the Actors Studio,* he recalled, "I'm afraid of previews, so I usually stand in the doorway. Around the time that little boy was killed on the raft, a man got up and began to walk out of the theater. The guy starts running. I go, 'Oh, my God—worse than a walkout, he's *running* out of the theater!' He got right next to me, went to one knee and threw up all over the carpeting in the lobby, went to the bathroom, came out five minutes later—and *walked back to his seat.* I said, 'It's a hit!'"

In 1817, in *Biographia Literaria,* when Samuel Taylor Coleridge coined the now famous phrase *willing suspension of disbelief,* which, he said, "constitutes poetic faith," he was laying one of the foundation stones of the Romantic Movement, which dominates all of the western arts to this day, and has found one of its most natural expressions in the craft of film.

Referring to the number of frames passing before the camera's lens, Jean-Luc Godard called film "the truth twenty-four times a second." Of course it's the *filmmaker's* truth, since he or she works with the editor, assembling the movie's thoughts—and yours.

But whether we know it or not—and we don't—we are active collaborators in this cinematic conspiracy, because without our persistence of vision—an optical term of art (now replaced by the even more mysterious *phi*) that has been employed to describe how we, the audience, make movies move by providing the trace of retinal memory that dissolves one frame into another—films would pass before us as an inanimate parade of stills, which is really all they are.

My passion for beginnings and my fascination with this arcane optical collaboration between editor and audience come together in my conviction that nowhere is the creative artist's power over us more nakedly apparent than in the opening sequences of films, after, during or sometimes before the titles. Orson Welles provides a striking example in *Citizen Kane* with a long montage in which his probing, subjective camera (one of the film's—his—many innovations) roams Xanadu, Kane's imperial estate, drawing nearer and nearer to a single lighted window in the mogul's castle, enters his bedroom and winds up, in the words of Mankiewicz and Welles's screenplay, in "A snow scene. An incredible one. Big, impossible flakes of snow, a too pictur-esque farmhouse and a snow man . . . The camera pulls back, showing the whole scene to be contained in one of those glass balls which are sold in novelty stores. . . . A hand—Kane's hand, which has been holding the ball, relaxes. The ball falls . . . onto the marble floor, where it breaks."

Over this is heard the voice of the dying Kane muttering, "Rosebud . . ."

And so begins, economically, intriguingly, what virtually every poll and list insists is the greatest film ever made.

W. C. Fields began many of his movies with scenes of child abuse—not abuse toward children, but *by* children toward his hapless character, so that when he turned the tables on the loathsome little creatures later in the picture, we not only wouldn't blame him, but would cheer him on.

Every Bond film begins with an utterly preposterous action sequence (to make all the action scenes that will follow fit comfortably, by comparison, within Hitchcock's waffling but workable theory of the "plausibles"); then follows Bond, striding debonairly through titles, to *that music,* and wheeling suddenly to fire a shot through a foreground title—at us, bringing the titles to a close with a smoothly descending curtain of fashion-red blood—*our* blood since, to paraphrase De Niro in another film, "There's nobody here but us."

That "other" film sports its own stunning opening sequence, delivering the vital information that the movie's point of view will be *Travis's* point of view, as his taxi navigates a hellish Manhattan, through roiling columns of steam bloodied by nearby neon with Scorsese's favorite color.

In *8 ½,* Fellini famously floated Marcello Mastroianni's tormented, blocked film director over a beach, his only link to reality the tether that tied him to . . . his press agent!—and the film's theme was established. In seconds. In the edit room.

To return from those masterful beginnings to the beginning of this book, with appropriate apologies for the shortcomings of my effort compared to the examples I've offered, I'll turn to Dickens for David Copperfield's final remark as he introduced his story: "To begin my life with the beginning of my life . . ."

Since the "life" of this book consists of the "anybody elses" who inspired it, I'll begin at the beginning of the life of *Inside the Actors Studio,* not because it is a matter of exceptional consequence, and certainly not because *I* am, but because it rendered the service of bringing the "anybody elses" and us—you and me—together, on the screen and now here in these pages.

If I may be permitted a final confession: I am a believer in universal causation, an assertion that is neither as pretentious (*pace* Will Ferrell)—nor irrelevant— as it may seem. Universal causation is the central principle of determinism, a philosophical stance that holds that everything that happens—physically, even psychologically—has a determinable cause. That's not very complicated, because most of us base every moment of our lives on that supposition, often without thinking about it. When we toss a ball or a hat or a child in the air, we assume it will come down, and behave accordingly—an attitude that is so deeply ingrained in us that, generally speaking, we perceive an inability to recognize any connection between cause and effect as a symptom of psychosis.

Clarence Darrow constructed his fabled legal career on a "hard" determinism that argued that no one could be considered "guilty," because the chain of cause and effect that had led the person to the moment of the crime (or Michelangelo to a particular brushstroke in the Sistine Chapel, or me to this word in this paragraph) decreed precisely and completely what the individual would do. Determinism's classic philosophical opponent, free will, argues that our choices are our own, freely made—to which Darrow and the hard determinists reply, "How can we speak of free will when our cognitive process at any given moment is, like the physical world, an unbroken chain of causes and effects, over which we have no control? Our decisions, like our actions," insists Darrow, "are predetermined and decreed by our experience."

There is a "soft" determinism, to which I subscribe, that argues that a choice can be seen as both free and caused, without contradiction. Leaving the matter there, I'll answer the question that is by now, perhaps impatiently, demanding an answer: What does any of this have to do with *Inside the Actors Studio*? The answer: everything, because I've elected to begin by responding to one of the questions most frequently asked me, how did it happen? The simple answer might begin: The first guest walked out on the stage on October 10, 1994—but that doesn't answer the question; it begs it, because it leaves out everything that *really* explains how it happened—and we're back to universal causation.

On May 4, 2004, when, after ten years, I stepped down from the deanship of the Actors Studio Drama School, the board of trustees of New School University marked the occasion at its dinner where I received the Founders Medal, which had been awarded only thirteen times in the university's history. Such an honor called for a response, and as I composed it, I found myself reflecting on a concatenation of people and events—a chain of cause and effect so direct and discernible that, I realized, any break in it, anywhere, at any link, would have meant that I would have had no occasion to write those words then—and would not be writing these words now.

All causal chains are infinite, since positing a "beginning" creates the contradiction of an uncaused effect. Religious philosophers have been wrestling with this uncaused prime mover argument for centuries, so I'll simply select an arbitrary link as starting point, with the stipulation that it is preceded by an infinite number of links that led to *it*, but are outside the purview of this matter.

To begin this proposition: If George Plimpton and Sarah Dudley hadn't married each other, I wouldn't be writing these words because there would have been no Actors Studio Drama School or *Inside the Actors Studio.*

To explain: In the first week of January, 1992, Sarah and George, who was, with the exception of my wife, Kedakai, the closest friend I've ever had, celebrated their December 31 marriage (a date doubtless chosen by Sarah so the notoriously absentminded George would remember their anniversaries) at the Colony Club in Manhattan. At the reception, Norman Mailer and his wife, Norris Church, pinned me to a wall and insisted that I come to the Actors Studio to see the work that they and the other Studio members were doing there.

They were longtime members of the Studio, and knew that I had been trained not by Lee Strasberg at the Studio, but by other exponents of the Stanislavski System, Stella Adler, Harold Clurman and Robert Lewis. All four of those innovators and leaders had emerged from the Group Theatre, the groundbreaking company of actors, writers and directors that had adopted the principles of Constantin Stanislavski and the Moscow Art Theatre in the 1930s, and, in so doing, effected revolutionary changes in American theater and film—changes that are today the norms and standards of acting, directing and even theatrical writing, as compared to the more formal, rhetorical, declamatory traditions inherited from the English theater, and often ritually imitated, before the Group Theatre made "fashionable" performance unfashionable.

But disagreements in their interpretations of Stanislavski's work and principles had divided the members of the Group Theatre and, after the dissolution of the Group in the 1940s, continued to provide lively, and sometimes rancorous, debate, with Adler, Clurman, Lewis—and Sanford Meisner, another prominent Group alumnus—on one side of the dispute, and Strasberg on the other.

As a young student of Adler, Clurman and Lewis, I was in no camp or faction, but had not attended the Studio, where Strasberg held famous sway until his death in 1982; though, of course, I had continual professional and social contact with most of the Studio members from the time I arrived in New York and began studying and working.

That evening in 1992 at the Colony Club, Norman and Norris pressed me hard, insisting that the Studio, now under the leadership of director and teacher Frank Corsaro, was doing the kind of exciting work I ought to see. "Observing" at the Studio is a privilege almost as zealously guarded as membership, but Norman and Norris insisted that my name would be on the list at the next session, and more to mollify them than out of genuine intent, I agreed to show up at the Friday session.

But when Friday arrived, work intervened, and there followed several weeks of calls from the Mailers and pledges by me, all of them broken—for various reasons that were genuine and more or less cogent.

The Mailers are the second link in this causal chain. If they hadn't attended George and Sarah's reception, electing, as they so often do, to remain in Provincetown with Norman on deadline, the chain would have been broken before it was begun. But it wasn't, and they are certainly among the heroes of this story, because finally—out of guilt, I suspect—I showed up for a session at the Studio, and mounted the creaky stairs of the onetime Presbyterian church that had been built in 1858, and has housed the Studio since 1955.

The next link is, of course, the Studio itself. When I arrived at the Playwrights and Directors Unit that day, the session was being moderated by Frank Corsaro and Arthur Penn. Despite the common misconception of it, the Actors Studio has never been a school. It has "members," not "students," has never charged tuition or granted a degree, and has scrupulously used terms like *session* and *moderator,* rather than *class* and *teacher,* for reasons that will become apparent in this account.

As I entered the session, Arthur Penn, whom I'd known for years, looked at me in surprise, then grinned and said, "Well, finally!"

That day in session, I worked (another Studio term), and when the session ended, Arthur grabbed my arm, took me to the Studio office, and said, "Jim's a member of the PD Unit."

Norman and Norris had been right: I was quickly and happily seduced, and began haunting the PD Unit, surprised at how happy I was to be back in the gym, flexing some muscles I hadn't used since Robert Lewis's workshop.

In the months that followed, I was asked by Corsaro to moderate the unit on several occasions, and finally, inspired by what I saw in the unit and in sessions, I decided on an experiment that, in ingenuity and importance, is at a remove of several light-years from Kuleshov's, but was nevertheless of great importance (far greater than I dreamed at the time) to me.

I made up my mind to test myself—and the Studio—to determine if we were as compatible as we seemed to be. The premise of the experiment was simple, based on assumptions about the Studio and concerns about myself. One of the myths about the Method—and the Studio—was that, while Stanislavski's innovations were suitable to the emerging theater and playwrights, like Ibsen and Chekhov, of his time, they were incompatible with, more accurately inimical to, the classics—Shakespeare, Molière, Aeschylus—and works of "style" from the pens of Goldoni, Sheridan, Wilde, Maeterlinck.

To this day the myth persists. It persisted in fact in me on *Inside the Actors Studio,* When I brought up the difficulties American actors have with Shakespeare's language, John Hurt retorted, "Let me say something. I think it's an unfortunate neurosis of the American actor, because it's not true. I've seen fantastic performances from American actors in classical plays when they haven't bothered about trying to talk with this ridiculous received accent that I've got. Use your own accent! The accent doesn't help to speak poetry. If you want to talk about that, what about Marlon Brando as Mark Antony? He made a lot of English actors look awfully silly."

But is it a myth? Was Hurt right and were the critics of the Method wrong? That was what I set out to test (several years before John Hurt came to *Inside the Actors Studio*): whether the Studio actors, and I as director, could navigate the shoals of high style.

For the test, I opened a drawer in my study, in which I'd stored a labor of love that had languished for several years. The labor began when, having been dazzled by *A Flea in Her Ear* at the Old Vic, the moment I returned to New York I acquired the complete works of the undisputed master of fin de siècle, boulevard farce, Georges Feydeau, who, when asked the secret of his success, replied, "It's simple. I just decide which of my characters should under no circumstances meet, then get them together as soon as possible."

Proceeding through the collected works at the pace my French permitted, I came upon an introduction to one of the volumes by the French playwright Marcel Achard, who insisted that, as celebrated as Feydeau's Belle Epoque farces were, bringing him international fame and his own table at Maxim's (where he can be seen in numerous paintings of the period), his comic master-pieces were the one-act plays he wrote late in his career, divorced and living the life of a bon vivant in a Paris hotel. "Renouncing," in Achard's words, the hidden doors and revolving beds, the coincidences, contretemps and coups de théâtre on which his fame rested, he trained his rapier wit and gimlet eye on a single subject: the institution of marriage.

In so doing, Achard said, Feydeau wrote for *himself* now, not for the public, a series of one-act plays, each of which focused on a different couple in a different place and time. "The characters change their names," Achard says, "but *only* their names," and when the plays are looked at side by side, Feydeau's intention becomes clear: one couple, one marriage, one relationship, from its innocent, charming beginning to its bitter (and equally hilarious) end. Achard added that it was Feydeau's ambition to publish the plays together in one volume titled *Du mariage au divorce,* but the syphilis that rewarded his happy hedonism with madness and death intervened.

Determining presumptuously to fulfill his intention, I set about translating the one-act plays into English, several of them, to my knowledge, for the first time. Then it occurred to me that by choosing three of the plays I admired the most, one from the beginning of the series, a second from the middle and a third from the end, I could accomplish Feydeau's purpose in a single evening, a single theatrical experience, under the title *Happy New Year.*

I chose for the test at the Studio my translation and adaptation of the first one-act, *Séance de nuit* ("Night Meeting"), in which innocent, authentic love is born out of the soaring Feydeauesque architecture of tangled misunderstandings and misdirected messages, as a would-be roué tries with mounting desperation to arrange an assignation in the private room of a Paris restaurant by telling his wife he's been summoned to an emergency meeting on New Year's Eve.

I cast the play with Studio members, and rehearsed it for several weeks, remaining scrupulously within the parameters of my training and theirs in the Stanislavski System (or the exercise would have been pointless), employing such central tenets of the System as action, sense memory and given circumstances to lead us into an organic exploration (yes, in a rollicking farce) of the characters the author had created and their intentions, moment to moment, in the play. Finally, I put it up in session for the Studio membership—a French, fin de siècle, boulevard farce at the Studio, for God's sake!

Fortunately, the actors were more than up to the challenge, the Studio's hallowed precinct, formerly dedicated to God and latterly to Strasberg (some members would fail to see a distinction), rocked with laughter (*merci,* Georges, *spaceeba,* Constantin), and the members perceived no violation of "the work" (the Studio's customary term for what the outside world calls "the Method").

I'd found a home.

Over the next year, I attended sessions frequently, "worked" occasionally (one waits one's turn in the cramped space of the Studio) and became so involved in the life and work of the Studio that, in 1994, I was elected to its board of directors.

From its inception in 1947, the Studio existed on a financial shoestring. Driven by an idealism that was artistically commendable but financially impractical, it had foregone such niceties as admission fees and dues in favor of an eleemosynary life that bordered on the ascetic. By 1993, as many cultural institutions faced destitution or extinction, the Studio's purity had brought it to a similar pass.

One night in the first week of April, at a particularly grim gathering in which, faced with continuing costs, mounting debt, no dependable income and official notice that we would be forbidden access to our elderly, beloved church unless costly repairs were instantly undertaken, we stared ahead at a bleak future that some of the participants felt threatened the forty-seven-year journey that had given the world some of its most influential actors, directors and writers.

Appealing to the membership, some of whom were famously affluent, looked problematic. The membership had been tapped so many times over nearly five decades they were tapped out. Even Paul Newman and Joanne Woodward, who had single-handedly supported the Studio for several years, had declared a moratorium on their generosity. Clearly, the Studio was at a crossroads—not the first one the Studio had faced in its history, but an undeniably compelling and disquieting one.

Some of the Studio members had been there from the beginning, forty-seven years earlier, and many of them had called the Studio their artistic home for decades, but the meeting ended in silence as we stared at one another across the table. Then, hopeless shrugs, then adjournment sine die.

I'd been a Studio member for only two years, but I shared some of the apprehension that hung over the room.

Sigmund Freud is said to have based his theory of the unconscious in part on a monograph by a mathematician who wondered why he sometimes went to sleep mulling a thorny problem, and awakened with the answer. Creative artists—writers, musicians—are familiar with the seemingly magical powers of the hypnagogic state, the dreamlike and sometimes fruitful state between wakefulness and sleep, and the hypnopompic state between sleep and awakening.

That night, after the meeting, I slept fitfully, and awakened with an idea so fully envisioned, not only in its broad outlines but in some of its finest details, that it would constitute the blueprint, virtually unchanged from that revelatory hypnopompic moment, of the concept and curriculum with which we would open the doors of the Actors Studio Drama School seventeen months later.

Which brings me to the next indispensable link in this chain—and hero of this tale and my life—my wife, Kedakai Turner Lipton. Although the link appears here, it belongs properly at the beginning of the chain, because, had I not met Kedakai at the ballet one evening and resolved to spend the rest of my life with her if she'd have me, the encounter with Norman and Norris at the Plimpton reception might have led in many directions, but not to these pages, and not to the Actors Studio Drama School and *Inside the Actors Studio,* because neither would have existed.

The reason I can assert that with such certainty is that, shortly after Kedakai and I married, she expressed a wish to give up modeling, at which she was very successful, for reasons obvious to anyone who has ever laid eyes on her, and fulfill a long-held dream to study design. That led her to two degrees at the Parsons School of Design, one in Environmental Design and a second in Interior Design.

During the years at Parsons, Kedakai so distinguished herself that, upon graduation, she was invited to join its board of governors, and that meant that when she attended dinners at the residence of Jonathan Fanton, the president of The New School for Social Research, of which Parsons was a constituent, I attended as her spouse.

Those evenings, presided over with grace and intellectual vigor by President Fanton and his wife, Cynthia, were memorable for a lively exchange of views, usually on the topic of the university lecture or event that had preceded the dinner.

On the morning that I woke with my notion, I asked Kedakai whether she thought Jonathan Fanton might be interested in it—provided, to begin with, that he remembered me and would take my call; and Kedakai, who is usually kind enough to tolerate my ideas, and who responded enthusiastically to this one, suggested something along the lines of nothing ventured, nothing gained.

The reason I wanted to propose my idea to Dr. Fanton, apart from the vivid impression of him I'd taken from those dinners at his residence, was the unique history of The New School for Social Research, which was founded in 1918 by a disaffected group of eminent Columbia University scholars led by John Dewey, James Robinson and Charles Beard as a protest against what they saw as a lack of academic freedom and the generally poor state of American education.

Joined by economists Thorstein Veblen and Alvin S. Johnson in a mission to create an independent, progressive alternative to the academic establishment, they built a revolutionary institution that found its boldest expression—and finest hour—when, under the leadership of the school's first president, Alvin Johnson, it participated in the rescue and reestablishment in America of two hundred artists and scholars who would have died at Hitler's hand. Many of the new arrivals found a home, and freedom, at The New School's felicitously named University in Exile.

Among them was the famed German director Erwin Piscator, who, with Bertolt Brecht, had developed the radical political concept of epic theater. Arriving in America in 1939, in the nick of time, he founded the Dramatic Workshop at The New School for Social Research. In the 1940s, with the dissolution of the Group Theatre, Stella Adler and Lee Strasberg accepted Piscator's offer and joined the Dramatic Workshop in their first teaching positions; and the Workshop's students—some of them performing on the stage from which *Inside the Actors Studio* would begin shooting fifty years later—included Marlon Brando, James Dean, Shelley Winters, Ben Gazzara, Walter Matthau, Harry Belafonte, Rod Steiger and Tennessee Williams.

That's why I called Jonathan Fanton.

Fortunately for this account, and for the many people who play a role in it—Studio members; New School administrators; Actors Studio Drama School students, faculty members and administrators; *Inside the Actors Studio* guests, staff and crew; the television audiences in America and around the world for the past thirteen years—he took my call.

"What if," I asked him, "someone could restore to The New School something of the luster it had when Erwin Piscator created the Dramatic Workshop?"

Fanton, a Connecticut Yankee known for his concision, replied, "Go ahead."

"What if I could persuade my colleagues at the Studio to create for the first time a degree-granting academic program?"

"Where's the pen and when do I sign?" Fanton said.

Armed with his interest, I headed for the Studio board—a matchmaker with no certainty that the other half of this proposed match would be receptive to what they might perceive as an intrusion on their treasured privacy.

From its inception, the Studio had been designed as a kind of cloister. In 1947, when it was founded by Group Theatre alumni, directors Elia Kazan and Robert Lewis and producer Cheryl Crawford, many of the most gifted and successful actors, directors and writers lived—and worked—in New York.

In the 1950/51 season, the theater set Broadway ablaze with eighty-five new productions, and off-Broadway was gleefully inventing and reinventing itself daily in a raucous tide that was spilling into every unused, unloved—but at least uncondemned—space in Manhattan. And New York was giving birth to the Golden Age of television, which provided an exciting experimental stage and showcase for its young auteurs, Paddy Chayevsky, Gore Vidal, Rod Serling and Reginald Rose, and its emerging directors, Sidney Lumet, John Frankenheimer, Arthur Penn and Sydney Pollack.

For the next decade, from 1950 to 1960, New York was indisputably the place to be, and every acting studio and school was jammed to the gunwales with actors chafing to answer the call of the theater and the voracious new medium of television, which needed them not only at night, in prime time, when the drama anthologies and series went on the air *live,* but in television's daylight hours where the soap operas—ten of them!—resided. In New York.

In the midst of this splendid ferment was the Actors Studio, harvesting some of the most exotic blossoms in this fertile field.

In the 1960s, when the burgeoning television industry headed west to the less costly and more available real estate of southern California, an exodus of actors, directors and writers would follow, but in 1947, most of the best of them lived in New York, where all the best teachers beckoned. What Kazan, Lewis and Crawford offered them was a refuge, a redoubt, out of the spotlight and the public gaze, where they could hone their skills, flex—and stretch—their creative and performing muscles, make their mistakes, fall flat on their faces—and *learn,* in a demanding precinct that could be nurturing without being indulgent, and critical without being judgmental, in the company of their peers, who—most important—were taking similar risks when their turns came.

In 1949, Lee Strasberg arrived, and the Studio entered *its* Golden Age, delivering to the world a dazzling array of artists, from founding members like Elia Kazan, Robert Lewis, Montgomery Clift, Marlon Brando, Maureen Stapleton, Jerome Robbins, Karl Malden, Herbert Berghoff, Eli Wallach, Mildred Dunnock, Paul Newman, Joanne Woodward and Shelley Winters to Martin Landau, James Dean, Steve McQueen, Jack Nicholson, Marilyn Monroe, Dustin Hoffman, Ellen Burstyn, Robert Duvall, Sally Field, Dennis Hopper, Julie Harris, Walter Matthau, Anne Bancroft, Christopher Walken, Lee Grant, Gene Wilder, Jane Fonda, Harvey Keitel, Sidney Poitier, Robert De Niro, Estelle Parsons, Al Pacino, Faye Dunaway, Sidney Lumet, Anthony Quinn, Eva Marie Saint, Arthur Penn, Alec Baldwin, Anne Jackson, Charles Durning, Cloris Leachman, Sydney Pollack, Charles Grodin, Roscoe Lee Browne, Olympia Dukakis, Ben Gazzara, Jon Voight, Geraldine Page, Mark Rydell, Holly Hunter and Gene Hackman.

The Actors Studio isn't a permanent repertory company like the Comédie Française, the Moscow Art Theatre or the National Theatre of Great Britain, with the incomparable histories of those institutions, or a stock company like MGM in its 1939 heyday when it claimed "more stars than there are in the heavens," but perhaps it can be asserted with reasonable validity that none of them could ever boast a marquee of the breadth and depth of the Studio's.

That roster was acquired incrementally over half a century, because, by design, the Studio was, and is, one of the most exclusive institutions in the world, not out of snobbism, but out of a sincere desire to set a standard that would make membership *matter.* All of its founders were busy, working professionals. They wanted the Studio to be different from their "other" lives—and every minute in it to count. So, to that end they erected barriers to membership that have become legendary. And true.

Jack Nicholson auditioned five times for membership, Dustin Hoffman six, and Harvey Keitel a staggering eleven times before he was accepted by the

Actors Studio. Since each rejection requires that the candidate go back to the end of the line and wait for as long as a year for the next round of auditions, Harvey's quest consumed ten years. When he acknowledged this on the stage of *Inside the Actors Studio,* the students, all of whom aspire to membership in the Studio, emitted a sound that was midway between a gasp and a cry of pain.

Martin Landau told our students that the year he auditioned for the Studio, two people were accepted, he and Steve McQueen. "How many auditioned?" I asked.

"Two thousand," he replied, and the students bleated like stricken animals.

Now, on April 14, 1993, I was on my way to the executive committee of the board to dare to propose that we open the Studio's doors, not to let the world in, but to let the Studio's process out, in a public academic setting, for the first time in forty-seven years.

The Studio had always been a loosely organized group whose members came and went randomly, showing up for a day, or sometimes for weeks at a time, depending on their work schedules and personal needs. On rare occasions in the first forty-seven years some of them had joined together ad hoc, to work on a specific project. Tennessee Williams, Edward Albee, Terrence McNally and James Baldwin had developed work at the Studio. In the 1950s, Michael Gazzo's *A Hatful of Rain* came out of improvisational experimentation at the Studio, and the Studio had even made wary overtures to Broadway, with mixed emotions ("Process, not production!") and mixed results; but for the most part, the members came and went as individuals, using the Studio, when it answered their needs, as a gymnasium. Now, I, a relative newcomer, was about to propose that the Studio reverse its time-honored formula and *use its members*—collectively—to answer *its* needs.

It sounds simple now, but it wasn't then—not because the Studio was stubborn or hidebound, but because for half a century it had had hard evidence that the austere privacy ordained by its charter in 1947 had served it well, and to a few of them I was suggesting that the Studio's walls—and the Studio's charter—be breached.

Laying my blueprint—and my cards—on the table, I demonstrated to them that, on the plan I envisioned, the Studio on Forty-fourth Street would remain sacrosanct—as reclusive, exclusive, sui generis and ornery as ever. The only difference would be that, in contradistinction to what was staring us in the face, it would continue to exist.

The heads around the table swiveled, the executive committee members stared hard at one another, and Victor Hugo's dictum that there is no idea so powerful as one whose time has come proved itself once more: The committee agreed to join me in taking the proposal to the full board.

A few days later, a majority of the board voted to break with forty-seven years of tradition, and raise the Studio's portcullis for a wary look outside.

On April 23, dispatched by the board as a lone scout, I returned to The New School for Social Research on West Twelfth Street, where Dr. Fanton had assembled a dozen of the university's officers and senior faculty in his eighth-floor office. Seated at one end of the long oval table, I began with "Three weeks ago, on my own initiative, I asked Jonathan Fanton if The New School might be interested in an affiliation with the Actors Studio." I offered some background on the Method, separating myths from reality, and the Studio: its history, its membership, the twenty audition requests it received every day, which might, I suggested, indicate a sizable applicant pool if this plan were to go forward.

Reviewing what I thought were the advantages to the Studio and to The New School in the affiliation, I suggested that in the Studio's case it was an opportunity to reunite under one roof and its own banner some of the most highly regarded acting teachers in the world, who for half a century had fanned out from the Studio to other institutions because it *wasn't* a school—and to place that faculty, teaching what the Studio had taught them, in an academic environment that had demonstrated its hospitality toward disparate disciplines—the University in Exile, the Parsons School of Design, the Mannes College of Music.

In The New School's case, I posed the advantage of adding to its academic landscape one of the world's most celebrated theatrical institutions, with the reputation and experience it had acquired over nearly fifty years.

I indicated potential synergies in the relationship, with the privilege of observer status at the Studio serving as an incentive to enrollment and retention in the school; and the possibility—not certainty but possibility, based on merit—of Studio membership after graduation offering to the Studio the prospect of enriching its roster with young men and women chosen in an admissions process as rigorous as its own and trained intensively for three years in its techniques.

I concluded by proposing to The New School what I had proposed to the Studio's board: a partnership between the two institutions that would create for the first time an Actor's Studio degree-granting program for actors, writers and directors, with every core course taught by a life member of the Actors Studio, here at The New School for Social Research.

After an hour of questions and answers, Fanton proposed a university committee, comprising the secretary of the university's corporation, Richard

Rogers; Associate Provost Dr. Robert Gates; Executive Vice President Joseph Porrino; and Dean Albert Landa, a former vice president of The New School whom Fanton had brought in as a consultant. At the meeting he introduced him to me as "the conscience of The New School," and in very short order he became mine.

Fanton left the meeting with instructions that we remain there in his office to "make this happen if it makes sense." In the next few minutes we arrived at a plan for the formal appointment of a committee from each institution to begin substantive discussions.

When I arrived on the sidewalk of Twelfth Street and started toward Fifth Avenue, I heard a voice calling, "Mr. Lipton! Mr. Lipton!" Turning, I recognized an attractive young woman who had been smiling nonstop at the conference table. "This," said Dr. Bea Banu, dean-elect of the university's Eugene Lang College, "is *hot!*"

Once again, I had the unexpected feeling of coming home.

When I reported The New School meeting to the Actors Studio board, it responded by appointing a committee to meet with The New School's representatives. The committee consisted of Ellen Burstyn, Norman Mailer, Paul Newman, actors Lee Grant and Carlin Glynn, director Arthur Penn, Shubert Organization vice president and studio treasurer Robert Wankel and me. Because I'd come up with this possibly harebrained notion, I was named chairman.

Over the next six months, the curriculum that took shape was to a surprising extent what I'd envisioned on awakening that morning in April: a three-year MFA program that would—uniquely among drama programs—train actors, writers and directors side by side in the principles of the Stanislavski System as they'd evolved at the Actors Studio.

From the first meeting between the two committees, it was apparent that the university looked to the Studio to create the curriculum. That was, in fact, the crux of the matter. We responded by constructing, at Ellen Burstyn's suggestion, an armature from Stanislavski's three historic books. *An Actor Prepares* provided the core curriculum for the first year: what Stanislavski called the work on "self," in which the conventions and clichés, the tensions and blocks that the inexperienced actor, or for that matter the untrained professional, brings to the work, are stripped away, and replaced by techniques that allow the actor unimpeded access to his or her own emotional truth.

We based the second year on Stanislavski's second book, *Building a Character,* in which the actor, using the lessons of the first year and an expanding array of exercises and techniques, moves from the familiar precinct of himself or herself to a new reality, the part—a "character" who is *not* the actor, but must be *inhabited* by the actor, organically, which is to say, from the inside out, discovering what the character wants at any given moment, and *doing* it, fusing the character and actor into one truth.

The third year was based on the posthumously published *Creating a Role,* in which the techniques used in the first two years enable the actor to find his or her place within the context of every scene and ultimately the entire play.

The curriculum we offered to the university and our students was supported by three pillars, the first of which was the decision to train actors, writers and directors side by side for three years. On the face of it, this may not seem remarkable, but all of us on the Studio's committee had come through the maze of theatrical training, in private classes and academic settings, and as we compared our experiences, and surveyed the field in 1993, none of us could find a circumstance in which the training of the three disciplines was fully, coherently integrated.

Many schools taught actors, some taught playwrights as well, and a few taught directors, but on the rare occasions when a school accepted all three, their curricula were kept meticulously discrete, and it wasn't uncommon for a playwright to complete a master's degree without having had to interface even occasionally—much less daily—with the other factors of the dramatic equation, the actors and director. The writers' academic lives were lived largely, sometimes exclusively, on paper, as if the work, like a novel or newspaper, were designed to be read.

This contradiction was addressed, definitively, I think, by Harold Clurman, whom I've mentioned earlier as one of the founders of the Group Theatre, and who will reappear importantly in this account. He figured importantly in my life then because, when he directed the all-star Broadway production of Lillian Hellman's new play *The Autumn Garden,* he cast me as the juvenile. I was then a student of his former wife, Stella Adler, and the conspicuous non-star in the cast, which was led by Fredric March and his wife, Florence Eldridge.

It was a heady experience: my first Broadway role, with that cast, in a new play by Lillian Hellman, directed by Harold Clurman. During the rehearsals, I spent every offstage minute jackknifed into a seat in the dark, empty theater, my knees propped against the seat in front of me, watching Harold, a god in the theatrical pantheon, working with the illustrious cast on the stage in what, for me, was a master class.

Class was abruptly suspended a week before the New York opening, when Lillian, impatient with the pace at which Harold and the cast were exploring the play, announced that she would be conducting the rehearsals from this point forward. Lillian's "rehearsals" consisted of restaging the play from start to finish. Weeks of often inspired work, arrived at with a lovely logic, were jettisoned by Lillian's nonstop mantra, yelled from halfway back in the house near me, still jackknifed in a seat, but poleaxed now as she shouted, "Never mind all that stuff. Just say the lines!"

The result was that the play became a kind of concert version in which, more often than not, gifted actors wound up at her instruction behind the furniture, gripping the backs of chairs ("Don't move while you're speaking!" was another of Lillian's mantras), reciting (the only word for it) her lines, to a refrain of "I can't hear you!" from Row Q—where, worst of all, she insisted that the lines sound exactly the way they'd sounded in her head when she wrote them ("Not 'What do *you* think?'" she'd insist, but "'What do you *think?*'"), and that the pictures she'd painted in her mind when she was writing be followed slavishly on the stage: "Turn toward the window when you say that. No, the other window. Slower."

Moment by moment, scene by scene, actor by actor, the life was drained from the play, as the actors became puppets—to Lillian's growing satisfaction. Her words were all that mattered, and now they were as crystal-clear—and cold and inert—as ice.

As I watched her butcher her own play, I asked Harold how he could stand by as Lillian turned the theater into a slaughterhouse. "It's her play," Harold said, his eyes distant.

"But—"

"That's the way it works," Harold said, his gaze still far from that place, far from me. "She's the playwright."

The play opened, a waxworks that left audiences and critics convinced that Lillian Hellman had written a bad play. Maybe she had, but when the play closed, the lesson I took from it was that we would never know what she'd written, because no one—not I, not the other actors, not the public, and, most of all, not Lillian—had ever seen or heard it.

The lesson was confirmed a year later when Lillian, emboldened by her directorial experience with *The Autumn Garden,* decided to eliminate the middleman altogether by directing her next production herself.

The play was a revival of her 1934 success, *The Children's Hour.* I wasn't there during rehearsals, but I suspect she used her now practiced techniques, because the play was so poorly received that some wondered what the critics had seen in it the first time around. This was unfair to Hellman: She was an important playwright, and *The Children's Hour* was an important play. Once again I wondered how anyone who wrote so well could be so tone-deaf.

It's my recollection that one of the newspapers invited Clurman to do a Sunday review of Hellman's production of *The Children's Hour*—perhaps in an effort to mitigate the daily critic's review of it.

Clurman's review was constructed, if memory serves, as a letter to Hellman that began literally with "Dear Lillian."

Clurman, who was a learned historian and, when he elected to write criticism, a critic on a par with Stark Young and Bernard Shaw, began by comparing the experience of European and American playwrights, pointing out that for hundreds of years European playwrights have *grown up* in the theater— literally, since the repertory system that prevails outside the United States provided apprenticeships in a permanent company of actors, writers and directors. The result, Clurman said, is that the European playwright is familiar and comfortable with the rehearsal process—and, in fact, with the actor's process because of daily eyewitness experience with the painstaking trial and error of it (which is what Hellman couldn't bear).

By contrast, Clurman said, for generations, Americans have had nothing remotely like that experience. Instead, the playwright meets the full cast for the first time at the first day of rehearsal, is party to the hectic four-week rehearsal period, and maybe two or three weeks out of town. Then the play opens, for a long or short run, it closes, and the entire company, from actors to stagehands to wardrobe mistresses, parts company never to meet again.

And when the playwright has found the courage, and the backing, to deliver another play, the process begins again, from square one, with a new group of strangers.

That is why, Clurman argued, most American playwrights never learn the fundamental lesson of theater: that what they have written *is not the play,* but the *text* of the play. Everything else that happens *after* they write "The Curtain Falls"—the casting, the rehearsals, the costuming and makeup, the director's imagination, the life experiences and training of the actors who must take the playwright's characters off the printed page and deliver them, via their own bodies and minds and understanding and attitudes and strengths and weaknesses, to the stage in three dimensions and recognizable life—all that, *plus* the writer's text, is "the play."

As we created the Actors Studio Drama School, we made up our minds that our playwrights would understand that—and so would our directors. Aware, and critical, of the fact that, in most schools, student directors complete their studies without ever experiencing the vital dialectic of working with a living, breathing playwright on the evolution of a new work, we erected the second pillar of our program, which decreed that, while our writers and directors would receive intensive specialized training in their crafts, in the first year of our drama school, all three disciplines would study the actor's craft side by side in the same classroom, since, as our catalogue ultimately presented it, "At the end of the day in the professional world of theater and film, when the writer, director, producer, scenic designer, lighting designer and stagehands step back, only the actor is left onstage or in front of the camera's lens to embody the skills—and hopes—of them all."

It would, we reasoned, make as little sense for a composer to write a symphony with no knowledge of what the various instruments can, or cannot, do, as it would for a playwright or director to create a play or film with no knowledge of the actor's process. The result would be Alice's misadventures in Wonderland . . . or Lillian Hellman's in the Autumn Garden.

Though this seems logical now, at least to me, it required a leap of faith for our entering students, which I tried to address each year in my first meeting with them at orientation: "If there remain in any of our directors and writers any questions about this concept, permit me to remind you that Elia Kazan, Sidney Lumet, Mike Nichols, Rob Reiner, William Shakespeare, Orson Welles, Ron Howard, Mark Rydell, Sydney Pollack, Clint Eastwood and Molière all started this same disreputable way. At his death in 1673, Molière was forbidden burial in sanctified ground because he had not formally renounced the profession of actor. There was such a public hue and cry that the Church relented to the extent of permitting his burial—but only after sunset. Even in this the Church was thwarted, since thousands of Parisians, following Molière's coffin to the cemetery, turned the night to day with their torches. So, you see? In the end, there's honor for all in the actor's craft."

The third pillar in our plan was the structure of our third year. Those of us on the committee who had studied in a formal academic environment were familiar with the usual culmination of an acting program, in which the students who have studied together are pitted against one another in a competition for the handful of leading roles in three or four plays. Such a system might work if a student who has labored hard for three or four years winds up playing Hamlet, but what about the student who has worked as long and hard and winds up playing the Second Gravedigger?

Most of us at the Studio came through the educational system developed by Lee Strasberg, Stella Adler, Bobby Lewis, Harold Clurman and Sandy Meisner, in none of whose schools was the student allowed, much less encouraged, to undertake "full-length" work. All of those teachers subscribed to the opinion that a developing talent can learn best by focusing on scene work, which provides a wide variety of experiences that challenge him or her in different ways on a manageable level, and that it is counterproductive to thrust the student into result-oriented production before the foundation has been carefully, thoroughly laid—and learned. Our reasoning was that, since that philosophy and those schools produced most of the first-class actors of the past fifty years, we might be well advised to follow it.

That was the thinking that led us to focus on shorter works that could be satisfactorily rehearsed and fully realized within the environment of the students' third-year schedule (and each student's level of development), and presented in repertory by our actors, directors and writers as their master's degree theses.

By producing three thirty- to forty-five-minute pieces in each week's program, we could offer the graduating actors anywhere from five to ten opportunities to test what they had learned—and reveal themselves to the public and the professional community—an exhausting, exhilarating, invaluable opportunity that wouldn't exist in a season of three or four full-length plays, and didn't exist, to our knowledge, in any other school.

The Repertory Season became the tent pole of our third year—and the heart and soul of our school. When we proposed it in 1994, we had no way of knowing that these radical concepts would prove acceptable—to the students or the academic community—but the fact that in the ensuing ten years the Actors Studio Drama School would become the largest graduate drama school in the country, establish the university's lowest attrition rate (less than 6 percent), and that more than eighty of its graduates would meet the Studio's notoriously stringent standards and be accepted to life membership, have led us to believe that they did.

Early in 1994, a ten-year agreement was signed by the Actors Studio and The New School, and on March 21, a lengthy and complex Proposal for Registration of our program, which Robert Gates and I prepared, went to the New York State Education Department in Albany.

At this point, as it appeared that we would in fact be opening our doors in the first week of September, reality set in for the Studio and the university: Faculty had to be assembled, the MFA program had to be staffed, space had to be acquired, recruitment had to begin. Processes that might normally consume a year or more would have to be compressed into a period of less than six months—which led to the next question: Who would lead the program?

Since, from the first day, I had been the hinge between the two parties, I was the recipient or author of every document and communication that passed between them, hundreds of pages that contained everyone's thoughts, concerns, hopes and expectations. In the course of producing this voluminous journal, I had, of course, addressed the question of leadership, and put forth a sizable roster of names, none of them mine.

Definitely and deliberately, none of them mine. All through that winter, I had been working, in whatever moments I could capture, on what I hoped would be my third Broadway musical, an adaptation of the film *My Man Godfrey.* By March, I'd completed the book and a third of the lyrics, and was looking forward eagerly to returning to it full-time.

That moment never came. As the accreditation proposal went off to Albany, and September loomed large and proximate, my colleagues at the Studio and our opposite numbers at The New School turned and stared at me, wordless but crystal-clear. My immediate response was "*Oh,* no!"—and their reply was "Okay, who else?"

My instant recitation of the eligible candidates was met with an implacable "This belongs to you. It's *in* you. Just get it started."

On May 20, 1994, after several weeks of serious soul-searching, I abandoned *My Man Godfrey,* the rights for which imposed a deadline I knew I wouldn't meet unless I walked away from the school, and accepted appointment as chairman of the MFA program. Working with the Studio's curriculum committee, I reached out to Studio members teaching all around the world, bringing them home to our school and its acting and directing students; enlisted the distinguished playwright and chair of Columbia University's Playwriting MFA to come to The New School and chair our playwriting department; assembled a voice faculty of teachers and singers trained in the techniques of the celebrated otolaryngologist Dr. Wilbur Gould and his successor Dr. Gwen Korovin at their Center for the Professional Care of the Voice; formed an alliance with the Alvin Ailey American Dance Center with the mandate that they create strong, healthy, supple instruments that would serve our students all their working lives; brought three distinguished scholars to our Theater History Department, which we'd included in our curriculum at the request of Paul Newman, who insisted in our committee meetings that he'd learned more about his craft in the Theater History courses at the Yale Drama School than in his acting classes.

During the months of joint meetings to create the curriculum and establish the terms of the partnership, The New School representatives had been at pains to ready us for the realities we'd be facing. We must be prepared, they said, for a much smaller entering class than we were projecting, and that was "perfectly all right; we're prepared for it," Dr. Gates said, pushing his reading glasses up the bridge of his nose, a gesture he alternated with fiddling fitfully at their outer corners until they slid down his nose, whereupon he'd push them up again with a bony finger.

Dr. Gates was preternaturally thin, possibly because of his insistence on walking eighty blocks to and from work every day, even in the dead of a New York winter. Formidably educated, with, as I recall, two Ph.Ds, he also had a disconcerting habit of lapsing occasionally and inexplicably, not to mention impenetrably, into long flights of German or Spanish, as if, somehow, his listener were as polyglot as he. One learned to wait patiently until he snapped back into English, with no apology or noticeable shift of gears or, for that matter, any loss of continuity.

Bob Gates is decidedly a hero of this story, because one of his tics was being wise, and another was being generous with his knowledge. He unobtrusively mentored me through the months before the school existed, and, after it did, indulged my frequent unannounced appearances, when I would lean in his open doorway until he turned from his computer, and then I'd ply him with questions. During that first year as chairman of the MFA, I measured my progress as a professional academician in inverse ratio to the (diminishing) number of daily visits to his office.

After all The New School's warnings about the size of our first class, none of us was prepared for what transpired. Since there wasn't time for the normal recruitment process, we depended on the eruption of newspaper articles about the affiliation of the Studio and The New School to inform the applicant pool that the Studio was at long last offering an academic degree in "the Method."

Applications arrived in a heartening stream—and then Charlie Rose invited a panel of us to his round table. Paul Newman, Ellen Burstyn, Norman Mailer, Frank Corsaro, Arthur Penn and I unveiled the plans for our school on *The Charlie Rose Show* . . . and the floodgates opened. Years later, when Charlie invited me for a solo visit, I acknowledged his role in launching not only the Actors Studio Drama School but *Inside the Actors Studio,* which wouldn't have existed without the school—and which sometimes competes with his show for potential guests.

We are very friendly rivals, and the night of my solo visit, I informed him and his viewers that in the fall of 1994, nearly every application we received, at the standard question, "How did you hear about us?" replied, *"The Charlie Rose Show."*

As the summer of '94 passed, too frighteningly fast, we read the submitted work of our writing candidates, and interviewed directing candidates. Most theater schools don't train directors, some perhaps because they're not equipped to, others because there are no rules for vetting a directing candidate. You can't go somewhere and watch them direct, and the young aspirants don't have portfolios and reviews. So, an in-depth interview is the usual compromise. An account of this mysterious procedure found its way into, of all places, *The New Yorker*'s "Talk of the Town," over George Plimpton's byline. Under the headline A FARCE ON THE UPPER EAST SIDE, George delighted in the confusion when a young man seated among the applicants turned out to be under the impression he was waiting to see the psychiatrist in the town house next door. George reported that I had reflected on the fact that he must have assumed that the other "patients" were *really* crazy, since every one of them saw himself as a director. "Everyone wants to be a director," George had me sighing.

During that frenetic summer of '94, as we assembled our acting faculty, they joined me in a round of auditions for the actors. In the short time between our announcement and what was to be the first day of classes, we auditioned two hundred candidates, applying the Studio's criteria, but with the understanding that the Studio is not a school—and a school is not the Studio.

The candidates who auditioned weren't ready to face the Studio's judges—and standards. If they were, they'd have had no reason to come to us. Stanislavski asserted that talent is inborn, genetic and can't be taught—but technique *can;* and the purpose of technique, he insisted, is to free the talent. So the criterion I proposed to our judges was: Do you as teachers have what these applicants need as students? Can this school find—and free—their unique talents?

Our applicants in the first year, and in all the subsequent years, came from every corner of America—and the world, as *Inside the Actors Studio* carried our message to 125 countries. For me, one of the most extraordinary facts about our students—who, it will become apparent, are the ultimate, indisputable heroes of this tale—is that they came to New York on their own initiative—and their own nickel—from Japan, Australia, Brazil, Greece, Turkey, Poland, France, Ireland, Sweden, Russia, England, Italy—often ponying up two airfares, since our catalogue informed them that we preferred scenes to monologues . . . for a five-minute audition!

Then, because academic policy proscribes admitting an applicant until all the candidates have been seen, they return to their homes—and wait. But, since the courage of these candidates never failed to move me, I developed a kind of provisional sidestep. When a quick conference with my colleagues indicated a sufficient interest in the auditioner, I'd ask that the candidate be brought back to the stage—especially if they'd come to us from halfway around the world—and invite them to sit on a center-stage chair for an informal chat. The chat often revealed as much as the audition had, and if it confirmed our interest, it always ended this way: "I can't tell you whether or not you've passed your audition, because we have more candidates to see."

A taut nod. "Of course."

"But I'd like to ask you a question."

A tight "Mmmm."

"Sit back. Relax. Put your feet on the floor. Let your arms fall. Open your hands. Wiggle your fingers."

"Mmmm."

"Blink."

"Oh—yeah."

"Breathe."

"Right."

"Good. Now, I'd like to know: If—you understand, *if*—we admit you, are you prepared to commit the next three years of your life to us, because that would mean we're ready to commit the next three years of our lives to you?"

Tears, nine times out of ten. Tears that coursed uncontrollably down male and female cheeks, choking off the "Yes!!!"

"Okay, we'll let you know in three weeks." But *we* knew, and maybe the student did too. I hoped so then, and hope so now, because those gallant souls faced a long, costly trip home and a nail-biting wait.

Full disclosure: I never—not once—asked the question unless we were certain the student would be admitted. Given the prohibition against premature notification of the applicant, this disclosure would seem to compromise future auditions—but it won't, because I'm no longer dean of the school, conducting the auditions. Someone else will have to fall in love with them.

In August, Albany responded: We were accredited, and could send formal acceptance letters to our admitted candidates, a relief as much to us as to them.

With my apprenticeship drawing to a close, and the real thing lurking around the corner, I met for the last time with Dean Landa. Al Landa is the kind of man whose native heft and wisdom bring the Buddha to mind, with good grounds on both counts. His round face is creased by a perpetual smile, no matter what his mood may actually be (as opposed to my natural mien, which makes me look, in my wife's view—and Will Ferrell's—like a particularly dour undertaker on an especially bad day, even when I'm seething with good humor).

In Landa's case and mine it's a mere matter of physiognomical architecture, for which neither of us can claim responsibility. It just worked out better for him. Like many people of ample girth, Al speaks in gusts, with sharp intakes of air between phrases. The result is a kind of punctuation that has the effect of adding gravity to each utterance, although normally his utterances need no added gravitas.

His knowledge of, and affection for, all the arts and the people who populate them were doubtless among the reasons Fanton assigned him to me as Pied Piper and Jiminy Cricket, two roles he filled to perfection.

Now, on this last day, as he prepared to push me from the nest, he had, he announced gravely—or as gravely as he could through that perpetual smile—two pieces of advice he said he wanted me to take with me and never forget. I was normally attentive to him; now I was riveted.

"The school's going to be a success," he said. "A *big* success."

I shifted uneasily, uncertainties surfacing.

"No!" Al said peremptorily. "A *very* big success. Bigger than you or The New School can imagine. And when it happens . . ."

"*If* it happens . . ."

"*When* it happens"—the smile was broader, the tone graver—"the university is going to be very happy. They're going to see a huge potential out there." He waved a plump hand at the window. "Students clamoring to sign up. And you know what they're going to want you to do?"

"No. What?"

"Expand!" gusted from him. "That's what they're going to say. Add classes. Add courses. Teach undergraduates. Put the Actors Studio label on courses in other divisions. Be an even bigger success! And you know what you're going to do? *Nothing!!!* You know what you're going to say? *No!!!* And why?"

He waited. So did I.

"Because," he confided, leaning closer, Buddha giving way to an Old Testament prophet, "the reason this MFA program is going to succeed is the same reason the Studio has succeeded. It's going to be *exclusive!*" The second syllable of the final word seemed to consume several seconds. "And you can't be exclusive without excluding. The word you're going to hear from the university, over and over again, is *grow*. Because they know—and you know—that you *can*. And what are you going to say?"

"No."

"Exactly! *Exclusive* isn't *snobbish*. It's *essential*! It's how the Studio got to be the Studio, and it's not negotiable."

He inhaled deeply several times, rasping as he caught his breath, then leaned close again. "Here's the second thing you mustn't ever forget." He paused, for breath maybe, or effect, or maybe because what he was about to say pained him. He took one more deep breath and said, "Jim . . . no matter what they say to you—about the curriculum, about the faculty—remember . . . it may only be about the money."

Having delivered his Two Commandments, my Old Testament lawgiver stepped aside and pushed me toward the Promised Land.

At last, Orientation Day arrived, and the first-year students drifted tentatively into the Tishman Auditorium, glancing nervously about and seating themselves randomly, discretely, leaving large gaps all around the theater as they waited, with understandable anxiety, for the formal program to begin. When it did, these were the first words they, or anyone, ever heard from our school, as I came to the lectern and studied them: "What's wrong with this picture?"

They glanced around the room, then looked back at me, perplexed. "All that empty space," I said. They hesitated, I waited, and finally a few of them got up and moved, filling some empty seats. "Too much empty space," I sighed, and more students rose, moving closer to the stage—and one another. But the house still looked like a half-completed jigsaw puzzle.

I shook my head and waited. More movement, but still no contiguity. I shook my head. And waited. Somewhat sheepishly, they resumed filling in the gaps until only a few empty seats remained. I waited. They shifted about, filling the last empty seats, until finally an unbroken mass of master's degree candidates that was at least geographically united faced me from the front of the house, empty darkness behind them.

"Beautiful!" I said. "For the next three years, this is how it's going to be. Get used to it." And I began my formal greeting: "To borrow the words of a much more significant person on a much more significant occasion, the world will little note what we say here today. But for the Actors Studio, this is a *very* significant moment. The Studio will note forever that, at 10:06 A.M., on September seventh, 1994, we admitted the first academic class in the forty-seven-year history of the Actors Studio."

There was a tentative trickle of applause from the students that swelled quickly to a thunderous roar. Onstage, our Studio members who had gathered to welcome these first students rose and gave them a standing ovation, which led to my next remark: "This odyssey, yours and ours, has now officially begun. How fitting that you should begin it to the sound of applause. Fasten your seat belts. You're in for a hell of a ride. And so are we."

The chain was complete. Each link had held. The adventure had begun.

CHAPTER Two

66 *Suit the action to the word, the word to the action.*

—Hamlet's advice to the players

Okay, what's the Method—and why should anybody give a rat's ass about it?

A fair question. I hope what follows is a fair answer.

First, of course, I admit to a bias that is, I suspect, obvious. I'm a vice president of the Actors Studio, was the founder of the Actors Studio Drama School and served for ten years as its dean, so I would hardly be filling these pages with encomia to Coquelin or Delsarte. Coquelin was a highly regarded figure in nineteenth-century French theater, who, in his book *L'Art et le comédien* ("The Art and the Actor"), argued strenuously and influentially for simulated rather than real emotions. I once heard Norman Mailer wryly describe a "Coquelin actor" as having the advantage that he or she could plan a post-performance dinner, down to the wines, dessert and seating plan, while emoting onstage in the third act.

François Delsarte was a nineteenth-century French teacher of acting and singing who published a classic of theatrical flummery in which photographs presented the gestures, like the back of an open hand to one's forehead, that would precisely illustrate and evoke feeling, each photo meticulously labeled with the emotion it represented. Memorize these gestures, Delsarte promised, and you're an actor.

Coquelin's representational approach to acting, with minor variations, was the only formal technique in western theater. There weren't conflicting views: It was the established church, and for centuries it didn't occur to anyone to challenge it. One cultivated a stentorian voice, with round vowels and pin-prick-sharp consonants, and a fine figure (male or female) that could be adorned like a dressmaker's mannequin. One posed in front of a mirror, then in front of the audience. One mimicked, one declaimed, one displayed. Above all, one *impressed.* A theatrical effect, once achieved, was repeated precisely, by rote, to the tiniest gesture, at every performance ad infinitum, with the result that the most successful actors wound up mimicking *themselves*—to torrents of applause when the familiar, anticipated moments arrived.

In Coquelin's world, acting had nothing to do with life; it had everything to do with *"acting"*—an exercise that was altogether self-conscious, self-involved, self-referential and, in the worst cases, self-reverential.

Amour propre was the actor's stock-in-trade—and the audience accepted it; in fact clamored for it, because, like any audience at any time, including our own, of course, it battened on what it was fed. And, truth be told, some of the proponents of this artificial style did it very skillfully, and could move an audience to tears or laughter as deftly as their modern counterparts.

The problem with that kind of performance was that it could go only so far before it ran into its self-imposed barriers. Simulated tears, complete with formulaic gestures (*vide* Delsarte), facial expressions and boo-hoo noises were safer than real ones because they didn't constrict the throat and choke the golden voice or, God forbid, smear the makeup, but the gap between "artifice" and "artificial" was perilously narrow, and often erased.

The schism between the dominant school of acting and its rare antithesis was limned definitively by George Bernard Shaw in a theater review I offer as evidence that, before he was a transcendent playwright writing his first play, *Candida,* at the age of forty, he was a transcendent critic of music in the *Star* and the *World,* under the pen name Corno di Bassetto, and a greatly feared—and respected—theater critic under the blunt byline GBS. On June 15, 1895, Shaw seized the opportunity to compare the two reigning actresses of the time, Sarah Bernhardt and Eleanora Duse, who, as good fortune would have it, were appearing simultaneously on the London stage, in the same role.

This week began with the relapse of Sarah Bernhardt into her old profession of serious actress. She played Magda in Sudermann's *Heimat,* and was promptly challenged by Duse in the same part at Drury Lane on Wednesday. The contrast between the two Magdas is as extreme as any contrast could possibly be between artists who have finished their twenty years' apprenticeship to the same profession under closely similar conditions. . . . [Shaw speaks of] the childishly egotistical character of [Bernhardt's] acting, which is not the art of making you think more highly or feel more deeply, but the art of making you admire her, pity her, champion her, weep with her, laugh at her jokes, follow her fortunes breathlessly, and applaud her—wildly when the curtain falls. It is the art of finding out all your weaknesses and practicing on them—cajoling you, harrowing you, exciting you—on the whole, fooling you. And it is always Sarah Bernhardt in her own capacity who does this to you. The dress, the title of the play, the order of the words may vary; but the woman is always the same. She does not enter into the leading character: she substitutes herself for it.

All this is precisely what does not happen in the case of Duse, whose every part is a separate creation. When she comes on the stage, you are quite welcome to take your opera-glass and count whatever lines time and care have so far traced on her. They are the credentials of her humanity; and she knows better than to obliterate that significant handwriting beneath a layer of peachbloom from the chemist's. . . . I grant that Sarah's elaborate Monna [sic] Lisa smile, with the conscious droop of the eyelashes and the long carmined lips coyly disclosing the brilliant row of teeth, is effective of its kind. . . . And it lasts quite a minute, sometimes longer. But Duse, with a tremor of the lip which you feel rather than see, and which lasts half an instant, touches you straight on the very heart; and there is not a line in the face, or a cold tone in the grey shadow, that does not give poignancy to that tremor.

. . . Obvious as the disparity of the two famous artists has been to many of us since we first saw Duse, I doubt whether any of us realized, after Madame Bernhardt's very clever performance as Magda on Monday night, that there was room in the nature of things for its annihilation within forty-eight hours by so comparatively quiet a talent as Duse's. And yet annihilation is the only word for it.

. . . Before long, there came a stroke of acting which will probably never be forgotten by those who saw it, and which explained at once why those artifices of the dressing-table which help Madame Bernhardt would hinder Duse almost as much as a screen placed in front of her.

Shaw explains that, after being turned out of her home by her father, Magda has achieved fame as an opera singer, been seduced and abandoned, and returned home, where she discovers that the father of her child, who is a friend of her family, has come to call on her. Shaw continues:

It must be admitted that Sarah Bernhardt played this scene very lightly and pleasantly. . . . Not so with Duse. The moment she read the card handed her by the servant, you realized what it was to have to face a meeting with the man. It was interesting to watch how she got through it when he came in, and how, on the whole, she got through it pretty well. He paid his compliments and offered his flowers; they sat down, and she evidently felt that she had got it safely over and might allow herself to think at her ease, and to look at him to see how much he had altered. Then a terrible thing happened to her. She began to blush; and in another moment she was conscious of it, and the blush was slowly spreading and deepening until, after a few vain efforts to avert her face or to obstruct his view of it without seeming to do so, she gave up and hid the blush in her hands.

... After that feat of acting I did not need to be told why Duse does not paint an inch thick. I could detect no trick in it: it seemed to me a perfectly genuine effect of the dramatic imagination.

I shall make no attempt to describe the rest of that unforgettable act.... There was a real play, and an actress who understood the author and was a greater artist than he. And for me, at least, there was a confirmation of my sometimes flagging faith that a dramatic critic is really the servant of a high art, and not a mere advertiser of entertainments of questionable respectability of motive.

Perhaps no critic has ever shown a more profound understanding of the actor's craft than Shaw did in this piece, in which he captured forever the contrast—and conflict—between the two disparate schools of acting.

While Shaw was learning from Duse, half a continent away, in Russia, a theater director was undergoing the same transformation—inspired by the same isolated group of dissidents.

For Constantin Stanislavski, the revelation was provided by the renowned Italian actor Tommaso Salvini, whom Stanislavski saw in a touring production of *Othello* in 1882, when Stanislavski was nineteen. As Duse's uncompromising honesty and authentic emotion would fling a door open for Shaw thirteen years later, Salvini's ability to fill Shakespeare's most volcanic moments not with bombast and pretension but with the genuine dynamics of human experience opened the young aspirant's eyes to possibilities he couldn't have imagined. When he wrote about it, he described it as "burning lava . . . pouring into my heart."

Both Salvini and Duse were anomalous artists, as rare and incongruous as an orchid in a cabbage patch. Their towering talents broke through the accepted orthodoxy: Bernhardt's beautifully—fastidiously—crafted artifice and studiously counterfeit emotions were the norm. And it was against that norm that Stanislavski, like Shaw, rebelled. And for precisely the same reason.

On June 22, 1897, Stanislavski and Vladimir Nemirovich-Danchenko, a critic and playwright who was, it turned out, as repelled as Stanislavski by the prevailing elocutionary, presentational acting style, met for lunch in a private chamber off the bustling main dining room of the Slavianski Bazar to share what they discovered was a passionate desire for a new kind of theater that would break with the fustian clichés and conventions of the past. Their fervid discussion ended at eight the next morning over breakfast. Out of those eighteen hours emerged the Moscow Art Theatre—and a revolution that would shake the theatrical world, and one day shape the world of film.

Production by production, rehearsal by rehearsal, virtually hour by hour, Stanislavski worked with his company to find empirical (one of his favorite words was *logical*) answers to the questions that were (literally) tormenting him—and the company. At a rehearsal of Turgenev's *A Month in the Country*, Stanislavski's attempts to apply his evolving techniques so unsettled Olga Knipper, one of the Art Theatre's leading actresses, that she burst into tears and fled the theater. The next day, Stanislavski sent her flowers and a letter that is quoted in Jean Benedetti's invaluable biography of Stanislavski: "At every point in the role, look for some desire which concerns you and you alone and banish all other vulgar desires concerning the audience. You will quickly find this inward work will carry you away. Once that has happened you will turn from something which is unworthy of true artists, the desire to serve and ingratiate oneself with the audience. In the same measure that you are not logical in that instance, you will become logical by being carried away by genuine feelings."

Clearly, a system was beginning to take shape. The "desire" Stanislavski commends to Knipper is unmistakably the Objective: what the character *wants,* translated to an Action, "which concerns you and you alone." But just as clearly, to Stanislavski, the resistance of the company's more established, and more inflexible, actors would impede its development, so he gathered about him the younger members of the company who were more open to experimentation and new ideas, and created what he described as not a school but a studio—which would become known as the First Studio of the Art Theatre—devoted to experimentation and research in the actor's craft, separated from it geographically but not ideologically. (Prophetically, the studio occupied a few rooms over a movie theater—in *1912*!) The fifty members of the young company—they included Richard Boleslavsky, Evgeny Vakhtangov and Michael Chekhov, who would become major theatrical forces—were working members of the Art Theatre at night, but in the daytime they belonged to Stanislavski, and it was on this canvas that he painted his System.

Stanislavski spoke repeatedly of his ambition to create a "grammar of acting," an idea seized upon and celebrated by Stella Adler half a century later when she said to her students, of whom I was one, "What happens when a housewife in Brooklyn goes to the butcher shop? She tells the butcher she wants sirloin, and he *gives* her sirloin. Not tenderloin, not filet mignon. Sirloin. And if she wants lamb chops—she *gets* lamb chops. Not pork chops, not veal chops. Lamb chops. Why? *Because she and the butcher speak a common language!*" She would pause for effect—Stella often paused for effect—then demand, "Why should you and I—and every other actor—not be able to communicate with each other *at least* as clearly, simply and specifically as the lady and her butcher?" And every one of us asked himself—and I still do—why not?

Stella Adler was a dedicated advocate of Stanislavski's concept of Given Circumstances. In our classroom, Stella was insistent: "Darlings [another Stella-ism], what happens when a bad actor is in trouble onstage? Nothing feels right. He knows he's losing his grip on the part. All he can hear is every cough and murmur in the audience. What does he do? He reaches for the biggest thing he can think of! He tries to gobble the whole part in one big desperate bite, hoping that will put him back on track. *It won't!* Listen to me, darlings, if you're in trouble, *concentrate*—concentrate on the *smallest* thing you can focus on. That vase on the table—is that a crack? Your partner's necktie—is that a spot? Something that you *know* is true. And real. It's yours, and once you own it, you can go on to the next small, *manageable* truth, and the next. The whole role is nothing but a chain of tiny truths *that you can believe in,* one after another. In the end, they'll lead you to a bigger truth, the truth of your character, of the play, of the playwright—the reason he wrote the play in the *first* place. You're his truth teller. And because *you* believe, *one tiny truth at a time,* the *audience* will believe."

But simply *saying* "truth" doesn't answer inevitable questions: It asks them. *Whose* truth—and to what end? Truth, on its surface so simple and straightforward, is, in fact, one of the most slippery (and precious) words in our vocabulary. When someone says to me, "One thing I am is truthful," I suspect instantly that "truthful" may be the one thing that person is definitely not. Under truth's banner (since no one ever marches into battle under a banner emblazoned "Lie!"), some of history's most monstrous crimes have been committed—and, of course, it has been the emblem of some of history's most glorious moments and creative expressions.

So, when someone unfurls the banner of truth, as Stanislavski did, we have a right to ask for a definition. And the definition Stanislavski gives is specific and verifiable. Occam would approve of the economy of "The truth in art is the truth of your circumstances."

Mike Nichols, who had studied with Lee Strasberg, emphasized this point on *Inside the Actors Studio:* "Look, there's only one question. It's differently answered in plays and movies but the question is 'What is this *really* like?' Never mind the conventions and the decisions we've all made together—and never mind, in fact, the script. What is it really like when this happens, when somebody seduces someone, when somebody kills someone, when somebody loses someone? What is it really like? And the only difference is that in the movie, the answers are less literal. Because 'What is it really like?' includes the unconscious, and includes our dreams. So, part of the answer in a movie can be from one unconscious to all the other unconsciouses."

Very early in his development of the System, Stanislavski postulated his theory of Action—what the actor is doing to accomplish an Objective—which is what the *character* wants at any given moment. That word *want* occurs often in Stanislavski's lexicon, and it lies at the heart of his concept of Action and Objective. Mark Rydell, codirector with Martin Landau of Actors Studio West in Los Angeles, and director of such films as *On Golden Pond* and *The Rose,* was a student at the Neighborhood Playhouse of Sanford Meisner, who was one of the most articulate and influential proponents of the concept of Action. On *Inside the Actors Studio,* this is how Rydell described it: "Meisner was very clear about what he used to call action problems. He knew about acting having to do with *doing* things. That is to say, you can always tell when an actor is *really* doing something or is *imitating* doing something. And if he's really doing it, everything comes with it. All you have to do to prove it is put someone in a closet and lock the door and tell them to get out. Well, if they really try to get out, in a minute they'll be flooded with emotion—because of the doing, and their inability to achieve their objective. You open the door and they're shaking, or in tears."

Rydell's illustration demonstrated Meisner's—and Stella Adler's and Robert Lewis's—contention that an emotion isn't an Action, it's the *result* of an Action. Here, emotion is reached not through an Emotional Memory exercise, discrete from text, rehearsal or performance, but entirely *within* the context of text, rehearsal or performance: Try to accomplish your action, Meisner would say, and the emotion will come; you never have to think about it.

From Objective, Stanislavski moved to the Super-Objective, the character's overall objective from the first to last moment of the play (or film). In this interpretation of the System, each of the Objectives, or Beats, along the way *must* be a link in the unbroken chain of the Super-Objective (that causal chain again), leading logically and inexorably to the Super-Objective's final destination, the *character's* final destination in the play. If not, this construct argues, it doesn't belong there: Either the playwright or the actor has erred, and the chain must be reconstructed.

Stella Adler used to illustrate this point with a metaphor: "You're on an ocean liner on the high seas." Stella enjoyed upper-class allusions and, some would say, illusions. "Bad weather is threatening, and the crew rushes to string a sturdy rope on the deck, the length of the ship. When the storm arrives and you're losing your footing, what do you do? You reach for that rope! That's what the Super-Objective is. In good weather, maybe you can proceed without it for a while, but the second you're in trouble, *that's what you reach for.* It'll get you where you have to go."

In the teens of the twentieth century, Stanislavski's vision gradually evolved into two components, work on the self, and work on the part, which formed the basis of his first two books. In time, it became so detailed that it could be depicted by Stella Adler in 1934, after her meetings with Stanislavski, in an elaborate chart that resembled a pipe organ. Robert Lewis was so impressed with the chart that he included his hand-drawn copy of it in a foldout in his book *Method or Madness.* Each of the forty pipes of the "organ" bore a word or phrase: "11—Action itself; 12—Magic 'If'; 13—Given Circumstances; 14—Beats." At the base of the ziggurat were the words "Work on One's Self" and, at its pinnacle, two stirring words: "The Part."

As the Moscow Art Theatre's fame spread, it began to tour, acquiring adherents wherever it brought its eye-opening offerings. The nearly universal absorption of the Art Theatre's theatrical behavior and ideology in the past three-quarters of a century makes it hard for us to understand how shocking those first international appearances were. The traditional, presentational theater was still firmly in place everywhere—*until* the Art Theatre showed up. When they packed their tents and moved on, the old ways looked, to some of the audience at least, quaint, artificial—and unacceptable.

The Moscow Art Theatre arrived in New York on January 2, 1923. Their opening night, with *Tsar Fiodor* at the Jolson Theatre, was described by Stanislavski, in a letter to his wife, Lilina, as the greatest success in the company's history.

When the Art Theatre sailed from New York on May 17, it left behind the seeds of its revolution in two teachers, Richard Boleslavsky and Maria Ouspenskaya, who founded the American Laboratory Theatre, where the very young, impressionable and gifted Lee Strasberg, Harold Clurman and Stella Adler were imbued with a philosophy—and a passion—that would fuel the next advance in this march when they and producer Cheryl Crawford founded the Group Theatre in 1931.

The Group Theatre has been richly, sufficiently chronicled. Suffice to say here that twenty-eight actors united their lives, their fortunes and their sacred honor in a venture that lasted ten years and altered the American theatrical landscape forever. Many of the actors and directors who emerged from the

Group have already appeared in these pages—and will reappear at upcoming milestones in this journey.

What is of consequence here is the rupture that developed in 1934 after Stella Adler's encounter with Stanislavski in Paris. When Boleslavsky inaugurated the American Laboratory Theatre in 1924, his emphasis was on the various techniques of Emotional Memory. In the next decade, Stanislavski would begin shifting to what he called Physical Action, at the expense of, and some would come to say in opposition to, Emotional Memory. But Boleslavsky and Ouspenskaya taught the System the way it had been taught to them.

In Stella's accounts, the first years of the Group Theatre were difficult for her because Lee Strasberg, who was the company's principal teacher, was thoroughly committed to Emotional Memory, a technique she found hobbling, stopping rather than starting her process. Seeking relief, she elected to spend the summer of 1934 in Paris with Harold Clurman, who was now her husband. Discovering that Stanislavski had arrived in Paris for a seven-week stay, she flung herself on him, demanding to know, as she related it to our class in her customary understatement, "why you ruined my *life!*"

Stanislavski's account describes a woman in panic, pleading for help. Stella, as anyone who ever knew her would attest, could be persuasive. In this instance, Stanislavski spent every afternoon for the next five weeks coaching her in a scene from *Gentlewoman,* the play directed by Lee Strasberg that had sent her, howling for rest and rehabilitation, to Paris.

It was there, during those five weeks, that Stella discovered, as she described it on her return to the United States, that Stanislavski had "abandoned" Emotional Memory, the technique that nearly deprived her of her sanity, in favor of his principles of Physical Action and Objective, which, if pursued correctly, according to Stanislavski as conveyed by Stella, would evoke (as Rydell's actor-in-the-closet was meant to demonstrate) whatever emotions were appropriate and necessary, without resort to a direct appeal to feelings through Emotional Memory.

It is not the province of this book to try to settle this controversy, which exists, with much less heat and perhaps a bit more light, to this day. What is of interest here is the array of consequences that flowed from the disagreement.

From the moment of Stella's return, the System raced along on two sometimes parallel, sometimes divergent tracks, one spearheaded, brilliantly and effectively, by Strasberg, the other led, with equal skill and fervor, by Adler, Meisner, Clurman, Lewis and Elia Kazan, who, more than the others, kept a foot in both camps, and today the Actors Studio and its drama school comprise a broad stream into which all the tributaries of the Stanislavski System flow freely and harmoniously.

A final question that may be hovering on the lips of the reader of these pages is "Why such a fuss? Look at all the great actors who just stood up and *did* it. Honestly, why study at *all*?"

A perfectly sensible question. One of the world's greatest actors, Laurence Olivier, went to his grave insisting that he had no need for the Method—or any other "system." What Lord Olivier didn't know was that Constantin Stanislavski would have agreed with him, since he never denied the role of genius, which, by definition, intuits what the rest of us must, often laboriously, unearth. In the introduction to *An Actor Prepares,* Stanislavski's American translator, Elizabeth Hapgood, notes that Stanislavski "is most ready to point out that a genius like Salvini or Duse [or Olivier] may use without theory the right emotions and expressions that to the less inspired but intelligent student need to be taught."

In *Building a Character,* Stanislavski expanded that statement with "A true creative state while on the stage, and all the elements that go to compose it, were the natural endowment of Schepkin, Ermolova, Duse, Salvini. Nevertheless they worked unremittingly on their technique. . . . Inspiration came to them by natural means almost every time they repeated a role, yet all their lives they sought an approach to it. There is all the more reason why we, of more meager endowments, should seek it."

Later in *Building a Character,* Stanislavski speaks of actors who "do not admit that laws, technique, theories, much less a system, have any part in their work. . . . The majority of them believe that any conscious factor in creativeness is only a nuisance. They find it easier to be an actor by the grace of God. I shall not deny that there are times when, for unknown reasons, they are able to have an intuitive emotional hold on their parts and they play reasonably well in a scene or even a whole performance. . . . But there are other occasions when for the same inexplicable and capricious reasons 'inspiration' does not turn up. Then the actor, who is left on the stage without any technique, without any means of drawing out his own feelings, without any knowledge of his own nature, plays not by the grace of God well, but by the grace of God poorly. And he has absolutely no way of getting back onto the right path."

Whether the course this chapter has followed is the right one, I can't warrant. But it is a path that has led an impassioned army of creative and performing artists to celebrated heights, some of them blessed with innate genius, some of "more meager endowments," but all fired by a determination no less tenacious than a surgeon's, a prima ballerina's or a plumber's to acquire at all costs the tools of their trades.

CHAPTER Three

❝ *Do you know that there comes a midnight hour*
when every one has to throw off his mask?
Do you believe that life will always let itself be mocked?
Do you think you can slip away a little before midnight?

—Søren Kierkegaard,
Epigraph in *Rainbow at Midnight,*
by Lawrence Lipton

My path to the world of the Actors Studio Drama School and *Inside the Actors Studio* was circuitous. At an important junction in my life, it wasn't supposed to lead in this direction at all.

In the beginning, I guess I was meant to be a writer. If not, why could I read (uncomprehendingly, to be sure) when I was one and a half? That claim is usually met with derision (with which there's a good chance it's being met at this moment), but I can only report what my mother told me. She was a teacher and my father was a poet, and my assumption has always been that he just couldn't wait for me to be able to read his poetry, so the reading lessons began in the nursery. I suppose, with enough effort and patience, you can teach an infant to do practically anything, as you'd teach tricks to a dog or an organ-grinder's monkey.

My mother wasn't given to what Mark Twain called "stretchers," and when I, as an adult, joined the doubters about my precocity, she offered two proofs. The first concerned a trip to the pediatrician that, according to my mother, nearly cost me my life as it was barely beginning. Since my father was a professional poet, we were always a little short of the ready, to put it bluntly—and mildly. Therefore, when a pediatric visit was scheduled, my mother, who had to be at school at the appointed hour, called upon her brother, who owned a car (which we decidedly didn't), to drive me there, wait at the doctor's office and, on his return, deliver me to the doorman of our apartment building, who would take me up to our apartment, where Mother would by this time be waiting.

Mother reported that her brother rolled down the window on the passenger side and handed me through it, an infant in swaddling, to the doorman. This was one of Mother's proofs, confirmed by my uncle: A package small enough to pass through a car window couldn't be older than a year and a half.

In Mother's account, I looked up at the doorman and read the name on his cap, "Lee Plaza," and the doorman dropped me (with, I think, arguable justification). Kids bounce: I was delivered to Mother only a little the worse for wear. The doorman may have taken longer to recover.

Mother's second proof involved bus trips up Woodward Avenue to her sister's house in the suburb of Ferndale. The bus then, as now, was lined with advertisements. According to Mother, I would sit on her lap, peering about and painstakingly piecing together the words on the ads, in a voice piping but piercing enough to draw suspicious stares from the other passengers, who, Mother said, probably thought she was a ventriloquist with a particularly lifelike dummy. She would smile awkwardly and turn me to face out the window. It didn't help. There were billboards out there, waiting for treble proclamation: "I'd walk a mile for a Camel!"

At three, I was "writing" poetry, in the bardic, oral tradition, every awful lay faithfully transcribed by my father. Fortunately, none survive.

At five, when I entered kindergarten, my mother received a call informing her with regret that her son appeared to be mentally impaired. When Mother arrived at the school in a state of alarm, she was offered a vantage point from which, unobserved, she could watch me in the classroom.

"See?" the kindergarten teacher said. What Mother saw was her son, wandering from one group of children to another as they applied crayons to coloring books, or constructed houses from blocks, or built sand castles. I would watch listlessly, my hands behind my back, then move on, in an unchanging cycle of indifference. "He won't even sit down," the teacher said.

Mother breathed a sigh of relief. "Give him a book," she said. "He'll sit down." They did, I did, and Mother went off to *her* school.

When I was six, my father disappeared one day, just vanished, was gone, without a prior hint or word of warning; and full responsibility for our survival fell to, and *upon,* my mother. (Decades later, this pattern of parental loss would emerge, as it will in this account, as a dominant theme of *Inside the Actors Studio,* to my surprise at first, but not for long, as it began to provide significant clues to the lives and drives of my guests, and to mine.)

With my father's defection, our economic condition went from fragile to fractured, and my mother and I moved into her parents' home in Detroit's inner city. For five important years of my life, I lived at 280 Hague Avenue in the kind of nondescript wooden house that looks like every other nondescript wooden house built in the Midwest between 1900 and 1940: See the houses with the big front porches in any Chaplin, Keaton or W. C. Fields movie. Ours sported wooden Doric columns on its porch.

My bedroom at 280 Hague was on the second floor, and since my grand-mother was always the first one up, my misty recollection of her is a pleasant one of a white-haired woman in an apron bustling about a big aromatic kitchen. I would run down the stairs, following today's scent—and the occa-sions I remember most vividly are those when I would arrive as she took a steaming apple pie from the oven and motioned me to the kitchen table, where she would cut two fragrant pieces of pie, fill two glasses with ice water and sit down next to me to enjoy what was the first, and virtually last, gourmet expe-rience of my childhood. Our customary bill of fare consisted primarily of the Midwestern staples: chicken, mashed potatoes, peas, biscuits. But, like the madeleine-entranced Proust, I'll never forget the contrast of the hot, assertive pie and the cold, neutral water.

Michigan's winters are legendary for their relentless grip. Earlier in these pages, I confessed to an inordinate fondness for Christmas. In my novel *Mir-rors,* I seized the opportunity to express my feelings through the character of a young woman: "You know what I like best about Christmas? It's so—whim-sical: normally sane people dragging messy, living trees into neat, dead rooms and using embarrassing words like *joy* and *merry;* choirs singing in banks, trumpets braying on street corners; janitors and bartenders hanging tinsel—everything you'd be fired, arrested, ostracized or committed for, any other time of the year."

Her words, my sentiments, formulated in adulthood, but formed in child-hood, trudging home on white snow under a black sky from a Fisher Theatre matinee, enchanted by the movie and the Christmas lights on Grand Boule-vard and Woodward Avenue—and by the conviction that suddenly this had become a joyful place and time: Christmas was around the corner . . . inevita-ble! One magical day in a decidedly unmagical year.

I harbored no delusions about Santa. My mother was a calm, confident atheist and my father a publicly outspoken one. I don't know when I first heard Mother's mantra, "No Santa at six, no stork at ten, no God at twelve," but it came as no surprise. And yet, somehow, when I was very young, in an unvoiced but undeniable compact, we both believed in the peaceable, hopeful reprieve of Christmas, and celebrated it fervently. On Christmas morning, I arrived at the fireplace before dawn to open the presents whose earthly, familial origins I knew, and counted them meticulously: Ten toy soldiers in a box equaled ten gifts, and a pair of socks two. By this means, I could measure the world's affection for me and, when the sun rose, could flaunt my bounty before the other kids in the neighborhood, who, I now suspect, applied exactly the same numeric formula to theirs.

Once again, I rely on my mother's recollection for an account that sums up that time in our lives. On a frigid night early in December, several of Mother's sisters and cousins were coming over to discuss the imminent holiday. Years later, Mother told me that she stoked the furnace with what, she discovered to her horror, were the last few lumps of coal in the basement. There was no more and at that moment no money for more—and the burly Michigan winter was just beginning to flex its biceps. And here came the family to plan Christmas.

In Mother's account, as the evening began, she listened distractedly, absorbed by the thought of the last embers dying in the furnace below, with her child lying asleep above, and no more coal or heat until . . . when? And no one to lean on, since the rest of the family was as afflicted as she. All, that is, except one.

The conversation burbled on, as unattended by Mother as the starving furnace, until her cousin Vera, whose husband was conspicuously, and uniquely, prospering, and who was known to put on occasional airs, said, "Listen, what's the point of going out and getting each other presents we don't want or need? Forget surprises. Why not just tell each other what we'd like?"

The idea passed instant muster, prompting Vera to continue. "Okay. For me, all I need is a sterling-silver grape scissors."

Something snapped in Mother, and haunted by the specter of the dying furnace, the empty coal bin, and me stiffening upstairs, she began to laugh. And, as Mother recounted it, the harder she tried to block the dual, dueling concepts of Vera's grape scissors and the impending Ice Age on Hague Avenue, the more uncontrollably she laughed. The startled family sprang to her rescue as she rolled convulsively off the chair and thrashed on the floor, engulfed by a flood of laughter and tears.

It was years before Mother, a proud and independent spirit, confessed to Vera and the others who had been there on that dark, distant December night that it was Vera's sterling-silver grape scissors that had threatened her sanity, and very nearly her life—and provided her with the therapeutic, cleansing laughter that helped her weather that winter and several more that would be no better climatically or financially.

And it was many years later, when Mother lived near me in New York under substantially improved circumstances, that she opened a gift from Detroit on Christmas morning and passed it to me with a wordless, eloquent smile. It was, of course, a sterling-silver grape scissors from Vera.

In my tenth year, as my grandmother lay dying, slowly and ingloriously, in the house on Hague Avenue, attended by Mother, the decision was made to spare me this experience by shipping me (literally) to Los Angeles for a summer with Mother's sister Marian and her family. Living as we do today in a world of nearly limitless options, it's hard to imagine a world in which there were so few. But that was the case, which meant that I would travel alone, cross-country, for three days.

I have an indelible memory of my mother, with me in one hand and my pint-sized suitcase in the other, nervously touring one railroad car after another, mysteriously looking for something—then stopping abruptly as she spotted a woman traveling with a boy about my age. Depositing me in the seat across the aisle from them, she waited, as nonchalantly as she could, until the woman noticed her, smiled, and asked if we were going all the way to Los Angeles. Provided with the opening I now know Mother was looking for, she replied that she wasn't, but I *was*—and waited, anxious, hopeful.

The woman obliged, volunteering to keep an eye on me, and expressing pleasure that her son would have company. Mother's relief and my anxiety mounted simultaneously as I eyed these strangers. Mother had no choice, and neither did I, and I have a recollection of her, when the final "All aboard" was sounded, backing out of the car with her eyes fixed on me and, I now know, her heart in her mouth. Years later she would say to me, "I don't know how I could have done that," and my reply was, "I do."

I was spared a lengthy and painful Hague Avenue death scene and, instead, spent my tenth summer in what to me was a tropical paradise, at the cost of an unnerving journey made not only bearable but providential by the discovery, on opening my suitcase, of a present Mother had packed in it. Unwrapping it, I found a Grosset & Dunlap edition of "*A Midsummer Night's Dream,* with the Famous Temple Notes . . . Copious notes and comments by One Hundred Eminent Shakespearean Authorities."

For three days the book was my steadfast companion, falling from my hand only when I fell (peacefully) asleep. Between the gray reality (for me) of Detroit and the sunny unreality of Los Angeles, I devoured every prefatory essay and footnote, and every word of the play that one of the book's commentators, Hartley Coleridge, noted was "all poetry, and sweeter poetry was never written." Three dreaded days became three enchanted days, thanks to Mother's forethought.

The book is still in my library, and opening it as I wrote this account, I discovered that it contained another of Proust's madeleines: my bookplate. All through my childhood, Mother's most frequent gifts to me were, unsurprisingly, books, in each of which I carefully pasted the bookplate she'd given me: a silhouetted man, perched on a book being hoisted by a crane to the top of a tall bookstack, with a space at the bottom for my proprietary, if spidery, signature: Jimmy Lipton.

On Hague Avenue, Mother began moonlighting nights and weekends, going door to door, selling *Compton's Encyclopedia.* The occasional commissions augmented her teacher's salary, but on an unforgettable Christmas morning, her real motive was revealed. In front of the fireplace was the premium she'd worked to earn: a free set of *Compton's.* For me.

Decades later, after Mother's death, as my wife and I sorted through the effects of a long and ultimately happy and successful life, we came upon a box that contained the outdated and until then forgotten set of encyclopedia, with my name embossed in gold on each precious volume . . . which may, in small part, explain why my book *An Exaltation of Larks* bears the dedication, "To my mother, Betty Lipton, who showed me the way to words."

I said this book would be about my heroes.

When I was twelve, the family had no choice but to sell my grandparents' house, which meant that Mother and I migrated farther west in the city, on our own now, to a small apartment in a neighborhood where we knew no one and, for some reason, there were few kids, despite the fact that we lived in the shadow of a large Catholic church. We moved in as the summer began, and once we were bestowed, Mother returned to her new post as a librarian, which was slightly but critically better paid than teaching in the public school system.

In that twelfth summer I became what is today called a latchkey kid, which simply meant that six days a week I was entirely on my own in the daylight hours. But once again, Mother's foresight provided. This time it was a typewriter, used and a little creaky but decidedly serviceable, brought home one night and placed before me on the kitchen table. Mother was silent, I was speechless and the typewriter was momentarily wordless. But not for long.

From that day forward, through every day of a simmering Michigan summer, the encroaching walls of that cramped apartment at 1935 Burlingame echoed back a relentless, rapturous clatter that produced, by September, three novels. Longer than short stories, and even novellas, they qualified as novels in everything but sophistication, craft and quality. But nonetheless, one of Mother's literary friends was so taken with them that she elected to pack them off to Grosset & Dunlap, the publisher of the *"Midsummer Night's Dream,* with the Famous Temple Notes," providing a tantalizing prospect: Shakespeare and I—the same publisher!

In the submission, I was identified as "an unpublished author," and for years I treasured a letter from a Grosset & Dunlap editor to Mr. James Lipton, informing me that my three novels didn't fit into their current list, but urging me to consider them my publisher and submit all future work to them.

That might have led, at the least, to another passionate summer of literary output, but destiny and a few of the more pragmatic members of mother's family intervened, inveighing against a summer of sloth like the last one. It was high time, they suggested to Mother, with some justification perhaps, that I begin to pull my weight in her ongoing financial struggle.

So, a job was found for me, and at thirteen I began my professional career, washing glass in nitric acid in a photoengraving plant in downtown Detroit. The plant was a cavernous space designed around what looked like a massive bellows camera that transmitted the images in front of its lens to a three-by-three-foot sheet of emulsion-coated glass that served as its film.

Once those huge glass negatives had rendered up the positive images that would appear in print, the glass was coated for reuse. Before the recoating, the exposed emulsion had to be removed by placing the sheets of glass in vats of nitric acid. In order to protect the plant's workers from the toxic nitric acid fumes, the vats were enclosed in a roofed shed in the middle of the room, with a sink and a single naked lightbulb hanging overhead. The shed was my place of employment.

I stood facing the sink, with a vat of nitric acid on one side and a tub of clear water on the other. One by one, as quickly as I could, I hauled the sheets of glass up from the acid and placed them and my hands in the sink under running water. Lifting the glass out of the acid required not only speed but great care, since years of use had broken their edges into jagged shards, waiting for me in the vat. Four or five times a day, the glass would get me, a distinctly unpleasant experience.

Rubber gloves were no solution, since the glass would have sliced through the glove, which would have filled with nitric acid, prolonging the unpleasantness. So the only remedy, such as it was, was yanking my bloodied hand out of the acid and plunging it under the constant stream of cold water in the sink until the bleeding stopped and I could go back to the vat for more glass.

Once the glass was in the sink, I rubbed it clean of the last vestiges of coating with blocks of charcoal, then delivered it to the tub of water, and reached into the acid vat for another sheet of glass.

Everyone who has studied even elementary chemistry knows that nitric acid is a test for protein, turning it yellow; and since I was then, and am now, in large part protein, I passed my thirteenth summer with bright yellow hands, like Mickey Mouse's, which led me to spend most of my time away from the plant with my hands plunged deep into my pockets.

August approached and, as the temperature in the shed soared and my spirits plummeted, I searched desperately for, and finally came up with, a palliative to my plight. Since the Detroit public schools offered Latin, which I'd taken eagerly, I would pass the rest of the sultry, acidic summer translating every popular song I knew into Latin. In the unlikely event that anyone reading these pages wonders what Cole Porter's "Night and Day" sounds like in Latin, here, to the best of my recollection, is the kind of Gregorian pop song that shrilled (my voice hadn't yet fully changed) out of my shed hour after hour:

> *Nox et dies,*
> *Tu es unica,*
> *Sola tu sub lunam aut sub solem.*
> *Sive prope me, sive procul,*
> *Non nullius momenti est, cara,*
> *Ubi tu es,*
> *De te cogito,*
> *Dies et nox, nox et dies.*

Shut away in the shed with my acid and glass, I was unaware of the fact that, as my repertoire grew, so did the ire of my coworkers, in equal—and, in retrospect, understandable—proportion.

"**Obnoxious** *adj* [Latin *obnoxious,* fr. *ob* in the way of, exposed to + *noxa* harm] akin to *noxious,* a: physically harmful to living beings; b: constituting a harmful influence on mind or behavior." *Webster's New Collegiate Dictionary.*

The inevitable day of reckoning came when the boss wrenched the door of my shed open to inform me that the workers were threatening to strike if he didn't stop me. The rest of the summer was spent under the lightbulb, in the fumes, fuming, in silence. September and school rescued me. But my childhood was emphatically over; and there has never been a moment, from that day to this, when I haven't been (more or less gainfully) employed.

My father is not one of the heroes of this account; neither is he a villain. I'm not sure *what* he is—or, in fact, who. And that may explain a great deal. From the moment he left when I was six, he was invisible, unreachable, unknow-able. For a while I clung to the hope that he would return as miraculously as he had vanished, but that illusion eventually faded away, to be replaced by . . . nothing.

I harbor no hard feelings: I harbor no feelings at all—which may be worse. But I have no way of knowing. After a long-distance divorce, Mother never remarried, and the notion of "father" remains to this day as mysterious to me as the runic alphabet or Planck's theorem.

For understandable reasons, Mother seldom mentioned my father. Once, when I asked about him, she recalled, without rancor, but without noticeable affection, the game they'd played for years, in which she challenged him with the most obscure words she could find in the massive *Webster's Unabridged*. He defined them unerringly, she said, with the exception of a handful of sesquipedalian (a word my father would have fielded effortlessly, and Will Ferrell will have my hide for) scientific terms.

In the wake of my father's decampment, my paternal grandmother under-took to compensate by inviting me to stay for a week each summer in her apartment near Chicago's Lake Michigan beaches, a privilege I prized equally for the annual sunburn and the chance to ask her about my father. On one occasion, she recalled the crisis precipitated by her husband's death of tuber-culosis when my father was fourteen. My grandmother told me, with still evident regret, that she had been trapped: My father, as the eldest of her three sons, would have to leave high school immediately for whatever full-time employment he could find.

When she informed the school, she said, a delegation composed of the entire faculty, led by the principal, arrived at her home to tell her he was the most gifted student any of them had ever encountered, and beg her not to take him out of school.

My grandmother described my grandfather to me as a would-be inventor whose efforts to construct automobiles that would challenge the Model T had left them penniless at his death. So, despite the importuning of my father's teachers, my grandmother replied that he would have to leave school at once and become the breadwinner.

She told me that, at the end of his first week of employment—on payday!—she waited eagerly in the window for his return. As he rounded the corner, she caught her breath at the sight of a package under his arm, and when he walked in the door, her fear was confirmed: He'd spent most of his first week's salary on books.

When he pleaded that he *needed* them, she struck a bargain with him: a quarter of his salary every week for books, three-quarters for her and the family. And that, she said, was how they lived until the second brother was old enough to step forward and take the financial reins.

At that point, my grandmother told me, my father took an entrance examination for the University of Chicago, and passed it, she said with understandable pride and exaggeration, with "the highest score in the university's history."

In the midst of one of those Chicago visits, my father unaccountably appeared one morning to pick me up from Grandma for the day. I have no idea where he came from, or where he went the next day, or for that matter for the next decade, but for that one day I was in the custody of this spectral stranger. There are large chunks of my childhood that are lost in the mists of time, but I remember every moment of that odd, uncomfortable day.

He took me to the dining room of the Blackstone Hotel for lunch. There was a lot of beef on the table, more than I'd ever seen: We were, after all, in the City of the Big Shoulders, Hog Butcher for the World. But I was young, skinny and nervous, and I ate little.

From there we went to a small, nearly empty movie theater to watch a gloomy Soviet movie with subtitles. I wondered if it was meant as a reading test. The next stop was a massive department store, Carson Pirie Scott, where my father watched judiciously as the saleswoman tried one sweater after another on my bony frame until my father pronounced a tan-and-brown cardigan perfect.

Finally, at dusk when we returned my grandmother's, he presented me with a Spiral Student Drawing Book, inscribed in pencil on its cover, "Jimmie—his Book." An accomplished artist, he'd drawn an ingenious alphabet, each letter anthropomorphized into an elaborate cartoon character—Mr. Hihat H, Miss Icy I, Mr. P. Palooka P, Mr. X. Xipilus X. When I returned to Detroit, I wore the sweater nearly every day—always with the studiedly casual remark that my father had given it to me—until it was threadbare and outgrown; but "Jimmie—his Book" is still in my library, its pages browning and unheeded until it was time to write *these* pages.

My father resurfaced in San Francisco when he married the writer Georgiana Randolph Craig, and created with her the nom de plume Craig Rice, a collaboration that produced a successful series of twenty-two mystery novels, one of which, *Home Sweet Homicide,* became a popular film, coauthored by F. Hugh Herbert and Craig Rice, and starring Randolph Scott, Peggy Ann Garner and Dean Stockwell.

But San Francisco, too, turned out to be a way station. With the emergence of the Beat Generation in the 1950s, my father found the perfect calling at last.

He had always been a rebel. In his twenties in Chicago, he had been one of the founders of the Dill Pickle Club, along with several fellow members of the celebrated Chicago circle of writers that included Ben Hecht, Carl Sandburg, Edgar Lee Masters, Sherwood Anderson, Harriet Monroe and Carl Van Vechten, the openly gay (in the 1920s and -30s!) novelist, critic, photographer and early champion of African-American culture.

Inspired by the nihilistic counterculturalism of the European Dadaists, the Dill Pickle Club set out to *épater* the American cultural establishment by acting up at public events, and offering the kind of alternative forms and behavior that had made the reputations of Tristan Tzara, André Breton, Marcel Duchamp and Man Ray.

My father made a smooth transition from nihilism to political radicalism, and then, when the Beats emerged in the fifties, fell into lockstep with them—though he might have maintained that they'd finally caught up to him.

When the Craig Rice collaboration, marital and literary, ended in divorce, he made a prescient beeline to Venice Beach, a sleepy seaside corner of Los Angeles cohabited by gooney-bird oil wells, bobbing monotonously up and down, and marginal-income retirees, moving monotonously down, with a sprinkling of artists attracted by the dirt-cheap rents. The community, prior to my father's arrival, was less generously described by the *Los Angeles Times* as "a seaside slum, an artists' colony surrounded by pimps, prostitutes, drug dealers and other outlaws."

Irresistibly drawn to such an environment, my father quickly became not only an inhabitant, but its spokesperson and poster-poet. Within a year of his arrival, the newly proclaimed (by my father) Venice West was one of the capitals of the Beat movement, and almost exclusively his domain, artistically and philosophically. San Francisco belonged to Ferlinghetti, Kerouac and Ginsberg, but Venice was emphatically my father's fiefdom, where he lived with his fourth wife, Nettie, and tens of thousands of books, which overflowed every surface in his house, and filled a two-car-garage-turned-library, every book, periodical, and tape recording meticulously catalogued in the Dewey decimal system.

His audiotapes were of particular importance, since, in 1956, he had begun pioneering the oral performance of poetry in a seminal essay, "Poetry and the Vocal Tradition," in *The Nation,* declaring, "The printed poem is to the poem what the score is to a piece of music." In short: incomplete without performance.

In Venice, my father lived the life of a literary lion, surrounded by a swelling community of artists, most of whom paid greater or lesser court to him. Under his aegis, the Venice West Café opened its doors on Dudley Street in

1958, with nonstop performances and exhibitions by poets and artists, infamous and unknown no longer. On nearby Market Street, the Gas House Gallery showed, and sold, the work of Beat artists, and the Grand Hotel offered lodging to the growing number of tourists who made Venice West an obligatory stop after my father's best-selling book *The Holy Barbarians* became one of the manifestos (and, for some, the bible) of the Beat Generation.

The book offered not only a literary exploration, but a philosophical credo, in which my father coined some of the terms of art of the Beat Generation, like *disaffiliation,* which he defined as "a voluntary self-alienation from the family cult [a precept I can affirm he honored steadfastly], from Moneytheism and all its works and ways"; and *dedicated poverty,* the latter of which may have been easy for him to say (or write), but was difficult to live by, as my mother and I could affirm, since he'd practiced these principles long before he preached them in Venice West.

My father's poetry wasn't an easy read: not quite as abstruse as Wallace Stevens's, but, to borrow a term from another of my father's bags: close enough for jazz. Consider this excerpt from *Fête de l'Âne,* subtitled "For Buridan's Ass" (the animal immobilized by pure reason, starving to death between two precisely equal bales of hay), in his poetic cantata *Rainbow at Midnight:*

THE HEIROPHANT

Now in the third hour
    They lead the beast to the enthronement
    garlanded with onion, the fool's rose

See him stand, between two bales of hay,
    the epiphenomenal automaton
    and bray his blasphemous Amen
    while goliards chant the office of the day.

THE POSTULANT

If rumor is to be believed, the mark
    upon his back is cruciform,
    whereon a veiled figure rides

But whether the Virgin or the Whore
    it is not given me to see

In matters antinomian the management
    is most discreet . . . I only know

I heard a voice and saw a lifted hand
    ignite a torch and put it to the veil

I think the voice cried Reason!
    and the hand was red

A mere illusion, surely, nothing
    to excite the press, and yet I swear

The air was sharp as urine and the noise
    like noises of the newly dead.

The poem concludes with:

CHORUS OF INITIATES

Who was it won the cap and bells
    with loaded dice? And why did no one
    but the ass behold the angel of the Lord?

Or hear a voice that cried:
    "The cock shall not crow
    till thou hast denied me thrice."

No one can say. But this I know:
    In the excitement that ensued
    the ass devoured both bundles of hay
    confounding the philosophers.

My favorite of my father's poems is at once the simplest and the cleverest. It was written to honor the "craft or sullen art" of Dylan Thomas when he died in 1953, and was included in a gathering of eighty-four poems by seventy-eight of the world's leading poets, published on the tenth anniversary of Dylan's death. A few of the chosen poets elected to write their tributes in Dylan's singular style. I think my father best captured his singing voice, his reckless romance with words, the rollicking allusions and even his impish hyphenated neologisms.

The poem, bluntly titled "Death of a Poet (for Dylan Thomas)," is in three verses. These are the first and third:

Let's strike a mean and say his life
Was half as holy as a priest's. He told
His beads with rosaries of loves

And walked unfrocked among the saints
Dispensing blasphemous indulgences,
Elfin and with silver shod
A tousled head all flittered with
The pollen of wild flowers, his spoor
The scent of unicorn, an antic god.

So young, so soon. Let's think of him
As one born swaddled in a winding sheet,
His life a brief rehearsal for eternity,
As one who broke the barriers of sense
And suffered all thereafter that one must
Who goes with onagers and deathless birds
Up to that high stone seat where one dies,
Goes mad, or wakes from dreaming to come down
Word-wild, song-struck and with a poet's eyes.

It's odd how often God turns up in my godless father's canon, and how drawn he is to the language and ritual of the Catholic Church. I should have asked him about it when I had the chance.

As Venice's reputation grew—in a city with an unquenchable thirst for the Zeitgeist—my father joined in the founding of L.A.'s first counterculture publication. Now that Los Angeles had an embryonic Greenwich Village, it was time for a *Village Voice.* It was called the *Los Angeles Free Press,* and it featured in each issue an incendiary column called "Radio Free America," written by my father.

This was the point at which I reencountered him, under significantly different circumstances from our previous visit. Both our lives had changed radically, and I was now in preproduction on my first Broadway musical, *Nowhere to Go but Up,* for which I'd written the book and lyrics. The producer, the composer and I had flown to Los Angeles for a run-through of the show at the Beverly Hills home of Ernie Kovacs and his wife, Edie Adams, because Kovacs had expressed an interest in directing it.

Ernie Kovacs was an astonishingly inventive television pioneer, exploring the comedic possibilities of the still-young medium in ways that, in my opinion, haven't been surpassed to this day. Television in the sixties possessed the curiosity and courage of a typical adolescent, and so did the still impressionable public, which enthusiastically embraced Kovacs's hilarious innovations. In the midst of his meteoric rise, he'd read the material our producer had sent

him, and invited the composer and me to perform the entire show in his living room for him, his advisors, his friends and potential investors—a classic
Broadway backers' audition.

As we prepared the two-hour performance of the entire show, in which the
composer, Sol Berkowitz, would play the music at Kovacs's concert grand, and
I would perform all the parts and sing all the songs, I debated whether or not
to invite my father, who was at that moment enjoying his own vogue (and
was, therefore, easy to find). I wondered whether this was the moment and
the way to reestablish our relationship—whatever that meant—and finally
threw caution to the winds and invited him.

On the evening of the run-through, the Kovacses' vast living room was filled
to capacity with *le tout* Los Angeles. Backers' auditions were routine in New York,
but not in Hollywood, and the Kovacs house was legendary for its grandeur, so
the run-through was a hot ticket, and the guests dressed as if for a red carpet.

Into this hotbed of Hollywood luxe came my father, accompanied, as it
turned out, by a band of his disciples, all of them, like my father, beaded, sandaled, unshorn and unshaven: dropouts dropping in.

My heart sank as they passed through the riveted crowd to a central couch, on
which my father sat, next to a stylish woman who put an involuntary hand on the
jewels around her neck as his acolytes sprawled on the floor in front of them.

There was no time to reflect on what I now regarded as my folly, since, at a
nod from Ernie, the composer struck up the first notes of the score and in a
few moments I began to sing—somewhat distractedly, since, as much as I
tried to avoid looking at my father, I couldn't help noticing his disapproving
scowl as he scanned the room, like Robespierre finding himself unfelicitously
in the Court of Versailles. It's not easy to throw yourself into a lighthearted
musical comedy performance when a voice inside you is muttering, "The revolution starts here."

No matter how enthusiastically the audience reacted, laughing at the
dialogue and applauding the songs, the glacier on the couch refused to thaw—
until midway through the first act when a comedy song brought down the
house, at which point I saw my father lean closer to the bejeweled woman and
murmur something to her. She nodded, and from that moment on, my father
was at one with the audience, joining in the laughter and applause, echoed by
his dutiful disciples.

The run-through was a success. Ernie signed on to direct the show, champagne corks popped, and when my father and his group had gone, I asked the
woman who'd been next to him on the couch what he'd whispered to her. "He
said," she replied, " 'This is the sharpest social satire since Swift.' "

In fact, *Nowhere to Go but Up* was a decidedly unseditious farce about two famous prohibition cops whose antics had kept the country laughing through the dry years, but once my father had decided that they, this show and I were *au fond* antiestablishment, hence crypto-Beats, we qualified for his guiltless approval.

High on the evening's results, Ernie piled his wife, several of their friends and our team into a Rolls-Royce the size and heft of a Brink's truck, for a celebratory supper at Scandia. Seated in the front seat next to Ernie, who was waving his ubiquitous cigar as he envisioned scenes on the stage, I heard Edie, in the backseat, chattering excitedly to a friend: "I couldn't believe it! There he was! In our house!" As I turned toward the backseat, she said, "Did you *see* him?" Then, abruptly: "Wait a minute. . . . Are you related?"

"He's my, uh . . . my father."

"Oh, my God!"

At dinner, as Ernie and I planned our meetings for the next week, Edie talked of nothing but my notorious father, and before we parted that night, she'd persuaded me, against every speck of better judgment I possessed, to lead a pilgrimage of Ernie, Edie and their friends to my father's pad for one of the evenings of poetry and jazz about which he wrote and, clearly, Edie avidly read, in "Radio Free America."

I called my father, a date was set for the next Saturday night, and all through the week, my phone kept ringing at the Beverly Hills Hotel. "Hi, Jim, Edie. Jack and Felicia Lemmon heard about it and they want to come. Okay?"

"Hi, Jim. Vincente and Denise Minnelli are dying to come with us. I said, yes. Okay?"

The numbers swelled for what was clearly perceived as an illicit (therefore daring, therefore worthy) pilgrimage to a dangerous netherworld.

On Saturday evening, a line of Bentleys, Aston-Martins, Jaguars and Ferraris assembled in the driveway of the Beverly Hills Hotel, snorting and pawing the pavement as my rented Ford was brought up to lead the regal procession to Venice West.

The evening went according to plan. The guests, who had dressed up for the event at the Kovacses', dressed down for this: I especially remember Vincente Minnelli in a lemon yellow sweater and monogrammed suede shoes, leaning forward, captivated by every anapest and trochee. Several poets, notably my father, read their work, nimbly accompanied by a jazz group. The poetry and conversation were spiced with the bluntest obscenities, scatologies and profanities, commonplace now, but deliciously scandalous then.

A Spartan buffet (dedicated poverty) was offered, and when some of the guests came upon the store of strong chemicals in my father's bathroom, the atmosphere brightened noticeably. Such a quantity and spectrum of drugs was consumed that night (but not by my father, who insisted he was always high enough "on life") that I wondered how the guests, some of them "liberated," I suspect, for the first time, would fare at work in the coming days.

In the short time I was privileged to work with Kovacs, when we went to lunch or dinner, he insisted on driving his wife's car, one of the new breed of "compacts," which he preferred to his lumbering Rolls.

A week after I'd returned to New York, our producer called me with news: Ernie was dead. Late the night before, he'd apparently fallen asleep at the wheel of his wife's car, the door of which popped open when he hit a tree, throwing him out, to die instantly.

I don't know what would have happened if he'd stuck to his Rolls—and our show—but in any event, *Nowhere to Go but Up* failed. In the years since, Sidney Lumet, who directed the show in his musical theater debut, has insisted to me that his inexperience was responsible for the show's failure. But Sidney's wrong. The show failed because the book and lyrics are two-thirds of a musical, and I just hadn't written them well enough.

I've refused every request to revive *Nowhere to Go but Up,* but I'll always be grateful to it for one thing: opening night.

The show opened on a chilly November night at the historic Winter Garden Theater, where Jolson had sung and, in the years to come, *Cats* would play 7,485 performances. But on that night when my show opened, I stood alone at the back of the theater, wrapped in a tuxedo and impenetrable gloom, dead certain that *Nowhere to Go but Up* would fail, deservedly, and slink off in the direction predicted slyly, if unconsciously, in the first word of its title.

As the couples hurried past my post at the rear of the orchestra, women in evening gowns, men in black tie (in the sixties, evening dress was de rigueur at musical opening nights), I had to fight the impulse to apologize to every one of them for my inadequacies, with which the poor innocents were about to be inflicted.

As the houselights dimmed to half, in sync with my mood, the survival instinct in me stirred. On similar dark occasions in my life, I'd devised a strategy for backing away from the brink by dividing myself into two quite separate beings, one who's in the mess, and one who isn't.

By this admittedly schizoid means, I was, in theory, afforded a dispassionate, objective observer who could talk sense to me—literally. Not aloud (which would constitute legitimate schizophrenia), but silently, sanely, patiently. Over time, I'd had some interesting colloquies with this alter ego—and one transpired in the Winter Garden Theater that opening night.

"Listen to me," the Other Me said.

"I'm listening."

"No! Listen! *Really* listen."

"I'm listening!"

"Good—you ungrateful son of a bitch!"

"Ungrateful . . . ?"

"Bet your ass. If a genie had popped out of a bottle five years ago, and promised you that, one night, you'd be standing in the Winter Garden, with the orchestra warming up, and the cast throwing up, and the curtain going up in front of a house full of people who dressed up, only—*only*—because you sat down one day and wrote, 'Act One, Scene One,' would you have said, 'Yeah, but it's gotta be a hit; promise me that or forget it'? Not a chance! You know what you'd have said? *'Just get me there.'*"

On the instant, the hovering clouds broke and scudded away, and somehow on that dark November night, the sun shone in the Winter Garden Theater. My tuxedo nearly burst with the elation and goodwill, toward everyone—even me!—that was surging through me.

And as good fortune would have it, at precisely that moment, an elegant pair of latecomers, dashing from the lobby and spotting the skinny young man in a tuxedo at the top of the aisle, made a logical assumption and thrust their tickets into my hand.

My mother had imparted to me her ardor for the arts, all of them, but our limited means meant limited access. In the case of the theater, a particular enthusiasm of Mother's, a solution was found. The Cass Theatre, one of Detroit's two legitimate houses at that time, economized by employing a chief usher who then chose volunteer ushers at a nightly shape-up. The reward was that, once the house was seated, the volunteers could watch the play from whatever vantage points they found.

It took me months of hopping up and down at the back of the Friday shape-up to attract the attention of the almighty chief usher. When he pointed at you, you were entitled for that night to enter a room full of musty maroon jackets, their cuffs frayed, their brass buttons dangling, but their promise dazzling, and pick one that more or less fit. I can remember the empowerment I felt the first time I emerged from that room, an usher! It was several more months of intermittent glory, picked one Friday, ignored the next, before, the chief usher's will be done, I joined the ranks of the true elite. No more shape-up: straight to the robing room every Friday, a professional, marching imperiously past the pleading plebes.

Through my high school years, I was at the Cass every Friday night during the season, escorting the theatergoers to their seats, then taking the place I'd claimed on the third step of the mezzanine stairs, which, I'd decided, was the best seat in the house.

To this day, whatever the event or venue, I can, unassisted, take my wife and me straight to our seats, a skill that still retains for me the tremor of investiture I felt at the Cass. So, when the elegant couple impatiently handed me their tickets at the Winter Garden, I didn't hesitate for an instant. Calling on the experience of a distinguished career, I said, "This way, please," scooped up a couple of programs from the stack at the top of the aisle, and led them to their seats, delivering them with a practiced "Enjoy the show!" just as the house went dark.

As I strode back up the aisle, my feet moving in blithe cadence with the first notes of the overture, I heard a *click!* It was a ring closing, clicking shut, linking past and present in a moment of startling clarity: an unbroken line from the Cass to the Winter Garden, from the usher to the author. *I got here.* Anything more than that would be lagniappe, icing on an already generous cake.

As I reread, and relive, these words, I have to admit that this would be a much better tale if *Nowhere to Go but Up* had miraculously carried the day with the critics. But it didn't. It failed, exactly as I'd expected it would. But at least it got me there; and it provided me with one of those circular constructions, the closing of the ring, of which I'm creatively and personally fond.

There will shortly be another.

Between my sixth year and my father's last, I was in his presence no more than a dozen times. One of those encounters was occasioned by the publication of his book *The Erotic Revolution,* a follow-up to *The Holy Barbarians,* and, as its title indicates, an ebullient, explicit sexual call to arms that advocated premarital sex (or private, consensual sex anywhere, at any time, in any circumstance); the abolition of all laws restricting heterosexual or homosexual conduct; the redefinition of marriage as an "optional" state; and universally legal, free contraception and abortion.

Needless to say, my father was once again in the spotlight, and when his book tour brought him to New York, he called and asked to visit me for the first time in my home. At that time, I lived in what was for me an ideal bachelor's apartment: a studio under the oxidized-copper eaves of a French limestone town house on East Seventy-third Street, between Fifth Avenue and Madison, one of New York's stateliest streets in one of its most elegant neighborhoods.

On the appointed day, my father was late, so I went to the street to corral him in the likely event that he'd strayed. As I looked up and down the block, he appeared, beaded, sandaled and thoroughly Beat, rounding the Madison Avenue corner and heading west, his head swiveling right and left, his countenance darkening with every fashionable home he passed. When he caught sight of me, his smile was forced. We shook hands formally, as always, and I invited him into the house. Staring up at it in silent disapproval, he mounted the front steps and entered the foyer, which led, I realized with belated misgivings, to a tiny elevator, whose rosy interior looked like the velvet lining of a Victorian candy box. Decadence upon decadence. I should have taken him up the stairs.

Too late. The elevator opened not into a public hall, but directly, exclusively, into my apartment, another haut monde contrivance that left my father shaking his head. But the worst was yet to come. As he stepped into the room, my father's head turned slowly, taking in the smoked glass, the baronial fireplace, the Venetian-glass sconces and chandelier, bourgeois horror-upon-horror (I was seeing it all through his eyes now). In the smoldering silence, I could read the classic parent's plaint that was etched on his stricken face: "Where did I go wrong?"

But at that point, a kind fate intervened: He glanced up at the ceiling. New York had just had torrential rains, and since I was on the top floor, the leaking roof had devastated my ceiling, discoloring the paint and leaving sectors of it hanging in ragged sheets. The painter was unavailable for a month, so my father, neck craning, eyes gleaming, was seeing it at its leprous worst.

The lines vanished from my father's forehead and his mouth turned up in a paternal smile. "Now, *that*," he said proudly, "looks like a writer's pad."

On January 28, 1974, my father wrote a letter to me that began, "Nettie and I wish you a somewhat belated happy New Year, but we rarely send cards out. You know of course that I am working on my autobiography and I find that I lack dates and other more exact information and wonder if you could take the time to give me some information. . . . I'm writing that segment of my autobiography concerning yourself and your mother, and I would like you to give me that information about your professional and personal life that you think would be suitable for this book."

The letter was signed, in a spectacular Freudian lapse, "With love from us both, Larry and Betty."

Apart from the fact that my father had signed "Betty" for "Nettie," the letter demonstrates the fact that we never settled on a term of address. Addressing me was easy: I was Jim or, when I was little, Jimmy or, as my father spelled it on the cover of his illustrated ABCs, Jimmie. But what was he? Neither of us could ever decide. I didn't know what to call him, and he didn't know what to call himself when he wrote or phoned. "Dad"? "Your father"? We never got around to it, and he and I settled, *faute de mieux,* for the default he chose: Larry.

The first time Kedakai met him, in his Venice home, she was struck by the fact that he and Nettie had to move stacks of books to provide us with places to sit, and, of course, by his beads and long hair; but what struck her most forcibly, she said as we drove away, was the way we behaved toward each other.

"What way?"

"I don't know exactly. I can't find the words." We drove in silence, away from Venice West, toward another world: Beverly Hills. Finally, Kedakai spoke. "Two writers."

"Two what?"

"Writers. It was like you and George Plimpton, or Norman Mailer, or Kurt Vonnegut. No, not that close. Like you and Jerzy Kosinski, maybe. Shop talk."

"That's all?"

"What did you expect?"

"Well . . . father and son?"

She turned and looked at me as if I'd lapsed into Chinese. "Did *you* think so?"

"I wouldn't know. But I thought you might. You've got a family."

She reflected a moment. "Acquaintances, that's what you were. Yeah, acquaintances. But definitely two writers—talking about work, *their* work, other people's work, writing. It's very interesting to listen to," she added reassuringly.

Now *I* was silent, navigating the 405. Finally, I said, "Jesus." (For the record, my favorite curse word.)

"I don't mean to hurt your feelings," Kedakai said.

"*What* feelings?"

"*That's it!*" Kedakai exclaimed. "Exactly!"

"That's what?"

"The answer to your question about the way you behaved: What feelings?"

Shortly after my father's 1974 letter arrived, I constructed a brief and, I thought, appropriate answer: "When you get to the part about me, why not simply print your January 28 letter to me? That tells the whole story in a nutshell."

My response was ready to go: The envelope was addressed and stamped. As an afterthought, I showed it to Kedakai. She shook her head. "You can't."

"Why not?"

"It's cruel. And pointless. Really. What for?"

As these pages make clear, Kedakai is much kinder than I, and often smarter. I agreed to a moratorium and finally, in June, as Kedakai doubtless knew I would, composed an anodyne letter that may have been just as revealing in its asepticism, beginning, "Dear Nettie and Larry," promising to send him at some unspecified future date the promotional material for my new musical, which would, I said, include a bio; and closing with a collegial "Hoping that you're both well and that the biography is humming along." Writer to writer.

A month later, in the second week of July, I discovered on the obituary page of *The New York Times* that a writer of my acquaintance had died in Los Angeles, before I could send him my bio, or he could finish his autobiography. I searched for sorrow, but couldn't find it, didn't know where to *look* for it. More my failing, I'm sure, than his.

Shortly after my father's death, Nettie proposed that his library go to me. But, since I'd been deeply impressed by the strength of their relationship, I contended that she was the proper custodian of his legacy, and so the library remained with her—fortunately, as it turned out, since there was great interest in it, and a spirited bidding war among several academic institutions, won by the University of Southern California for a substantial figure that went into a trust fund from which Nettie was able to draw when she fell ill. The fund covered the costs of her care for the rest of her life, as well as a permanent USC scholarship in my father's name. And his library is intact and invaluable at USC.

In 1996, when New York's Whitney Museum and Minneapolis's Walker Museum organized an exhibition called "Beat Culture and the New America," a Whitney curator, seeking rights for the exhibition and the book that would follow it, called to ask me for the name of my father's literary executor. I said I had no idea, but would try to find out. Since Nettie had long since died, the only source I could think of was the widow of my father's brother, who said she'd investigate.

A week later, a manila envelope arrived in the morning mail. It contained a note from my aunt and two documents: Lawrence and Nettie Lipton's last wills and testaments. My father, in the kind of businesslike legal language he had mocked all his professional life as "square," had appointed Nettie his literary executor, with the stipulation that, on her death, the responsibility would pass to me. Nettie's will affirmed his wish, and as I sat at my desk, staring down at the two documents, I wondered whether this cup would have passed to me had I not turned out to be the sharpest social satirist since Swift.

Over the years I've fielded numerous requests to reprint his work, from the Whitney, of course; from the *Chicago Review* for my father's essay "The Poetry of Kenneth Rexroth"; and, of greatest significance, from the permissions manager of the Library of America, who explained that "our permissions budget allows $17.50 per page, for a total of $87.50 and two copies of the publication."

I granted the permission, and in March 2002 a check arrived in the mail, made out by the Library to James Lipton, The Estate of Lawrence Lipton, for $87.50. I raced upstairs to brandish it at Kedakai. "This is money! From my father! For me!"

I've never cashed the check. I haven't framed it either: far too melodramatic and self-pitying. It's just there, still in its envelope, in my Lawrence Lipton Executor file: the only penny of financial support I ever received from him—if one doesn't count the cost of a cherished tan-and-brown sweater from Carson Pirie Scott.

Mother lived a full, productive and, in all the important respects, triumphant ninety-four years. When I moved to New York, so did she, where she had an outstanding career as second in command of B. Altman Company's prestigious Rare Book, Map and Fine Binding Department on Fifth Avenue until she was in her seventies; then continued to preside serenely over a mini–literary salon for her friends and mine in her apartment near Riverside Drive.

She was so popular in our circle that a hundred of her admirers showed up when Kedakai and I invited them to celebrate her eightieth birthday in our home, where composer Cy Coleman and I serenaded her with songs from the musical we were writing—which prompted Lena Horne, who rarely consented to sing at her own parties and, in my experience, *never* sang at anyone else's, to say to me, "I'd like to sing for your mother."

Cy stayed at the piano, and after a moment's consultation with him, Lena smiled at my mother, who was seated at the far end of the grand piano, and began to sing, "Don't know why, there's no sun up in the sky—stormy weather . . ."

That began the parade. Burton Lane played and sang songs from his scores for *Finian's Rainbow* and *On a Clear Day You Can See Forever.* Sheldon Harnick, halfway through his lyric for "Sunrise, Sunset," from *Fiddler on the Roof,* forgot the words, and from a nearby couch, Joanna Simon's operatic soprano picked it up without missing a beat. Tammy Grimes sang Brecht/Weill. Betty Comden and Adolph Green sang—no, performed; just singing was never enough for them—classics they'd written with Leonard Bernstein, Jule Styne and Cy Coleman.

It went on for hours. For Mother.

When her career at Altman's was cut (in her view) short, she volunteered to teach remedial reading in the New York public school system, which she did industriously until a school supervisor found her gasping at the top of several flights of stairs and, with undisguised regret (and a public ceremony to celebrate her service), sent her into a second retirement at the age of ninety.

All her life, Mother had an unshakable penchant for worrying (which somehow coexisted compatibly with the sturdy optimism and penetrating sense of humor that saw her through some menacing storms). The story was told in the family that she once walked into a roomful of relatives wearing a dark frown and, when someone asked, "What's wrong, Betty?" replied, "I'm worried about something, but I can't remember *what*." To which a sister replied, "That's all right, Betty. As long as you're worried."

On May 7, 1980, I produced at the White House an entertainment to inaugurate the independent cabinet status of the Department of Education. My proposal for the event, which President Carter enthusiastically endorsed, was to invite the participating artists to dedicate their performances to the teachers who had most influenced them, and to bring the teachers with them, to be honored that night at the performance, each one with a Presidential Citation, presented onstage by the artist and the president.

Because President Carter admired Loretta Lynn, and she'd appeared in his Inaugural Gala, I invited her back to Washington for this occasion, with her favorite teacher. A week after she'd agreed to come, she called me, near tears, to "confess" that she shouldn't have accepted the invitation because the truth was she'd never been to school at all.

"But someone must have taught you *something*," I insisted.

"Well, sure," she said.

"Who?" I asked, suspecting I knew the answer.

"Well . . . Mama . . ."

"Bring her," I said; and the president wholeheartedly approved the decision.

On the night of the performance, in the course of the cavalcade of illustrious poets and painters and dancers and musicians and their mentors, Loretta's turn came. She performed with her usual canny simplicity, then invited her mother to the stage, where the citation was read and the framed presidential document was presented to her. Each of the mentors had spoken, and now it was Clara Webb's turn. She stammered once, then raised the citation to shield her face from the audience, tears welling. President Carter stepped forward and took her in his arms as the audience cheered her, and Loretta beamed. It was that kind of evening and, during the four years that I was periodically in its service, that kind of White House.

As I'd prepared the Education celebration, I'd reported to the president that my mother was by any sensible measure a distinguished educator, and he'd insisted she be invited. Late that evening, after the performance and the dinner, with the Marine Concert Band playing, and hundreds of guests milling about the White House, Kedakai and I lost track of Mother and finally found her sitting alone on a brocaded couch outside the Red Room, frowning at Rosalynn, who was posing for a picture with two of the evening's artists, poet Richard Wilbur and sculptor Louise Nevelson, under the Kennedy portrait.

"What's wrong?" I asked Mother.

"I'm worried."

"Of course, but about what?"

"Rosalynn, having to clean up after all these people."

As I reread the pages of this chapter, it's odd how I, who was so confident in the second paragraph of this undertaking that "this book won't be about me," have dwelt so resolutely on recollections that seem to violate that pledge.

Arguably, even this chapter is fundamentally about the promised "anybody elses" who have shaped me, but I'm too present in it for my taste. The only excuse I can offer is that it's harder than I thought it would be to confine myself to the shadows. On *Inside the Actors Studio,* since I'm responsible for the edit, I can remove myself with a flick of the editor's wrist. It's not as simple in a book that includes chapters of remembrance like this one, where occurrences and reflections that I thought had been safely dispatched to oblivion come sidling back, demanding attention. For example, Detroit, a benign and honorable place, turns out to be, for me, "Detroit," an unsettling, quotation-marked concept.

But maybe there's hope of deliverance, even for as stubborn a case as mine.

In the fall of 2001, a delegation arrived in New York from Wayne State University, which was founded in Detroit in 1868, and is today one of the nation's foremost urban educational institutions. With thirty-three thousand students, it is the equivalent in the Midwest of the City University of New York. The delegation was led by Linda Moore, dean of the College of Fine, Performing and Communication Arts, and their principal purpose in coming to New York, she explained, was to meet with me, an announcement that came as a surprise, since I'd long since reconciled myself to the fact that the university had utterly forgotten me.

In the seventies, my cousin Liz had sent me the Wayne State catalogue, which contained, as a motif on nearly every page, linguistic terms from my book *An Exaltation of Larks,* without attribution. As I wrote the admissions director, the terms did in fact have an author for whom, a cursory review of their records would have revealed, the university could take credit. My letter wasn't acknowledged.

So, it was with understandable curiosity that I sat down to lunch with the Wayne State delegation in a restaurant near the university where I now served as a dean. Wayne State's former apathy had apparently given way to interest as the goal of their mission was revealed: an invitation to join the governing board of the College of Fine, Performing and Communication Arts.

From the boot to the boardroom, at an improbable stroke. The delegates explained enthusiastically how I would be brought to Detroit for periodic meetings . . . and that was when their voices began to fade, crowded out by other voices, other times.

I hadn't been back to Detroit for twenty-five years—for reasons I couldn't begin to explain to Dean Moore and her colleagues. So, I sat across the table from them, impaled on the horns of an exquisite dilemma: On the one hand, the thought of returning regularly raised specters I'd banished with difficulty and had no intention of resurrecting; on the other hand, how could I explain why I was spurning their goodwill without sounding, legitimately, like an insufferable snob or an ungracious boor?

My lunch remained untouched as they pressed their suit, singing the university's praises until, ridden with guilt at this waste of their time, I raised a hand and stumbled through a makeshift explanation of my misgivings that was interrupted by the dean's gentle question, "Unhappy memories?"

I clutched at the helping hand. "It's not Detroit's fault. Good city, good people . . . it's just . . . me. You understand . . ." I ended lamely, hopelessly.

"Of course."

"Isn't there *anything* you miss?" one of the delegates asked.

A moment's reflection yielded, "Yes. Sanders hot fudge and Vernors ginger ale."

The luncheon ended in an amicable standoff: They were gracious in defeat, and I walked back to my office, awash in self-loathing and relief. A week later, a large box was delivered to my desk. It was packed with jars of Sanders hot fudge (incomparably smooth, from the Detroit ice-cream emporium that invented the ice-cream soda 130 years ago) and cans of Vernors ginger ale (distinctively aromatic and incomprehensibly unavailable in New York).

The care packages kept coming, uninsistently, with no strings attached, but bearing an unmistakable, though always unspoken, message.

Then, a few months later, Dr. Irvin Reid, Wayne State's president, called to inform me that the board of governors had voted—unanimously, for the first time in his experience at the university, he said—to award me an honorary Ph.D.

Obviously forewarned by the delegation, he added that all I had to do was appear at the commencement in Detroit's Cobo Hall, receive the doctorate, deliver a commencement address to twenty thousand graduates and guests, and head straight for the airport.

Fed up by now with my temperamental antics, I wasn't about to waste another moment of Wayne State's time. "I'd be honored," I said.

I assumed that by that bold stroke I'd finally crossed the Rubicon—or at least the Detroit River—until the middle of the night before my flight when Kedakai shook me awake because I was screaming, "No! No!" I sat up in bed, awake, aghast, the nightmare still vivid: I was alone in a room. A man approached me and asked casually, "Is that window open?" I said yes, and he walked nonchalantly to it and jumped out, which triggered my horrified cry.

The two characters weren't hard to identify, since I've often appeared in a dual role in my dreams, as myself and as myself observing myself (a sign, perhaps, of incurable solipsism). In my twenties, I had a frequently recurring dream in which I lay in bed in my bedroom on Hague Avenue. The room was exact and unmistakable. The dream always began as I woke in it, opened my eyes and didn't move. All around the bed, on straight-backed chairs, everyone I would see that day (that was a given) sat stiffly, silently, staring fixedly ahead in what appeared to be a choreographed ritual. At the foot of the bed stood one more person, who ceremoniously handed me the mask I would wear that day. Once the mask was between me and the eyes of the figure at the foot of the bed, who was manifestly the other I, offering today's disguise, I reached up and surreptitiously slipped off the mask I was already wearing—the one that prevented even me from ever seeing me—and slid the day's mask into place.

A curiously hermetic nature for someone who would ultimately make a career of trying to draw others out, to the point where the French magazine *Télérama* described *"la méthode de l'omniscient doyen"* as *"mi-confession, mi-analyse* (half-confession, half-analysis)." My only defense is the one offered by the character in Rabelais's *Gargantua and Pantagruel* who, when accused of not following his own advice, sniffs, "I am like the signpost that points the way to Paris without ever going there itself."

I have a weakness for untestable theories, one of which is that somewhere in every single person on this planet resides the same genetic fragment that animates the poetry of Eliot, Frost or Milton. I believe, in short, that a poet lurks in everyone. The proof? Persuade any truck driver, electrician, vagrant, banker, convenience store clerk, doorman, accountant or cop to describe his or her dreams, and you'll be witness to an intricate web of wildly imaginative constructions that, however surreal, are rich in metaphor, synecdoche and metonymy, the vital stuff of poetry. Tossing words and ideas about like a manic juggler, swapping images at warp speed, jumbling fears and hopes, then reinventing them in vivid flashes and revelatory strokes, the dreamer may never have heard of the poetic secret of compression, but at night when the unconscious rules, he or she wields it with the ease and grace of Keats at the Urn, Matisse at the easel, or Federer at the baseline.

The conviction that the most sensitive and compassionate of arts unites us all gives me hope for the race when the headlines don't.

A few hours after the nightmare, despite its shrill warning, I jumped through the yawning window into an airplane bound for Detroit. Detroit is unmistakable from the air because of Woodward Avenue, which bisects it, running due north from the river—and Canada, which is, illogically, south of Detroit because of the way Ontario slides under the thumb of the Michigan mitten.

My cousins Jean and Ann met me at the airport and took me directly to a cousins dinner, a sizable affair, since not only did my mother's parents have eleven children, but so, give or take a kid or two, did the rest of my grandparents' generation. It goes without saying that the dinner featured, without prompting, Vernors ginger ale and Sanders hot fudge.

Late that night, Ann drove me to the Detroit Athletic Club, where the university had arranged for me to stay. When I lived in Detroit, the DAC, off-limits to everyone but its elite membership, was as remote and exotic as Camelot, especially since I swam on my high school team and the DAC was reputed to house the city's best pool, a supposition I couldn't corroborate since I'd never been privileged to test the waters. But now, through the vagaries of time and fate, I was being welcomed to the DAC by a smiling desk clerk who handed me a thick packet, which I assumed contained instructions to the gym, the dining room . . . the pool.

In my room, I prepared for bed, then glanced again at the packet I'd dropped on the desk. Maybe there were messages from Wayne about tomorrow's ceremony. I opened the packet and started. On top of the pile, a letter that had been forwarded from my office was crowned by a blue, white and red insignia incorporating France's new, younger Marianne, over the words *Liberté * Égalité * Fraternité* and *République Française*.

Below that, *Ministère de la Culture et de la Communication* crossed the page in an elegant cursive font.

At the left were two words: *Le Ministre.*
Then:

Monsieur,
J'ai le très grand plaisir de vous annoncer que je viens de vous décerner
le grade de chevalier dans l'ordre des Arts et des Lettres.

The letter, explaining that knighthood in the Order of Arts and Letters was awarded to honor cultural contributions in France and the world, was signed by the minister of culture, Catherine Tasca.

Within moments I was on the phone to Kedakai, who, in a patent effort to buoy my frequently flagging spirits (and make sure I got on that plane), had been jollying me for days about the doctorate. Knowing I was now in the line of fire, she was unusually cheery. "Hi, Doc!"

"Forget the 'Doc,'" I growled. "It's 'Sir' to you. I've been knighted."

The next morning I was picked up by Rick Rogers, the former secretary of The New School, who'd helped establish our drama school there and was now president of a flourishing school, the College for Creative Studies, in the vibrant cultural center that contains the Detroit Institute of Arts and the Wayne State campus. At his invitation, I was to tour his campus, and lunch with him at the DAC before the commencement.

His college, which, not surprisingly, had a substantial automotive-design component, and was strongly supported by Detroit's auto manufacturers, contained vast, airy classrooms filled with students sculpting automobile-size, avant-garde works of art that were in fact swooping, lunging mock-ups of the cars we may one day drive.

When we finished the tour, an hour remained before our luncheon reservation, and Rick asked, "Anywhere you'd like to go? Anything you'd like to see?" My answer was instantaneous and as unexpected by me as by him: "Yes!"

"Where?"

"Can we go someplace in your car?"

"Sure. Where do you want to go?"

"North on Woodward. I'll direct you."

As we drove north, the years spooled away with each passing block. Some landmarks had vanished, replaced for long stretches by sullen emptiness on Woodward's barren, abandoned flanks. But once we crossed Grand Boulevard, the familiar sights snowballed. To the west, the spire of the Fisher Building rose, a changeless monument to every Saturday afternoon of my childhood in the picture palace it bestrode: the Fisher Theatre, its marquee still promising marvels, but living ones now: It had replaced the Cass and Shubert Lafayette as Detroit's legitimate theater. As we swept by it, I wondered how it acquired its ushers.

Now every block was familiar, remarkably unchanged, many of the small buildings looking tired and discouraged; but they had looked tired and discouraged then. Inner city then, inner city now. Sacred, bleeding heart. *Plus ça change . . .*

"Slow down," I said.

Euclid Avenue . . . Philadelphia . . . Hague.

"Turn right."

Every brick was in place, every tree. As we crossed John R, I wondered why it had never occurred to any of us to ask, "John R *who?*"

Half a block later, I said, "Stop." I got out and stood on the sidewalk. Rick emerged on his side and leaned on the roof of the car, silent. "This is where I lived," I said. "Two eighty."

Rick and I stared at the house. It was smaller than I'd remembered, of course: I'd grown. But in every other respect, it was unchanged: the wooden porch, the Doric columns, the brief lawn in front, the shrubbery, the sidewalk where the handle of my Radio Flyer wagon had bounced back and gashed my forehead, occasioning my first stitches and the scar above my right eyebrow that Michele O'Callaghan, *Inside the Actors Studio*'s makeup person, camouflages before each shoot.

I looked up and down the street. It was, if anything, more genteel than it had been then. Detroit, like every aging industrial city in the post–World War II years, grew like an amoeba, outward, in suburbs, as its aspiring middle class fled the inner city, ceding it to an economic class on its own trajectory up from a lower depth.

The result was the urban demographic doughnut, minority at its center, white in its outer circle, with suburbs spawning rings of exurbs for those prosperous enough to flee the suburbs, in a never-ending cycle of escape and exclusion.

When Mother and I lived on Hague Avenue, Detroit's inner city was already in transition. On Hague itself, and on all the streets around us, upwardly mobile blacks were eyeing and buying the homes that upwardly mobile whites were leaving. Some of the neighborhoods to the east of us were already blighted then, filling with people trapped in a cycle of poverty that discouraged aspiration.

Now, on this balmy day in the spring of 2002, Rick and I stood in the center of an entirely black community that radiated out for miles until it fetched up at the suburban wall that contained it.

As I stood silent on my peak in Darien, a black woman came distractedly down the block and started up the steps of the house next to 280 (the Faust house once upon a time), and stopped abruptly as she saw us standing stock-still, anomalous, on the sidewalk. After eyeing us in silence for a moment, she came to a decision and descended the steps to ask us, politely but plainly, "What are you doing here?"

"I used to live here. This was my home." She was silent. "I haven't seen it in a very long time."

Her body language sent a less guarded signal. "Has it changed?"

"Not much. I'm surprised. The whole street. It looks the same—maybe a little better. You're taking care of it."

She surveyed the street, studying it through our alien eyes, then turned back to us, indicating the north-south street to the east. "Don't go across Brush. That's nothing but drugs and guns. They see you there, you won't come out."

"Thanks." I looked up at 280. "I'd like to go inside. Who lives there?"

"A minister."

"Oh." I started toward the porch.

"A Muslim minister." I looked at her. "He's not there. I saw him go out." Her words were uninflected, but I came back to the sidewalk.

"I'd love to see the backyard." She shrugged, friendly, noncommittal, and started back up her steps. "Thanks for the information," I said. She nodded and went into the Faust house (hers now, of course, but old habits die hard). I looked at Rick. "Want to see our backyard?"

"Sure."

We went up the walk that flanked 280 on the east. I glanced at the house to the left—Renee (not Renée, Ree-ny) Smith's house, and at her bedroom window, opposite mine, where we used to lean on the sills and chat about whatever eight-year-olds chat about.

The backyard was precisely as I remembered it: a small square of grass, bordered by flowers and fences, and intersected by a narrow cement walk that led to the back fence and the alley where the tougher neighborhood boys hunted rats in garbage bins by flinging open the lids and spearing the startled animals with sharpened broomsticks *pour le sport*. One makes do.

Just behind the house, I stopped and pointed at the back fence. "You know what it meant to hit a homer over that fence?" I studied it. "Now we could flip quarters over it." Rick nodded. I pointed up at a window above the kitchen door. "That was my room. There used to be a porch outside it. We called it the verandah. I guess it fell down." I moved closer to the house and tried to look into the dining room, but it was in deep shadow.

Returning to the front of the house, I elected to go up on the porch and, cupping my hands around my eyes, peered into the living room in search of the fireplace where my creative accounting had made for some bountiful Christmases. But the room was too dark to reveal itself, and as a passing car slowed at the spectacle of this outsider spying on an innocent citizen, I backed away from the window.

At the top of the porch steps, I looked down at Rick, waiting patiently on the sidewalk. "Two more minutes?"

"Sure."

Rick got into the car. I stood on the porch, not sure what I was going to do with my two minutes—or why I wanted it. I'd seen all I could see. Two eighty Hague hadn't disappointed. It was so remarkably unchanged that I could imagine turning around, twisting the knob on the front door and walking into the musty little foyer where the mail waited each morning, then pushing open a second door and turning left into what the family called the library because it contained tall, standing bookcases with heavy leaded-glass doors that used to open with a promising quiver on the mysteries and marvels of my childhood, including and especially some ancient French primers from which I labored to teach myself French. Sometimes I stood on my verandah, the primer in hand, declaiming to the empty backyard in the tongue I assumed this magical language sounded like.

Now, a lifetime later, on the front porch, abruptly, still not knowing why, I sat down on the top step, precisely as and where I'd sat countless times when I was six, seven, eight, staring out at Hague Avenue. What I saw then, I saw now: the line of houses across the street; the tree in front of 280, which was always home base for hide-and-seek; the broken, bumpy sidewalk that had uncomplainingly borne our streaking bikes and cheeky chatter. . . .

Then, suddenly, I knew why I'd come back to Hague Avenue this morning. It turned out that I was looking for something, and, sitting on the step, I found it. In a few hours Wayne State, my university, would confer on me the honorary degree of Doctor of Humane Letters—and last night I learned that the Republic of France had invested me with the title of *chevalier de l'ordre des Arts et des Lettres*—two data that pale to invisibility next to the achievements and honors of my countless betters—but, to me, at this moment, perched on the top step of the porch at 280 Hague, man and boy together again, together *at last,* gazing tranquilly at the street with our arms over each others' shoulders, they were the last links in an unbroken chain, completing one more circle, from me on the porch at 280 Hague once upon a time . . . to us on the porch at 280 Hague now. We got here.

Click.

The ring closed.

I stood up, walked to the curb, got into the car with Rick and drove away from Hague. But not from the past, because I didn't have to anymore.

CHAPTER Four

66*Beginners, please!*

—The British equivalent of America's
"Places, please," signaling curtain time

One of the questions I frequently ask my guests on *Inside the Actors Studio* is "When did it start for you? What was the spark?" The answer is often a grade school play, with the initiate proclaiming, "I am the Spirit of Leafy Green Vegetables: eat me daily."

But some of the beginnings are more intricate—and interesting.

Dustin Hoffman began his career as Tiny Tim in Dickens's *A Christmas Carol.* In his account of it on *Inside the Actors Studio,* he told us, "I'm supposed to get on the table with the crutches and say, 'God bless us, every one.' There was a kid in the ninth grade who was a senior, Bob Schwartz. He's in the show, and he says, 'I dare you to get up on the table and say, "God bless us all, God damn it."'"

"Did you do it?"

"Yeah. Got suspended again."

Anthony Hopkins told us that his father, denouncing him as a layabout, ordered him out of the house, so, "I walked into the YMCA one night. They were rehearsing a play. I asked if I could join in. They gave me a part in a sort of religious play. I played a saint. My first line ever spoken onstage was, 'Blessed are the meek, for they shall inherit the earth.' And I felt very comfortable onstage. I thought, 'Well, maybe I'll do this for a living.'"

For Barbra Streisand, inspiration came through television, specifically, commercials. "My cousin Laurel and I would call people up from the phone book. And I would say, 'If you can answer this question, we will send you a thousand dollars.' And so we would ask them questions and then I'd say, 'I have to interrupt you now and do a commercial.' And the commercial was Fab. Remember Fab soap? I remember speaking to this woman; I said, 'Do you use Fab?' And she said, 'Oh, I use Fab, and the suds go all over my floor and it's just wonderful!' Imagine that? The suds go all over her floor, she's telling me. She liked Fab. We used to send them fake money in an envelope."

In time, theater replaced television in Barbra's expanding world: "The first time I ever went to New York to see a show, I was fourteen, and I wanted to see *The Diary of Anne Frank.* I remember that moment, coming out of the subway for the first time, coming into New York City from Brooklyn, having never been there before. That corner of Fiftieth Street and Broadway, that subway station—I came from the IRT—and, my God, I'm going to the theater! We saw Susan Strasberg. The ticket was a dollar ninety-eight. I sat up in the top row of the balcony, and thought, 'I could play that part. I'm Jewish. What else *is* there? You're Jewish. Play the part.'"

Given Jane Fonda's lineage, it should come as no surprise that her epiphany took place on the French Riviera, from a source unlike any other in the history of the series: "I went swimming with Greta Garbo, skinny-dipping, to be exact. Is that the summer you're referring to?"

"Yes. Anybody who saw Greta Garbo naked has caught my attention."

"She's so Swedish, she just got down to the bottom of the stairs in the freezing cold Mediterranean and took off her bathrobe—and she was naked. She was beautiful and athletic, but she wasn't perfect! And I thought, my God, you can be loved even though it's not like *Playboy.* And I just remember treading water there and her looking at me and saying in that Ninotchka voice, 'Are you going to be an actress?' And me saying, 'No, no, I'm not. I'm not talented.' And her saying, 'Well, you're pretty enough.' I almost drowned."

Billy Crystal busked for coins in his living room: "All the relatives would go around and give you change. It was a rough room. You'd put the money on your head. And when your head was filled up, the show was over."

"But how would it stick?"

"You were sweaty and you'd just go . . ." He slapped remembered coins on his forehead. "A good show was a dollar fifty. If you got a dollar fifty, you were doing really well."

Al Pacino was inspired by Ray Milland in *The Lost Weekend.* "I didn't know what I was seeing, of course, but I was taken with the energy of it, the excitement. He's an alcoholic and he hid the bottle somewhere. He goes into a frantic search for it. I found that very interesting as a five-year-old. And I would perform it."

"For whom?"

"For anyone who would listen. My mother was always dragging me out, saying, 'Sonny, show these people *The Lost Weekend,* do *The Lost Weekend* for them.' And I would do *Lost Weekend,* this frantic search. I never understood why they were laughing. They were looking at a five-year-old do it—but I was very committed."

A few years later, Al began making grand entrances when he came home from the movies: "I would come home every night and perform something. I'd open the door . . . till one time I fell. I was on a first-floor fire escape. I fell on my head as a nine-year-old. It explains a lot."

But, for Al, the defining moment arrived in a gloomy theater in his native Bronx: "It was seeing Chekhov's *The Seagull,* by a wandering troupe of players. They were at a place called, I think, the El Zamir Theater. It was an old vaudeville house. And it sat about three thousand people and there were about twenty of us in the audience, and there was this troupe, performing *The Seagull.* I must've been fourteen, fifteen. I was stunned by it. I was shocked. I was transformed, and . . . it was over. It changed me.

"And then, I went to school. It was at Forty-sixth Street, the High School of Performing Arts, and I went to get a malted milk or a coffee, and there behind the counter waiting on me, was the star of the show, *The Seagull.* Ain't that the way it is? Right?

"And I looked at that guy and I said, 'Man, I *saw* you!' Well, he couldn't believe it. 'I saw you in *The Seagull* and you were great!' He said, 'Oh, thank you, thank you!' It was like meeting a great athlete or something."

On *Inside the Actors Studio,* Michael Caine recalled that, when I produced a Royal Gala Performance in 1985 to celebrate Bob Hope's eighty-second birthday, Michael came onstage at London's Lyric Theatre to address Bob and Prince Philip in the Royal Box: "There was this little Methodist preacher called Reverend Butterworth who built this youth club in my area, and he used to drag guys like me off the streets to come and do something. It wasn't just to play Ping-Pong or anything like that. There were amateur dramatics, which, of course, is where I got the whole thing.

"Bob used to come and do a show at the Prince of Wales. He was from Elton in Kent, and the money from that show used to come to our club. When I was fourteen, I was the boy designated to welcome Bob to the club—and take the check off him. When he gave me the check, he said, 'If I'd known how much money this kid was gonna make, I'd have adopted him.'"

Martin Short told us that he'd begun with a television show, of sorts, in Canada, when he was fourteen: "It took place in my attic. I had an applause record." When our students laughed, Short glared at them. "And I suppose fourteen-year-olds out there didn't have applause records?" He amended it. "It wasn't a *real* applause record. It was *Sinatra at the Sands.* I would take the section after he finished 'Chicago.'"

He cupped a hand over his head. "I had one of those gooseneck lamps, like so—and suddenly, I was lit! I'd come out, open with a song. Meanwhile outside, people my age were going, 'Oh, the whole world's watching'—you know, protesting Vietnam. And I'm in my attic going, 'Wonder why it's such a cuckoo day.'"

"When did your show air?"

"I couldn't do a show every week because it would conflict with my film career."

"I understand."

"It's so sad to admit. Tragically sad. I would alternate with Andy Williams. Eight thirty, Mondays, NBC. Andy wasn't happy about it, but I was a bigger star."

For Mike Myers, the first inkling came when he was four: "It's my first memory. I've wanted to do this my whole life. Kurt Vonnegut talks about having a sense of your life. Your peephole opens, like an iris opening in a film. Your first memory is kind of like, whoo, here I am! And since that time, I've wanted to do this."

For Martin Scorsese, of course, the revelation was cinematic: "In 1950, my father took me to see a film called *The Magic Box*. It was made for the fiftieth anniversary of British cinema. Robert Donat played the inventor of cinema in England. And in that film he shows Maria Schell the persistence of vision: that you could draw little figures on the edge of a book. And if you move an arm just a little bit more in each drawing, and then you flip them, it looks as if they're moving. So I started to do that, on the telephone books. In 1950, there were some wonderful television shows, and I started drawing my versions of those on panels."

"You were storyboarding."

"Storyboarding, yes."

Russell Crowe's parents were movie caterers in Australia: "I visited a lot of movie sets and TV sets when I was young. When you're a little kid—we're talking 1969, 1970—it was hugely exciting, you know. The props guy would lend you a helmet for half a day, and, man, I was off! Give me that helmet. I'm in the bush! It was really interesting for me as a kid 'cause I'd get to explore the sets and start to realize that not every door went somewhere, you know? I was in this whole artificial world, and that's wow! That's cool!

"They gave me a part in this show *Spyforce*. There's footage of me as a six-year-old, wearing a football jumper from a team called South Sydney, which is red and green stripes. So, it's like, you can't miss me—you know what I mean? I can remember what was going through my head, but to see my face and see whether or not that process as a six-year-old was actually coming to the surface is very interesting. And funnily enough, it *was*—which is quite weird 'cause I remember having very, very serious thoughts about it, you know? What was the history of my character and all that sort of stuff." He shot a glance at the grinning students. "I'm serious!"

Since UCLA didn't give a journalism degree, Carol Burnett settled for joining *The Daily Bruin,* and majoring in English. "And then, I was just drawn to the theater department—so I could take the playwriting courses. That would be my excuse, but I knew down deep I really wanted to get up and be onstage. Then, I did a one-act which was a student-written. It was about a hillbilly family, so all I did was draw from my great-grandmother and my grandmother. I played a hillbilly woman, and they laughed a whole lot, and . . . I just felt at home.

"All of a sudden, I was popular, which I hadn't been. I was kind of a nerd in junior high and high school, and really shy—and now guys were coming up and asking me for dates, and I thought, 'This is a really nice kind of thing that's happening here.' They said, 'Gee, you were funny, and we liked you,' and, oh, I just started to bloom. *I* started to like me."

"You've described that discovery as being a drug, a high. To hear people laugh."

"It was. It's an amazing adrenaline. It's healing. There's a healing power that happens to you, and also happens to an audience, there's no question about it."

Christopher Reeve, heroic in his wheelchair, in his first public appearance after the accident that had left him a quadriplegic, spoke to our students—eloquently—on each exhalation of his respirator: "What started it for me, I was sitting in a science class in fourth grade. And somebody came from the Princeton Savoy Arts. They were looking for somebody to sing a townsboy in *Yeomen of the Guard.* I had a fairly decent voice when I was a little kid—I don't know what happened to it—but as a boy soprano I was pretty decent, and I raised my hand—to get out of science class more than anything else.

"I auditioned and I was accepted, and suddenly I found myself over at the McCarter Theatre in the middle of this wonderful company. In one week, you could see an actor like George Hearn play the lead in Pirandello's *Enrico IV,* and George in *Of Mice and Men,* then play Malvolio. All in the same week! And these transformations, these complete characterizations of such different style, were magic to me and I wanted to be part of it."

Philip Seymour Hoffman, in whom *Inside the Actors Studio* takes a modest but justifiable proprietary interest because he was invited to our stage before the public—or the profession—had realized he was one of the most remarkable actors of his generation, identified the person who had ignited the spark: "It was my mother. When I was in seventh grade I started going to a theater called Geva in Rochester, New York. It's now kind of a prominent Equity house, but then they used to bring in actors from New York and put on new plays and American classics. The first play I saw there was *All My Sons*. It was the first professional play I actually saw. They might've been awful, but I was in seventh grade and I thought they were brilliant. I thought the whole thing was brilliant. And I couldn't understand why everyone didn't just do this every night. It was amazing! These people are up there going through all this stuff for our benefit? There was something so extraordinary about that!

"So my mom would take me. I became the season-ticket holder with her. I was really short at the time, and it was general seating, and she was a notoriously late person. She would show up at like five of eight, and the people would be lined up on the street. I was about four eleven till I was in eighth grade, so, I'd wheedle my way through everybody to the door of the theater. They'd open the door and I'd run in, sit in the front row, center, and slap a *Playbill* down next to me. The whole theater would fill up, then my mom would walk in and sit in the front row, center, next to her little son."

Tom Hanks also looked back to someone who had lit the creative spark for him, albeit inadvertently. When I asked him, "Who is Dan Finmore?" he replied, "Dan Finmore! Oh, my!"

"Why 'Oh, my'?"

"Dan was one of those guys in high school who was good at everything he attempted. He was Dracula in *Dracula*. The title role! I was a classically disinterested sophomore, not good at much of anything. And because I knew Dan, I went to see the play. I was sitting out there with a bunch of parents—and then Dan walked out in a cape, and I just thought, 'Boy, I wanna do that!' Even before anybody said any lines, I wanted to be allowed access to the inner sanctum of whatever was going on up there."

"That was the turning point?"

"Yeah. If a moment of absolute selfish envy can be viewed as the turning point. I didn't even know what it entailed, really. I just wanted that special attention."

Gabriel Byrne's reflections on our stage were thoroughly, unmistakably Irish in tone and tenor: "I was always in awe of actors. Always. For some reason, I associated magic with actors. I remember seeing a very famous old Irish actor—I was a student—and he was almost blind, walking down Baggett Street, dressed in a jet-black wig, with makeup on, and a silver cane and long yellow gloves and a little flower in his lapel. And he had one of those old, Victorian actor-voices. I remember thinking to myself, '*That's* an actor. That's what an actor *looks* like. That's what an actor *is:* something different, some-thing strange, something magical, something that ordinary people *aren't.'*

"I think life and acting are two very different things. I think acting is one thing, and life is another, and one shouldn't be lived at the expense of the other. In a strange, bizarre way, it's almost the wrong profession for people who go into it. I don't mean that in any facetious way. I think of actors as chil-dren in a way. And a great many of them are like wounded children, who seek, at some deep level, an approval, some kind of universal approval. So, it took me a long time to make that decision that I would become an actor. And, it's taken me a long time to embrace the fact that I *am* an actor."

In my case, which I readily, emphatically, admit is in no way comparable in quality or degree to the cases cited here, the creative impulse was present—in my three dreadful twelve-year-old novels, on the third step of the mezza-nine stairs at the Cass Theatre—but effectively checked in Detroit by my growing resolve to set off on a path antipodean to that trodden by my father.

The arts, while an acceptable avocation, would never do as a vocation. By the age of fifteen there was simply an unvoiced, unexamined assumption that I would pursue a profession that was sure to raise my father's eyebrows and ire: the law. There was never a moment when I made a conscious link between my vocational choice and my father. Year after year, he was as far from my thoughts as from my presence. It's only now, in retrospect, as I prepare these recollections for a public forum, that the whole picture comes into focus.

Once I'd been released from the acidic confines of my shed, I moved up professionally to the position of copyboy in the cavernous, clamorous city room of the *Detroit Times,* one of the three newspapers Detroit could then boast, this one the local incarnation of the powerful Hearst empire. The tele-types of the three main wire services, AP, UP and INS, were confined to a far corner of the city room, in order to muffle their constant clack and the clang-ing bells that would summon a copyboy to distribute the breaking news to the appropriate desks.

A small nearby room was the exclusive domain of a single teletype: the Hearst wire, which was, I was given to understand, connected directly to San Simeon, the California Taj Mahal of the eponymous William Randolph Hearst. As the wire service teletypes banged and rattled and shook in their room, the Hearst wire lay majestically dormant, waiting for the moment when the western giant stirred, at which point it would shudder to life and begin to disgorge a communication that always began with the compelling words, "Chief says . . ."

Even its clanging bells were different, announcing in a distinctive, insistent cadence that the chief had been moved to engagement. As I advanced through the copyboy ranks, it became my privilege, and mine alone, to drop whatever I was doing at the sound of the apocalyptic tocsin, race to the Hearst wire, rip off the inches, or yards, of imperial will, and deliver the flapping edict at a run to a (very) select group, as the city room paused to watch.

One such occasion produced one of the heroes of my life promised on the first of these pages. The fact that I think I remember his name as Mr. Knight may speak to the editorial disposition of memory, but I can see him clearly, sitting erect and nattily dressed (in marked contrast to everyone else on the floor) at his desk in the editor in chief's office, separated from the city room by glass partitions that made his presence continually visible to us and, more important, ours to him.

In this instance, he was the only one to receive the Chief-says, and, since I was the sole Hearst wire sentinel, he and I were the only two at the paper to know that Chief wanted a story critical of the A & P grocery chain (an important advertiser) killed, spiked, consigned to oblivion in the Hearst papers.

Abiding by custom, I entered the editor's office without knocking, laid the copy in front of him without being bidden and heedless of what he was doing, then stood back and waited, as still as a ball boy at Wimbledon. The editor read the communiqué, sat back for a moment, then rose, wordless, left his office and headed down the corridor that led to the managing editor's office, the bishop on his way to the archbishop, to fling down the gauntlet.

When he returned fifteen minutes later, he gestured me back into his office, where he said, "When the bulldog comes up, bring it to me. Nobody else. Understand? One copy. To me."

I nodded, and as I left, he did something I'd never seen before, and have never seen since, not even in the best pressroom scenes of Hecht and Mac-Arthur. In full view of the now silent, staring city room, he went to the coat stand next to his door, put on his hat and coat, returned to his desk and sat down to wait for the bulldog edition, the day's first run—the test. The Moscow Art Theatre's Michael Chekhov taught his actors to search for the Psychological Gesture, a behavioral pattern, large or small, that revealed the character in an illuminating instant. I've never seen it more tellingly demonstrated.

In the middle of the city room, there was a large round hole through which a dumbwaiter hoisted the first copies of each run from the press room to the city room, announcing each arrival with a distinctive bell that summoned the copyboys to distribute the papers across the floor, an event of no great moment in normal circumstances (except to the occasional reporter who might be checking a promised byline).

But this, of course, was no normal circumstance. From my stand next to the inert dumbwaiter, I could see the usually frenetic city room, reduced to a still life, every head turned toward the immobile figure seated outlandishly at his desk in his hat and coat. No one but he and I knew the cause of the crisis, but one message was clear to everyone on the floor: We might be about to lose our leader. As I watched him across the frozen landscape, I could imagine the transcontinental phone lines sizzling between the managing editor and the chief, archbishop and pope, deliberating, decreeing.

Finally, after what seemed like hours, and was no more than a few minutes, I was alerted to the clangor from the elevator rising out of the hole next to me, less by its distinctive racket than by fifty bodies jumping in unison as the city room leapt back to life. Every head snapped from the editor in chief to me.

Summoning whatever maturity and gravity I could find in a sixteen-year-old soul, and, I suspect, enjoying this rare moment in the spotlight, I turned—slowly—picked up the top copy on the dumbwaiter, savoring the warmth and fresh-baked aroma of the newsprint, and walked—oh, yes, walked—past my breathless colleagues, their fates cradled in my arms, entered the editor's office without knocking, and laid the paper on his desk.

Over his shoulder, I could see the front-page headline. I don't remember the exact words, but it was approximately, U.S. INVESTIGATING A & P.

It was at that moment that I realized I'd pretty much stopped breathing too. Now I inhaled deeply—and so did the city room—as, without comment or change of expression, the editor in chief rose, went to the coat stand, hung up his hat and coat and returned to his desk, to a wave of cheers that drowned out the teletypes.

I didn't realize I was still standing next to him until he glanced at me, heedless of the plaudits and plainly curious at what was keeping me there. I spun and dashed back to my everyday duties that were never everyday again—because that morning I had learned two of the most important lessons of my life: First, that the most valuable word in the English language is *no*, exercised judiciously and with conviction when *yes* is not an option; second, that *principle* is not negotiable, and standing up calmly, firmly, for a carefully considered and sincerely held principle isn't merely the wiser course—it's the only course. And once that concept is accepted, it's also the easier course.

As these pages will show, I've tried, not always adroitly or successfully, to apply the lesson my editor taught all of us in that city room; and, in the years since, have sometimes had occasion to suggest to my colleagues and our students that they consider it. It goes without saying that it's not a panacea or a guarantee of success, but in my view since that fateful morning, abandoning it is a guarantee of failure, even if the day appears to be won.

In sum, I learned all I would ever need to know about integrity that morning at the *Times*—and added a hero to my private pantheon.

I found another hero that year, Jim Trainor, the city editor of the *Times*. His name, and the profound impression he made on me, are preserved in my depiction of him in my novel *Mirrors*, where he appeared as himself, in all his gruff glory:

> Jim Trainor was a large man, vertically and horizontally, crippled in one leg, so that his progress across the newsroom floor resembled the passage of a three-masted schooner in a heavy sea. Every day when he arrived at his desk in the huge room, a quiet, brilliant reign of terror began.

If Trainor is himself in *Mirrors*, it requires no imaginative leap to divine Chris's identity.

> Jim Trainor was Chris's mentor and model. Trainor worked in shirtsleeves rolled to just below the elbow; Chris worked in shirtsleeves rolled to just below the elbow. Trainor lived by a classic newsman's code; Chris lived by a classic newsman's code. "Journalists," Trainor would occasionally sneer, "work for magazines. But," and his voice would soften, "newspapers are written by newspapermen."

One of the reasons the *Times* had employed me as a copyboy was that my application had included several stories I'd written for my high school paper, the *Central Student,* a publication modeled stylistically on New York's *Times* and *Herald Tribune.* The quality of the *Student* was consistently recognized by the Columbia University School of Journalism, and its fledgling journalists were welcome at Detroit's three newspapers.

When I rose to the rank of coeditor in chief of the *Student,* the *Detroit Times* took note, and I received journalism's classic first writing assignment: an obituary. Reeling at the magnitude of the honor, and calling on the lessons learned at the side of our journalism teacher, Spencer Fishbaine, I approached the city desk, where Mr. Trainor was wedged into his slot, brusquely bringing order from chaos.

"Uh . . . Mr. Trainor?"

For what felt like an eternity, he opted not to take note of my hovering presence. Finally, shifting his weight to one side of his crowded, creaking swivel chair, he peered up at me, waiting without undue interest and clearly anxious to return to the bustling matters at hand.

"I've been assigned an obit," I said calmly, maturely. He was silent, incurious, impatient, so I went for the jugular: "What style would you like it in?"

That was when the earth stopped turning, and as he stared impassively at me, I felt as if I might fall off. Wished I would, in fact. Maybe a headfirst dive through the hole in the middle of the city room would end this agonizing impasse. But at last his lips moved.

"Your own inimitable," he said, and jammed himself back into his slot.

The *Times,* like the photoengraving plant, was simply a means to an end. I owned a Newspaper Guild union card because it was obligatory, but journalism wasn't the way I'd chosen. I was going to be a lawyer, and the *Times* was a better way of keeping body and soul together than washing glass in nitric acid.

I wrote, as required, in school; I wrote the occasional obit at the *Times* . . . but any further in that direction lay danger. The stolid security of a lawyer's life for me. The arts—theater, movies, music—were spectator sports, no more. I dabbled, confining myself to a class play in high school, but no harm done: It was a puerile play, poorly performed and quickly forgotten.

The Catholic Theater, on the other hand, was an acceptable outlet for an appetite I didn't define and barely acknowledged. The Catholic Theater was one of Detroit's best amateur groups, and since there were never enough men in the company, I fell into some choice assignments.

One night, after a performance, a hefty man named Ernie Ricca came backstage to introduce himself as a professional director, a rare calling in Detroit. "Have you thought of acting professionally?" he asked.

"No" was the instant, automatic answer.

"Why not?"

"This is just for fun."

"Good."

"I've *got* a job."

"Where?"

"The *Times.* I'm a copyboy."

"You want to be a newspaperman?"

Too quickly again: "No." Then, "I have to make money, to go to school."

Ernie, a gentle, amiable man, smiled. "You can make money as an actor."

He'd said the magic word. And opened a door with an acceptable excuse. "How much money?"

"Depends." He grinned. "More than the Catholic Theater."

I said I'd think about it, and he gave me his phone number.

A few days later, impelled, I was certain, by a financial interest, I called and we met again. He suggested I join AFRA, the American Federation of

Radio Artists. But joining the union required an initial cash investment that brought me up short, literally and figuratively. "It's worth it," Ernie said.

Laying my cards on the table, I told him what I was earning as a copyboy. "I know these things take time," I said, "but eventually—not this week or this month, but *someday*—do you think I could make more as an actor than I'm making as a copyboy?"

Ernie smiled. "I can practically guarantee it."

Under the wing of Ernie and his wife, Jeanne (heroes, of course), I soon outdistanced my meager earnings at the *Times*.

With television still far over the horizon, especially in the media backwaters of the Midwest, Detroit offered the rare homegrown theater production, but most of a Detroit actor's income came from radio, and most of that from WXYZ, the radio station owned by George W. Trendle, who had created three popular national radio programs, *Challenge of the Yukon, The Green Hornet* and, of greatest importance, *The Lone Ranger,* which aired every Monday, Wednesday and Friday from coast to coast. By the time I arrived at "those thrilling days of yesteryear," the show was an American institution.

The young actor who had originated the part of the Lone Ranger's nephew, Dan Reid, had outgrown the role and moved on, and a search was on for a replacement. The program was populated by a small stock company of actors who doubled and tripled in every episode, delivering twenty characters for the price of seven or eight (George W. Trendle was, in the words of S. J. Perelman in another context, "a slow man with a piaster"). Rollie Parker, a member of the cast with whom I'd worked in the Catholic Theater, proposed me to Chuck Livingston, the director. I auditioned, and found myself, three nights a week, in the rambling mansion on Grand River that had been converted to radio station WXYZ.

The program was broadcast live, twice each night, at seven thirty for the East Coast and Midwest, and at ten thirty for the West Coast. In between the broadcasts, I could retire to an empty studio to do my homework. A perfect arrangement, paying better than the *Times* and making more modest demands on my schedule.

As I resurrect that time, it surprises me how vividly I remember some of that group: big, gruff Paul Hughes, who played the basso bad guys (and also, to his profit and chagrin, barked the role of the sled dog, King, in *Challenge of the Yukon*); Rollie Parker, who looked and sounded like Humphrey Bogart and was the best actor of the lot; Gillie Shea, short, stout and Irish, the classic sidekick; John Todd . . . dear, gentle John Todd, who played Tonto.

John was English, very old by my lights, portly and bald, with a feathery corona of white hair. Always immaculate in a suit and vest, from which an elk's tooth dangled, he looked lost in the hurly-burly of that studio, where the action moved so fast that the scripts were printed on legal-size paper, and dropped to the floor by every actor, a page at a time (there was no time to turn them), so that at the end of a broadcast we looked snowbound.

I was told that John had been touring with a fly-by-night Shakespearean company that went broke in Detroit, stranding its actors—just as Trendle was launching *The Lone Ranger* in the 1930s. Times being what they were, the entire company showed up to audition for the radio show, and John Todd left the stage for the sage, little dreaming that he'd be saying, "Ugh" and *"Tai, kemo sabe,"* for the rest of his career, and his life.

Away from the microphone, he was the quintessential English actor, well- and soft-spoken in an impeccable English accent; and between the broadcasts I contrived to spend most of whatever free time I had with him, transfixed by his lavish, sometimes lickerish, often riotous account of a life in the theater that I'd hitherto known only from the third mezzanine step of the Cass.

He was, in the words of Gabriel Byrne to me decades later, "what an actor *looks* like . . . what an actor *is,*" leading me behind the curtain to the hallowed boards he'd once trodden—as a student, then as a practitioner, of the classical tradition. I was the eager audience he'd left far behind him when he donned buckskin and feathers. For two and a half hours every Monday, Wednesday and Friday, we were meant for each other.

By the time I met John, he was approaching seventy—and still not resigned to the role of a taciturn Indian, grunting brief phrases in a manufactured, meaningless tongue. I was a fascinated witness as he campaigned relentlessly for an occasional double, commensurate with his history and talents.

Finally, we arrived one afternoon to find the usual huge stack of scripts waiting for us—with John's name listed twice on the cover sheet, as Tonto, of course, and as Titled Englishman. John glowed and Chuck Livingston breathed a sigh of relief. It was a substantial part: The Titled Englishman was England's most celebrated marksman. By the end of the first page we could all see where this was going: He would challenge the Ranger to a contest—and lose, nobly and gracefully, to the superior shot. But along the way to that fateful confrontation, he would journey west on a train with his daughter, enabling the writer to provide the T.E.—and John—with a scene in which he spied a rabbit bounding along next to the lurching train. [SOUND: TRAIN WINDOW BEING OPENED] "My rifle! Quick!" the T.E. cried, and his daughter handed it to him. [SOUND: RIFLE SCRAPPING ON WINDOW FRAME (Remember, this was radio) AND RIFLE CLICKING HOME]. "You'll never hit it!" from the daughter. T.E.: "We'll see! [SOUND: A SHOT] T.E.: "A *hit!*"

Or so it was written. But John wasn't as young as he once was, and he hadn't said anything but "Ugh" in months, so, at rehearsal we heard:

"You'll never hit it!"

"We'll see! A *hit!*"

[SOUND: A SHOT]

Chuck Livingston, in a control room that looked down though glass on the studio, pushed the talk-back button. "John."

"Yes?"

"You have to wait for the shot and *then* say, 'A hit!' "

"Didn't I?"

"No. You said, 'A hit!' before we heard the gunshot."

The problem was that the *Lone Ranger* set was compartmentalized: The actors in the big studio gathered in a circle under a single hanging mike, shedding pages like leaves in a windstorm; the director in his aerie, peering down at us through soundproof glass, throwing cues like Toscanini; the bucking train, the clacking tracks, the creaky window and all the sound effects all the time (including the great horse Silver's toilet-plunger hoofbeats) being produced by three sweating boys (yes: boys; George W. Trendle never saw a corner he couldn't cut) in a separate room, invisible to the actors but visible to the all-seeing director. The gunshot was produced by a sound-effects record on a turntable in the control room, audible to the director and the listening audience, but inaudible to the actors. Perfect synchronization was imperative.

"The gunshot, *then* the line," said Livingston. " 'We'll see,' *pause,* 'A *hit!*' Got it?"

"Got it."

Under the best of circumstances, patience wasn't Chuck Livingston's long suit; and when repeated efforts and increasingly frantic cues from the director failed to yield anything but miraculous hits before the trigger had been pulled, we could hear Chuck's fist hammering the talk-back button down. "John!!!" John peered up at Chuck through his thick glasses. "Have you got a pencil?" Chuck demanded. John stared up at the control room. "Somebody give John a pencil!" A pencil was produced. "Now, *there,*" Chuck said, as if lecturing a child, "in front of the words 'A hit!' write 'CUE'—capital letters: 'CUE.' Then, you *can't* forget to look up at me, and I'll cue you. Right?"

"Right!" John said, meticulously marking the page.

One more repetition and all went according to plan.

"We'll see!"

[SOUND: A SHOT]

John looked up; Livingston thrust a finger at him, like a pitcher delivering a fastball.

"A *hit!*"

A collective sigh gusted through the room, and a few minutes later we went on the air for the East Coast: The engineer at the turntable in the control room spun "The William Tell Overture" (public domain, long out of copyright: George W. Trendle knew how to count his musical pennies); Fred Foy proclaimed, "A fiery horse with the speed of light, a cloud of dust and a hearty 'Hi-yo, Silver' . . . the Lone Ranger!" and we were under way—live. Since the show was live, there was no margin for error. But all went well: the pages tumbled, Chuck Livingston danced in his fishbowl, hurling cues like lightning bolts—and John's moment arrived. "My rifle! Quick!" the Titled Englishman exclaimed.

[SOUND: RIFLE SCRAPING ON WINDOW FRAME AND RIFLE BOLT CLICKING HOME]
"You'll never hit it!"
"We'll see!"
[SOUND: A SHOT]
"A *cue!!!!!!*"

It was many months before John was once again entrusted with a double, a small one with no attendant sound-effects; and in the meantime, three times a week, he, the Lone Ranger and I rode off into the sunset with a hearty "Hi-yo, Silver!" "Gittum up, Scout!" and, from me, in an obbligato a full octave above them, "Come on, Victor!"

John Todd was Tonto, the faithful Indian companion, to the end of his life: He'll be John Todd, the wry observer and theatrical Scheherazade, spinning intriguing tales, to the end of mine. A hero.

After I left *The Lone Ranger,* and Detroit, for military service, I encountered the show only once more, under unusual circumstances. In 1989, I was commissioned by Aaron Spelling and ABC to write a Movie of the Week about the magazine *AlaskaMen.* Susie Carter, a spunky, inventive Anchorage resident, had created *AlaskaMen* in a bold effort to redress the gender balance in Alaska, where there are eight men to every woman, with an even wider gap in the more remote communities. From first page to last, the magazine was a frank advertisement of Alaska's rugged male population, with photos, biographies and a mailing address at the magazine. Each issue was distributed to women in the Lower Forty-eight, and worldwide, some of whom answered Susie's invitation to come to Alaska to meet a chosen AlaskaMan. Not quite the mail-order brides of the Old West, it was nonetheless unmistakable evidence that Alaska's reputation as America's last authentic frontier is hard-earned and well deserved.

Obviously, Alaska would be a principal player in the story I was commissioned to tell, so it was essential that I pay it a visit; and since I was on deadline, I arrived in Anchorage in the heart of the Alaskan winter.

The story I was constructing called for various locations in the vast

Alaskan landscape, and in December, there was only one way to make the survey. With what amounts to one major highway and one rail line snaking north from Anchorage, Alaska challenges the traveler in the most clement of times, but in December, blanketed top to bottom in snow, it offers only one option, the air, with the result that a view of Anchorage from above reveals the startling spectacle of a Piper or Cessna in nearly every driveway.

I had a second, equally compelling motive as I scheduled my itinerary. To every aviator, the expression *bush pilot* conjures up not only dashing glamour, grit and guts, but evokes a profound respect for these navigators of the most difficult environments on the planet. No airspace offers more challenges and hazards to the voyager than Alaska, with its volatile, violent weather. So, the moment I signed on to write the film and make the survey, my course was set: I would, for one week of my life, fulfill a pilot's dream: I would fly the Alaskan bush in December.

Susie Carter put me in touch with Bob Curtis, a bush pilot who bore the imposing handle the Bald Eagle of the Yukon, and was indebted to her since he'd recently married for the fifth time, courtesy of Susie's *AlaskaMen*.

Of indeterminate age—I judged him to be somewhere in his seventies—he owned an Aeronca 15 AC Sedan that had been built in 1956. Constructed of Irish linen over the fuselage and empennage, with metal wings, it was powered by a 180 HP Lycoming engine that would transport us at eighty-five statute miles per hour, with a range of four hundred miles (in dead air, which we were unlikely to encounter). Like every general aviation aircraft in the state, its undercarriage provided wheels, floats or skis, depending on the destination and time of year. In December, skis were the only appropriate footwear.

We met at dawn on Anchorage's Lake Spenard, the frozen surface of which had nearly disappeared under a mantle of aircraft of every shape, color and condition. The Eagle's Aeronca was no more or less noteworthy than any of the others. Weathered, coddled, patched and cherished, it was a bush plane. That was all that mattered.

Since I'd be flying the plane, the Eagle briefed me, noting offhandedly that all the gyro instruments were out, and that, once we were aloft, I shouldn't bother setting the heading indicator, "because it'll only recess." When I asked how we'd hold our heading, he replied that we'd fly the whole route VFR, by pilotage, using ground references with which he was familiar after fifty-one years and some thirty thousand hours of flying the bush, getting our directional guidance from the magnetic compass—which, I reflected, has many more tricks up its sleeve than recessing. But I said nothing. As the plane's owner, Bob Curtis was pilot in command; and he was the Bald Eagle of the Yukon.

As I reached for the strut to swing myself aboard, he added that there were no deicing boots—"Oh, and no transponder. I've got one at home, but I forgot to bring it."

For some strange reason, none of this news (which, under any other circumstance, would have grounded the plane—and *me*) discouraged me at all. If anything, it made me all the more eager to begin the adventure. Somehow, I reasoned, the bush was *supposed* to be like this.

Grabbing the strut again, I climbed eagerly into the right seat and strapped in, noting that at least the plane had seat belts. There was one more "by-the-way": As we turned into the wind and began the takeoff roll, the window in the door next to me began to flap violently, prompting the Eagle to inform me that the latch was broken, so I'd have to hold it shut manually during takeoffs and landings. "At altitude," the Eagle said equably as he rotated the Aeronca and it labored aloft, "the slipstream keeps it closed."

The route I'd chosen was the Iditarod Trail, site of the annual Alaskan dogsled race that traverses the most formidable terrain in the state. To be frank, that was what attracted me to it. The Iditarod Trail begins in Anchorage and ends in Nome, and our flight plan called for making it through the Alaskan Range's notorious Rainy Pass in time to spend the night in the tiny gold-mining village of McGrath. With the brief Alaskan day ticking away, we arrived at the mountains; and as the pass loomed ahead, massive and formidable, so did the weather, turning, as it does in Alaska, or in any bush environment, on a dime. We were flying into the teeth of a snowstorm. The pass was treacherous in the best of conditions: a long, narrow corridor near the top of the range, with canyon walls of jagged ice, frequently no more than fifty feet off our wingtips on either side, and a five-thousand-foot drop below—the whole environment vanishing completely in brief whiteouts as the snowfall intensified.

I'd taken the controls for most of the flight, with Bob confining himself to takeoffs and landings, for which the unfamiliar skis disqualified me. The pass was one of the challenges I'd looked forward to, and as we entered it, Bob, bravely or foolishly, said the hallowed words, "Your airplane," and settled back with his arms folded over his ample paunch, and his feet on the floor, off the rudder pedals.

White-knuckled but in a state of indescribable elation, I steered the pitching plane through the maze, mile after unforgettable mile. And then, half an hour into the pass, the engine coughed and quit cold.

In the stunning silence, I glanced at the Eagle, who hadn't stirred. His eerie calm told me either that he was an utterly resigned fatalist, or knew something about his plane that I didn't know. I fervently hoped it was the latter.

After a few moments, as the powerless plane began settling slowly into the frigid abyss, the Eagle leaned forward and peered at a yellowed plastic tube that emerged from the Aeronca's high wing and entered the engine through a hole in the cowling. In the air, I'd encountered one more "by-the-way": The plane contained no gas gauge. Instead, the Eagle kept an eye on the plastic lines as we switched back and forth from the tank in one wing to the tank in the other to keep the plane in balance. We'd recently switched from the finally depleted right tank to the left one, which in theory contained enough gas to take us to our destination. But the left gas line was conspicuously empty.

"Right aileron," the Eagle said, more casually than was, in my view, appropriate. I twisted the yoke, putting us into a right bank that headed us toward the jagged right cliff-face. Assuming that the Eagle knew what he was doing (what choice did I have?), I held the bank as the canyon wall loomed.

"Left rudder," the Eagle suggested in the ominous quiet.

I pressed my foot into the left rudder pedal, balancing the forces of the right aileron. That realigned the plane's axis with the center of the pass, on course, but left us in a slip, flying forward at a rakish thirty-degree angle, one wing down, the other up. One of the consequences of any slip is a rapid loss of altitude, which was the last thing I wanted to do in this instance, but the Eagle's glacial calm was somehow contagious: He was, after all, in his element.

We waited, my eyes following his to the empty gas line, which hovered above us with the left wing, as the plane, gliding on its right side like a side-stroking swimmer with one arm stuck inexplicably up in the air, sank relentlessly toward the narrowing gorge below.

"Steepen it," the Eagle said.

I looked at him. He was expressionless, his eyes on the unresponsive gas line. With what was now a pure act of faith, I steepened the bank to forty-five degrees from vertical. Needing no prompting, I jammed the rudder hard left to maintain course. Obedient to the laws of aerodynamics, the plane glided forward—and sank faster.

My faith in the Eagle—and his in the Aeronca—turned out to be justified. After a few moments, gravity overcame whatever was blocking the gas line, blue avgas burbled down it into the engine, which ignited, cleared its throat and burst into full-throated roar. No airplane engine has ever sounded louder—or more beautiful.

I corrected the slip, resumed straight and level flight, pushed to full throttle, and began a climb to take us back to our former altitude. A glance at the altimeter told me we'd lost more than a thousand feet. As we arrived at altitude, it registered on me that it was still snowing hard and the plane was pitching and yawing in the wind, but no flight has ever felt silkier.

Glancing at the Eagle, his arms folded across his stomach, his eyes half-closed, I reflected on the fact that he'd never lost confidence in his plane, and I considered asking him if he'd been sure the slip would work. Had it happened before? And what if the slip *hadn't* worked? Would there have been another plan? But he appeared to have resumed his nap, so I dialed in the only navaid on the Sedan's Spartan instrument panel, a lonely (and welcome) VOR indicator, and set the CDI on a TO course for the McGrath VOR.

By the time we emerged from the pass, we'd used up our meager allotment of daylight, but the snow was abating, and the ferocious winds of the pass were behind us. When the McGrath runway lights appeared in the distance, I began what was now a routine descent to the traffic pattern altitude that I found on the wrinkled chart we'd stowed in the side pocket of the right door, the one with the broken window latch. I reflected, with a faint shudder, that the window had remained closed (as the Eagle had predicted) even when we lay on our right side during the slip.

As I neared the TPA, on course for the runway, the Eagle, who, like any bird, appeared to have a built-in altimeter, roused himself and sat up with an affable "My airplane."

I released the yoke and a minute later the Eagle greased the landing, the skis chattering on the runway's packed snow. As we deplaned, I went suddenly, totally, inexplicably blind. Snatching off my Ray-Bans, I discovered that my first exhalation hadn't merely fogged them; it had coated them on both sides with an opaque layer of ice. It was my first experience of thirty degrees below zero.

We encountered two uniformed Alaskan Airlines pilots who had elected to land in McGrath and stay overnight, rather than challenge Rainy Pass in the storm. When they learned we'd just flown through it, one of them brought a hand to his cap in salute. The other confined himself to rolling his eyes. Since it's an aviation axiom that there are old pilots and bold pilots, but there are no old, bold pilots, the second flyer's reaction may have been the more appropriate.

With a permanent population of four hundred, McGrath provides limited accommodation. Bob Curtis and I spent the night next to the runway in the Miner's Café, Inn and Gaming Room, an establishment that consisted of a small restaurant on the ground floor and three minuscule, bare rooms and a bathroom upstairs. The gaming reference, I assumed, was a relic of what must have been a colorful past. Bob and I took two of the rooms, and when it was time to shower the next morning, I was relieved to discover that, despite the minus thirty degrees outside, the Miner's Inn maintained a comfortable seventy degrees inside.

Dawn was still distant when we showed up in the hotel restaurant, which looked like, and served as, a diner for the airport. Bob finished his breakfast and went out to the runway to gas the plane and prepare for departure, and I remained at the table to sip my orange juice, reflect on yesterday's extraordinary adventure and review the flight plan for today's leg to Mount McKinley and Talkeetna. At that moment, the radio station that had been providing background music through the dining room's speakers switched to drama: an episode, the announcer explained, from a classic radio program that had been recently remastered and released.

The low-cost but high-energy opening chords of "The William Tell Overture" snapped my head up. Fred Foy's stentorian "Return with us now to those thrilling days of yesteryear. The Lone Ranger rides again!" nailed me to the back of the banquette. Paul Hughes's rumbling bass, Gillie Shea's Celtic cackle, Brace Beemer's plummy baritone, the note of nobility-brought-low (for the Indian and the actor) that I could somehow always hear in John Todd's Tonto—it was all there, *they* were all there, alive again and bringing the western frontier to life, in 1989.

And then, suddenly, Dan Reid was there, *I* was there, my adolescent voice, reedy and ready for adventure, issuing from the speakers, ignored by the other diners in the room, but heeded by me in the Miner's Café, Inn and Gaming Room in McGrath, Alaska, up to my Ray-Bans in *real* adventure on a real frontier.

Click.

Even during the *Lone Ranger* years, performing at night, going to high school, then the university, in the daytime, acting was still only a part-time job, subsidizing school and helping Mother pay the bills. I was, I kept telling myself, going to be a lawyer, for which the university was preparing me. That was the reality; that was all that mattered.

Wayne had a drama program, but I gave it a wide berth, focusing on the courses that were preparing me for a new and very different life. There were, of course, the traditional literature, language, science and history courses, the typical stuff of liberal arts, but in all the time at Wayne, I never set foot on the stage of the university's Bonstelle Theatre. I had meticulously subdivided my life: actor by night, student by day, and the barrier that separated them was secured by a Gordian knot.

The sword that cut it was, quite literally, a sword: military service. In that era of the draft, the only alternative to the potluck of the lottery was the voluntary option. Following the bent that would one day find me next to the Bald Eagle of the Yukon, I applied for flight training and was assigned to Keesler Field, in Biloxi, Mississippi, where, over a period of days, I underwent the battery of tests, written, physical, psychomotive, designed to find the few candidates considered eligible for pilot training.

Of the hundreds who went through the tests with me, fewer than ten qualified. I was one of them. And then I arrived at the simple, pro forma, final step: Just get on the scale, record your weight and proceed to the desk where a beaming officer covered in a fruit salad of medals would offer you a hearty handshake and the precious papers that declared you a cadet pilot and officer candidate.

Awash in the magnitude of my accomplishment, I mounted the scale, then started to step off it, but the airman who was adjusting the sliding balance said, "Hold it." He rebalanced the scale, then shook his head and told me to step aside. There would be no handshake, no papers: I'd washed out—at the last millisecond, after days of travail and triumph.

"What's the matter?" I demanded.

"Didn't make the weight," the airman said.

"*What* weight?"

"The minimum. You've gotta weigh at least a hundred and twenty pounds."

I looked at the scale. One hundred eighteen (*sic*). "You're gonna wash me out for *two pounds?*"

The airman shrugged me off and turned to the next candidate.

"*Two fucking pounds!?*" I yelled, attracting the attention of the officer at the desk. He came over.

"What's the problem, soldier?"

"Sir, I passed everything! You've got my papers there. He's washing me out for two pounds!"

The officer glanced at my papers, checked my scores, and studied me, prompting me to persist: "Two pounds!"

"Tell you what," the officer said. "We've got another group coming through tomorrow morning. Eat a big meal tonight; eat a *couple*. Come back tomorrow, and we'll see."

"Yes, sir!"

Keesler Field was divided into squadron areas, each containing several barracks, with each individual barracks constituting a flight. I went back to my flight, where my fellow trainees, none of whom had qualified, were waiting to welcome the conquering hero. I raised a hand to interrupt their cheers. When I explained the problem, and my deadline, I was inundated with a chorus of advice. Intense debate finally arrived at a consensus: bananas, eat nothing but bananas; then, tomorrow morning, drink as much water as you can swallow—and, most important, between now and the weigh-in, don't go to the latrine, no matter what!

All day long, I was plied with bananas by my support group, but that evening, I came up with a little extra insurance. Each candidate was naked at the weigh-in but, as a safeguard, could carry his wallet on the scale. "Silver dollars!" I exclaimed to the barracks. "How many of you carry lucky silver dollars?"

Several were produced. I tucked them into my wallet: They were invisible—and weighty. Not yet weighty enough—but there was still room in it. The members of my flight fanned out through the squadron area (for obvious reasons, I couldn't be trusted to move from my bunk), looking for silver dollars. Finally, the wallet couldn't hold another ounce of silver.

The next morning, when I stepped gingerly on the scale with my wallet and belly packed, the airman's eyes widened as he slid the balance farther and farther to the right. Finally, he simply yielded to the overnight miracle and waved me toward the waiting officer, who handed me my papers with a broad grin.

After all that, I didn't get my wings. Not in the service. With no war to fight, hence no casualties to be replaced with the newly recruited and trained, the government came to us with an offer. Explaining that the training we were undergoing was the costliest in the military, they offered us the option of completing it and getting our wings and lieutenant's bars, but with the obligation, then, of a four-year reenlistment, to amortize the cost of the instruction. The alternative option was to take an immediate honorable discharge, another hearty handshake and a return to civilian life.

Reasoning that I could complete my flight training as a civilian, without the four-year obligation, and fulfill my patriotic commitment by saving my country a lot of money, I opted for self-determination—which turned out to mean a brief return to Detroit. Having tasted life (albeit a limited and strictly regulated one) elsewhere, I looked eastward, toward New York—to Columbia University, or perhaps New York University, where I could complete the study of the law and keep my destined date with convention, routine and security.

I headed for New York without a backward glance—and without an inkling that I was embarking on a journey that would consume ten difficult, challenging, exhilarating years—in precisely the direction I'd shunned to that moment.

Now, at last, my education would begin.

CHAPTER Five

Assez vu. La vision s'est rencontrée à tous les airs.
Assez eu. Rumeurs des villes, le soir, et au soleil, et toujours.
Assez connu. Les arrêts de la vie.—O Rumeurs et Visions!
Départ dans l'affection et le bruit neufs.

Seen enough. The vision appeared in every air.
Had enough. City sounds, in the evening, in the sun, and always.
Known enough. Life's halts.—O Sounds and Visions!
Departure in new affection and new noise.

—"Départ," Arthur Rimbaud

I n New York, waiting my turn at the enrollment doorstep of the crowded universities, I immediately addressed my perpetual need: finding part-time employment that would subsidize school, pay the rent, put food on the table, and supplement Mother's income. She had moved to New York when I did, found her destined place in the rare book department of B. Altman's, and moved into an apartment not far from mine on the west side of Manhattan.

As I examined my options, it became clear that the most practical route to employment was the one I'd followed in Detroit. I was, after all, a professional actor: I belonged to the union (which was turning into AFTRA, the American Federation of *Television* and Radio Artists), and I had my Detroit credits on my résumé. Enough for a start, I thought.

I was wrong. Within a few days I discovered that New York was swarming with young actors who looked upon acting not as a part-time subsidy but a full-time job—a vocation, a mission, an obsession. I was now, I realized with a shudder of apprehension—and comprehension—on a very fast track.

New York at that moment was a hotbed of theatrical exploration. Dustin

Hoffman described it on *Inside the Actors Studio:* "During those years, the fifties, early sixties, New York was a mecca of acting education. The giants were teaching—Sandy Meisner, Stella Adler, Bobby Lewis, Lee Strasberg. You called it going to temple to learn our craft. I'm sorry I didn't get to study with Meisner. That's whom Bob Duvall studied with, and he loved him. I'm sorry I didn't get to study with Stella Adler, because she was this extraordinary expert on scene study and breaking down Ibsen and Strindberg.

"We'd get on the street corner and Duvall would say, 'Strasberg's full of shit—sense memories, waah, waah, waah!'" It was Dustin mimicking Duvall mimicking the cliché of a self-indulgent "Method" actor. The students howled with glee at this irreverence in a Method shrine. Dustin continued, in a dead-on impersonation of Duvall extolling his teacher: "'Meisner, Meisner, Meisner! Improvisation, improvisation! Repeat the words, repeat the words.' And we would almost get in fights over whose teacher was the best," Dustin concluded. "There was passion, you know."

There was. It was everywhere, all over the city, all the time. Elsewhere in the fifties, actors might be talking about managers, agents, casting calls, restaurants, clothes and cars, but in New York, the conversation seemed to revolve exclusively, and often combatively, around teachers and exercises and theories and yesterday's class and today's revelations.

As Dustin indicated, battle lines, dating from the schism of the thirties, were drawn, and the debates raged.

In the classroom session on the first night of *Inside the Actors Studio* in 1994, when one of our students asked Paul Newman, "What are your expectations of us?" Paul replied, "To be as well prepared in the craft that you've chosen for yourself as you can possibly be. There's nobody that can control the circumstances outside of this hothouse you're in, but I'll tell you one thing: You're more likely to have a better chance coming out of here than you are in anyplace I can think of. Primarily because there is that insistence on the literature of theater. There's insistence on the fact that you have to use your body and your voice. And more than that, there's an insistence that you be immersed, seven days a week, sixteen hours a day.

"These people who come to New York and think they're gonna blister the place by having a two-hour session twice a week, and then sit in the drugstore, have not much to look forward to. Of the possibilities that are available to you, this is probably about as good as you're gonna get—so that you'll go out there as well prepared as you can be."

When Giampiero Iudica, an Italian student, asked, "You've talked about character, talent. What else do we need?" Paul replied, "I think tenaciousness is the single most important thing you can have, whether it's acting or directing, playwriting or making salad dressing or spaghetti sauce. Mostly because I've seen people with a tremendous amount of talent, whose instincts are impeccable, whose instrument is accessible and fluid and available to them—and who simply think that's enough.

"It isn't! And unless you can combine that with a fierce determination to build it to whatever optimum of excellence it can find for itself, you're really cheating yourself and you're kidding yourself, and it will come back and bite you. I've seen very gifted people who just piss it away, or they abuse themselves or their bodies or their gifts, and it all just disappears. It's tragic. I resent those people, incidentally, more than anybody because I figure if I'd had that combination, man, look out!"

Paul was modest—and smart. And Dustin was right: There was passion, and everyone was a student of *someone.* Except me.

I'd naively blundered into a cauldron of unbridled experimentation and self-examination. Standing at the edge of it, I was dismayed, but I reasoned that I had no choice. If I was ever going to reach my goal and stand before the bar, I would have to arm myself for the combat that was swirling all around me. In short, I would have to show up at auditions ready to compete with these seasoned gladiators.

The landscape that Paul and Dustin described was the one I faced. In nearly every building west of Broadway and north of Forty-second Street, there seemed to be a teacher soliciting the aspiring actor's custom. It was a bewildering prospect. But several names stood out. They were, of course, the ones on Dustin's list. And the one I chose, after several weeks of nervous investigation, was Stella Adler.

Stella was the product of an acting dynasty. In the teens of the twentieth century, Manhattan's Lower East Side was the serendipitous beneficiary of the prejudice and pogroms of Eastern Europe, filling to overflowing with the "wretched refuse" that would enrich America's art, education and commerce.

Second Avenue was the Lower East Side's Broadway, lined with bustling theaters that the journalist Lincoln Steffens declared superior to the English-speaking theaters uptown, and the Adlers were this society's royalty. Stella often used her family to illustrate an acting principle. When an actor in the class stopped a scene in annoyance because a prop was missing, Stella exploded—something she did with some frequency and a kind of odd aplomb. "Why did you stop?!"

"The prop was missing."

"*So?!!*" The student stared, nonplussed. "*Use* it," Stella exclaimed, coming out of her seat to face us from the front, another frequent occurrence. "When my sister Celia was appearing on Second Avenue—in front of a full house [the

Adlers always seemed to play to full houses]—she was supposed to shoot her cheating husband. The gun was in a drawer in the kitchen table. She pulled out the drawer. No gun!" Stella's voice had dropped to a throbbing whisper. The class was mesmerized. "What did she do? Did she *stop the scene?*" The question didn't merit an answer. "She did what any normal human being in that situation would do. She went looking for the gun, ransacking the kitchen, opening every cabinet, every drawer. It was *nowhere!*" Italics were Stella's frequent weapon of choice. "The prop man had *messed up.*"

None of us had the courage to ask what the philandering husband was doing as she flailed about, searching for the means of his extinction.

"Did she stop the scene?" Stella demanded. "Did she apologize to the audience? Did she leave the stage?" Scorn dripped from every word. *"No!* The circumstances demanded that she kill this monster. By whatever means possible. That's what the play wanted. That's what her character wanted. That . . . was . . . the . . . only . . . reality." She had slowed to a thudding cadence. "All she had were the given circumstances—this man—in this kitchen: He had to die! She looked around the room again. There was nothing there. . . . AND THEN SHE SAW IT!" Stella spoke fluent Upper Case. "On the kitchen table—a pot of strawberry jam! She didn't hesitate. She ran to the table, scooped out the jam, and THREW IT AT THE BASTARD." Stella hurled the lethal jam at us, screaming, "DIE!!!!" with no less conviction and naked truth than she would have brought to Lady Macbeth or Medea.

In the profound silence, our collective breath couldn't be heard, because we'd stopped breathing. Stella gathered herself and proceeded. "The jam hit him in the middle of the chest—a big red stain—and he fell back—DEAD." Her eyes swept us. "Do you think anybody noticed? Do you think one person in that packed house cared that it was jam? *No!* Why? Because *the actor* believed. So, *they* believed."

And so, from that day forward, did we.

For all her outbursts, airs and affectations, Stella's grasp of the craft was steely, her expression of it was often scientifically specific, and every illustration she offered, no matter how far-fetched initially, always ended in a rapier-sharp point.

During the first months of our training, the exercises she employed were silent. Words, she explained, would come when we were ready for them: first our own in improvisation, then, when and only when she felt we could be trusted with them, a playwright's words. So, for months, we worked like galley slaves, in arduous silence, straining to the beat of the pilot's drum and the occasional crack of her whip.

In one of Stella's favorite early exercises, she assigned to each of us a painting, which we were to study, absorb—and ENTER, to put it in Adlerese Upper Case. Each of us was to select a figure in the assigned painting and find that person's action: What was that person doing at that instant, and why was he or she doing it? Then, we were to prepare an exercise in which *we* would do it, which would, if organically executed (i.e. with our own total belief in it), place us inside the character—and the painting.

Simple. And, for beginners, an unnerving challenge. One of the actors in our class was assigned a painting, by Manet, if I recall, of a man in a boat, leaning on an oar, looking quite serious, perhaps even a bit menacing.

The actor's turn came. He took the small stage in front of the class, and began the exercise in silence, glowering, grimacing and shooting threatening glances around the room.

"STOP!!!" The offense had warranted both Upper Case *and* italics. The actor sat frozen in his imagined boat. "What in God's name are you doing?" Stella demanded.

"I'm doing the guy in the painting. . . ."

"What does *that* mean?"

"He's fierce—so *I'm* being fierce."

A fatal misstep! Stella was on her feet in a gossamer swirl (she always dressed for class, trying to make the point to us that the class, like the theater, was a sacred precinct). Advancing to the stage, she towered over the actor, crouched in his "boat."

"You're *'BEING'* fierce? Just how do you do that?"

"Well . . ." His hands flopped about him in a helpless gesture.

"You can't *'BE'* fierce!" Stella exclaimed. "*Nobody* can *'be'* fierce." She made a "fierce" face that Delsarte would have applauded—an empty, imitative "indication" of the real thing—then bent back over the student. "We don't 'be'—we *do*! That's *all*! You *do* something—something specific, something you believe, something you own, something *the character wants to do*—then we, the audience, will decide whether you're fierce or not. Do you understand?"

The student stared up at her, cowed (she was a tall woman in any event). Stella impatiently gestured him back to his place in the class, and took stage alone. We were about to witness an illustration. Stella drew a long, deep breath, and seemed to grow even taller. A big, powerful woman stood before us.

"When I played Zinida, the lion tamer, in Andreyev's *He Who Gets Slapped*—on Broadway," she emphasized carefully, "I wore a lion skin and carried a whip. On opening night, I was in the wings of the Booth Theater, alone, preparing for my first entrance." This solitary preparation was another sacred tenet of the system Stella espoused. "Suddenly, I was aware of someone next to me, tugging at my elbow, INTERRUPTING MY PREPARATION."

Stella paused, still aghast at the magnitude of the offense. "All I could see, down there in the dark, was this blue hair. It was Theresa Helburn."

Theresa Helburn, who did in fact have electric-blue hair, was a tiny woman of a certain age who, with Lawrence Langner, ran one of Broadway's most powerful producing organizations, the Theatre Guild.

"I couldn't believe she was doing this," Stella growled. "I said, 'What do you *want*?!' And she said"—Stella paused, barely able to voice the sacrilege—"she said, 'Remember, Stella—be fierce.'" Another disbelieving silence, then: "I said to her, 'I don't have to "be" fierce, Terry. *You* don't walk around trying to "be" fierce—and you scare the shit out of *me*.'"

Point taken by the actor in the boat and all of us in Stella's remarkable presence.

Stella's interpretation of the Stanislavski system was breathtakingly simple, crystal-clear and took as long to fathom as any powerful, comprehensive concept. But, once understood, organically, in the marrow of the actor's bones, it was capable of giving birth to such transcendent talents as Robert De Niro, Harvey Keitel, Marlon Brando, Melanie Griffith and Benicio Del Toro. When he was on *Inside the Actors Studio,* De Niro said, "At the Dramatic Workshop, I stopped for about six months and then I started again when I was eighteen, and that was with Stella Adler. She was very inspirational. What she did very, very well was the 'conservatory of acting'—Stanislavski, *Building a Character.* I think that was really, really important for any actor. I can't see how you wouldn't be made aware of that." He paused, reflecting, then smiled. "There was a bit of pomp and splendor blended into it. . . ."

"*Plenty* of pomp and splendor," I offered.

"But at the end of the day," De Niro said, "she was really good, a good teacher. I always give her credit for having a big influence on me and making it, 'It's not about neuroses, or *playing* on your neuroses; it's about the character and the *tasks* of the character. You're not going about it as if it's all about *you,* and how *you* would do it. It's about the character and being faithful to the text, the script.' Breakdown was something that I had not seen, other than with her. Script Analysis, breakdown, was a really good class, in terms of seeing something for what it *is*—from photographs, then through a text, a play, and breaking that down. And *not fictionalizing,* but just taking whatever you get from that and making your choices, *based* on what you picked up from that."

"She said something to us when I was studying with her," I recalled. "I wonder if she said it to you: 'The talent lies in . . .'"

Bob seized it. "'The talent lies in the choice.' Yeah, that was it."

On our *Inside the Actors Studio* stage, Harvey Keitel recalled, "Stella was a trip. I mean, I always felt she was an artist. I could listen to her all day and watch her all night. She, to me, epitomized the word *artist.* She possessed such integrity and such knowledge, such wisdom, such respect for the theater. It was just enormous. And she was a witch."

I asked, "Haven't you said something about what happened when an actor told her he was feeling content about his work?"

Harvey laughed. "That was my favorite. She said, 'Dahling, only cows are content.'"

"Do you feel she gave you a craft that you use to this day?"

"She was a tremendous craftsperson. She was just a genius at the craft. Scene Analysis was a brilliant class, her character work was extraordinary. Those two areas were just extraordinary."

Stella's influence spanned generations. When Benicio Del Toro, one of the shining lights of the generation behind Keitel and De Niro, was on *Inside the Actors Studio,* I asked him about his experience with Stella.

"When she came to the West Coast it was an event, number one. I think I was nineteen; I was probably the youngest in the class. You had to be recommended to be in it. It was a scene class, which was more 'performance.' People used to pay to see the class. The theater was full, but only the first row was the people going up on the stage and getting hammered. Hard. I remember very, very clearly what she said. The first scene I did was from *Does a Tiger Wear a Necktie?* And she stopped the scene immediately. She said, 'Put your shoulders back right now! You're a man. You ceased to be a boy when you were seven. Play the man.' To this day I do that, I try to play the strength of the character.

"Then I did *Zoo Story.* The talk in the class was that, if she liked the scene, she would let it play all the way to the end. If she didn't like it, she'd stop. So I started doing the scene, and halfway through the scene, I'm thinking, She's not stopping! Three-quarters into the scene—she loves it. At the end of the scene, I'm going, like, I am the man! Everybody got up and started clapping. They were fooled like I was.

"She told everybody to sit down and she said, 'Mr. Del Toro—do you like big parts?' And I go, 'I guess.' She goes, 'Well, you ain't ready yet.' And she was right. I'm absolutely sure she was right. I probably screamed and raved a lot through the scene, and didn't have an idea of what this guy was and who he was, where he was coming from, what he wanted, where he was going."

Benicio described doing another scene in her class, from Arthur Miller's *A View from the Bridge:* "She walked me through it, and what I got out of it was, you've got to investigate the text. What is the thing that your character *wants,* and why?"

It is generally acknowledged that Stella's masterpiece was Marlon Brando.

That was one of the many reasons that, from the day *Inside the Actors Studio* was born in 1994, I wrote innumerable letters to Marlon, importuning him as a charter member of the Studio to join the show's roster. I invite participants twice a year, in August and December, before each school semester, and though the years went by without a murmur of acknowledgment from Marlon, I persisted.

Then, finally, an acknowledgment, albeit an ambiguous one. One morning, my voice mail at the school office offered up a familiar voice: "Jim Lipton? Marlon Brando." There was a long pause. "Oh—I guess it's eight o'clock in New York. You've gone home." Another long pause. "You've got some great signature! Heh-heh-heh. So long."

"What do we do?" my secretary asked.

"Nothing."

"But, it's"—she waved a trembling hand at the telephone—"Marlon Brando!"

"Got his number in the Rolodex?"

"No, of course not."

"Then, we wait."

We didn't have to wait long. Two weeks later, I walked into my office to find my secretary waiting anxiously, her face flushed. "There's someone on the phone. He's been waiting for fifteen minutes."

"Why didn't you tell him to call back?"

"He said he wanted to wait."

"Who is it?" I asked as I went into my office.

"Marlon Brando" came the breathless answer from the anteroom.

I'd encountered Marlon a few times when I first came to New York, and as I reached for the phone, I flashed back to a particularly memorable occasion when he, his closest friend Wally Cox and I went to lunch at a tacky diner, where he and Wally ordered New England clam chowder. One New England clam chowder looks pretty much like another, but he and Wally seemed to prefer each other's lunches as each reached slowly across the table, groped about in the milky broth like a mechanical claw scrabbling for prizes under glass in an arcade machine, scooped clams out of the other's bowl, then, wordless, brought the dripping prize to his mouth in some sort of grave ritual.

I picked up the phone. "Hi, Marlon."

"I'm never gonna do *Inside the Actors Studio.*"

"Then, why are you calling me?"

"Your letter *said,* 'Call me.'"

"It said, 'Call me if you want to do the show.' Why would you call me if you don't?"

He doubled back to clarify his initial declaration. "Strasberg and the Studio were always taking credit for me. They had nothing to do with it. Stella was my teacher."

"Stella was *my* teacher. Come on the show and we'll talk about her."

"Why do you want me? For the greater glory of the show?"

"Maybe the first year, maybe even the second, but we've had a lot of great actors on the show. No offense intended, but we're doing okay without you."

A long silence. I waited. "Then, why do you want me on the show?"

"Do you want bullshit or the truth?"

"The truth."

"Because you're the best actor I've ever seen."

A longer silence, then, "That's very flattering."

"No, it's not. You wanted the truth, and the truth isn't flattering or *un*flattering. It's not flattering because you've told me you won't do the show, so I've got nothing to gain, and it's not unflattering because it's just a simple fact."

He was silent—waiting apparently—so I went on. "I'm not talking about *Streetcar,* or *Truckline Café,* or even *Candida.* I saw you in *I Remember Mama.*"

Marlon made several stage appearances. *Truckline Café,* by Maxwell Anderson, was directed by Harold Clurman. *Candida* paired him with the theater's reigning queen, Katharine Cornell. *Streetcar,* unfortunately, marked his last appearance on the stage, and *I Remember Mama* was his first. In it, he played one of the children in a Norwegian-American family. I was brand-new in New York and gorging on theater from the cheapest balcony seats, and *I Remember Mama* was a highly praised Broadway hit.

"There was an actor onstage, playing Nels," I said to Marlon, "and he scared me to death. It sounded as if he didn't know his lines."

On Mulholland Drive, Marlon chuckled.

"The minute the lights went up for the first intermission, I looked at the bios in the program—so did a lot of other people in the audience—and I thought, 'Oh, that explains everything.' You remember what you put in the *Playbill?* 'Marlon Brando was born in Calcutta, India.'"

Marlon chortled appreciatively.

"So, I relaxed in the second act. The poor guy was struggling with the American accent. That assumption lasted about five minutes. Something *else* was going on. I didn't know what it was, but by the third act, all I knew was I'd never seen anything like it before. A door was opening. I didn't have any idea where it went, but I knew I was going to try to go through it. A lot of other actors felt the same way. You changed acting. For everybody. Forever."

A very long silence, then, from Mulholland Drive: "What do you know about the American Indian?"

"Only what Princess Sasheen Littlefeather told us when she accepted your Oscar. You want to discuss it on *Inside the Actors Studio*?"

He appeared to want to discuss it on the phone, then and there, with me. And a broad variety of other subjects in a long, rambling discourse. At one point he lapsed into a lengthy disquisition in Spanish. When I could get a word in, I said, "Marlon, I don't understand Spanish."

"I'm talking to my maid."

Finally, after forty-five minutes, during which the subject of my invitation never came up again, I said, truthfully, "I have to go into a meeting."

"Oh, okay." And he was gone. As *Inside the Actors Studio*'s viewers know, he never appeared on *Inside the Actors Studio.* I regret it. I knew what Stella had taught him, and we could have conducted a class in the Gospel according to Stella that would have honored her craft—and his. And maybe opened a few more doors.

In Keitel's, De Niro's and Del Toro's accounts, Stella's focus is clear: to define the actor's task always in terms of an active (as distinctly opposed to passive), doable (which is to say practical) verb, expressed in the infinitive: to persuade him; to evade attention; to evade attention *at all costs* (in a stronger action); to seduce her; to get him out of my life; to poke holes in her story; to win over his parents; to make them see the folly of their ways; to forge a new path.

The word *act* comes from the Latin *actus,* "a doing," and *actum,* "a thing done," both words derived from the past participle of *agere,* which means, quite simply, "to do." An actor, Stella would insist, is a "doer."

And all of it, every action, justified (believed) organically, from within, from the actor's own experience, from the actor's unique, inimitable soul.

In Scene Analysis, Stella divided each action into beats—briefer actions that proceeded to the moment in the play (or film) where, clearly, a new beat began—all the beats linked to, and adding up to, the larger action; and all the character's actions (or "objectives") tied firmly to the character's Super-Objective, a doable action that ruled the actor's performance from curtain-up to curtain-down, or Fade In to Fade Out.

The character's emotions, Stella insisted, would flow naturally, strongly— and unforced—from the actor's pursuit of each action in the face of the obstacles placed in its path by the artful playwright (once again, as Mark Rydell demonstrated in the example of the actor locked in the closet and given the action "to get out!").

To the end of his life, Lee Strasberg remained committed to the pursuit of emotion *qua* emotion, and produced some of America's greatest actors through his skillful use of Stanislavski's early emphasis on sense memory. Stella also taught sense memory, but hers was employed simply to build the chain of truths in which she fervently believed, unbroken by even the smallest falsehood.

So, in one of her sense memory exercises, we cleaned and polished a delicate art object that wasn't there. We "remembered" it through our sense of touch. One false moment, and she was on us ("Congratulations! You just *broke* it!"), making us repeat the exercise over and over until the object was visible, palpable in the classroom.

Stella's insistence on small truths leading to larger ones was graphically illustrated when, in my second year in her class, she invited me to accompany her and her brother Luther to an off-Broadway performance of *Macbeth.* I arrived to find Luther seated in the center of the first row. The two of us waited for Stella, and as the houselights dimmed and I peered anxiously toward the back of the theater, Luther murmured, "Don't worry; she'll be here."

The house went dark, and this being off-Broadway, a troop of soldiers in medieval armor came tramping raucously down the aisle from the rear of the theater. Luther turned, touched my arm and nodded significantly toward the end of the line, where Stella, inappropriately dressed for battle, but completely caught up in the spirit of the warriors, was waving her fists and joining in the boisterous hubbub. As the troops mounted the stage and disappeared into the wings, leaving the stage to the witches, Stella, having made the "entrance" that Luther obviously anticipated, peeled off and slid into her seat next to me with a mellifluous "Good evening, darling."

Then followed what was one of the most painful (literally and figuratively) theater experiences of my life. The performances on the stage were monuments to the kind of indication and declamation that Stella had dedicated her life to combating. What made the experience even more painful was that I was seated between Stella and Luther, one of whom was clutching my right arm, the other the left, and each time there was a conspicuous example of bad acting they would react—without exception simultaneously, which shouldn't be surprising, given their genetic and professional kinship—by digging their aggrieved fingers deep into my arms. As a result, the puzzled audience was treated to the spectacle of this shadowy figure (me) repeatedly rising and falling in the front row, as the pain brought me out of my seat.

Nevertheless, even in this alien environment, there was an acting lesson to be learned. At one point, Macbeth was handed a prop tankard. A subaltern "filled" it with wine from an obviously empty pitcher. The actor playing Macbeth then raised the tankard in a grand gesture, and tossed off the wine in such a way that, *had* there been any liquid in the cup, he would have sloshed enough on himself to melt the glue of his beard and the joints of his cardboard armor.

Never one to miss a pedagogical opportunity, my teacher leaned to me and whispered stertorously, "He can't drink a cup of wine—but he can play Macbeth!"

For the first year of my study with Stella, I didn't question the conviction that I was doing this to enhance my chances to land acting assignments, and that the acting assignments existed for the sole purpose of permitting me to pursue a law degree.

But as I fell deeper under the sway of this sorceress and the world into which she was leading our class, the allure of torts and civil procedures and real property and antitrust—and even the anticipated majesty of constitutional law and the excitement of litigation—began to fade into a distant void and dim resolve to avoid . . . what? Oh, yes: the perils of a life like my father's, a life lived somewhere in the realm of the arts, a life . . . like this.

The long war with what I saw as the baser side of my patrimony ended in neither truce nor treaty; it just became irrelevant when, one day, without fanfare or forewarning, I wakened to the incontestable fact that, unsolicited, exercise by exercise, discovery by discovery, my avocation had become my vocation. I had no notion, and certainly no great expectation, of what I might achieve in this new direction; I only knew that I could no longer maintain the fiction that this life I was living, fervently, twenty-four hours a day, was a way station to something different and more suitable.

For better or worse, it was the way I was going to go, and from that point on, my training was frankly intended to enable me to work not part-time toward a greater goal, but full-time, full-bore, for its own sake; and nearly every day of the next decade of my life was devoted to the pursuit of the most elusive, maddening and enchanting of quarries: craft.

On the strength of Stella's training, I began to act in television, playing the young Michelangelo sculpting the *David*, on CBS's *You Are There*, directed by Sidney Lumet; in theater, off-Broadway in *Dark Legend*, based on the novel by the psychoanalyst Frederic Wertham, in which he psychoanalyzed Hamlet through the contemporary case of a young man, whom I played, who had murdered his mother and her lover; and on Broadway in Lillian Hellman's *The Autumn Garden*; in film roles in *The Big Break* in America and *Wheel of Fire* in Europe; in soap operas, principally *The Guiding Light*, which subsidized my continuing acting studies and my work at night in the theater.

When I concluded Stella's two-year course, she asked me to stay for another six months, to assist her in class and in a project she was directing, *Johnny Johnson*, the Kurt Weill musical that had been unsuccessfully mounted by the Group Theatre in 1936, under Harold Clurman's direction, then Lee Strasberg's. Stella's purpose was to show them both how it ought to be done, and in exchange for my assistance in the direction, I was offered six more months in class, and my choice of any of the play's roles. When that reprieve ended, both Stella and I had run out of excuses: The fundamental stage of my education was over. Suffering immediate withdrawal, I looked for the next. It came, fortuitously, in the form of an announcement that electrified the acting community: For the first time in the career that had begun with the Group Theatre, Harold Clurman had elected to teach a private class. It was instantly the hottest ticket in town. Admission to his workshop was by audition or Harold's invitation, and he was deluged with applications. Since I'd been directed by him in *The Autumn Garden,* I entered by invitation.

The workshop met twice a week, from eleven thirty p.m. to one thirty in the morning, to accommodate many of the students who were working in the theater. At that time, before television had abandoned its initial base in New York for the more spacious and less costly venues of Los Angeles and convenient proximity to the film industry, taking a legion of actors with it, many of the best actors lived in New York—and a sizable number of them wound up in Clurman's workshop.

In his autobiography, Elia Kazan described Harold Clurman's application of the Stanislavski system:

> I learned from Harold that a director's first task is to make his actors eager to play their parts. He had a unique way of talking to actors—I didn't have it and I never heard of another director who did; he turned them on with his intellect, his analyses and his insights. But also by his high spirits. Harold's work was joyous. He didn't hector his actors from an authoritarian position; he was a partner, not an overlord, in the struggle of production.
>
> He'd reveal to each actor at the onset a concept of his or her performance, one the actor could not have anticipated and could not have found on his own. Harold's visions were brilliant; actors were eager to realize them. They were also full of compassion for the characters' dilemmas, their failings and their aspirations.

In the introduction to *The Collected Works of Harold Clurman,* the editors, Marjorie Loggia and Glenn Young, quoted an assessment of this theatrical master by author Irwin Shaw: "His wild harangues on acting, politics, drama, sex, theater, which he delivered wherever he happened to be—backstage, at Sardi's, in hotel rooms on the road, with a play in Boston or Washington, at the Russian Tea Room, on the movie sets in Hollywood—all came out in the same eloquent tumble of words and the same unflagging zest and wisdom."

For four years, I was one of the beneficiaries of that maelstrom of enlightenment. In his later years, when he taught the workshop, Harold was a fleshy man, doughy of form and feature. His nose was bulbous, his cheeks gelatinous, his lips full and sensual—the "sense" being both *common* sense and rare as it issued from them in a stuttering torrent. His words never seemed able to keep pace with his racing thoughts, and as he sat facing us, usually perched on the edge of the little stage at the front of the classroom, growing more and more excited with each explosive idea, he would rub his pudgy hands together with such vigor that I wondered if the friction might not someday produce fire.

Stella Adler was the greatest technician I ever worked with; Harold Clurman was the most inspiring person I ever met. At the end of each class, we were always too stimulated to go home. It was one thirty in the morning, but sleep was out of the question. We wanted more, and when there were no more scenes left to dissect, we begged for an anecdote, because Harold Clurman was, as Irwin Shaw noted, the most willing, and best, talker on earth.

One night, after scenes *and* anecdotes, two A.M. loomed, and we were still refusing to leave. Harold threw up his hands. "What *else* is there to talk about?"

"Weren't you a play reader for the Theatre Guild in the twenties?" a student asked.

"Yes."

"Well, God—that's when the Theatre Guild was producing O'Neill and Synge and O'Casey and Sherwood!" the student said. "So, if you were the Theatre Guild reader, you must have discovered some amazing plays."

"Yes," Harold said, and shifted his thighs on the edge of the stage. In addition to all his other remarkable attributes, Harold appeared to be so prodigiously endowed that, from pelvis halfway to knee, his left trouser leg dwarfed the size of his right one—a fact of considerable interest and frequent private comment in the class.

"What was the *best* play you ever read at the Theatre Guild?" the student asked, and the class leaned forward in perfect unison.

"I'd have to say there were two," Harold said reflectively.

"Tell us!" came from the class in chorus.

Harold settled himself and gave his palms a brisk, preliminary rub. "The second-best began, 'Act One, Scene One. A provincial French house, 1802. Outside, a storm rages. Snow beats against the window. In the darkness, a fist pounds on the door. A man and woman sit up in bed. The woman lights a candle, the man goes to the door in his nightshirt. He opens it and a man, covered in fur and snow, staggers into the room. The couple struggles to close the door against the howling wind and drifting snow.'

" 'Doctor,' " the man cries, " 'come quick, the baby's being born!' "

With a zest that belied the late hour—ours, not the play's—Harold launched into an account that had the wife begging her husband not to go out into the storm, and the husband insisting that he couldn't shirk his duty, throwing a fur coat over his nightshirt, pulling on his boots, seizing his medical bag, and plunging into the night with the caller.

" 'Act One, Scene Two. Six hours later,' " Harold said, and recounted the man's return at dawn after a harrowing journey in which, he tells his wife between restorative drafts of brandy, the horse drawing the sleigh fell into a ditch, and the two men plunged on afoot until they reeled into the house where the pregnant woman waited.

Harold rocked on the edge of the stage as he quoted the doctor's account of his journey back, alone, falling over and over again, thinking each time he'd never rise, finding the still warm body of the dead horse in the ditch, and huddling next to it until he'd regained enough strength to lurch back to the house.

Harold stood for the finale, his eyes ablaze: " 'That's terrible,' the wife exclaims, 'You could have died out there!' "

Harold slowed, fully possessed now by the doctor: " 'It doesn't matter. *Nothing* matters—because that child I brought into the world tonight' "—the doctor's, and Harold's, voice trembled—" 'that child . . . was *Victor Hugo!*' "

Harold sat back down on the edge of the stage, delivered of the memory and basking in the approving roar from the class.

"That was *second*?" a student gasped. "What was *first*?"

Harold reflected, then spoke reverently. "The first? I never went beyond the title page. Because nothing could equal it. It said, 'Act One, Scene One: Ten million years before the first living creature crept out of the primordial ooze. Act One, Scene Two: Two weeks later.' "

Harold mimed closing the script in his ample lap, and sat back with a beatific smile. We went home content that night, and slept the sleep of the innocent.

Harold always assigned the scenes we worked on. He frequently steered me toward the classics and works of style, and increasingly, he proposed that I direct the scenes in which I or others acted, so that I had the advantage of being taught by him as both actor and director.

When two actors brought in a scene that the class found utterly incomprehensible, to the point where one of the students demanded to know if the actors had been speaking English, Harold asked us whether we could guess the playwright. We were shocked to learn that it was the work of the master of clarity and logic, George Bernard Shaw.

The scene was the Interlude from Shaw's *The Apple Cart,* and Harold explained that he had assigned it because of its notorious difficulty. "In most productions of *The Apple Cart,* the Interlude's omitted," Harold said. "I want to see the scene again. Jim, direct it for you and Nina, and bring it back to us."

Nina was Nina Foch, one of the remarkable galaxy of stars in that workshop. We'd recently married, and maybe Harold thought we'd bring something personal and useful to the roles of King Magnus and his mistress, Orinthia, in her boudoir.

As we worked on the scene, we found it a model of Shaw's acrobatic intellect, summed up in one of Magnus's speeches when Orinthia demands more of his time and attention: "Do not let us fall into the common mistake of expecting to become one flesh and one spirit. Every star has its own orbit; and between it and its nearest neighbor there is not only a powerful attraction but an infinite distance. When the attraction becomes stronger than the distance the two do not embrace: They crash together in ruin. We two also have our orbits, and must keep an infinite distance between us to avoid a disastrous collision. Keeping our distance is the whole secret of good manners; and without good manners human society is intolerable and impossible."

Framing this austere view in the sharply contrasting context of what the scene in fact was—a midday sexual "interlude," as the title bluntly asserts, in which the king arrives cheerfully to claim his droit de seigneur—we explored its sexuality in ways that other actors might not have elected to. Since, uniquely in Shaw, the playwright's voice and philosophical fireworks can be heard in the voice of every character—speaking through both the munitions manufacturer, Andrew Undershaft, and his Salvation Army daughter, Major Barbara; animating both the martyr Saint Joan and her tormentor Pierre Cauchon, the Bishop of Beauvais—we undertook to honor Shaw's Fabian dialectic and our Stanislavskian imperatives, couching the scene—literally—in the dramatic intentions Shaw has given his lovers: Orinthia's, "To make him leave his wife, the Queen, *in any way necessary, intellectually or sexually*"; and Magnus's, "To have Orinthia *on my own terms—but at all costs, to have her!*"—conflicting actions that end with iron logic in the playwright's stage direction, which describes the scene as "scandalous."

We had two obligations: the "scandalous scene" the playwright called for, and the crackling clash of ideas he expressed, as always, through the two characters. That was the scene we brought back to the workshop, to the satisfaction of the teacher and the class, which roared with laughter—and, mirabile dictu, comprehension—at what it had previously taken for gibberish.

I present this not as a testimonial to my talent, such as it is and is not, but as a blueprint of the approach that Harold and Stella taught us to employ, and that Nina Foch applied with notable distinction to her movie and stage careers, to an equally important teaching career at the University of Southern California, and as a sought-after coach to a generation of film actors.

Harold conducted the workshop for four years, and when he closed it, I found myself once again bereft. Clearly, I'd turned into a perennial student, and was reconciled to it, more accurately, content with it. Once again, I was bailed out by a former member of the Group Theatre, Robert Lewis, called universally and affectionately, Bobby.

Bobby was diminutive, plump, with a head as round and glossy as a bowling ball, and a perpetual impish grin. He was manifestly gay at a time when people went to great pains to mask their orientation. Bobby didn't. It was uninsistent but unequivocal.

Perhaps it was his sexual persuasion that influenced his theatrical sensibility. As his fellow Group members marched to the proletarian beat of plays like *Waiting for Lefty* and *Awake and Sing,* Bobby's heart was in the highlands. Literally. His first directorial effort on Broadway was William Saroyan's lyrical *My Heart's in the Highlands,* and he forged a notable career with stylish works like *Brigadoon, The Happy Time,* Truman Capote's *The Grass Harp, The Teahouse of the August Moon* and *Witness for the Prosecution.*

The title of Bobby's book, *Method or Madness,* encapsulates his approach to the craft: a never-ending effort to separate the wheat from the chaff, fact from fiction, widespread misconceptions about the Stanislavski system from its down-to-earth application.

On the general principles of the system, Bobby sided strongly with Stella, promising in his book to answer "the question as to whether or not the point of the Method was to reproduce our 'real life' on the stage, and who wants it? Had not Stanislavski himself said, 'An authentic "fact" and genuine reality do not exist on the stage! Reality is not art. This last, by its very nature, needs artistic invention.'"

In the belief that when students chose their own scenes, they served up nothing but softballs, Bobby followed Clurman's example of assigning the scenes he thought would engage each student's strengths and weaknesses. The reading of the assignments was an anxious occasion. Since we were certain they revealed Bobby's opinion of each actor's progress from one level of challenge and difficulty to the next, they were the equivalent of grades in a conventional academic program. Like Harold, Bobby pushed me toward the classics and works of style, and on the night Bobby, consulting the assignment list in front of him, said, "Jim Lipton, *Hamlet,* the arras scene," there was a murmur from the class—and my constricting heart.

As insurance against potential failure, I asked Mildred Dunnock to play my mother, Gertrude the queen. It's emblematic of that remarkable time in New York that Dunnock, who had climbed Broadway's heights keening, "Attention must be paid!" as Willy Loman's wife in *Death of a Salesman,* and was wreathed in honors for her work onstage and in film, was a constant, attentive student in Bobby Lewis's class, and willing to play Gertrude to the Hamlet of a young actor who was, to say the least, not in Lee J. Cobb's league.

At one of our many rehearsals, upon reaching the moment when Gertrude cried, "O Hamlet! Thou hast cleft my heart in twain," and Hamlet replied, "O! Throw away the worser part of it, and live the purer with the other half," I was so overcome by Gertrude's infidelity to my father—and to me, her son—that I burst into tears. The harder I tried to quell it and continue, the more bitterly I wept. Unable to stem the torrent and blinded by it, I fell to my knees and cried helplessly for what felt like five minutes.

Finally, as my breathing steadied and my vision cleared, I looked up to find Millie where I'd left her, standing in the center of the room, silent, expression-less. After a moment, she said matter-of-factly, "Well! Now that we've got that out of our system, shall we play the scene?"

When we put the scene up in class, the waterworks were gone, replaced by more interesting and revealing behavior. As Bobby Lewis famously remarked, "If crying were acting, my Aunt Rivka would be Eleanora Duse."

Toward the end of the two years I spent in Bobby's workshop, Bobby sat on the stage late one night, staring sadly at us. "What's wrong, Bobby?" one of the students asked.

"I was just thinking what you're going to have to put up with."

"Yeah—auditions, rejection, waiting tables . . ."

"Worse," Bobby said. "The problem is that when acting is very good—like that"—he gestured at the actors who had just concluded a beautifully acted scene—"it looks exactly like walking and talking. And *everybody*"—rising ire pushed him to his feet on the stage—"every common, ordinary soul on this planet walks and talks. The better you are, the easier it looks, so, all your lives, cretins are going to walk up to you and say, 'I saw you in so-and-so, and you know what? That was *me*! *I* could've played that part! Like that!" Bobby snapped his fingers. "And you know what you're going to want to do? Strangle them."

He scanned the class, engaging every gaze. "Do it," he said evenly, "strangle the sons of bitches," and left the stage for the night.

If the 1930s were, in Harold Clurman's apposite phrase, "The Fervent Years," the fifties and sixties were, in New York, in our calling, "The Fertile Years." This account would be incomplete without reference to two of the other masters of the Stanislavski System. Fortunately, *Inside the Actors Studio* has contributed to the preservation of their invaluable legacy.

Sidney Lumet, *Inside the Actors Studio's* fourth guest, an early member of the Actors Studio, and the director of *Serpico, Dog Day Afternoon* and *Network,* spoke to our students about his training with Meisner. "Sandy Meisner was the best acting teacher I ever saw. I studied with a great many teachers, but nobody like Sandy. He put it very simply. Acting is doing, and therefore, one doesn't deal with the mood or the feeling. In other words, one doesn't deal with it in result terms. One deals with it in an active verb form, and assuming that you've chosen the proper action, the feeling will be stimulated in you to communicate itself to an audience. It's a technique that I am firmly convinced works."

Sydney Pollack, the director of *Jeremiah Johnson, The Way We Were, Tootsie* and *Out of Africa,* and a co–artistic director of Actors Studio West, both studied and taught with Meisner. "It was," he said, "a watershed experience for me to bump into a guy like this at that particular point in my life. I had never had the experience of someone who was so succinct and perceptive and crystal-clear about any art form. I don't know if you've ever had the feeling where you heard somebody say something that you feel you've thought before, but never *knew* you thought it. You want to stand up and say, 'Yeah, yeah, yeah, that's right!' When I finished that, I came back as his assistant and spent the next five or six years teaching, which is really what ultimately led me to directing."

I asked Sydney about Meisner's famous Repetition Exercise.

"He was adamant about the sense of connection that has to exist between two actors—and how really dependent you are on the person that you're working with. But it takes a long time for that to become truly organic. And one of the ways he made it concrete was to literally force you to mimic each other in a way that removed from your concentration anything but the other person, because your job was literally to repeat what you saw being done. It was a terribly simple but very, very beneficial exercise. I say, 'One,' you say, 'One.' I say, 'Two,' you say, 'Two.' I wink and you wink. It's nothing. But if we sat here for an hour and did it, what would happen to both of us would get pretty wild." Seeing the look on my face, Sidney concluded, "I'm not gonna do it!"

Lee Grant, an Academy Award winner for her performance in *Shampoo,* a co-artistic director of the Studio, and one of the creators of the Actors Studio Drama School, told our students, "The great thing about Sandy was that he was very acerbic, very tough, very honest, very clear, and he sent you off, out of the nest. He did not try and hang on to you. He did not try and make you a sycophant all of your life. The kind of lessons he gave me were like life pre-servers. The most important was breaking down a play so that it was not a mysterious thing for me anymore. I mean, acting is such a mystery. If you're given a place to go and a lifeline to go to it, it lets you work through the mys-tery. You have an objective, you have action, so that the emotion comes out of it. You're not working on your emotion, you're working on what you *want*. Everybody wants something every minute of their day. When you go to the market, you want something, and therefore you go about getting it in a certain way. Well, it's the same thing in acting: You want something; and how badly you want it is what makes you theatrical, and interesting and exciting."

Alan Alda, one of our most articulate guests, summed up this approach to the actor's craft with, "I don't think you should be allowed onstage unless you are trying to get something—unless you *want* something. There should be a sign up in the wings: WHAT DO YOU WANT?"

He was equally emphatic—and clear—on a subject that would come up repeatedly over the years: the essential difference between what the public thinks of as "listening" and what it means in the actor's lexicon. "We all know listening is important. To me, listening is being able to be *changed* by the other person. It's not waiting for your cue; it's not 'When are they going to stop, so I can talk?' It's *letting them in,* letting them get inside you, letting them have an effect on you. Then you don't have to act! You listen to them, and they *make* you angry. You listen to them, and they *make* you fall in love with them. It's wonderful."

Both Eli Wallach and Anne Jackson, husband and wife and consummate members of the Actors Studio, studied with Meisner. Eli said, "I got a master's degree, and then I got a scholarship, as Anne did, to the Neighborhood Play-house. I went to audition, and I did a drunk. And Mr. Meisner said, 'Well! It'll take you twenty years.' And I thought, 'Does he know who I *am*? I've just come up from Texas, where I did *Liliom*." Eli sighed. "It took twenty years."

Anne said, "I think what I came away from Sandy's classes with was the sense that acting was not showing off, was not striking an attitude. You *acted.* You *do* something. You come into a room to get something, you get it and you leave. Or you don't get it, and you get thrown out. But you come on the stage in order to do something, and you get off as soon as you've done it. Don't linger."

I reminded Joanne Woodward that she'd said, " 'For two years I was slapped down, torn apart, and taught how to act by Sandy Meisner.' What did he teach you?"

"Fear. I'd been acting all my life, and all I knew was, you acted, whatever, you know? And it was a terrible, terrible trauma to do that. And I'm sure I never succeeded as far as Sandy was concerned. I found, finally, that it took me years and years—and the thing that I learned most from him was: It will take you twenty years to be an actor."

"He was famous for that."

Joanne nodded. "He said, 'It's like trying to play a violin. It takes you twenty years to learn how to put your finger on the fret without thinking about it.' And I swear to God I know exactly what he meant. It took me until *Rachel, Rachel.* One day I was doing a scene, and I realized, 'I didn't think, I didn't plan, I didn't prepare, I didn't do *anything*!' I was *in the moment,* I played the scene, and it was what I wanted it to be."

Joanne received an Academy Award nomination for *Rachel, Rachel,* which was directed by her husband, Paul Newman. It was one of four she received. She won the Academy Award for her remarkable performance as Eve White, Eve Black and Jane, the three "faces" of a woman afflicted with multiple personality disorder.

As anyone knows who has ever taken the time to watch the *Inside the Actors Studio* credits at the end of each episode, the program is produced by In the Moment Productions. When I created the series, I assigned the copyright and all its revenues to the Studio in perpetuity. In the Moment Productions is the instrument of that authority, and one of the means by which the decision we made to open the Studio's doors at a parlous time in 1994 has assured the Studio's healthy existence beyond the lifetimes of any of us who participated in that effort.

In the moment is a term of art, used often by Meisner, that means being completely committed, living totally, comfortably and without distraction in the given circumstances of that moment in that play or film.

In my long wandering in the groves of theatrical academe, I never studied with Meisner, but his definition of one of the central elements of our craft has, I think, never been equaled. I learned early, and remained convinced, that actors, playwrights, screenwriters, directors—all of us, individually and collectively—are in the "conflict" business every working moment of our lives. Every dramatic work, whether designated comedy or tragedy, is an examination of the collision and resolution of conflict. It can be lighthearted or heartrending, an entire work, a scene or a brief exchange of dialogue, but it is the engine that moves every dramatic endeavor.

I was told once that Meisner, facing a classroom of directors, asked them to define conflict. Most of them rushed confidently back to 350 B.C and Aristotle's *Poetics,* which spelled it out: "Tragedy is the imitation of an action; and an action implies personal agents who necessarily possess certain distinctive qualities both of character and thought; for it is by these that we qualify actions themselves, and these, thought and character, are the two natural causes from which actions spring, and on which all success or failure depends."

There was a comfortable consensus in the room. Conflict, the directors were certain, was nothing more nor less than two opposing actions, each one (if the author's construction is sound) the obstacle to the fulfillment of the other; and the collision between them is conflict.

In the account I was given, Meisner listened patiently until the class had come to its conclusion, then said, "Fine. Except for one thing: You've left out the key ingredient." The directors looked at one another, but no one came up with a response. "Everybody leaves it out," Meisner sighed. "I'll give you an illustration that I hope you won't forget. There are two brothers. One wants to devote his life to Quattrocento art in Florence, Italy; the other wants to be a Major League second baseman. And they're Siamese twins."

I suspect the directors were as struck by Meisner's parable as I was when I heard it.

"You left out the *glue,*" Meisner said. "Any hack can create two conflicting actions and toss them onstage. The literature's *full* of them. But what forces the characters to *deal* with each other? What prevents one of the characters from just saying, 'I don't need this. I'm outta here,' and walking out of the room—and the play? The *glue!*" Meisner declared. "You don't stay in the scene and fight it out because the author says you have to; you stay because the *character* says you have to. Because it's so well constructed that you have no choice! *The glue!*" Meisner repeated. "If you're a writer, write it; if you're a director, direct it; if you're an actor, act it. And don't forget it!"

That insight alone made me regret that I didn't add two years to my quest, in Meisner's scholarly company.

This appraisal of the theatrical giants who bestrode our profession's academic Golden Age would, of course, be incomplete without a stop at the Actors Studio itself for a visit with the imposing figure who directed its course for thirty-three years. Since I had no firsthand experience with him, I'll return once again to the wellspring that informs these pages. Needless to say, the name Lee Strasberg came up often on the stage of *Inside the Actors Studio.*

Our sixth guest, Sally Field, regaled us with colorful memories of Strasberg. "A wonderful person and actress worked on *The Flying Nun* with me. Her name is Madeline Sherwood and she was a very key player at the Actors Studio. One day she put her arm around me and said, 'I want you to come with me.' I said, 'All right,' and she took me to the Actors Studio. This was in Los Angeles. Lee Strasberg used to work at the Actors Studio West six months of the year."

"Who was there at the time?"

"Jack Nicholson was there all the time, and Ellen Burstyn and Shelley Winters and Bruce Dern. And it wasn't long before I signed up to do a scene. We'd prepared a scene from Sartre's *Respectful Prostitute.* Now, if you can imagine, I'm doing *The Flying Nun* in the day and at night I'm doing *The Respectful Prostitute.* I had no idea what it was about."

"What did you think those men were doing when they gave you money after?"

"Oh, I understood that part. I just didn't understand Sartre's words. I didn't know what the play was about and I didn't know how to work. But we worked and worked and worked and we prepared this scene, and it was one of the turning points of my life, right up there with having children, because we were to do this scene for ten minutes. Lee let the scene go on for forty-five minutes! And he said something to me . . . he said, 'You were quite brilliant.' And I almost said, 'What? Say it again!' And it allowed me to be where I am today."

"But didn't you stop going to the Studio?"

"Oh, yes. One day I had done a scene, a one-act play with another actress, and I remember feeling this kind of, like, cockiness. *Now* I know that any time you feel that, you're in trouble! He turned to me . . ." She paused to glance uncertainly at me. "This is television. Can we say all the words that we really say?"

"Yes."

"Can we *really*?"

I said, "Yes," and unleashed a firestorm.

"He asked what I was working on, and I said, 'Well, I was using my father.' And he said, 'When are you gonna quit this shit?'

"I said, 'What?' And he said, 'When are you gonna quit this goddamn *shit!*'" Sally trembled on our stage as she must have trembled then. "Lee never yelled like that, ever. *Ever.* He stood up and he started screaming at me. 'I am so fucking tired of this shit!'

"First of all, I was embarrassed. Because I had, like, 'cocky' written all over me. And he was red in the face, screaming at me. And I started to cry. And then I thought, 'I don't *want* to cry. I'm angry!'

"I said, 'How do you know? How do you know it's full of shit? How do you know it's full of shit?'

He said, "I DON'T BELIEVE YOU WERE FUCKING WORKING ON YOUR FUCKING FATHER!"

I said, "YOU CAN'T TELL ME WHO I AM! I WAS WORKING ON MY FATHER!" I was screaming back at him, and I stood up and I said, "WHO THE FUCK ARE YOU TO TELL ME WHO MY FATHER IS?" And I'm like crying, and screaming, my nose is running down my face, and I'm desperately trying *not* to cry. I don't *want* to cry! My nose is running. . . . 'You . . . can't . . . tell . . . me . . . who . . . I . . . am!'"

As she sobbed operatically on every syllable, the students' laughter swelled to thunderous applause. Caught in the memory, Sally looked at them, startled, then steadied herself. "So . . . I kind of, you know, got my little belongings and tried to pick up myself up as if, 'Well, you know, I'm really just as good as I was a minute ago. I really still am his pet, he really likes me, and I . . . I . . . I really . . . you know?' And I threw myself in the car and I went home and I was catatonic. It was devastating to me. It was DEVASTATING. And I didn't go back for a while."

Like Stella, Sally spoke fluent italics and Upper Case.

Dennis Hopper, *Inside the Actors Studio*'s seventh guest, called his experience with Strasberg "by far the most important time of my life." Explaining Strasberg's use of sense memory to the students, he said, "Sense memories are just hearing something that isn't there, seeing something that isn't there, smelling something, doing something that you've experienced. Stanislavski talked about standing in the corner for five minutes and not thinking about a white bear. The second you're in the corner, you think, 'I'm here not to think of a white bear.' So you can't win at that game.

"You tell a friend how your mother slapped you one time, but that doesn't mean anything; you don't have the emotion that happened when your mother slapped you. So, the only way you can do that is to stop thinking about what it was, get in this relaxed state and then go through your senses. What was I wearing, but not what was I wearing—can I *feel* what I was wearing that day? Can I hear anything that was happening that day? Not what was happening, because that's a conscious thing that's going to shut you off, but going through your senses, your smells, your seeing, your hearing, your touch. Something is going to hit and it's going to bring back the emotion.

"We did the song and dance, where you stand and sing. You know 'My Funny Valentine'?" Dennis began to sing protracted, vibratoless notes. "Myyyyyyyy fuuuuuuuuuuuuu-nnyyyyyyyyy vaaaaaaaaaalentiiiiiiine. So, then you're relaxed and Strasberg would say, 'You're real and we're real. You're real and we're real.' That's the song exercise. And then to do the dance, you start doing the same thing, but it's like a rag doll, a rag doll dance. It doesn't have any kind of form. It's just to see if your body's working with your voice."

I asked Dennis if he used sense memory.

"It's the best! Especially in film. In plays, you have to prepare way off, at the beginning of the act for when they bring the telegram that your father is dead. So, you have to do your emotional memory and carry it through and let it go at that moment. But in a film, you can do it a few seconds ahead. Or just before the camera rolls. And it's more effective, I think."

Some of the most celebrated film actors of the past fifty years, from Jimmy Dean, Montgomery Clift and Maureen Stapleton to Jack Nicholson, Ellen Burstyn, Dustin Hoffman, Anne Bancroft and Al Pacino, have been delivered by Strasberg, which leads me to think that Dennis made an important point: Strasberg's interpretation of sense memory, with its emphasis on the invocation of emotion at will, may be ideal for film, where the actor is summoned from his or her trailer after hours of waiting, and asked to deliver the most emotional scene in the movie—without the buildup, step by step, action by action, of a theater performance.

Ellen Burstyn, who earned six Academy Award nominations, and won an Oscar, employing Strasberg's techniques, spoke fervently of him on our stage.

"I made up my mind to leave California, move back to New York and study with Lee Strasberg, and that changed my life."

"How?"

"For me, it was a life-changing experience, because—it's hard to describe this—but I felt he took me seriously, and I hadn't had that feeling before. Anywhere. He listened to me in a way that I hadn't ever been listened to, that I hadn't listened to *myself.* I was a pretty, silly girl. I got by on my looks a lot, and I did okay, doing that. But he looked beyond that, and, and saw my humanity. And I hadn't ever been seen like that. And that changed my life. It changed the way I thought about myself, and it changed the way I thought about acting, and it changed the way I looked at other people. I took life more seriously because of him. That was a very great gift to me."

"Technically, what did he stress to you?

"He always stressed relaxation, commitment—the commitment to an impulse. He taught me how to listen *inside,* to know when an impulse was rising up, and snatch it and pull it out and express it, rather than what I had been doing until then: Anytime something rose up that was unaccounted for, I put it down. I had an idea of how something should be shaped, how the character should be, and whatever rose up that wasn't according to that idea I discarded.

He taught me how to listen to those unbidden thoughts or feelings or impulses that came up, and to appreciate that they are coming from a deeper place than my everyday mind conceptualizing about the part. That taught me to listen in a different way, to listen inside instead of outside."

One doesn't normally associate Mike Nichols with Lee Strasberg, but he was a devoted student. "In class there was a girl doing a scene, and Strasberg said afterward, as he said to all of us, 'What did you work for?' And she said, 'Oh, the night and the spring and the romance.' And he said, 'Do you know how to make fruit salad?' She said, 'Yeah,' and he said, 'How do you make it?'

"She said, 'I get an apple and I peel it and cut it up, and I get an orange and I peel it and cut it up, and I get a banana and I peel it and cut it up, and I mix them together.' And he said, 'That's right. You can run over the fruit in a steamroller or you can sit in front of it for hours and say, "Okay, fruit salad!" But you will never *have* fruit salad till you pick up each piece of fruit, peel it and cut it up.' And that is certainly what our jobs are. There's just no question about it: It's a series of small, specific tasks. I think of my work as sort of like cleaning a floor: You clean this little piece here, and then you move over and you clean the next part and the next part."

Harvey Keitel, a copresident of the Studio, and one of Strasberg's staunchest proponents, said, "He taught me something that was one of those lessons that have stayed with me all my life. We were doing a sensory class. I had not done much work in that area. I was always shy about it and I felt it was silly, you know?"

The students laughed and Harvey grinned at them. "You recognize that, huh? So, I was up there taking a shower."

I said, "For the benefit of those who are not among the initiate, it doesn't mean he was up there naked, under water. It's an exercise."

"I was dressed!" Harvey said. "So, I'm up there doing it, and people were encouraging me, 'Do it, Harvey, try and do it.' I'm trying to feel soap, morning, and thinking, 'Oh, Harvey, you jerk, this is embarrassing, embarrassing!' I get done and Strasberg asked me what I thought about it, and I said, 'I just don't believe anything.' And he asked the people, and they all said, 'Well, *we* believed it. We believed the water. We believed the soap.' And I'm sitting up there thinking, 'You're such fools. How could you possibly believe that? It's so silly.' Then he started to talk to me about it. He said it was very good. And I started asking questions. But this? But that? And finally he screamed at me, 'Just *do* it!! If you do it, you will understand it!' And he was right. I kept doing it, and it was *in the doing* that I understood what he meant. And now it informs all my work."

Harvey studied the students, and added, "In Dante's *Inferno,* there's a passage where Dante is sitting next to Virgil, and they have to get from here to there, and the terrain is filled with these monstrous creatures. Dante is scared, and he doesn't want to go where he has to go, for fear of being annihilated by these creatures. Not wanting to admit his fear, he says to Virgil, 'Are you sure we should try to cross this space?' And Virgil replies, 'The only answer I give you is in the doing. A just request is best met in silence.'"

Jane Fonda told us about her first meeting with Strasberg. "I was twenty, twenty-one, and I got to know Susan Strasberg. We would play chess on the beach in Malibu, and she would say, 'Why don't you join Lee's classes?' And so, finally, I did. I went and met him at the house in Malibu where he was living with Paula, his wife. She was coaching Marilyn Monroe on *Some Like It Hot*. I was so scared he wouldn't accept me that I convinced myself I didn't care. He said to me later, 'You were so boring and proper.' I said, 'Well, why did you take me into your class?' And he said, 'Because of your eyes. I could see something else in your eyes.'"

When Dustin Hoffman came to *Inside the Actors Studio,* like Jane Fonda, he recalled his first encounter with Strasberg. "Of course, I knew about the Studio. My God, the Studio, you know? Monty Clift and Brando and Kazan and Strasberg! It was legendary. That was the whole fantasy. I couldn't get in the Studio, but I heard that Strasberg had private classes at Carnegie Hall. You had to write a letter first. I wrote a letter. It's on Central Park West, I think, where he lived. And I remember walking in the day he was interviewing students. You're just petrified. These shelves and shelves and shelves of books on the theater. Extraordinary! He was a theater man more than anything else. It just came out of his pores.

"I had this two-minute interview, three-minute. I can't remember what the hell it was about. I was just so nervous. And then I found out I was going to be accepted, but it was in two years." The students groaned, and Dustin looked out at them. "I waited two years. And I went—seventy-five people in class. They didn't have a stage. Lights were on the actors and he sat in the first row. And you sat there for weeks, until you got up to do a sense memory for ten minutes."

Dustin chuckled at the memory. "But it was worth it—to hear him talk about the theater, to hear him talk about the Berliner Ensemble. I wasn't a student. I didn't go to college. But I got an education. His passion was overwhelming."

In the past century, perhaps no teacher, with the exception of Stanislavski himself, has put his stamp so thoroughly on an institution as Strasberg did on the Studio. And in the six decades of the Actors Studio's existence, perhaps none of its members can be more closely identified with Strasberg and his techniques than Al Pacino. Al is one of the copresidents of the Studio, and when he came to the *Inside the Actors Studio* stage, twenty of my nearly five hundred blue cards were inscribed with questions about Lee Strasberg. The first was, "What was he like as a man?"

"To me, he was sort of like a relative. My relationship with Lee changed. It went from being so scared of him to hugging him all the time because we became actors together, and once you work with someone, when you're in the trenches, it changes the dynamic. That's when Lee and I became very close friends. But before that, he was very imposing. He had an aura about him, and it was good for the Studio, because there was a distance between him and everybody else, and it had a real power.

"It was exciting to work for him because he was so interesting when he talked about a scene or talked about people. One would just want to hear him talk, because things he would say, you'd never heard before. In his last days, he made me an ice-cream soda. And it was really good, like one you get in candy stores when you're growing up. And afterward, he said, 'You want me to teach you how to make it?' I said, 'Well, that's not necessary.' He said, 'Not necessary? How are you going to have it again?' He was so interested in how things happened.'"

I asked, "What are one or two things he taught you that you use in your work?"

"He taught me something that I don't do enough of. I forget it sometimes. I wish Lee were around to remind me. He said, 'Sometimes, don't go as far as you can go.'"

"Stay well within yourself?"

"Stay well within yourself, absolutely."

"Do you use affective memory when you work?"

"It's extremely helpful at times. Over the years, I've developed a way of working. The whole idea of being 'personal' is very important—to find that *in you* that you can relate to the play."

I asked Al about acting with Lee Strasberg in *Godfather II,* in which Strasberg played Hyman Roth, who bore a resemblance to real-life crime lord Meyer Lansky.

"I loved acting with him."

"Does he live by the rules when he acts?"

Al grinned. "No way! He's an actor. He's one of us, you know." In the audience, Ellen Burstyn burst into laughter. "He put all of that away, and was just one of us." Al paused to reflect, then resumed. "He had such a great understanding because . . . he loved actors so much." Al's voice shook slightly.

The eight and a half years I spent under the capacious wings of Stella Adler, Harold Clurman and Bobby Lewis constituted the core of the educational program I was devising. I had no choice but to assemble it myself, since no university or acting school could offer training of that caliber. I was becoming a classroom addict, earning my living in theater and television, but resolutely filling every offstage or offscreen moment with study, fitting the academic pieces together in a decadelong pursuit of the elements of craft.

During my first year in Stella's school, I began voice training with Madame Eva Gauthier, a legendary teacher who taught in an apartment lined with photos of the opera singers she'd trained. I followed her lessons with several years of intensive work with Arthur Lessac, whose book, *The Use and Training of the Human Voice,* is dedicated to his student roster, which has included Martin Sheen, Beatrice Straight, George Grizzard, Faye Dunaway, Michael Douglas, Nina Foch, Frank Langella, Peter Scolari, Morris Carnovsky and Linda Hunt.

Lessac had devised an ingenious system for the training of the speaking and singing voice. I zealously studied both, interweaving his twice-weekly lessons with my other classes.

At the same time that I began the study of voice, I elected to add another arrow to my quiver with the study of dance. I harbored no ambitions or delusions about becoming a dancer: I simply saw dance—and voice—as vital adjuncts to the training I was receiving from Stella, Harold and Bobby.

There was nothing unusual in this: Actors have traditionally trained the voice and body. Stanislavski and the Moscow Art Theatre placed strong emphasis on these external aspects of the craft. But the Russian actors found their voice and body training *at* the Moscow Art Theatre; I found mine through a personal quest, piecing together what I perceived as a comprehensive, compatible curriculum.

If there is a premonitory gene, I suspect I lack it. Just as I left Detroit for New York without a clue to what I would actually find, and began working with Stella under the benighted impression that her classes were a means to an unrelated end, I began the study of dance as one would join a gym, for the exercise.

One of the glories of all the arts is their seductive guile: They open the door to you like an impassive maître d', then close it behind you like Mata Hari on the make. Whatever I thought I was going to find in a dance class, I found instead a surprising interest, then a fascination, then a determination, then an unquenchable passion—not only as a witness but as an enthralled participant.

My first dance study was with Hanya Holm, the German-born dancer and choreographer who became one of the pioneers of modern dance in America.

A small, bustling, high-spirited woman, she found a special niche in the theater, as choreographer of *Kiss Me Kate, My Fair Lady* and *Camelot,* and her school was a modern-dance mecca.

I enrolled for Hanya's classes and soon found myself sweating and stretching and learning five mornings a week under her jolly, demanding tutelage. Professional ballet training begins at the age of six or seven; modern dance training can begin later (which is why some colleges offer it), because it doesn't require ballet's "turnout," which must begin early in order to twist the knob at the top of the thighbone around in the hip socket, an agonized angstrom at a time, until, after hundreds of thousands of pliés and battements, the knees face sideways, permitting the leg to rise in a graceful extension that grazes the dancer's ear with an arched instep—without dislocating from the hip. Since female bone stops growing at fourteen, and male at sixteen, I had clearly passed the point of no return, and modern dance was the only prescription.

When Hanya didn't teach the class, her pupil and disciple, Alwin Nikolais, did. Nik was himself a choreographer of great distinction, and when my reckless zeal attracted his and Hanya's attention, he, Hanya and I became friends, a friendship that endured to the ends of both their lives. Dance is a salubrious discipline: Hanya died at ninety-nine in 1992.

Given my insatiable thirst for instruction, it was inevitable that the seed that had been planted by Hanya and Nik would sprout. Piqued by my putative ineligibility for ballet, and encouraged by my progress in modern dance, I signed up for ballet classes with Ella Daganova, who was the foremost teacher of Cecchetti, the technique developed in the nineteeth and early twentieth centuries by Enrico Cecchetti, who trained Pavlova (with whom Daganova had danced), Nijinsky and the dancers of the Maryinski and Ballets Russes.

After two years with Daganova, I was emboldened to enroll at the Fokine School in Carnegie Hall, which had attracted the dance world's attention with the sudden emergence of a young American teacher to whom the dancers of Ballet Theatre and the New York City Ballet were flocking.

His name was Benjamin Harkarvy. Though barely in his twenties, he was balding and, not to mince words, fat, looking anything like a dancer—but it was in overcoming his dance disabilities that he had developed an innovative approach to classical ballet that was the talk of New York's dancers.

His classes were packed, and I breathed a sigh of relief when I was admitted. The years that followed (while, on a parallel track, I proceeded from one acting teacher to another, and underwent my vocal training) were a blissful blur of glissades, chassés, assemblés, entrechats quatres (on good days sixes), cabrioles and jetés.

Harkarvy was as advertised: a born teacher, inventive, inspiring and rigorous in his demands and approach. I studied with Harkarvy for several years, until he embarked for Europe, where he served as ballet master of the Netherlands Ballet, and was one of the creators of a celebrated dance company, the Nederlands Dans Theater. He was director of the Juilliard Dance Division from 1992 until his death in 2002.

In the interest of full disclosure, I should admit that, while my devotion to ballet was genuine and elevated, there was another compelling motive.

For all the years that I studied it, I was surrounded in class by lissome young women in skintight clothing, performing slow, sensual movements in front of a mirrored wall. Of all the classical arts, dance is the most frankly erotic—when it chooses to be, and sometimes when it doesn't. I tried to describe dance's sensual roots in my novel *Mirrors,* asking, What is a classical pas de deux, in *Swan Lake* or *The Sleeping Beauty* or *Giselle* or Jerome Robbins's *Afternoon of a Faun,* but "the basic configuration of dance and life: one male, one female, squared off face to face, one on one."

And here I was at the barre, in tights, constrained only by a dance belt, executing a grand plié in second position behind an exquisite eighteen-year-old danseuse in an identical inviting position.

Granted, there were other men in the class, every one of them more prepossessing than I, not to mention a far better dancer—but *not one of them,* for their own good and cogent reasons, shared my reveries about these silken, *neglected* nymphs.

The field was clear and open! And I stood with Yeats: "How shall we know the dancer from the dance?" If these young women looked like this, and moved like this, and stared at their captivating bodies in the mirror like this, hour after hour, day after day, chances are they *were* like this. And, often, that turned out to be the case. Not to put too fine a point on it, for several concupiscent years, I thought I'd died and gone to heaven.

Driving myself relentlessly to make up for lost time, I trained almost to the professional level, in a class that included some of America's most renowned classical dancers. Exactly as I'd stopped thinking of my acting classes as adjunctive to another career, so I stopped considering dance a means to something other than its wondrous self. I didn't lose touch with reality: I would never qualify to dance a step on a stage. But I no longer saw the classroom as a gym. I loved watching dance, and I loved doing it, as well as I was able. Like the real dancers around me, after the explosion of vertical jumps that ended each class, I left the classroom drenched in sweaty elation.

Unexpectedly, my dance training helped me breach the last barrier to the creative life I'd shunned in my teens. Stella, Harold and Bobby had banished every taboo but one—the most threatening one. I accustomed myself to acting and directing without anxiety or guilt—but *writing* was what my father did, and so, from the age of eighteen through my mid-twenties, I confined myself to my university assignments, dutifully delivering what was required, but scrupulously avoiding anything that could be construed as a product of the creative imagination.

However, my voice training, my absorption in dance and the propulsion toward directing in Clurman's workshop were nudging me in a distinct direction. Without forethought or conscious design as always, I awoke to the fact that acting, plus directing, plus singing, plus dance added up to four of the seven essential ingredients of the theatrical form that was America's unique gift to the world's stage, the Broadway musical.

The three missing ingredients were the play, the lyrics and the music. One of my last literary outbursts, before I lowered the creative curtain at the age of eighteen, was a spate of lyrics in high school, written to the music of a prodigiously gifted fellow student, Laurence Rosenthal, who would go on to the Eastman School of Music, to the tutelage of Nadia Boulanger in Paris, to a string of Oscar nominations and Emmys for his film and television scores, and, ultimately, to Broadway with me, as the composer of our musical *Sherry!*

Now, as uninvited impulses stirred, I acquired a 1679 edition of the complete works of Molière and, on an impulse, began translating *The Doctor in Spite of Himself,* as a pure exercise, or so I thought. But as the translation emerged, it began to be interrupted by song fragments, or at least the words of songs; and finally, bowing to what felt like the inevitable, I enlisted Laurence Rosenthal, whom I'd reencountered when he was studying with Boulanger and we were both living in Paris, to set the lyrics to music.

The last barrier to the forbidden life fell without a sound. I was writing—indisputably and without noticeable ill effects. As I've retraced the journey that brought me to this moment—in exactly the way I ask my *Inside the Actors Studio* guests to do, looking for the moments and events that shaped them—the only logical explanation I've been able to come up with for the feelings and behavior that ruled me for a critical decade of my life is the adversarial relationship with my father. This discovery, for whatever it's worth, is one of the unintended consequences of this undertaking.

Once Laurence Rosenthal had agreed to provide the music for *The Doctor in Spite of Himself,* in a creative fever I converted the translated play to a musical book, completed the score with Larry, and offered the project, as book writer, lyricist, director and choreographer, to the Theatre Guild—run by Lawrence Langner and Stella's blue-haired nemesis, Theresa Helburn.

Within forty-eight hours, they accepted it for their summer theater, the Westport Country Playhouse, which served the Theatre Guild as a tryout house for their more experimental offerings, providing them with a relatively low-cost "out-of-town" venue.

I cast the popular comic actor Jules Munshin, who had played one of the three sailors, with Frank Sinatra and Gene Kelly, in the film of Leonard Bernstein's *On the Town,* as Sganarelle, the hapless doctor in spite of himself, and Betsy Palmer, who costarred with Jack Lemmon in *Mister Roberts,* as the object of Sganarelle's lubricious interest.

In an (entirely unnecessary) effort to give the work authenticity, Larry's inventive work was advertised as the music of Jean-Baptiste Lully, the composer who provided the music for Molière himself in the seventeenth century.

The show was such a resounding success that Langner and Helburn proposed me to Jerome Robbins as codirector of his first Broadway directorial assignment, *Bells Are Ringing,* starring Judy Holliday. Robbins, not unexpectedly, or unwisely, declined and went solo, but, thanks to Molière and the Theatre Guild, I'd been launched as a director—and a writer—*pace pater meus.*

The show also launched me as a choreographer, since Walter Terry, one of the most influential voices in American dance as dance critic of the *Herald Tribune,* happened by the Westport Country Playhouse and published a glowing review of my choreography. The review attracted the attention of Lucia Chase, the codirector of Ballet Theatre, who invited me to choreograph a work for the company.

Beginning the process with the music, I chose a work by Darius Milhaud, *Le Boeuf Sur le Toit.* Used at one time to score an unsuccessful French ballet called, in English, *The Nothing-Doing Bar,* with a libretto by Jean Cocteau, it was one of Milhaud's polytonal works, strongly informed by his infatuation with jazz. When I found a photocopy of Milhaud's original manuscript at the New York Public Library, I discovered his note at the top of the first page: "Written to accompany any Charlie Chaplin film"—and in that instant I had my ballet.

I called it *Charlot,* which is what Chaplin's tramp is called in France and everywhere outside the United States, and I choreographed it on several of the stars of Ballet Theatre, Enrique Martinez, Violette Verdy, Sallie Wilson and Ray Berra, with a large corps dancing the characters one encountered in a Chaplin film. I placed the ballet in a park, with Martinez, a wiry, *demi-caractère* dancer, as Charlot; Violette Verdy, one of the company's most lyrical ballerinas, as the inevitable flower girl; Ray Berra, a powerful technician, as one of Chaplin's archetypal villains; and Sallie Wilson, who normally danced the DeMille and Tudor narrative roles that required strong acting talent, as a nursemaid in the park who becomes enmeshed in all the tangled plots.

Assisted by Gemze de Lappe, the dancer who had been Agnes DeMille's muse, then her assistant, I rehearsed the cast at intervals for several weeks, bringing the ballet close to completion when the company left for a European tour. We were to resume rehearsals immediately on their return, but halfway through the tour, I got a call from my cast, assembled around a phone and all shouting at once. It seemed that Lucia Chase, who not only codirected the company with Oliver Smith, but financed it from her considerable personal fortune, had, in one of the fits of pique for which she was famous, announced that she was closing her checkbook—and the company. Ballet Theatre was about to become extinct. And with it, *Charlot*.

Understandably desperate, the dancers were urging me to find a new "Lucia"—or even to *be* a new "Lucia"—and save the company—and the ballet, which they wanted to perform.

When the company returned, the newspapers were full of the drama of its demise, and after some time, Chase was persuaded to resume her financial sponsorship. The company reassembled, but reassembling the cast, which was caught up in the company's frenzied effort to rehearse and remount the Ballet Theatre repertoire after its layoff, proved to be a daunting challenge, despite the dancers' wish to preserve *Charlot*.

It quickly became clear that remounting the ballet would require more time from the overburdened dancers, Gemze and me than any of us could provide. Like the little tramp at the end of each film, *Charlot* skipped away, gamely twirling his malacca cane, to an indeterminate fadeout.

It was neither a career-altering failure, though God knows it might have been, nor a career-altering success, though there's a slim chance it might have been. What it was was the conclusion of one chapter and the emphatic beginning of another.

*6 6The force that through the green fuse drives the flower
Drives my green age.*

—Dylan Thomas

Ten years went by in a flood of academic exploration. While I was probing the mysteries of acting and directing and modern dance and ballet and the Italian art song and the Broadway ballad, and testing what
I'd learned on the stage and screen, I augmented my curriculum at several of
the city's universities with the continuing study of French and literature and
philosophy and symbolic truth-functional logic (Wayne University had taught
Aristotelian categorical logic) and art- and music-history and filmmaking,
always for credit in order to pit myself against the course's exams.

As I made my way through the groves of academe, I became fully engaged
in my various pursuits full-time.

A film called *Wheel of Fire* took me to Europe. When I was ten, I used to
spend each Saturday afternoon at the J. L. Hudson Company, where my
mother ran a circulating library in the book department, which occupied half
a city block *(autres temps, autres moeurs)* of one of the largest department
stores in America.

After browsing the library for the weekly stack of books Mother would
check out for me, I'd roam Hudson's dazzling bazaar, always winding up for at
least an hour, leaning on the counter of the Ask Mr. Foster Travel Bureau, gazing longingly at the posters of exotic places—Africa, London, Rome, Paris—
that might as well have been Mars.

Wheel of Fire was scheduled to be filmed in Greece, where I would play the
leading role, but the director phoned me when I arrived in Paris, instructing
me to remain there, at the company's expense, while they continued to wend
their way through the Greek bureaucracy as they prepared the shoot.

Faced with this ultimate hardship assignment, I tried to disguise my joy.

On my first night in Paris—my first night anywhere outside the United States, apart from Windsor, Ontario—I asked the concierge of the Hôtel Duminy to recommend a nearby restaurant, and he pointed me toward Chez Pierre à la Fontaine Gaillon. As I walked there on an early March night, the Paris streets were dark and cold and wet and indescribably beautiful. Everywhere I looked, the posters of the Ask Mr. Foster Travel Bureau smiled back at me.

Because it was March, there were no tourists crowding the streets. Paris was still recovering from the trauma of the war years, which is to say, it was still in many respects the Paris of the twenties and thirties, when it was the cynosure of the civilized world.

When I arrived at Chez Pierre, it was nearly empty. On this first night of a startling new life, I took my place on a banquette, and as I picked up the menu, I hoped the waiter wouldn't notice that my hand was shaking. When I'd ordered dinner in my college French (I would have been more comfortable, and comprehensible, in Latin), I was suddenly confronted with a mysterious creature: my first sommelier.

Desperate not to be perceived as gauche—or louche!—I scrutinized the wine list he'd handed me, recognized nothing, put it down and said, as casually and world-wearily as I could, "I think, tonight, I'll just have your *vin rouge ordinaire.*"

The sommelier paused for an instant, then nodded and vanished. I was relieved when he reappeared with a red wine *en carafe.*

I was halfway through my dinner, and beginning to feel French to my fingertips, when the eponymous Pierre showed up and, seeing me—and seeing *through* me—came to my table with a smile to ask if I was enjoying my dinner. I replied smoothly that I was. Glancing at the carafe, he asked what wine I'd ordered, and I committed my first gaffe. "I ordered the *vin ordinaire.*"

He drew himself up. "We don't *serve vin ordinaire.*"

"I—well, I—well, that's what I ordered," I sputtered—exposed as a parvenu on my first night in Paris!

Taking pity on me, he summoned the hovering sommelier with a snap of his fingers, and asked for a glass. Filling it from my carafe, he took a sip—and his face fell. "Oh, *monsieur,*" he exclaimed. "I'm so sorry!"

"Why?!"

"This wine," he said, staring at it as he swirled it slowly, "is for certain occasions."

Feeling very uncultivated and American, I asked, "Such as?"

Still staring at the wine with narrowed eyes, he said, "You have just learned that your mother is ill," and directed a questioning glance at me. I shook my head and he resumed the litany. "Your favorite uncle has been arrested for an unspeakable perversion." I shook my head. He continued, on one long, unbroken breath now, glancing at me for each disavowal: "Your rich aunt has died—and left you out of the will. You've discovered that your mistress is deceiving you." (We were entering uncharted waters; seeing my expression, he veered to a less sophisticated track.) "Your dog has been run over. You've lost your last sou at *chemin de fer*. You've contracted a venereal disease. . . ." There were more, but those are the ones that stick in my memory.

Finally he ran out of citations—or breath. "None of them? Nothing like that?"

"No," I said, abandoning a terrible performance (I could hear Stella screaming, "INDICATING!"), and opting for my only remaining option, honesty. "It's just the opposite. This is my first night in Paris—in Europe! I've never been so happy in my life!"

His eyes lit up. "Ah!" He snapped his fingers and murmured something to the sommelier, who hurried away and returned in a moment with a bottle of wine, which he opened with a flourish and poured into two new glasses. Pierre sat down at my table. "Now, taste *your* wine." I took a sip of the first wine. He pushed my water glass to me. "A little water. Now—*this* wine." He sipped from his glass as I followed his instructions. It was a thunderbolt. I'd never sampled two tastes side by side. Even to this neophyte, the two wines were now as unlike as syrup and vinegar.

"Which one do you prefer?" Pierre asked.

"This one!" I said, brandishing the new glass.

"Of course," he said, regarding the wine deferentially as he revisited his litany. "Your mother was ill, but you've just learned that she's going to recover. Your favorite uncle has been cleared of all charges, with an apology from the little girl. Your rich aunt has died—and left you *everything*! You've got a fabulous *new* mistress! Your dog has been run over—but by you in a brand-new Citroën. You've made a killing at the racetrack. Your worst enemy has contracted a venereal disease. . . ."

Pierre remained at my table, and a man who was watching the spectacle with evident amusement from an opposite table got up and joined us. The three of us polished off the favored bottle of wine as the newcomer, who was a Swiss businessman in town for two days, explained that he'd bought two of the best seats for the Folies Bergères, and had come to Chez Pierre in hope of finding a young woman who might be interested in his company. "But . . ." he said, gesturing at the empty restaurant.

Pierre, our genial boniface, genially suggested *"notre ami américain."* The Swiss concurred, and my first evening in Paris ended at the Folies Bergères, the charms of which hadn't been so much as hinted at by the posters lining the walls of Ask Mr. Foster. Clearly, I concluded, Mr. Foster had led a pathetically sheltered existence.

In less than twenty-four hours, I had been blooded.

When I was finally summoned to Greece, it was evident that the production was in serious trouble. Each time the right people were paid off, the producer moaned, the government fell, and there was a new pack of bureaucrats with their hands out. The Greek people were another matter—quite simply the kindest people I'd ever encountered.

Since the production was once again stalled, I was at liberty in Greece for nearly three months, installed in the Hotel New Angleterre on Othos Ermou in Athens, and exploring Attica and Sparta in the producer's car, which he lent me, out of guilt, perhaps, at the endless delays.

I toured the Greek Isles. On Mykonos, which I'm told is today as crowded and chic as Capri in season, there was only one primitive hotel, which I couldn't afford. I stayed instead in a private home that, in place of a front door, had a beaded curtain, so that the water carrier could enter in the middle of the night and fill the tall clay vessel just inside the entrance with fresh well-water.

Liberated in every conceivable way from the constraints of the past, I fulfilled an amorphous childhood dream and ran away with gypsies—in the company of an exquisite young Greek woman who shared my fascination with gypsies, and was in flight from an arranged marriage to a wealthy businessman in the Anglo-Egyptian Sudan. With her family in hot pursuit, we made our way north in my producer's handy car, following our gypsy band until we parted company with them at Delphi on the slope of Mount Parnassus.

There may be a Hilton in Delphi now, but in those distant days there was only one accommodation. A bent local woman, garbed in the requisite black, seemed to own a cliff face, into which several caves had been cut. They were reached by a tall ladder that she provided, after payment of the night's tariff. Each cave contained candles, a bed, a basin, towels and water jars, which was sufficient to our needs. The cave we were assigned contained a religious picture, which under our illicit circumstances seemed unbefitting. My companion crossed herself before it, then covered the Savior's penetrating gaze with a towel.

The only exit from the cave was via the ladder, which required summoning the hotelier with shouted exhortations from the mouth of the cave. We stayed for two days, visiting the rock on which Apollo's oracle had perched in previous millennia, counseling visitors, some of them, I suspect, in situations not unlike ours.

We ended each afternoon in Delphi on our own perch, above a stone wall that contained two stone spigots, channeling freshwater from Parnassus, one at shoulder height for the citizens, one at knee height for their burros. Our wall commanded a view to east and west of mountains growing purpler and purpler as they marched into what appeared to be an infinite distance.

From the valley below, the inhabitants of Delphi toiled up the winding road in a daily ritual, remounting Parnassus with their burros, each one carrying a bright yellow sheaf of wheat. When they arrived at the fountain, as their forebears had, we assumed, two thousand years ago, they paused to slake their thirst at the higher spigot, as their animals lapped eagerly at the basin below. And, this being Greece, not one person was too hot or tired or thirsty to pause before drinking to smile and say, *"Kalispera"* ("Good evening"), to the enchanted refugees on the wall.

I can report that my companion suffered no ill effects from our reckless adventure. Apart from our happy confederacy with the gypsies and the people of Delphi, her act of rebellion convinced her family that the arranged marriage was a serious mistake. How the fellow in the Anglo-Egyptian Sudan took it, I never discovered. And didn't much care in those sunny, feckless times.

As the movie remained stalled, I made my way into Sparta to visit Mycenae, where the House of Atreus stood, its stone foundations still laid out like a blueprint on the Mycenaean acropolis. Employing a 1905 Baedeker, I arrived at the Gate of the Lions, where a wizened gatekeeper directed me to Agamemnon's palace. There, I found, in Baedeker's words, the stone steps up which Agamemnon walked to his death at the hands of his wife, Clytemnestra, and her lover, Aegistheus, when he returned from Troy.

That night, waiting for dinner at La Belle Hélène (of course), a hotel that Baedeker (in 1905) correctly called "the worst accommodation in Europe," I wandered into a neighboring field, where I found a dozen shepherds hunkered in a circle, chatting animatedly while, around them, their sheep grazed, each animal's neck dangling a bell so that the flock sounded a constantly shifting, otherworldly chord.

To the west, the sun was setting in the (then) unsullied air of Greece, in a riot of silvers and greens and pinks and crimsons, framed by a parade of silhouetted cedars on the surrounding hills. Abiding by the prevailing Greek spirit of bonhomie, the shepherds, each one holding a hand-carved crook, gestured me to join them.

I'd discovered that one of the advantages of Greek travel is that, wherever one goes, there is the likelihood of finding at least one English-speaking citizen who has retired to his native land after thirty or forty years of operating a restaurant in St. Louis or San Diego. The one in this circle had served souvlaki and saved his money in Cleveland. Another shepherd spoke French; and, with time on my hands, I'd reverted to type and was taking daily instruction in Greece's art and language.

The moment I'd settled into my place, the shepherds leaned forward as if they'd been waiting for this moment all day—or all year—and the English-speaking shepherd nodded toward the acropolis and asked, "Did you go up on the hill today?"

"Of course. That's why I came to Mycenae."

"You saw Agamemnon's house?"

"Oh, yes. I walked up the steps."

"You saw the bathtub where he was killed?"

Baedeker had led me there. "Yes."

The entire circle leaned further forward, every eye on me, as the shepherd purred, "Why do you think she did it?"

I couldn't believe my ears. "You mean Clytemnestra . . . ?"

"Of course."

"Why did she kill Agamemnon?" The entire circle nodded. Feeling myself sliding into a time warp, and unable to believe that I was blithely uttering these words, I said, "Because he sacrificed their daughter, Iphigenia, to get wind for his sails, so he could sail to Troy."

The circle opened like a flower, rocking back on its heels and roaring with laughter at my naïve response. I glared at the shepherds, annoyed: We were talking about the Trojan War, for God's sake! We were hanging out in an Elysian field at sunset discussing Agamemnon's ten-year campaign to reclaim Helen, the face that had launched a thousand goddamn ships when she ran off with Paris, as if . . . as if . . . !

My interlocutor, taking pity on me, revealed their hand: "Then, why do you think Electra had to get Orestes out of town in such a hurry? Because *those kids knew exactly what was going on between their mother and Aegistheus,*" he confided in a conspiratorial whisper.

I reeled. Aegistheus was Clytemnestra's lover; "those kids" were the Electra and Orestes of my drama classes. Returning from exile as a man, Orestes would consult the Oracle at Delphi, in the very spot my friend and I had consulted her, and return to Mycenae to join with his sister in killing Clytemnestra and Aegistheus—and launch Western literature.

Past and present had merged in a single, surging stream—in this field, lit by the setting sun, and accompanied by the music of a hundred bells, where this whole history was nothing more nor less than neighborhood gossip, as alive and real now as it was in 1200 B.C., when Agamemnon returned from Troy. Homer didn't get around to it until five hundred years later in *The Iliad* and *The Odyssey*. Since the House of Atreus was seven hundred years old when Aeschylus saw it, he saw exactly the same ruin I'd seen this morning, minus only La Belle Hélène . . . and here we were—*here I was*—nattering on about it as if it were yesterday. Or today.

Granted, not a lot had happened here in Mycenae in the 3,200 years since Agamemnon climbed those steps I'd climbed today—certainly nothing as interesting. Maybe these shepherds had a right. Maybe *I* had a right, but it still felt peculiar.

The shepherds joined in, insisting vociferously that all that talk about revenge for what Agamamnon had done to Iphigenia at Aulis was just a cover-up for Clytemnestra and Aegistheus's *real* motive: to get Agamemnon out of the way—permanently, so they could continue the adulterous affair.

The shepherds sat back, resting their case, waiting for me to yield and stop perpetuating the nonsense that had fogged the air of this case for three millennia. I guessed they figured that if they could make one convert their day had been well spent—and I wondered how many times they'd lain in wait here for the next candidate to emerge from La Belle Hélène.

When the dinner bell sounded at the hotel, and I rose to return to the worst accommodation in Europe, one of the shepherds reached out and handed me his crook, perhaps because I'd been such a malleable initiate. The crook hangs prominently in my study to this day, the carved dragon coiled on its crest reminding me every time I glance at it of a magical evening when a circle of generous shepherds shared with me the whole, unvarnished truth of Homer's odes and the plays of Aeschylus and Euripides.

When there was no longer any gainsaying the reality in Athens, *The Wheel of Fire* folded its tripods and C-stands, and I returned the car to the producer who, in a fit of rage at the film's fate, shoved it off the pier as it was being loaded on the freighter that would have returned it to the States. I daresay the Greeks hauled the wreck out, but, since it carried me to some of the most provocative experiences of my life, I like to think that it still rests in the azure waters of the Aegean, a memorial to a remarkable time and place and a seminal adventure.

I returned, on my own now, to Paris, and spent the better part of the rest of that year there, undergoing the rites of passage that Paris uniquely affords, falling happily in with the community of American literary expatriates who were studiously following in the footsteps of Hemingway, F. Scott Fitzgerald and Gertrude Stein.

A number of us met weekly at a salon we'd set up in the living room of one of the better-heeled, hence better housed, of the group. It was customary on these Sunday afternoons for everyone in the circle to exhibit the week's work.

Poets read poems, novelists read the latest chapter, composers premiered sonatas, singers performed Puccini.

On one occasion, a stout young woman who'd come to Paris to study opera declined to sing when her turn came. Sacrilege! No one had ever refused to join in the sacred ritual. Thinking she wanted to be coaxed, a chorus of persuasion arose, but she was adamant. So was the group, until finally, red-faced, she blurted out, "If you must know, I'm wearing a new girdle and it's so tight, I *can't* sing!"

She spoke in French, in which the word for girdle is *gaine*. The room went silent, and finally one of the writers in the corner drawled, "Well, your *gaine* is our loss." As with any masterful pun, respect demanded silence, not laughter. The room was in such awe that no one was willing to follow the *jeu de mots*, and the afternoon ended on that stirring note.

Since I was no longer on an expense account, the question of keeping body and soul together came up, as it had so often in my life. From the photoengraving plant to the *Detroit Times* to *The Lone Ranger,* I'd shown some agility, but here in Paris a work permit was virtually impossible to acquire: There was at that time barely enough work for the French.

Rescue came, as it so often did in my life, from an unexpected quarter. On first arriving in Paris, I'd met a young Frenchman who had introduced me to all the blandishments of Paris. My age, he was an experienced and invaluable, if unorthodox, guide. In the course of one evening's prowl, we found ourselves, at his suggestion and with my enthusiastic agreement, in the red-light district, Paris's famed Rue Pigalle, where we were besieged on a cold March night by a clutch of clientless *poules,* competing to offer the most exotic delights.

My friend Fernand was an experienced hand. When two of the *filles* offered to demonstrate their love for each other, Fernand struck a bargain, and the four of us repaired for the demonstration to a room in the hotel that housed them and their colleagues. I'll ascribe to myself neither concupiscence nor consternation. Suffice to say, to my then untutored eye, the performance was matchless.

When they concluded, they offered additional services, which I declined on the grounds, to which I still subscribe, that if you have to pay a partner for sex, you don't deserve it. Thoughtful, artful seduction, I reasoned then, and believe now, is the price one partner pays for the privilege of the other.

When Fernand and I came down the hotel stairway, he grabbed my arm suddenly and steered me toward a curtained opening. Pushing through it, we arrived in a bar—to a chorus of protests from the *filles* and their *mecs* (a less pejorative term than pimps; *vide Irma la Douce*), for whom it served as a private club in which to drink Calvados, munch on artichokes, gossip about their kinkier clients, play bezique, a card game from which pinochle descends, and enjoy some hard-earned R & R.

The walls had been painted by the artists of neighboring Montmarte (in return for cost-free affection, I suspect) with a remarkably convincing *station de Métro.* At one end of the room, a trompe l'oeil subway train rushed at us from the dark depths of a tunnel.

Civilians were strictly barred from the *station,* but Fernand's rough Parisian argot and attitude gained us enough time to slide into a booth, from which we refused to move. The result was a standoff: We were ignored, and repeated requests for service went unanswered—until the two *filles* Fernand had recently employed, who had been dressing upstairs, walked in and elected to join us in our booth. That brought the *patron,* a burly man who spoke the impenetrable French of the Auvergne region, to our table, where he took orders for us and our newfound friends.

Their names, we discovered, were Régine and Mickey. Régine, who sat next to me, was blond and young, with the kind of fresh beauty that adorned the beaches of the Riviera. She was in fact Cannoise, and had come into the *milieu* in order to earn enough money to return to Cannes and open a perfume shop. It turned out that she, like many of her colleagues, was very frugal, living simply and banking every sou against the day when she would be able to realize her dream.

In time, I discovered that she allowed herself one financial indiscretion a year, leaving the Pigalle district for the Avenue Montaigne and its renowned houses of couture to buy a designer dress for a single occasion: church on Easter Sunday. Out of respect for the Church, and an authentic religious conviction, Régine eschewed church every other day of the year, convinced that her presence would be hypocritical as long as she remained in the *milieu*—but Easter was sacred, and she dressed appropriately—and beautifully; I saw her collection of dresses.

Once I'd been admitted to the inner sanctum of the putative hotel on Rue Pigalle, I returned to the bar nearly every evening toward midnight for supper with my friend. It was an unusual relationship: She was sexually available, of course, for a price, but not to me because the thought of buying her now revulsed us both. On the other hand, availing myself, free of charge, of her professional services felt to me like cynical, backhanded exploitation, and would have raised God knows what questions for her at the end of her long day's work or, worse, between clients. I'd learned that what these professional temptresses offered was, for them, anything but sexual, no matter what their clients persuaded themselves.

One night I brought Régine a bird in a cage that I'd won on a wheel of fortune in the Place Blanche, and several of the *filles* wept at the tender gesture. Another night I arrived with a bouquet of yellow roses that evoked cries of distress from the *filles* in the bar. Yellow flowers, they told me, are a sure sign that a man is deceiving his woman. Given her professional life and our relationship, Régine could hardly be defined as "my" woman—but that wasn't how the *filles* saw it as they ceremoniously dumped the flowers in the trash and forgave me my youthful, American ignorance.

A few days later I was summoned to Greece. I thought the Delphic interlude might put the matter of Rue Pigalle and Régine to rest, but when the movie was canceled and I returned to Paris, I barely took time to dump my luggage at the Hotel Duminy before heading for Pigalle.

Everything was as it had been, in every way. Régine and my friends welcomed me back; the artichokes and Calvados were on the house that night, and life in the *milieu* resumed. Of course, Régine and I immediately found ourselves back on the horns of our dilemma. It made for some interesting conversations and occasional tension. Sometimes Régine thought we should, and sometimes she didn't, because she feared I'd begin to be like any other "client," rather than forever "different."

This was certainly different from any relationship I'd ever had, and either in spite of it or because of it, our friendship flourished, and I now became a fully accredited denizen of the *station,* as unexceptional as every other member of the club.

In addition to Régine, there were some remarkable women in that bar. At that time in Paris, still not far removed from the austerity of the war years, unemployment among men was endemic, and in a society like France's, women weren't encouraged to compete with men for the finite number of jobs. The result was that their opportunities were severely circumscribed. One of the few areas open without restriction to women was what was called discreetly by the French, "the middle," the *milieu.* It wasn't only open without restriction; it was open without censure. Prostitution was legal in France, and strictly regulated, with weekly medical examinations. Some of the bordellos, in more elegant districts than Pigalle, were legendary for their luxury and refinement, and the *filles* were as pampered and prized as geishas.

Educated women, who had elected not to starve to death while waiting for employment in their chosen fields, had simply entered the *milieu* as a stopgap. Young married women whose husbands were floundering in that difficult time, or whose children were in danger of going hungry, came into the *milieu.* And when they'd achieved their financial goal, they left and went straight back into polite society, without stigma or a whisper of opprobrium.

On the one occasion when I asked Régine the inexcusable question "Why do you do this?" the businesswoman in her answered patiently and straightforwardly, "I make more money than my banker does."

It seems very hard to believe now, in this atrocious age of drugs and disease and enslavement, but for a time in Paris, for a broad stratum of women, many of them utterly indistinguishable from the rest of the city's population, the *milieu* wasn't just a viable option; it was the only option.

One night, I arrived at the bar with a large bouquet of flowers and very bad news. Taking Régine to a corner booth, I told her I would have to return to New York. Sitting back on the banquette as if I'd shoved her, she asked, "Do you want to go?"

"No, of course not."

"Then why are you going?" I was silent. She rubbed a thumb and forefinger together. *"Pas de fric. T'es fauché."* No dough. You're broke. I shrugged. "I knew," Régine said.

"How . . . ?"

"The other night, when I asked you to buy us some Gitanes at the *tabac*— you remember? You made an excuse and we sent a *chasseur.* I said to myself, he's running out of money."

I sat back in the booth, out of arguments and ideas. "I've got my ticket home, and enough for this week's rent. That's all."

She leaned across the table with a gentle smile and said, "I've been thinking about it since then, and the problem is solved." Her smile was radiant. "You'll be my *mec.*"

When I recoiled at the idea of delivering clients to her bedside, she laughed and waved the thought away. No, she'd leave that to the *chasseurs. I,* she said, clearly proud of her ingenuity, would be a *spécialiste,* delivering tourists for exhibitions like the one at which we'd met—and receiving the customary commission, she added with the crispness she always employed when discussing *le business.*

When I continued to struggle with the idea, she took my hand in both of hers and said, "Jeem . . . don't you see? This way you'll be able to stay in Paris. We'll be together, like this. For a little longer?" She waited, proud of her inspiration and certain of her logic.

My mind was racing. Hadn't Stella emphasized that we had to experience life in all its variety? Hadn't Harold and Bobby? Every one of my teachers had argued that, in the end, we had nothing but ourselves to bring to any role, and the richer and broader our life experience, the richer and broader our interpretations would be. And, I reasoned, an experience like this would never come again. . . .

Of course I was indulging in the common practice of providing ex post facto reasons to shore up a decision already taken. Régine had had me with "Jeem. . . ."

Now there was the matter of accreditation. In the formalized hierarchy of the *milieu,* one didn't simply declare oneself a *mec.* Even here, rank had its privileges—and presumption its penalties. A soi-disant *mec* would evoke the enmity of the real articles. Not advisable.

When I arrived at the *station* the next night, Régine was waiting for me at a center table, surrounded by *filles,* all of them beaming at me over an open bottle of champagne. Permission had been granted—and, with it, a reprieve.

America faded into an indistinct future. I was now a working member of the community, just like the Parisians I saw leaving for work in the morning and returning each evening with baguettes of bread under their arms. For a person who had grown up convinced that he didn't quite belong in the world in which he found himself, I was completely at home in this peculiar circumstance. To this day, from the moment I arrive in Paris, I feel instantly and thoroughly at home.

My life took on a comfortable regularity. It had structure and a daily routine. In a sense, it was more conventional and bourgeois than any life I'd ever known (though I suspect my father would have approved of *this* conventionality). I even had an office of sorts, in the Place de l'Opéra, on the sidewalk outside the American Express office next to the Café de la Paix, where I could count on finding a large congregation of tourists, most of them American, eager to sample the fabled delights of Paris. The sidewalk echoed with the shouts of jostling guides offering expert personal tours to Notre Dame and the Sainte-Chappelle and the Eiffel Tower.

I offered a different delight, in a quieter, more discreet voice. And the tourists, who in their secret hearts of hearts had come to Paris *hoping* that an opportunity like this would present itself, were, to put it mildly, receptive.

Régine and I did a thriving business. The tourists were understandably nervous about entering Paris's most notorious quarter, so, like all the other guides, I offered personal service. My clients would meet me at the appointed hour and I would take them to Rue Pigalle for what was called in the profession a *cinéma cochon,* a "dirty movie," but was, of course, a live, and lively, exhibition. Because Régine insisted I have special privileges at the establishment, I was allowed to bring my clients, almost all of them nervous, excited young middle-class couples from Middle America, into the *station,* where they sat gingerly in the booth with me, picking out the *fille* to team with Régine upstairs.

I offered them a full bill of fare: two women or a man and woman. A man and woman was much more costly than two women: the law of supply and demand—not to mention the law of diminishing returns; the women could perform countless times each day, the men only two or three.

The men were summoned from a bar at the corner where they waited, drinking Pernod, smoking Gauloises and reading sports magazines, for a summons to one of the street's lineup of hotels.

Once my clients had made their choices, we mounted the stairs to one of the rooms, each of which featured ornately flocked crimson wallpaper, a large rumpled bed with a heavy, carved headboard, a couch and a couple of chairs covered in red velvet and, behind a curtain, a bidet. In retrospect, viewing the scene through the eyes of my young clients from Baltimore or Memphis or Des Moines, those rooms must have looked like the eighth circle of Dante's Inferno (which at least placed me in the respectable company of Dante's guide, Virgil)—or Paradise.

As the clients' personal guide, I was obliged to stay with them. That was an essential ingredient in the package: They wouldn't have shown up, or would have fled in terror, without it. Besides, they needed translation when, as most of them finally did, they made timid requests of my performers for what they called "er . . . positions."

When we arrived in the room, I deposited the couple in the velvet couch, where they sat primly on its edge, like students in a particularly strict school. Régine and the appointed partner proceeded to the bed and the performance began. It was my first experience as a producer, and I have to say that, in the many times this ritual was performed, I never had a complaint from the audience.

At the end of each performance, there was the traditional invitation to join the performers in an (expensive) encore, and occasionally the clients accepted.

At the end of a night's work, I would often walk from Pigalle to my apartment in the First Arrondissement. Paris's summer nights are brief. At the city's northerly latitude, the sun sets at ten p.m.; and at three in the morning, which was the hour I was usually on my way home, a mysterious interlude of milky, magical light separates darkness from dawn. Sometimes I would detour to the flower market on a bridge between the Right Bank and the Île de la Cité, where fresh flowers cascaded from the span like waterfalls, to buy water lilies for my bidet, a device that went unused, since Régine was insensate in her bed in Pigalle after a workday of entertaining half a dozen clients—a dozen on a good (*sic*) day.

I offer this account not as a defense of my conduct, nor as an apology. I'd intended to leave the matter out of the book entirely, but Arthur Laurents, the playwright and author of one of the finest libretti ever devised for a musical, the masterful foundation he laid down for *Gypsy*, outed me in 2000 in his autobiographical *Original Story By,* in which he described attending one of my exhibitions with a group that included Farley Granger. Arthur has colored the event, which featured a substitute *fille* because Régine was indisposed (periodic *hazard du métier*), with a lofty auteur's hauteur in an unfamiliar setting; but apparently the experience made a sufficient impression on him to warrant two pages in a book that was crowded with the major incidents of his life. And Arthur elected to name names, which is to say, mine. His prerogative, but it made any reticence in these pages pointless and precious.

Besides, the entire episode nearly popped out in, of all places, the classroom of *Inside the Actors Studio* when Julia Roberts was our guest, and I asked her whether she'd gone to the sources in her preparation to play the streetwalking prostitute in *Pretty Woman.* "Yeah," she said emphatically.

"Where?"

"Hollywood."

"Talk to them?"

"Yeah."

"Were they nice?"

"Oh, yes. Very. Horrible, horrible stories, but fascinating girls, and they were really nice to me and told me a lot of things, and it was incredibly helpful. A lot of the things that they said to me we ended up incorporating in the script, so it was really valuable time spent. One of the writers on this script was a woman named Barbara Benedict, whom I sat down with and, at length, went over the stories I'd heard and the conversations I'd had, and she put a lot of it into the script."

Then I took the fatal step. "Once upon a time, for reasons that will not be stated tonight, I did some research also on the subject of prostitution. This was in Paris. And . . ."

I couldn't continue. Julia jackknifed in her chair and the students exploded into what may have been the loudest and most sustained laughter in the history of the show. Taken aback, and reminding myself that I was the students' dean, I added hastily, "It's not what you think!" It didn't help. The laughter redoubled and Julia threw herself back in her chair, convulsed. I tried joining the joke with a lame "It's worse."

It didn't help. I could barely be heard over the tumult as I tried to turn the debacle in an academic direction: "But what I did learn was . . ." Gales of laughter. I persisted, with what I hoped was an effective disclaimer: "This was a long time ago, before drugs and disease had turned everything so horrible. But I learned that . . ." I couldn't hear myself in the uproar. More than a little angry now, I gritted my teeth and plodded on: "I learned that . . ." Julia was trying to quell her laughter with some water, and the microphone was picking up her teeth chattering on the rim of the glass. Nothing would deter me. "I learned that the whores I knew in Paris were . . ."

That was it! The students went mad. For reasons unknown to me to this moment, I persisted. "Now, come on! I'm *going* somewhere with this!" The students stamped their feet in glee, and Julia dipped her fingertips into the glass to splash water on her crimson face. "They were the most businesslike people I ever knew," I yelled over the hubbub. "The one thing they very seldom did on the job was enjoy themselves. They all saved their money, and I'll bet you five bucks, Julia, that when you talked to these women in Hollywood, they were also saving, and they had goals."

Trying to help me out, Julia muttered "Mmm-hmm" through tightly compressed lips, as the students' laughter rolled on, unabated.

Grabbing the lifeline Julia had thrown, I said, "Usually they're very specific. A beauty shop, right? Or . . ."

I was running on empty again, so, pitching in valiantly, Julia offered, "In fact I was going to say that, but I felt I was going on too long with that little topic—but they all had a very specific goal for the future, and it was absolutely going to be theirs."

Under the mistaken impression that I was out of the woods, I reached back and called on Régine to rescue me. "I knew one woman who bought only one dress a year. She went to Balenciaga or Dior and had a beautiful dress made for Easter, for church. It was the only expense she allowed herself in the whole year. . . ." I looked helplessly at the cackling students. "That's the truth." The room exploded in new waves of laughter, and I slumped back with a beaten "Getting a lot of laughs I didn't intend."

So the matter ended—on the stage. But it has remained one of the mysteries of *Inside the Actors Studio,* raising occasional conjecture among the students and even letter-writing viewers. Julia and I have never had occasion to discuss it, but—Julia, in the event you read these pages, now you know. So, for better or worse, does everybody else.

For some reason that I don't pretend to understand, that time with Régine and the circle at the *station* persists. In the late sixties, when the world and I were removed by what I thought were light-years from the Pigalle of Régine and Mickey and me, I arrived in Paris to propose a project to Peter Ustinov. One of my closest friends was a young woman named Nina Georges-Picot, whom I'd met, with her sisters, Flor and Olga, when their father was the French ambassador to the United Nations. Now, in Paris, at dinner with Nina and her family on the Avenue Foch after a day of meetings with Ustinov, I choked on my *biftek* as Nina exclaimed impulsively, "Poppy! Did you know that Jim was a *mec*?"

The remark eradicated any other topic at the table, and when the evening ended, I found myself yielding out of sheer exhaustion and with profound misgivings to the three sisters' entreaties to throw a party for all my French friends in my old haunt.

Fully expecting that the statute of limitations had run out and I'd find a McDonald's at our Pigalle headquarters, I showed up to discover that the train was still running in the *station,* and that the bar and its contemporary inhabitants were in fact available for hire in toto on a normally slow night. Trapped by the fact that a gleeful Nina was hopping up and down at my side, I booked the *station de Métro* and the *poules,* and Nina rushed home to send out a blizzard of invitations.

I invited some American friends who were in Paris at the moment, and on the appointed night, what looked to me like *le tout Paris* showed up. There was a liberal sprinkling of counts and countesses, and, at the vortex of the affair, standing head and shoulders over the other guests, Nina's father, Ambassador Guillaume Georges-Picot, inexplicably dressed as if for a diplomatic reception, standing tall and ramrod straight with a polite smile on his face and a champagne glass held delicately between thumb and forefinger, as the *poules* circled him with undisguised curiosity.

My instructions to the *patron* had been: hors d'oeuvres and champagne, served by the *filles*—and no hanky-panky, under any circumstances. The purpose of this evening, I stressed, was not sexual; it was social. I'd pay for the *poules'* time as if they were delivering the usual product, and fully compensate the hotel for the nonuse of the rooms upstairs—*but,* I insisted, my guests were to be offered nothing—repeat, *nothing*—but food and drink. Since the remuneration was equivalent to any other night at the establishment, without the usual wear and tear on the merchandise, the *patron* was only too happy to comply.

I was greatly relieved to find that the party was going off without a hitch: My guests, French and American, were intrigued by their surroundings, and not a bit patronizing toward the young women who were serving them with fastidious, if slightly starchy, refinement. Thanks to Nina, Flor and Olga's insistence, I'd brought off the nearly impossible coup: a Parisian party with an entirely novel theme.

My fear that I would be indelibly tarnishing my reputation vanished. I'd forgotten: This is Paris; these people are French. All around me I could see admiring glances, and Flor Georges-Picot, who was a ravishing teenager, hugged my arm, emitting squeals of ineffable joy.

A triumph, but then . . . some of the *filles* grew restless. The plan had been explained to them, but they were, after all, professionals; they'd been paid full value for their time—and they weren't *giving* full value. A true professional considers lack of interest an insult, and these professionals were no different in that regard from—well, say, actors. They began to *want* to be noticed. They began to coquette—and finally, to my horror, they began to ask the classic question: *"Tu viens, chéri?"* ("Coming, darling?") And they would nod toward the stairs. There wasn't an extra franc in it for them, but there is such a thing as professional pride.

I hurried to intervene, but my guests were enjoying the attention. And most of them were French. Still, no one accepted the invitation—that is, no one French. Suddenly, one of the Americans headed for the stairs, with a delighted girl on each arm. Her husband, who was elsewhere in the room, smiling at the blandishments of a *poule,* gasped and headed her off with a hoarse "What are you *doing*?!"

"Well, I thought . . . ," she began blithely, but his withering glance cut her off, and sent the *filles* flying. And, watching the drama unfold, I wondered whether, if he'd come alone to the party, he might not have ventured up those stairs.

The party ended without further incident and to great acclaim—and the fact that these words are appearing on these pages means that Barbara Walters gave me permission to include them. I'm not sure what would have happened to her upstairs, but I'm absolutely convinced that it was the insatiable journalist, not the insatiable woman, who wanted to sample a new experience. Barbara's intrepidity that night is one of several reasons (the others will be revealed later) why she is one of the heroes of my life.

Sometimes the past just won't go away—which may mean that it shouldn't. In the summer of 2002, my production team and I embarked for Paris to shoot two episodes of *Inside the Actors Studio* at the Opéra Comique, one with Juliette Binoche, the other with Jeanne Moreau.

We began the trip with a survey of Paris—to the scenic spots I recommended for B-roll and my intros. On this occasion, I was the standard tour guide, leading my troupe to the Champs de Mars with its incomparable view of the Eiffel Tower, to the *butte* of Montmartre with its panoramic view of Paris, to the quai de la Tournelle for the best view of Notre Dame's flying buttresses . . . but Christian Barcellos, the Bravo executive responsible for our show, kept pestering me for the *other* tour, the one to the environs I'd hinted at in the Julia Roberts episode.

Finally, when we'd run out of locations to scout, with hours of summer sunshine still on tap, I directed our driver to Pigalle, where we disembarked for a walking tour of the famous street. The fronts of the buildings had changed—there was much more chrome and neon—and the *poules* were stacked in picture windows like puppets, tapping on the glass with their long, painted nails and beckoning us inside.

The *station de Métro* was finally gone, and even from the outside my former haunt was unrecognizable. As we made our way back to the corner where our driver waited next to the car, we passed the cavernous bar where the male stars of our exhibitions used to hang out, waiting for a call.

A *chasseuse* on the sidewalk shrilled at us, inviting us into the bar. As we proceeded to the car, I felt a restraining hand on my arm. It was the *chasseuse,* who had darted forward to grab me. She peered up at me for a long moment, studying me intently, and finally queried, *"Tu achètes ou tu vends?"*

"What did she say?" my companions asked as I detached myself and approached the car.

"Ask him," I said, jerking a thumb at our bilingual driver, who was grinning broadly.

"'You buying or selling?'" the driver chortled.

"Once a *mec,* always a *mec,*" Christian observed with undisguised pleasure as we drove away from Pigalle.

In the car, I was silent, lost in thought, reflecting that in the year 2002, sex-for-sale had become wholly anomalous. I'd learned that it was never, by any stretch of the imagination, romantic—but, I tried to persuade myself, for Régine it was intended as a means to an honorable end outside the *milieu,* and for me it had afforded a reprieve when I needed it, and a genuine adventure, without harmful consequences—that I knew of.

Was I rationalizing? Diligently—even comforting myself with the thought that Rimbaud ended his life as a rich gunrunner in Africa, and Wallace Stevens was the vice president of an insurance company. One does, I told myself, what one must, and there are more grievous sins than a brief stint in the *milieu.* Flawed reasoning, I daresay, but it was all I had at my disposal on that pensive drive across Paris.

Of one thing I was certain: The world had changed so radically that a party like the one I'd given in the sixties was now unthinkable. Prostitution, in any guise and every respect, had become simply dreadful and unconscionable, in every corner of the globe, including, of course, Paris.

As my mind raced back and forth between past and present, I recalled that, even then, in my salad days and Régine's on the Rue Pigalle, there were times when the *filles* lurched into the bar with horror tales that made even that seasoned troupe blanch.

Such an occasion finally earned me unconditional acceptance by my colleagues in the *station de Métro*. Régine, a couple of *mecs* playing cards in a corner, several *filles* and I were eating artichokes (for some unknown reason the specialty of the house; maybe they were plentiful in the Auvergne) when one of the young women whom we all especially liked came dashing into the room in tears, followed by a beefy American, reeling drunk and hurling invective at her. We learned from her, in French, as he continued railing at her in English, that he'd refused to pay her and, to punish her for whatever he saw as her shortcomings, had opened her purse and pocketed the rest of her night's earnings—all of which was, in this precinct, a cardinal sin.

This kind of thing happened occasionally—it was always a client in pursuit of free fornication—but usually the miscreant was out the door before the *fille* could enlist help. This moron had followed her into the bar, on the theory that the language barrier would shield him.

It didn't. Neither combative nor versed in donnybrook, I'm the last person anyone would want at his side in a brawl, but this time, before I knew it, I was on my feet, responding to the buffoon in kind—and in his own language. As I recall, my first words, uttered in a ringing register that would have received an ovation from Arthur Lessac and Mme. Gauthier, were "Hey, asshole!" It got the American's attention.

Calling upon every lesson learned from Stella, Harold and Bobby, I assumed a persona none of them had ever asked me to play. I'd seen bits and pieces of this brute in the movies and on the stage, but I was on unfamiliar terrain. In a split second, I decided that my action was "to recover my friend's money," and the first beat of it was "to scare this drunken oaf to death!"

Of course, I had surprise on my side because the last thing he'd expected to find in this den of French iniquity was someone who spoke his language, in the vulgate. I took him for a New Yorker. Okay, I'd be from Brooklyn. Red Hook!

"You hear me, asshole? You listening to me? This little lady says you stole her money!" I left the booth and advanced on him. He must have outweighed me by a hundred pounds—but I had justice on my side and genuine, righteous wrath. Stella was right: Play the action and you won't have to go looking for the emotion. "Where's the money, you prick?"

"I never touched her money." But in a classic psychological gesture, he was backing up.

"You wanna lose it?"

"Lose what?"

"Your prick, you prick! Take a look around." I pointed at the *mecs*. "You know what these guys are? Algerian!!" They weren't, and it wouldn't have mattered much if they were, but I thought it was a nice touch, given the headlines about the fierce Algerian resistance to the foreign *pieds noirs*—and Stella would have found it imaginative. It was time for a new beat in my action. "Let's see your passport!"

His hand leapt protectively toward a pocket. "What for?!"

"We're gonna roll it up and shove it up your ass! How're you gonna explain *that* to Immigration? Or the little woman?" I added, noting the glint on his left hand. This was good. Too good to lose. I was making mental notes.

His head swiveled toward the two *mecs,* who didn't understand a word I was saying but were clearly awestruck by the volcanic depths of this docile American who'd never done anything more aggressive in their presence than have a quiet supper with Régine at the end of an honest night's work.

"What're you looking at *them* for? They're just waiting for one word from me."

Oh, *very* good! His hands were flying in and out of his pockets, spilling francs and dollars. I started scooping them up.

"Wait a minute!" he whined. "Some of that's mine."

"How do *I* know what you owe her?"

"Ask her!"

"I don't speak French. Did you get a blow job? That doesn't come cheap. And if she swallowed the smoke, that's extra!" His hands flew back to his pockets and more money appeared; then his arms fell limply to his sides.

"Where's her bonus?" I demanded.

"Bonus!"

"For the aggravation!!!"

He reached into his pocket, withdrew some francs, dropped them on the pile at his feet, and pulled his pockets inside out. "That's all I got."

"Let's see your watch." He looked even more stricken. "Never mind. Get outta here." As he sprinted for the exit, I yelled, "And stay away from our women! They're too good for you!"

It may have been my best performance. Ever.

That night Régine insisted we make love, and we did. A month later, with classes looming in New York, I left for America.

Every time I go to Cannes, I take a walk, hoping to come upon a *parfumerie* called Régine's, but I've never found one.

CHAPTER Seven

❝*The difference between the almost right word and the right word is . . . the difference between the lightning bug and the lightning.*

—Mark Twain

Once I'd ended ten years of self-imposed writer's block with *The Doctor in Spite of Himself,* I returned to the calling that had begun at the age of three, been abandoned at eighteen, and has continued nonstop, with modest distinction but boundless zeal, from the day of its resumption to this moment as I write these words.

Like many of our *Inside the Actors Studio* guests, I found myself in the thick of the Golden Age of television that has already made an appearance in these pages, an exhilarating time when Paul Newman and Robert Redford were cutting their acting teeth, Sidney Lumet and Sydney Pollack were acquiring their formidable directing skills, and the likes of Paddy Chayevsky and Gore Vidal were turning television into a haven for fresh, inventive writing.

Making up for lost time, I churned out a deluge of pages. My first two teleplays were bought immediately by *The United States Steel Hour,* which was produced for TV by the Theatre Guild. The second of them, *The Charlie and the Kid,* told the story of a tramp clown—a "Charlie," after Chaplin—and his running battle with anxious social workers to keep his adopted son with him in a traveling circus.

I was attracted to the subject as a circus buff, but my knowledge of that world was limited to the circus library I'd collected. As I would do years later in Alaska, I went looking for firsthand experience, and found it with the fourth-generation circus family of Trevor Bale, a wild-animal trainer and the father of a brood of tumbling, climbing, leaping, dangling kids who, like the "kid" in my teleplay, traveled with the circus and appeared in it as soon as they could toddle into the ring.

When I joined the circus—and the Bale family—for a week of research, Elvin Bale was a six-year-old learning to hang by his heels over a pile of mattresses and pillows, and when his father took his wild animals and spangled family to Ringling Bros. and Barnum & Bailey, all of them, Elvin, his sisters, Gloria, Bonnie and Nita, and their mother went to work on the show (not "in" it; the Bales spoke Circus).

In time, Elvin rose to the top of the Greatest Show on Earth—literally— cavorting without a net at the top of the arena on his whirling Wheel of Death. Risking his life as many as three times a day, Elvin became, in Ringling's customary, but in this case fully justified, hyperbole, "The World's Greatest Daredevil," as his sisters put dogs and elephants and horses through their paces below, his mother was carried around the arena in an elephant's mouth, and his father cracked his whip at a cageful of tigers, wearing a plastic nose because his had been bitten off by one of them.

Each year when Ringling Bros. and Barnum & Bailey came to Madison Square Garden, Kedakai and I would gasp with the crowd at Elvin's death-defying stunts—and our nephew, Tommy Demers, would be scooped up and whisked away by Elvin before the performance, to reappear, in a suit of armor and state of enchantment, on a caparisoned pony in the parade called, in proper circus parlance, spec.

Elvin survived the Wheel of Death unscratched, but on January 8, 1987, at the Chipperfield Circus in Hong Kong, performing his human cannonball act, a miscalculation sent him flying out of the cannon and over the air bag at the other end of the arena, breaking his legs and back and paralyzing him from the waist down.

We still thrill to him each year, when the Cole Brothers Circus, which he governs from his motorized wheelchair as the show's touring vice president of operations, pitches its big top next to the Elks Lodge in Southampton, Long Island. Kedakai and I round up every kid we can dragoon, and still cry unabashedly when our charges show up in spec, grinning, waving, enchanted—and secretly plotting to run away and join the circus. They don't fool me for a minute.

The Charlie and the Kid was a successful television film that led to others, but, for me, its greatest gift was providing me with the circus family I will have all my life, and one of the promised heroes of this account.

When my schedule no longer permitted dance classes, I switched to the Pilates System. Today, it's ubiquitous and trendy, and nearly every Hollywood mansion is fully equipped, but then it consisted of an Eighth Avenue studio full of wooden beds, straps and springs called Universal Reformers—unique machines presided over by their inventor, the physical culturist (which was what he was called when he arrived from Europe in 1926) Joseph Hubertus Pilates.

Joe claimed to be directly descended from Pontius Pilate, which I always considered a dubious distinction, but Joe was a powerful man with a short fuse, so I never questioned him about it.

I trained with Joe for years, and when he died in 1967 at the age of eighty-seven, several of us bought the Pilates name and method in order to protect his widow, Clara, a powerful little sparrow whom we adored. When Clara died a few years later, I delivered her eulogy, and our group transferred all rights in the system to Romana Kryzanowska, who was, in our view, Joe's legitimate successor.

As it turned out, Joe had never bothered with such niceties as patents and copyrights (not to mention, as we discovered when we sought to bring order to Clara's life, income taxes), so our effort to keep the Pilates name and house intact was thwarted; it proliferated unimpeded, with numerous competing claims of purity and authenticity. I'm convinced that, at the foundation of all this smoke, there's a genuine fire: Joe was definitely onto something, and I still try to start each day with his mat work, taking guidance from the photo-copied manual he gave me, titled "Return to Life Through Contrology," which shows photos of Joe at sixty going methodically through every move of his thirty-four floor exercises, from "The Hundred" (which Teri Hatcher demon-strated on the floor of our *Inside the Actors Studio* stage) to the dreaded—and immensely effective—"Teaser" (which I demonstrated and discreetly edited out of the show).

While Pilates, which was the only exercise system George Balanchine ever endorsed for his dancers, provided some of the exercise I was no longer get-ting from daily ballet classes, I found it couldn't replace the rush I'd become addicted to in dance. As was the case increasingly now, I found my outlet on the page, in a novel about dancers called—it will come as no surprise—*Mirrors,* which has already made an appearance in these pages.

When I delivered the manuscript of *Mirrors* to St. Martin's Press, they did what publishers do, sent the galleys out for blurbs. One that came back imme-diately knocked me flat, first, because it came from one of the incontestable heroes of anyone who's ever pulled on a ballet slipper, Bob Fosse, who in one year won the Oscar for the choreography and direction of *Cabaret,* the Tony for the choreography and direction of *Pippin,* and the Emmy for the choreog-raphy and direction of *Liza with a Z;* and second, because of what he chose to say: "Mr. Lipton has obviously observed Broadway musicals and dancers of varying dedication and ambition carefully. He has written about them with compassion, humor, sensuality and great authenticity. The all-night dance rehearsal scene was so real my muscles ached after reading it."

Gwen Verdon, the peerless Broadway dance star, wrote, "Dance and dancers are usually mute. But now, at last, we have a spokesman. No book or ballet has ever moved me as much as James Lipton's *Mirrors.*"

During that heady time, my phone rang one afternoon, and a voice rasped, "You son of a bitch!"

"Who's this?"

"Paddy Chayevsky." I knew he'd been sent galleys, and my heart sank at the obviously adverse reaction of the three-time Oscar winner. But my spirits began to rise with his next words. "You kept me up all night. I started to read your book after dinner, and at eleven I called Fosse and asked him if he'd read *Mirrors,* and he said, 'Yeah,' and I said, 'Is all this stuff true—is this what it's honest-to-God like?' and he said, 'Every word of it.' So, I relaxed and kept reading and I couldn't put it down till I finished the last page this morning."

"Jesus!" I exclaimed. "Do you want the publisher's phone number?"

"I don't give blurbs," Paddy said, and hung up.

Paddy Chayevsky and Bob Fosse were Damon and Pythias, inseparable and incomparable. Like many dancers, Bobby barely finished high school, and like many writers, Paddy was chronically overweight and underexercised. That made them a perfect pair: Paddy was Bobby's Apollonian side, and Bobby was decidedly Paddy's Dionysian side.

When Bobby had the open-heart surgery he chronicled in *All That Jazz,* Kedakai and I visited him in the hospital a few days after his operation, where we found Paddy and writer Herb Gardner facing his bed in chairs. They'd discovered that the heart monitor beeping over his head could function as a laugh meter, and, in a lively competition, were taking turns telling jokes to the agonized patient who, between fits of laughter, kept bleating the classic post-surgery plea: "Please!!! Don't make me laugh!"

When Paddy died, suddenly and inexcusably at the age of fifty-eight, Kedakai and I attended his funeral. A procession of public figures went to the dais above the casket to celebrate Paddy, but every person in the huge room was waiting for the final speaker: Bob Fosse. When his turn came, he mounted the steps slowly, then turned to face us in his invariable attire: chinos, suede desert boots and a black silk Meledandri shirt.

After a pregnant silence, he began slowly in his thin tenor. "As most of you know, Paddy and I were friends." He paused for a long, hushed moment—during which collective breathing would have been heard, had anyone been breathing—then resumed. "When I had my operation, we made each other a promise. I told him what I wanted him to do at my funeral, and he told me what he wanted me to do at his. Of course, we both thought I'd be the one to collect on the promise." Again he fell silent, staring down at Paddy's casket, then, looking out at the congregants, he said, "I hope nobody will be offended, but Paddy loved this—and a promise is a promise."

And, with no introduction or accompaniment, Bobby began to dance on the dais above the casket—a very slow, soft-shoe pavane, performed with great solemnity and in utter silence—except for the staccato eruptions of mourners unable to control their feelings.

A few years later, Kedakai and I were invited to Bobby's sixtieth birthday party at his house in Quogue. On the night of the party, I was in the Los Angeles apartment we kept year-round for my increasingly frequent, extended working trips, so I couldn't attend it, but Kedakai called me at midnight her time, when she got home. It had been a wonderful party, she said. From her report it sounded as if Bobby had been in an oddly euphoric mood, demanding that, since it was a significant birthday, each of the guests stand up and say something nice about him.

Accustomed to, and fond of, Bobby's quirky moods, the guests, according to Kedakai, complied. At first, she said, it was hilarious, and the raucous crowd was enjoying it, but by the time it came around to the fifteenth person, the tone had darkened, and by the twentieth speaker, it was, in Kedakai's description, "a little bizarre."

"Didn't the tributes sound like eulogies?" I asked.

"Yes. Exactly."

"He was staging his own funeral!"

"I guess he didn't want to miss it," Kedakai observed. "But he was having a great time, and he kept saying, 'Your turn,' so everybody went along with it."

"What did *you* do?"

"I didn't want to say *anything,* but he kept insisting. And, finally, I saw a way out of it. I said, 'There's been enough talk. I just want to dance with you.'"

"What did he do?"

"We danced. And all of a sudden, it was a party again."

Kedakai was Bobby's last dance partner. A few weeks later, after the final dress rehearsal of a revival of *Sweet Charity* in Washington, Bobby delivered his traditional opening-night message to the dancers, "Okay, kids, tonight you're going to Tap Dance Heaven," left the theater with Gwen Verdon, and fell dead of a heart attack on the sidewalk.

Bobby and Gwen—and Kedakai—are the reason I dedicated *Mirrors* to "my wife, Kedakai Turner Lipton, who did me the small service of redefining the universe . . . and to every dancer I have ever known."

When *Mirrors* was published, the *New York Times* critic wrote, "*Mirrors* begins and ends with the word *vibrant,* and if what goes on in between vibrated any faster, the novel would fly apart in your hands. . . . Its authenticity and good humor make *Mirrors* more than the literary equivalent of *Fame* and *A Chorus Line.*"

A few days after publication, I got an excited call from my literary agent: "Steven Spielberg has offered us half a million dollars for the film rights to *Mirrors*!" As the negotiations proceeded, Beatrice Straight, who was acting in *Poltergeist,* which Spielberg was producing, called me to say, "On the set today, Spielberg walked by me with a book in his hand, and I saw the title. It was your book! I said, 'That book was written by a friend of mine. Why are you carrying it around?' He said, "I carry it all the time. It's my next picture.'"

A few years later, the lyricists Marilyn and Alan Bergman told me that, at that time, they'd received the book from Steven with instructions to read it at once, since he was preparing to direct it, and might want some songs.

E.T. had just been released, confirming Steven's place in the Hollywood firmament, and he came under enormous pressure to direct a sequel to *Raiders of the Lost Ark,* which had come out the year before *E.T.* Employing the acute sixth sense that sets him apart from nearly every other director, Spielberg switched from *Mirrors* to *Indiana Jones and the Temple of Doom,* and I accepted an offer to write and produce a film version of *Mirrors* for NBC television.

The *Chicago Tribune*'s television critic wrote that *Mirrors* "deserves applause, and when this dancely drama ends, people should stand up and shout, 'Bravo.'"

I hope I will be forgiven if these pages sometimes sound like an advertisement of myself, but I hope, also, that they are sufficiently balanced by the false steps and bad news I've reported. I've set myself the same task I set my guests on *Inside the Actors Studio:* to retrace *all* the steps that have shaped me—and there were a few peaks among the valleys.

Mirrors led immediately to an overture from Dick Clark Productions, which had been trying unsuccessfully to convert Barry Manilow's three-minute song "Copacabana" into a movie.

The song yielded little: three first names and a place, the Copacabana, where Lola danced, Tony tended bar, they fell in love, and there was a fight with someone named Rico. From this, I fashioned a two-hour screenplay,

weaving into it songs from Manilow's catalogue, creating a story with a beginning, middle and end, a large cast of characters, settings as far away as Havana,
and extensive histories for Tony, Lola and Rico that shaped them and the
narrative.

On the day before principal shooting began, Barry invited me to his home
for dinner, and asked me to read the entire script for him, playing Tony.

"You mustn't mimic me," I said. "That would be the *worst* thing you
could do."

"I won't. I promise," he said. "But this is *your* Tony. You created him. I want
to get your take on him." For the next two hours, Barry sat silent, intent, as I
read the teleplay aloud, pausing only when he asked an occasional question.

When *Copacabana,* the movie, aired on CBS, *People* magazine called it "a
daring step forward," *The Washington Post* described it as "darn near perfect,"
TV Guide's critic, Judith Crist, listed it as one of the Ten Best TV Movies of
1985, and Barry Manilow called me to express his undying gratitude.

A few months later, Waris Hussein, who won the Emmy for his direction
of *Copacabana,* and who lived in London, called me in indignation to report
the London opening of the stage version of *Copacabana* that bore an indelible
resemblance to the story, structure and characters I'd created, though the
names on the marquee and in the programs, he said, credited Barry and his
lyricists as the authors of the book.

When Barry moved the production to America, the Writers Guild and I
caught up with him, and appropriate legal measures were taken. Suffice it to
say that, since these pages are intended to celebrate the heroes of my life, in
the interest of honesty and candor, it's incumbent on me to make clear that
Barry Manilow is not remotely one of them.

My second Broadway musical, *Sherry!,* was based on *The Man Who Came
to Dinner* by Moss Hart and George S. Kaufman, and in order to acquire the
rights, Laurence Rosenthal and I had to agree to write two-thirds of the score
on spec. On a date set, we would perform the work for the executors of the two
estates, Kitty Carlisle Hart and Anne Kaufman Schneider, and they would
have the option of granting us the musical stage rights or shutting us down,
voiding everything we'd written. It was a draconian bargain, but understandable since *The Man Who Came to Dinner* was one of the most popular, and
profitable, plays in the Kaufman and Hart canon, and this was only my second Broadway musical and Larry's first.

As we worked on the score, Larry was summoned to London to write and
record the score for *Becket,* the Richard Burton, Peter O'Toole film, and in
order to meet our deadline, I had no choice but to follow him, find lodging,

and share Larry's time and talents with the producers of the movie. Since this was the London of Carnaby Street and the Swinging Sixties, it was, like my Paris sojourn, anything but a hardship post.

Larry finished his *Becket* assignment (which earned him an Oscar nomination), and we met our deadline. The run-through was scheduled for Kitty Hart's legendary apartment on East Sixty-fourth Street, and when Larry and I arrived, the spacious living room was packed with lawyers and agents—theirs and ours—and miscellaneous friends and advisors who would help Kitty and Anne make their fateful decision.

Larry sat down at the concert grand where, both of us suspected, the likes of Gershwin, Berlin and Weill had entertained the Harts' guests on previous occasions. Fast company. I noted with concern that Larry's hands were shaking as he brought them to the piano keys. But I needn't have worried: In addition to his formidable creative skills, Larry was a concert pianist, and as he played the score and I sang it, performing all the parts, Sheridan Whiteside, his secretary Maggie, her suitor Bert, the flamboyant actress Lorraine Sheldon, the audience responded warmly, then eagerly, and by the fourth number, Larry and I were rounding third base, headed for home.

When we'd presented the last number, the audience, led by Kitty and Anne, sprang to its feet and the rights were ours. The gamble had paid off, and waiters and waitresses burst into the room bearing trays of champagne and caviar. As they emerged, I muttered to Larry, "What do you suppose would have happened to all that stuff if we'd bombed?" As a matter of fact, what would have happened to *us*? But such mundane concerns were swept away in the general joy.

We cast the show with the actors we wanted: the dry, acerbic George Sanders, who, it turned out, had a trained singing voice, as the dry, acerbic Sheridan Whiteside, whom Kaufman and Hart had modeled on their fellow member of the Algonquin Round Table, the dry, acerbic Alexander Woollcott; Broadway's reigning soubrette, Dolores Gray, as Lorraine; and one of Broadway's reigning ingénues, Elizabeth Allen, as Maggie.

When we left for our first tryout at the Colonial Theatre in Boston, we were awash in good omens and high expectations. Around Broadway, the inside word, in a word, was *hit*.

After a tech rehearsal at Boston's Colonial Theatre, I returned to the Ritz Carlton in high spirits to find the phone ringing in my room. It was the stage manager, informing me that George Sanders was locked in his dressing room, and would talk to no one but me.

Galloping across a snowy Boston Common, I assumed that I'd been selected by George for whatever this privilege was going to turn out to be because he'd spent weeks in my apartment learning the songs from Larry and me, so he knew me better than anyone else in the company.

In the theater, I was led to George's dressing room by the ashen stage manager, who simply pointed at the door, from behind which came the sound of uncontrolled sobbing. I knocked on the door. The only response was continued sobbing. I called out, "It's me, George. Jim. You wanted to see me?"

There was a moment of silence behind the door, then the scrape of a chair. I gestured to the stage manager, who left, and the door opened to reveal an inconceivable sight: the majestic, imperious George Sanders trembling and weeping like a helpless child.

In the course of a few very painful minutes, I learned that he and his wife, Benita Hume, had received word that day that she was terminally ill, with only a few months to live. I'd come to know Benita as well as I knew George, since she was frequently in my apartment during the song session, and she, George, Larry and I often dined together afterward. She employed a cane because, she said, of recent surgery, but she seemed in glowing spirits and health.

Now George was pleading with me to get him out of the show as soon as possible, so they could go away together for the final months of her life. "Of course," I said. "Can you open the show in Boston?"

He agreed to do that, but his emotional state was so fragile that we had to cut his numbers to skeletal fragments of what we'd written. Abiding by the show business commandment "Never complain, never explain," we offered Boston the bowdlerized version of our show, and the critics reacted appropriately, lamenting the desecration of *The Man Who Came to Dinner*.

The recasting of the role, and rehearsal of Clive Revell, the new Whiteside, couldn't be accomplished in time to restore the show for its Philadelphia opening, so we opened with the by now poleaxed George to the same devastating reviews. The word went back to New York: *Sherry!* was breathing its last.

Finally, a few days before the end of the Philadelphia run, Clive Revell took over, in a radically revised show, since it had to be tailored to him, and he'd arrived with a new director, the gifted Joe Layton, who, nevertheless, was bringing a new and very different sensibility to the project.

Benita died a few months after George left the show, and George committed suicide in Spain five years later, leaving a notorious note: "Dear World: I am leaving because I am bored. I feel I have lived long enough. I am leaving you with your worries in this sweet cesspool. Good luck."

I would love to have seen his Sheridan Whiteside. And I'd have loved to have seen the show we'd written that had raised such high hopes in the theater community at the gypsy run-through before we left for Boston. Unfortunately, neither circumstance was in the cards.

Revell and Layton worked valiantly in the short time we had left between George's departure and opening night in New York. But the harm had been done, and the show we presented in Kitty Hart's apartment was never seen— in Boston, Philadelphia or New York.

The New York critical reaction to what was left of it ranged from enthusiastic to lukewarm. Unfortunately, the lukewarm reaction was from Walter Kerr, the all-powerful critic of *The New York Times,* who confessed that he'd never been a fan of *The Man Who Came to Dinner,* a singularly discouraging note at such a late date.

The score fared well in the notices, and a popular recording of the title song went to #3 on the *Billboard* charts, but the show closed before we could record a cast album. Three decades later, the opportunity would arise to describe what happened to *Sherry!*

The morning after any Broadway show ends its run, two things happen: The set is loaded onto trucks and taken to New Jersey, where it is unceremoniously burned (storage being too costly); and the show's score, every note, every orchestration, every sheet of music, which has been stacked throughout the run for safekeeping on the musicians' stands in the orchestra pit, is carefully packed in a trunk and sent to the writers' publisher.

A month after *Sherry!* closed I got the first of what would be many offers for a production of the show. My call to our publisher was routine: Open the trunk and deliver copies of the hundreds of pages of musical orchestrations to the producer making the request. Chappell's response was *"What* trunk?"

The three-month search that followed that chilling response was fruitless, and led me to the only possible, and heartbreaking, conclusion: The trunk had been put on the wrong truck and burned with the set in New Jersey.

For the next thirty-two years, every offer of a *Sherry!* production was met with the same dolorous response: "Sorry, the score is lost." Then, in the fall of 1999, I got a call from Robert Sher, a record producer who said he'd heard a pirated tape, recorded by one of those musical comedy buffs who sneak into theaters with tape recorders in their laps to record, however indistinctly, shows that are about to close. "It's a great score," he said, "and I want to make a cast album."

For perhaps the hundredth time, I recited the sad litany of the lost score, and prepared to hang up when he said, "Maybe the composer could reconstruct it from the pirated tape."

"It would take years to put those orchestrations back together, and he's got a life to live and a living to earn," I replied, and when Sher tried to press his case, I said, "Look, the wound has finally closed. Don't reopen it."

But Sher's call had struck a resonant chord, because when Bernadette

Peters appeared on *Inside the Actors Studio* a short time later, I mentioned the lost score to her, and said, "You know, if we ever *did* put *Sherry!* together again, you'd be perfect for the role of Maggie." Bernadette said she'd love to hear the score, which only succeeded in reawakening melancholy memories.

A few weeks later, on New Year's Day, 2000, I encountered *Inside the Actors Studio* alumnus Nathan Lane, who was about to open on Broadway as Sheridan Whiteside in *The Man Who Came to Dinner,* which prompted me to mention the lost score. "I'd love to hear it," Nathan said, and the wound ached again.

A month later, Kedakai and I went backstage to visit *Inside the Actors Studio* alumna Carol Burnett. A glutton for punishment, I brought up the lost score again, observing that she was born to play Lorraine Sheldon, who, I explained, had several comedy numbers, including the title song. "Oh, I'd love to hear it!" Carol exclaimed, which led me to call Robert Sher with the bitter complaint that, thanks to his call, the wound was wide open again. Sher said, "You know, the Library of Congress is the great repository of the musical theater. Maybe there are a few scraps of sheet music there that would inspire Larry to start reconstructing the score under these circumstances. I know the curator. I'll call him."

"Don't," I insisted. "It's over." But he'd hung up.

An hour later, he called back to ask, "Are you sitting down?"

"Why?"

"It's there," he said. "The trunk is in the Library of Congress. Nobody's opened it in thirty-two years. Everything you guys wrote, Jim—it's all there."

In time, we learned that on the morning after the show closed, the musicians' books, containing the entire score, had been taken from the stands and packed in the handiest trunk, a large, painted stage prop that had made a brief appearance in the show; and because it was painted with manifestly fake straps and locks, it was sent not to the publisher's offices but to its warehouse in New Jersey, where it languished until the nineties when Warner Music bought Chappell Publishing, and cleared out its warehouse, sending its historic Porter, Kern and Gershwin manuscripts, along with our peculiar trunk, to the Library of Congress, where our trunk's contents were duly noted and stored, on the assumption that Warner/Chappell had sent them there for the same reason they'd sent the rest of the archive. Larry and I weren't notified, since the archivists assumed logically that Warner/Chappell had sent the material at our instruction. And so the score languished, untouched and unnoticed until the intrepid Robert Sher (one of the indisputable heroes of this narrative) called the curator.

When I called Larry in San Francisco, I used Sher's opening gambit: "Are you sitting down?" What followed was one of the happiest phone calls of Larry's life—and of mine.

With the blessed assistance of the curator, Mark Horowitz, we retrieved the score, and it *was* all there, every number that was ever in or out of the show, from first rehearsal to opening night in New York, every note, every page of music, every orchestration, in mint condition.

Over the summer of 2000, Larry Rosenthal and I reconstructed the show that had never been seen or heard. Then, one night in August, we performed it in my home, with Kitty, now ninety, and Anne in attendance, leading the applause as they had in Kitty's living room, in front of Nathan Lane, Bernadette Peters, Carol Burnett, Bruce Lundvall of EMI, and the usual assortment of friends and colleagues. And that night, just as the crowd at Kitty's had, long ago, everyone said yes—Nathan, Carol, Bernadette and Bruce, for Angel Records.

Tommy Tune joined the cast to play Beverly Carlton, Kaufman and Hart's homage to Noël Coward, and in the spring of 2001, Sher, Larry, our musical director Marvin Laird and I went to Europe, to record the reexamined and reorchestrated score in the keys of our stars—with an orchestra composed of fifty-two classical and jazz musicians in Bratislava, Slovakia, and sixty-two in Prague.

Returning with the orchestral tracks of what is, to my knowledge, the largest pit orchestra in Broadway history, we delivered the tracks on CD to our cast, together with a CD we'd recorded when Larry and I performed the score for them at my home.

When Nathan arrived at his first rehearsal with Larry and me, he sang the role of Sheridan Whiteside, which is larger and more musically demanding than the one he played to acclaim and perfection in *The Producers,* straight through, flawlessly, from first note to last. When Larry and I stared at him in astonishment, he saw nothing remarkable in his feat; but doing effortlessly what others must struggle to do is one of the definitions of genius. When Bernadette arrived for her first rehearsal, she matched Nathan's achievement.

So did the rest of the cast when we gathered in a New York studio—Nathan, Bernadette, Carol, Tommy, Mike Myers, another *Inside the Actors Studio* alumnus, who joined us in the second-act role of Banjo, Kaufman and Hart's portrait of Harpo Marx, a supporting cast that included Phyllis Newman, Tom Wopat, Siobhan Fallon, Lilias White, Keith David, me as Whiteside's dithering doctor, and a full chorus of singers and dancers. To my knowledge, the *Sherry!* cast album is the only CD ever to credit a choreographer.

The *Sherry!* CD was released in February 2003, thirty-six years after its

Broadway opening. For me, it was worth the wait to hear Nathan delivering, definitively, Whiteside's beguiling/infuriating self-regard in the opening chorus of the nine-minute eleven-o'clock number, in which he muses alone on Banjo's advice that, if he wants to rescue Maggie from her romance with a local newspaperman (and, not incidentally, retain her services as his secretary), he marry her himself:

(Speaking)
Marriage . . . Mr.—and *Mrs.*—Sheridan Whiteside . . . Hmmm. Why not?
There's room on my Christmas card. And the wedding would make a
beautiful Easter broadcast. God knows I've squeezed the last drop out of
the Resurrection.
(He begins to sing)
Yes, why not
Marry the girl myself?
Intriguing!
Incredible though it seems to be.
Of course she's getting much the better of the bargain,
But then, she always
Has got the best of me.
To fall in
Love with the girl seems too impulsive,
And yet, if I really must,
I may.

She makes an excellent Martini
And she very seldom cries.
And when she's gay,
The Milky Way
Sparkles in her eyes.
The sparkle in her eyes
Can make a man blink
And make a man think
He'd marry the girl himself today.

So why not
Marry the girl myself?
Enchanting!
Why didn't I think of this before?

It's such an entertaining way to spend the winter . . .
And maybe summer . . .
And maybe even more!

By God, I'll
Marry the girl in Chartres Cathedral.
Stokowski will lead the Mormon Choir.
I'll get Matisse to do the flowers
And Antoine to do her hair,
And as for me,
I will be
Dressed like Fred Astaire!

Yes, dressed like Fred Astaire
And wreathed in a smile,
I'll march down the aisle
As women go wild
And tear their hair.

I hold no brief for the worth of *Sherry!* but at least I have the satisfaction that comes once or twice in a career (if one is lucky) of knowing that the work that exists is everything it could have been—thanks to this company of heroes.

A few days after the Broadway production of *Sherry!* closed, I was seated at my desk, contemplating a dilemma familiar to most writers: Now that my latest effort wouldn't provide an income, after two years of speculative dedication to it, how would I pay the rent and provide food for the table?—a riddle I'd been wrestling with, on and off, since I was thirteen.

As I stared blankly into space, my gaze slowly focused on a small pile of detritus that had been accumulating on a corner of my desk for years: matchbook covers, backs of envelopes, scraps of paper napkins and menus and notepaper, on each of which was lovingly transcribed a term comprising four words: invariably an article, a singular noun, the preposition *of* and a plural noun. Collectively, each set of four words identified, and in a poetic or amusing stroke of inspiration illuminated, a group of things.

I first encountered these constructs, as has everyone else who employs the English language, as coinages so common that they didn't attract my attention. They were simply everyday figures of speech—*a gaggle of geese, a school of fish, a pride of lions, a host of angels, a bevy of beauties*—and, in a more fanciful vein, *a barrel of monkeys, a hill of beans, a dose of salts, a plague of locusts, a quiver of arrows, a tissue of lies* and *a can of worms.*

For years, I took them for granted, which surprises me, looking back, because writing lyrics, as a certifiable genius like Stephen Sondheim demonstrates every time he picks up his pen, begets a profound respect not just for language, but for individual words, since the unique flavor and particular sense of each of them must survive the test of floating naked before us on musical notes, supported by the music but, equally, supporting it. We can read, if we wish, at two hundred words a minute, but half notes and whole notes parade past at their leisure, and in the kind of seriously intended, artfully crafted song America gave to the world for half a century, woe betide the careless or inapposite word that thuds into the delicate design.

In short, it's impossible to practice the profession of setting words to music without falling head-over-heels in love with them. And yet, the poetry lurking in *a pride of lions* went unnoticed by me until the day—an auspicious one, as it turned out—when it occurred to me to ask, "Wait a minute—*why* is it a *pride* of lions, and who decreed that it *should* be?"

Tracking down the answer to that question—and the flood of questions it precipitated—set in motion a voyage that entailed years of discovery, and led finally to the most fulfilling professional experience of my life.

On that day at my desk in 1968, as the pile of scraps swam into focus, I shuffled through the collection of four-word expressions that had accumulated over the years. My only purpose was to while away a few moments admiring them again. On the desk near the inscribed scrap pile lay a business card. I turned it over to find the term I'd written on it, but its back was blank. Turning it right-side up, I recalled its having been given to me by a friend, Richard Grossman, who had been a senior editor at Simon & Schuster, and was now setting up his own publishing company.

I recalled, too, that, a few months earlier, when I'd run into him on the street and inquired at his disconsolate aspect, he'd explained that his marriage had just broken up, and with the holiday season looming, he was feeling utterly lost. My response was to invite him to my mother's Thanksgiving dinner, and he accepted instantly.

The salons I've described at Mother's usually involved word games of various sorts after dinner. Mother's favorite was "Dictionary," which was a variation on the one she'd played with my father, but in recent months I'd been injecting into the mix a game based on my newfound passion for these collective terms. In addition to the authentic terms, like *a murder of crows,* that I'd been unearthing in a still random search, I'd begun inventing some, like *a lurch of buses, a slouch of models* and *an acne of adolescents*; and my game at Mother's consisted of presenting the guests with a list of groups, like *dentists* and *decorators,* and offering points for the most inventive terms—*An acre of dentists? A tantrum of decorators?*

On an impulse for which I'll be forever grateful, I dialed the number on Dick Grossman's card and, when he came to the phone, said, "Do you remember that game we played at Mother's Thanksgiving dinner?"

"Of course."

"I want to turn it into a book."

"Meet me at the Players Club for lunch tomorrow. One o'clock," Dick said.

At the Players Club, we agreed on an advance that was sufficient to finance several months of intense research. My first forays into this terra incognita confirmed my suspicion that these must have been authentic hunting terms, and that ignorance of them would have subjected a fifteenth-century gentleman, whose principal pastime was hunting, to ridicule. My search led me deeper and deeper into the past, to the splendidly named "books of courtesy," medieval and fifteenth-century social primers, each of which contained its own list of the proper, accepted terms of the hunt—and each of which had to be tracked to its lair.

I found the earliest list, containing 106 terms, in the Egerton Manuscript, which dates from about 1450. From there, my search led me to the two Harley Manuscripts, with 48 terms in the first and 45 in the second, the Porkington Manuscript, with 109 terms, and the Digby and Robert of Gloucester Manuscripts, each with 50.

I would recount the adventure in the book I'd elected to write on the subject of this odd linguistic habit that is unique to the English language:

The subject was of such importance that, in about 1476, within a year of the establishment of printing in England, a printed book, *The Hors, Sbepe, & The Ghoos,* appeared, with a list of one hundred six terms. But by far the most important of the early works on the subject was *The Book of St. Albans,* written by Dame Julianna Barnes in 1486, with its one hundred sixty-four terms.

Some of the seminal sources were visible, with considerable cranking, on microfilm at the Forty-second Street Library of Humanities and Social Sciences, but my pursuit of the mother lode in *The Book of St. Albans* took me to the majestic Main Reading Room of the British Museum, where, having provided the obligatory scholarly bona fides, I was issued a temporary reader's ticket, just like the ones that had served Oscar Wilde, George Bernard Shaw,

Rudyard Kipling, H. G. Wells, Mahatma Gandhi, Karl Marx, over a period of twelve years as he prepared to write *Das Kapital,* and V. I. Lenin, furthering the cause.

At the British Museum I learned that some of its great volumes were first among equals, which is to say, they weren't brought to you; you were brought to them—in the depths of the museum, where you were escorted to a small room with only one entrance. Overhead, a bright light illuminated a table at which you sat, waiting for a uniformed guard to deliver the requested volume and retreat a few steps to the door, where he remained as long as the book was in your possession.

I have no firsthand knowledge of the way Van Cleef & Arpels conducts its business, but I've been given to understand that when jewels exceed a certain value, they are shown in a similar inner room, with a guard at the door.

In any event, the experience is guaranteed to impress you with the value of whatever is placed in your hands. In my case, it was the end of a long quest— and the beginning of a matchless adventure. *The Book of St. Albans* yielded up the definitive list that included not only the anticipated *gaggle of geese* and *pride of lions* but such unexpected flights of literary imagination as *an unkindness of ravens, a murmuration of starlings, a rag of colts, a skulk of foxes, a leap of leopards, a tidings of magpies, a charm of finches, a shrewdness of apes, a knot of toads, a parliament of owls* and *an exaltation of larks,* which gave me, the instant I happened on it, the title of my book.

The study of this eccentric and, to me, fascinating, corner of the English language grew, unexpectedly, into a meditation on our linguistic legacy, which I confessed with "The heart and soul of this book is the concern that our language, one of our most precious natural resources, is also a dwindling one that deserves at least as much protection as our woodlands, wetlands and whooping cranes."

The Book of St. Albans provided continual astonishments, which I shared with the readers of *An Exaltation of Larks:*

It may surprise you, as it did me, to discover that, of the 164 terms in *The Book of St. Albans,* 70 of them refer not to animals, but to people and life in the fifteenth century, and every one of these social terms makes the same kind of affectionate or mordant comment that the hunting terms do.

By 1486, the terms were already a game, capable of codification; and if you think the social terms were casually intended and soon forgotten, be advised that the ninth term in the *St. Albans* list is the perennial *bevy of ladies,* and the seventeenth term in the list is none other than *a congregation of people,* appearing between *a walk of snipes* and the eponymous *exaltation of larks.* The social terms are scattered throughout the list, with nothing to distinguish them from the hunting terms.

The Book of St. Albans delivered fifteenth-century flights of fancy like *a pontificality of prelates, a superfluity of nuns* (prefiguring the Reformation), *a discretion of priests, a disworship of Scots, an illusion of painters, a rascal of boys, a foresight of housekeepers, a melody of harpists, a riffraff of knaves, a skulk of thieves* and *a herd of harlots,* which is the seventh term in the canonical St. Albans list, 125 positions ahead of *a school of fish.*

To me, the importance of these terms was twofold: their poetry and their authenticity. I tried to convey it in the book with:

> The thesis of this book can be summed up very simply: when a group of ravens flaps by, you should, if you want to refer to their presence, say, "There goes an unkindness of ravens." Anything else would be wrong.

The term *a sege of Hayrynnys* (a siege of herons, poised hungrily at the water's edge) in the Egerton Manuscript provided, for me at least, a significant clue to one of Shakespeare's nagging riddles, addressed in July 2006, in *The New York Times* by Ben Brantley, its drama critic: "So is he or isn't he—mad, that is? In Shakespeare's *Hamlet* that's what everybody asks everybody else about its title character, and scholars and theatergoers have continued to pose the question for more than 400 years." In March 2007, *The New York Times* reported soberly and at length on "The Trial of Hamlet," at the Kennedy Center, presided over by no less a personage than Supreme Court Justice Anthony M. Kennedy. Enlisting the testimony of eminent jurists and literary scholars, the trial attempted to find Hamlet either guilty of murder or innocent by reason of insanity. My (uninvited, but I believe pertinent) testimony can be found in *An Exaltation of Larks:*

> Herein lies a clue to one of Hamlet's more mysterious utterances, "I am but mad north-northwest; when the wind is southerly, I know a hawk from a handsaw." By Shakespeare's time, the common tongue that had turned *"Route du Roi"* into "Rotten Row" had corrupted the insulting "He doesn't know a hawk from a heronshaw (heron)" to "He doesn't know a hawk from a handsaw"—a mark of churlish ignorance of the language of hunting. Since herons fly with the wind, a southerly wind makes them easy to distinguish by putting the hunter's back to the sun; hence Ham-

let's cryptic hint to his childhood friends Rosencrantz and Guildenstern that his madness is feigned.

I rest my case.

Of the hundreds of contemporary terms, some of them, I like to think, might have received Dame Julianna's endorsement: *a chisel of repairmen, a flush of plumbers, a ring of jewelers, a lot of realtors, a score of bachelors, a freeze* (archaic: *frieze*) *of virgins, a mews of cathouses, a handful of gynecologists, a rash of dermatologists, a click of photographers, an unction of undertakers,* (in a larger group) *an extreme unction of undertakers.*

In November of 1968, on the publication date, I mounted my bike, and, brimming with the optimism—and naïveté—of a fledgling author, toured every bookstore in mid-Manhattan, pretending, of course, to be a buyer in pursuit of "that book everybody's talking about, *An Exaltation of Larks.*" Needless to say, no one was talking about it, and not a single bookseller had ever heard of it.

Crushed, I peddled uptown in the darkness that was gathering—on the streets and in my soul—stopping, as a last dubious resort, in my neighborhood bookstore on Madison Avenue just south of Sixty-fourth Street, where the owner, irascible in the best of circumstances, looked up from the cartons of books he was laboriously unloading for the Christmas season.

"I thought the door was locked" was his amiable greeting.

"There's this book . . . ," I said.

"Which book?"

"An Exaltation of Larks."

"Never heard of it," he muttered. When I stood rooted to the spot, too disheartened to move, he growled, "Can't you see I've got *work* to do?" and I left with my tail tucked neatly between my legs.

Enter—or rather, reenter—Barbara Walters, who was then one of the hosts of the hugely influential *Today Show* on NBC. She'd had Laurence Rosenthal and me on the show, performing a number from *Sherry!* and now she called to invite me on the show with *An Exaltation of Larks.*

I arrived at daybreak on a morning in late November to find the entire *Today Show* set decorated with flying silver larks, suspended from the studio grid, and Barbara and her cohosts, Hugh Downs and Joe Garagiola, armed with copies of the book and their own lists of terms to contribute to what Hugh Downs declared "the only book I truly couldn't put down."

There were five thousand copies of the book—somewhere in the country—in the first printing, and by the end of that day, there were none left. A few days later, Tom Guinzburg, who owned Viking Press, which had absorbed Dick Grossman's company, called to tell me that, in an effort to meet the two hundred thousand outstanding orders, Viking was printing and binding *An Exaltation of Larks* seven days a week, and shipping the books with the binding glue wet to bookstores across the country clamoring for their allotments.

And then the reviews came out. Herbert Mitgang of *The New York Times* called the book "a garden of verbal delights." Raymond Sokolov, *Newsweek*'s critic, wrote, "Lipton has performed all speakers of English a great service. If there were an English Academy, he would surely deserve election," and the *Wilson Library Bulletin* declared, "You'd sooner part with *Roget*'s or *Bartlett*'s than lose Lipton's."

CBS television reported the *Exaltation of Larks* phenomenon in a five-minute feature on its *Evening News*. Strong meat—but all of it was eclipsed on Christmas Eve 1968, when I left my apartment and went to the corner of Madison Avenue in a driving rainstorm, trying desperately to protect the armful of lovingly wrapped Christmas gifts I'd ventured out to deliver. Anyone familiar with New York knows that my chances of finding a cab on a holiday eve in the rain were slim to nil, but I was short of options: Tomorrow was Christmas, and these soggy gifts had to get to their destinations.

As another forlorn wayfarer appeared on the opposite side of Madison, clutching a similar sopping Christmas offering and peering up and down the avenue for a taxi, I did what any seasoned New Yorker would do: headed south to intercept any taxi that chanced to be moving north in search of a passenger. It's dog-eat-dog when New York's weather turns inclement.

As I plodded south, my spirits sinking with each disintegrating Christmas wrapping, something caught my eye as I passed it: the bookstore I'd slunk out of in embarrassment a month earlier. It was closed at this late hour, of course, the last Christmas shopper gone, but the store window bore the final vestige of the holiday season: an enormous sheet of brown wrapping paper, three feet high and six feet across, its jagged ends attesting to the frenzy with which it had been ripped from a roll somewhere in the store. Whatever books the store was featuring in its window had vanished behind the huge, improvised sign on which was scrawled by a patently desperate hand, YES! WE HAVE AN EXALTATION OF LARKS.

For the rest of the city, fighting over *a dearth of taxis* (these venereal terms do tend to sneak in unannounced) in the torrential rain, Christmas Eve was a washout. But for me, standing stock-still in front of that bookshop window with my back to the street, the rain had stopped and, miraculously, the sun had appeared, as it had once before in the Winter Garden Theatre, bathing the street, the sign and me in a golden glow.

I didn't care if a taxi never came. If it *had* come, I would have waved it on: This was the only place on earth I wanted to be, just like this, staring at a messy scrap of paper bringing Christmas tidings of comfort and joy.

In the years since *An Exaltation of Larks* was published, it has never been out of print, going through several expansions and numberless editions—including one now as I write this book—and has progressed, in Viking Penguin's doubtless biased words, from a perennial to a classic.

An entire shelf in my library contains nothing but books that have excerpted or quoted it. It's become a standard reading assignment in creative-writing curricula. It's a staple of *The New York Times* crossword puzzle. And it is still, and will always be, my letter to the world. And none of this might have happened if Barbara Walters hadn't launched it on the wings of those silver larks.

CHAPTER Eight

His eyes look like two holes burned in a blanket.

—Irna Phillips, *The Guiding Light*

During the long learning years, I supported myself with acting jobs on and off-Broadway and on prime-time television, and increasingly with directing and writing assignments. But the solid, steady financial mainstay of that crucial decade was the institution that has sustained some of our most celebrated actors in their formative years: soap opera. Not "daytime drama," not "daytime serial." No, the unadorned words for the unadorned thing: "soap opera," so named because the monarchic cleaning-product manufacturer Procter & Gamble, aiming straight at the heart of the American housewife, elected to sponsor, own and produce some of the prime members of the species.

To put it plainly, my work in soap opera underwrote my acting, voice and dance training, and provided me with the luxury of accepting low-paying, or unpaid, theater roles that were a vital part of my education. It paid for my philosophy and literature and French and filmmaking courses. It bought my books and recorded music, and theater and ballet tickets, and concert tickets. Most important, it bought me *time*—to grow and grow up (I'm still trying to collect on the latter dividend).

Among the several themes that have emerged on *Inside the Actors Studio,* soap opera has held its own with parental loss, struggles with addiction, mentors, Oscar experiences and tattoos.

Why? Because for the actors who have elected to remain in New York to study and work in the theater, it provides a perfect fit: soap opera in the daytime, theater and classes at night. That's been the case since prime-time television journeyed west, followed by a caravan of actors facing financial facts; and it's safe to say that, without the soaps, the theater would be confronted with a depleted talent pool. The relationship between soap operas and the theater is one of our profession's best-kept secrets and most important synergies.

The names of some of the *Inside the Actors Studio* guests who had soap opera careers might come as a surprise to anyone unfamiliar with our series—or daytime television.

In his appearance on our stage in his wheelchair, Christopher Reeve affectionately recalled his career on *Love of Life,* describing the experience as "taking us back to the old touring companies."

I asked him the name of his character.

"Dan Harper. I was a bad guy."

When I asked him whether he found that soap opera viewers can't seem to separate the actor from the role, he replied, "I was in a restaurant and this woman came up to me, took a vicious swipe at me with her handbag and said, 'How dare you treat your mother that way!'"

Tommy Lee Jones, an actor one doesn't normally associate with the soaps, is an alumnus of *One Life to Live.* He was unequivocal about the experience.

"It was wonderful. Yeah, it was wonderful because I was able to pay rent, and I could not have done those twelve or fourteen plays that I did in the seven years I lived here if it had not been for the soap. What else did it do?" he mused. "You know, I'd never performed for over five hundred people in my life, and I remember on the first day, looking at one of the producers and saying, 'How many people do you think will be watching us on TV today?' She said about thirteen and a half million, and I thought, Whoa! It was really hard to get your mind around that idea. It was a good way to learn to not pressure up."

He summed it up with "It's kept a lot of us going, kept a lot of us alive, and thank God for them. And it's something that happens every day, which is really, really good for actors. If you believe in theater, and you believe in acting, it's important to the quality of cultural life that our actors stay busy. I kept auditioning for plays, and the casting director would say, 'We think you're a really good actor, but we need more of a box-office name.' The message was 'You're not famous enough to get this role.' So, my question was 'How do you *get* famous?' And they would point to the soap opera stars who were getting jobs on Broadway."

Laurence Fishburne made his soap opera debut—and TV history—at the age of eleven, as a member of one of daytime's first black families. "It was incredible for me—for a couple of reasons. First, because I was suddenly in the presence of real actors. Al Freeman Jr. used to come up to me every day and go, 'Concentrate, kid!' because I was goofing around. But what *really* impressed me was watching Tommy Lee Jones work, because Tommy Lee and

I were on the same show. You'd come in in the morning—it'd be seven o'clock; we'd have these read-throughs—and Tommy would just be beside himself, ripping through the pages going, 'I can't possibly say this!' And he'd rewrite the things that didn't make sense, and demand that things be made clearer, and that his character have proper motivation. It's something that stuck with me—that I wound up doing later on, without even realizing that I'd learned to do it there."

Kevin Kline recalled vowing when he arrived in New York that he would never, ever do a commercial or a soap opera "because they demeaned the art of acting, and great acting comes from playing great parts in great dramatic literature. After about six months of unemployment, someone said to me, 'You know, artists have to eat. That's one of their first duties: to eat.' I was offered a recurring role in a little thing called *Search for Tomorrow.* At three hundred dollars an episode! And it was a six-block walk from my house. I went in at eight in the morning, got out at three, and then, as my agent said, 'You know, you can work now, off-Broadway or on Broadway or off-off-Broadway, and be an artist. You can support that habit by doing this work which you think is so demeaning.'"

Martin Sheen was on *As the World Turns* and *The Edge of Night.* Julianne Moore also appeared in *The Edge of Night,* playing "Carmen Engler, a Swiss-French girl. She was Swiss-French because they couldn't decide where she was from. First, I was French; then they said, 'Well, if her father is Swiss, maybe she's Swiss.' So, the accent would kind of go back and forth. But it was so exciting. I was so happy. It was a job."

As the World Turns offered Julianne an even greater challenge, "playing Franny Hughes, who was the daughter of the chief of staff of the hospital. The chief of staff of the hospital always has a daughter. And she's always in trouble."

"And on that show somebody's always named Hughes," I said. "That was the family—"

"Yeah. That character had been born on the show. And they wanted to bring me on and make Franny Hughes bad for the first time. And it didn't fly! People got really upset, and they had to do a major character shift. For two months I was snapping at people and wearing sexy clothes, and then one day I came in and all my clothes were pink and white and very demure. They just changed it. And then they spun her off into her half sister Sabrina, who was English and wore a wig and glasses and contact lenses and all that kind of thing, and I was kidnapped. . . ." As the students responded with laughter and, by now, profound understanding, she continued. "I had amnesia. I slept with my own boyfriend, you know? Because he said it was dark and he couldn't tell the difference. That was my favorite line. Yeah, the lights are off. How can you tell?"

"For this miraculous double role, I believe you won an award."

"I did. I won a Daytime Emmy. It was nice."

Perhaps the last name one would associate with *soap opera* is the august Morgan Freeman, but he, too, put in his time, as the architect Roy Bingham on *Another World,* who, as Morgan recalled, "eventually got married, and went off to Europe on a honeymoon and never came back."

Salma Hayek occupied a prominent place as the eponymous Teresa in the torrid world of the *telenovela* in Mexico. If American audiences come to feel they own their soap opera characters body and soul, the Latin American audiences take it even further. "Teresa was a schemer," Salma told us. "And she was a social climber. I am living in this house with the professor and the sister, and I have lied about my background. And my mother comes to visit me in the show, and I pretend she is my maid. And I am in a restaurant with my real mother and my family. And this woman takes her purse [clearly the weapon of choice among soap opera fanatics], comes over to my table, and starts hitting me with her purse. 'Bad daughter! Bad daughter! You're going to go to hell! It's terrible, what you did to your mother—because of her background!' And my mother is like, 'What did she do? What did she do?' And the woman is trying to hit me. And I'm like, 'Wait a minute. Get ahold of yourself!'"

Salma described the furor when she left the adulation she was enjoying in Mexico to begin at the bottom in Hollywood. "Why would I leave Mexico, if I was doing so well? They just couldn't understand that I would leave a successful career in Mexico, to work in the United States as an extra. And so, they started making all kinds of theories."

"Like what?"

"Like I was having an affair with the president of Mexico, and we had a fight, and I *had* to leave the country."

Susan Sarandon valued her time on a short-lived serial called *A World Apart.* "I think it was great because I hadn't studied acting, and this was kind of a combination of theater and film, because basically you're performing live, but you're dealing with all this equipment. On *World Apart* I was the one that everything happened to. I can't even begin to tell you the things that happened to me as the character, but I learned a lot, and I worked with good people."

"Didn't you also do a stint on *Search for Tomorrow*?"

"I did. Yeah, that was a really good one because the main character, who'd been on for about fifty years, was being held captive in a cabin, and she'd lost

INSIDE *INSIDE* | 173

her sight. I was always at the Laundromat. I was always calling my mom at the Laundromat. Mostly my boyfriend was the bad one. My boyfriend and I were brought in to kill the guy that was keeping her captive in this cabin. And then she ran out to get help, and fell off the cliff and got her sight back."

"Right." Nothing could surprise us at this point: Our soap opera suspension of disbelief was unqualified and infinite.

Susan resumed without missing a beat, as caught up in her narrative as we were. "It didn't end there. We went into town and my boyfriend became her gardener. Now, there was something vaguely familiar about this guy to this woman, but of course she couldn't recognize him because she'd been blind."

"Of course."

"It ended with a big shoot-out in a kids' park. They made the whole set. Now, the only problem was that the guy that played my boyfriend was not used to doing soap. He was a theater actor and it was very stressful for him to learn all these lines, you know, every single day."

"Mm-hmm."

"So, in the last episode, my boyfriend had everyone at gunpoint. He wept through the entire show. And everyone thought it was brilliant. That's when I learned about tears, because it had nothing to do with what was going on. He was actually having a nervous breakdown. But they thought it was brilliant."

"Sounds good to me."

My exchange with Teri Hatcher on the subject of soap operas was the briefest in the show's thirteen-year history.

"You ever do a soap opera?"

"For about two minutes."

"Why two minutes?"

"I was fired."

"What was the soap opera?"

"*Capitol.*"

"I was writing it."

Meg Ryan was a soap opera star of the first magnitude on *As the World Turns.* When I asked her her character's name, her dazzling smile appeared, and she pronounced every syllable with evident pride. "I was Betsy Stewart Montgomery Andropoulos. That's everyone I was ever married to."

"Tell us about Betsy."

Meg settled into her chair, clasping her hands as she warmed to the subject. "Well—they got me on the show, and they gave me like this little family tree, which is a very complicated kind of diagram of how everybody was related to everybody. It was insane. And then they said to me, in kind of hushed tones, 'You know, your mother, your *real* mother, died falling up the stairs.' And I thought, 'That's it! She's a complicated babe, honey.' I mean, she went *up* . . . ?"

"Did they ever explain it?"

"No. It was left for me to think about—for a long time. But then every time Betsy would do something totally out of character, which happened often during the writers' strikes, I'd go up the stairs. *Up*, that's right, because her mother died going up the stairs. It explained a lot; it was useful."

"Were you ever kidnapped?"

"I have to defer to you. Was I?"

"Well, *everybody* was. On a soap opera, you're always kidnapped, eventually."

"That's true. True."

"And you were pregnant."

"Yes!"

"But not by your husband."

Gripping the armrests, Meg came half out of her chair. "No! Because he was both sterile and impotent. But he thought I wouldn't get it, you know? Like he thought I could just . . ." Meg sprawled back in her chair, overwhelmed by Andropoulos's presumption. "It was unbelievable!"

"Wasn't he also psychotic and a paraplegic?"

"Yes!" We were soaring side by side, caught in the same histrionic whirlwind. "He was faking the paraplegia!"

"Oh."

"And I was pregnant!"

"Was he faking the impotence?"

"I don't think he was faking the impotence," Meg said, her brow knotted in serious reflection.

I'd done my homework. "But then you got pregnant."

"Yes, by my Greek construction-worker lover. In Spain," she added pointedly.

Meg's wispy voice could barely be heard over the convulsive response from the students in the audience. But I was on a mission. "You got pregnant in Spain."

She nodded emphatically. "In Spain, that's where it happened."

"Didn't Mr. Andropoulos wind up in a jail in Greece?"

"Eventually, on another remote trip," Meg said gravely.

Then, still treating the subject as seriously as she had her years of study with the famous Method teacher Peggy Feury, she observed, "You know, the other thing that happened on the soap opera . . ."

"What?"

"I really fell in love with actors. It was so much fun to be around these people because everybody was so out front with all their stuff. There was such a soap opera in this studio on East Seventy-sixth Street."

When Meg recited her string of married names on our stage, I remarked wanly, "On *The Guiding Light,* I romanced or married everybody on the show but my mother."

During the Stella Adler/Harold Clurman years, I joined the cast of *The Guiding Light,* which can be found in the *Guinness Book of World Records* as the longest-running soap opera in current production and the longest-running program of any kind in television history. Since I appeared on it, it has mysteriously lost its article and become simply *Guiding Light,* and when I joined it, in media res, it was already an institution.

I was brought aboard for a brief romance with Kathy, the show's ingénue, played by Susan Douglas, who introduced me breathlessly to her family and the audience as Dick Grant, her high school's basketball star. The fact that I am five feet, nine inches tall on a good-posture day didn't deter the show's legendary creator, Irna Phillips, who was accustomed to having her way—and had probably never seen a basketball game in her life.

Dick Grant was created casually by Irna for a single, specific dramatic purpose, to break Kathy's heart by leaving town—and the show—in a few weeks, which I did dutifully and with some regret, since, like all the actors who testified years later on *Inside the Actors Studio,* I appreciated the payday.

But Irna, who lived in Chicago, in the bosom of the heartland citizens at whom her art was aimed, and who watched the show every day in her living room through their eyes and with their sensibilities, had a habit. When an actor who'd been cast in New York appealed to her on her screen in Chicago, wheels were set in motion: If she disliked the actor, he or she met an untimely and sometimes unseemly end; but if she *liked* the actor, intriguing things began happening to the character, and the role grew exponentially.

Irna was notorious for writing only three or four weeks (and sometimes, when she was seriously dilatory, as few as two weeks) ahead of the show's live shoot-date. The result was that her new predilections would become quickly evident on the screen—and to the viewers, who were her unquestioning coconspirators and collaborators.

I had caught Irna's attention: the high school basketball star who had broken Kathy's heart had captured Irna's. She notified New York, and I was hastily contracted to return to the studio in a month, whereupon I, and several million viewers, were participants in what can be most generously described as a miracle as Kathy's doorbell rang, she opened the door, innocent, unwitting and still heartsick, and gasped, with Middle America, at the sight of Dick Grant back in Springfield, explaining calmly—and in as low a vocal register as I could manage—that I'd come back to serve my surgical residency at Cedars Hospital.

No one—not Kathy, not Procter & Gamble, not the show's devoted followers—noticed, much less complained, that the recent basketball star had graduated from high school, earned an undergraduate degree, completed med school and served an entire medical internship in four weeks. It was an Irna Phillips fait accompli, not her first, not her last, and not even her most audacious.

In Julianne's and Susan's and Meg's accounts on *Inside the Actors Studio,* the tangled soap opera webs rival Iago's, and no one could weave a web more tangled, ingenious and intriguing than Irna. She possessed an undeniable genius for plot—but when it came to clothing the intricate plots in dialogue, her muse fled in panic.

Since Irna created both the bible (the reverent term soap opera's developers long ago invented for its long-term story) and every day's script, she had no choice but to dictate the dialogue, at breakneck speed, to her longtime, long-suffering secretary, Rose Cooperman, who would arrive at Irna's apartment each morning (in Chicago's frigid winters in the floor-length mink coat, identical to Irna's, that Irna had given her at some point to atone for some minor mistreatment).

When the script arrived in New York, Ted Corday, the show's director, and the cast would assemble around a table to rewrite large chunks of it, adhering faithfully to Irna's baroque story lines. Each day, when the show went off the air, the phone would ring in the control room, and through the glass, we could watch Ted Corday wince at some of Irna's more caustic comments, especially when he—or the cast—had had the temerity to rewrite one of her favorite lines.

The conflict came to a head one day when the scripts that awaited us on the table required one character to describe another's exhausted state with "Look at him. His eyes look like two holes burned in a blanket."

"Cut it!" Ted exclaimed, and around the table, pencils were diligently plied. When the show went off the air that day, the control room phone rang instantly, and Ted looked exceptionally pained as he listened to the caller. We couldn't hear him, but he seemed to be fighting back—a rare occurrence and, apparently, a declaration of war. Two or three weeks later, when we received the script that Irna wrote the afternoon of the contretemps with Ted, one character described another's eyes as looking like two holes burned in a blanket. "Cut it!" Ted growled.

The battle was joined. In every day's script, someone was charged to say, "His eyes look like two holes burned in a blanket." Gender no longer mattered—sometimes it was "her eyes"—nor did characterization, motivation, plot or, finally, sense. Every day, someone was supposed to say it, and every day no one did. Irna no longer bothered to dispute it by phone: She simply wrote it in, relentlessly. Clearly, she considered it her "To be or not to be," and the philistines in New York would eventually have to see the error of their ways.

What came to be known as "the battle of the blanket" raged for months—and then Easter, the season of redemption, arrived. Irna, who was not, I strongly suspect, a pious person, nonetheless honored her viewers' beliefs with scrupulous celebrations of the important religious holidays. Initially, the title *The Guiding Light* had a religious connotation, since the show's first leading character in the 1930s was a minister. So, Irna wrote an Easter episode that was restaged each year with, at its center, a lengthy sermon delivered by an authentic minister, borrowed for the sacred occasion.

The cast looked forward to it because it was what we referred to lovingly as a "brass ring," which is to say, there was no homework, nothing to memorize the night before: All we had to do was show up for dress rehearsal, and take our designated places in the church's pews to listen, silent and reverent, to the sermon written by Irna early in the show's history on the Seven Last Words of the crucified Jesus.

The sermon was unvarying, and our only assignment was to look rapt as the cameras roamed our faces, since each year the director placed us strategically so that the current closeted lovers, feuding families and mortal enemies were fatefully side by side. Irna's web was never more tightly woven than in those pews on the show's Easter Sunday morning.

In the "battle of the blanket" year, at the dress rehearsal, we sat idly in the pews with some of the actors absorbed in books and magazines on their laps as the minister began, "And at about the ninth hour, Jesus cried with a loud voice, saying, 'My God, my God, why hast thou forsaken me?'"

The dress rehearsal droned on, with occasional stops as Ted, on the loudspeaker from the control room, adjusted his cameras to better reveal the scene's tortuous subtext. None of us were paying close attention as the minister preached Irna's version of the Seven Last Words: "At the foot of the cross, the soldiers, indifferent to the suffering of the man from Galilee, cast lots for his tattered garments. Distant thunder rumbled and on the horizon lightning flickered, causing one of the soldiers to look up. Suddenly, he grasped the arm of the soldier next to him, exclaiming, 'Look!' All the soldiers followed his trembling finger, which was pointed upward at the cross as he gasped, 'Behold His eyes! They look like two holes burned in a blanket!'"

Now it was the turn of the actor playing the minister to look up in astonishment as the entire congregation shot into the air as if the pews had been booby-trapped. Staring in disbelief, he watched us writhe on the floor, howling, clutching one another and gasping for breath, apparently as indifferent to the suffering of the man on the cross as the soldiers had been. Worse, we somehow found it screamingly funny!

Ted Corday's voice crackled over the loudspeaker, reassuring the man of the cloth: "It's okay, it's okay. A private matter. Nothing to do with the sermon. Keep going, please. Continue the sermon. And *please,* people, get back in the pews. We're running way behind schedule!" When we stared up at the control room, Ted snapped, "The 'blanket' line stays! So, cut the crap and cue the minister."

The floor manager cued the shaken cleric who, eyeing the congregation warily as it struggled back into the pews, declaimed, "Then said Jesus, 'Father, forgive them, for they know not what they do,'" and reeled back from the pulpit as a torrent of laughter struck him from the helpless congregation.

"Okay, okay!" the loudspeaker brayed. "I've got my shots. Go to makeup, and report back for air."

We made it through the live show, barely, hoping against hope that the viewers would attribute our quivering lips to a valiant effort to control emotions evoked by the beauty of Jesus's—and Irna's—Seven Last Words.

In the aftermath, Ted explained to us that it was his Easter gift to Irna, but we knew that the war was over and Irna had won. Maybe Jesus's eyes still look like two holes burned in a blanket in the annual Easter sermon, and the show's fans—make that the show's "addicts"—are none the wiser and all the happier for it.

And, as our soap opera alumni have indicated on *Inside the Actors Studio,* soap opera stars are revered by their fans in ways that even movie stars are not.

That's how *The Guiding Light* provided me with one of the most prized friendships of my life, when Nina Foch, whom I'd met in a television version of Thornton Wilder's *The Skin of Our Teeth,* called me from California to ask me to show her apartment to her friends Lena Horne and Lena's husband, Lenny Hayton, who were finding it difficult to rent an apartment in New York in that still biased time.

When I lived in Paris, I'd once spotted the couple shopping on the Faubourg Saint-Honoré, and since I was of the firm opinion that Miss Horne was hands down the most beautiful woman on earth, and a dazzling artist, I forewent an entire afternoon of recruiting tourists outside the American Express office to follow the couple at a discreet distance as they strolled in and out of one elegant store after another.

Now, years later, standing on the sidewalk in front of Nina's apartment, I was in an understandable state of excitement as the couple rounded the corner and headed toward me. I showed them the apartment, then watched them go with the same unvoiced veneration I'd felt in Paris.

The next day, I got a call from Miss Horne, who had called Nina in Los Angeles for my phone number. "Lenny said I shouldn't bother you," said the honeyed voice, "but I've got to know. You *are* Doctor Grant, aren't you?" As hard as it is to believe, her voice was trembling. When I said yes, the voice at the other end of the line screeched at Lenny Hayton, "I told you so, Daddy!" Then, back in the voice I knew so well, she said, "I can't believe I'm actually talking to you."

Explaining that she belonged to a large circle of devoted *Guiding Light* viewers, she invited me to their hotel suite for drinks Saturday night, and asked if I'd mind if she invited a few friends—in my honor. Not believing my ears, I accepted.

On Saturday night, I arrived at their door, which was opened by Lena, smiling that incomparable smile, and leading me into a large living room so packed she had to force our way through it, clutching my hand and whispering that every person in the room was my devoted fan, and that none of them could believe it when she invited them to meet me.

As the awesome, awestruck crowd parted before us, an unoccupied armchair was revealed at the other end of the room, with a table next to it on which untouched hors d'oeuvres, a glass of champagne and an unopened pack of cigarettes (my brand; she must have asked Nina) waited. When Lena had seated me ceremoniously in the chair, the crowd, now silent, gathered in a large semicircle, with some of them, including Lena, the legendary cabaret singer Mabel Mercer, and Fran Allison of the inimitable *Kukla, Fran and Ollie*, seated on the floor, literally at my feet.

The Q & A began: "What's Papa Bauer like?" "Will you and Kathy get back together?" Some of it was advice, offered as if we never saw any scenes but our own: "Look out for that nurse, Janet. She's got her eye on you." Some of it consisted of naked pleas for future story lines, with the excuse that "I'll be in Europe for two months, and I won't know what's happening!" I explained that none of us in the cast knew what was happening next; it was Irna Phillips's policy. "What's *she* like?" came the chorus.

The exchange continued for more than an hour until dinner was served; and that encounter began a long and close association with Lena and Lenny, and her daughter Gail, that in time had nothing to do with *The Guiding Light* or Lena's illustrious career, as it turned into a splendid friendship.

It was during the *Guiding Light* years that the last barrier between me and my father's nefarious lifestyle crumbled and I began writing for the theater and prime-time television. All my ventures, and my continuing classes, were subsidized by the soap, for which, like Tommy Lee Jones and Julianne Moore, I am unequivocally, and unapologetically, grateful.

My increasing focus on writing, and the imminent production of my first Broadway musical, necessitated my leaving the shelter of *The Guiding Light.* Having long since completed his residency, innumerable romances and two marriages, and having become a renowned surgeon with "golden hands," Dr. Dick Grant, like Morgan Freeman's Roy Bingham, "went off to Europe . . . and never came back."

When my dark and revelatory opening night at the Winter Garden Theatre left me at rock bottom with, literally, "Nowhere to Go but Up," and no idea how to begin the ascent, it was Bob Short and Ed Trach of P & G who appeared out of the blue with a surprising offer. Irna had expanded her CBS horizons with the phenomenally successful *As the World Turns,* and when she created still another soap, this time for NBC, called coyly, *Another World,* P & G felt she had overextended herself, and persuaded her to turn the head-writing reins over to someone she could regard as a protégé: her erstwhile favorite, Dr. Dick Grant, and, as luck would have it, me.

What followed was another period of intense, compressed and invaluable education, as I assumed the backbreaking duties of a soap opera head writer, with Irna looking over my shoulder, at P & G's request and mine.

Although Irna's empire was based in New York, she remained steadfastly in Chicago, which meant that meetings, which were frequent, required hasty flights from Cincinnati for Ed Trach and Bob Short, and from New York for me. Irna usually contrived not to be feeling well when we arrived, with the result that the meetings took place in her ornate bedroom, with Irna propped coquettishly in something fluffy against a pile of pillows on her bed, and the P & G contingent and me ranged around the bed on chairs.

I was new to the process, but Ed and Bob had been observing this ritual for years. One night, after a long meeting in Irna's bedroom, when they and I returned to the Ambassador East for dinner in the Pump Room and an appraisal of the evening's proceedings, I asked them whether it had ever occurred to them that we were players in an elaborate charade. "You know what we are, don't you?" I asked, and Ed nodded wearily and replied, "Sure, Irna's boyfriends."

"You don't mind?"

Ed shrugged and spread his hands. "She delivers the ratings."

In the first months of my stewardship of *Another World,* I made many trips to Irna's bedside for consultation and counsel. Given the responsibility to turn out five thirty-minute episodes every five days, the equivalent in pages of a feature film a week, fifty-two films a year, the interruptions to my relentless routine could be jolting, but the discomfort was mitigated when I was invited to join the elect, with full rights and privileges, at Hefner's Playboy Mansion, which was then located in Chicago, not far from Irna's apartment.

On my first visit to the mansion, instructed by a liveried butler to remove my shoes and proceed across the white carpets and up the grand staircase to the massive double oaken doors, I came face-to-face with a brass plate that read, *"Si Non Oscillas, Noli Tintinnare."* I have never been more grateful for my years of devotion to Latin, not to mention my apprenticeship on the Rue Pigalle, as *"Si Non Oscillas . . ."* dissolved to "If you don't swing, don't ring."

I pressed the button with what can be conservatively described as alacrity, and the doors swung open to reveal a seraglio of bunnies and centerfolds, many of them, as I would learn, fresh from the cheerleading squads and parochial schools of Iowa, Arizona and Florida, lolling on a field of massive couches as strolling waiters and waitresses plied them and Hefner's guests with an endless stream of food and drink, all of it presided over by a praetorian guard of suits of armor around the perimeter of the vast room.

Some mornings, when I arrived at Irna's bedside after a late evening at the mansion, she expressed concern at the toll my writing schedule seemed to be taking on me, but I assured her I could handle the workload, quickly opened my notebook and revealed to her my latest diabolical designs for the citizens of Bay City. When Irna was particularly taken by one of my ideas, she would lean forward from her pillows to beat her little fists into the bedspread, laughing delightedly and with a mentor's pride at the ingenuity of this chip off the crafty old block.

Irna possessed several secrets, but the key one was what she called her "squares": a sheet of paper that had been divided by Rose, with pencil and ruler in this pre-personal-computer era, into small squares, like a game board—which is exactly what it became as Irna, giggling with glee like a Scrabble player placing a Z on a triple-letter space, filled in a square with a particularly cunning development.

The days of the week ranged across the top of the page, and the character names appeared in a column down its left side. With this system, Irna knew at any given moment what every character was doing with—and to—every other character, and this was the means by which she would weave her web, moving her characters about on the board like puppets, to suit each new, nefarious notion she came up with. The same technique, magnified, could tell the soap's story consistently in every act and scene of each episode, enabling Irna, and every writer she trained, to keep dozens of soap opera balls aloft, to the amazement and pleasure of the daytime audience.

In the course of the decade following my service on *Another World,* on my own and using what Irna taught me, I head-wrote a covey of soap operas: *Guiding Light* in two two-year tours; *Love Is a Many Splendored Thing*; *Return to Peyton Place*; *The Best of Everything,* which I created for ABC; and *Capitol.*

In the last years of her career, Irna trained three writers, all emerging at the same time. I was the runt of the litter. The two who mattered, and whose work matters today, are William Bell and Agnes Nixon. I chose to leave the soap world, and they remained—and reigned. Bill Bell, who died in 2005, was the creator of *The Young and the Restless* and *The Bold and the Beautiful.* Aggie Nixon created *One Life to Live, All My Children* and *Loving.* Their five shows have been on the air collectively for 154 years, so, clearly, Irna taught them well, and they learned well.

They were right to stay, and I was right to go. But I'm deeply indebted to that world because it quite simply made everything else possible until the night in October 1976 when Leonard Bernstein called, and everything changed again.

CHAPTER Nine

66 *The image of the president is truth,*
Wisdom's message his rod.
The home of the president is the White House,
And the president's power is God.

—Muhammad Ali, Jimmy Carter's Inaugural Gala

Kedakai and I were lying side by side in bed (we were married by this time), watching *Monday Night Football,* and I was exercising my God-given right to hurl imprecations at Howard Cosell, when the phone rang. The voice at the other end of the line said, "Hi, Jim. Lenny." I waited for more. "Aren't you surprised to be hearing from me at this hour?" Bernstein asked.

I glanced at the clock, which read midnight. "Yeah," I said, "a little. What's up?"

"I can't keep a copy of *An Exaltation of Larks.*"

"Why?"

"People see it on my coffee table, and open it, and steal it."

"Put it in your bookshelf."

"They'll find it."

"Okay, I'll send you five copies, and you can put one on the coffee table and keep four in reserve."

"They'll all be gone, and then what?"

"You'll notify me, and I'll send you five more. Ten."

"What's *that* about?" Kedakai whispered.

"You know that letter you sent me about 'The Star Spangled Gala'?" Lenny asked.

"Yeah."

"I keep it on my night table, and when I need inspiration, I read it."

"The Star Spangled Gala" was a benefit performance in 1976 at the Metropolitan Opera House. Between 1973 and 1975, Broadway star Gwen Verdon, who had a house in the Hamptons, as did Kedakai and I, had persuaded me to write, produce, direct and host a series of gala dance events to benefit East Hampton's cultural center, Guild Hall.

Gwen was one of the most seductively persuasive people I've ever known, onstage or off, so when she became aware that I'd begun executive-producing the soap operas I was writing, she took me firmly by the hand and led me into producing for the stage. Then, once she'd solved Guild Hall's financial problems, Gwen saw another opportunity. In the wake of New York City's financial crisis of the mid-1970s, public money for such fripperies as art and culture was in very short supply, and the newspapers reported the imminent demise of the New York Public Library of the Performing Arts at Lincoln Center, America's leading performing arts archive and research center.

That was all Gwen had to hear. Placing her powerful dancer's hand on my arm, she led me to Lincoln Center, where it was agreed that I would write, produce, direct and host a series of gala performances in the library's Bruno Walter Auditorium, starring Gwen and everyone we could co-opt. The galas worked, selling out and raising money—but not nearly enough. The auditorium was small and the library remained in mortal danger. In an audacious moment, I proposed to produce a gala for the benefit of the library at its neighboring four-thousand-seat venue, the Metropolitan Opera House.

The enterprise required months of preparation and a worldwide flurry of appeals and exhortations, with the result that, on May 9, 1976, the Metropolitan Opera's massive curtain rose on what was then, and perhaps is still, the largest gathering of performing artists ever presented on its stage. It was called "The Star Spangled Gala," and the morning after the performance, Clive Barnes, *The New York Times* dance and drama critic, wrote, "James Lipton's 'The Star Spangled Gala' opened with the divine Twyla Tharp, ended with the equally divine Julie Harris, and crammed as much in between as to make a club sandwich seem like a fortune cookie."

Elizabeth Taylor and Vice President Nelson Rockefeller were my onstage hosts. Shirley Verrett sang "Una voce poco fa." Jean-Pierre Rampal came from France to perform Mozart's Flute Concerto in D, then played Debussy's "Syrinx," which was, in Clive Barnes's description, "sensuously performed and choreographed by Martine van Hamel." Gwen Verdon and Chita Rivera gave the sold-out house Bob Fosse's brand-new dances from *Chicago.* Judith Jamison danced Alvin Ailey's—and her—signature work, "Cry." New York City Ballet's reigning stars, Suzanne Farrell and Peter Martins, performed Balanchine's

"Tchaikovsky Pas de Deux." And Mikhail Baryshnikov and Natalia Makarova danced the "Don Quixote Pas de Deux."

In Clive Barnes's words, "It must surely go down as a gala-person's gala." But for me, and, as it would turn out, for Barnes, what mattered most that night was a piece created by choreographer Jerome Robbins for the occasion. When I embarked on this reckless venture, one of my goals was to persuade Mikhail Baryshnikov, who had recently defected from the Soviet Union, and had appeared only once in the New York area, at the Brooklyn Academy of Music, to make his Manhattan debut in the gala. When he agreed, I set out to persuade Jerome Robbins, who towers over the American choreographers of his time and, in my view, ranks, with Balanchine, among the greatest choreographers of the past century, to create an original piece for the occasion for Baryshnikov and Makarova, who had also recently defected from the Soviet Union.

Robbins was notoriously difficult to enlist in any project, but my ace in the hole was the knowledge that, like most dancers, Robbins had left school at an early age, had become an autodidact, educating himself at the New York Public Library, and, in gratitude, had donated to the library in perpetuity a percentage of his royalties as director and choreographer of *Fiddler on the Roof*.

Now, when I asked him to join in the effort to save the Library of the Performing Arts, he agreed. I solicited foundations to finance the production cost, Jerry began rehearsals with Misha and Natasha, and the Met sold out at extravagant prices within hours of the announcement that the evening would include a Jerome Robbins world premiere, created for Makarova and Baryshnikov in his debut performance.

Jerry's genius was a matter of public record; so was his reputation for being, on occasion, difficult and quixotic, to the point where he sometimes canceled major projects at the last moment because they weren't meeting his stringent standards. So, I wasn't surprised when I got a heart-stopping call from him a few days before the gala, informing me that I'd have to take the piece out of the program.

"Why?"

"Natasha's a very slow learner. We won't be ready."

"You know that the house is sold out, and this premiere is one of the reasons."

"It's not ready—and I don't know if it's any good."

"There's a lot at stake, Jerry. I'll have to notify the ticket buyers, and some of them may cancel." Jerry was silent. Knowing his history of self-doubt, I ventured, "Maybe it's better than you think it is."

There was another silence; then Jerry said, "Can you come to the State Theater tonight?"

"Of course."

"We'll be in the rehearsal room on the top floor at nine o'clock. But if I *do* change my mind, I want to notify the critics. They can't write about it. I don't want them to *mention* it."

"You won't notify the critics. I will. I'll write a letter explaining that they owe it to you and the dancers not to review it."

"I'll want to see the letter."

"I'll bring it with me."

As the elevator took Kedakai and me to the top floor of the State Theater, we could hear the New York City Ballet orchestra and the thump of the dancers' feet on the stage below. In the rehearsal room, we found Jerry, Misha, Natasha, the pianist and two chairs with their backs to the mirror. Kedakai and I took our places, feeling a bit like royalty at the Maryinsky, and the pianist struck up the Chopin music to which Jerry was choreographing.

The piece was called *Other Dances,* since it continued Robbins's previous Chopin exploration in his acclaimed *Dances at a Gathering,* and it contained four Chopin mazurkas and a waltz. Jerry leaned on the piano, watching in silence, as Misha and Natasha danced the work from start to finish.

When it had concluded, Natasha retired, gasping and sweating, to a corner of the room to light a cigarette. Misha walked to Kedakai and me and stared down at us, toweling sweat and waiting. "It's good," I said. "It's very good. It's better than that." Misha nodded, and joined Natasha to light a cigarette. I went to Jerry, who was waiting for me at the piano.

"Do you have the letter?" was all Jerry said. I produced it and handed it to him. He read it, said, "Take out the part about the *Fiddler* royalties," and handed it back.

"I'd like to do one other thing."

"What?"

"Tear it up." I indicated Misha and Natasha, still gasping and smoking in the corner. "It's a major work, Jerry. Don't make me deprecate it."

Jerry stared at me. "Natasha still hasn't got some of it." He paused, studying the dancers, then said, "I'll see how it goes tomorrow, and I'll call you tomorrow night if we've still got a problem. Will there be time to send the letter?"

"Yes."

"*If* I decide to let it go on at all," he added ominously.

The next night I said to Kedakai, "We're going to a movie."

"What movie?"

"I don't care. I just want to get out of here."

When we got home, there were no phone messages.

And in his review of "The Star Spangled Gala," after describing what he called the evening's "great performances," Clive Barnes wrote, "However, that is not why Mr. Lipton's wonderful fund-raising gala for the Performing Arts Research Center of the New York Public Library deserves to be remembered. What was really unusual was that the gala unveiled a masterpiece. . . . It was a piece of genius."

In the years since the gala, *Other Dances* has become one of Robbins's most popular ballets, finding its way into the permanent repertories of the American Ballet Theatre, New York City Ballet, the Paris Opera Ballet and the Royal Ballet, among others; and Baryshnikov has called "The Star Spangled Gala" a turning point in his career.

And the indomitable Gwen had succeeded in two objectives: She had enlisted me in the campaign to save the Library of the Performing Arts, which was in fact threatened with extinction, and remains today the world's leading performing arts research center, and she had turned me into a working producer.

Leonard Bernstein was one of the artists I'd tried to enlist in "The Star Spangled Gala," and because I knew his cultural roots and predilections, my letter to him had gone back to the dire consequences of the burning of the Library of Alexandria. That was the letter he referred to that night in 1976 as I lay in bed contemning Howard Cosell.

"Honestly," Lenny insisted, "the letter's inspiring."

"Lenny," I said, "why are you calling me?"

His tone changed. "I need you."

"For what?"

"Are you going to vote for Carter and Mondale?"

"Yes."

"I'm doing the big fund-raiser—in Washington—and the Democratic National Committee is producing it—and they don't know fuck about producing. It's going to be a catastrophe! You've got to come in and take it over!"

"They're not going to allow that."

"They will if I say so," Lenny muttered.

"When is the event?"

"Ten days."

"You're kidding. I'm working, Lenny."

"You've *got* to! It isn't just the election that's at stake; it's my reputation!"

"It's out of the question."

"What are you doing tomorrow night?"

"Nothing that I know of."

"I'm conducting at Carnegie Hall. There'll be two seats for you in my box."

"Lenny, I can't just drop everything and . . ." But he'd hung up.

After the concert the next night, Kedakai and I accompanied Lenny to a supper in his honor at the Dakota. As the guests assembled, he took my arm, led me into a study and closed the door. "You're not leaving this room until you've said yes. My goddamn *life's* at stake!"

Nine days later, the gala concert, which I'd redesigned from stem to stern, transpired in Washington, featuring, among other attractions, Rosalynn Carter, speaking the narration in Aaron Copland's *Lincoln Portrait,* under the baton of a beaming Leonard Bernstein.

During the intermission, Tom Beard, an official of the Inaugural Committee, came backstage to ask me, "Will you do our Inaugural Concert?"

"I will if you get him elected," I said.

They did, and I did.

Shortly after the election, I met with the Inaugural Committee, led by its chairman, Bardyl Tirana, and Gerald Rafshoon, representing the president-elect. When I realized they were expecting the traditional Inaugural Gala, a splashy performance in an eighteen-thousand-seat arena for the party faithful, with the best seats going for ten thousand dollars each, I asked them, "Didn't you guys just get Carter elected on a populist platform? Do you really want to launch his administration with a ten-thousand-dollar-a-seat party for fat cats?"

"What choice do we have?" Tirana asked.

"Television," I said. "It's the most democratic medium ever devised. Free in every home. Why doesn't Jimmy Carter begin his administration by sharing his gala with the American people?"

Clearly tempted, Tirana said, "But the gala has to pay for the whole Inaugural Week."

"We'll get a license fee from a network, like any other television show, and I'll turn all the revenues over to the Inaugural Committee."

Carter and the committee agreed, and handed me the Presidential Gala. I returned to New York owning it, to all intents and purposes. CBS bought the show at the end of November, and I had from then until January 19 to cast, write and produce the first Presidential Gala ever televised.

After the cultural community's long alienation from the White House during the Nixon years, casting Jimmy Carter's gala was like uncorking an especially lively champagne: The artists' responses came gushing out, and on Inaugural Eve, the first television broadcast ever to originate from the Opera House of the Kennedy Center presented to the live audience and the American people a gala celebrating not President-elect Jimmy Carter but, at his insistence, the people and spirit of America. The celebrants were, among others, Paul Newman, Joanne Woodward, Linda Ronstadt, Aretha Franklin, Warren Beatty, Leonard Bernstein and the National Symphony Orchestra, Chevy Chase, Dan Aykroyd, Bette Davis, Paul Simon, Shirley MacLaine, Mike Nichols, Elaine May, Redd Foxx, Jean Stapleton, Carroll O'Connor, Jack Nicholson, Freddie Prinze, Loretta Lynn, Muhammad Ali, the Alvin Ailey American Dance Theater, Frederica von Stade, James Dickey, Beverly Sills and John Wayne.

I had exactly six weeks in which to engineer this coup, at a time when every hotel room, limousine, restaurant, airline reservation—in short, every facility and service in D.C., Virginia, Delaware and Maryland—was solidly booked by the delegations pouring in from every state in the union. Now, suddenly, I appeared with the customary first-class requirements for food, housing and transportation of an army of superstars and their support staffs.

There isn't room in these pages for an account of how this miracle was wrought. Suffice to say that every star wound up in a royal suite in the hotel of his or her choice, my limousines and drivers came from as far away as Florida and Illinois (my staff could always recognize a car containing one of our stars by the road map clutched anxiously in the driver's hand), and my sizable technical crew wound up in accommodations fifty miles from Kennedy Center.

Since I wrote all of the show's original material, with the exception of one sketch written by Herb Sargent, the only way I could prepare the cast in six weeks was to barnstorm the country, meeting with each of them, wherever they were, to present the material I'd prepared for them, revise it if they wished, rehearse them, and bank the segment against their arrival in Washington.

The entire gala was modular, with each piece ready to be slid into place on the Kennedy Center stage on January 19. The theme of the evening, which the president-elect had strongly endorsed, reversed the traditional format of tributes like this. The president was seated with Mrs. Carter and the Mondales in the Presidential Box of the Opera House, and each of the performers spoke not of him, but *to* him, on behalf of one of his constituencies, young people, older people, women, Hispanics, blacks, students, challenging the president-elect to respond to their needs and goals and dreams.

As the material evolved, I sent word to Carter, asking whether he would mind if some of the evening's humor, not all of it reverential, was aimed at him, and the word came back, "Aim it!"

With that authorization, Shirley MacLaine opened the evening singing the lyrics I'd written to Cy Coleman's "It's Not Where You Start, It's Where You Finish":

When it started in Plains,
Superior brains
Said, "Jimmy, don't be silly.
Listen to brother Billy.
Stick to pickin' peanuts.
Politics is a game
Strictly for the famous.
North of the Mason-Dixon,
You're gonna need some fixin'.
So, you better be sure.
Reflect before beginning.
Do you want to endure
Two dozen months of grinning?
Try smilin' through,
'Jimmy who? Jimmy who? Jimmy who?'"

In the course of the song, Shirley observed:

The early returns were sort of thinnish.
The papers said your show was a flop.
But it's not where you start, it's where you finish.
And you went and finished on top.

Later, she sang:

That hundred-to-one shot,
The one with the grin,
Well, whattaya know!
He had the chutzpah to win.

And she reminded him of his naval career:

A seasick lieutenant
Was headed for grief.
Tomorrow at noon
He'll be commander in chief.

As the evening progressed, nothing was sacred. Dan Aykroyd, as chief justice, administered the oath of office to Chevy Chase as Carter, and the two
ended ballroom dancing around the Kennedy Center stage.

At my request, Nichols and May, reuniting for the first time in years, revised their sketch "Mother," in which an astronaut is reduced to babbling babyhood by his hectoring mother, to a conversation between Jimmy Carter and his mother, Lillian, on the eve of his inauguration. On *Inside the Actors Studio,* Mike Nichols recalled that "Miss Lillian was *not* amused," though the president-elect conspicuously was.

Perhaps the most respectful voice on the Opera House stage was that of John Wayne, who had certainly not voted for Jimmy Carter. But when I learned that he had written Carter an eloquent letter wishing him well, signed "The Loyal Opposition," I asked Carter if I could invite Wayne to read his letter in the gala, and the response was "Absolutely."

The Inaugural Gala was a heady experience for all of us. For several days we felt as if we were at the center of the universe—and in some respects we were. There were so many stars roaming the Kennedy Center during our three days of rehearsal that the six hundred people involved in all the levels of the production stopped taking note of them—until two latecomers showed up, John Wayne and Muhammad Ali. Then, a silence fell over the bustling Opera House, and everyone turned to stare, including the stars who were onstage or lolling in Opera House seats watching the rehearsal. When Wayne walked onstage, it was immediately evident that royalty had arrived, and when Muhammad Ali and his entourage emerged from the wings, even John Wayne's head snapped around.

Marty Pasetta, who normally directed the Oscars, was in the production truck far below the stage level, moving his cameras and setting his shots, and I was onstage, putting in place the modules I'd been preparing for six weeks, directing the performers and shaping the performance. In the routine I'd established, a runner informed me as each star arrived at the Opera House, and we met onstage to begin the rehearsal. Ali, who was one of the few participants I hadn't worked with prior to his arrival, was surrounded by a cordon of very large men in the neat business attire of the Nation of Islam, and as I shook hands with him, I was reminded of the boxers' custom of protecting their most valuable asset from strangers eager to demonstrate their powerful handshakes by offering a hand as limp as a dead fish.

In addition, Ali's eyes were half-closed as if he'd just wakened or was halfway to a nap. His entourage offered no explanation, so I decided to begin working with him backstage, offering, "Would you like to see your dressing room?"

Ali nodded drowsily and we proceeded to the dressing room floor, where he slumped into a chair and promptly closed his eyes completely. His entourage drew up chairs in a semicircle behind him and stared at me, silent.

Finally, Ali ended the impasse. His chin still on his chest and his eyes still closed, he murmured, "What do you want me to do?"

It was the cue I'd been waiting for. Seizing my notebook, I asked, "You know who Freddie Prinze is?" Ali's chin moved on his chest, which I took to be a nod. "Well, he does an amazing imitation of you, and at the end of his monologue he's going to do it, and I thought it would be a great entrance if you came out on the stage behind him while he's imitating you, so the audience could see you, but he couldn't. When he hears the audience laugh, he'll turn around, and you can box with him and chase him off the stage and then begin *your* part of the program."

Ali's eyes opened. "You mean you want me to walk out and go . . ." He stood up, not only wide awake, but transformed into the electric Muhammad Ali I'd seen at weigh-ins and news conferences, bug-eyed, wide-mouthed and bellowing, "I AMMMM THE GREATEST OF ALLLLLL TIIIIIME!!!"

He went silent and sat down, open-eyed but sedate, and at a vast remove from the explosion I'd just witnessed. "Is that what you want me to do?"

Unable to believe that I'd just seen Muhammad Ali deliver a stunning imitation of Muhammad Ali, I stuttered, "Well, I . . . I thought . . ."

He shook his head. "I can't do that."

"Why not?"

He waved a hand at the open door of the dressing room. "The president's gonna be out there, right?"

"Yes."

"Can't do that in front of the president."

"But you can. That's the way he wants it—no holding back—everybody can be himself." Ali frowned, and a startling thought crossed my mind: If Ali can imitate Ali, maybe *that* Ali isn't Ali at all, but a part he plays when it suits him. Maybe being himself has absolutely nothing to do with the colorful character that has made him the most recognizable figure on earth.

Ali was ahead of me. "You said I'd do '*my* part of the program.' What's that?"

Treading eggs now, I essayed, "Well, everybody's talking to him up there in the box, more or less saying whatever they'd *want* to say to someone who's about to be president of the United States. I thought you might want to write a poem."

Utter silence. Finally, Ali said, "I can't do that."

Another surprise. Maybe the poems were part of the act. Maybe other people wrote them, and he simply recited them at the appropriate moment. But given the at least fifty-fifty chance that I was wrong, how could I voice such an assumption?

"Not enough time?" I asked, and he was unresponsive.

My mind was racing, sorting options. Finally settling on the possibility that his poems were collaborations, I ventured, "I'm writing the show. Would it help if we threw some ideas back and forth . . . ?"

"Yes," Muhammad Ali said.

His response was galvanizing. "I've got rehearsals till late tonight, and all day tomorrow. The only time I've got is six o'clock tomorrow morning," I concluded apologetically.

"Fine," Ali said.

"You're sure."

"Yeah. Roadwork time."

Of course! He's a boxer. "My place—at the Watergate Hotel?"

"Yes."

I scrawled my room number on a piece of paper, handed it to one of his entourage, and sat back, relieved. But the group didn't move. Ali appeared to have gone back to sleep. I wondered what the protocol was: Does one simply get up and walk out on a dozing world champion?

Once again, Ali solved my problem. His eyes opened, and his lips moved. "The face of the president is open," Ali intoned.

I wheeled on my assistant, Martha Millard. "Start writing!" She opened her notebook and began taking the dictation as he continued.

The eyes of the president are bright.
The lips of the president are never closed.
The head of the president is upright.

The quatrain came out calmly and steadily, in polished meter and without a pause for revision or a fumble for rhyme. He sounded as if he was quoting a meticulously memorized poem, but of course, there was no way he could have known what I would ask of him. It was unmistakable: He was improvising comfortably in rhyme and meter.

When he finished the quatrain, he fell silent. Assuming that he'd concluded his poem, I instructed Martha to read it back to us. He listened with his eyes closed, and the instant she uttered the last word, he opened his eyes and resumed.

The soul of the president is flaming.
The heart of the president is warm.
The president has neither fear nor doubt
Through rain and storm.

When he paused, I nodded at Martha. She read the second quatrain aloud, and once again her last word triggered his first.

> The image of the president is truth,
> Wisdom's message his rod.
> The home of the president is the White House,
> And the president's power is God.

The poet sat back and said, "Let's hear it again." Martha raised her notepad, but before she could speak, Ali began reciting the poem, from memory now, without prompting until he hung fire for an instant on "rain and storm."

When he finished, he nodded satisfaction, and I asked, "Is that it?"

"That's it," Ali said.

I turned to Martha. "Go to the office, type it out and bring it back—one copy for me and one for Ali." Martha raced out the door and as we sat in silence, waiting for the hard copies, Ali looked at me. "You think it's good enough?"

Again I stared at him in disbelief. "Good enough?!"

"Well, it's the president."

"Listen to me," I said. "Most of my friends are writers—some of them are famous writers—and not one of them could have done what you just did."

When Martha returned with Xeroxed copies of the poem, Ali took one and rose with his entourage, one of whom said, "We got an invitation to the White House."

"We're all invited there, the whole cast, after he's sworn in. We'll be the Carters' first White House guests. You're coming, aren't you?"

Catching Ali's glance, the spokesman said, "Yes, all of us," which evoked a sudden thought. Surveying his entourage, all but one of whom had the look of bodyguards, I asked carefully, "Are any of you by any chance packing?"

There was a pregnant silence until the spokesman, after another glance at Ali, said, "Yes."

"In that case," I said, "may I suggest that you leave your heat at the hotel? Every inch of the White House is under electronic surveillance—as you can imagine—and a weapon would set off alarms," I concluded, glancing at Ali, who replied, "Of course."

When he'd left, and I returned to the stage to work with my next performer, Ali's spokesman appeared in the wings, signaling to me. I walked to him and he said, "Muhammad sent me back."

"Any problem?"

"No. He told me to ask you if you meant what you said about nobody else being able to do what he did."

"Absolutely. I've never seen anything like it."

At the concert, the Ali the audience knew snuck out of the wings behind Freddie, got a roar from the audience and, capering and yelling, boxed Freddie off the stage. Then, the Ali the audience didn't know turned to the Presidential Box and said with quiet dignity, "I wrote something and dedicated it to Mr. Carter. Soon I'll be able to say, 'Mr. President.' It's entitled 'The President' "— and brought the audience to its feet with his poem.

Several months after the gala, Ali invited Kedakai and me to spend a weekend with him and his wife, Veronica, at their home in Chicago, which we did. In the course of that memorable weekend, Kedakai and I invited Ali and Veronica and Mr. and Mrs. Herbert Muhammad to a night of ballet at the Chicago Opera House, where, unfortunately, one of the doyennes of Chicago society snatched him away from the rest of us and seated him ostentatiously in her box a city block from the stage; we attended a Nation of Islam dinner, where we were welcomed as Ali and Herbert Muhammad's guests; and were escorted to the rumpus room in Ali's basement, where he preached nondenominational sermons to us from stacks of handwritten three-by-five cards that he selected with care from a catalogued file cabinet, asking my opinion of the literary merit of some of his favored constructions.

Calling Muhammad Ali one of the heroes of this account is a tautology: As the world has come to realize, *Ali* and *hero* are synonymous.

One of the last elements I put into place as I was preparing the New Spirit Concert was literature, which I felt had to be represented. I wanted to have an Inaugural Gala poet laureate, who would write a poem for the occasion, as Robert Frost had written a poem for John F. Kennedy's inauguration, which he couldn't read in the bright sunlight at the swearing-in. I asked Mr. Carter if he'd like to choose the poet, and to no one's surprise, he selected the great Southern voice, James Dickey.

I contacted Dickey's agent, Theron Raines, and was told that Mr. Dickey would be honored to participate; and he showed up in Washington with a beautifully crafted poem called "The Strength of Fields." Our musical director, Donn Trenner, composed elegiac music to be played by our orchestra as Mr. Dickey read his poem.

At the dress rehearsal, when Mr. Dickey's turn came, he tottered—there is no other word for it—out of his dressing room, up the stairs and onto the stage, where he began not with his poem but with an explanatory introduction to it . . . that rambled on for fifteen minutes in slurred slow motion. The music Trenner had prepared ran out after seven minutes, which was the time allotted to our poet laureate, and the pit musicians had to scramble back to page one of their books and begin again, in what began to sound like a perpetual loop.

Then, Mr. Dickey got to the poem, but whatever he'd been consuming was really kicking in, so he slowed to a crawl, dwelling on every word of the poem—for another fifteen minutes, as the musicians in the pit scrambled back to the beginning of the music again. In the production truck, my staff and the CBS executives were tearing their hair, not just at the exhibition on the stage, but for another much more important reason.

When I sold the New Spirit Concert to CBS on behalf of the Inaugural Committee, I proposed what was then a revolutionary idea: The gala would begin in Kennedy Center at seven P.M., and would air on CBS at nine, giving us a two-hour cushion between the live event and the telecast. Beginning at seven, I would be stationed in a production truck below the stage, connected by phone to a bank of editors in New York who were receiving our feed with time code, enabling me to edit the show as it was being shot, polishing the performance and keeping it to time.

The system seemed foolproof, but James Dickey unchecked, consuming not seven but thirty minutes, would eat up nearly a quarter of our lead time, leaving us, if there were any other delays, perilously close to a live feed to the network, with no margin for error and no opportunity for judicious editing.

At the end of the dress rehearsal, the CBS executives and my staff turned to me, and I said, "Don't worry. I've got an idea."

I found Dickey relaxing, to say the least, in his dressing room, which was redolent of esters. Pulling up a chair, I said, "It occurred to me that you might know my father."

"Who's 'at?"

"Lawrence Lipton."

"Certain'y do. Fine poet."

Having presented my credentials, I proceeded to the point. "Beautiful poem."

He smiled affably. "Thanks."

"It's *so* good," I said, "that I think you're doing it a disservice."

"Oh? How so?"

"The introduction. Utterly unnecessary. The poem speaks for itself. Introducing it with all that explanation makes it sound like you're *apologizing* for it. It's unfair to the poem."

"I never thought of that! You really think so?"

"*Everybody* does. You're hurting the poem!"

"My God! Don' wanna do that!"

I stood up. "So—just the poem."

"Of course. What was I thinking of!"

"No harm done," I said magnanimously, and returned to the truck, mission accomplished.

When the Inaugural Gala began promptly at seven on the nineteenth, Shirley delivered the opening number with her customary charm and verve, Paul Newman introduced the evening's theme with the powerful simplicity he brought to his screen roles, and we were under way. Far below the stage, I manned my post in front a bank of monitors as Marty Pasetta worked his magic, conducting twenty cameras like Toscanini on the podium.

Everything proceeded on schedule and according to plan: Using the time code that united us with the edit room in New York, Bob Wynn, the show's line producer, and I were able to polish and trim as we went along. And then Bette Davis pronounced the words I'd written for her, "While the entire spectrum of America's arts couldn't be crowded on our stage, the written and spoken word *must* share the stage with music and dance," and introduced our poet laureate, who lurched out of the wings, peered at the distinguished audience, and said, "I thought you'd prob'ly want to know something 'bout what you're gonna hear . . ." and proceeded with not a fifteen-minute but a twenty-minute exegesis of his poem.

"Start cutting!" I yelled over the phone to the editors in New York. When Dickey had finished the introduction, he began the poem—at a snail's pace, pausing at one point, to remark, "Oh, that was good!" and repeat the stanza with lip-smacking relish, as the pit musicians returned frantically to the beginning of the music. "Keep cutting!" I yelled at New York.

In the end, what America and the world heard was the seven-minute peroration of James Dickey's poem, beginning, "Now, as I walk the night and you walk with me . . ." and concluding exquisitely, if at a leaden pace, with:

Lord, let me shake with purpose.
Wild hope can always spring
From tended strength.
Everything is in that.
That and nothing but kindness.
More kindness, dear Lord of the renewing green.
That is where it all has to start;
With the simplest things.
More kindness will do nothing less
Than save every sleeping one

And night-walking one of us.
My life belongs to the world.
I will do what I can.

A few days after the gala, Martha Millard came on the intercom at my office in New York. "James Dickey's agent is on the phone."

"Okay." I sighed. "May as well get it over." I picked up the phone. "Hello, Theron."

"Mr. Lipton," he said, "I have two words for you."

"I know," I said. "The second one is *you.*"

"That's right," Theron said, "and the first one is *Thank.*"

The president-elect had chosen our Inaugural Concert poet laureate wisely, albeit rashly. Nearly two decades later, in our first episode of *Inside the Actors Studio*, Paul Newman filled in the backstage details of the James Dickey saga.

"There was a bottle of tequila under the stage, wasn't there?" I said. "Tell me the truth, at last."

Paul grinned. "When I got to the theater, I found out that I was to occupy a dressing room with Duke Wayne. When I got to the dressing room, it was nine thirty in the morning, and he's just had a little tiny cup of tequila and water. And he said, 'Would you like something?' and I said, 'I don't think so, but I'll have some tea.' And Dickey came in. He said, 'What're you having?' And Duke said, 'Well, I'm having some tequila and water.' And Dickey said, 'You are?' And Duke knew what was going to happen. He said, 'You want one?' Needless to say, Duke was the class act of that whole show. Mr. Dickey was stumbling around, but, by God, Duke was straight as an arrow and had been going with him cup-for-cup all day long."

"All these years I've been blaming Nicholson and Beatty for it!"

"No," Paul said, "it was Duke."

Because I'd seen John Wayne's letter, and knew what he was going to say—and because he was John Wayne—I put him next to closing in the concert, where he said in his patented drawl, "I've come here tonight to wish you Godspeed, sir, in the uncharted waters ahead. Starting tomorrow at high noon all of our hopes and dreams go into that great house with you. We are with you. I am privileged to be present and accounted for in this capital of freedom to witness history as it happens, to watch a common man accept the uncommon responsibility he won fair and square by stating his case to the American people, not by bloodshed, beheadings and riots at the palace gates. I know I am considered a member of the opposition, but keep in mind, the *loyal* opposition—the accent on loyal. I'd have it no other way."

The New Spirit Concert was the first Inaugural Gala ever televised, and, occurring as it did on the eve of the swearing-in of the thirty-ninth president, it was in a real sense the first public utterance of his administration, so I felt a profound obligation to try to get it right. Whatever these artists expressed on the Kennedy Center stage, it was my responsibility as the event's executive producer and writer to make certain that the words I wrote for them reflected the principles, ideals and, to the extent that I could divine it, the sensibility of this newcomer to the political stage.

And since I'd learned over the years that the first and last moments of any creative presentation are usually what the public remembers, I was faced finally with a creative dilemma: With that incomparable cast, how, and with whom, should the evening end?

As little known as Jimmy Carter was when he appeared on the national scene, one of the things that became quickly apparent was the strength and depth of his religious conviction. That was one of the reasons, apart from the company's internationally acknowledged brilliance, that I invited the Alvin Ailey American Dance Theater to perform its signature work, *Revelations,* which was born out of Alvin's religious upbringing in the churches of rural, black Texas.

And it was one of the reasons I wanted to end the concert with Irving Berlin's anthem to the country and his faith, "God Bless America." But the way in which the song could be employed eluded me, and began to torment me, until the rehearsal week in Washington when, suddenly, I saw the finale clearly. I'd been concentrating on how big I could go; now I realized that the only way to top everything that had happened on our stage was to go very, very small.

Through ASCAP, the songwriter's association, of which I'm a member, along with most of America's composers and lyricists, I was able to reach Irving Berlin's assistant, Hilda Schneider, and describe to her what I'd envisioned: At the end of the concert, after all the performers and performances, the stage would go pitch-black, and then a pinspot would illuminate a pair of hands on a piano keyboard, center stage. The hands would begin to play, and the spot would iris out, revealing Irving Berlin at the keyboard, playing and singing his song to the president-elect and the Kennedy Center audience and America and the world, joined finally by our orchestra and the entire cast—and the Opera House audience—in "God Bless America."

"Oh, my God!" his assistant said. "It's wonderful but—you know, he's eighty-eight years old. He never goes out."

I did know, because for several years I'd been his neighbor on Beekman Place. But, I thought—I hoped—that this request might draw him out of his seclusion. "I'll take it to him," his assistant said.

The next day she called to say, "Mr. Berlin said to thank you. He loves the idea—he really does—but he just can't. You understand." Her own regret was audible.

"Of course."

In Washington, I could no longer postpone a decision. Whatever the finale would be, it had to be planned, orchestrated and rehearsed. What was holding me back was that I couldn't relinquish the notion of focusing the scale of the performance down to that pinspot. But on whom?

And then I realized that the only person who could possibly command that moment as the composer would have was already a member of our cast. I described the finale to her, and on January 19, when John Wayne left the Opera House stage, the ensuing darkness was pierced by a sliver of light that illuminated a familiar face in the center of the enormous Opera House stage, and Aretha Franklin began to sing "God Bless America" without accompaniment. Just that face and that matchless voice, singing the song as reverently as I, or Irving Berlin, or the president-elect could have hoped.

As she sang, the spot widened, revealing her alone on the stage. Then, section by section, our pit orchestra began accompanying her, joined by the National Symphony Orchestra in full array. From the wings and from upstage, the Howard University Choir, the five United States Service bands and our cast filled the brightening stage with hundreds of performers, singing with Aretha; and finally, at a signal from Leonard Bernstein, the entire audience joined in, the three-thousand-strong ensemble creating the most joyful noise I've ever heard, or ever expect to hear.

In the production truck, I told New York to let the number run to credits, pulled off my headphones, sat back and watched the monitors in relief and wonder.

There was to be one more unforgettable moment that night. The day before the gala, our friend Jane Lahr had called from New York with a last-minute request. "It's probably too late—but you know that John Lennon has been living in complete seclusion since the Nixon people went after him. Nobody's seen him outside the Dakota. He's very excited about Carter, and he wants to come out—publicly. They want to know if they can come to the gala."

I said, "Jane, I've held one pair of tickets and one Watergate suite in reserve in case of a last-minute emergency. This qualifies. Tell them they've got them."

The next night, at our postperformance dinner in the Kennedy Center Atrium, I had the extraordinary experience of introducing my mother, my wife—and John Lennon and Yoko Ono—to the president-elect and Mrs. Carter.

Gwen Verdon and Lenny Bernstein, one twisting one arm, the other the other, had gotten their way: I was now a full-fledged producer. I realized at that point that producing was the one discipline I hadn't studied, but had drifted into, as most beginning producers do, to fill a looming vacuum. There are more competent actors, directors and writers out there with, in Arthur Miller's famous words in another context, "a smile and a shoeshine," than theater, film and television can accommodate, but there is a chronic shortage of authentic producers sensitive to the sometimes inimical organizational, financial and creative needs of a proposal or project.

When my customary practice of looking for a school that could fill a gap in my education yielded no results, I took the only available course, attaching myself, unannounced, uninvited and at a polite distance, to a role model: in this case to the producer of films like *Serpico, Dog Day Afternoon* and *Scarface*, Martin Bregman. He was patient, forbearing, and has remained my friend and mentor to this day.

A few weeks after the Inaugural Gala, I got a call from a USO official in Washington, who said, "You know, the public thinks we're a government agency, but we're not. We're completely dependent on private funding. And when it's peacetime, the public forgets about us completely. But that's when we're needed the most, because everybody's forgotten about the troops too."

"I understand, but why are you calling me?"

"Can you do for the USO what you did for the president?"

"You mean a television special?"

"Yes."

"I don't think so. The networks have preferences. . . ."

"You mean stars."

"Big stars." The caller's disheartened silence was so eloquent it inspired a thought that would reverberate for the next twelve years. "But there's a guy who was associated with you for thirty years."

"Of course. But not lately," said the caller.

"I think he's about to turn seventy-five," I said. "If you can get him to give you his seventy-fifth birthday, I can't imagine a network saying no."

"I'll get right on it" was the electrified answer.

A few days later, I got a second call, telling me that they'd enlisted Bob Hope's friend General William Westmoreland, who had taken him for what my caller described as "a walk in the woods." Bob Hope, I was told, had accepted my suggestion and given the USO his seventy-fifth birthday, and the USO was hereby giving it to James Lipton Productions.

As I'd "owned" President Carter's Inaugural Gala, I now "owned" Bob

Hope's seventy-fifth birthday, with the understanding and agreement that I would turn all its revenues over to the USO.

When I offered the special to NBC, the network with which Hope had been associated for nearly half a century, I told them in a moment of hubris that if this show was successful, it was my intention to turn Bob's birthday into a national holiday, with a special every Memorial Day Weekend, near which Bob's May 29 birthday always fell.

For the seventy-fifth birthday special, I teamed with Gerald Rafshoon, who was now President Carter's communications director, and it was agreed that the telecast would include a White House reception with our cast and the Carters, and that we would return to the Kennedy Center Opera House, which was now a prime television venue following its debut with the New Spirit Concert.

Since the show was to be a birthday tribute to Hope, it would have been unseemly if he'd sought or received his usual executive-producer credit, or participated in the casting and writing of the show as he normally did. James Lipton Productions, not Hope Enterprises, was the production company, and I was, in name and fact, the show's executive producer, the first executive producer of a Bob Hope show other than Bob in his career. Bob, who customarily began every Bob Hope show with a monologue, would be seated in the Presidential Box, and would come to the stage only at the end of the evening for acknowledgments and thanks.

I'd been preparing the show for several weeks when my office phone rang and a jaunty voice I'd been listening to since I was a child said, "Hi, this is Bob Hope."

"How do you do, Mr. Hope."

"How's it going?"

"Great."

"Shouldn't we meet?"

"Absolutely. Can we set something up? I'd like you to know my plans."

Following the MO I'd devised for the Inaugural Gala, I'd become once again a peripatetic producer, traveling from guest to guest, setting the material, banking it and moving on. Since I was planning a California trip the next week, Bob and I set a date to meet.

As I would years later with *Inside the Actors Studio,* I'd been immersing myself in Bob Hope's life and career. I showed up at his home on Moorpark in Toluca Lake lugging a suitcase full of the books by or about Bob Hope that I'd acquired. Sitting with him at a table overlooking his wife's garden and his putting green—a table that would become one of the loci of my life for the next twelve years—I reviewed my plans, for the show and him, and he repeatedly nodded approval.

In the course of the meeting, I said, "You know, this isn't the first time we've met."

Hope, who prided himself on a prodigious memory—not just for tens of thousands of jokes—sat back and studied me. "Really? I don't recall. . . ."

"I think I was eight. You were making personal appearances with a movie. I don't remember for sure—maybe it was *My Favorite Brunette,* and you were onstage at the Michigan Theater. You invited the audience to come to the stage door for autographs—"

Bob broke in, polite but firm. "It was *My Favorite Blonde* and it was the Fox."

"Oh." I'd just enrolled in Bob Hope 101.

"Did you get an autograph?"

"Yeah. As a matter of fact . . ." I stopped, hesitant to pit my memory against his.

"What?"

"There was a long line. You were sitting just inside the open stage door with a note block, signing your name, tearing off the sheet of paper and handing it to the fan without looking up. I remember thinking, 'I don't want to get a sheet of paper like everybody else. I want him to look at me.' So when my turn came . . ." I paused again.

"Yeah?"

"I said, 'How much is this autograph worth?'"

"How old were you?"

"Eight or nine, I think."

"Not bad," Hope said, and hummed a little tune, which, in time, I would learn to interpret as a sign of his pleasure. Then he asked, "Did I look up?"

"Yeah, and said, 'After my next picture, nothing.'"

Hope smiled and hummed a little louder. I ventured further. "I was wondering"—as he had once before at the Fox Theatre, he glanced at me—"if you'd sign one of these books."

"Sure." He reached for the book, reflected, and signed it with a flourish. I didn't look at it until I got back to the hotel. He'd written, prophetically as it turned out, "To Jim Lipton, Here we go again—38 yrs later. Bob Hope." The autograph he gave me at the Fox had long since vanished, but needless to say, I still have, and treasure, this one.

The obligatory centerpiece of the seventy-fifth birthday special was, of course, a carefully compiled and edited montage of Bob's USO years, especially his Christmas shows. We'd contracted with a noted documentary producer to assemble fifteen minutes, and I wrote its narration for, of course, John Wayne, who had agreed instantly to do it.

But in the weeks preceding the special, Wayne fell desperately ill. Already fighting cancer, he underwent bypass surgery to place a pig valve in his heart. As the weeks went by and we waited for news of his recovery, it became more and more apparent that he wasn't going to be able to come to Washington for the show, although no one called from his office to cancel the appearance. Finally, as we reached the point of no return, I called Hope and said, "Wayne's not going to call. I've got to let him off the hook."

"Of course," Bob said.

Since I'd dealt with Wayne's office during the Inaugural, I called his secretary and companion, Pat Stacy, and said, "Listen, I'm calling for Bob and all of us. We know how much Duke wants to do the show, and you know much we want him to, but please tell him that the only thing that matters now is his full recovery—without any outside pressures or obligations. Tell him not even to think about the show. Everybody understands, and we all send him our love, and we'll be thinking of him that night, and we'll see him soon when he's back up to speed."

"I'll tell him," Pat said.

Five minutes later, she called me back. "You really know the Duke."

"Why?"

"This is his message. 'Tell Lipton there's no way on God's earth I'm not doing this show. Tell him to figure it out and get back to me.'"

"That's it?" I asked.

"That's it," Pat replied, and I could hear a smile in her voice.

I conferred with my director, Bob Wynn, and we arranged to send a crew to Wayne's house the day of the show, and project him by satellite to the Kennedy Center, so he could narrate the USO film live.

On my last trip to California before the show, Kedakai and I drove to his home in Newport Beach to review the script I'd written and sent him. At his home, we waited in the living room, whose enormous picture windows framed a living Dufy of multihued sailboats coasting about the bay. When the Duke came into the room, we caught our breaths. He had changed radically since striding onstage at the Opera House, a master among masters.

He moved haltingly, breathing with audible effort and reaching out for support from the chairs he passed. We sat down and he took out the script I'd sent him and laid it on the table between us. There were penciled notations on it, and I opened my notebook, ready for comments.

"Who wrote this?" Duke asked.

Bracing myself, I said, "I did."

Duke spread his big hands on the script, stared at it for a moment, and said, "It's beautiful." I breathed easier. "There's only one thing wrong with it," he went on. "I don't know how I'm going to get through it. I love that son of a bitch so much."

He looked up at me, tears streaming from under his reading glasses. He took them off, pulled a Kleenex from a box on the table, covered his face, bent his head, and cried very hard, without shame or, it began to seem, surcease.

I was only in John Wayne's presence a few times, but there was never an instant when you weren't aware of his power, though he did nothing to remind you of it. At that table in his home, a surreal thought flew into my mind: We're sitting here waiting for John Wayne to stop crying.

And that's what Kedakai and I did for what seemed like five minutes, but may only have been two. Finally, without comment, the Duke wiped his glasses, put them back on, picked up the script, and began rehearsing it with us.

On the night of the show, the USO segment went off smoothly, with our film and John Wayne, looking—well, like John Wayne—in front of the fireplace in his Newport Beach living room, sharing an immense screen on the Opera House stage.

A three-hour time slot is normally reserved for such earth-shaking events as the Oscars or the Super Bowl, but NBC's daring decision to preempt its entire prime-time schedule for our show turned out to be astute. *Happy Birthday, Bob* was the most-watched program of the week, with a 27.1 rating and 47 share—which is to say, 47 percent of all the viewers in America who turned on their television sets that night tuned in to our show on NBC—and in our last half hour, the share reached a stratospheric 50 percent.

These were attention-getting statistics, even for Bob Hope, and within a few days of the show, NBC had committed to what would turn out to be the second of twelve of the annual Bob Hope birthday specials I'd promised. By the time Bob's eightieth birthday loomed, the show was a television institution. In March of 1983, Bob called me with what he described as "a great idea for the eightieth. Cleveland!" I was silent. "Whattaya think?"

"Cleveland?" I replied incredulously.

"I grew up there when we came from England." Bob sounded hurt.

"I know that—but this is a big birthday, Bob. Shouldn't we do something special?"

"Cleveland's special," Bob insisted.

When I hung up, my mind was racing. I've never been in Cleveland, and I'm sure it's a worthy city, but each year I racked my brain to come up with an unusual venue, and somehow, Cleveland didn't feel special enough.

In the ensuing days Bob kept calling to ask, "What's happening with Cleveland?" and my invariable reply was "Working on it, Bob," but what I was in fact working on, with increasing desperation, was an alternative so intriguing that it would dislodge Cleveland from Bob's scenario.

Suddenly, a few minutes after one of Bob's calls, I had an answer, maybe *the* answer. In the five years since the first birthday special, Hope's great friend Ronald Reagan had dislodged Jimmy Carter from the White House. I still had the White House switchboard number in my Rolodex, so I dialed it and asked for Mike Deaver, the deputy White House chief of staff, explaining that I was calling from the Bob Hope show.

I found over the years that the Bob Hope name was, when necessary, an open sesame. Within moments, Deaver was on the line. I explained my idea and he said, "I'll call you back." An hour later my phone rang. "You've got a deal."

Dropping the phone into the cradle would have wasted a precious second. I pressed the cradle button, got a dial tone and called Bob in Toluca Lake. "How's Cleveland going?" he asked.

"Fine—but I've had an idea. Will you listen to it?"

"Yeah," he replied suspiciously, and I launched into my pitch.

"Picture this: two guys in their shirtsleeves, sitting on a couch with their feet on a coffee table, talking over old times and everything that's going on and taking a look at the future."

"What's so special about that?" Bob demanded.

"Nothing—unless the two guys are you and Ronald Reagan in the Lincoln Bedroom."

"You think we *could*?" Bob exclaimed.

"I think I *did*. I didn't want to try it on you till I'd talked with the White House. . . ."

"What did they say?"

"Mike Deaver says we've got a deal. We could cut from the bedroom to the Kennedy Center. . . ."

Cleveland vanished in an explosive "How about that!!"

I booked the Kennedy Center and began casting the show, bringing in Don Mischer, the reigning director of spectacles, to take the technical reins. As our plan for the show became public, calls from PR representatives and agents began flooding in—and I kept saying, "Yes," and Bob kept saying, "Great!"

Finally, the show had swollen to such proportions that I called NBC. In addition to the changes in Washington, NBC had undergone a change at the top in the years since 1978: A remarkable young man named Brandon Tartikoff was now running NBC, taking it to unparalleled heights. He agreed to see me.

Tartikoff occupied a small, unprepossessing office in the Burbank studio complex—by design, I suspect: He was, for our, or any, business, a remarkably modest, straightforward chief executive. When I arrived, the small space was filled with his staff members. I put in front of him a chart (not unlike Irna's "squares"), which showed at a glance my cast and our two-hour show, segment by segment. "Looks great," Brandon said.

"One problem."

"What?"

"Unless I cut every performance down to two minutes, there's no way I can fit all this into the format."

"What do you want me to do?"

I indicated the chart. "Help me decide which stars to cut."

Brandon smiled and turned to the head of business affairs. "Give Jim the third hour."

When I got back to the office, I called Bob. "Happy birthday. You've got a three-hour show."

"How about that!!"

The Kennedy Center shoot was scheduled for a Friday night late in May. When Bob arrived in Washington, I said, "We're set for the Lincoln Bedroom Thursday. I've written the piece to make it sound like you're staying there."

"I *am* staying there," Bob said matter-of-factly.

Of course. What was wrong with me?

On Thursday afternoon we brought our cameras and lights into Mr. Lincoln's— and, at the moment, Mr. Hope's—bedroom, which is next to the family quarters on the second floor of the White House. Don Mischer was in a mobile unit outside the building, and I was in the room with Bob and the president, directing the two men, with Mike Deaver at my side.

I'd provided Deaver with a list of topics, and once Bob and the president had doffed their jackets and taken their places on the couch, I sat cross-legged on the floor at their feet with the list in my lap. The two men looked at me and I said, "Gentlemen, would you begin with some of your memories of Hollywood in the forties and fifties." And they were off, two actors, after all, who'd heard their cue, easy with each other, comfortable, funny and accustomed to each other's company.

Each time they'd given me all I needed of one topic, I proposed another. One of the items in my list was a reminder that Ronald Reagan did a classic Jimmy Stewart imitation. I prompted Bob to ask the question that I knew would lead into it, and the president of the United States responded like a trouper.

The last two lines of the scene were scripted. On a cue from me, the president was to say, "Well, tomorrow's a big day for you, so I'll let you go to sleep in Mr. Lincoln's bed there." Then he was to cross to the door, open it, turn back and say, "Oh, by the way, on behalf of the American people, I'd like to wish you a happy birthday," and exit, closing the door behind him—at which point in the finished, edited show, we would smash-cut to the Opera House of the Kennedy Center as the military bands of the five services marched onto the stage and the Hopes and Reagans entered the Presidential Box. In the Lincoln Bedroom, after forty-five minutes of dialogue, we completed my list and I said, "Thank you, gentlemen. Mr. President, we have to relight for your exit. It'll take about fifteen minutes."

"Fine," the president said, settling back on the couch to trade jokes with his old friend. Not just jokes: dirty jokes. Very dirty jokes. They vied with each other, roaring at each other's offerings and rushing to offer a competing story. The only joke that is repeatable in this, or nearly any, company is one of the president's: "This guy walks into a bar," Mr. Reagan said, "and orders a drink. He's already pretty far gone, and when he sees a woman at the other end of the bar, he calls the bartender over and says, 'Tell the douche bag I'd like to buy her a drink.'"

The president was playing all the parts: the sodden patron, the affronted bartender. "'Pardon me, sir,' the bartender says. 'This is a respectable place. We don't refer to ladies as douche bags!' The guy says, 'I tol' ya to offer the douche bag a drink!!' And just to shut him up, the bartender goes over to the woman and says, 'The gentleman would like to buy you a drink. What would you care for?' And the woman says, 'Just vinegar and water.'"

As the jokes grew raunchier, I heard a sound at my side, glanced down and shuddered. The forty-five-minute conversation had been feeding into a Nagra sound recorder, which had been placed on the floor next to me—and the reels were still turning. Because Don and the crew were in the truck, and the sound track was being coded with time-of-day, it hadn't been turned off during the break, so that the time codes would be valid when we resumed.

Every filthy joke had been impeccably recorded on that tape. The lighting director signaled that all was well, and I cued the president. "Well, Bob," he said, "tomorrow's a big day for you, so I'll let you go to sleep in Mr. Lincoln's bed there." He crossed to the door, delivered his final line and exited. A moment later, the door popped open and the famous head appeared. "Was that okay?"

"Yes, sir, it was perfect." Then, not quite believing my ears, I heard myself say, "That's a wrap, Mr. President."

As we were cleaning up, one of the Secret Service agents who had been overseeing the shoot came to me. Recalling each other from the Carter days, we exchanged greetings; then, he indicated the Nagra and said, "May I have the tape?"

Alarmed at the sudden specter of delay, I said, "But we have to have it transcribed tonight so Bob and I can do a paper-edit tomorrow. We're on the air in four days."

"You'll have it back tonight," he said evenly, and extended his hand.

As I prepared to leave the Lincoln Bedroom, Bob, who would not be with Don and me at the edit in New York, said, "When are we going to see the transcript?"

"There's been a slight delay. We won't be able to give the audiotape to a stenographer till sometime tonight, and we'll be rehearsing all day tomorrow. The only time we'll be able to go over it is after the performance tomorrow night."

When the Secret Service agent returned the tape to me Thursday evening, and exactly eighteen minutes of it were blank, I said, "Remarkable coincidence," and rushed it to a stenographer for transcription.

The moment the Opera House curtain came down Friday night, the cast, crew, network executives and Washington nabobs headed up to the Atrium for an after-show dinner. During the performance I'd been handed the transcript of the Lincoln Bedroom scene, and the moment I left the production truck, I went looking for Bob to lead him to our Opera House production office, where we could work on the transcript. I was told he'd headed for the party, so, transcript in hand, I arrived in the Atrium, where Brandon Tartikoff intercepted me with "Giving you that extra hour was the best decision I've made since I came to the network."

As I searched for Bob in the crush, Don Mischer approached. "Shouldn't we be on our way to the airport? If we don't start editing by three A.M. . . ."

I brandished the Lincoln Bedroom transcript. "I can't leave till Bob and I have cut this from forty-five minutes to six—and I can't find him."

A runner pushed through the crowd. "Mr. Hope just called. He's looking for you."

"Where is he?"

"The White House."

Of course. I went to a pay phone, dialed the White House switchboard and asked for Mr. Hope. Bob answered. "Where are you?"

"Trying to find you."

"Come on over."

"To the White House?"

"Yeah."

"Do you know what time it is?!"

"So what?"

"So what happens when I walk up to the guards at one in the morning and tell them I've got an appointment in the White House?"

"I'll let 'em know you're coming," Bob said, and hung up.

A runner arrived from our Opera House office, wheeling my airline carry-on, which was crammed with the script and every note we would need in the edit. With my crew in pursuit, I headed for my car, which was poised for the race to the airport with my luggage in its trunk.

"Not yet," I told the driver. "The White House. The northwest gate." As I clambered into the car, I shouted back at a production assistant, "Stand by in the office! If I get arrested, the driver will call you."

At the northwest gate, the guards nodded and opened the gate, put my carry-on through X-ray, returned it and directed me to the famous walk where network journalists, microphone in hand, talk to the nation with the White House as a backdrop.

Arriving at the portico, I found another familiar Secret Service agent waiting. He led me into the foyer where Mother had once worried about Mrs. Carter. As he took me to the broad stairway to the second-floor living quarters, he spoke softly. "We'll have to be quiet. The family's asleep."

"I understand."

He pointed at my trolley. "You can leave that here."

I hesitated. "Will it be safe? The entire show's in there. If anything happened to it . . ."

"Mr. Lipton, if it's not safe here, where *is* it safe?"

"Of course. Sorry. I haven't had much sleep this week."

I opened the carry-on, extracted the transcript of the bedroom scene, and we climbed the stairs. Tiptoeing past the first family's living quarters, I entered the Lincoln Bedroom to find Bob sitting on the edge of the martyr's bed in his pajamas, humming, I was happy to hear, a little tune.

"Got it?" Bob asked. I handed him the transcript and sat down next to him.

The agent said, "If you need anything, call me through the switchboard," and headed for the door.

"As a matter of fact . . ." I said, and he paused—"I haven't had anything to eat since yesterday. Would there be something?"

"The kitchen's closed," the agent said, "but I'll have a look."

The next hour qualifies as one of the most thoroughly surreal experiences of my life: sitting on Abraham Lincoln's bed next to a man who was inarguably one of the most celebrated and, to many, most beloved, beings on earth, editing a scene we'd shot with the president of the United States—who was sleeping, peacefully I hoped, a couple of walls away.

Bob and I wielded pencils, and the debate over what to cut and what to keep was sometimes lively. At one point, when Bob suggested cutting one of the president's remarks about President Lincoln, I said, "You know, some people think this room is haunted—by him." I tapped the bed. "How do you think *he'd* feel about it?" I shrugged. "It's up to you: You're the one who's sleeping here tonight." Bob never struck me as a superstitious, or particularly religious, man, but he yielded the point and the line stayed in the show.

The Secret Service agent appeared with a green apple and an apology: "This is all I could find." I accepted both gratefully.

When we'd finished working with the transcript, Bob wished me luck in the edit. I tiptoed back down the stairs, retrieved my carry-on, said good night to the agent and headed down the long walkway to the northwest gate, outside which my car and driver waited. Halfway to the gate, it occurred to me to turn around and look at the White House. There was only one illuminated window in the West Wing, and as I watched, it winked out, leaving the facade in shadow under a full moon in a clear sky.

There was no *click,* because nothing remotely like this had ever happened to me before. Or would happen to me again. That, of course, was the point. I took a long, deep breath, savoring one of the top-ten moments of my life, and proceeded to the northwest gate, which swung open to let me get into my car and drive to the airport, exhausted and fulfilled.

The success of the birthday show led to another astonishing adventure. On a March night in 1979, Kedakai and I were in Jean-Pierre Rampal's dressing room after one of his Lincoln Center concerts when I idly picked up a phone to check with my answering service. In those days the answering was done by live human beings, one of whom reported that the White House had called.

"What did they want?"

"They said Bob Hope called them for this number, and they were asking permission to give it to him."

"The White House was asking *my* permission?"

"Yes."

"What did you do?"

"I told them they could give him the number. I hope I haven't . . ."

"No, no. It's fine. Has he called?"

"Yes. He left a number."

I dialed it, and when Bob answered, I asked, "Why did you call the White House for my number?"

"I'm on the road and I didn't have my phone book with your number in it."

"But you know the White House number by heart."

"Sure." There were some things about which Bob had no sense of humor. They were too obvious to be funny.

"What's up?" I asked.

"I want to go to China. And I can't get in. Nixon has tried, Kissinger has tried. Will you try?"

"Sure, but—why do you want to go?"

He seemed shocked by my naïveté. "I shot the first special in the Soviet Union, and I want to be the first American entertainer in China." *Res ipsa loquitur.*

Working with Bob, I'd come to realize that one of the things Bob's political detractors didn't understand about him was that being a Republican or a conservative, both of which he certainly was, took a distant second place to who and what he really was: a comedian.

Comedy was more than an article of faith: It *was* his faith, taking precedence over every ideology—and every bias. Though he never made a point of it, Bob was the first star to include in his television stock company comedians who were black and female. To this day, most of the female comedians acknowledge that it was Bob Hope who opened a door that was previously tightly locked. The only question Bob ever asked was, Is it funny?

In my experience with him, it was the only criterion he ever applied to any person, place or event: Will it make the audience laugh? It applied indirectly to me, because the success of our shows gave him and his humor an unexpected platform late in his life. There was a significant age gap between us, and since I'd come to his attention through my relationship with a Democratic administration, he knew there was a political gap as well.

He knew, and accepted without question or criticism, the fact that I'd marched against the Vietnam War, and late one night, on one of our walks, he brought up the heat he'd taken for his Vietnam USO shows. "I *hated* that god-damn war—and everything that was going on over there—but as long as there was one American soldier in Vietnam, no one was going to keep me away!"

Now, without a qualm or second thought, he was determined to take his act to the heartland of Asian Marxism. "See what you can do about China," Bob said. "Maybe the White House can help."

The next day, I called Gerry Rafshoon at the White House, and he said, "We're not what you need. Your best bet is a private organization called the

U.S.–China Arts Exchange at Columbia University. The guy in charge is Schuyler Chapin. . . ."

"I know him!" I said. "Thanks."

Schuyler was dean of the Columbia University School of the Arts. I'd first encountered him when I produced "The Star Spangled Gala," and lately he'd been in the news as the creator of an educational and cultural exchange program with which the Chinese collaborated more comfortably than with government agencies. When I called Schuyler, he said, "I'm leaving for China Friday. Can you give me a letter?"

I did, and two weeks later I called Bob. "There are two visas at the Chinese Embassy in Washington."

"How about that! Go!!"

Hope Enterprises footed the bill, and in April 1979, seven years after the Shanghai Communiqué pledged the U.S. and China to work for "normalized relations," and within weeks of the establishment of the first U.S. Embassy in China, I arrived in Beijing with Bob Wynn, whom I'd signed on as director.

We were met at the airport by Chi Chin, a small woman in a Mao jacket who informed us that she had been assigned by the Ministry of Culture to be my interpreter. Indicating a woman smaller than she, she said, "Comrade Law will get your luggage," and we sat down in an anteroom to wait. Interrupting our conversation, I said, "Since I've only been in China five minutes, the last thing I want to do is make trouble for anybody—but you sound exactly like my neighbors in New York."

Chi Chin smiled. "I went to the City and Country School in Greenwich Village until I was fifteen."

"What are you doing here?"

"When the Chiang Kai-shek government fell in 1947, my father came with my mother and me to be part of the new China. My brother stayed behind."

"Have you been back to New York?"

"No." I detected a faint note of regret, but elected not to pursue it.

With Chi Chin in charge, we were driven to the Peking Hotel, a complex of three buildings that were begun in 1900. It was, Chi Chin informed us, "the best first-class accommodation in Beijing." Later that day she would confide that it was the *only* first-class accommodation in Beijing. It wasn't La Belle Hélène but in the Old Wing, to which we were assigned, it was only a few cuts above it.

Chi Chin, who was one of the heroes of our China experience, argued with the front desk until they transported us three decades forward to the New Wing, which was decidedly of the 1930s but, more important, looked and felt like a movie *about* the 1930s—noirish, romantic and tantalizingly remote. At my request, and with Chi Chin's relentless insistence, the New Wing would become home to Bob and our troupe when they arrived, and while I understand that Beijing today bristles with not just first-class but world-class hotels, I'll be forever grateful that I lived for several weeks in the Peking Hotel when it and China were the storybook place I'd hoped to find.

On my first morning in Beijing, I was escorted to a Ministry of Culture meeting with a large delegation of Chinese officials—or, as Bob Wynn, an excellent director and the right man to join in the scout for our Chinese locations, insisted on referring to them, suspiciously, warily, invariably, "Communist" officials. They were manifestly both, and that was what shaped my proposal. With Chi Chin at my side, translating, I said, "There are many people who could come to you now with a proposal like ours, and all of them are unquestioning supporters of normalization between our countries. So are the people who will read what they write or watch what they broadcast."

Taking a deep breath—and the bull by the horns—and assuming that the Chinese had done some homework on the subject of Bob Hope, I said, "Mr. Hope represents the *other* side of American society, those who are *opposed* to normalization—and socialism—instinctively and politically. If I may suggest, *they* are the Americans who should be reached, and this is the best opportunity you'll have to do that.

"If someone whose political views are known to be supportive of normalization were to present a television program like the one we propose, the public that would watch it would come to it already convinced. In America we call it preaching to the converted. But if Bob Hope returns to the United States with a favorable account of his experience in the People's Republic, millions of Americans who might never *think* of watching a program about China will tune in only because they trust Bob Hope, and wonder why he, of all people, went to China.

"And what will they see? He's not a politician or a journalist. He's an entertainer, which means his job is to entertain, and you can be sure that, if he comes to China, he comes to entertain—and *be* entertained. That's what he'll take back with him: a cordial encounter between two cultures, a kinship of Chinese and American artists.

"That's what every single one of his shows is about: laughter and high spirits and celebration. Look at his movies. Look at his television programs. That's all you'll see. And if the millions of Americans who will watch this program see Bob Hope enjoying himself in the People's Republic—which is what Bob Hope does wherever he goes—they may form a different opinion of China—and normalization."

The next day I called Bob. "Tell Dolores to pack. You're off on the road to China."

"How about that!!"

For the next week, with Chi Chin at our side, Bob Wynn and I scoured Beijing, picking locations—the Great Wall, the Marble Boat, Tiananmen Square, the Peking Opera, the Forbidden City. Nothing was off-limits, and it became clear in the days following my meeting with the Ministry of Culture officials, who were now our official hosts, that the word had gone out: China's wonders were available to us.

By now it should be evident to anyone reading these pages that I sometimes go in deliberate search of the surreal. What could be more thoroughly surreal than negotiating for the Great Wall of China? Sitting across the table from my Chinese opposite numbers, I explained through Chi Chin that I wanted to begin our three-hour show on NBC with Bob Hope on the Great Wall, singing one of his signature songs, with words I was writing for this special occasion.

Their response was instantaneous: The Wall had never been used for such a purpose in two thousand years. It was out of the question.

"But the Wall is the perfect symbol of China's indomitable history," I said. "How can we tell our story, or yours, without it? We want to show America something more compelling than a picture postcard."

The officials conferred, and Chi Chin shot me a quick smile. A moment later she translated the formal permission.

I had two missions in China: to acquire our locations and find our Chinese cast. Touring the performing centers of Beijing and Shanghai, I enlisted China's premier acrobats, the stars of the Peking Opera, the Shanghai Puppets, the Shanghai Circus with its performing pandas. In Shanghai we attended a performance at its Comedy Theater, where our Shanghainese translator, seated next to us in the audience, nearly drowned out the actors onstage. Not only did the rest of the audience not mind, it applauded us politely every time we laughed. And backstage after the performance, I cast the team of Yuan, Hong and Li, three buoyant vaudevillians in the mien of—well, Bob Hope.

Back in America, Hope and I cast our American contingent and I prepared to lead a troupe of forty performers and crew to China, four times the number the Chinese had initially agreed to. One night in the first week of June, Baryshnikov, who was now with the New York City Ballet, approached Kedakai and me at our table in Elaine's Restaurant. When I replied to his casual "What's new?" question with "We're going to China at the end of June," Misha's eyebrows rose.

"You want to go?" I asked, and he replied, "Of course!"

When his emphatic answer prompted me to ask why he was so interested in China, his response surprised me. "It's the only Communist country I can go to without being arrested. It would be like going home—without jail." The next day I called Bob, and while he wasn't entirely familiar with Baryshnikov's work, he had a sharp eye for casting coups.

As our departure date neared, I moved into place at the Hope office in Burbank, where I got a call from a crestfallen Baryshnikov. "I can't come."

"Why not?"

"The company's summer season in Saratoga. I'm dancing."

"What if you asked Balanchine?"

"I can't do that. You know Mr. B."

"What if *I* asked him?"

"You can try, but it won't do any good."

That afternoon, in the living room overlooking Bob's putting green on Moorpark, I told Bob that Misha was canceling. By this time, Bob was fully aware of Misha's star power, and intrigued at the prospect of taking a world-famous Soviet defector into a Communist country that was only too happy to poke a stick at the Russian bear. "Why?" he demanded.

I explained about the New York City Ballet season at Saratoga—and Balanchine's notorious hold on his dancers. "Aw, c'mon, he's a great guy!" Hope exclaimed.

"Who is?"

"Balanchine."

"You *know* him?"

"Of course. The Ziegfeld Follies of 1936—at the Winter Garden. I sang 'I Can't Get Started with You' and he was the choreographer. . . ."

"Would you ask him?!"

"Sure. Where is he?"

"I'll find him."

With Hope at my elbow, I grabbed the phone and called the New York City Ballet office. Balanchine was unavailable, they said, but they put me through to Lincoln Kirstein, cofounder with Balanchine of the company. When I explained that Bob Hope was trying to reach Mr. Balanchine, Kirstein replied, "George is in the hospital for some surgery. He's been very depressed. This would be a tonic." He gave me the number of the phone next to Balanchine's bed. I dialed it and heard a nasal "Yessss?"

"Mr. Balanchine, Bob Hope would like to speak to you."

I handed Bob the phone. "George! How are you? I hear you're under the weather."

I was then privileged to listen to a spirited conversation between Bob Hope and George Balanchine as these two *anciens camarades* resumed their relationship without missing a beat, trading recollections and howling with laughter at what sounded as if it had happened forty days, not forty years, ago.

Lincoln Kirstein was right: It was a tonic. I could hear Balanchine cackling wildly at the other end of the line, particularly when he and Bob went through the chorus line—as it appeared they had in 1936—chorine by chorine. Hope's powers of recall were, as always, prodigious. "No, George. Suzie was the little brunette in the middle. Claudine was the big blonde with the . . . Yeah, yeah!"

Surreal.

Two minutes later Bob was insisting, "No, George! That was Opal. She was *yours*. Mitzi was mine. . . . Oh. Yours *too*?!" As Bob rocked back in laughter, it dawned on me that he might forget our mission, so I scrawled "Baryshnikov!!!" on a piece of paper and pushed it across the table.

"Oh, yeah. George—this guy Brrshynikoff—I need him the first week of July."

I'm convinced that it's thanks to Suzie and Claudine and Opal and Mitzi that Baryshnikov got to go to China.

In the second week of June 1979, our caravan departed Los Angeles International Airport for a five-week shoot in China. After an overnight stay in Tokyo, we left Narita for Beijing on a Japan Airlines flight. As always, Bob and Dolores occupied the forward right seats in first class. Whenever Kedakai and I flew with them, we were assigned the forward left seats. Now, as we crossed the East China Sea, I glanced across at Bob and Dolores, who were playing gin rummy. Laying down a card with evident satisfaction, Dolores began to sing to Bob. "I'd love to get you on a slow boat to China." He joined in, and as they continued to play, singing softly, I acquired an insight into a marriage that endured for sixty-nine years, despite everything Bob (who admitted publicly and often, "I'm no angel") might do to jeopardize it.

A few minutes later, I got up and leaned over them, pointing out the window. "There's China." The cards fell as Bob lunged at the window, pressing his nose against it like a kid outside a candy shop. One of the things I admired most about Bob was precisely that childlike eagerness and curiosity. It was a hallmark of his career and his life, and from the day I met him to the last time I saw him, it was always there, belying his years and overriding his slick professionalism.

On the ground in Beijing, as the plane taxied toward a portable stairway, I saw a small fleet of limousines detach itself from the terminal and head for our destination, accompanied by several troop carriers and a sizable contingent of soldiers. As the plane wheeled on the tarmac, Bob saw the greeting committee through his window and sprang into action, yelling, "Don, I need you!" toward the rear of the plane.

Don Marando was a key member of Bob's team, his makeup man. On hearing a familiar cry, he jumped up and pressed forward into first class, makeup box at the ready. Leaning past Dolores, Don applied a quick swipe of pancake to Bob's face, and daubed the crown of his head with the brown makeup that filled in some of the bare spots on it. The entire maneuver took less than sixty seconds, and Bob was standing with a broad smile and the golf club he wielded like a scepter when the airplane door opened and a squad of soldiers entered.

As Bob stepped forward, an officer extended an arm, barring him from the aisle and clearing the way for a delegation of Japanese businessmen in identical black suits carrying identical black briefcases who swept past us, descended the stairs, were greeted ceremoniously on the ramp, entered the limousines and were whisked away, flanked by the military escort.

At that point, the last soldier left the plane, brusquely gesturing to the rest of us to disembark. I couldn't bring myself to look at Bob, patted down and tarted up by Don's expert hand, standing there with his scepter—without a living soul to pay him court.

Since we were in the first row, Kedakai and Dolores proceeded down the stairs to the deserted ramp, followed by Bob and me. As we descended, I heard Bob mutter, "Damn!" and turned, ready to accept his displeasure. "Why didn't we arrange to have our camera crew out there!" he growled.

"For what?"

"To shoot the arrival! What an entrance! Big fuss—cars, military escort—and I come marching out—and everybody's gone! Can you imagine the *laugh* that would've got?"

I thought: Of course; nothing matters but the laugh. First, last and forever: a comedian.

Instead of the unwelcome mat at the airport, our special opened on a breathtaking shot of the Great Wall of China. On the day we shot it there was a last-minute hitch when the custodians, who'd been informed that we'd be shooting, dug in their heels as I looked up at the Wall, teeming with Chinese tourists, and explained that we expected to have the Wall to ourselves while we shot.

That, the custodians insisted, wasn't anywhere in their instructions. These people, they insisted, had as much right to be on the Wall as we did. I argued that they would be staring into the cameras, maybe even standing in front of them—but what I was privately concerned about was that they would park themselves in front of the cue cards we planned to paste on the interior surface of the wall, out of the camera's view, but well within Bob's.

"Not in two thousand years . . ." was wielded, but Chi Chin and I took the head custodian aside and I reprised my by now well-rehearsed, but nonetheless sincere, plea for a chance to present China in the best possible light to the American public.

For the first time in two thousand years, a half mile of the Wall was cleared, and Bob Hope and I and our crew took temporary charge of it. One of the most treasured photos on my study wall is of Bob and me, bedazzled grins on our faces, two solitary figures on the only man-made object visible from space.

A few minutes after the picture was shot, Bob Wynn called, "Action," and Bob Hope emerged from a parapet and sauntered toward the camera, twirling his golf club like Charlie Chaplin's cane, and singing the lyric I'd written to one of his trademarks:

> *Hey, we're off on the Road to China*
> *With fun and adventure in mind.*
> *The Seventh Wonder of the World*
> *   is here beneath our feet.*
> *Compared to this, the Road to Mandalay*
> *   is obsolete.*
>
> *We're off on the Road to China.*
> *Who knows what we're going to find!*
> *Like Marco Polo long ago,*
> *   we enter starry-eyed.*
> *We're ready to be Pekingesed*
> *   and hot to be Shanghaied.*

Two choruses and two hundred feet of Great Wall later, Bob neared the camera, singing:

> *Let's meet on the Road to China.*
> *We've nothing to lose but our cares.*
> *We're half a world away from old New York*
> *   and London town.*
> *We're doing pretty well for people*
> *   standing upside down*
>
> *It's time for the feast to begin.*
> *Our table's set with China,*
> *So let's all dig in!*

There were a number of musical numbers in the show, each to be shot in a famous setting, and as with any filmed or videotaped number, the vocal tracks had to be prerecorded as protection against the locations' ambient sound. Our orchestral tracks were prerecorded in L.A., but the cast was scattered around the country until they assembled in Beijing, so we knew we'd have to record their voices in Beijing.

On a limpid June night in Beijing, we piled into Bob's car for a trip across the city to the German-equipped sound studio Wynn and I had found on our survey. The Cultural Bureau had provided us with several cars and drivers. Our stars' and mine were converted taxis. Bob's was a Red Flag limousine, manufactured in China (as were our small sedans). On the streets, the Red Flag was literally that: a signal to the public that a very important Chinese or foreign dignitary was passing by. The car looked like a 1936 Packard, with curtained windows, bud vases, jump seats and a partition between the front and rear seats. On this occasion, Bob, Crystal Gayle and Caroll Spinney, who had brought his character of Big Bird to China for our show, were packed in back, and Kermit Love, who by chance shared a name with the frog and who was responsible for getting Caroll in and out of the huge Big Bird costume, was seated in the front seat next to the driver.

It was Beijing's evening rush hour, and the streets swarmed with cars, motorbikes, buses, trolleys and a sea of bicycles, the whole mass moving at the pace of barely molten lava. Because we were in a Red Flag, we were the object of the crowd's attention, and at a top speed of ten miles an hour, close scrutiny was easy. Face after curious face peered in each window until, comprehending why the Red Flag featured curtains, we drew them.

Not that the crowd would have recognized Bob. China had been cut off from everything American since the Japanese occupation at the beginning of World War II, and the revolution in 1947 had slammed any doors that might have opened, in either direction. Two Chinese generations had grown up with as little knowledge of us as we had of them. When I returned from the survey, Bob kept referring to me as Marco Polo, and there were times when that was exactly how I felt.

Now, perched on a jump seat in the airless backseat, I felt a tap on the shoulder, and jumped as I turned to find myself nose-to-nose with Oscar the Grouch, glowering at me over the back of the front seat. Behind Oscar, the Santa Claus face of Kermit Love was beaming as he manipulated the puppet he'd designed, and whom Caroll played.

"I didn't know you'd brought Oscar along!" I said.

"Do you think he'd have let us leave him behind?" Kermit demanded, as his hand, in Oscar's, patted my head.

From my vantage point I could see how Oscar worked. Inside his head, Kermit's right hand was operating the mouth and blinking eyes, while his left hand wore Oscar's freely moving arm like a sleeve and mitten.

"May I put him on?" I asked. Instantly Oscar vanished, and I was left with Kermit's stern visage. Having come to know Fran Allison and Burr Tillstrom, her puppeteer partner—and through them Bil Baird—I should have known better than to make such a request. The genius of puppeteers resides in their inextinguishable belief that their creations are real. In the years I knew Burr Tillstrom, he would greet Fran and me as we entered with "Well! You won't believe what Kukla did today!" And although Fran sometimes went into the room where the puppets were arrayed—or stored—or lived—I was never invited through that door.

Now I'd crossed the line, and I turned abjectly to Caroll, who *was* Oscar. "I'm sorry, Caroll."

"It's okay."

"No, it's not. It was stupid." I turned front to the still aggrieved Kermit. "I'm sorry, Kermit."

From behind me I heard Caroll's voice say, "Let him put Oscar on," and I spun back to say, "No! You're bailing me out, and you don't have to. I know better."

Caroll, a tall, skinny, gentle man, was insistent. "No, I mean it. I'd *like* you to do it."

I jumped again as something was draped over my shoulder and I turned to find a limp Oscar there. With Kermit's help, I entered Oscar's head and arm, and suddenly he was animate, glaring (since that's his only expression) at the other passengers, opening and closing his eyes as I wiggled my fingers in the rings I found in his head, flapping his jaw as I moved my thumb in his chin, and gesticulating busily with his—our—free hand.

All of this with Caroll's Oscar-voice filling the Red Flag. I've seldom felt so empowered. Oscar and I took one look at the drawn curtains and we darted to them. I drew them back, and Oscar's head and arm popped out of the limousine—to the astonishment of the bicyclists and motorists surrounding us, trying to catch a glimpse of the august personage being chauffeured across the city.

Now, suddenly, they were confronted with a glowering, wild-eyed maniac, yelling, *"Ni hao ma!"*—"Hello, how are you!"—to them, waving like a demented royal, and offering to shake hands with petrified passersby. To right and left, drivers slammed on their brakes, bicycles toppled, children shrieked in terror or joy and came running after this Red Flag from outer space.

Inside the car, my colleagues had twisted to peer out the rear window at the chaos we were leaving in our wake. Because of the crawling traffic, there was no danger: The entire contretemps took place at the pace of a stately walk.

One of the things we learned about China in 1979, when its political system was showing the first trickles of a spring thaw, was that anything resembling whimsy was not in its nature. And Oscar the Grouch was *nothing* but whimsy—whimsy personified, magnified and purified.

The younger the citizens we passed, the more quickly they adjusted, and, finally, we were trailing a parade of kids, capering and laughing and leaping up to brush Oscar's furry fingertips.

The mad journey across Beijing lasted half an hour, and if there was one thing that gave me more joy than watching those magically liberated kids, it was glancing at Bob Hope, kneeling backward on the rear seat of a Red Flag limousine in Asia's Communist capital, laughing like—and with—the pursuing children, and pounding his fists on the ledge behind his seat in innocent, uncontrollable glee.

Definitely, definitively surreal.

CHAPTER Ten

❝ *Oh, let a man of spirit venture where he pleases*
And never tip his golden cup empty toward the moon.
Since heaven gave the talent, let it be employed!

—Li Po, Tang Dynasty

From the moment the Ministry of Culture endorsed our visit to China, Bob began pressing me about where and for whom he would do the monologue that, for him, was the raison d'être of any Bob Hope show. The moment our dates were set, and I realized that we would be in Beijing on the Fourth of July, I had the answer: Utilizing Bob and our cast, I would produce the first Fourth of July Gala in the four-thousand-year history of the Middle Kingdom. That would enable us to invite not only a Chinese audience, but the Beijing diplomatic colony, all of whom understood English and would, I assured Bob, be an ideal audience for his jokes.

As Bob listened to my idea, he hummed, and I breathed a sigh of relief. But I knew that producing a gala in Beijing could prove more daunting than producing one in New York or Washington, so, the day after our troupe arrived in Beijing, I contacted the brand-new American Embassy, and presented my plan to the first American ambassador to the People's Republic, Leonard Woodcock, who agreed to sponsor our gala. Now I had everything but a venue, and three weeks to put the entire event together—while we shot the rest of the show from dawn to dusk every day.

There was only one venue in Beijing that could accommodate our offering, the Capital Theatre on Wangfujing Street in the downtown district. As my car rolled to a stop in front of it, a finger tapped on the window next to me. I lowered it and an open, friendly face that would become an important part of my life in China, and America, popped into it. "How do you do," the man said in impeccable Oxonian English. "My name is Ying Ruocheng, and I'll be your interpreter."

As we made our way into the theater, I asked him if he'd acquired his English in England, and he smiled faintly through the cloud of cigarette smoke that perpetually wreathed his head and said, "I've never been outside China."

In an upstairs office, he translated for Bob Wynn and me as we negotiated for the theater, its technical crew, its stagehands, its box office facilities— everything we would need for our gala performance. He was so linguistically adroit, and so clearly versed in the theatrical process, that we began speaking in virtual tandem, Ying translating a beat behind me.

As he escorted us back to the car, I learned that he was an actor and director in the Beijing People's Art Theatre. What he didn't mention was that he was the leading actor and director of the company, and that it was China's most important theater, under the direction of China's leading playwright, Cao Yu.

As we emerged into the bright sunlight of a hot June afternoon, I rephrased the first question I'd asked him. "Why is your English so much better than mine?"

With the deference and modesty that seem to be an ingredient of the Chinese character, he denied it was, but explained that his grandfather, Sir Vincentius Ying, had founded Furen University in Beijing in 1924, and that his father, who had been educated in England, had become a professor of English at Furen, and had introduced Ying to English and English literature.

"Is your father still an educator?" I asked.

"No," Ying replied. "He died ten years ago. He was a dean at Taiwan University." I glanced at him through the cloud of smoke and he concluded evenly, "He left in 1949, on the last plane for Taiwan."

"And you stayed."

"I was a young student—full of ideals."

I wanted to ask how his ideals were faring, but I was learning that the people with whom we were working, like Ying and Chi Chin, couldn't yet afford the luxury of the free speech we take for granted.

At the car, I said to Ying, "Listen, I've had an idea. I have to talk to Mr. Hope—but if I want to reach you, can I call the theater?"

"Certainly."

The theater was near our hotel, and the instant I arrived, I headed for the Hopes' suite, where Dolores promptly opened the steamer trunk of American staples she'd brought along to sustain her husband and all the rest of us. In addition to Bob's prune juice and bran cereals, it was packed with tins and boxes and packages of every conceivable comestible need, with which she plied the entire company, from stars to grips, as she'd been doing, I suspected, for Bob's entire peripatetic career.

I declined Dolores's offer of canned fruit and cookies, and got down to business with Bob. "I've solved the problem!"

"What problem?"

"Your monologue."

"I thought it *was* solved."

"The theater's going to be great. It's the translation."

"You said the diplomats understand English."

"They do, but half the audience will be Chinese. Isn't that what you wanted?"

"Yeah—but we'll project the monologue with slides. That's how we did it in Russia."

"I've got a better idea."

"Like what?"

"Simultaneous translation. I met this guy at the theater. His English is better than yours or mine—and he's an actor!"

"He's Chinese?"

"Of course. He'll be standing right next to you. You'll speak; then he'll speak—"

"Impossible!"

"Why?"

"You can't tell the same joke twice."

"You can if it's in two different languages!"

Bob's only response was to pick up a stack of typescript and thrust it at me. "Here's the monologue. Give it to the guy. Tell him to translate it and put it on slides."

I made one more attempt. "Bob—every time you turn on the TV, you see simultaneous translation. You'll look like the president!"

"Put it on slides," Bob said, and plucked a candy bar from Dolores's cornucopia.

On the night of the gala, the Capital Theatre was packed to the rafters, and as Bob and I had requested, half the audience was Chinese and half came from the diplomatic compound. Ambassador Woodcock welcomed the audience to the two hundred third birthday of American democracy on behalf of our embassy and our people, and introduced "America's ambassador of fun and laughter, and one of the best-known Americans of this century . . . Bob Hope!"

Bob made one of his patented entrances to tumultuous applause and launched into his monologue. Two minutes—and ten jokes—into it, he was in trouble. Following his instructions to the letter, Ying had translated the monologue and put it on slides, and it was now being projected, according to plan, on the proscenium above Bob's head. The result was that, after each joke, one laugh arrived from the diplomatic community, and a second laugh occurred after a five-second delay when the Chinese audience had absorbed the overhead projection—and Bob was halfway into the next joke in his customary rapid-fire delivery.

Worse, half the audience wasn't looking at him, but was craning upward to read the subtitles, which would, of course, look preposterous in the all-important reaction shots our cameras were recording for the telecast. Bob slowed, speeded up, paused, resumed, then stopped dead with a heartfelt cry: *"Jim!!!"*

"Yes, Bob," I replied serenely from the wings.

"Where's that guy?!!!"

"That guy" was standing next to me, as I'd instructed him to do, so that all I had to do was give Ying Ruocheng a push, and he walked out onstage to stand next to Bob, who signaled the master of his cue cards, Barney McNulty, who was crouched on the orchestra floor in front of the first row, to flip back to the first card. As I strolled back into the wings—humming, as I recall—Bob began the monologue from the top—to waves of in-sync laughter.

What had been heading for disaster veered back to a triumphal 4/4 march, with the two men riding the laughs and their instant relationship like the stage-wise veterans both were.

The best moments were unscripted. At one point, Bob described the spectacular Forbidden City as "Caesars Palace without slot machines." Ying, who had been going with Bob's incomparable flow, delivering the Chinese version as fast as Bob delivered the English, began in Chinese, then slowed and turned to Bob with a helpless "What's a Caesars Palace?"

Half the house fell apart—and so did Bob, which was something I'd never seen him do onstage. "It's a little spot where they take what the IRS didn't get," Bob said, and resumed with "I spent some time on the Marble Boat at the Summer Palace. The emperor thought it wouldn't float, and then Billy Graham showed up."

Once again, Ying launched into his translation and skidded to a halt. "Who's Billy Graham?"

"An advisor at Caesars Palace," Bob said, and laughter engulfed the Capital Theatre.

It wasn't exactly Bob and Bing—but Bob and Ying was turning out to be a satisfactory alternative on America's two hundred third birthday.

A couple of minutes later, in the classic Bob Hope tradition, Bob said, "I love the Great Wall of China. It's the greatest job of construction this side of Raquel Welch."

Again, a torrent of Chinese, an abrupt stop and a turn to Bob. "Who is Raquel Welch?"

"She also plays Caesars Palace," Bob said.

No matter where Bob was in the world, his monologue writers stuck to subjects familiar to his core American audience, and the Chinese or Russian or French devil take the hindmost. And this night, at the Capital Theatre, Bob and Ying, combined, made most of it work splendidly. Toward the end of the monologue, Bob, describing the mai tai cocktails the cast and crew were consuming at the hotel bar, said they came in three strengths, "premium, unleaded and regular," and turned with what was now evident pleasure to watch his interpreter unravel. But Ying didn't. Delivering the joke with eloquent body language, he got one of the biggest laughs of the night, and Hope rocked back on his heels in surprise, then took Ying's hand in a congratulatory handshake.

After the performance, in the Hope suite, where Dolores had taken the scotch out of the trunk, I asked Ying in a private moment how he'd managed to get such a big laugh with a joke the Chinese couldn't possibly comprehend, and he replied, "The same way I did with a lot of others—by finishing with 'That's a joke. Laugh.'"

He grinned, sipped his scotch, puffed on his cigarette and added, "If that didn't work, I said, 'For Chinese-American relations—laugh!'"

One of the highlights of the gala required no translation. When Baryshnikov signed on, he said, "What do you want me to do?" and I said, "Dance a pas de deux. I'll figure out where." Of course, the gala was the perfect venue, and on July Fourth the entire audience was waiting, breathless, for a glimpse of this international phenomenon. I had told Misha, and my Chinese colleagues, that this was our opportunity to demonstrate the universality of art, obliterating national and political boundaries at a bound—literally—with a Chinese ballerina and her Soviet/American partner at a Fourth of July celebration on a Beijing stage.

Misha decided he would dance the second-act *Giselle* grand pas de deux, and since he would be performing at Saratoga until the last possible moment before joining us in Beijing, he asked me to select the Chinese ballerina. His last words to me were "Remember, Jim—not too tall."

Because the Chinese had long since cast out the Russians and the Russian repertoire, and because, like Ying and his fellow actors, the entire Central Ballet Company, including Madame Dai Ailian, its director, had been banished to the countryside to feed pigs and raise rice during the Cultural Revolution, Madame Dai had to search the company's ranks to find someone old enough to reconstruct the *Giselle* choreography and style for the dancer in preparation for her performance with Baryshnikov.

I chose a brilliant young dancer, Zhung Wenlian, and the Central Ballet trembled at the prospect of this honor that had leapt into its life. On the day that I delivered Misha to the company's headquarters for a rehearsal with Zhung, as he changed from street clothes to tights and T-shirt in a parlor they'd assigned us, I asked if he wanted me to check out the rehearsal studio, and he said yes.

A few minutes later I came back with a sobering report. "It's a huge studio—with a sprung-wood floor. There's a pianist and a grand piano. . . ."

"Good," Misha said, stretching his back.

"One thing, though." Misha paused and looked at me. "I think that every ambulatory dancer in northern China is in that room. They're sitting on the floor, ten deep around the walls. Some of them have brought their children."

"To watch the rehearsal?"

"Yeah." We stared at each other. "It's up to you. If you want them to leave, I'll be the bad guy."

He frowned for a long moment, then said, "Okay—but explain to them, I've got to warm up. Yesterday I was sitting on a plane for twenty hours. I'm stiff like wood. They're dancers; they'll understand. I don't need a big studio. Just half an hour anywhere. *But no audience.*"

"Of course."

I left the room to find Madame Dai Ailian (ballet tradition trumps political doctrine: To her students, and to me, she was addressed as "Madame," not "Comrade"), a delicate sparrow, hovering in the hall. Like Chi Chin, she'd been born elsewhere, in Trinidad in her case, and had grown up in London, studying ballet and Graham technique. And like Ying, she spoke an English far more elegant than mine. "Is everything all right, Mr. Lipton?" she asked anxiously.

"Yes, it's fine. But Misha needs a warm-up, and naturally, he wants to do it alone. Any studio will do—"

I stopped. She had put her hand on my arm. "Mr. Lipton, please understand something. We haven't just been waiting for this moment since you told us you were bringing him here. We haven't been waiting for this since they let us come back to Beijing and dance again. We haven't been waiting since we created the company twenty years ago. We've been waiting all our lives. Please—don't take him away from us for one minute."

I stared at this tiny woman, who appeared to be in her late seventies, but whose grip on my arm was painfully firm. "I'll speak to him," I said, and she released me.

Back in the parlor, I told Misha what Madame Dai had said, and after another long, reflective moment, he shrugged, threw a towel over his shoulder, and said, "Let's go."

Misha was used to—probably inured to—ovations, but when Madame Dai threw the door open and he walked into the room, the roar that greeted him knocked him back a step, and its palpable force continued to batter him as he crossed to the barre, tossed his towel over it, and assumed a first position. Then, instant silence, broken only by the sound of the dancers scrambling back to their seats on the floor.

As Misha lowered himself into a demi-plié in first position, the dancers whipped out notebooks to write, "Eight demi-pliés in first position"—as if they hadn't done exactly the same thing that morning, and every morning of their lives from the age of six. But Baryshnikov was doing it, before their eyes, and it had to be solemnly recorded by each of them.

When he had finished the warm-up, Zhung was brought in, in a long romantic tutu that had been hastily created by the company's seamstresses for this *Giselle*, Madame Dai informed me. The two dancers rehearsed the entrée, then the adagio with its soaring lifts; then Misha coached Zhung in her variation. One of the glories of ballet is that not only is movement universal, but its spoken language is, too, Chinese dancers responding to *pirouette en dehors* as readily as French or Russian dancers. Misha and Zhung communicated freely from the moment they stepped on the floor together.

Misha was attentive and patient, rehearsing her over and over, making adjustments and suggestions, demonstrating for her. Throughout the rehearsal, Madame Dai sat cross-legged on the floor next to me, and at one point, as Misha stood close to the ballerina to guide her arms through a movement, she tore her rapt gaze from him to sag against me, sighing, "Oh, God, if only I were ten years younger."

A moment later she leapt up, ran out of the room, and returned with a pair of pointe shoes. "The only pair of Capezios in China," she said to me as she waited for a break in the rehearsal. "No one's been allowed to wear them because our shoemakers are going to take them apart. We've got to find out why they're so much better than ours. But she can't dance with Baryshnikov in those shoes!" she said emphatically as the surging waltz stopped for a moment, and she rushed out on the floor to put the Capezios on Zhung, who stared down at them as if they were the Red Shoes.

Only two parts of the dance remained to be rehearsed: the man's variation and the coda. There was, of course, no reason for Misha, jet-lagged and spent by the long rehearsal, to rehearse his variation, and the pianist began practicing the opening chords of the coda. But Misha walked to the piano, spoke quietly to him and returned to the center of the room. A moment later, the pianist struck up the music of the male variation and Misha soared into Central Ballet history, cleaving the air above the seated dancers' heads, dancing full-out and as passionately as I had ever seen him dance before an audience of thousands.

The echoes of all his past ovations were drowned out by the ring of dancers screaming their surprise and joy and gratitude. When the variation ended and Misha stood drenched and gasping in the center of the room, the tumult only swelled, ricocheting like gunfire off the trembling mirrored walls; and I was reminded once again why I am more deeply moved by dance and dancers than by any other art or artists.

My workday in China began at five a.m., so that we could be on the location by first light. We would shoot until last light, and return for a dinner meeting at the hotel, where my staff and I went over the details of the next day's schedule. At ten p.m., as the others dragged themselves off to bed, Chi Chin and I headed for one of the hotel's conference rooms, where the Ministry of Culture delegation, sometimes as many as twenty strong, waited around an immense table with the next day's schedule and script.

At each night's meeting, we would begin by dealing with any logistical problems that they or my team and I foresaw, and then the delegation would turn to its leader, a taciturn, rotund man with the look and gravity of the Buddha, and cheeks so round there was little room left above them for his eyes. For weeks, I couldn't see them, and I remember wondering what he was able to see through the tiny aperture of his lids.

But apparently he wasn't hard of seeing, because when his turn came, he would peer down at his translated copy of our script, and the questioning would begin: What is Elvis? Where are the Beverly Hills? Who is Big Mac?

I realized that they were looking for a line or joke that might contain a veiled disparagement of China, which would sound entirely innocent to them but would be apparent to an American audience. I didn't blame them: If I was Marco Polo, they were the vulnerable Kublai Khan who welcomed him.

When the delegates conferred audibly and openly among themselves, Chi Chin would translate their remarks to me—and at the end of the evening, as she walked me to the elevator, she would add details, nuances and interpretations she'd left out in the conference room. Chi Chin was a gentle, quiet woman—and she was putting herself at serious risk. If the ministry thought, or, God forbid, knew, that she was going beyond the narrow purview of an interpreter—and even counseling me privately—she would have paid a heavy price. But Chi Chin and our troupe had come to like and respect each other, and, as a genuinely loyal citizen of the People's Republic, and the only one among the group assigned to us who had any idea of what its impact could be in the country where she'd grown up, she was determined to see this venture succeed, and was willing to take risks to ensure it. For China.

The danger to her was real, first, because Chinese criminal penalties were then, and still are, summary and severe, and second, because she and I soon realized there was a doctrinaire member of the delegation, Oh Yang, who, unconvinced that our presence was beneficial, or benign, would have seen—and reported—Chi Chin's support of us as treason.

Oh Yang was gaunt and dyspeptic-looking. On the table in front of him, there was always a tin of Chinese pills, which he poked through and popped at regular intervals. His English was limited, but sufficient to hold Chi Chin in careful check as she translated the delegation's discussions for me. Our mistrust of Oh Yang was confirmed when Ying Ruocheng confided in us that it was Oh Yang who had denounced him to the vigilantes of the Red Guard during the Cultural Revolution, resulting in three years of imprisonment for him and his wife, and the exiling of their daughter, Ying Xiaole, to Inner Mongolia, leaving their eight-year-old son, Ying Da, to survive on his own.

I was mystified by Ying's astonishing forbearance toward this onetime theatrical rival who had cleared a path for himself when he was a journeyman and Ying a star by engineering Ying's imprisonment and the demolition of his family. I was even more mystified by a political system that could engender such an atrocity.

Each night at about one a.m., after my meeting with the delegation, Chi Chin would tell me what had actually been said, and where the pitfalls might lie; then I would return to the room where Kedakai was sleeping, turn on the dim light (there were no bright lights in China) at the table in the corner, write whatever dialogue would be needed the next day, based on my meeting with the Chinese, and fall into bed at two, to rise at five.

In Shanghai, we were housed in its only first-class hotel, the Jin Chiang, an Art Deco jewel built in 1929, when Shanghai was one of the world's great cosmopolitan centers. President Nixon had stayed at the Jin Chiang when he and the Chinese signed the normalization communiqué, and Bob was assigned the Nixon suite.

On one of our last nights in China, Bob and I were in the living room of his suite. Dolores had gone to bed, and when we'd finished our meeting and I got up to leave, Bob said, as he often did, "No. Sit down." I always assumed it was the years in vaudeville that shaped Bob's circadian rhythm. When he wasn't on location, he slept until eleven A.M., and at the hour when most people were retiring, he was at his most vigilant and, like an overstimulated child, reluctant to call it a day.

That night in Shanghai, as we had before, and would so many times in the next decade, we unwound with stream-of-consciousness conversation. Bob leaned back in the couch, rested his head against the ubiquitous antimacassar, closed his eyes for a moment and said something that brought me out of my own reverie: "God, I'm old."

"What the hell are you talking about?"

"Don't bullshit me. I can count."

"Do you know what I hear from every one of the Chinese? How old is Bob Hope *really*? They refuse to believe you're seventy-six."

"*I* believe it," he said without opening his eyes.

I'd never seen Bob like this, and I tried to change course. "We gave the Chinese your bio, and this morning one of them asked me if it's true you do a hundred personal appearances a year."

"What'd you tell him?"

"'Yes,' of course. And he wanted to know why." Bob was silent, his eyes still closed. "I've wondered too. Why do you do it? All the travel, the hassle . . ."

I stopped because he'd opened his eyes and sat up, shocked by my naïveté. "That's when I'm alive. If I didn't do that I'd be . . ." I saw his lips start to form the word *dead,* but before he could utter it, he shifted to "sick."

A few minutes later we said good night, and I left him sitting in the room where his longtime friend Richard Nixon had opened the road to China on which we'd marched.

In the United States, I discovered that the Road to China didn't end at the China Sea: It continued to reverberate in my life and Kedakai's for years—to this day, in fact, as I write these words. Like many of my experiences with Bob Hope, it altered my life perceptibly and permanently. A few months after we'd returned from China, I had a call from Linda Hope, one of the Hopes' four children, to whom Bob had assigned a producing role, telling me that Hope Enterprises was subsidizing a trip to Los Angeles for Chi Chin and her ten-year-old daughter, Wen Wen. I volunteered to underwrite the second stage of Chi Chin's journey home, to New York, where she reunited with her classmates from the City and Country School.

Chi Chin returned to California, not China, and lives today in San Francisco, near Wen Wen, who sailed through the California public school system, Mills College and the University of San Francisco, earning, it somehow goes without saying, an MBA, and winding up in the higher financial reaches of the city's business community.

For several years after our China trip, Kedakai and I exchanged Christmas cards with Liu Maoyou, our young Shanghai translator, who, like Chi Chin, had taken grave risks on our behalf. His cards always contained a letter expressing his determination to study in America. Then, in one of our Christmas exchanges, he announced that he'd received a student visa and was on his way to UCLA.

He left behind his wife, Li-ling, and his two-month-old daughter, Jia Jia. I saw him every time I was in Los Angeles, and on one occasion, he told me with great excitement that his wife and daughter, now three, would be joining him.

Liu and Li-ling had left large families behind, whom they planned to visit regularly, but in 1988, when the Tiananmen Square incident exploded on China and the world, Liu, being a true patriot who was deeply devoted and uncompromisingly loyal to China and its people, immediately joined the bands of Chinese students across America in a protest movement that so alarmed China's ruling class that Liu's activities landed him high on the (ironically named) Red List of Chinese citizens marked for arrest the moment they set foot in China.

That more or less settled the matter of where their future lay, and over the years, every one of my trips to Los Angeles has included a visit with my adopted, and adoptive, family. As Liu and Li-ling prospered in business, Jia Jia, who arrived without a syllable of English, glided smoothly into her father's alma mater (two generations of Lius at UCLA in twenty years!). Graduating with a degree in communication studies and psychology, she was instantly hired as a news editor by the *O.C. Post* in Orange County.

I probably don't have to add that the Liu family restored my flagging faith in the American dream, and that they and Chi Chin and Wen Wen are among the reasons I wrote this book, which is to say, they are its—and my—heroes.

There is another Chinese member of my personal pantheon, and his name, of course, is Ying Ruocheng. Days after *The Road to China* was aired, I got a call from a producer saying that he was preparing a miniseries on Marco Polo, and that the part of Kublai Khan was proving very hard to cast. He said they'd heard about this fellow who did a comedy routine with Bob Hope on my show. Did I think he could play a serious role like Kublai Khan?

"I think he could play King Lear," I replied bluntly. "Where are you? I'll send you a videotape of the show."

Ying got the role, and made such an impression in it that Bernardo Bertolucci cast him in the key role of the prison governor who becomes the ruler's mentor in *The Last Emperor*, and subsequently as the Tibetan lama Norbu in *Little Buddha*.

As Ying's international reputation grew, he led tours of the Beijing People's Art Theatre to Europe, playing one of his signature roles in Lao She's *Teahouse*, and when he and Arthur Miller joined their considerable forces for the historic production of *Death of a Salesman* in Beijing, his adventures found their way into the front sections of newspapers around the world. With Ying providing the translation, playing Willie Loman and assisting Miller in the direction of the play, *Salesman* opened triumphantly at the Capital Theatre in the spring of 1983.

Fortunately, the public relations campaigns for Ying's American films brought him to America, and the friendship that had begun in Beijing flourished in New York in our home and in the Broadway theaters, which we haunted side by side. *Cats*, with its actors singing the Eliot poems he'd grown up with, showed him theatrical possibilities he hadn't known existed, he said.

One night at Elaine's, on his first trip to America after *The Road to China*, I spotted someone across the room, went to her table, and asked if I could introduce Ying to her. Since she'd seen the show, her response was ebullient. I went back to our table and led Ying across the room. "This," I said, "is Raquel Welch."

"Sit down!" she commanded and, in the ensuing half hour of lively conversation, much of it about their mutual friend Bob Hope, with whom Raquel had toured the world, made it clear to Ying, as he observed when he returned to our table, that there was considerably more to her than "the greatest job of construction" this side of the Great Wall.

When Ying's wife, Wu Shiliang, accompanied him on one of his trips, they spent a weekend with Kedakai and me at our summer home in East Hampton, and at a party in their honor, George Plimpton arranged a display of Chinese fireworks that he launched from the surface of our pool; and the next night, at a cocktail party crowded with writers and journalists, when I mentioned to Susan Alsop, the wife of the columnist Joseph Alsop who had accompanied Nixon to China, that Ying's father had been a prominent member of Taiwan University's faculty, she said that her husband had spent considerable time at the university and might have encountered him.

Pushing my way through East Hampton's beau monde to Ying, I told him what Susan Alsop had said, and he sprang out of his chair to follow me to Susan, who led us across the room to her husband.

Ying is a Chinese equivalent of Smith, so Alsop asked, "What was your father's first name?"

"Aloysius."

"I was his student!" Alsop gasped. "He was my mentor!" Ying sat down abruptly, as if his legs had given out. Alsop drew up another chair and the two men, knees touching and faces close, talked excitedly for an hour, their often overlapping voices indistinct to Susan and me under the animated Hamptons buzz that surrounded them.

Driving to our house from the party, Ying sat silent in the darkness of the backseat. On the only occasion I had heard Ying mention his father, I'd detected a distinct note of regret, which I attributed to the fact that Ying seemed to hold traditional Chinese views—especially toward family. The Yings had been China's most prominent Catholic family, a fact that doubtless precipitated the elder Ying's departure in 1949—and made Dolores Hope Ying's most enthusiastic advocate in 1979.

Driving with us through the Hamptons, Ying began to speak softly about the gulf between Taiwan and China—and father and son—calling it "China's tragedy." In the beginning, he said, there was sporadic correspondence, but in 1952 his father's letters stopped, and he had no further word of him until 1969, when he learned that Aloysius Ying had died. Ying's most fervent wish, he said, was to visit his father's grave, to which the Chinese government had finally agreed, but which the Taiwanese government prohibited.

Now, suddenly, in this most unlikely circumstance, he'd had the only first-hand news of him in nearly three decades, and in the darkness of the backseat, I could see a match's little flame tremble as he tried to light his cigarette.

In China during the eighties, Ying's career soared as he translated a flood of Chinese works into English and international books and plays into Chinese, guiding them into print and to the stage. In 1986, he was appointed vice minister of culture, a post he held until shortly after the Tiananmen Square incident, when the government distributed to every official a loyalty oath denouncing the students, which Ying refused to sign.

It cost him his government position and threatened his freedom once again. I called Arthur Miller and proposed that we set up a Ying Watch that would set in motion an international protest if he were arrested. Arthur agreed, and within a few days a small but influential ad hoc army stood silently by, waiting for marching orders.

I had Ying's home number in Beijing, but Arthur and I agreed that in the event his phone was being monitored, we'd be adding to his problems if we called him. With the help of our Chinese friends in America, I was given the phone number of someone brave and friendly who lived within sight of his house and could give us weekly reports of his comings and goings, which, we were relieved to learn, were unimpeded.

When he died, it was as an honored elder statesman who had, in the words of England's *Guardian*, "from 1978, with the opening up of China, played an important role in transforming his country's cultural life, encouraging international exchange and urging creative freedom for writers."

Arthur Miller was so impressed by his experience with Ying that he made him the subject of a book, *Salesman in Beijing*, on the cover of which Arthur and Ying loom over the Capital Theatre in a collage of photographs taken by Arthur's wife, Inge Morath. The copy in my library contains two inscriptions. The first reads, "For Kedakai and Jim—and the spirit that makes it all possible. Arthur and Inge." The second, in a bold, flowing hand, reads, "For Kedakai and Jim: Who were two of the first 'Salesmen' in Beijing and who showed me the way to meaningful cultural exchanges between our two peoples. Yours with love, Ying Ruocheng, July 8, 1984, in East Hampton."

In December 2003, when I learned that Ying had died, I felt what I couldn't feel when I got the news of my father's death: deep, unchecked grief at the loss of a member of my family.

Sometimes I wonder where Chi Chin or Wen Wen or Liu or Li Ling or Jia Jia would be if Bob Hope hadn't touched their lives. How different would Ying Ruocheng's life have been? How different would mine be?

In the years following *The Road to China*, I arrived annually at the Hope house on Moorpark, to plan another adventure. In the middle of April I would move into Hope Enterprises' executive producer's office for six weeks. We would shoot a birthday show—somewhere in the world—in the third week of May, rush back to Los Angeles to edit it over the usual three or four hectic days, and deliver it to NBC on the morning of the airdate.

For a dizzying dozen years, Bob and I and our itinerant troupe of stars roamed the world, to the Kennedy Center and the White House twice, to Los Angeles, New York, West Point, the Air Force Academy, Annapolis, the deck of the aircraft carrier *Lexington*, London in a Royal Gala for His Royal Highness Prince Philip, and Paris in the year of the French Bicentennial, where Bob was awarded the Legion of Honor. Three times the birthday show was at the top of the week's Nielsen ratings; it was in the top five six times and in the top fifteen ten times. The London show carried NBC to its first victory in the May sweeps since 1969.

But as I've taken this look back at the years with Bob, I've realized that what stands out most vividly isn't the grand events or once-in-a-lifetime excitements, but, rather, a very small, private memory. Because of Bob's show business–shaped daily timetable, it was his custom to work at night until about eleven or twelve, then take a walk before retiring. Night after night, year after year, our meetings would end with "Let's go for a walk." The ritual was invariable: I walked with Bob in New York, Palm Springs, Beijing, London,

Paris. And as we walked, we talked—about whatever came to mind. The unvarying routine relaxed Bob and freed him—completely.

Publicly, Bob was, like most stars of his time and generation, polite, professional and necessarily guarded: His conduct was for, and on, the record. But at midnight, on Park Avenue, Chang'an, or the Champs-Élysées, with no one but me in tow, he was unbuttoned, unconstrained and much more candid than I.

No subject was off-limits, no thought censored. By him. I mostly listened. Or prompted. One night, in London, as he talked about his family's flight from English poverty in Eltham to American poverty in Cleveland, I asked him whether he ever had nightmares about being poor again. (I had wakened shaking the previous night—but I didn't preface my question by saying so.) "Of course," he said.

"Do you think it'll ever go away?" I asked hopefully.

"Nope," Bob said, and traveled back, with me at his side, to his childhood in Cleveland. I'd heard the routine he did on the subject, in his act. This was different: There were no jokes as he recalled his hard-drinking father and his dedicated mother, whom he and his six brothers called ma'am, and who stoically held the family together by taking in boarders.

Of all our walks and talks, the one that stands out took as its setting the deserted streets of Palm Springs, under a canopy of stars so thick and lustrous they looked as if they might collapse and smother us in diamonds. Bob had examined all the shop windows that interested him, and it appeared we'd run out of conversation as well, but Bob wasn't ready to call it a night. Casting about for topics, we came up with the hoary filler: If you could live in any other time and place than this, what would it be?

Bob considered the court of Louis XIV—provided he could be Louis; I mulled Periclean Greece, Quattrocento Florence and Elizabethan England, rejecting them all finally for the poor quality of their medical care—then suddenly I stopped dead with "I've got it!"

Bob turned to me, waiting, and I said, "I'd like to have been a star in Hollywood in the nineteen thirties."

Bob's response was unequivocal. "It was paradise."

The next hour was one of the most entertaining of my life, as Bob strolled through the desert night, recalling Hollywood's Golden Age. "We didn't *know* it was paradise. We just took it for granted. Everybody else had problems. The country was broke, but we were doing okay—and no taxes!" Bob's eyes glittered in the starlight.

He relived riotous croquet games with Chaplin and Fairbanks and Pickford and Harpo. He described Will Rogers galloping along the bridle path that bisected Sunset Boulevard—and that recollection reminded him of the

Beverly Hills Hotel. "You know why they built those bungalows? To keep their stars out of trouble. Privacy!" he confided with a wink. "What happened back there was nobody's business. The studios made sure their bread and butter stayed out of trouble. And if you got in trouble, they got you out." In Bob's account, Hollywood was alive and young and (moderately) innocent again, MGM was making good on its boast of "more stars than there are in the heavens," the Trocadero and the Brown Derby were crowded with America's idols, Palm Springs was a remote, private oasis for those fortunate few.

Fred and Ginger danced across the desert floor that night, and Hope and Benny brought the populace together in front of their radios to laugh their troubles away. Plumbing his phenomenal memory, Bob replayed his favorite radio shows—monologues that told the story of that time and place, sketches with Bing and Skelton and Edgar Bergen and Charlie McCarthy. "Can you imagine? A ventriloquist—on radio!" he exulted.

As magically as the shepherds of Mycenae had revived the Greece of 1200 B.C., Bob resurrected the Hollywood of the thirties. It wasn't surreal. It was better than that. It was *real:* I discovered I was right about the blessings of being a star in Hollywood in the thirties, because that night in Palm Springs one of them ebulliently took me there.

When Bob died on July 27, 2003, two months after his hundredth birthday, I was asked by Dolores to speak at his memorial ceremony. The ceremony fell on a day when I was shooting an episode of *Inside the Actors Studio,* a commitment that couldn't be canceled or postponed, so I sent the words I would have spoken as a letter of condolence to Dolores and the family. Gary Smith, the television producer, who was organizing the memorial, called to ask me if he could read what I'd written at the ceremony, and I consented gratefully.

My tribute began, "There are a few—a very few—people who are, quite simply, life changers. Bob Hope is preeminently one of them. He changed my life—effortlessly, uninsistently, profoundly—simply by permitting me to share some of his matchless adventures."

And it ended with a respectful bow to Dolores's unshakable religious faith: "Bob was first, last and fundamentally a Pied Piper who had been put on earth in a tireless quest for the most elusive and precious of prizes: free, open, hearty, happy, life-restoring, hope-restoring laughter. Thank you, Bob, for the magic carpet ride. Heaven knows where you and your carpet are now. On second thought, perhaps heaven *does* know. Bon voyage, my friend, my teacher. The magic carpet ride is just beginning."

As I was writing those words for Bob's memorial, I was struck by the disheartening thought that, in the dozen years I spent in his orbit, I'd never said them to him. But now, as I write these words, I've realized that on one occasion, I did.

Bob's eighty-fifth birthday fell in the middle of a writer's strike, which meant that neither I nor any of his battalion of writers could lift a pen or strike a key. As the show's executive producer, and a member of the Writers Guild, it was my responsibility to respect the embargo, which I did to the letter of the code.

But the code contained an exception: It covered only spoken words. For some reason (that I've sometimes regretted), lyrics—and lyricists—exist outside the Writers Guild's purview. With no objection from the guild, I enlisted Cy Coleman, the composer of *Sweet Charity, Little Me* and a parade of standards like "Witchcraft," "The Best Is Yet to Come" and "It's Not Where You Start, It's Where You Finish," which Shirley MacLaine had sung, with my words, to Jimmy Carter, to compose an original score with me.

Persuading himself that the end of the strike was just around the corner, Bob refused to sign off on my plan. Finally, ten days before the shoot date, with the biggest birthday-show cast I'd ever assembled waiting in the wings, and not one word on paper, I confronted Bob with the unanswerable argument that, in a wilderness of canceled shows, we were about to become another casualty— unless he allowed me to deliver to the cast—and him—a musical special.

Bob yielded, and Cy arrived eight days before the shoot date. In the course of the next week, working eighteen hours a day, Cy and I wrote six musical numbers, the equivalent of a Broadway first act. I would write a lyric between four and ten A.M. and deliver it to Cy, who would work all day on the music while I went to the Hope office to prepare the rest of the three-hour show. At six I would return to Cy and hear his music. We would rehearse the song, fine-tune it, then drive to the recording studio I'd put on twenty-four-hour standby, where he would play the new song and I would sing it. Runners waited to rush dubs to the guests who would sing the number in the show, and to Bob's music director, Bob Alberti, who would orchestrate it overnight. Cy and I would block out the next song over a late dinner, and at four the next morning, I would begin writing the new lyric.

Once we'd completed the six songs, I had one more lyric to prepare. Every year I would write tailored words to "Thanks for the Memory," to close the birthday show. However, this time, Bob wasn't in his usual place onstage to sing it, but at a table with Dolores in the enormous ballroom we'd created in NBC's largest Burbank studio, so I suggested to Bob that someone else sing it, to him.

"Who?"

"Well, I was thinking . . . Nancy Reagan."

"Call her!"

I came back to Bob later that day. "Mrs. Reagan says she'll do it. But she wants to know what charity we're doing the show for. What'll I tell her?"

"Hope Realty," Bob said, straightfaced. Money wasn't funny to Bob.

Mrs. Reagan came nonetheless, and with Cy at the piano, I taught her the lyric I'd written for the occasion. Since her entourage included a White House photographer, I received a photograph of the two of us working together, inscribed, " 'Thanks for the memory'—and all the help."

Cy and I were nominated for an Emmy for the song we'd written—in one frenetic day—for Lucille Ball (in what would be her last performance before her death) to sing to Bob Hope. Since I wasn't allowed to write spoken words, each song dealt with an aspect of Bob's life. This one was called "Comedy Ain't No Joke," and I realized a few sentences ago that that was the occasion when I tried to thank Bob for what he'd taught me. It was Lucy's voice, but I know now that I was speaking. To Bob. About Bob.

Lucy delivered the first chorus to the hundreds of birthday guests in the huge studio.

So you think that it's fun to be funny,
Just a barrel of laughs night and day,
In a world that's eternally sunny,
With a life that's all work and no play.

Just because we can make it look easy
Doesn't mean it's a carousel ride.
So we cackle and crow,
And go on with the show,
Although we are dying inside.

Comedy is a serious business.
Comedy is an art.
Comedy is a matter of miming
And timing
And playing a part.

When you're frantic'ly trying to please,
Sweating bullets and down on your knees,
And you see your career
Disappearing in smoke . . .
Comedy ain't no joke.

Comedy is a serious business.
Comedy is a test.
Comedy is a grin ear-to-ear,
Even when you're severely depressed.

It is making 'em laugh till they cry.
It's the pits and the ultimate high.
It's the art of pretending you couldn't care less,
A lighthearted laugh when your life is a mess,
It means "Go for the gold"
When you're going for broke . . .
Comedy ain't no joke.

In the last chorus, Lucy made her way down the steps from the stage and walked to Bob at his table.

Comedy is the noblest profession.
Comedy is the truth.
Comedy is a slap on the knee
And the key to perpetual youth.
It is banishing ev'ryone's blues.
It is praying and paying your dues.
When you talk about hard work
And talent and scope,
Comedy is Bob Hope.

CHAPTER Eleven

❝ *Well, well, well. What's going on here?*

—Christopher Reeve, *Inside the Actors Studio*

W hat these pages have gradually made clear to me—and long since, I suspect, to the reader—is how much of my life has been devoted to assembling a family. As hard as it may be to believe, it wasn't something of which I was fully aware until I began this endeavor. Inured from childhood to a family unit of two, I adopted the defensive posture of disdaining the conventional blandishments of "family."

But now, of course, I'm aware of the labyrinth of families that have emerged in these pages—not only Bob and Dolores and Ying and the Lius and Chi Chin and Wen Wen and my circus family and the Mortemarts, who are waiting in the wings, but Stella and Harold and my fellow Studio members and the students and faculty of our school and my *Inside the Actors Studio* team. I've gone, without realizing or planning it, from a blithe disregard for family to a profound appreciation and apparently ceaseless search for it.

The central figure of my family and my life has already made a number of important appearances in this narrative. She is, of course, my wife, Kedakai Turner Lipton. Because I've sometimes woven our story into the fabric of *Inside the Actors Studio,*, and because Kedakai's genetic blend of Japanese and Irish has produced a person of arresting beauty and serenity, I'm sometimes asked how we met. The circumstances were unusual.

In 1970, I was a model of solipsism, the archetypal loner, leading a contented bachelor's life in Manhattan, pursuing my professional pleasures by day and my personal pleasures by night. Little more prepossessing then than I am now, I nevertheless seldom lacked company—not family, and I fear not really companionship, but inarguably company.

In those happy, indulgent times, I had a recurring nightmare in which, to put it bluntly, I was getting married. In a panic, I would fight my way out of sleep and reach out for reassurance to whoever was that night's resident on the other side of my bed. Not an attractive portrait, I admit, but a clear indication of how sunk in self I was.

One afternoon in January 1970, I arrived for a meeting with my agent, and waited next to his desk, since he was on the phone. A young film actress, who was at that moment the object of considerable public and professional interest, came through the door and stopped to wait on the other side of his desk.

Recognizing her and, like a good many other Americans, developing an immediate interest in her—and being, in those freewheeling times, brazen—I said, "Would you like to have dinner tonight?"

She studied me for a moment, then said, "Yes," at which point our mutual agent hung up and introduced us. That night she moved in with me—temporarily—since she was (A) married and (B) scheduled to leave for her home in Los Angeles the next day.

In the morning, she called her husband to explain that some important meetings would delay her return. Because she was recognizable, we didn't leave my apartment for two days and nights, which didn't aggrieve either one of us.

On the morning of our third and what we understood had to be our last day together, we were reading the *Times* when she reacted to an article about the premiere that night of a Jerome Robbins work, *In the Night,* to Chopin nocturnes, at New York City Ballet. She would, she said, give anything to see it. We stared at each other, trapped in our illicit seclusion. Suddenly I saw a way. "I've got it! I'll order tickets. We'll get out of the cab a block from Lincoln Center and separate. I'll pick up our tickets and walk past you in the lobby and slip you your ticket. We'll happen to be sitting next to each other in the theater—nothing wrong with that. And then we'll leave separately and meet where we got out of the cab and come back here."

The plan sounded foolproof, so, that night I joined the line at the will-call window in the lobby of the State Theater. My friend was standing casually near the ticket taker a few yards away. As I waited, I glanced idly at the door from the plaza, where, among the crowd pushing in, I spied Paul Leperq, an investment banker and prominent dance patron.

Next to Paul was a very young Eurasian woman, dark hair cascading down her back to her waist and a face of such startling beauty that, I realized, I wasn't the only person in the crowd staring at her. As she and Paul moved toward the end of the line in which I stood, I knew—not thought, not suspected—*knew* that this was the person with whom I would gladly spend the rest of my life.

Of course, that sounds like a tired cliché, but apparently, in an instant, I was ready for precisely that cliché, and nothing else, nothing less. The eleven sybaritic years, the anticommitment nightmares, were washed away in a tidal wave of what felt like—and turned out to be—authentic, abiding love.

As Paul and his companion joined the end of the line, I turned to the person behind me and said, "I'm waiting for someone. Why don't you go ahead of me." The moment the offer was accepted, I turned to the next person behind me—and by this process the gap between Paul and me shrank quickly. Unfortunately, the young woman with him, who had grown more beautiful with each forward step they took, wandered away just as I made way for the last interposed ticket buyer. Paul and I greeted each other, I picked up my tickets, he picked up his, his directed him to go left and mine directed me to go right, where my friend was waiting.

In the Night was performed early in the program, to permit the critics to scurry away and make their deadlines for tomorrow's paper. When I suggested we go out to the Grand Promenade, my friend wavered, but, on a new and not very admirable mission, I proposed we go up the aisle separately, and run into each other casually and innocently.

My plan was based on a long acquaintance with Paul. Since he was one of New York's most energetic and successful bon vivants, a position to which I also aspired, our competitive paths had crossed frequently. Paul was tall, athletic, cultured, extremely French, wealthy, with a crown of golden hair—a Greek god in short—none of which I was. In any mano a mano face-off, I would be at a distinct disadvantage—but my previous encounters with him had revealed an important flaw: No matter whom Paul was escorting, no matter how spectacular she usually was, if you were with an attractive woman, Paul wanted her too. He would figuratively, and sometimes literally, elbow you out of the way, to take her aside and invite her to his retreat in the Bahamas, which was often a successful preemptive maneuver.

In sum, I was counting on Paul—and he didn't let me down. In the Promenade, I managed to move my friend into his line of vision, and instantly he struck, hurrying toward us with the marvel in tow. Introductions were exchanged, and recalling my friend's dance career, he engaged her in animated conversation, his back to me and the only person of consequence in that throng.

In the course of the intermission, I discovered that she was with Paul because his girlfriend (of the moment) was dancing with the company tonight. Superb news! I learned that the name Kedakai Turner meant she was half-Japanese and half-Irish . . . but the intermission ended too soon: Paul and Kedakai went left; my friend and I went right. As we headed down the aisle, she whispered, "Do you know what that guy did?!"

"What?"

"He invited me to the Bahamas for the weekend!"

"No!"

"Keep him away from me!"

"You bet."

But at the next intermission, I persuaded her that I would run interference for her in the Promenade, and Paul, always resourceful, found us in a corner and struck again. This time, I learned that Kedakai was a model with the Wilhelmina Agency—and I was armed with the vital information.

The next morning, moments after my friend's tearful departure for the airport, I raced for the phone, called the Wilhelmina Agency and left a message for Kedakai Turner.

It goes without saying that Paul Leperq isn't the antagonist in this drama; I am.

Kedakai and I met for dinner, and a few days later, on the first morning that Kedakai was in my apartment when my secretary arrived, she strolled into my office, sipping a cup of coffee, and I introduced her to Joanna. It wasn't the first time I'd introduced someone to Joanna at ten A.M., but this time she behaved differently. I invited Kedakai to sit down, the three of us chatted, and Joanna kept stealing glances at Kedakai. Finally, she flattened her hands on her desk and said, "I'm just going to say it! You'll have to excuse me for staring at you. You're the most unusual-looking person I've ever seen."

Kedakai shook her head over her coffee. "No, I'm not."

Now *I* stared at her. Our relationship was less than a week old, so I exercised some care. "Kedakai, if someone said you were the most *beautiful* person they'd ever seen, I could understand your denying it—even though I would disagree. But how can you say you're not unusual?"

Kedakai was unfazed. "Because it's true."

"Prove it!"

She put her cup on the coffee table and leaned forward. "Two or three times a day, when I'm out in the street and I stop at a red light, a man will come up to me and say, 'Sorry to bother you, but you look just like someone I know.'"

Now both Joanna and I stared. Finally, I blurted out, "And from this you conclude that there are a lot of women like you walking around out there?"

"Of course," Kedakai said placidly, picking up her coffee cup.

Anyone who knows Kedakai can attest to the fact that she, with little reason to be modest, is a person of unwavering modesty—just as anyone reading these pages can attest to the fact that I, with every reason to be modest, am

With Mother in the backyard at 280 Hague on what, from our attire, appears to be a special occasion.

A young dreamer, always with pen in hand, hair in face, and something far away in mind . . . like the dreamer in the image below.

Lawrence Lipton, future rebel, Beat poet . . . and highly unconventional father.

Mother, lost in *her* dreams, an expression I saw often and remember fondly.

The moment when the prospect of a life in the law yielded to a radically different path.

Newly arrived in New York, 140 pounds of muscle and bone, scanning far horizons from a rooftop tarbeach.

My life-changing teachers, Stella Adler and Harold Clurman.

The ballet student: an interest that became an obsession.

On *The Guiding Light,* where
Dr. Dick Grant was renowned
for his golden hands—and his
torrid, turbulent romance
with Kathy (Susan Douglas).

With Joan Lorring in the
Broadway production of
Lillian Hellman's *The
Autumn Garden,* directed
by Harold Clurman.

Directed by Sidney
Lumet on CBS's
You Are There, as the
young Michelangelo
sculpting the David in
his own image.

Starring in the film
The Big Break with
Gaby Rodgers.

How many men can claim to be the husband of Miss Scarlet? It's unnerving, however, to discover that your wife committed the murder in the library with the candlestick.

Kedakai in the crown and gown of a Chinese empress.

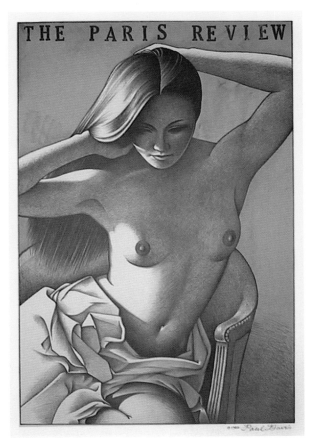

A lithograph of Kedakai by Paul Davis for George Plimpton's *Paris Review* magazine. I am proud to say that the poster, the chair, and the astonishing woman in it are still in my living room.

Presenting President Carter and Gerald Rafshoon with videotapes of the Inaugural Concert, which I had written and produced.

With President Carter and Diana Ross, who wanted to return to the Oval Office when she realized she'd taken a picture with her shades parked on her head. But there were no take-twos in the White House.

Mother and Kedakai with Mrs. Carter the night I produced a White House evening honoring America's educators.

Arrival in Beijing, June 1979, with Bob Hope bearing his trademark golf club. To the right is Oh Yang, who would turn out to be trouble.

On the Great Wall, with Bob about to perform the first musical number on its venerated surface in 2,000 years, singing the words I'd written for him: "We're off on the Road to China, with fun and adventure in mind."

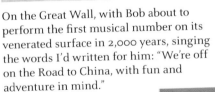

On the road with Bob Hope at the conclusion of a Royal Gala in London. From the left, Julio Iglesias, HRH Prince Philip, Chevy Chase, Marvelous Marvin Hagler, Bob and me.

A souvenir from Mrs. Reagan, recalling her performance of the lyric I wrote to "Thanks for the Memory" for Bob Hope's eighty-fifth birthday.

To Jim Lipton
"Thanks for the Memories and all the help- my best
Nancy Reagan

Preflighting the Aeronca at dawn on the Iditarod Trail, Alaska, December 1989.

The cliff face off the wingtip in Rainy Pass, Alaska, moments before the engine died.

Two treasured friends: my mother and George Plimpton.

Kedakai and her guys,
Kurt Vonnegut
and my godson,
the Count Severin
de Rochechouart
de Mortemart.

A rite of summer:
Flying to Provincetown,
Massachusetts, where
Norman Mailer, who
led me to the Actors
Studio, awaits
us at the airport.

Smiling as I pilot a 172
down the Hudson River
VFR corridor. Piloting any
plane, anywhere, tends to
make me smile.

The startling picture Kedakai took as I flew us down
the Hudson a few months before 9/11.

A good day at the Hampton Classic on the gallant Chico.
Every day over fences is a good one, win or lose.

My blue cards—in a black-and-white drawing!—by the incomparable Al Hirschfeld.

When Will Ferrell showed up on
our stage, I was beside myself.

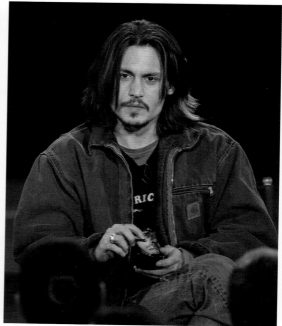

Johnny Depp, fearlessly rolling a cigarette
that evoked cheers from the students in our
smoke-free university.

Billy Crystal, bringing the
fine art of comedy to what he
pronounced "a good room."

The polymathic Mike Myers, who
gave us equal parts of scholarship
and humor, described himself as a
site-specific extrovert.

Spending the evening this close to Angelina Jolie—and her tattoos— is one of the rewards of hosting *Inside the Actors Studio.*

A Simpson at last, with yellow skin, three fingers, a severe overbite, funny things to say and an amazing company of players to say them to.

An infinity of Simpsons. From left, Bart, Homer, Marge, Mr. Burns, Apu, Lisa . . . and everybody else in Springfield.

Jamie Foxx,
playing, singing,
enchanting.

Robin Williams, mesmerizing
our students and a few million
viewers around the world.

Robin in the most renowned moment
in the show's history: improvising
with a pink pashmina to create an
automobile emerging from a car
wash.

Charlize Theron studied ballet until she grew too tall for her partners—like me, somewhere back there, supporting her on her five-inch heels.

Our Actors Studio Drama School master's degree candidates enjoy unique perks—like dancing with John Travolta.

Russell Crowe, ruining his bad-boy reputation with a thoughtful, eloquent classroom session.

Dave Chappelle, on our stage at two in the morning— indefatigable, incomparable.

Dustin Hoffman, our two hundredth guest. In the foreground, five hundred blue cards chronicling his remarkable career.

Chris Rock, intense, in gear, in charge.

When Tom Cruise was on our stage our students discovered how effortlessly fame and decency can coexist.

not. Though there's nothing Kedakai can do to rescue me here, in life it's my frequent hope that her behavior will serve as a counterweight to mine.

To add immediate further evidence of my deficient modesty quotient: A month after we met, Kedakai moved out of her apartment and into mine. And eight months later we were married. And anyone who doesn't think that's arrant bragging doesn't know me or has never been in Kedakai's radiant presence.

The night we were married, we left for a honeymoon in Europe. In Paris, we discovered that the Netherlands National Ballet, which was now under the direction of my former teacher Benjamin Harkarvy, was appearing at the Théâtre des Champs-Élysées. Glancing across the lobby during the first intermission, I found Paul Leperq staring incredulously at us. Crossing the lobby, he said, "What are you doing here?"

"We're on our honeymoon."

His eyes widened. "Where are you staying?"

"The Trémoille."

"I'm leaving Paris tomorrow. I'm sorry we can't have dinner."

The next afternoon when we returned to our hotel, virtually every surface in the living room of our suite was banked with flowers. Paul is *definitely* not the antagonist of this tale.

A month after we returned from our honeymoon, the Nederlands Dans Theater arrived in New York, and Kedakai and I gave a party for them to which the entire dance community was invited. Early in the evening, I was seated at the desk in my study across from Neil Simon, who asked me how Kedakai and I met, to which I replied with the account that began with my manipulations at the State Theater and ended at the Théâtre des Champs-Élysées.

The writer in Neil prompted him to ask, "Did that guy ever find out the whole thing was a plot?"

"Not till this moment. That's Paul Leperq on the window seat behind you."

The writer whirled. "Well? What have you got to say?"

Paul, in a masterful demonstration of the French art of savoir faire, leaned toward me and said, "Do you still have that actress's phone number?"

Kedakai brought many gifts to my life, not least the robust Irish-American family into which she had been adopted at birth. The Turner family came complete with a father who was a cop (of course), an archetypal Irish mother (translation: she tippled) who, after adopting Kedakai, had given birth to two children, Martha Ann and Jimmy. When the family came into my life—or, more accurately, I came gratefully into theirs—Martie had married Tom

Demers and produced Tommy and John Robert (the name John was an anomaly in this family: Our holiday tables were crammed with Jims and Toms). In the years since I joined the family, Tommy and John Robert have begotten four offspring (need I mention that there is a Tom among them, but, thank God, no additional Jims).

In short, the Turners taught me about family. But one gap remained. Just as I have no concept of "father," all my life I've listened enviously to brothers and sisters laughing, teasing, bickering, sharing, and wondered what *that* felt like. Imagining a relationship one has never had is like trying to imagine a color one has never seen.

Finally, thirty-five years ago, I found the closest thing to a brother I've ever known. When George Plimpton died in September 2003, Charlie Rose invited several of his closest friends and colleagues to gather around Charlie's table and talk about him. I remember predicting that, in one way or another, I would think about George every day of my life, and I have. And do at this moment.

When George turned fifty, it occasioned an explosive celebration among his friends and colleagues, who were legion, and among the authors and poets who had seen their first or most famous work published in *The Paris Review,* the literary magazine he had cofounded in Paris in 1953, fresh out of Cambridge, and which he carried, creatively and financially, long past the normal life span of a publication with far-reaching influence but a peak circulation of ten thousand readers.

The birthday celebration took place in the only conceivable venue: the most famous literary salon since Gertrude Stein and Alice B. Toklas set up shop at 27 Rue de Fleurus for the Lost Generation of Hemingway, Pound, Sherwood Anderson and Thornton Wilder. George's salon was located on East Seventy-second Street in—no, not "in," it *was,* night and day, fifty-two weeks a year—George's living room and adjoining poolroom, overlooking the East River. Its parties were legendary, but none of them had ever compared to this one, as George turned fifty. If a tidal wave had risen from the East River and destroyed the building and everyone in it, America would have become in that instant a second-rate intellectual power.

One after another, America's literary lights stood on a makeshift podium next to the piano at the north end of the packed expanse, saluting George with cutting wit, scholarly allusion, reckless irreverence and deeply felt, exquisitely expressed respect.

Two weeks before the event, George's wife, Freddy, had called me about my part in the program. "You're writing something, right?"

"Yes. It's nearly done."

"I need one more thing."

"Oh?"

"There's a birthday present I've always wanted to give George."

"What's that?"

"A naked girl jumping out of a birthday cake."

"I see." She was silent. "Why are you telling *me* this?"

"Well, *you* know, Jim . . ." She paused, waiting.

George and *The Paris Review* had been coeval with my Paris sojourn, and apparently at some point he'd spilled the beans to his wife. "Freddy," I said, "I've been out of that business for a long time...."

"You're my only hope!" burst from the phone. "Please! You've *got* to! For George!"

Oddly, it was Kedakai who came up with a solution, reminding me that our friend Janie Kawaguchi, whom we'd met when she danced with the Joffrey company in one of my East Hampton galas, was currently featured on Broadway in Kenneth Tynan's *Oh! Calcutta!* the audacious revue written by Nobelist Samuel Beckett, John Lennon, Sam Shepard, Jules Feiffer and Tynan.

"Janie's doing the nude ballet," Kedakai reminded me.

When Janie consented to jump out of the cake, the writer, director and producer in me collaborated on what struck me as an inspired notion. I called Freddy. "Okay, I'm doing it, but this is my swan song."

"It'll be the grand finale of the whole evening!"

"Hold on. I've been thinking. Anybody can produce a naked girl from a cake—"

"No, they can't, Jim. Only you—"

"Never mind that. Our friend Janie Kawaguchi is in *Oh! Calcutta!* and her boyfriend plays guitar in the band. She says she'll bring him along—so, when she jumps out of the cake, her boyfriend will start to play the opening number where the cast sings and dances in these big robes, flashing the audience, then takes them off—and they're all naked. Janie comes out of the cake, dancing, in the robe."

"I love it!"

"Wait! We rent an ape costume."

"What for?"

"Janie's in it." I didn't bother explaining to Freddy that nothing amuses me more than someone in a gorilla costume, like the three apes in Ernie Kovacs's famous Nairobi Trio. All I said to Freddy was "The gorilla's wearing the *Oh! Calcutta!* robe, and it dances and vamps to the music—and everybody thinks, 'That's it—a gorilla striptease!' Funny?"

"Yessss," Freddy said uncertainly.

I delivered the coup de grâce. "That's *not* it! The gorilla drops the robe and dances naked—in its fur. Then the gorilla whips off its head. And there's Janie—that beautiful face, her long hair tumbling out of the head. Then—zip!—she drops the ape suit and you've got your naked lady, dancing for George on his fiftieth."

"I absolutely *adore* it!!" Freddy screamed.

On the birthday night, after the dazzling parade of speakers, a team of *Paris Review* interns staggered out of George's study carrying a huge cardboard cake to the pool table. At the other end of the room, Janie's boyfriend and the *Oh! Calcutta!* pianist struck up the tune, and everything went precisely as planned, with George strategically placed by Freddy in front of the table. When Janie, pale, slender and utterly naked, danced out of the fallen ape suit, the assemblage gasped, then cheered wildly, which inspired Janie to leap off the table into George's arms. Bedlam! One of my most successful productions.

Early the next morning, my phone rang. It was Freddy. "Jim, we're at the airport." I prepared to reply modestly to a torrent of gratitude and praise. "We're on our way to Barbados."

"Good."

"You've got to help me!"

"With what?"

"George's parents were there."

"I know. We talked."

"*After* the gorilla?"

"No. Why?"

"His mother was very upset."

"Now, look, Freddy, you were the one who wanted the naked lady!"

"You think I'm going to tell them *that*?!"

"You want to blame it on me?"

"That's not the problem. Shirley Clurman was there. You know she works for *People* magazine."

"Freddy—I didn't invite Shirley; *you* did!"

"She brought a photographer. I'm sure there's going to be a picture of the girl jumping on George in *People*—and George's mother will die! She'll drop dead on the spot!"

"Well, call Shirley."

"I can't."

"Why not?"

"I told you—we're on our way to Barbados. They're announcing our plane! Call Shirley. Explain what's at stake!"

"Now, listen, Freddy . . ." But I was talking to a dial tone.

A few hours later, I got a call from the Barbados airport. "What did Shirley say?"

"She said it's a First Amendment issue."

"*What?* Has she ever read *The Paris Review*?! George practically *invented* the First Amendment!"

"She won't budge."

"Budge her! *Please!* I'll call you from the hotel."

She was gone again. When I called Shirley Clurman, she said, "Jim, we're a family magazine. Do you think we'd do anything to jeopardize our place next to the supermarket cash register? There are going to be *twenty* pictures, every one the size of a postage stamp."

Freddy wasn't happy about the postage stamp compromise, but I told her it was the best I could do, and firmly washed my hands of the matter. When the magazine came out, there were in fact twenty postage stamp–size pictures—and one glorious full-page photo of Janie Kawaguchi, from the rear, naked as the day she was born, leaping into the arms of the delighted guest of honor.

George's mother, a woman of infinite grace, ultimately forgave me, and George (who, needless to say, didn't mind in the least) had the last word, as always, when he commissioned Paul Davis, the acclaimed poster artist of the New York Public Theater, who had won awards with his painting of Kedakai for China Seas Fabrics' advertisements, to create a *Paris Review* poster, which prompted Davis to produce a stunning lithograph of his favorite model, nude to the waist.

The poster hangs in the Plimpton salon on East Seventy-second Street, and in our home, and on the wall at Elaine's Restaurant, next to a bust of George, in a memorial to our departed friend. Elaine usually seats my guests and me at the table under it, where I preside beneath my wife's graceful form with understandable pride.

Years after the historic fiftieth birthday party, Freddy ended what the world looked on as a golden union by vanishing one day with a man she would shortly marry—and as shortly divorce. A broken George, whose voice I barely recognized, called to ask if Kedakai and I would come and stay with him in Sagaponack. We left within the hour and spent the next ten days in his house, barely letting him out of our sight, and retrieving him when he rose in the middle of the night to wander the village roads.

The breach ended as well as it could for Freddy. When she was alone again, George, who had sold the house in Sagaponack, bought a house in Bridgehampton that could accommodate Freddy and, in the summer when they visited, their children, Taylor and Medora, and they rebuilt a viable friendship.

In time, Sarah Dudley entered George's life and all the lives that orbited it. When he and Sarah decided to marry, they invited Kedakai and me to dine with them at the River Club for a formal Plimptonian announcement, which we saluted with corresponding formality and unalloyed enthusiasm.

In the course of the dinner, George regaled us with tales of the meetings of the Mayflower Society, where, he said, as the names of the boat's passengers are read, "you stand up for each of your ancestors."

"So, you have to stand up twice?" I asked.

"Yes," George said, "and Sarah has to stand up three times."

"Jesus," I said, "that's half the manifest."

Contemplating this patrician lineage, I recalled sitting with George and Kurt Vonnegut in a bar one night, reflecting silently on my conviction that, apart from the obvious genetic deficiencies that separated me from them and Norman Mailer, I would never be in their literary league because they, and virtually all the important writers I know, were serious drinkers (a polite euphemism) and I wasn't. (Norman credited his literary genius to his abundant head of hair, and he had me there too.) That night in the bar, George had to leave, and Kurt and I remained. Kurt studied the white-thatched Giacometti as it ambled out and muttered, with undisguised affection, "There goes the last gentleman."

George bore his breeding lightly. On the occasions when he prepared dinner, the menu was invariable: macaroni and cheese, from the nearest available package. I think, if he could have, he'd have taken it from the freezer and eaten it like a Popsicle.

At the same time, he was America's most coveted dinner guest. For good reason: George could talk to anyone, on any subject, knowledgeably, entertainingly. Kedakai and I used to hold boxing nights in our home. We would order up the fight on pay-per-view, and twenty or so aficionados and fighters and trainers would show up. George ran the betting pool (which Kedakai won so often the crowd thought it was a fix), and on one occasion George and Mailer sat in the front row, commenting spiritedly on the fight, as they had at the Ali-Foreman Zaire fight in the great *When We Were Kings* documentary.

When George and Freddy lived on Sag Main Road, Kurt Vonnegut and Jill Kramentz lived next to them, and Kedakai and I lived on the same road, a mile north. Kurt and I got into the habit (of immeasurable value to me) of exchanging whatever we were writing for comment. One day Kurt showed up at our house with the galleys of his new novel. When I'd read them, and we sat next to his pool to talk, I said that there were elements in the book that reminded me strongly of Erasmus's *The Praise of Folly*.

Kurt said he'd never read it, and asked if I had a copy. I delivered to him from my library a special boxed edition of the book with the sixteenth-century title *Moriae Encomium* on its cover. Two weeks later, Kurt called to invite me over to talk about the letter he'd enclosed with the book when he sent it back to me in New York. When I told him I hadn't received the letter or the book, he reacted as if I'd announced the death of a close friend.

The Postal Service was no help, and for months Kurt gave me an agitated running account of his visits to bookstores wherever he went in the world in search of that distinctive cover. I told him that any edition of *The Praise of Folly* would do, but he insisted that he was going to replace *that* one.

A year later, Kurt called me triumphantly from San Francisco. "I've got it!" On his return to New York, he handed it to me—no trusting the post office this time!

The next day I called Kurt. "Guess what showed up in the mail this morning! My *Moriae Encomium*, with the year-old postmark, and your letter."

Kurt had written:

Dear Jim—

As I've said many times, my friends educate me in the liberal arts, since I was educated as a chemist. Friends told me what to read, and on occasion it was as though they had told me to stick my prick in a light socket, so to speak: *Candide, Lysistrata, Theory of the Leisure Class, Kapital,* and on and on. I now add *The Praise of Folly* to that very short list. How could I have missed it until now?

When you said Erasmus and I were kindred spirits, I supposed he was a skeptic about codified religious beliefs. Before I read him, I expected him to be like Voltaire, whereas he is brilliantly respectful of scripture, wishing, apparently, only that the translation be exact. I am particularly grateful for his scholarship in detecting that the notion of the Trinity in some translations was a fraudulent insertion, a self-serving anachronism.

Cheers, old friend—

The letter ends with his trademark signature: his name incorporated into a cartoon of himself, a cigarette protruding from his bristling moustache.

I volunteered to send the new book back to him, so we'd each have one; and those books, one in my library and one in his to the end of his shining life, stand as twin encomia to a singular writerly act. Cheers, old friend.

When Sarah gave birth to twins, George solemnly appointed me godfather to both. I think, typically of George, who was both invariably generous and notoriously vague, he'd offered similar appointment to several friends, with the result that on the baptismal day, there was a goodly crowd around the baptismal font of the Cathedral of St. John the Divine.

The dean himself presided over the ceremony, and later, at the luncheon in the historic East River apartment, he and I found ourselves perched on the edge of the pool table where Janie Kawaguchi had cavorted in the buff, and each issue of *The Paris Review* was lovingly assembled.

The belated realization that I, a nonbeliever, was charged with overseeing the religious instruction of two defenseless human beings may have been what triggered an oddly antic and I fear disrespectful mood. "I want you to know," I said to the dean, "that while *some* godparents"—I waved a hand at the crowded room—"may not take their religious duties seriously, I intend to begin Laura and Olivia's instruction with the Manichean Heresy." When he eyed me uncertainly, I went for the theological jugular. "And when they begin school, they'll be the only children in their class who will know that the Immaculate Conception refers not to the birth of our Lord and Savior Jesus Christ, but to his mother Mary's birth without the stain of Original Sin."

"We're probably the only two people in this *room* who know that," the dean said approvingly.

I took a cucumber sandwich from the tray next to me on the pool table and bit into it with entirely unwarranted satisfaction.

On September 7, 1994, the first students arrived at the university . . . and, in the circular construction to which I've demonstrated my partiality, we're back where we began, a lifetime—*my* lifetime—ago, at the birth of the Actors Studio Drama School.

Once we had assembled our full-time faculty of Studio members, and guest teachers who could commit to four Fridays for a workshop, one category remained: those Studio members and colleagues whose lives were so circumscribed by their work schedules that they could give us, if they were willing to participate, only one evening.

I set out to enlist them, sending dozens of letters, explaining and describing our school, and inviting them to come for one evening—that was all—to teach our students. There would be nothing to prepare, I promised them: that would be my job. All they had to do was show up on the appointed night for an interview that was designed to provide these young people who were at the threshold of the life they'd chosen with a kind of telescopic glimpse of the path ahead, with all its twists, turns, vicissitudes, joys, perils and possibilities.

I explained that the audience in front of them would be composed of our master's degree candidates and members of the public, whose series subscriptions would go toward our students' financial aid, and that the subject of the interview would be the craft our students studied and they practiced. There was no talk or thought of television: It was a live event, a class in our curriculum for the benefit of our students.

The response to my letter startled and heartened me. Paul Newman said yes, as did Alec Baldwin, Sally Field, Dennis Hopper, Shelley Winters, Arthur Penn, Sydney Pollack. Because our students came to us as actors, writers and directors, and because they studied a spectrum of disciplines, including voice and movement, and would have to adapt to a variety of styles, techniques and systems all their working lives, I reached out beyond the Studio, to people I'd worked with, knew and respected, and in those first months, Stephen Sondheim, Neil Simon and Stanley Donen accepted my invitation.

With a sheaf of acceptances in hand, I sent word back into the professional world from which I'd come. It was a simple message: "These are the people who are coming, and it's possible that they may say something worth preserving. The only way to preserve it is with cameras and microphones." In an existential leap of faith for which I'll be forever grateful, the young, small Bravo cable network stepped forward.

Now, suddenly, we were an academic class, a live subscription event *and* a television series, owned, at my insistence, entirely by the Actors Studio, and licensed, like any other television series, by the network. The day after the contract negotiation was concluded, I got a call from a network executive asking, "By the way, what's the series called?"

"I've got someone on the other line. I'll call you back," I sputtered, and hung up. I had no one on the other line. What I had was a problem. In the hurly-burly of putting together our TV staff and crew, and booking equipment—not to mention admitting our first academic class as chairman of the MFA—I hadn't paused to give "the series," as it was identified in the contract, a name. Now, seated at my desk at the school, brow knotted, I asked myself, "What *is* it called?"

I was still covering a sheet of foolscap with names—*Onstage!—Lights! Camera! Action!—Backstage*—when the phone rang. The network executive's voice trembled. "Listen—we've got a *TV Guide* deadline! If we don't tell them what it's called right now, the Bravo space'll be blank!"

The words came out instantly and automatically: *"Inside the Actors Studio."*

"Got it! I'll tell Publicity."

I hung up and wondered *why* it was called *Inside the Actors Studio*. "Well," I told myself in one of my alter-ego moments, "it's obvious: You're inviting all these people *inside the Actors Studio* to teach the Studio's students, and the public's being invited *inside the Actors Studio* to witness the interaction."

It may have been obvious to me, but it hasn't been obvious to every member of our television audience. I still get viewer letters from self-appointed custodians of the Studio's torch demanding to know whether Anthony Hopkins and Martin Scorsese and Robert Redford and Vanessa Redgrave are Studio members, and, if not, what are they doing there! All I can do is sigh and say, (A) I wish they *were* members, and (B) I'm eternally grateful to them for interrupting their busy schedules to come *Inside the Actors Studio* to teach our students, whose education would be the poorer for want of their instruction.

In the short time between Bravo's bold acceptance of our show and the first taping, I had some critical decisions to make. Over the years, as an independent producer whose fate hung on the success or failure of every venture, I'd created for myself a series of checkpoints, intended to test the value of any idea I came up with. The first checkpoint was the question "What's the franchise? Why should anyone pay attention to this offering? What can they get here that they can't get elsewhere?" If the answer was "Nothing," I abandoned the project.

Now I was venturing into a jungle, on a path littered with the bones of those who had preceded me. To this day, interview programs and talk shows turn up like mayflies in summer—with about the same life expectancy. What, I asked myself, could possibly raise the profile of our classroom above the teeming competitive landscape, with every inhabitant clamoring for the attention of a public whose habits were already ingrained?

Those questions led me into a necessarily brief (the premiere was looming) but essential internal debate, and these were the answers I came up with.

Before moving into the academic world, I'd been a guest on most of the interview shows with which *Inside the Actors Studio* would be competing— and they all had one thing in common: Several days before the scheduled appearance, mine or anyone else's, a young subaltern would show up with a tape recorder and a long list of questions, the answers to which were typed out and delivered to the show's writers—those five or six or ten names in the closing credits—who chose the answers they liked, and delivered them to the host with the questions that would trigger them.

Then, when you arrived for the show, you found the segment producer who had done the preinterview waiting with a script that contained, you were told pointedly, the answers you'd given—and the questions you would be asked to lead you into them. You didn't need to be told that you would stray from the script at your peril, since this was all the information the host had.

Obviously, shooting five shows a week, these hosts have no choice but to work this way—and they do it extraordinarily well, producing a witty, seamless result that looks entirely spontaneous, employing skills I don't possess.

My hat is off to them—and, revising the axiom "If you can't beat 'em, join 'em" to "If you can't beat 'em, take a different path," I made up my mind that, alone among America's interview/talk shows, *Inside the Actors Studio* would employ no preinterview, no segment producer with a tape recorder, no script waiting for host and guest.

That left me with the sobering realization that I would have to do the research, all of it, myself. It was a fateful and, at times—when exhaustion threatened to flatten me—a nearly fatal decision because, combined with my decanal duties at the school, it chained me to my desk seven days a week, fourteen hours a day, from September to June, with two days off, Thanksgiving and Christmas.

The preparation for every guest who comes to our stage takes two weeks. For better or worse, every one of the three to five hundred blue cards on my desk has been written by me, distilled in my computer from a mountain of raw material unearthed from libraries, the press and the Internet by Jeremy Kareken, an immensely talented graduate of our school.

One of the few things I brought with me from my brief flirtation with the law was a fundamental axiom of the art of cross-examination: Never ask a witness a question the answer to which you don't already know. (Consider the fiasco of O. J. and the gloves.) What I do for two weeks is shape the raw material in my computer into a narrative, with a beginning, middle and end. As I prepare for each guest, I look for, and somehow always find, a unifying thread— the Super-Objective Stella taught me to look for—and that enables me to break the narrative down into the objectives and beats of the guest's life and career.

Each card contains the information that may inform the guest's answer, and once I have that, I write the question that will take me, our students and our audience there.

I may be putting too fine a point on all of this. Every host has his or her own system, and some of them achieve results I can only dream of. This just happens to be my way of working, and sometimes it has served me and the guest well. After thirteen years, I'm convinced of one thing: Eliminating the preinterview pushes the guest and me into a conversation, the course of which neither of us can predict. I sometimes think of *Inside the Actors Studio* as a circus tent with a high wire at the top and rope ladders at its opposite ends. As the evening begins, the guest goes up one ladder and I climb the other and we meet up top, on the wire—for four or five hours—with no net.

Sometimes—rarely—the evening lasts three hours, more often four, sometimes five—two to three hours with me in the interview, one to two with the students in the classroom segment. I literally threw Spielberg, Robin Williams,

Billy Joel, Tony Hopkins and Barbra Streisand out at twelve thirty in the morning on the grounds that "these kids have to go to class in a few hours!"

The fact is that these encounters are so seductive for both guests and students that I have no doubt they would often stay all night if I'd let them. When Dustin Hoffman arrived at Pace for his seminar, he'd watched the show often, so he knew its reputation for both depth and length. "Who holds the record?" he demanded.

"Barbra. Nearly six hours."

"I'll break it," he said forthrightly. And he did.

I made two decisions as I shaped the show. The first was that there would be no preinterview. The second was that *Inside the Actors Studio* would be about craft—not gossip, the most valuable commodity in talk show television and the surest way to quick returns in the life-and-death ratings race. I was warned that this focus on craft could be a fatal mistake, and wiser heads counseled that the safest route would be the customary one: brief, preferably funny, anecdotes, juicy personal tidbits and slightly salacious tales out of school. *In* school, of course, on our stage.

With the backing of the Studio, I stuck to my guns: If we were to fail, we would fail on our own terms. I harbored no delusions. I'd produced television shows with consistent shares in the thirties and forties, and had learned what it took to get us there. I knew that cable television's universe was much smaller and in theory more select, but, still, I didn't conceal the fact—from Bravo, the Studio or myself—that sticking resolutely to the subject of craft might make us too dry for any television audience.

What I didn't anticipate was the fact that asking my guests to relate—and, more important, relive—the moments that shaped them as people and as artists would blow the hinges off the doors they normally keep firmly closed in public, and make *Inside the Actors Studio* not the most arid talk show on TV but one of the most intimate and emotional, to the point where foreign newspapers and magazines usually referred to me as "confessor" or "psychoanalyst." In France, the headline above a *Télérama* story read, NO STAR RESISTS HIM, and a *Paris Match* headline said, HE STRIPS THE STARS NAKED.

But all of that lay ahead in a decidedly unknown future when *Inside the Actors Studio* resolutely set sail under its own colors on October 10, 1994.

The first guest on our stage was Alec Baldwin, a Studio member who had received a call from Paul Newman supporting my letter with "Lipton may be onto something."

Paul would be our first guest on the air, on April 26, 1995, because Bravo wanted to launch the series with the Studio's president—and one of its founding members. But Alec was the first to put a foot in our untested waters.

Alec's counsel to the students was unsparing. "I say to people, 'If you want to be an actor, you must really understand how much you love acting. It's like oil exploration. You have to have this passion that translates into this great patience. Because you're going to get to do so little of it.'

"I have two types of friends—friends who are rich and famous actors, and actors who make a living. Every now and then they make a commercial, do a film, a small film, a supporting role in film, a little television—they do theater, theater, theater, theater, theater. They can make a living. And they can *live*. They're *actors*. That's what acting is. I say to people, 'Do you want to be an actor, or do you want to be a *famous* actor?' If you want to be a famous actor, I feel sorry for you because it takes so much drive. You have to back up and run and smash your head against the door again and again and again and again and again.

"I say, if you want this careerism thing, you're going to find out that you're just not going to do that much acting. In the movies, it's so piecemeal. You shoot a movie, it's twelve, thirteen hours in a day—and maybe, *maybe* you actually get to act forty-five minutes out of the day. And the rest of it is"—Alec whistled—"devastating."

Tough love. True love. In the very first *Inside the Actors Studio* evening, and in every successive class, the students were forewarned: The life they'd chosen wouldn't be easy. It didn't discourage them. It seemed, in fact, to energize them and, since our school's attrition rate remained below 6 percent for a decade, even inspire them.

Paul Newman was the second guest on our stage, and a few days before his October 24 date with us, he called me to ask, "May I set up a screening of my new movie for the students?"

Needless to say, it was an offer I couldn't refuse, and the afternoon of Paul's appearance, our students—a scant six weeks into the pursuit of their master's degrees—found themselves lounging like stars or moguls in the leather armchairs of Paramount's New York screening room; and that night Paul brought the film's director, Robert Benton, with him to our school.

I was in the makeup chair when Paul arrived in our green room. My eyes were closed as Michele O'Callaghan applied makeup to my eyelids, and when I felt her normally rock-steady hand freeze, I opened my eyes to find myself staring into Paul's cobalt blue irises in the mirror as he leaned a forearm on my shoulder and grinned at me.

Aiming a thumb at the face next to mine, I said to Michele, who was appropriately transfixed by it, "You see that? That's what God intended me to look like. See what you can do about it."

Looking back at these first episodes as I have done to write this account of them, I'm startled by their appearance. All through the fall and spring of that first year, the guests and I occupied two chairs that, on my instruction, my staff had literally swiped out of a nearby classroom a few hours before Alec arrived, and the glass table on which my cards rested went back to the green room after each shoot, where it normally bore a telephone.

Our initial license fee from Bravo, which at that point reached fewer than twenty million homes, was so low that the borrowed chairs and table, in front of improvised screens, constituted our entire set; and our titles featured the doors of the Studio swinging open (for the first time, get it?), concealing the two Studio members who were tugging at offscreen wires to open them.

But as I revisited the first episodes, I was equally surprised at how many of the elements that became the hallmarks of the series were in place at the beginning. From its first moment, under titles, the program's mood was set by Angelo Badalamenti's haunting music, which exists because Angelo, who composes the scores for all of David Lynch's films, and wrote what is to my mind the most evocative score in television history for *Twin Peaks,* served with me on the governing board of the National Academy of Television Arts and Sciences, and on an impulse one day as we left a meeting, I asked him to compose and record the theme music for our new show. He did, and over the years we've received countless inquiries about its origin, and requests for a recording of "the full score," on the assumption that it is excerpted from a classical work.

The Pivot Questionnaire was there from the outset, as a tribute to Bernard Pivot, since it was he who showed me (and I daresay anyone else who was fortunate to see his programs on France 2) the real possibilities of the talk-show format.

And, most surprising, the face-to-face encounter between the guest and the students, without my interposition, was there from the first episode, albeit in the informal framework of a postinterview get-together over coffee and cake, which is all it was meant to be until it evolved organically and inevitably into a full-fledged continuation of the onstage seminar because the students and guest were too stimulated to end the exchange.

On our stage, Paul was one of the most self-deprecating guests we would ever have, insisting that "I don't know what I have a gift for except tenaciousness. I always wanted to be a jock, and I skied and boxed and wrestled and played football—badly, all badly. I could only dance with one person; that was Joanne. I had no physical grace. The only thing I ever found any grace in was an automobile. Which I guess is why I got hooked on that.

"I never felt that I had *any* gift at all to perform. But it was something I wanted badly enough that I just kept after it. Someone asked me once, 'Liken yourself to a dog.' And, I thought, terrier. My dog Harry knows how to work over a bone. And I think that's a pretty accurate assessment of the way I work. Of course, I was very resentful of people who were instinctive and intuitive, whose instrument was readily available to them and whose life experience prepared them for that. Mine didn't seem to, and to try to find what it took to make me available and accessible was the largest trajectory I had to travel. And it's just recent, actually, that . . ." He paused.

"That you've arrived where you've wanted to be?" I asked.

"Yeah. I don't like watching my early films at all. Some are worse than others, but—"

"You're not knocking *The Silver Chalice,* are you?"

"Well, I think I'm the only guy that ever took out an advertisement in the *Los Angeles Times* with a funeral wreath around it apologizing for what was happening on NBC at eight o'clock. And the worst thing, of course, is that it backfired. Everybody wanted to know what I was apologizing for, and the film had the best ratings they'd ever had. So I don't do that anymore."

In an effort to dispute his disparagement of his early work, I said, "Most of us who've watched your work all these years were filled with admiration almost from the beginning, excluding of course *The Silver Chalice*—with the cocktail gown."

He corrected me. "Oh, no, no, no, no. I had a cocktail *dress.* Nero had a cocktail *gown.*"

Speaking of his historic teamwork with Robert Redford in *Butch Cassidy and the Sundance Kid* and *The Sting,* Paul said, "When I was shooting *Nobody's Fool,* the local radio station called and said, 'If you'll do a radio interview, we'll give five hundred dollars to your favorite charity.' We'd just shot in a hospital and the nurses were trying to raise a thousand dollars for their Christmas party and they were five hundred bucks short, so, I said yes.

"The guy said, 'Why haven't you done another film with Redford?' And I said, 'For fifteen years, Redford and I have been trying to find something that would measure up to the movies we did, and we simply haven't been able to do it.' And the guy said, 'Why don't you do *Indecent Proposal II* with Redford?' And I said, 'Uh, exactly how would that work?' And he said, 'Would you shack up with Redford for a million dollars?' And I didn't even wait. I said, 'Like a rocket. Are you kidding? I'd shack up with a gorilla for a million dollars.' And he said, 'What about a male gorilla?' And I said, 'Add ten percent.'

"Of course, that hits the newspapers. And, apparently, Redford got a call.

The reporter said, 'Newman has said he would shack up with you for a million dollars.' And the guy said there was a long pause at the other end of the line, and Redford said, 'Not enough.'"

In the first year, for the session between the guest and the students, we moved to what was literally a classroom. It had been created in the 1930s for Martha Graham when she taught at the New School for Social Research, and since it was a large space on one level, it enabled the guest and students to meet at close quarters. In the course of the Paul Newman session, a student named Jason Powell asked Paul about the scene in *The Verdict* in which he knocked Charlotte Rampling down with a vicious punch. "As soon as you walked in there," Jason said, "you seemed to have something on your mind, an objective or intention, an active verb. It was something clearly on your face, and she read it. It was almost like you guys had a dialogue—but no words. What was going on?"

Paul said, "I was concerned about the comedic element of that thing. You walk up to a girl and you go . . ." He stepped forward and stopped in front of Celeste Walker, a young woman who, it should be remembered, had arrived at our doorstep six weeks before this moment, and gestured to her to rise. When she shrank back in her chair, her classmates raised an uproar, chanting "Improvise!" to her.

Paul took her trembling hand and brought her to her feet, suiting the action to his words. "I mean, if you really walk up to a girl who has betrayed you, if you walk up to her like this, and look at her, and launch off and belt her"— he mimed a punch, and she fell back in perfect sync, to an ovation from her classmates—"there's a great chance for comedy," Paul said, intent on the lesson. Repositioning Celeste and himself, he continued, "There is *no* chance for comedy if you walk in the door, and you see her, and you start from back there. I had forty feet to move before I got to her, and if your intention was very clear, she had to know what was coming. It was a choice, and I think it was right."

Later that night, over supper, I speculated to my staff, "What do you suppose will happen when Celeste's mother calls her and asks how school is going, and Celeste says, 'Well, Monday afternoon I saw Paul Newman's new movie in the Paramount screening room, and Monday night Paul and I improvised a scene from *The Verdict*'?"

My assistant, Anjanette Clisura, was smart and practical. "Her mother will think she's snapped, and drag her back home—and we'll lose a good student."

O ur third guest was neither actor nor director, nor was he a member of the Actors Studio, *pace* the Purity Police who have appointed themselves the protectors of our tradition. He was there because our students were being ridden hard and put away wet in several arts, among them the important contemporary skill of singing and *delivering* a musical performance. And he was there because, with all due respect to Will Ferrell, who has been known to portray me as given to hyperbole, I have actually used the word *genius* only once in thirteen years, when I brought our third guest to the stage with "In 1831, upon first hearing Chopin's music, Robert Schumann said, 'Hats off, gentlemen. A genius.' Hats off, ladies and gentlemen, Stephen Sondheim."

The only criterion I use in inviting guests to *Inside the Actors Studio* is: Does this person have something to teach our students? Steve had a great deal to teach them. When I asked him if he stood by his statement "I've always thought of lyric writing as a craft rather than an art; music is more challenging, more interesting and more rewarding," he replied, "Oh, sure. Because music's abstract, and it's fun, and it lives in you. Language is terrific, but the English language is a difficult tool to work with. Two of the hardest words in the language to rhyme are *life* and *love*. Of all words! In Italian, easy. But not English. Making lyrics feel natural, sit on music in such a way that you don't feel the effort of the author, so that they shine and bubble and rise and fall, is very, very, very, very, very hard to do. Whereas, you can sit at the piano and just play, and feel you're making art."

Reflecting on my own labors, I said, "The *love* rhymes are *shove, above, dove, glove* and *of.* That's all we've got."

"*Live* isn't easy either," Steve said. "You have *give, sieve* and then you're in a lot of trouble."

Continuing the mutual commiseration, I said, "The English language has forty-two single-syllable sounds; French has twelve. That's why Molière was able to write those alexandrines, couplet after couplet, without ever straining for a rhyme."

"It's also about open vowel sounds. The Italians have it all over us because everything is *ahhhhhh*! Try to sing *me* on a high note. And *me* is a very useful word."

"Or *him*," I groaned.

"Exactly. Short *i*'s are terrible. Singers will tell you that their throats close up."

We moved from words to music when I offered, "I've heard you say that you don't want to work at the piano."

"If you're too good a piano player, as some composers are, the music may become flavorless and glib," Steve responded. "And if you're not a very good pianist, your fingers limit you to the same patterns." He volunteered that he had "a very good right hand, but a left hand like a ham hock. If you force yourself away from the piano, you come up with more inventive things. I force myself to write in different keys that I haven't written in for a while. For me—and I find it's true of most composers—the sharp keys are the enemy and the flat keys are the friends. Flat keys somehow are more welcoming. But I force myself, quite often, to write in sharp keys—just to get away from the pattern. I think it's very important to try to write away from the piano."

That night, in addition to an invaluable lesson in the nuts and bolts of writing for the musical theater, Steve's songs were performed on our stage to illustrate the points he was making. It's fitting that the Sondheim lesson end with an example of what happens when everything goes resoundingly right. In *A Little Night Music*, the world-weary courtesan Madame Armfeldt laments,

> *In a world where the kings are employers,*
> *Where the amateur prevails and delicacy fails to pay,*
> *In a world where the princes are lawyers,*
> *What can one expect, except to recollect*
> *Liaisons.*

One of her recollections leads her into a summation of her philosophy and, I suspect, Steve's.

> *At the palace of the Duke of Ferrara,*
> *Who was prematurely deaf, but a dear . . . ,*
> *At the palace of the Duke of Ferrara,*
> *I acquired some position,*
> *Plus a tiny Titian. . . .*

> *Liaisons! What happened to them,*
> *Liaisons today?*
> *To see them—indiscriminate*
> *Women, it*
> *Pains me more than I can say.*
> *The lack of taste that they display.*
> *Where is style?*
> *Where is skill?*
> *Where is forethought?*
> *Where's discretion of the heart?*
> *Where's passion in the art?*
> *Where's craft?*

The delicate plosive tympani of the *p* and *t*'s in "Plus a tiny Titian," and the sly antepenult rhyme in "indiscriminate/Women, it" would be sufficient to qualify the song for theatrical art-song immortality, but when one adds to it what Madame Armfeldt—and Steve—are saying and feeling (in an ingeniously inverted double entendre, not progressing from the standard apparent innocence to sexual innuendo, but moving in the opposite direction, from the art of sex to art itself), and the natural, conversational ease with which it is expressed—all of it floating on the music of a bewitching waltz (in a score written, like *Der Rosenkavalier,* entirely in 3/4 and 6/8)—the magnitude of Steve's achievement becomes, in my opinion, inescapable. I think that history will record that Sondheim has spent his creative years in a realm that is beyond the reach of any of his contemporaries; and our students, in the first semester of their three years with us, were privileged to spend an evening in that realm with him.

For me, the most remarkable thing about these craft forums is that they are ineradicable: The two hundred master's degree candidates the public sees in that audience will carry with them for the rest of their lives the four or five hours they have spent with each of the forty to fifty artists who have come to teach them during their three years with us. In an effort to thank our guests, I have written, "Your seminar will play an active role in two hundred personal and professional lives. Assuming that these students have forty working years ahead of them, forty years times two hundred lives comes collectively to eight thousand years during which this information can be processed and used. I think that's a very substantial contribution, not just to our students but, if fortune smiles, to what they'll offer the world."

That is not hyperbole: It is a mere statistic.

—

If Paul Newman did us the inestimable service of validating *Inside the Actors Studio* for everyone who elected to follow him, and Stephen Sondheim lent it credibility, Sally Field gave it a unique and, it turned out, permanent style.

The reader of these pages has already encountered her uninhibited description of a battle with Lee Strasberg. When I asked her for her favorite curse word—bearing in mind that Paul Newman had dodged the question with "I have such a wealth of them, I really don't want to discriminate," and Alec Baldwin's curse word had been the inoffensive *ass-bag*—I expected a no less sanitized answer. Instead, she doubled her little fists, beat them on the arms of her chair and, as if liberated from an exceptionally strict girls' school, hollered, *"Motherfucker!!!"*

She had set the bar, and everyone who followed had to meet her high standard.

She also set the bar for candor, withholding nothing from our students and our television audience. With both Paul and Alec, my first questions addressed them as adults, beginning their careers, but Sally elected to double back, describing the frightening physical challenges her father, a stuntman and, briefly, a Hollywood Tarzan, had leveled at her, which evoked for me what I thought was an innocent question about retreating from the pressure into her room.

The floodgates opened. "This is all going to get very dark here. My career was so difficult; so much of it was a very hard struggle. A wall would be placed in front of me periodically, and it was only my anger that broke through it. I realized as life went on that I wasn't just an angry little person; I was *furious,* I was so deeply angry. And the more I could become in touch with how furious I was, the more it could drive me forward. Instead of colors that are conceived of as dark, you know, sad or angry, they would be colors that would move me. Mostly, I think, it drove me into places that I would have been frightened to go to. I was very shy, and it just gave me an attitude: I didn't care. I *had* to get in there! And so I always felt that it was my anger, that friend, that had carried me places I wouldn't have gone otherwise."

Our jolted students were listening, openmouthed, to the demure Flying Nun with whom they'd grown up.

She wasn't finished. In the classroom, a student, clearly worried by Sally's description of the nude scenes she'd played on-screen, said, "Hi, my name is Michelle. My question regards nudity—the burden that the industry puts on women. I was told that was the reality of the business. Do you think that's true?"

"I don't really know whether it is or not," Sally said. "They haven't asked me to take my clothes off for quite some time. But you know what? I have to tell you honestly, what difference does it make? That's what I feel. It's all about the work. If it's a piece of garbage, don't do it. But who cares? *Who cares?* It's one thing if it's a porno film and there's, like, you know, insertion of some form." The class roared. "Then you have a moral question. But I personally don't know what the big deal is about taking your clothes off. I wish somebody had asked me to take my clothes off."

A young man yelled, "Take your clothes off!" and Sally grabbed the bottom of her sweater and pulled it up to her chest. As the tumult grew, she said, "Now, *that* was the *old* Actors Studio days. And if it *had* been, I *would* have. And there would probably be three or four of you out there that would be nude already."

The students had been through our routine university orientation: Now they were undergoing a much more realistic one.

A moment later, a student said, "Hi, my name is Liz Sherman. Upstairs you were talking about, when you first get a script for a movie, you begin to hurt yourself. Were you talking about emotional memory work?"

"Yeah. Emotional memory work and all sorts of tools I've invented, myself, that if I told Lee about now, he'd probably yell at me again. Before I even begin the work, if I'm going to do a drama, I have little tools I've taught myself to use to sort of raw myself up. I just feel myself taking little razor blades to my insides, and it hurts like hell. It isn't focused on any particular place; it isn't sad, or angry. It's just gonna be available and it's gonna be right on the surface, and it's gonna be painful—and I wish I didn't have to do it.

"Now I know enough to hold back at rehearsal time. Don't go in certain areas that are gonna be raw; don't go for 'em until the 'now,' that very 'now,' 'cause in film that 'now' is, like, once. It's not take twelve. I don't care what Dustin Hoffman says. It's not take four hundred and fifty. It's a 'now'; it just happens once, usually, and that's what you're looking for—some instinct, some third eye I have, because I've worked in front of a camera for so long. I feel the set's starting to get ready. I'm coming to the set and I feel the raw parts start to bleed, where I haven't even asked it to, it's just time, it's time, it's time . . . and then my hands start to shake and I don't know exactly where I'm gonna go. I just know that whatever happens, I'm available."

Hamilton Oliveira, a wonderfully eccentric student from Brazil (who is today a member of the Actors Studio), picked up on Sally's grim theme: "I understand plenty about what you say about hurting yourself, 'cause I do the same thing to myself. If I'm doing a scene, a little exercise or whatever it is, I start hurting myself. And I hurt myself during my sleep and I wake up hurting myself and I go to sleep hurting myself, but it seems to me that's the only way I can live."

He stopped, choked by tears, and Sally said, "I don't think there's anyone in here who doesn't understand how much it hurts, and how much you want. And you know what? That will never, ever, ever go away. And don't look for it to go away. And if it goes away, then become a cabdriver. I mean it seriously. Because that hurt is what will drive you on. And hope there's something behind the hurt. If you cry and cry and cry, there's something else behind the hurt that's more productive, that'll move you further. The hurt's just the easiest one for you, for whatever reason. Some people get angry easier than they hurt. But you hurt easier. And you'll just keep hurting. That's all. And someday you'll get paid for it. And that will hurt because it won't be enough."

The class Sally had brought to helpless tears dissolved into helpless laughter—and Sally had given *Inside the Actors Studio* a threshold every subsequent guest would have to step up to and over. From the Sally Field episode onward, there was a standard of deportment that precluded "performance." What our students expected—and got—was the person unadorned, with nothing to sell, nothing to gain and, everyone finally realized, nothing to lose. These students had chosen to risk their lives in a precarious profession: They deserved nothing less than the unvarnished truth, and that, for thirteen years, is what our guests have given them.

Even if some of the shier guests arrived with a protective persona—or at the least a patina—the atmosphere of the classroom, and the tradition that Sally established, quickly made it anomalous—and unnecessary—and any pose was abandoned in the interest of an honest exchange with a trusting and vulnerable audience.

The students also shaped the show—with their commitment. Other audiences our guests faced, in various circumstances, came to be entertained: Our audience came to learn and even to emulate—a sobering responsibility for the artists on our stage. "Acting" in front of this audience was out; just being in the moment was in. And Paul, Alec, Stephen and Sally led the way.

Our first episodes began airing in April of 1995, and in October 1995, Bravo invited us to a meeting to open negotiations for a two-year extension of the series beyond the period covered by our first contract. The Bravo executive opened the meeting by putting the network's cards on the table. "It may not be a very smart negotiating position, but we'd like to tell you that you've defined Bravo. *Inside the Actors Studio* is our signature show." He paused, then added, "How shall I put it? You are to Bravo what *Beavis and Butthead* are to MTV," which I took to be a compliment.

The detailed negotiations, like all such television transactions, moved glacially through the next few months; and then, in March 1996, the network called to ask for a meeting at my home with a woman who had conducted focus-group research on *Inside the Actors Studio* for the network.

On March 19, the focus-group person, whose name I omit to protect the innocent—not her, us—arrived with a sizable contingent of Bravo executives. The atmosphere was cordial as I was placed in front of my television set. The Holly Hunter episode was put into my VCR and a printout of the focus group's reactions to every moment of it was laid across my lap like an accordion-folded electrocardiogram.

The Bravo executives spread out around the room, a little uncomfortably I thought, as the focus-group person took a chair next to me, smiled amiably, and began interpreting the printout as the videotape rolled in front of us. "You see?" she said amiably, tapping the printout. "The focus group doesn't like all this talk about 'craft.'"

It was a moment before I could reply; then I summoned, "But our guests do. That's why they come to us. A number of them have said so publicly."

One of the Bravo executives pointed toward the unfolding readout. "But according to the focus group, that's not why the *viewers* come."

I turned to him. "Does the focus group think the viewers will show up if the stars don't? How will the network feel about that?"

"Why don't we look at the rest of the research," one of the network people suggested diplomatically.

In the next few minutes, every one of the show's pillars was toppled: no "craft talk," no directors in the guest chair, no writers—and above all, no students on the screen!

"How do we do that?" I asked. "We're in a school."

"You don't have to *say* it's a school. It could be *anywhere*." The researcher looked pleased with the ingenuity of her proposal.

"But what happens when the students and the guest get together in the classroom after the interview?"

"Oh, *no classroom!*" the researcher proclaimed.

I looked at the Bravo executives, who stared impassively back. The researcher leaned close and whispered cozily, "Why don't you just cut it?"

At that point, on the TV in front of us, I began asking Holly the Pivot Questionnaire and the researcher dug a rigid finger into the printout with such force that it almost punched through to my thigh. "They definitely didn't like *that!*"

For a long moment the only sound in the room was Holly answering the contemned questions. I broke the silence with "So, you're saying—"

The researcher raised her hands defensively. "*I* don't say *anything*, Mr. Lipton. The focus group does the talking."

"Right. So, the focus group says, no craft, no school, no students, no classroom, no writers, no directors and no Pivot Questionnaire."

"Right!" the group exclaimed in chorus, relieved that I was getting the message.

"What's left?" I asked, fighting a wave of bone-deep weariness.

Clearly, this was the moment the researcher had been waiting for. She sprang into action. "They want fast, funny anecdotes and film clips."

I waited, then essayed, "Anything else?" She shook her head. "But that's what they get on all the other shows," I said.

She beamed. "Exactly!"

"Then why would they bother to watch *us*?"

Her smile remained firmly in place. "I don't offer opinions, Mr. Lipton. I simply lay out the facts."

In a distant, unforgotten past, my editor in chief sat literally and figuratively upright in the *Detroit Times* city room, clad in hat, overcoat and marmoreal rectitude, mutely, immutably pointing the only way.

I turned off the VCR.

"But there's more," the researcher said.

"No, there isn't." I stood up and looked at the network group. "Thanks for coming."

There was an awkward exit, and I called my colleagues on the Studio's governing executive committee to explain that what I had just done virtually guaranteed that *Inside the Actors Studio* wouldn't be renewed. The series provided the Studio with essential revenue, and it certainly played an important part in my life, but to the Studio's credit, the committee agreed to forefeit the income rather than permit the confiscation of its name by an anonymous vox populi recruited, as such creative collaborators often were, in a shopping mall.

As dean of the Actors Studio Drama School, I also met with the president of The New School, Jonathan Fanton, and told him that the Studio and I were walking away from what had turned into one of the university's most valuable assets, attracting students not only to our school but to all the divisions of the university.

"There's no room for compromise?" Jonathan asked, his voice tinged with rue.

"Sure, if I scuttle the students and the school. But if they go, I go."

He stood up, came around his desk and shook my hand.

In the ensuing weeks, there were sporadic approaches by the network, always sticking resolutely to the findings of the focus group. And, as resolutely, I stuck to the other lesson I'd brought with me from the city room: The most potent word in the English language is *no*. By the end of the summer, with a new season looming, and immediate commitments that had to be made to our guests, our subscribers and our students, we faced the fact that *Inside the Actors Studio* was extinct.

Enter one of this narrative's heroes, Charles F. "Chuck" Dolan, a visionary entrepreneur who had founded HBO, then, when he sold it to Time, Inc., created one of the country's largest cable systems, Cablevision, which owned Madison Square Garden with its teams, the Knicks and Rangers, and three cable networks, American Movie Classics, SportsChannel and Bravo.

Chuck Dolan's daughter, Debbie, was one of the country's top riders, which meant that every year, in the first week of September, he and his family cheered her on from a table in the Grand Prix tent at the Hampton Classic. In 1995, Kedakai and I were assigned a table near the Dolans, to which we invited the choreographer/director Pat Birch and her husband, Bill Becker, an Eliot House classmate of George Plimpton's at Harvard who, like George, had headed for Europe on graduation, to Oxford in Bill's case, where he earned a Ph.D. with a dissertation on the plays of W. B. Yeats. Bill had returned to America to assume the presidency of Janus Films, which provided all the networks, including HBO when Dolan was there, with the work of the great French, English, Italian and Swedish filmmakers.

When Bill and Dolan spotted each other, they jumped up for an enthusiastic reunion. Bill looked back at me and said, "Of course, you know Chuck." When he realized we'd never encountered each other, he said, "Chuck, you two ought to meet. You have a mutual interest."

"Oh? What's that?"

"Inside the Actors Studio."

Dolan's face lit up, and as I rose to shake his hand, he said, "Isn't that show amazing? This guy sits there with these cards and he knows everything. There's nobody like him on any other network. Do you know him?"

On this hot, sunny day at the Classic, I was wearing a T-shirt and jeans, a baseball cap and sunglasses. As Dolan spoke, I took off the cap and glasses. He slowed, then veered. "That's you?"

"Yes."

The Dolan family and Kedakai and I spent the rest of the Classic week together at our adjoining tables, rooting for Debbie, who won the Grand Prix. In the course of the week, we discovered that, in addition to *Inside the Actors Studio,* we shared two passions, jumping horses and flying airplanes; and when the Classic came to a close, Chuck promised to come to a taping of the show.

A year later, in September 1996, on Grand Prix Day at the Classic, we greeted each other, and he apologized for not having been able to attend any of our tapings during the previous season. "But you can bet we will *this* year," he said.

"Afraid not," I said. With no option but the unpleasant facts, I told him that the negotiations had broken off, and the show was effectively canceled. As he stared at me in undisguised dismay, the competition began in the ring, and he said, "I'll call you tomorrow."

Early the next day, my phone rang, and after I'd given Dolan a brief account of the impasse, he asked me to put the details in a letter and messenger it to him, which I did that afternoon. At midday the next day, I got a call from one of the Bravo executives who had attended the March 19 meeting. "I want you to understand one thing," he said. "I had nothing to do with that focus-group stuff!"

That afternoon, our lawyer got a call from Bravo's lawyer, and in short order a revised, unobjectionable contract (that would prove to be of lasting benefit to both parties) was on his desk. I never saw the focus-group person again, but Frances Berwick, whom I had met for the first time at that meeting in my living room when she was newly arrived from England, became the network's liaison to the show and its most consistent and valuable supporter during the decade that followed that perilous moment.

In February 2000, Chuck and Helen Dolan attended the Harrison Ford taping, and a few days later, I got a letter from him that concluded, "We are never so proud of Bravo as when *Actors Studio* is on."

Whatever *Inside the Actors Studio* is, whatever it has achieved, whatever its virtues and faults, it is an inarguable fact that none of it would exist if Chuck Dolan hadn't mounted up (maybe it was one of Debbie's horses) and ridden to its rescue.

———

When we began the series, I worried that, since we would be working within if not a narrow, at least a confined compass, the episodes might in time become repetitious. I've never heard a complaint, from our guests or our audience, that it happened, and as the years went by, I realized why: Since my goal was to try, at least, to gain a glimpse of each soul in that chair opposite me, and since it's safe to say that no two souls on this earth are identical, we have been faced with an infinite spectrum of being, belief and behavior.

That said, if no two people are alike, some are certainly more *unlike* the rest of the species than others. I believe that Christopher Walken, a longtime member of the Studio, and one of our second-year guests, stands near the top of that list. He is, for want of a better label, a genuine exotic.

When I asked him to explain this perception of him, he replied offhandedly, "I come from the country of Show Business. I grew up in dressing rooms in musicals, with gypsies, you know. Wild, crazy time. Great. Great."

"When you graduated from Professional Children's School, who handed you your diploma?"

"Gypsy Rose Lee. Her son was in my class."

A clue to Chris's elusive quality emerged when I asked him about his approach to the soliloquies in his portrayal of Iago. "To whom are you speaking?"

"This is very good. I mean to talk about it because I think that everything I do in the theater is influenced by my beginning in musical theater. I've always felt that at the end of the cast list of any play, the last character on the list ought to be the audience, because the audience is a palpable presence in the play. I've always felt that way, and in musicals I guess I got accustomed to it. My relationship to the audience is just as real as my relationship with anybody I'm talking to on the stage. If it's in a play or *Saturday Night Live* or whatever, the audience is there."

"Do you think of yourself then as a 'performer'?"

"Yeah."

"To you, it's an honorable word."

"Absolutely."

As with every Studio member who came to our stage, I asked Chris how he got into the Studio. His reply evolved into a valuable acting lesson.

"I was a kind of apprentice there for a long time. I would go there and do whatever they wanted me to do. I'd help them as a stagehand. I'd do little parts in scenes. I think I must have been doing that for ten years. Then, I auditioned and got in. I may have gotten in just because they were so used to having me around.

"In session once, I was doing a scene from *Death of a Salesman,* and in the middle of it, somebody in the back dropped a huge box of dishes. Made a big crash. And afterwards, Strasberg said, 'Well, that was okay, but somebody dropped a big box of dishes during your scene.' I said, 'Yes, I know.' And he said, 'Well, you didn't even blink.' And I said, 'Well, yes, I was concentrating.' He said, 'You can't do that. That's bad acting. You can't ignore life. Everybody in the room jumped and you looked as though it didn't happen.'

"That really stuck with me. It was very valuable, particularly when I came to do movies, because there's always that element of life interfering with you. I'm playing a scene with you and a glass gets knocked over and we both go to pick it up, and the dialogue suddenly comes alive and it seems real. It's just like life. That's what he meant, and he was right. It was a great lesson."

"How much of Chris Walken is in every role you play?"

"Everything. I can't imagine being somebody else. And anything I play, my reference is completely from the planet Show Business. I don't know anything about anybody else. People I've known all my life, my family, my brothers, I don't know. I only know me."

I made a final attempt to pin down Chris's unique persona. "You've spoken of the advantage of being a 'Chris Walken type.'"

"There's a certain kind of part—it's sort of my specialty."

"In other words, if they want a Chris Walken type . . ."

"Not too many places you can go." His furtive smile flickered. "I'm sure the 'villain thing' has something to do with what I look like. What I sound like. The fact that I've been in show business all my life, you know, I have that stamped on me. I think 'strangeness' can easily equate, by way of the camera, with 'menacing.' I think that's all it is." Chris, the students and I settled for strangeness.

In the greenroom before the taping, the subject of boxing had come up, and when I discovered that Chris was an avid fight fan, I volunteered to arrange an evening at Madison Square Garden, since Cablevision owned both the Garden and Bravo. The next big fight night found Chris, George Plimpton and me in the Garden's box. George's unmistakable figure always attracted attention, but on this night, with Chris seated in the box, too, the crowd's awareness increased exponentially. Clearly, a "Walken sighting" was worth two of George and several thousand of me.

After the fight, we repaired to the Garden's VIP suite for a few minutes to let the crowd disperse. George ordered his customary Dewar's, and by the time we arrived at the corner of Eighth Avenue and Thirty-first, the streets were nearly empty. As we peered down Eighth for a taxi, our view was abruptly blocked by an encircling ring of young black men who stared at us in silence. George, Chris and I glanced at one another, then turned back to the impenetrable circle, waiting for whatever fate had in store. After a moment, one of the group pushed into the circle to belly up to Chris. His face inches from Chris's, he said, "Man—you are the coolest white man in America."

As he stepped back, and the ring opened politely to let us hail a cruising cab, I muttered to Chris, "That may be the best compliment you'll ever hear."

Nathan Lane inaugurated our third year with an *Inside the Actors Studio* first. When I asked him, "Is there anger in comedy?" he replied, "Anger! Oh, a huge amount of anger! I've got a steamer trunk with the rage that I feel!"

"Are you being serious?"

"Oh, absolutely! *Most* of humor is based on anger. I'm a very angry little man." Over the students' delighted laughter, he allied himself with another short person. "Look at Napoleon. Why do you think he did all that stuff?"

"He was hilarious," I volunteered.

"Oh, he was a funny guy." Nathan stuck a hand into his jacket. "When his hand was in here, he pulled out a big pig bladder and hit people over the head with it. He *invented* that."

I persisted obtusely. "Are we being serious or are we joking?"

"Wait!" Nathan declared. "Can I have some water?"

Reaching for the pitcher always at the ready on a small table next to me, I filled a glass and handed it to him. Clutching it, he said, "I remember when they said, 'Napoleon, we're sending you to Elba.'" Taking a long sip of water, he bellowed, "'*Elba!!!*'" and water sprayed across the stage, my desk, my cards, me and the first two rows of the audience.

Mopping my cards with a hastily produced tissue, I exclaimed, "And I poured that water! What an idiot I am!"

Daintily flicking water from his vest, Nathan asked, "Am I the first person from the Actors Studio to do a spit take? The Danny Thomas spit take?"

He was, and it is one of the most celebrated and widely appreciated moments in the history of the show—though it became known as the Nathan Lane spit take, a term of art not previously part of the Stanislavski lexicon.

That night, I made a final, feeble attempt to snatch academic order from the students' riotous response: "So—seriously, *is* there?"

"Anger?"

"In comedy, yes."

"Absolutely! I'm telling you, that's one emotion I'm truly in touch with. I'm angry about everything. I'm angry 'cause I'm short. I'm not a tall, blond, Scandinavian person—I'm *very* angry about *that*."

On *Inside the Actors Studio,* the lessons have come in all sizes and varieties. But they show up often at the most unexpected moments. Our students and our audience have learned to keep their eyes and ears open, despite the dire predictions of the researcher and her focus group—who, if they chose to stick around after Chuck Dolan pulled us back from the precipice, may have found Nathan both entertaining and enlightening.

I'd met Christopher Reeve in the equestrian world, and when I heard that one of the limited number of pleasures available to him in the difficult new world in which he was immured was watching *Inside the Actors Studio,* I reached out to him and he responded enthusiastically, sending word that, whatever it took to get him to our stage, he would be there.

It was far easier said than done, since it meant transporting him and his respirator-equipped wheelchair from his Westchester home to the university on West Twelfth Street, then raising the chair and him to our stage with a forklift. In addition, his team explained to me that one of the reasons he ventured out of his home so infrequently was the pack of paparazzi stalking his every move: Chris was determined that they would get no pictures of him being carried, an inert object in his wheelchair, from house to van or from the van to his destination. An even greater concern, I was told, was that the paparazzi might get a picture of him going into spasm, an uncontrolled, and uncontrollable, effect of the paralysis that looked, my informant said grimly, like electrocution.

On the night of the taping, we'd acquired the forklift and arranged for Twelfth Street to be closed to traffic. The university's security was keeping the baying paparazzi at bay a block away, and we had erected curtains around the front of the school, so that Chris's van could be backed up to the theater entrance, and the wheelchair lifted out of it in complete privacy.

The plan proceeded like clockwork, and Chris arrived in the greenroom without incident. He was accompanied by a team of four, one of whom was his wife, Dana, an actress and singer of ethereal beauty and selfless devotion. Chris sat in his wheelchair, his hands flat on the arms as if pasted there, the breathing tube in his neck, the respirator soughing behind him, and an absolutely beatific smile on his face. We reminisced about the fabled East Hampton Artists/Writers charity softball game in which, one year, I'd played my usual lackluster game at second base and he'd been voted MVP. Then Dana said, "Chris has been spasming a lot today."

I turned to her for more, but she was silent. At a loss, I said, "Look, we don't have to go ahead with this. . . ."

"Yes, we do!" It was Chris behind me, every syllable riding emphatically on the respirator's exhalation.

I stood between Chris and Dana, in a no-man's-land of ignorance. Finally, I suggested, "If something happens, we can close the curtains."

"No." Chris again, smiling, firm.

Since he could turn his head only five degrees to right or left, I moved in front of him, still trying to understand what I apparently needed to understand. "Okay . . . before we begin, I'll explain to the audience that something *might* happen. . . ."

"No." Calm. Very firm.

I looked at Dana, out of ideas. She smiled. "If anything happens, we'll handle it."

"Okay. Fine. If you're comfortable . . ."

"I'm comfortable"—Chris's voice sighed on its airy current—"and very happy to be here."

The interview went with surprising ease. Since Chris could speak only on the respirator's exhalation, he was able to gather his thoughts during the machine's inhalation. The result was that he was one of the most articulate guests in the show's history. Before each edit, I'm provided with a transcript of the evening, prepared by mysterious but amazing trolls somewhere in Manhattan who spend their nights crowned with headphones, transcribing every word, every stumble, every *uh* and *er* exactly as it transpired onstage. I've been told, but don't know for certain, that most of these amanuenses are moonlighting actors, and that *Inside the Actors Studio* is the most coveted gig the transcription company offers.

When I began editing Chris's transcript, I was struck by the fact that he spoke in closely reasoned, gracefully expressed paragraphs, complete with semicolons, colons, independent, subordinate and relative clauses. I offer in evidence, and will rest my case with, his response when I asked him about one of the 150 plays he'd appeared in before turning into Superman, this one called *A Matter of Gravity*.

"Well, people say I acted with Katharine Hepburn. I acted *near* Katharine Hepburn. I adored her and still do. I played her grandson onstage and this translated to offstage as well. We went on the road for about seven months; and what I loved about her—I remember many things I'll cherish for a lifetime—but one thing was her stunning way of playing 'opposite.' She would laugh when you'd think she would cry, or cry when you'd think she would laugh. So, I never knew what was going to happen next. I think all the great actors are like that: Gene Hackman, Vanessa Redgrave, you never know what's going to happen next. And it's always *right.* I think that that danger, that risk, is what makes them so fascinating to watch and be with."

Because this was Chris's first public appearance since the accident, I'd asked him in the greenroom whether he wanted to put any time restrictions on the evening, and clearly exhilarated by this return to a stage, he insisted there be none.

About ninety minutes into the interview, it happened. There were no signs; there was no slowing down, no verbal hesitation; Chris simply glanced at me sidelong—the only way he *could* look at me—and then his entire body convulsed. His legs kicked violently off the footrest, his arms flailed against their restraint, his head toppled forward from the headrest and, from where I sat, the breathing tube appeared to have popped out of his neck.

Throughout the interview, Dana and the support team had stood in the wings, watching, waiting, and now they sped to the wheelchair, moving in a striking display of perfectly coordinated order, surrounding him, shielding him from the audience, each of them addressing one of the assaults on his writhing body, with Dana in front of him, bending over him, tending to him, talking softly, steadily, to him, as the breathing tube was reinserted.

Because I had been forewarned, I didn't react as anyone normally would, but simply remained in place, obviously aware of the crisis, but watching it in a state of suspended animation that may have looked like equanimity to the shocked audience, but was one of the most difficult roles I'd ever attempted. Apparently it was a successful performance, because the students and subscribers, taking their cue from me, maintained a benumbed calm after an initial horrified gasp.

What got them—and me—through the experience was the next stunning development. As the team around Chris continued their rapid, well-rehearsed drill, restraining and recapturing his flailing body, a voice issued from the theater's speakers. It was Chris, his wireless microphone still pinned to his shirt, his tube reinserted, his respirator providing him with the vocal wherewithal: "Well, well, well. What's going on here? A little problem. Nothing to worry about."

For two harrowing minutes, Chris kept everyone going with genial reports from the front, helping *us*, reassuring *us*, rescuing *us*. "Ooookay, looks like we're getting there. Won't be long now."

From my position next to him, I could see the urgency of the struggle as the team repositioned his head on its rest and taped the breathing tube to his neck, but the voice on the theater's speakers might have been describing an especially tranquil croquet match. "Juuust about there. Couple of seconds. Yep."

As the team stepped back, their vital mission accomplished, Dana and Chris, in profile to me, exchanged a gentle, lingering smile that was the most exquisitely romantic psychological gesture I have ever seen: Romeo and Juliet, young, in love and forever united. Then, Dana and the team returned to the wings, Chris turned his head five degrees toward me and said, "Now—where were we?"

And at that moment, I thought, but didn't say, "Mister, you *are* Superman."

The next morning, I found a knot of students outside my office door with no agenda other than their inability to shake what had happened the previous night and their need to talk about it—with one another, with me.

We went into a nearby classroom, and I tried to explain that they had witnessed something Chris had hoped no one but his family would ever see. "I think you should remember something for the rest of your lives. Chris didn't just share his life with you. He didn't just share his career with you—and his craft. He shared that spasm with you. So, someday, when you're in a play or a movie that you're *sure* is going to sink and take you down with it, and you don't know how you're going to get through it, I've got two words that'll put things back in perspective: Christopher Reeve."

Chris died seven years and eleven months later, before the research on which he was counting, and to which the Christopher Reeve Foundation has contributed nearly $100 million, could raise him and thousands of other men and women with spinal-cord injuries from their wheelchairs. And in an unthinkable twist of fate, Dana Reeve died a year and a half later of lung cancer.

Chris and Dana are many things to many people, but to me and two hundred students who were privileged to spend a few hours in their presence in November 1996, they are Romeo and Juliet, young, in love and forever united.

CHAPTER Twelve

❝ *I think if you want entertainment, you get a couple of hookers and an eight ball.*

—Sean Penn, *Inside the Actors Studio*

Firefighters watch *Inside the Actors Studio*. I can assert it categorically because every time I encounter them, they not only bring up the show, they discuss it in knowledgeable detail. I presume that's because, as firefighters hang around the fire station waiting to save our lives, they spend a fair amount of time in front of the television set.

Late one winter night, when Kedakai and I had left the garage where we park our car and were trudging toward our house, we passed four fire trucks lined up in the street as the crews packed their gear after dealing with whatever had summoned them. The exchange began with a familiar cry from the first truck: "Hey, Lipton, what's your favorite curse word?"

Alerted, the rest of the truck's crew turned and began hurling questions and comments: "Did you have any idea what Robin Williams was going to do next?" "The *Simpsons* show was the best! The whole house was on the floor!" "You think Kevin Costner could've played pro ball?" "What's your wife got against tattoos?"

The quiz continued from truck to truck, and finally, as we neared the end of the block, the firefighters gave the show a standing ovation that brought the street's startled residents to their windows.

One afternoon in December of 1996, the fire alarms went off at The New School for Social Research, and everyone, students, faculty and staff, was herded to the street, to wait, shivering in the bitter cold, for the firefighters to check the building out.

As we huddled across the street from the main building, my assistant pushed through the crowd to press a phone message into my hand. "Mike Nichols is trying to reach you." This antedated the cell-phone era, so I went to the phone booth on the corner and dialed the number on the slip of paper. "We were channel surfing last night," Mike said, "and all of a sudden, there you were with Steve Sondheim. It was extraordinary."

"Mike, I've been writing to you for two years."

"I know."

"Does this mean you're going to do the show?"

"I'm thinking about it."

I returned to the building just as word came that the firefighters had declared a false alarm, and a thoroughly chilled and surly mob surged toward the doors. As it arrived, the university's head of security apologized for the long wait, explaining that, once their job was done, the firefighters had insisted on a tour of the auditorium where *Inside the Actors Studio* was shot.

On February 10, 1997, Mike Nichols came to our stage. He has already, for good reason, made several appearances in these pages, but there were some moments in that evening that can't go unrecorded. One began when I said, "For most of us, the Holocaust is a distant and incomprehensible horror. But I'm sure not for you. How many years did you live in Germany before you left?"

"Seven."

"I think that Adolf Hitler became chancellor when you were two."

"Sounds right."

"You came in 1939?"

"Mmm-hmm."

"I understand your mother was ill. She couldn't come with you and your brother?"

"She came a year later."

"In 1941?"

"Right. The *Bremen,* the boat I was on, was two weeks before the *St. Louis,* the boat that couldn't land anywhere and got sent back."

"Do you ever reflect on that?"

"Always. I feel like this is all borrowed time. It's a strange thing—as time goes by, it's with me much more, rather than less. There were years, decades, that I didn't think about it. And then I did. And now I do almost all the time."

Since Mike had developed his comedic skills in an improvisational group, and since improvisation figures importantly in our curriculum, I asked him what took him back to Chicago after studying with Strasberg in New York.

"Well, I couldn't make a living of any kind. I'd run through all the sort of Howard Johnson type jobs, and, I was, not to put too fine a point on it, starving. And Paul Sills by that time, together with Elaine May and a few other people, had started Compass in Chicago, which was a cabaret, and he said, 'Why don't you come back and work with us?'"

"Did you adapt to improvisational theater quickly after Strasberg?"

"Slowly. All I did was cry for the first two months."

"Why?"

"Because that's what I had learned at Strasberg. I was very truthful, you know? They would come in and say, 'All right, get your hands up,' and I would say, 'Why are you pointing your finger at me?' Truthfulness is not what you're looking for when you're improvising comedy."

"But in speaking of the Compass, you've used a very Stanislavskian term: You've spoken of learning to find the spine of a scene."

"Well, when you're making up a scene for people who've got a lot of beers in their hands, you learn, in a painful and memorable way, what an audience expects. The first thing coming at you is the unspoken 'Why are you telling me this?' It's very powerful. And you'd better have a good answer. Now, interestingly, 'Because it's funny' is a good answer. But if that *isn't* your answer, get another one and make sure it's strong and clear or you're gonna be this schmuck sitting up there trying to think of the next line. That pressure turned out to be fantastically useful and educational, because slowly it teaches you what a scene is; it teaches you that, if we're doing an improvisation and you say black, I'd better say white."

"Back to Aristotle. Conflict."

"Exactly. Create a conflict as soon as you can. Elaine had a motto: When in doubt, seduce. Which is a very good motto. Though you're better off if you're a man and woman onstage. But still, it's a very good thing to fall back on. You've got to make something happen. Jokes aren't going to do it. You've got to create a situation. There has to be something you want, and the other person has to oppose it. And slowly into your blood are absorbed these primal rules of drama because you've got to do it or you're making a fool of yourself onstage."

As hard as it may be to believe, I turned Julia Roberts down when she asked to be on *Inside the Actors Studio*. Not because I wasn't more than eager to sit three feet away from her for a few hours, but because, by the time she'd made the request in the fall of 1996, all of our slots were taken. She waited—more patiently than the students and I—until February 24, 1997, when she strode on the stage to a riotous ovation.

In the past thirteen years, some of the most beautiful women on earth have graced our stage, and, for me, one of the revelations of this series is how self-effacing (literally) they are. When Julia spoke of her arrival in New York shortly after graduating from high school, I asked her, "Did you try some modeling?"

"To no success. I mean, it was horrible. I was not terribly attractive."

I assumed she'd misspoken or I'd misheard. "You weren't very interested."

She persisted. "I wasn't very attractive."

"Pardon me?"

Over a burst of laughter from the audience, Julia tried to set the record straight. "Well, I've sort of grown into my cuteness."

The only response I could muster was "I don't know what to say to that."

A few minutes later, when we were talking about Julia's first important role, in *Mystic Pizza,* I said, "In the credits they show pictures of young people who are presumably all of you at an earlier age. The young woman in glasses, is that you?"

"Mmm-hmm."

"That one was you?"

"Yeah, yeah. Why do you say it like that?"

"Because it looked like you, a little bit—"

"I told you I was not attractive. I had glasses—"

"Are we going to have to deal with this all evening?"

"I had buck teeth and the whole thing."

Aware that several hundred men in our audience and, I daresay, several women, were falling hopelessly in love with Julia, I came to her defense. "I thought you were very cute."

"Thank you," she said demurely—and patently unconvinced.

Moments later, the debate resumed as I recalled that shortly before joining the cast of *Steel Magnolias* as Sally Fields's doomed daughter, she had had a close brush with death. "You'd been swimming," I said.

"Did you call my mother?" Julia demanded.

"She said you were extremely attractive from the day you were born," I shot back.

"She *would*!" Julia retorted.

I turned for support to the students. "Isn't this something? I'm reassuring Julia Roberts."

"It's nice. I'm taking great comfort," she said, and sounded as if she meant it.

Over the years we've had a number of descriptions of the Woody Allen experience. Julia recounted hers in his musical film, *Everyone Says I Love You.*

"Well, first of all, he's *Woody Allen,* so you're completely nervous and just wanna die. And, of course, the first time I met him I was sick, so I was off to a good start 'cause he was like, 'Get away, Typhoid Mary!' But he's just the most sweet and charming man, and very specific. As a director, he does not mince words. It starts off, 'Do whatever you want, just say whatever you want, this is what I'm thinking: It goes from here, and we go around here. . . . ' It's really more about moves; he sort of tells you where he wants to you to move.

"He says, 'You know the story; just be somewhere in that general vicinity.' But, of course, he's Woody Allen. He's written this great script, so you're not gonna change a word of it. And all my scenes were with Woody, so can you imagine me just going off and saying whatever I want? As a person, he's very different. He's sweet and funny and, and . . . Woody Allen."

Her face darkened. "But as a director, he sort of terrified me. The very first day I *knew* I was gonna be fired. I was *horrible*. I was about to cry. I felt like I was seventeen years old and I was terrible. We're doing a scene, and we had camera problems and it was getting late, and I knew that Woody had a dinner reservation and he was hungry and we had to do this scene and it was just the two of us and it was this big camera move.

"And the camera finally gets it right, and Woody, he doesn't say, 'Cut'; he says, 'Okay.' He goes, 'Okay, the camera finally got it right, and I was okay, and you're terrible.'" Some of the students laughed and some of them recoiled empathetically. Julia continued, caught in the grim memory. "So, Woody says, 'Let's just go back to the beginning.' I was like, 'Oh! Oh! I was terrible!' I couldn't believe it. I mean, I *could* believe it, but he just, like, *said* it, just like that, like it was no big deal: 'You're terrible.' Oh, my Lord! So I go back to my start mark, shoulders shaking, trying to not be terrible."

By now all the students looked as stricken as she. "And I just proceeded to screw it up over and over again; I pronounced words wrong at that point—I was completely falling apart. And then by some miracle, the last take, *seconds* before his dinner reservation, it was great. It was! I mean, it just *went,* you could feel it, it was like a dance, it was fabulous. And he goes, like, 'Okay,' and leaves.

"So, I go home that night and I'm thinking, 'They're gonna deport me from this country. Woody is gonna have me carried out in the night.' So, the next day, I had to go to work, and there's this scene where I have to kiss him, and I thought, 'Oh, great! Now I'm gonna be a bad actor and I'm gonna be a bad kisser. He's totally gonna fire me. I was convinced of it. So, we do this scene and I'm all dressed up, and he comes up behind me and he knows all these secrets about me—"

"The character does," I interjected.

"I was just about to say that. The character. He knows that if you blow on this girl that I'm playing, if you blow on her shoulders, she becomes aroused. And so he comes up behind me at this party, and I have my back to him and I can hear him, and I want to laugh so bad 'cause I can hear him. . . . *Phhhht!*" Julia's legendary lips fluttered as they emitted a loud, moist gust.

She looked out at the students, rocking back and forth in their seats, drowning her out. "I know how funny it is, but I'm trying to be really straight-faced. So, I'm thinking, 'He's blowing on my shoulders; this is my fantasy for men to do this to me,' and I whip around, and I gather him up in my arms, and I'm also towering over him, so I'm looking down at this sweet face of Woody Allen, with his little glasses, and he's looking up at me, and he goes, 'You're hurting me.'" It was a perfect, plaintive Woody Allen whimper. "And I hadn't even kissed him yet!"

O n a pleasant night in April 1997, Billy Crystal gave our tiller a mighty push and sent us off in a new direction. From the moment he arrived on our stage, everything changed. Many of our previous guests had made us laugh, but Billy saw our stage—and especially our young, smart audience—as a bully comedy pulpit where he could bound back and forth between the moments of introspection for which the show was by then known and pure stand-up, on his feet at the edge of the stage, leaning convivially out over the rollicking audience.

Billy not only revised our tradition, he began a brand-new one that has become an *Inside the Actors Studio* staple. One of the vows I made when I created the show was that I would never ambush a guest. If my blue cards include a request for something outside the show's normal parameters, like dancing or singing or mimicry or re-creating a character, I obviate the possibility of embarrassing the guest in front of the audience by asking permission before we go onstage. In the greenroom with Billy, I asked him if I could interview some of his best-known characters. When he didn't respond immediately, I said, "It's okay. I'll understand if you don't want to. We'd be improvising—"

I stopped because he had raised a hand. "What the hell," he said, "you're from the Actors Studio. If they can't improv, who can? Let's give it a shot."

Onstage, I summoned the Latin lover Fernando whom Billy had created when he heard Fernando Lamas respond to Johnny Carson's "You look good" with "Well, you know, John, I would rather look good than feel good." In Billy's skilled hands, Fernando became a talk-show host whose trademark greeting to every guest was a sincerely insincere "Dahling, you look mahvelous!" When I asked Fernando about the three questions he asked guests like Mr. T and Hulk Hogan, Billy morphed into the silky Fernando to respond, "Where are you going for Passover?"

"Right," I said. "The second question is very appropriate for this group."

"Do you yearn to go back to your roots in the theater and direct?"

"And the third one?"

"What is your definition of love?" Fernando purred.

"Now, Fernando . . ."

"Yes, dahling . . ." He shifted gears. "Jim."

"Yes?"

"I got to tell you . . ."

An alarm bell sounded, and I tried to beat him to the punch with an awful truth. "I do not look mahvelous."

"No. Jim, dahling, you look . . . studious!" He poked a finger at my stack of blue cards, and the students cheered to see their dean one-upped.

Billy's description of Meg Ryan's orgasm scene in *When Harry Met Sally* was a highlight of his—or anyone's—evening with us.

"Meg was very nervous. You have thirty-five extras in Katz's Delicatessen, and you're going to have an orgasm all day—from a lot of different angles. She's a very shy person, and this is a difficult scene to do with the director's mother sitting right there."

"*Really?* Rob's mother?"

"Yeah. That's Estelle Reiner, sitting there, ready to tell the waiter, 'I'll have what she's having.'

"So, Meg's very tentative, and Rob is impatient with her. She tries it a couple of times, and Rob's going, 'No, no, no! Come on!' 'Cause we knew we had a great thing here, and she was holding back. He says, 'No, Meg! It's got to be like *this*!' And he sits down, and he has an enormous orgasm. I mean, he's pounding the table. Spice balls are flying off pastrami. Gherkins are becoming pickles!"

"Swelling," I volunteered.

Billy was receptive to the suggestion. "*Swelling!* It's just unbelievable." He hammered the arms of his chair. "Boom! Boom! Rob's a big guy and it's loud and he's screaming. Finally, when it's over, he pulls me aside, and goes, 'I just did something bad.' I said, 'No, that was great.' He says, 'No, you don't understand. I just had an orgasm in front of my mother.' "

In Billy's classroom session, when a student asked him whether he'd consider doing a one-man Broadway show, Billy answered prophetically, "Tonight was another convincer for me to get my ass into town and start doing what I set out to do, which is be funny in front of people. I know it sounds odd, but with the squeals and laughter tonight, I feel juiced up."

Two weeks after the taping, I got a call from Billy in the Czech Republic, where he was shooting his new movie, exulting, "I just called to tell you I'm still high from that night."

And on December 5, 2004, Kedakai and I were Billy's guests at the opening night of his Broadway one-man show *700 Sundays,* which went on to break the box-office record for a nonmusical and earn him a Tony. When Billy returned to our stage in 2007, and we recalled the student's question in 1997, he said, "It *did* start something," and described the show's genesis as a pursuit of "something like this, like *Inside the Actors Studio,*" first with Martin Short, then with David Steinberg, evolving finally into the solo show that opened on Broadway: an enterprise born, in my biased view, in our classroom.

Anthony Hopkins brought two worlds to our stage: the classical English tradition and an approach that can be described only as American—or Stanislavskian. That was one of the reasons I was so pleased when he accepted our invitation. Here was an actor who embodied—and united—in one highly regarded artist the two dominant approaches to our craft.

Describing his training in London, he said, "I went to RADA, the Royal Academy of Dramatic Art. I was a young student. There was a guy who'd trained with Stella Adler and a few others, and he wanted to go over to England to learn the English system. He left after about two terms, he couldn't stand it there; but I was so impressed by what he did, because he was such a detailed actor, he was so real. I used to hang out with him. We'd go and buy books, Boleslavsky's *The First Six Lessons,* and Bobby Lewis's book, *Method or Madness,* and Michael Chekhov's *To the Actor*—and then Stanislavski, *Building a Character* and *Creating a Role.*

"I was so fascinated by it. That's what I wanted to be. He used to come here, to the Actors Studio, and I used to ask him, 'What's it like there in the Actors Studio?' And he'd talk about people like Brando and Montgomery Clift. They were such talismans to me—so it's a great honor for me to actually be here tonight—thirty-six years later!"

The unique fusion of the two schools in him was evident as he talked about Olivier's counsel to him when he was a member of the National Theatre: "I've played Shakespeare, quite a lot of it, but I find it very difficult. I tend to break up the verse. Olivier was very helpful to me because he told me, 'Don't break it up. When you break it up, you break up the thought.' He said, 'Breaking up the verse, you break up the action. You break up the through line, the objective.' He used to say, 'The objective is *there*—in the speech.'"

For me, one of the pleasures of *Inside the Actors Studio* is the opportunity to compare the views of two guests, on two different occasions, describing the same event or person, their discrete views sometimes lending the show an intriguing *Rashomon* quality.

Tony Hopkins and Chris Reeve shared a valuable counselor. Tony encountered her when he made his movie debut in *The Lion in Winter.*

"I remember going on set—thirty years ago this month!—and my first scene was with Miss Hepburn. I don't get nervous. I think nerves are a waste of time. It's insecurity, kind of an excuse. But I was a little intimidated by Ms. Hepburn. We rehearsed the scene, and she said, 'Tell me, do you like the camera?' I said, 'What do you mean?' She said, 'The bread-and-butter machine, do you like it?'

"I said, 'Well, yeah,' and she said, 'Then, why the hell do you play the whole thing with the back of your head to it? You do that and I'll steal the scene from you. I'll probably do that anyway.'"

When Tony had arrived that night with Lois Smith, who was then a partner in the public relations firm PMK, Lois had advised me that, since Tony was booked on a very early flight to England the next morning, it was imperative that we finish as close to ten as possible. I assured her we would.

But as Tony conducted the student session with obvious relish, he studiously ignored Lois Smith waving at him from one side of the theater and me from the other.

The transcripts from which I do the paper edit of each episode of *Inside the Actors Studio* and the thousands of feet of videotape we've rolled in five and sometimes six cameras at each shoot contain identical time codes that enable us to locate every moment I've chosen when we get into the edit room. The code is time-of-day, so I can assert that at precisely fifty-seven minutes, forty-nine seconds and twenty-five frames past ten P.M., prompted by Lois's frantic signals, I stepped back to center stage to say, "Now, listen, this man's flying to England tomorrow. He's been very generous to us—"

"Oh, I'm okay," Tony interjected. "I'll answer the rest of the questions quickly." Across the theater, I saw Lois grab a pillar for support.

At 11:07:15 and seven frames, I stepped between Tony and the students, and Lois dashed out of the wings to take his arm and lead him firmly offstage. In the greenroom, as Tony wiped away his makeup, Lois and I made plans to get some childhood photos from his family home in Wales. When we'd exchanged the necessary data, we turned back toward the makeup mirror, and Lois gasped. Tony was gone—and excited voices from the theater alerted us to where he might be. We dashed back to the stage and, of course, there was Tony, out in the house, surrounded by the students, once again engaged in an animated exchange.

Lois turned to me in despair, and I spread my hands helplessly. Since the transcript, with its time codes, stops when the cameras do, I can't provide the precise moment of Tony's ultimate departure, but I can attest to the fact that

that night our students learned what it truly means to be an actor, and to love it with every particle of your being.

T he same might be said of the guest I introduced on February 9, 1998, with "The simple facts are simply staggering. Eight Academy Award nominations—more than anyone except Laurence Olivier and Spencer Tracy. Two Academy Awards for *Mister Roberts* and *Save the Tiger,* making him the first actor ever to win both Best Supporting and Best Actor Oscars. Twelve Golden Globe nominations. Three Golden Globe Awards for *Some Like It Hot, The Apartment* and *Avanti.* The Golden Globe Cecil B. DeMille Award. Two Cannes Film Festival Best Actor Awards for *The China Syndrome* and *Missing.* The Venice Film Festival Best Actor Award for *Glengarry Glen Ross.* The American Film Institute and Screen Actors Guild Life Achievement Awards."

That was what Jack Lemmon brought to our stage.

In interviews, I am invariably asked, "What's the most surprising thing that's ever happened on the show?" and this is my invariable answer: "I try to get my guests to say their most famous lines on our stage—for our students. I tried, and failed, to get Robert De Niro to say, 'You talkin' to me?' I succeeded in getting Tom Hanks to say, 'Life is like a box of chocolates.' There was a line I wanted Jack Lemmon to say when we were talking about *Days of Wine and Roses.*"

The exchange that followed from that provided us with the most surprising— and one of the most famous—moments in the history of the series. It began with my description of several of the gripping moments in the film. "The scene with the baby when you break down; the scene where you wreck the greenhouse, looking for the bottle; the straitjacket scene; the motel scene with Lee Remick; the scene on the table under straps—but for me, there's no moment that equals the one where he stands up in the AA meeting—with a simplicity that I commend to you all, every actor in this group—and says to them . . ."

I paused and turned to Jack. "The first lines at the AA meeting. Remember?"

I waited, hoping to hear them. With characteristic generosity, Jack responded. "Yeah. My name is . . . And I'm an alcoholic."

I looked at the students, gratified. "You see? As simple as that."

To my left, Jack continued, so quietly that it sounded as if he were speaking to himself: "Which I am, incidentally."

I turned back toward him. "Who?"

"Me."

I didn't want to misunderstand. "Are you talking as Clay now or . . ."

"No. As Jack Lemmon. I'm an alcoholic."

There followed the longest silence in the history of *Inside the Actors Studio.* We simply stared at each other, and the audience was immobile. When Jack sat back, electing to leave it at that, I moved on.

In the greenroom before the classroom session, Jack's wife, Felicia, told me, "That's the first time Jack's said it in public."

Jack provided our students with another unforgettable moment when he indicated me and said, "I was saying today, I hope he asks me what I think about acting. And what it means."

"That's what I'm doing."

"That's what you're doing," he spluttered, "and I'm trying to come up with an answer." The students laughed. "No," he said firmly. "I know exactly." He spoke of the work his daughter Courtney was doing with human rights organizations, distributing medicines around the world, and observed, "I think of how proud I am of what she does. And then I think, 'You, you schmuck, you're an actor—what're *you* doing?'"

He looked out at the students with an expression that seemed, oddly, as sad as glad. "But I'm wrong. I'm wrong. Because I had forgotten something. And a while ago, I realized it. It is a glorious profession. Not just a nice one. It is a *glorious* profession. And as Shakespeare put it, it is truly noble. The reason being that at some time or other—I know I've had chances; I don't know if I've been successful at it—at some time, every actor, all of us, are put in a position that very few people on the face of the earth are put in, where you can actually change somebody's life. You can move them and enlighten them, using the bricks the author laid—and make them think about something they never would have thought about before, if they had not seen that performance.

"Sure, you want the applause. And sure, I wanted all the kids at school to love what I was doing. That got me going. *But that's not what it's all about.* It's all about what happens to the *audience,* not to the actor."

‍

Susan Sarandon came to our stage with a body of work that included five Academy Award nominations and a Best Actress Oscar, but as usual when she faced a young audience, the film they were most eager to hear about was *The Rocky Horror Picture Show.*

"That's probably what's going to be in the time capsule," Susan moaned. "Of all the films, that'll be the one that lives the longest. Everybody's always trying to make me defensive about it, but I loved that film! You know," she added pensively, "my fantasy is, if anyone ever does assassinate me, it's going to be a parent who's had to drive their child at midnight to the mall. I get some of the worst letters, saying, 'I'm not going to give my daughter her allowance at college till she sends back those corsets!'"

When I asked Susan about the arresting opening scene in *Atlantic City* in which Burt Lancaster spied on her as she rubbed lemon on her breasts to get rid of the smell of fish, she said, "God knows how that fish smell ever got to my breasts. But, okay, it was a European thing. And it worked."

"It launches the movie," I said. "Everything happens because of that."

"I've often wished I'd rubbed something else on me," Susan said wistfully, "so people would stop sending me lemons. It should have been dollar bills, or some fabulous perfume that I would get for the rest of my life. Instead of lemons. I'm always finding lemons!"

When I asked Susan about the frequent demands for nudity in contemporary films, she said, "I don't like to make rules about what I will or won't do. Until *The Hunger,* I hadn't had one of those generic tumble-around-and-try-to-hide-behind-the-other-person's-body love scenes that are in a lot of movies. All the things I've done have been very specific, so that makes it easier. I've never been incredibly comfortable, just walking around naked.

"I think that nipples upstage you, anyway. No one's listening to anything you're saying for the first fifteen seconds. You know? So why would you do it? Right?"

The students responded with an ovation, and she resumed. "I don't know that it's so easy to be sexy, naked. What do you have to work with? For me, what's interesting about love scenes is what happens to lead up to the love scene, and what happens after the love scene. Everybody kind of knows what happens *during* the love scene."

The students gave her another enthusiastic hand.

As we discussed Susan's Academy Award–winning performance in *Dead Man Walking,* directed by Tim Robbins, I asked her, "Is it easier or harder to be directed by someone with whom you live?"

Susan, who is nothing if not frank, replied, "You know, I could talk about another director that I lived with."

"Are we naming names here?"

"Louis Malle. When you're living with a director, and you're working with that director, and six people have been giving that director problems, you know you're not going to be the one that's gonna walk. Tim and I had, I'd say honestly, maybe five pretty ugly days that had nothing to do with artistic differences. Now, I've had five really bad days on movies where I *wasn't* living with, or even sleeping with, the director. But Tim and I never blew up in front of everybody, and I knew that if we could get through it, we would be in an even better place than where we were."

Susan's refreshing candor had emerged earlier, when she described how Tim got his first important acting role as the rookie pitcher in *Bull Durham.*

"Kevin Costner could have been so competitive with Tim. The brilliant thing about that film is that everybody found their niche. I mean, Ron Shelton needed an asshole—across from Kevin Costner. And Tim's the *best* at being an asshole." She turned toward the students as they laughed. "Really. He's brilliant at that."

A few weeks later, when Tim was our guest, Susan showed up in our audience, seated with the students, and when the evening ended, I found her in the greenroom with him, challenging his choice of *pussy* as his favorite curse word. As I entered, she was insisting, "*Pussy* is *not* a curse word!"

"It's not *your* curse word," he riposted.

There followed a lengthy, spirited, civil semantic debate that failed to settle the matter, but did offer an insight into the chemistry of this charismatic couple.

In Susan's classroom session, when Coy Middlebrook, one of our directing students, asked for her definition of a good director, she replied, "I think everybody's got to be a grown-up. Come out of their trailers when they're supposed to, do their job, show up knowing what they're supposed to do. And I think the director has to be prepared, and a lot of times, directors aren't. It's like any profession: There're good ones and there're bad ones, and if a shoot goes smoothly, it doesn't necessarily mean the movie's any good."

She surveyed the students, then leaned closer, confiding, "This is one of life's little ironies. A terrible shoot can produce a good movie and an absolutely blissful shoot can make a boring movie. It's just like the orgasm, which is God's way of showing you He has a sense of humor."

B y the time Meryl Streep came to our stage, she had already broken an *Inside the Actors Studio* record: No actor had been spoken of more often or more reverentially by our guests than Meryl. Since I knew that our students were waiting eagerly for an insight—*any* insight—into her formidable gifts, and that she was famously cautious about discussing them, I elected to let Joseph Papp, who had launched her career at the New York Public Theater shortly after she received her MFA from the Yale Drama School, open the subject for us.

"Joe Papp said, 'There are very few people I would call pure actors. Meryl is one.' You said a few moments ago that sometimes you don't know how you get in 'that zone.' Can you define the zone?"

"Well . . . I'm not real articulate about this subject because it's like church for me, and to some part of me it's like approaching the altar. I feel like the more you talk about what it is, the more likely something will go away. I mean, there's a lot of superstition in it."

I remained silent, prepared to concede to her qualms, but abruptly she resumed. "But, I do know that when I'm in the zone I feel freer, less in control, more susceptible. Not completely!" she amended the statement, laughing. "I don't know; I'm always accused of being a technical actress and I think probably I'm the *least* technical actress in the world, in what people think of as 'technical,' because I really have no way of talking about what we're talking about.

"I mean, honestly, I come to each job with an open heart, trying to do my best, and with some connection to a character that I don't completely understand, but I know that she lives in me—and I don't question it, I *have* it, it's a thing that's undeniable, and I know I can't make a wrong move if I just hold on to what I know is true, knowing what I know is real for me—and *that's* what is real for me."

Liberated by her forthrightness, I suggested, "But it must start in you *somewhere.*"

"It starts in a word or a phrase in a script somebody sent you. It has to do with the day that you got it, whom you're mad at that day, whom you're in love with. It has to do with context and music and all sorts of things. You know?" She brightened, inspired. "It's like falling in love! You meet a character that way, and then you're connected."

A few minutes later, discussing *Silkwood,* in which Meryl was directed by Mike Nichols, I asked, "How did Mike work with you as a director?"

"Well, he said that everything that I did was right. No! He's—oh, God!— basically, he's very, very good at what he does because you don't realize that you're being manipulated, but you're being manipulated up the wazoo! You know what I mean?"

"Mm-hmm."

"So, I don't have any sense of how he shaped and molded me, but he did it in a nice way, not in a bullying way."

"Now, turning it around and looking at it from Mike's point of view, this is what Mike Nichols saw as he was seeing what you just saw: 'Directing Meryl Streep is much like falling in love: It has the characteristics of a time which you remember as magical and creative but which is shrouded in mystery.'"

These crossroads where force fields sometimes collide are, for me, among the paramount virtues of *Inside the Actors Studio.*

Later that evening, I said to Meryl, "I have a whole arsenal of fatuous questions, as many talk-show hosts do."

"Well, I have fatuous answers," she said, "so, fine."

"I'm going to spare you most of them. But, since more than fifty percent of our actors and directors and writers are women—"

"Really? Oh, good."

"—I *will* ask you for a word of advice to women who will be going into this profession, *from* a woman in this profession."

"I'm so encouraged that that's the proportion, because I think that's what we need. But it's hard. It's not hard to make the first movie. It's hard to make your second, third, and fourth—to sustain, to make what *you* think is important in the world and *they* feel might be marketable in the world. That's something I deal with all the time.

"Even though most of the people that go to the movies are women, and most of the people to whom advertisers skew their money on television are women, somehow woman-stuff in the movies is . . . well, let's say that the range of offerings is less than it could be. And I think that's a mystery. It's a very deep mystery, but maybe you'll be able to fix it.

"I think there's some great complicity that we all share in. It's a very deep thing. I don't think it has to do with marketing. I think it has more to do with where men and women are with each other right now than anything else. But you just have to do what you think is good, and keep slugging it out and trying." She sat back and stared at the students for a long moment, then glanced at me and sighed. "That's pathetic, isn't it?"

"No."

"But it's true." She turned back to the students. "You just have to keep your dream. If you lose it and get cynical, you die."

It will come as no surprise that Sean Penn began his evening with us by breaking a rule. A few minutes after arriving on our stage, he pulled out a pack of cigarettes and lit up, which was by this time prohibited in many public places, and was a flagrant violation of the university's stern policy—which is doubtless why the students gave Sean a lengthy ovation.

In the first years of *Inside the Actors Studio,* once I had stopped worrying that the show might become repetitious, I concentrated on ferreting out what it was that made each of our guests unique, and with Sean, as I had with Chris

Walken, I tried to locate the source of his novel and fascinating approach to his craft. I suspected we might find it in his training with the legendary teacher and member of the Studio, Peggy Feury, whose name had been brought up on our stage by Anjelica Huston and Billy Crystal.

When I asked Sean about his work with her, he said, "I had misgivings, frankly, about the notion of studying at all. I think somewhere in my mind I equated it with going to a therapist. I felt that there were instinctual things that might be tampered with. I had a high level of mistrust. So initially I went in with the idea of, Let me see what this is. And then Peggy had such an effect on me! I found out, really, how limited I was, with those instincts I'd prized so much."

"What was the routine there?"

"For the first year it was four days a week, five hours a day. And you would spend that much time away, with rehearsals of the scenes you were working on."

"I've read that you used an expression—maybe you got it from Peggy: the uncommon thought on the common matter."

"Mmm-hmm."

"What does that mean to you?"

"I can't quote this verbatim, but there's a poem by Charles Bukowski that I think articulates it fantastically. It's about a seven-year-old boy on a train. This man is sitting next to the boy, and the two of them are looking out the window at the Pacific Ocean. At a certain point, the little boy looks to the man and says, 'It's not beautiful.' And the man thinks, it's the first time he realized that he didn't find it beautiful either—that there was a conditioning that oceans are beautiful, and that he'd been looking out, thinking that's what he was seeing—until this little boy said, 'It's not beautiful.'

"I think that's the spirit of an uncommon thought on a common matter. It's somehow just breaking through all of that conditioning that doesn't always apply."

It's probably apparent that this account, like *Inside the Actors Studio*, is as revelatory of my biases as of my guests'. One of mine is a partiality for the uncommon thought, in Sean and any other actor. Nothing in a performance impresses me more than unpredictability. It was a central component of Brando's gift: We never knew what he was going to do next. There was no way to outguess him, so we simply surrendered to the unpredictability—and inevitability—of his choices.

The same is true of Sean Penn: Like Brando, he is a dangerous actor who constantly threatens our complacent expectations. And no matter how startling his choices, he somehow convinces us that they couldn't be otherwise.

His creative principles appear to be ruled by the same steely logic. A question I asked toward the end of the evening evoked one of the most often-quoted moments in the series' history. "In 1991, you made two important transitions. One was away from acting, and the other was to directing. It's easy to understand why a gifted actor would turn toward directing, but," I asked, "why would a singularly gifted actor, still very young, turn against acting?"

A look of pain flickered across Sean's face, and it was a moment before he replied. "I think as much as anything else it's bad luck. By bad luck I mean directors, scripts, things that made it an often agonizing process. I don't mind giving a lot to something, but I mind it not giving anything back. Something happened, I'm gonna guess around 1974, from when I was a filmgoer to when I later became a participant. Something happened in movies, which I think affected even the good filmmakers. The status quo had to do with a kind of 'impress the audience.' I didn't come up as an actor in a cinema of expression. I came up in a cinema of 'impress.' And I think that at a certain point I started to feel that I was staring at hotel room ceilings, wondering what I was doing with my life. Not diminishing what I felt I could do as an actor so much as whether there was any value in what you could work as an actor *in*.

"I've heard all the debates about films. You know? People very happily and proudly say, 'There's room for entertainment, strictly for its own sake.' I disagree with that. I think if you want entertainment, you get a couple of hookers and an eight ball."

He tried to continue, but was drowned out by an ovation that eclipsed the students' salute to his cigarette. When he could be heard again, he said, "Film is too powerful a medium to be just that. There's got to be some kind of human sharing in it, some kind of growth. There's got to be some kind of journey and risk taken, so that it's exciting not only for the audience but for the participants."

He had to stop again because the students were cheering.

Sean was, quite simply, one of the most poetic guests who ever came to our stage. Listen to him answer a writing student's question about Charles Bukowski's effect on him: "I think the thing that impressed me most about him was he was not 'irreverent.' He was 'without reverence.' After a hard night of sex and drinking, he was us before the shower, on the toilet, sick, tired, brokenhearted and on the way to work. He found poetry where nothing was necessary to heighten. You didn't have to create a world that started with Overture."

I remember, sitting on the sidelines as I always did during the classroom session, catching my breath when he said that—and holding it as he continued in a free-flight of poetry that Bukowski might have admired, and I envied.

"He was able to find poetry that's similar to what I think John Cassavetes did—that there's drama and poetry in people's lives—*as* we live them—that it's not necessary to heighten something, because heightening something, whether it's in literature or in the movies—*particularly* in the movies—is dangerous. Or destructive. 'Dangerous' maybe makes it too important. The idea is that you're exhilarated in the theater, but when you walk out and you feel more *alone,* then . . ."

He paused, his gaze narrowing, darkening. "Then, the director has crossed us. I don't think there's any room for a film like that, as entertaining as that might be. Even when we think back and want to excuse it—'Well, when I was a kid, I saw a movie like that and I loved it'—I think that we're less people than we would have been had we not seen it. And so that's what I love about the people that found poetry without creating a world we can't touch."

I n August of 1998, Sidney and Pytie Lumet invited Kedakai and me to see *There's Something About Mary* at the East Hampton Cinema. From May to September, the Hamptons are so awash in the privileged refuse of the teeming shores of Los Angeles and New York that, on any Friday night in August, the line outside the East Hampton Cinema can give the line on the red carpet at the Cannes Film Festival a run for its money.

Once inside the theater, since the Lumets had provided the tickets, I volunteered to join the end of the line that snaked back and forth around velvet ropes and stanchions at the refreshment stand. I was listening idly to the sound of trailers issuing from several theaters when I heard a voice from the head of the line say, "The morning after I saw you and Holly Hunter on your show, I called Holly and said, 'I learned more about you in that one hour than in all the time we've spent together.'"

I turned and found Steven Spielberg looking at me from the counter, as an attendant scurried about, delivering armfuls of popcorn bags to several trays in front of him.

Shameless when it comes to recruiting candidates for the show, I said, "I've been inviting you to *Inside the Actors Studio* since the day we opened our doors."

"I know," he said, "and I'd love to come."

We were calling across several tentacles of the line, and the usual lobby buzz had stilled as the refreshment customers listened to me say, "What's your schedule?"

"Let me take a look," he said, pulling a datebook out of his pocket.

As he leafed through it, I reflected on the fact that, if there is one thing more sacred than Friday night at the movies in East Hampton, it is the pop-corn line. Cutting into it or slowing it down is generally acknowledged to be the fastest route to Southampton Hospital—and we had stopped it cold. Since Steven's trays were full and the attendant was waiting for payment, one-third of the available counter space was effectively shut down, and it was time for the riot to break out.

But there wasn't a peep out of the line, which led me to suspect that as many as half of them either had, or hoped to have, projects on Spielberg's desk. We were as safe as a piglet at Passover.

"I've got to go to Europe to promote *Saving Private Ryan.* Can you get me in around Thanksgiving?"

Every head in the popcorn line swung to me. "We have two dates," I said, and there was a collective sigh of relief. "But I'm not sure what they are." The sigh petered out and the heads swiveled toward Steven.

"Call me," he said.

"Where?"

"I'll give you my private number."

As he and I heard the click of several ballpoints, Steven reached for one of those coupons that reward you with something you want if you'll invest in a sufficient number of high-priced snacks you don't want, wrote on it and leaned across the frozen line to hand it to me.

On Monday, I called the number on the coupon. A woman answered. "Hello." No more.

"I'm sorry . . . I thought I was calling Steven Spielberg's office."

"You are." She waited.

"Oh." I told her what had transpired at the popcorn line, and she replied tranquilly, "Well, Steven must have meant it, because this is the number he calls me on. You're the only person besides Steven who's ever called it." She was, it turned out, Steven's remarkable young aide-de-camp, Kristie Macosko, who deftly arranged our encounter.

As I prepared my cards for his visit, it occurred to me that one of the explanations for his extraordinary success is that he doesn't watch movies in the sterile isolation of a screening room (which I daresay he has in his home and his office), but stands in line for his tickets—and his popcorn—and experiences movies with an honest-to-God audience.

On our stage, when I asked him about the first glimmerings of his calling, Steven described an introduction to the moving image that echoed what Martin Scorsese told us. In Steven's case it came when he was assigned a Dickens classic in school. "How do you require a child of twelve to read *A Tale of Two Cities*? So what I did was, I made little stick figures in the dog-eared section of the book, one frame at a time, different positions, and I would riffle them. I just did flip books, and saw these images come to life and that was the first time I was actually able to create an image that moved. On the pages of that classic!"

Over the students' laughter, I said, "It was the best of books, it was the worst of books," and the laughter turned to groans.

As we discussed *Jaws,* I expressed admiration for Steven's canny strategy of making us wait an hour for our first glimpse of the shark. "The wonderful thing about the sea as a device," I said, "is that you can't see underneath that water. The surface of that water could harbor anything, and all through the picture, once you've established the fact that there's a shark out there, just seeing the surface of the water is much more terrifying than seeing something swimming around underneath it."

"I don't know of anything more terrifying than off-camera violence, off-camera suspense," Steven replied. "You have to give the audience credit. They probably bring with them to the movie theater collectively more imagination than any of us behind the scenes put together. They come in there with their imaginations and implore us as filmmakers to allow them to *use* it!"

"For me," I said, "it's the difference between suspense and surprise, because with suspense the audience is allowed to be two steps ahead of the characters, and they begin to worry. But once the surprise happens, it's over. There's a sexual reference that says it: Satisfaction is the death of desire."

"That is great! Yeah, yeah!" Steven exclaimed. "It's basically expecting the audience to bring a level of imagination to the experience that is better than the experience you have provided for them."

Spielberg is not only a creator of film but a creation of film: It inhabits him so thoroughly and unself-consciously, informing everything including his everyday discourse, that when I asked him about his work with John Williams, he said, "John goes off for six, seven weeks of writing, and about the seventh week I'll get a call from him—'Do you want to hear the music on the piano?'—and I am there in no frames."

As he said it, I could see it: an abrupt cut from Steven at home to Steven standing next to Williams's piano—in no frames.

For me, one of the most gratifying moments of the past thirteen years occurred when I asked Steven about the climactic scene of *Close Encounters of the Third Kind.* "Your father was a computer scientist; your mother was a musician. When the spaceship lands, how do they communicate?"

Steven was silent for a moment, a slow smile appearing. "That is a very good question. I like that. You've *answered* the question."

"They make music on their computers," I said, "and they are able to speak to each other."

"Sure. You see, I would love to say I intended that, and I realized that was my mother and father—but not until this moment . . ." He paused to make way for the students' laughter and applause, then concluded with, "But thank you for that."

When we talked about *Raiders of the Lost Ark,* I asked him if he used more short lens than usual on the film, and he replied, "I use a lot of short lens on most of my films."

"Why?"

"Because I like master shots. Sometimes I like the audience to be the film editor—let the audience choose who to look at from time to time. You know, I don't like films that are all close-ups or cut too fast, so you can't catch your breath. And in a lot of my movies I like to do not only one master, but three or four masters in the same scene. It just gives you, the audience, more geography, to know where stuff is."

Looking for an explanation of his remarkable technical economy, I asked him, "How long did you shoot *Raiders*?"

"We shot seventy-four days."

"What was it supposed to be?"

"About eighty-six."

"You came in ahead of schedule."

"Way ahead. I wanted to get out of Tunisia so bad!"

"How many setups a day?"

"I was averaging about thirty-five a day."

When I asked Steven if he edited his films electronically, he recoiled. "Never!" then laughed and began singing, "Tradition, tradition!" from *Fiddler on the Roof.*

The problem with electronic editing, Steven said, is that, in his opinion, "it doesn't look like photography. The whole electronic process infuses so much light onto the screen that you're not getting the contrast, you're not seeing the highlights, the light areas compared to the darkness. And also it doesn't smell like film; it smells like an electronic lab. There's a whole different odor in the air.

"But when you're actually opening up trim boxes and taking film out—granted, Mike Kahn and I can make four cuts electronically to every one cut I can make on the Moviola or KEM—but it gives me time while they're pulling the trims to walk around, catch my breath and think about what I'm doing. The technology isn't pushing me. It's not shoving me to make decisions when

I'm not ready to make them. I need those seven or eight minutes where they're pulling down the trims and showing them to me on the Moviola to think about what I'm doing."

When I asked Steven why his actors so often stare past the camera at something beyond it, he replied, "I find it interesting to watch people thinking. That invites us into their thought process, like a magnet. Once a character spends a little time not running the lines but thinking, it draws us into 'What are they thinking about?' And once again, it respects us. And allows us into the filmmaking process, allows us to become participants in the story, not just observers."

For reasons that may be obvious—or irrelevant—I was, like millions of other moviegoers, deeply touched by the loneliness and isolation of the alien in *E.T.* When I asked Steven how he had elicited such remarkable performances from the two children in the final scene, he replied, "Well, I can tell you how that happened. I shot *E.T.* in complete continuity; I mean *religious* continuity, from the first shot to the last shot. I have only done that a couple of times in my career. So, that was the last time the actors were ever going to see E.T. Ever. And—it was cruel—but I went to Henry Thomas, who was already on the verge, and I said, "I just want you to realize when you're saying good-bye to E.T. that this really *is* good-bye, because this is the last time you will see him.

"And I meant it, and it was true. I didn't say his dog was dead. I didn't say E.T. was dead. I just said, 'You're not gonna see him.' It took eight hours to shoot those scenes and Henry was in that zone for eight hours. And so was Drew."

"So was E.T.," I said.

"And *he* was. Or she was. I get in trouble by saying 'he' with E.T. I've gotten a lot of letters about that."

"Have you determined the sex?"

"E.T. is a plant."

"Okay."

"E.T. is a botanical garden unto himself. Or herself."

When I asked how long the *Schindler's List* shoot had been, he said, "Seventy-one days, seventy-two, something like that."

"You've said, 'The faster I work, the better I work.'"

"Yeah, it's true."

"Why?"

"Because I'm seeing the movie playing before my eyes. I'm actually seeing the movie unspooling, unreeling, before me. If I shoot slowly—like on *Jaws*, I couldn't see the movie for a long time—I had to get into the editing room to figure out what kind of a movie I had. But with this movie, or with anything that I'm very passionate about, I try to shoot it as quickly as possible because I get to see it. If I can get thirty-five, forty shots in one day, that's the equivalent of something like five and a half, six minutes of cut footage eventually.

"And I can see the movie *happening.* I can see the performances. I can see the story being told. I can see all the moments being strung together like a string of pearls. When I shoot a movie slowly, just the opposite happens. I start to lose my objectivity and I start to become very critically subjective, and that's the death of it, of the art form, for me."

Steven told us that shooting some of *Schindler's List* at Auschwitz had affected him so profoundly that he had sought help from a friend. "I called Robin Williams for a comedy fix. I said, 'Robin, I've been crying for half an hour. Make me laugh.' And he would keep me on the phone for an hour and I would be dying of laughter. Just dying of laughter. He's the greatest friend to have, I'll tell you. You can't have a better friend than Robin Williams."

In the classroom session, one of the students asked, "How much of the potential of your spirit or your creativity did you sense within you before you were Steven Spielberg?"

"Zero. Zero. None. Never. Never. I simply wanted to take what scared me out of me so I would no longer be frightened, and be able to look at it. And then, because I'm a bit of a monster, I wanted everybody else to be afraid of what I used to be afraid of."

The students laughed and burst into applause. "So, for me," Steven continued, "it was just a form of therapy, a form of getting it out of my life and putting it square in the middle of yours. Which is why, in a strange way, I am so knocked out being here with all of you. This has just been a tremendous evening. Tremendous evening for me. And at the same time it's been somewhat of a self-conscious evening, because I don't think of myself or see myself the way you may. I don't see myself that way at all. I don't see myself as a famous person. I know I *am.* I'd be dumb to say I'm not. Because, you know, I sign my name a lot. And not just to some American Express cards."

He studied the students, then resumed, slowly, thoughtfully. "But if I ever see myself the way you see me, then I have to retire. I can't work anymore. Because that's when I'll start copying myself, I'll start cloning, I'll no longer have a subjective experience filmmaking. I'll simply be imitating the person that you think I am."

At 11:50, I tried to release Steven, but he insisted on continuing. At 11:57, I intervened again, and when both Steven and the students protested, I said, "Steven is willing, but we're running out of videotape." At 12:04:22:26 on the time code in our cameras, Steven said, "I'll never forget you for this. Thank you for inviting me. Thank you so much. Oh, man! I love you guys so much," and left, with obvious reluctance.

B ecause the students of the Actors Studio MFA are taught every aspect of the dramatic art, including its most esoteric and elusive component, comedy, I've never lost an opportunity to bring a master of comedy to them. When Jerry Lewis showed up on April 12, 1999, in fine fettle and febrile form, I asked him about the screeching character he'd inhabited—or who had inhabited him—for years, the one he usually referred to only as The Kid.

"How old is The Kid?"

"Nine."

"He's also sometimes called 'The Idiot,' is he not?"

"Well, yeah, because when I'm sitting with a production crew they have to be clear about which hat I'm wearing. If I'm wearing the writer's hat, that's one discussion. If I'm wearing the director's hat, that's another. If I'm wearing the actor's hat, it's another. And if it's the producer's hat, it's another. But all of those hats are always talking about our moneymaker, The Kid, The Idiot. Whatever we called him, they always knew who I was talking about."

"So, sometimes you do think of him as 'him.'"

"Oh, yes, without question. Because if he were sitting here with you now, he'd be up in the rafters throwing bananas at you."

He'd opened the golden door. "I'm glad you brought that up." The students whooped in anticipation of meeting The Kid. "I have an interest in moments like this. Do you think, Jerry, with your permission, and with his, that I could speak to him?"

Jerry the film professor turned to the students. "Remember *Three Faces of Eve*?"

Turning back to me with The Kid in charge, he shrieked, "Hiii!"

"That has force!" I said to the students, then turned to The Kid. "Tell me something."

"Yeahhhh?"

"Do you go to the movies?"

"I go to the movies a lot."

"Have you ever seen Jerry Lewis?"

"Yeah."

"What did you think of him?" The Kid was silent. Feeling a glow of satisfaction at the prospect of gaining the upper hand, I leaned chummily toward him. "Tell me frankly, Kid. Be honest. Don't hold back." There was no response

on the stage, and out in the house, the students roared at the growing likelihood that the dean was being drawn into a trap. Nonetheless, I persisted. "Go
ahead. Speak." A perceptible note of desperation was creeping into my voice.
"It's *okay!*"

Finally, when the answer came, Jerry was sneaking back into the persona in the
chair opposite me. "Well, you know why I like him?" The Kid answered quietly.

"Why?"

"Because he gets paid for doing what I get punished for."

It was still the nine-year-old voice, but the distance between The Kid and
Jerry was narrowing fast. "There's a certain iron logic in that," I said, then
headed for the target to which all the other questions had been designed to
lead. "Does he make you laugh?"

"Yes. When he's funny."

We weren't quite there yet. "Is he ever not funny?"

"Yes. There's a lot of times he's not funny." The seventy-three-year-old man
almost shouldered aside the nine-year-old Kid. "Oh, Christ, there are times!"
The two beings opposite me reflected for a moment; then The Kid seized the
reins again. "Oh, yeah! I can tell you about some nights when he thought the
audience were Arabs and they knew what he was!"

When the audience's raucous response had subsided, I said, "My final question is, what do you want to be when you grow up?"

The Kid vanished, leaving Jerry Lewis alone in the chair to respond can-
didly, "Nine."

J ust as I am constantly trying to provide our students with guests who
practice the mysterious and important trade of comedy, I maintain a watch
for musical artists who can complement our students' voice and musical performance training. Billy Joel and his band had been with me when I led a
contingent of seventy performers and their road crews to Cuba for the "Havana
Jam" in 1979. Like *The Road to China,* it was the first American venture into a
tightly closed environment.

For three days and nights—on the stage of the Carlo Marx Theater—
American and Cuban performers alternated in an exchange that bridged—
and banished—politics. The Cubans whom I met, and with whom I worked,
seemed solely interested in two subjects, both of them major American
exports: baseball and music. So, the "Jam" was a resounding success, to the
dismay, I suspect, of the Soviet apparatchiks, who were then still in incongruous evidence on every street corner in Havana.

When Billy was submitted to me as a potential guest, I leapt at the opportunity, and on our stage at the university, where I arrived to find him already there, checking the grand piano we'd put in place, we greeted each other like veterans of a distant victorious battle where he had ended his explosive performance with a variation on his customary farewell: "Don't take no shit, Havana!"

On *Inside the Actors Studio,* Billy proved to be a superb teacher, in the chair next to me and at the piano. When I asked him if he enjoyed the writing process, he said, "I enjoy the initial moment of creation. The Promethean moment. The birth. But not the labor and not all the push, push, and the postpartum depression. And the child rearing, and the toilet training and all the things that go with it. No."

"Steve Sondheim said here that the flat keys are the writer's friends and the sharp keys are his enemies. Do you have favorite and unfavorite keys?"

"Yes, I do. I think A is cold. Very cold. I rarely write in A. C is easy, but C is like eating a sandwich with Wonder Bread. You know? It's light. It's fluffy. No nutrition. But it's always there if you need it. I love B-flat! I'm not all that familiar with some keys. I didn't practice my scales enough when I was young, so, the more flats or sharps in the key, the more complicated it becomes. Sometimes, I feel like I'm going to Egypt, and I don't speak the language. So, I look for relatives.

"I love E-flat! When I'm in E-flat—the fourth of E-flat is A-flat. Now you're starting to get into some heavy stuff. And you gotta talk Arabic. So, I'm in E-flat now. Okay! There's B-flat! Now, that's a cousin of F, who's related to the C family, those Wonder Bread people that we all know. I think of writing in terms of 'I gotta find a relative somewhere.' And I pull chords out of keys that really don't belong there only because I'm in Egypt and I gotta talk to somebody who speaks English! So, I'll somehow try to make my way to C—or F—out of E-flat. It's not the most scientific method of writing, but it sure helps to do a progression."

"When you're writing for Billy Joel the singer, do you try and stay away from long, sustained round notes?"

"I don't write well for Billy Joel the singer."

"Why?"

"I don't think of myself as a singer." He refuted the students' laughter with "I just don't!"

"First dumb thing you've said on this stage tonight," I protested.

"I know people have said, 'But I *like* your voice.' It's all subjective. I don't like my own voice. I'm always trying to sound like somebody else. I'm trying to sound like Little Richard. I'm trying to sound like Ray Charles. I'm trying to sound like the Beatles. I'm trying to sound like anybody but that little schnook from Levittown. I don't *like* his voice. But in a way it's made me a more inventive writer, because I can think of being *anybody*. I don't have to just write for me. I get *tired* of me. I like *other* people."

I asked him how he categorized his music. "Eclectic? Rock? Pop? None of the above?"

"Everything. There're elements of classical music in my songs. If I take almost any song—say, 'Uptown Girl'—it could be . . ." His fingers drew rippling Mozartean figures from the keyboard.

"Or take . . ." He sang, " 'Oh, oh, oh, oh, for the longest time.' It could be . . ." The music floating out of the piano was as caressing as a Chopin impromptu, and both Billy and the students were so intrigued by it that he played it through to a finish and an ovation. Returning from the piano, he said, "The vernacular that was popular when I grew up was rock 'n' roll. I was born at the perfect time. Rock 'n' roll was music for everybody. It was a viable career. It was a way to express yourself and make a living. Everybody was doing it. And we were hearing the voice of Black America. The soul of our country was coming out with this music. Everybody loved the stuff and we were all swept up in it."

Billy expressed the conviction that well-written music could be adapted to any period. "Had I not been born during the rock 'n' roll era, I would have written music in another era. Copland was taking Puritan themes. ''Tis the Gift to Be Simple' is a Puritan hymn, arranged for the twentieth century. This is the great thing about music: this incredible flexibility, this incredible fluidity. It crosses all kinds of lines. Racial. Ethnic. National. Sometimes we look down on our own culture and say, 'Ah, what is it? It's all pop. It's all crap. It's garbage. It's Hollywood. It's this. It's that.' Our music is *American*! It reflects all the different kinds of music."

Over a burst of applause, he concluded the lesson with "We're mongrels. We're mutts. So what! We're Americans!"

The applause swelled to an ovation.

‒

When Tom Hanks came into our greenroom in September of 1999, his first words were "Steven said, 'Wait till you meet those students!' " Since Spielberg's affection for our students was already a matter of record, I wasn't surprised that when he'd urged Tom to appear on *Inside the Actors Studio*, he'd commended them. As a matter of fact, by 1999, I had made it a practice to alert our guests that the audience they'd be facing was in no way the conventional claque of fans, but, rather, a knowledgeable audience of master's degree candidates whose response would be, if anything, louder and more forceful than anything the most rabid fans could deliver. "Be prepared," I would say. "You'll be able to *feel* it—literally."

When Tom walked out on the stage and the force of the students' ovation rolled up over the footlights, he looked at me and nodded.

The first thing we got on the record was that Tom had distinguished antecedents. "The name Hanks prompts an obvious question," I said. "Since Hanks is not a common name, and Nancy Hanks was the mother of Abraham Lincoln, are you by any chance related to our sixteenth president?"

"Yes, I am," Tom drawled. "I am a descendant of Abraham Lincoln's mother, Nancy Hanks Lincoln. My father's people came out to California from the hills of Kentucky, and all the time I was growing up I knew that Nancy Hanks was some sort of distant relative."

In the interest of historical accuracy, I provided, "One of the sons of Thomas Hanks, who was an ancestor of Nancy Hanks, was the great-great-great-great-great-great-grandfather of tonight's guest."

For obvious reasons, our students are interested in our guests' training. Tom's spoke with strong feeling about a mentor. "I signed up for the drama class in my junior year of high school. And everything after that was just more fun than you could possibly imagine."

"So, you were happy with that."

"Yeah! What *is* high school really but spending most of your time avoiding getting beaten up—either physically or emotionally. And when you can find a haven for people who are kind of *like* you, just by the natural passion you share, you get to know each other. That's what happened to me in Mr. Farnsworth's drama class."

"Rawley Farnsworth."

"Yeah. Truly the most influential man in my history."

"How so?"

"He let us go. He had us doing real plays. He wasn't like the English teacher who had just gotten the drama class. He had a great passion for this. And because of that, he had us working on things that bona fide actors worked on. He was empowering us."

That night, when we arrived at Tom's Academy Award–winning performance as Andrew Beckett, the gay lawyer dying of AIDS, in *Philadelphia*, I asked him how much weight he'd lost for the role, and he replied, "It was thirty-seven pounds, I think. And you know what? It wasn't enough. For what it truly does to the body, I should have lost another twenty."

I said, "I've read a statistic that there were fifty-three gay men who appeared in various scenes in that movie. And within the next year . . . Do you know the end of that statistic?"

"There's only a handful that are left," Tom said.

"Forty-three died in the next year," I said. "You must have got to know some of them."

"Well, the camaraderie that exists on any film is something that becomes quite palpable. In the first transfusion scene, I happened to be seated next to a guy—he was way down the line. He had lesions on his face; they were quite visible—and he weighed almost nothing. I was asking about how he was living and what it was like and where he worked. He worked at a noodle company; he made noodles. I asked him how his employers treated him, now that he had AIDS. And he said, 'They've been the most wonderful group of people you can imagine. I go to work every day, even when I'm on my oxygen.'"

Tom slowed, his voice beginning to rasp. "He'd . . . he'd wheel in his tank of oxygen and go back to his same place in the noodle factory. . . . You"—he stopped to clear his throat, and continued with difficulty—"you end up having those kind of conversations with people that . . ." There was another, longer silence, then, "It's a hard movie for me to watch now . . . 'cause I remember the guy from the noodle fact—. . . and he's right there." He shook his head as though he could somehow dislodge the memory, then gave up and gave in. "They last forever, you know, these movies." He reached for the water glass on the table next to him, but it was too late: The tears fell.

I suggested that when Tom won the Oscar for his performance as Andrew Beckett, his acceptance speech had "gone down in the annals of Academy history."

"Yeah, yeah." He laughed.

"To whom did you pay tribute?"

"To Rawley T. Farnsworth. I wanted to communicate to three billion people out there that the greatest thing that has happened to me as a professional is that when I was in school I came under the tutelage and inspiration of a man who was gay."

"Did he know you were going to say it?"

"I called him two nights before, and I said, 'Well, look, Mr. Farnsworth, here's the deal. I actually think I have a shot at, you know, having my name called. And if they do, can I mention your name?' And he said, 'Well, I think it would be wonderful.' And I'm glad I had the chance to do it."

In the classroom session, Denise Lyons's Irish roots showed in her lilting brogue and her question about self-expression and the dignity of the human spirit. "How do you feel it's all going to tie in together for you as an artist?"

Tom replied, "What I want to do in the course of whatever my artistic output is, is have people in the audience recognize themselves up there, because that's what I'm looking for when I go to a movie. I really want it to be about our lives and how we do what we do. Because I think, by the natural laws of God's green earth, there is dignity in that."

The classroom session had begun at ten forty-five, and Tom must have found the truth in Steven's assessment of the students, because the session ended after midnight. Tom's valediction was "There's nothing greater than saying, 'I am a professional actor, and I will be till the day I die.'"

The more than two hundred guests who have come to our stage have brought with them an atlas of ethnicities and enough religions to turn our seminar into a seminary. Some of the family trees bear more branches than others. When I asked Michael Caine about a scholarship he'd won as a child to a school with the mysterious name Hackney Down Grocers, he replied, "Hackney Down Grocers was basically a Jewish school. I'm Church of England. In America that would be Episcopalian. And I was educated by Jews. So, I have this dichotomy: My father was a Catholic, my mother was a Protestant, I was educated by Jews, and my wife is a Muslim."

For Michael, as for so many of our guests, parental loss figured prominently in the shaping of him. When I asked him if he had been with his father at the end, he said, "Yeah. My father died of liver cancer. He was a big drinker and smoker, and he died when he was fifty-four, in a hospital called St. Thomas's which is right opposite the Houses of Parliament. He was suffering terribly, and I went in and said to this chief surgeon, 'Can you give him something just to, you know, end it, for Christ's sake?' This is forty years ago, and the doctor said to me, 'Good God, no! I couldn't do that!' And then he said, 'Come back at midnight.'

"I went back at midnight. I always remember it because the hospital's right opposite Big Ben, and Big Ben was striking midnight. And I looked at my father and he just died at midnight. The doctor was standing there, and I looked at him, and he gave this sort of slight smile, and I knew that he'd done it. He'd done it.

"And then the nurse gave me everything that my father owned. It was in his pockets. She gave me one and nine pence, ha'penny, which is about thirty-five cents. And that's all he had.

"That night I changed very much. I was determined to make something of myself. I had a very hard time becoming a successful actor. I had ten years of real slog in the theater. Real slog, trying to get bigger parts—and it was only the memory of that night that kept me going. When everybody, including all your friends, from the kindness of their heart, tell you to give up because they know you can't do it, you really need something to put a steel rod up your back. And my dad's death was always the steel rod for me."

There was undisguised grief in his voice as he said, "He never owned *anything*. He used to rent a radio. *Rent* a radio! Now, with the money he rented that radio for he could've bought *thirty* radios over the years." He paused in dark reflection, then continued resolutely. "The poor can't afford cheap goods or cheap deals! That's what I learned when I was young." He looked sternly at the students. His voice rose. "That's where you get trapped! You can't afford to be trapped in that!" He broke off, startled by his own fervor, then sat contritely back. "Sorry about that."

The room was still. "Thank you," I said.

"All right," Michael replied quietly.

Once again I was astonished at what our guests are willing to share with our students.

Michael told us about the premiere of *Zulu*. "It was my first big movie. I was a completely unknown actor till that happened, and I wanted to take my mother to the premiere. But she wouldn't come. I said, 'I'll get you an evening dress; I'll get you a mink coat, the jewels, everything. We'll go to the premiere.' And she refused to come. So, I went to the premiere with a very beautiful girl. We got out of the limo and we were walking in, and I saw my mother in the crowd, watching."

He nodded as the students gasped, then continued. "It was the most unbelievable moment for me. I didn't know whether to laugh, cry . . . I didn't know *what* to do. I just got very angry—very angry that she wouldn't come with me and she came all that way on the bus and stood in the crowd and watched me going in."

In December 1998, one of the most powerful PR agents in Hollywood called to ask if I could book one of her clients immediately, and edit the episode in time to broadcast it a month later. I responded that there were no slots left, but in the ensuing days, she continued to look for a way to cut the knot and work the client into our schedule.

Finally, I asked her why it was so urgent, reminding her, "We begin shooting again in February."

"Too late!" she exclaimed.

"For what?"

There was a note of pity in her voice. "You don't know, do you?"

"Know *what*?"

"The studios and the agencies have decided *Inside the Actors Studio* is one of the most influential shows on the air. Out here, they watch it at night and talk about it at lunch the next day. We think our client has a shot at an Oscar nomination, and this show is the best way to get it."

In December 2006, Liz Smith noted in her *New York Post* and syndicated column: "If you were trying to win your client an Oscar, what would you do? Go to *People* magazine, ask this column to burble on, take ads in *Variety*, slip it into Page Six in the guise of sexual innuendo, approach *Vanity Fair*? None of the above. What you *should* do is get James Lipton to set your star for one of his rare interviews *Inside the Actors Studio*. No kidding!"

The show's Oscar influence has been acknowledged in a *TV Guide* cartoon headlined "The Oscar Campaign" in which Wilson, the ball washed up on the beach with Tom Hanks in *Cast Away*, was making what were depicted as the obligatory stops: a trade ad in *Variety* and, in successive panels, appearances on *The Early Show*, Chris Matthews's *Hardball*, and *Inside the Actors Studio*, where he confided in me, "Of course, more than anything, I want to direct."

In the cartoon's last panel, Wilson lost the Best Supporting Oscar to Julia Roberts's Wonderbra, but our other guests did better.

In 2000, the *Inside the Actors Studio* episodes of three of the four Oscar winners, Russell Crowe, Julia Roberts and Benicio Del Toro, had been broadcast by Bravo during the Academy voting period; in 2003, all four of the acting honors went to guests we'd aired during the voting period, Sean Penn, Charlize Theron, Tim Robbins and Renée Zellweger; in 2004, I celebrated at the *Vanity Fair* Oscar party with three of the four winners, Jamie Foxx, Morgan Freeman and Cate Blanchett, all of whose episodes we'd aired when the Academy members were casting their votes; and in 2007, ten of the Golden Globe winners and ten of the Academy Award nominees were alumni of *Inside the Actors Studio* whose episodes were aired during the voting period.

K evin Spacey came to us in December 1999, laden with critical praise for his performance in *American Beauty*. Noting that he was on record as saying he transformed himself physically for every role, I said, "This was a major physical transformation. How did you do it?"

"Trained!" he replied with a groan. "I had a trainer. I had a gym. It traveled with me everywhere. I ate right. I took more pills than you can imagine—supplements to change the way your metabolism works and the way you digest. And this guy just beat the shit out of me every day. The oddest part of that was that I had to get in the best physical shape from day one, because we were on a very short schedule. It would often be the case that in the morning we were shooting the schmo Lester, and then in the afternoon I had to work out for some later scenes. We created the early Lester through posture, makeup, costume—you know? You put on a suit two sizes too big for you, and you walk like Matthau."

"All this because he listens at his daughter's bedroom door and hears the young cheerleader about whom he's obsessing say that if only he were a bit more buffed, he might have a chance with her," I said.

"There's not a guy that don't understand that," Kevin observed.

In the classroom session, a student rose. "Hi, Mr. Spacey. My name is Jeff Margolis and I'm a second-year actor. Last year you came to talk to us about *The Iceman Cometh,* and, as a *Glengarry Glen Ross* fan, I asked you if you could tell me to go to lunch three times. And I thought we would take that a step further today. I brought a copy of the sides of just that scene."

The students hooted gleefully at Jeff's audacity, and passed the sides forward to Kevin as Jeff pressed ahead. "I'll play Alan Arkin's part here." When Kevin received the sides, Jeff, beet red, said, "You know—just for Christmas?"

"I wanna know when you graduate. That's what I wanna know," Kevin said.

"If you—if you *want* to."

"All right. Go ahead."

"Okay. We'll start with"—Jeff flapped his hand, which was trembling so hard he couldn't read the side—"we'll start once *that* goes away." Grasping the sides with both hands, he asked, "You wanna be Williamson?"

"Yeah, I'll be—" Kevin responded, then caught himself as the students laughed and applauded their classmate. "You know, I got asked that question once and I said yes. All right, go ahead."

"Okay." Jeff took a deep breath and plunged into the scene. "I work here! I don't come in here to be mistreated!"

"Go to lunch, will ya?"

And they were off. The scene built to Kevin's "I'm trying to run an office here. Will you go to lunch? Go to lunch! *Will you go to lunch?!*"

The students cheered the fulfillment of Jeff's dream. Kevin would fulfill one more dream that night. When he'd answered the Pivot Questionnaire and I started to move on to the classroom session, he stopped me. "Wait! You know what? I've answered a question inappropriately. Could you ask me the question, if I were ever to do anything other than acting? If you could ask me that question again."

"Okay. Kevin, what profession other than yours would you like to attempt?"

"Well, when I was a kid, I always wanted to play Santa Claus, and I was never big enough. And that's what I would like to do. I would want to be Santa Claus." The students began to cheer as, unseen by me, a delegation emerged from the wings, led by our producer Mike Kostel, carrying a large framed portrait. Of me.

"This is an original Hirschfeld," Kevin said. "It was commissioned as a Christmas gift from Bravo and your community here. Merry Christmas."

Kevin introduced Margo Feiden, the gallery owner representing Al Hirschfeld, whose caricatures had adorned the Arts pages of *The New York Times* for seventy years. She recalled an occasion when she'd heard me confess to aspiring, like everyone else in our profession, to be drawn by Hirschfeld, with no expectation of meriting it. She pointed to the lapel pin Hirschfeld had drawn. "And there are the pilot's wings."

"My pilot's wings and my blue cards," I said, staring in disbelief at the portrait. One of Lipton's Laws states that no surprise party has ever actually been a surprise—but this was a surprise.

Feiden explained that Hirschfeld's lifetime chronicling the performing arts had made him an avid viewer of *Inside the Actors Studio.* That's why, she said, this drawing was unique. To begin with, this master of black and white had colored my blue cards blue. Hirschfeld's legion of admirers knew that he always embedded his daughter's name in the drawing, appending a number next to his signature to help the public ferret every "NINA" out. Feiden pointed at the number at the bottom of this drawing: "+1." As Kevin and I leaned closer to the drawing, we discovered its secret: There was a "NINA" concealed in the hair above my left temple; and in the hair over my right temple, Hirschfeld had drawn "JIM." It was, Feiden told us, another rare Hirschfeld tribute.

At the end of the classroom session that night, a student asked Kevin, "Can you help us appreciate this early experience, these lean years, these very difficult years leading up to the ultimate prize that hopefully most of us will receive?"

Kevin's answer was plainspoken and priceless. "There *is* no prize out there. The only prize is *this* one." He indicated the theater around us. "And what you feel and what you want to accomplish as you start out in what could be lean years or fat years. To be ambitious and to want to be successful is not enough. That's just desire. You have to know *what* you want. And understand why you're doing it. And dedicate every breath in your body to achieving it. If you feel that your particular talent is worth developing, is worth caring for, then there's nothing you can't achieve, and no matter how many apartments you get kicked out of, there is no one, no matter how negative, who can stop you from doing it.

"Trust yourself and trust your friends. They can be as much a teacher for you as anybody here or anyone who's privileged enough to come here and speak to you."

Bravo aired Kevin's episode of *Inside the Actors Studio* during the Oscar voting period, and he won the Best Actor Award, and Michael Caine won the Oscar for Best Supporting Actor, keeping our string intact.

CHAPTER Thirteen

66*Tonight we are going to cook octopus balls!*

—Robin Williams, *Inside the Actors Studio*

B y 1999, *Inside the Actors Studio* had begun an international journey that would ultimately take our guests and students into 125 countries. This expansion had many consequences, not least the fact that candidates in Europe, the Near East, Asia and Latin America, seeing our students—and our school—in joyful, fruitful action, applied in such numbers that in time they comprised nearly a quarter of our student body.

As our international exposure mushroomed, reviews and news stories flowed back to us. I waited with special interest and some anxiety for the French reaction, for three reasons: first, of course, because I still thought of Paris as a second home; second, because the French, who invented the neighborhood cinémathèque, are such knowledgeable cinephiles; and finally, because they can be so harsh in response to what they see as the encroachment of American culture.

So, when my assistant laid in front of me an inch-thick packet of reviews sent by Paris Première, our French network, I braced myself, literally, gripping the edge of my desk, as white-knuckled as I had been in Rainy Pass.

The review I most looked forward to—and dreaded—was the one in *Le Monde,* the French equivalent of *The New York Times,* and the paper for which I had the most respect when I lived in Paris. I leafed through the packet—and there it was, *"Le Monde"* in its distinctive, authoritative typeface over a review that consumed half a page, with a picture of Mary Tyler Moore and me on our stage.

"Si on a raté le générique," the review began—"If one missed the opening titles, one sees only a small, very ordinary theater"—my heart began to sink—"rows of well-behaved students and two armchairs in bad taste in the center of an empty stage."

The review fell from my fingers. Bad taste! The two *"fauteuils de mauvais goût"* were our pride and joy, recently purchased after a long search, for *a thousand dollars each,* to replace the chairs we'd stolen from a classroom. They were all we could afford and all we could offer—and they weren't good enough for the *rafinés* tastes of *Le Monde* and its critic. My regard for *Le Monde* sank—but not as fast as my regard for our show.

Some of our guests insist they never, under any circumstances, read reviews. I am not of their number. I picked up the bad news, resumed reading—and gulped hard. The next words were, *"Ça commence mal!* This is beginning badly!" It would get worse—instantly. *"Un petit homme sans allure*—A small, nondescript man [Me!], with a tight smile [Yes! True! Kedakai's mantra is, "Smile more!"], comes out to occupy one of the two chairs and place his notes on a little table."

Okay. A brief reprieve: no harm no foul. "After having reviewed the career of his guest, the host [*"animateur"* in ominous quotes]—he scarcely seems to deserve the title, his performance is so stiff—[Oh, my God! I hope nobody on the Rue Pigalle is reading *Le Monde*]—extends an arm toward the wings and the still unoccupied armchair, offering a ritual: 'Ladies and gentlemen, please welcome . . . [The greeting was in English].' "

"One could be expecting the most old-fashioned talk show in the history of television. [I was suicidal.] But for those who didn't miss them, the opening titles had forewarned us that we shouldn't necessarily rely on appearances. [A ray of hope?]

"Superimposed on the titles were a parade of faces: Marilyn Monroe, James Dean, Paul Newman, Jack Nicholson, Robert De Niro, Dustin Hoffman, etc. Yes, we're in New York, at the Actors Studio, prestigious crucible of theater and cinema for more than half a century.

"Then," the critic wrote, *"la magie opère*—the magic happens. [I took a very long, very deep breath.] An hour of pleasure and intelligence. [My hand shook, but for an entirely different reason.]"

The critic wasn't quite through with me. *"Le petit homme sans allure* [*Moi!*] turns into an admirable interviewer. [*Moi?!*]"

"James Lipton," the sensitive, perspicacious critic wrote, "is a vice president of the Studio, heir to Elia Kazan and Lee Strasberg, who founded this unique conservatory under the influence of 'the master' Stanislavski. Facing him, the cream of the acting and directing world take turns in the other *fauteuil de mauvais goût.* [Okay, okay, no critic is perfect.]

"Each one shares his experience, and seems to say here what he has never been able to say in any other show or interview. The encounter ends with audience questions, and we can attest that everyone, on the stage and in the theater, takes care to maintain the level and reputation of the institution.

"So, here, at one and the same time, painlessly and with good humor, is a masterful course in English—American—and in theater and film."

I laid the review down, and as they had in front of the bookstore on Christmas Eve a lifetime ago, the clouds broke, and once again the sun shone brightly.

When Harrison Ford arrived on our stage in February 2000, his credentials were impeccable: He was indisputably the most successful actor in the history of motion pictures; seven of his films comprised 25 percent of the highest-grossing movies ever made, and in *Empire* magazine's list of the Top 100 Movie Stars of All Time, he was ranked number one.

And he was Indiana Jones. Still, of all the guests who have appeared in the series, no one has ever been as visibly frightened. Over the years, I developed a gauge of our guests' comfort. For want of a better title, I call it the Back of the Seat Test. The guests and I sit at an angle to each other, in order to enable the close-up cameras to get a clean shot of each of us. As a result, from where I sit, I can see the guest in profile in the chair.

The calm ones sit down and settle comfortably back. The nervous ones perch on the edge of the seat like dutiful students facing an exam for which they fear they may not have sufficiently prepared. That isn't the atmosphere on our stage, but some guests bring the expectation with them, and my first task is to dispel it.

That's where the Back of the Seat Test comes in. Because of the chairs' angles, if the guest is sitting rigidly forward, I can see a sliver of light between his or her back and the back of the chair. Since I have no way of predicting its occurrence, I include in the first twenty or thirty cards for each guest one or two of the questions that may evoke a "How did you know that!"

That's usually the point at which the sliver of light vanishes. For reasons I don't fully understand, the realization that I've done my homework seems to reassure—and, more important, relax—nervous guests, and they sit back—and we're off.

Not only did Harrison sit rigidly forward, but we could see his hands shaking. Early in the evening, I asked him, "Whose was the first voice heard on WMTH-FM?"

"I know the answer to that. Or I *think* the answer to that is . . . me."

His uncertainty made me ask, "Is it apocryphal?"

"It's one of the many things I wouldn't have been able to remember but for the fact that I sat down and read a book about me."

A few minutes later, he came back to the subject. "As I was reading that book the other day it reminded me—"

I broke in. "This is the book you read to refresh yourself on your past?"

"Yes, sir. Yes," the dutiful student replied.

"Why the hell didn't you call me? I would've told you a few things."

"That would have spoiled our fun here tonight."

Harrison added some ingredients to our ethnic mix when I asked him about his parents.

"My mother is Russian Jewish and my father is Irish Catholic."

"Do you feel that in any way that's influenced you? As a person? As an artist?"

"As a man, I've always felt Irish. As an actor, I've always felt Jewish."

When we came to the Indiana Jones films, I said, "Lucas has hinted that you were a model for Indiana Jones almost from the beginning. But he didn't want to confuse it with the *Star Wars* films."

"I didn't want to confuse it with *Star Wars* either."

"Indiana's a more complex character certainly than Han Solo."

"Well, he's a lot smarter than Han Solo and the breadth of the character is so much greater."

"He's also a very vulnerable action hero. Although, I think all of your action heroes have some vulnerability in them. Is that by design?"

"Yeah. Absolutely by design. I always thought that the whole idea of it—'it' being acting—was to try and establish an emotional relationship with the audience. To give them someone they could feel along with, feel the story *through*. So, I wanted fear to be an element. I wanted vulnerability. I thought it was more interesting. I also thought it would allow for more fun, that there would be humor in it."

Once again we reached a crossroads. Like Meryl Streep, Harrison had been directed by Mike Nichols, in Harrison's case in *Working Girl*. When I asked him what it was like to be directed by Mike, our students heard, "Well, Mike is a charming host and one of the most brilliant manipulators of actors. You never feel his hand on your shoulder, or pushing you in any direction. He's so clear and insightful, and so good that he leaves no marks on you. You just do the right thing and you don't know how you've done it or why you've done it. But Mike has made that the only choice you could make. And you think it's all your idea."

With Chuck Dolan, the president of Cablevision—and my fellow pilot—sitting in the front row next to his wife, it was inevitable that I would ask Harrison, "What attracted you to flying?"

"When I was in college, I wanted to fly, and I ran out of money before I got a chance to solo. Now I was riding around in airplanes—the studio was shuffling me back and forth—and I'd sit up front with those guys and watch what they're doing, and just wanted to learn how to do it. I hadn't learned anything with that much complexity in a long time, so I didn't know if I'd be able to actually do it."

"How long ago did you start?"

"About four years ago. I was fifty-four when I started to fly. As you know, there's a lot to learn. But I just fell in love with the skills and the responsibilities."

"That's the main thing," I said. "The responsibilities."

"Yeah, yeah! All this stuff we pretend to do in movies, you really *are,* out there."

"You're PIC."

"Yeah! Pilot in command! It's become a really important part of my life. And it's gotten me into the company of a whole new bunch of people whom I admire. And I love what it looks like from up there. And I love the machines."

I asked Harrison about the planes he owned.

"I've got a Husky. It's a little fore-and-aft two-seat tail-dragger. I've got a de Havilland Beaver like the one in *Six Days, Seven Nights.* A different one," he added hastily.

"Yeah."

"I have a Bonanza B36TC, and I have a Cessna 206. And I used to have a helicopter. I'll have another one soon."

Here was an occasion where I knew the answer before I asked the question. "What happened to your helicopter?"

"It . . . uh . . . it broke."

The students laughed and I turned to them. "He's not telling you. This is the *real* Indiana Jones."

"I broke it," a hangdog Harrison said, age no more than ten.

In the classroom session, Harrison, who had begun so uncertainly, vied with Sean Penn for the position of Actors Studio Drama School poet laureate. A young woman said, "My question is about you being known as a somewhat private person in real life—whether that has ever affected your ability as an actor to extend to your character the intimate side of yourself that we all strive to give to each character we portray. Has it ever hindered you?"

"No. I am a private person in my private life. In my working life, I expect to grant my audience complete and total access. Everyone's got a backstage pass—you know? You have to be willing to live in front of people. *Live* in front of people. Let them see the good, the bad, the ugly, the weak, the strong—the conflicted, the terrible. You've just got to be willing to do that.

"For me, one of the great things about movies, one of the redeeming things about acting, one of the things about acting that gives me the greatest satisfaction, is the opportunity for that emotional exercise—that investment to the point where it produces true emotion. When that happens to you, you feel that it's not about you; it's about the continuity between you and the rest of your race, it's about being human, and it's about sharing that humanity, and coming to *know* that humanity. It's among the most important moments of my life, being able to do that. The true ambition is to give yourself to that moment. And that's no conflict with my privacy."

Like a bullfighter who doesn't eat the day of a corrida on the theory that, if he's gored, the surgeons will want an empty abdomen, or a fighter who wouldn't think of filling his stomach before going fifteen rounds, or an actor who waits until the curtain falls to think about food, I confine myself to no more than a bowl of soup or an apple and some cheese on shoot days.

The result is that when we wrap at eleven or midnight, I'm struck, suddenly and often forcibly, with the realization that it's been twenty-four hours since I've had anything like a real meal. Over the years I've discovered that many of my guests, faced with four or five hours on our stage, follow the same Spartan regimen, so I've fallen into the habit of inviting my guests to join Kedakai and me for a late supper. Which means, at that hour of the night, Elaine's.

The principal draw was, and is, Elaine herself, a woman of imposing physical and societal heft who created not only a restaurant but a world. If George Plimpton conducted America's private literary salon, Elaine conducts the public one. I have a theory, as resistant to proof as most of my theories, but stubbornly clung to nonetheless, that were it not for the fact that Elaine, whose appetite for writing and writers is as insatiable as her evident appetite for food, had not allowed two generations to run tabs between their advances and their royalties, America's literary mainstream would have shrunk to a trickle because most of its practitioners would have starved to death.

The great publishing houses should erect a monument to Elaine, because she, often in their place, has kept America's literary population alive for half a century.

There is a reason, apart from hunger pangs, that the guest, Kedakai and I often head for Elaine's after the shoot: The guest and I are simply too wired after four or five hours on the high wire to go home and go to sleep. We need decompression and Elaine affords it. When Harrison, Kedakai and I arrived at our table, Harrison slumped into a chair and said, "I have a confession to make. I didn't tell the students the truth."

"About what?"

"My planes. There's another one."

"Oh?"

"A Gulfstream."

"Why didn't you mention it?"

"Sounds like bragging."

Later, he said, "I hope I was making sense tonight."

"You certainly were."

"Good. I haven't slept for three nights."

"Why?"

"Nerves."

"You mean the show?"

He nodded. Apart from that, for more than an hour we traded flying stories over our pasta. Kedakai and Elaine conducted an animated independent conversation.

·

Because the Actors Studio MFA trains actors, writers and directors, guests who combine two of those disciplines, and sometimes three, are of great value to our students. Spike Lee brought all three gifts to our stage. Selfishly perhaps, for my own edification, I began with the writer.

"When do you write?"

"In the morning."

"How long do you write?"

"Two hours. Can't do more than that."

"What do you write on?"

"Three-ring loose-leaf binder paper. Longhand."

"How much rewriting do you do?"

"A lot. But the bulk of my rewriting is done once we start rehearsals. It's amazing when you write something and you think it's great, but when you hear the actors say the words, a lot of times it's terrible."

"Do you allow them to change things?"

"Yes."

"You *encourage* them to change things?"

"Certain actors," Spike replied emphatically.

It was Spike Lee the director who provided us with the most startling moment of the evening as we discussed *Malcolm X*. It began calmly and innocently when I asked him, "What did Warners want you to cut the film to?"

"They did not want it to be three hours, that's for sure."

"What did you do?"

Spike seemed to hesitate for a moment. Then he said, "Here's the story. The budget we had for *Malcolm X* everybody knew was not adequate. We knew it, the bond company knew it, and Warner Brothers knew it. And, you know, you have to pay the piper; that day comes when you run out of money, and the bond company says, Okay, what are we gonna do now? We said, 'Look, we told you from the beginning this wasn't enough.' Warner Brothers wanted us to cut the film down from the three-hour length. They said, 'Unless you cut the film, there's nothing we can do.'

"Contractually, the film's now in the hands of the bond company. So, everybody on the postproduction staff, including the editors, got a registered-mail letter saying, 'You are fired, and your service is no longer needed.'

"So, here we are in postproduction. We started September, finished before Christmas, but we still had to go to Africa, to shoot. So they said, 'You don't have to go to Africa. Just shoot the Jersey shore.'" Spike looked out at the students. "In January!"

"At the pyramids," I offered.

"At the pyramids," Spike confirmed. "I tried to become a student of Malcolm and Malcolm always talked about self-reliance—that black people have enough resources, that we have to start relying on ourselves. I knew Warner Brothers wasn't going to give us any money, so I made a list of all the prominent African-Americans I knew I could call on the phone and say, 'Look, we need some money.'

"So, my first call was to Bill Cosby. Bill wrote a check. Then, I called Oprah Winfrey. She wrote a check. Then, I called Magic. He wrote a check. Then, I called Michael Jordan—told him how much Magic gave." Over a roar of laughter from the students, he drew the moral. "'Cause you know money's competitive. Then, I called Tracy Chapman. Janet Jackson. And you know, everybody . . . they wrote these checks knowing that . . . that . . . that they weren't gonna get the money back. . . ."

That was when it happened. He had slowed and leaned forward. I assumed it was to collect his thoughts, but when he straightened, his glasses had filled to the brim with tears, which spilled down his cheeks. The students were as shocked as I: This was Spike Lee, who in his films seldom cracked a smile, much less shed a tear. This was Spike Lee, the personification of cool . . . crying in front of five hundred people!

He struggled unsuccessfully to compose himself, as he said, "It could not be a tax write-off. But they knew that this film was important. So . . . so, they wrote the checks and they said, 'Spike, make the film you want to make.'"

For some mysterious reason, when the public is impressed with an emotional moment on the stage or screen, it refers to the phenomenon as "real tears." "He cried real tears!" "She cried real tears!" in contradistinction, presumably, to tears induced by a caustic spray or someone whispering, "Your dog died."

Nothing in *Inside the Actors Studio*'s history has been a greater surprise to me than the volume of tears shed on our stage. Contrary to what some may think, these moments are impossible to stage, or even to predict. When Sharon Stone was with us, we were discussing a teacher whose name had come up often on our stage. "Would you talk to our students about Roy London?"

"It would be my greatest pleasure. He was the most astonishing teacher, in the best sense of the word, teaching us that it's not all the things that are right and wonderful about you, but the things that are *wrong* with you, the things that don't work, and don't fit in, the things that make you unique, that make you yourself, that are your true gift to the world."

Because I knew of Sharon's work for AMFAR, the American Foundation for AIDS Research, I tried to introduce the subject with "What happened to him?" Her response was both expected and unexpected.

"Roy died . . . from AIDS. And . . . I think this happens to people when they are dying: They kind of go and come back. I was with him, and he went. And suddenly, he was back in his body. And he was as startled as I was, I'm sure. And he said, 'It's so beautiful. It's just so beautiful.' And I expected him to say, you know, 'The white light, the thing.' And I said, 'What?' And he said, 'It's all about love.' Poof!"

The "Poof!" ushered in such a cascade of tears that I felt obliged to apologize to her for raising the subject, but she pressed ahead. "It's so moving, because . . . what he said was that he wished he could teach one more class." She clapped her hands impatiently, as if to stifle another emotional display, and concluded with a matter-of-fact "So, there you have it."

It was the memory of his mother that brought Danny Glover, a big man, powerful and, in films like the *Lethal Weapon* series, impregnable, to tears on our stage. "My mom," Danny said, "she's an incredible woman, she had gone to have her cards read, and she told me, 'You're going to do a role in 1983, in September, that's going to be about you in a way. And it's going to be such an important role in your career.' She said this in April!"

Later, as we discussed his role in *Places in the Heart,* I recalled his mother's prophecy. "You said your mother told you what the cards had prophesied for your brothers and for you."

"Yeah."

"But didn't mention herself."

"Didn't mention herself."

"What happened on the day you got the role?"

"The day that I got the role, uh, my . . . um . . . my mom died in an automobile accident. And so . . ." He broke, cried hard for a moment, then wiped his eyes and rallied with "So the work is a tribute to her."

I am always awkward in this circumstance, but I did my best. "This *moment* is a tribute to her."

"Yes."

I was caught unawares again when we were discussing the most effective scene in the movie, in which Danny's character, saying good-bye to Sally Fields's, abruptly hands her one of his few possessions as a farewell gift.

Danny nodded. "A handkerchief." He swallowed hard. "It was my mother's handkerchief."

As the dam broke a second time, I said, "I'm sorry! I didn't mean to push you into that."

"Boy, I tell you," Danny said through a mixture of laughter and tears, "you are—you are fifteen years removed, and you . . ." He turned to the students with a plea. "How do you ever stop missing your mom?"

Billy Bob Thornton belongs in the sui generis category with Chris Walken and Sean Penn. A gentle, generous man, he nevertheless marches to the beat of his own drummer, even in grief. When I said, "I believe there was another loss, in 1988," he replied, "Yeah. That's the second time I went insane. My brother was two and a half years younger than me. All the pictures on the wall are of me and him. He's the kid I grew up with. He was brilliant, and to this day I feel guilty that it was him and not me—because anything that I'm able to do in this stuff, I always feel like he deserved it, because he was truly a brilliant person."

"Where is Jimmy buried?"

"He's buried in Alpine, Arkansas. I . . . I actually feel more peaceful when I go to that cemetery than anyplace else."

"Isn't there a bench, facing his grave?"

"Yeah. It says, 'To everything there is a season.'"

"You can sit on that bench?"

"Yeah. I sit on that bench. . . ."

"You feel okay?"

"Yeah."

"You've said, 'I don't think I've ever been happy, without being sad.' Is that the case?"

"Absolutely. Yeah."

Burt Reynolds's public persona is quick, clever, glib, devil-may-care. What happened on our stage was in sharp contrast. "You've described your father as a very tough man," I said.

"Yes. He's ninety-four years old, and I wouldn't fight him with an ax. He was quite a hero in the war, and then when he's chief of police, and you're the *son* of the chief of police—it's like being the son of a preacher, you know? You can go one of two ways, and I went the other." The students, always sympathetic to rebels, laughed appreciatively.

"I was always in trouble. He arrested me one night and put me in jail."

"You've said, 'My parents always rationed overt affection in front of us.' True?"

"We didn't ever kiss, and . . . my father, when . . . uh . . ." He cleared his throat, which failed to stanch the tears. "Uh . . . later on in years when . . . I . . . I had the courage, I said, 'I . . . I love you . . . I love you, Pop . . . ' and he said . . ." He cleared his throat again, this time in imitation of the incoherent sound his father had made in return, then translated it for us. "Which, if you slowed it down on a record . . . would be 'I love you too.' "

When the students laughed uneasily, Burt sprang to the defense of his father. "He *can't* say it. He's from another era, another time. But now . . . my father and I are . . . uh . . . we hug each other." He wiped his eyes and concluded painfully, honestly. "But he still can't say it."

Not the Burt Reynolds any of us knew. But that was becoming par for the course on *Inside the Actors Studio.*

One of our guests cried for happiness, just as helplessly as any of the guests who had cried for sadness. In January 2004, when I asked Kate Winslet, "What happened last December twenty-second?" she glowed and said, "I had a baby! His name is Joe Alfie Winslet Mendes."

"And his father is?"

"Sam Mendes."

"We feel a certain proprietary interest in Sam Mendes because when Steven Spielberg was here, he said, 'There's a young director. We're signing him to do a movie.' The rest is history."

"Yeah, he's really . . . wonderful, he's . . . I'll start crying in a bit 'cause I'm so emotional about . . . we've just had the baby and . . . and . . ." She gave up and blubbered.

"Why would it make you cry?" I asked inanely, but she was too far gone to hear me.

"He's—he's really wonderful," she said to the students. "It's just, you know, an amazingly emotional time and I'm seeing him being this wonderful father. . . . Sorry! Oh! Excuse me."

"But that's *nice,*" I said, making my usual futile effort to help.

"Yeah," Kate bawled. "I'm very, very happy. Sorry! I'm very happy right now."

The students, as helpless as I, burst into laughter and loud applause, to which Kate replied, "Oh, God!!! Have you got any gin? Maybe *that'll* calm me down."

Like Billy Bob Thornton, Queen Latifah had lost a brother, and she sought a similar consolation. "You've described visits to your brother's grave," I said. "What happens when you go there?"

"Well, um . . . Why you start with me, James Lipton!" The students laughed and I picked up another card, but she kept going. "It's the only cemetery that I don't feel uncomfortable or spooked by—because so many of my family members are in this place, and my brother's there, and it's the closest I can get to him."

She came to a halt, searching a pocket for a tissue. "You about to have the makeup people coming out here!"

"But your description of it was very touching. Couple of beers, pour one on the ground . . ."

"Yeah. You know you can't take one without pouring some out for those who ain't here. So, I would go buy two beers and go up there and . . . and . . . sit and talk. . . . Why you start this? Damn!"

"We don't have to go on."

"Well, I'm crying now, so I'm messin' up my makeup anyway, so—no, it's cool." She steadied herself and continued. "When things would get too hectic for me to handle—my anonymity's starting to be gone and people know who I am—it would get heavy sometimes, so I would just go up to where my brother was buried and sit on the ground, look at the sky, talk to God, drink a brew, talk to Winky, cry, laugh, pray, you know? And then, I would be all right. Now can I get that makeup lady out here?"

She changed her mind. "Can I get a tissue at least?"

I handed her some tissues from the table with the water pitcher. "Thank you. That's gonna make things much nicer. I'm not that high-maintenance; I don't need my makeup lady. Just a little tisha. That's T-I-S-H-A, tisha." She blotted her face daintily. "Okay, that's better."

In the classroom session at the end of Spike Lee's evening, he offered the students some valuable counsel. "In no other profession in the world do people have to deal with rejection as you do. Your worth—let me not use the word *worth*—your talent, all the stuff that you can do, might have nothing to do with whether you're right for the role. You'll be told you're too short, you're too tall, your nose is too big, it's too small, get some butt, get some breasts, lose some butt, lose some breasts. It's a very, very tough business. But if this is what you want to do, if this is what you love, then you're not going to let that stop you."

On the nights Kedakai and I go home after the shoot without stopping at

Elaine's, Kedakai says good night and goes off to bed, knowing that, after a bowl of soup or an apple, I will sit down in our living room without television or reading material at hand, to wind down, alone and silent, thinking of nothing, looking at nothing, just staring into space, coming back down to sea level.

After our evening with Spike, I sat in the living room, reflecting on his last words to the students, summed up in the brutal honesty of "In no other profession in the world do people have to deal with rejection as you do."

That jarred a memory of the many times people—friends, strangers—have asked me if actors are as "vain as they seem," a question guaranteed to arouse my ire—and a response to the effect that, by and large, actors have, not sturdier, but far more fragile egos than any equivalent group in any other calling.

The explanation lies in Spike's summation. How many jobs does the average adult hold in a lifetime? Five? Six? How many times is the average person hired, fired? How many times does he or she have to begin again from square one—as the average actor does after every job? How many traumatic periods of unemployment does the average person face? How many times in a lifetime does anyone in any other walk of life have to face the kind of rejection Spike described: You're too short, you're too tall . . . ?

How many times does an actor go through that emotional meat grinder? Fifty times a year—if the actor is lucky enough to be offered that many opportunities, with the possibility—the likelihood—of fifty nos a year. Fifty rejections with, in Spike's words, "nothing to do with whether you're right for the role." In an average career, that can add up to two thousand rejections.

And not only in the "average" career. As our students learn from even the loftiest of our guests, that was the experience of most of them before they became "overnight successes."

Sylvester Stallone, a wealthy man and bona fide star, told our students about *his* overnight success. The character of Rocky, it turned out, was a metaphor. "I guess Rocky was born out of frustration because we may never see the best actors. They don't make it because quite often their instrument is so sensitive, with the amount of rejection one takes, and the constant bombardment to the ego, they just self-destruct or they leave the business. So, I thought, if I could somehow put together all the frustrations in life and my inability to be recognized as an actor, in the embodiment of a fighter—because that's basically what we're doing, we're constantly fighting the odds—it might translate."

Stallone was one of those rare guests who brought all three disciplines, acting, writing and directing, to the actors, writers and directors in our school, but most of all, I wanted them to hear the saga of *Rocky,* not only as metaphor for the actor's life, but as a parable of the kind of crucial decisions our students would someday have to face. Sly's tale began in the cheery language of a fanzine.

"I delivered the script and they said, 'Very nice. We're going to buy it from you. We're going to give you twenty grand. And we'd like to have Ryan O'Neal play the part—or Burt Reynolds.' I said, 'Oh, God, I really have my heart set on this.' They said, 'But no one knows you.' I said, 'I understand that, so I'll work for free.' They go, 'It doesn't work that way.'

"They said, 'Well, would you take eighty grand?' I said, 'No.' They said, 'Well, you know, we're also going to send it to Redford. And if he wants to do it, we're going to give you two hundred grand.' I said, 'Well, that's a lot.'"

He stared out at the students. "Understand, I had sold my dog because I couldn't afford dog food, you know what I mean? The car cost forty dollars, and I couldn't even put gas in it. We used it as a storage room. It never left the driveway."

"I've read that you had a hundred and six dollars in the bank," I said.

"A hundred and six bucks between me and oblivion."

"And they were now offering how much? Two hundred thousand?"

"It was at two hundred. So, Redford showed some interest, and so did John Boorman. They said, 'Okay, would you take three hundred?'

"I go home to my wife and say, 'Oh, my God!' Now, you understand, it was so hot in the kitchen in this little place that she used to get a bloody nose cooking, from the heat. So, we could've used the money. We were really down and out—and we're talking down and out! But—I can't do it. I can't do it! I know it maybe sets us up for the rest of our lives, but . . .'"

He shook his head in remembered anguish. "My life is an open wound. It's a mystery, and I hate that. I can't live a mystery for the rest of my life. But I can't do it. I can't look in the mirror. I go, 'You've come this far. Your whole life! You can't *sell* it!'

"So, they said, 'Three hundred thirty thousand. And then finally, they said, 'Three sixty,' and I said, 'Let me explain something. Don't make the movie. Don't make the movie, because I'm never going to sell it.'

"And they said, 'You're crazy!' I said, 'I understand that, but I'm never going to sell it.'

"So, they came back and said, 'Okay, fine, you can do the movie. You're going to get paid three hundred forty dollars a week. And that's it.' And I said, 'Fine.'"

"What did they give you for the screenplay?"

"The minimum: twenty grand. After taxes and the agent, I cleared about eight. I was more than happy, really more than happy."

When Matt Damon was on our stage, he described a similar circumstance when a bidding war erupted for *Good Will Hunting,* the screenplay he'd begun as an exercise in a class at Harvard and completed with his boyhood friend Ben Affleck in a desperate effort to create roles for themselves in an indifferent Hollywood. "Was there pressure for you guys not to play the roles?" I asked.

"Oh, yeah," Matt replied. "People kept saying, 'This is unprecedented. Nobody knows who you guys are; you can't do this.' And our answer was 'Sylvester Stallone.'"

Matt and Ben won the Academy Award for their screenplay, and Matt was nominated for an acting Oscar; and Sly Stallone's tale had a famously happy ending, as romantic and unlikely as Rocky Balboa's. But, needless to say, these two tales are notable because they're atypical. The typical experience is not ego building, and I believe that what the public takes for vanity is the result of a lifetime of being required repeatedly to sell the only product the actor has: himself or herself. And when the buyers say no to the actor, they're saying no to the *person*. The skin doesn't thicken; it thins, and what the public perceives as veneer is body armor.

Mike Myers brought five hours of what he proudly called "silly" to our stage. It was, he explained to the students, traditional in his family. "Silly was big for my dad. If my dad had written a treatise on life, it would've been in praise of silly. 'Silly is an underrated art form,' my dad would say. 'It's hard to be silly, and it's important to be silly. Silly is a state of grace,' is what my dad would say. 'Silly is you in a natural state, and serious is something you have to do until you can get silly again.'"

Mike's mother qualified too. "My dad knew when he was being silly; my mom is just silly. She's very nutty, my mom; she has no sense of internal monologue. Everything that's in her head comes out. We'll be driving along and she'll say things like, 'Ants don't like cucumbers. Termites *do* like cinnamon. In fact, most of your exoskeletal pests don't like condiments of any sort. Do you know a termite could be starving, you put down cinnamon, he wouldn't thank you for it.'

"She's just odd, my mom. I love her to death, I do, she's really, really great, but—you know how the day is long? That's how nutty she is."

At this point we knew we were in for a significant experience. We didn't realize quite *how* significant.

For one thing, no guest has ever been more generous in allowing me to interview his characters. We began with one of his most popular *Saturday Night Live* creations, Linda Richman, who was, he informed us, based closely— *very* closely—on his mother-in-law.

I said, "I wonder, Mike, if you would mind if I spoke to Linda for just a moment."

He morphed instantly. "Oh—okay."

"Linda, you and I have something in common. *Coffee Talk* and *Inside the Actors Studio.* I think sometimes the public probably can't tell the two shows apart. How did you become a talk-show host?"

"Well, the first time I saw you, and you came out, pink as gum, I loved you. I saw you there, talking to Christopher Walken . . . and I got a little *verklempt.*" Immersed in Linda now, he turned to our audience as Linda customarily turned to hers when she was *verklempt.* "I'll give you a topic. James Lipton is neither a lip nor a ton. Discuss."

Mike's generosity that night was boundless. I said, "Another of your most popular characters is Philip, the hyper-hypo. How did you invent him?"

"Well, as a child, I was extremely hypoglycemic. I would eat chocolate and then I would have to be restrained. I ate chocolate at Expo '67 and ran into the Soviet Pavilion. I left a vapor trail and my parents thought I'd defected. Sometimes when I eat a lot of chocolate—like I did before this interview," he added significantly, "I'll just say anything that pops into my head."

Throwing caution to the winds, I said, "I wonder if I could have a word with Philip."

Instantly, Mike was the squirming, screeching Philip. "Yes, you can have a word with Philip!"

"Philip, how old are you?"

Philip held up four fingers. "I am this many years old. Hey! I don't think about you when you're not here, you know."

Philip—and Mike—are masters of non sequitur, and twisted Cartesian logic. "Are you named after soup?" Philip demanded. "Are you filled with potatoes and whatnot?"

To the tune of "London Bridge Is Falling Down," Philip sang us a song about a stegosaurus, then asked if he could comb my hair, an offer I deflected with "I can't help noticing that you're not wearing your helmet or your harness tonight."

"No, I am *sans chapeau.* I am without my harness. Which I think ultimately will be a mistake." He veered again. "I followed you home once!"

"Me?"

"Yes, I wanted to see if you had pop bottles. But you didn't."

"I might have given you some chocolate."

Philip peered across at me, his right eyelid at perpetual half-mast, and delivered one of his signature lines. "You're the devil." He leaned closer to confide, "My mom says I'm not supposed to have chocolate because I have an adverse reaction in the islets of Langerhans, which is the area that produces insulin within my pancreas."

"A lot of our students would think you're a very lucky kid because you get to play with girls like Nicole Kidman and Kim Basinger. Does that have an effect on your metabolism?"

"Hel*lo*!" Philip declaimed. "I'm presexual!"

"Oh."

"My responses are not gonadal! My love for her would be familial and aesthetic. Duhhh! Mr. Man, Mr. Soup Man, Mr. Soup Man, Mr. Soup Man. Are you married to a ladle?" He turned to the students to confide, "He was attacked once 'cause he was soup. He was a-salted." He fell back in his chair, legs and arms limp. "Sugar dip! Must, must, must get sugar. Need sugar. Talking in taciturn way until get sugar."

He clutched the glass of Coke on his side table and took a long draft, then sat up, restored. "Full sentences!"

Addressing Mike, I said, "Are some of these characters, any of them, all of them, a way of exorcising demons, of expressing yourself in ways that you wouldn't dare do otherwise?"

"Well, yeah. I think I'm a situational extrovert. I'm a site-specific extrovert. I'm not always extroverted."

"Are you ever introverted?"

"I'm *mostly* introverted."

"Are you really?"

"Oh, yeah. Not right *now,* or you'd have a really crappy interview. But I'm not like Sybil. It's not like, 'I'm Mrs. White now,'" he said in Sally Field's Sybil voice. "When I feel like being silly, I'm silly."

One of the things the students and I have learned about comedic artists like Billy Crystal and Robin Williams and Mike Myers is that the extraordinary scope of their intellects provides them with an encyclopedic, instantly available frame of reference as they skip merrily from the islets of Langerhans to creative evolution.

When Mike and I were talking about the Austin Powers films, I said, "There's a lot of bathroom humor in Austin Powers, including a character named Number Two. The British are nuts about it."

"And so am I. The thing I like about British comedy is that there's a wide range of what they'll find funny. Like the juxtaposition of two unlike things now perfectly meshed together. Henri Bergson said that comedy was the realization of your own mortality in that instant. For example, if you slip on a banana peel, you're no different than matter: Matter is inanimate, and you're subject to the laws of gravity like anything, which means that you are dead, and that's why you laugh. And I think poo-poo is funny. Know what I mean?"

"From Bergson to poo-poo."

"It doesn't matter. That's what my point is: I don't judge. Smart joke, not-smart joke—it's funny or not funny, as far as I'm concerned."

When he turned his analytical eye to the craft of comedy, he said, "I think it was Woody Allen who said that comedy sits at the children's table. And I think it should *always* sit at the children's table. That's fine because I think comedy is an appropriately modest art form that shouldn't necessarily take itself so seriously. The thing I admire about great comedic acting is that it's ninety-nine point nine percent commitment and one molecule of judgment or exaggeration. That's the proportion of distancing to commitment that I think marks a great comedic actor. Someone like Peter Sellers has maybe an electron of judgment, but it's just enough to know that it's comedic."

As usual, when the evening ended, the guest and I were hungry and too wired to call it a night, so Mike and I, in a group of eight, headed for Elaine's. Once we arrived, the site-specific extrovert made way for the introvert, and Mike, while amiable and engaged, said little, as seven of us carried the conversational ball for hours, with Mike's occasional pointed contributions.

A week later, my assistant tottered into my office with an enormous gift basket piled high with edibles and potables, every one of them a Lipton product.

The attached note said: "Dear Soupy, Thanks to you & your students for an awesome experience, before the meal . . . & after."

Melanie Griffith had to cancel her first date with us. She was supposed to come shortly before Thanksgiving, but a week before the scheduled date, I picked up the morning paper to read that she had checked herself into rehab for a recurring drug problem. At noon that day, I got a call from her PR representative, Robin Baum, who confirmed the newspaper report, and told me that she had Melanie on a second line, from the rehab center. Melanie had insisted, Robin said, that she call me.

"Tell her we understand," I said. "It's okay. The only thing that matters is Melanie."

"You *don't* understand," Robin said. "She's coming."

"To New York? To us?"

"Yes."

I could hear Melanie's voice, faint but urgent, issuing from Robin's second phone: "What's he saying?"

"Can you wait a week?" Robin said. "Just one week?"

"But won't she need time . . . ?"

"She'll be out of rehab in ten days, and then she just needs a couple of days at home."

I could hear Melanie's voice issuing from the other phone. "Please!!!"

"Of course," I said.

She showed up on the new date, eager, a little jittery, and, to put it mildly, welcome. Melanie is normally gentle and vulnerable: On this night she was visibly fragile—and as valiant as Joan of Arc.

Onstage, she was gracious, bright and fascinating, describing a childhood as the daughter of one of Alfred Hitchcock's muses, Tippi Hedren, living among Hollywood legends. "I meant to bring this to you because it's so beautiful," she said. "I have an autograph book. Charlie Chaplin drew his little tramp—it's a real collector's item now. And I had Marlon Brando, who wrote, 'To a beautiful young lady I hope to see again and again.' I loved that!"

"And he meant it. How old were you?"

"I was eight."

"Maybe he didn't mean it."

"So—Marlon Brando, Charlie Chaplin, Sophia Loren, who became like my idol. I thought she was really a woman. She was wonderful with me, and very patient and beautiful."

"So, it was not your average childhood."

"I guess not."

At the age of eighteen, Melanie played Joanne Woodward's daughter in *The Drowning Pool*. She told us, "I have a picture of Paul Newman and me on that set and he's gesticulating with his hands, and it looks like he's saying something very poetic to me. But actually, what's he's saying is, 'You have to go to acting school! You have to learn your craft.'"

She responded by enrolling with Stella Adler. "She was unbelievable and powerful," she said, then echoed De Niro. "She made me understand that it wasn't about me, it wasn't about my part, it was about the story—and if you picked up a glass of water, how did that character do that? She was so scary and fabulous and enticing and mysterious—all at the same time, wasn't she?"

"Yes, she was."

"I did *Waiting for Lefty* in front of her, and afterwards, she said, 'You are going to be a great actress . . . But you cannot play that part.' She was awesome."

"Do you use what you learned with her?"

"Absolutely."

Since her recent relapse and rehab had been in the press, and there had been speculation about whether she would in fact show up at our school, and hordes of paparazzi were waiting for her when she arrived, I asked her in the greenroom if she wanted to talk about that part of her life. She replied with what I learned was her favorite word: "Definitely."

Onstage, I said, "One would have thought that in the wake of personal successes like *Something Wild* and *Working Girl,* your life would be on a very even keel."

"Yeah. One would have thought . . . one would have thought. . . ."

"That was when you checked yourself into the Hazelden clinic?"

"That was right after *Working Girl.* Can I smoke a cigarette?"

"Yes."

"If we're going to get to this part, I'm going to smoke a cigarette."

The cigarette got the usual hand, but not for the usual reason. The students applauded her guts.

As she lit up, I said, "*That's* a dangerous addiction."

"Yeah, I know. Well, one addiction at a time."

"I've asked this naïve question before of Jimmy Caan and Richard Dreyfuss, Ed Harris. With so much going on in your lives, so much that's wonderful and so much to lose, how does it happen you put yourselves at such risk?"

Melanie was patient with me. "It's not something that you intend to do, you know. When I put myself into Hazelden in 1988, it was to quit drinking and to quit doing cocaine. And then, just recently, I had to put myself in someplace for pain pills, which were prescribed by a doctor. It was not my intention to get hooked on those things. But I think that what happens with us is that—at least I can speak for myself—I am a sensitive . . . in that I mean that I feel everything really strong. . . . It makes me want to cry." She fought threatening tears. "I feel things very strongly. And I think in my youth, I used alcohol and cocaine in order to cover up the pain that I felt."

"What pain?"

"*Any* kind of pain. Like the pain of the emptiness inside that you don't know how to fill really. I can fill a *character* great, but I don't know how to fill myself, you know? And therein lies the rub." She chuckled at the allusion. "So, that's something I'm working on."

"How are you doing?"

"Seventeen days and counting."

The students cheered.

As we prepare to edit each show, we ask the guest to send us their personal memorabilia—family photos, yearbooks, souvenirs. Jack Lemmon had lost most of his personal effects in a California mudslide shortly before he came to *Inside the Actors Studio.* But when we went into the edit room, a photo album arrived—the only one that had survived the debacle—entrusted to the express mail service and to us.

Holly Hunter sent us a package with a note: "Jim—I'm placing sole responsibility for the safety of these five pictures with you. Have fun in the editing room."

The day we went into the Griffith edit, a package arrived. I opened it to find myself confronted with Charlie Chaplin's tramp and Marlon's flirtatious note: Melanie had put her album in our hands.

⚊

I'm often asked, "Who was your favorite guest?" It is, of course, the one question I will never answer. Assuming that I had a favorite, I would hardly risk offending more than two hundred guests by selecting one. But the truth is, I don't have a favorite. Since my criterion for issuing an invitation is, Does this guest have something to teach our students, I have many favorites for a wide variety of reasons.

Some guests are shier than others, some bolder, some take longer to relax and let go, some arrive in overdrive, some are exceptionally articulate, some exceptionally impassioned, but none of them has ever failed to fulfill the program's purpose: to pass whatever information, experience and expertise the guest possesses across the footlights to the students and through the camera lenses to the public.

If I were to keep track of each comment, solicited or unsolicited, that I receive, every show from 1994 to the present would turn out to be *someone's* favorite, some shows, admittedly, with more admirers than others, but no show would fail to make the list. That said, it's no secret or surprise that the show most often and enthusiastically mentioned by the public is the Robin Williams episode.

Robin delivered so much talent, gusto, brilliance and unbridled joy to our stage that Bravo asked for a two-hour special episode. But even with the added time, the public saw only two-fifths of what our lucky students did. For five hours, Robin was in his chair, out of his chair, running around the stage, climbing the proscenium arch (literally), singing, dancing, doffing one persona and donning another at warp speed, inventing, entrancing, beguiling, bewitching—reanimating Arlecchino, Punch, the Lord of Misrule.

Robin came onstage at 7:07 p.m.—and took over—with, I don't hesitate to say, my full cooperation. At 7:16, I managed to ask my first question.

By 7:23, I'd worked two questions into the thrilling pandemonium, and was preparing to ask a third, when Robin sprang out of his chair and leaned over my table to peer at my lapel pin, saying, "I have to fix this. Hold on."

He rotated the pin 180 degrees. I rotated it back. "No, that's the way it's supposed to be."

"You want the eagle upside down?"

"Yeah."

"It's supposed to be like that?"

"That's AOPA."

"Ay-OH-Pa?"

"Airplane Owners and Pilots Association, and for some reason, the wings slope down."

"But you want it going into the ground?" He leapt to his feet and addressed the audience, reeling drunk in the time it took him to reach the footlights. "I'd like to welcome you to the AOPA. We also have AA-AOPA, so, if this is your first time flying a plane on alcohol, I'd like to welcome you. Oooh-kay, let's go over a couple of features in the plane. The wet bar's here." He sobered up and looked at me, savoring the acronym. "AOPA?"

"AOPA."

"AOPA . . ."

"And that's the way they make their wings."

"They make their wings going down?"

"Yep."

"That's reassuring. Like a Parachuters' Association with just strings." By now, he was barely audible over the laughter and applause. "Welcome to the National Association of Free Fall. We have a meeting. So far, no one's attended. But we're hoping for more people next week." He looked at me, still enjoying the word. "AOPA."

"AOPA. In fact, I'm going flying next weekend. Would you like to go flying with me?"

"*Oh,* yeah! Yeah, buddy. What do you fly? Is it a two-engine plane?"

"No. Single."

"Single engine. Even *more* reassuring."

In July 2001, I received a letter from Phil Boyer, the president of AOPA, saying, "What a hilarious interview with Robin Williams on *Inside the Actors Studio*! I shared the AOPA excerpts with our employees during a recent 'hangar session.' As you can well imagine, the audience roared. I would like to include those excerpts as part of my presentation during Pilot Town Meetings I conduct across the country." We sent him the material and I assume that, from that day to this, the Pilot Town Meetings begin with Robin's besotted aviator.

Just as Robin's episode is often singled out by the public, there are five minutes of it that constitute the most famous tour de force in the history of the series. Like every other moment that night, it began innocently: We played back for Robin and our audience what happened when I asked Billy Crystal if there was anyone he envied, and he replied, "Robin Williams. He has a boldness and a fearlessness that's an exploration of his mind. You go, 'Wow! Look at that!' You know, if I was fast tonight, he'll be faster."

That prompted me to say to Robin, "All of us admire the lightning-fast physical reflexes of great athletes. For those of us who haven't been blessed with your gift, how do you explain the *mental* reflexes that you deploy and are deploying tonight with such awesome speed? Are you *thinking* faster than the rest of us? What the hell is going on?"

He stood up and improvised a five-minute stand-up on what appeared to be one breath. It was filled with wild flights like "It's all part of the mind that is a three-and-a-half-pound gland that pumps neurons constantly and deals with itself by responding to stimulus. That's what we're *designed* to do, evolving slowly. Even Darwin's going, 'I had *hopes*. I had such high hopes!' And now they're spilling oil in the Galápagos, and there's turtles wandering around going, 'Don't you *get* it? This is a testing ground!'"

The turning point—for him, for *Inside the Actors Studio*—was when he said, "But the real fun is when you actually take things from people in the audience." Scanning the front row, he zeroed in on a young woman with a pink pashmina in her lap. "Darling, you look lovely and I love what you put together tonight. Let me borrow your little shawl. We've never met before, have we?"

He draped the pashmina over his head and was instantly Indian. "I came to Bombay last year. You know, I have directed fifteen movies in Bombay. I am very excited about my musical. It is a lovely musical called *Whose Sari Now*. I have written this magical thing and I do them all now. My other one is 'Bindi, Bindi, Bindi-bowl'—and 'Tika-Tika-Tika-Te.'"

He pulled one edge of the scarf across his face, covering all but his eyes, changing accent and gender. "I would like to welcome you to Iran. Help me! Help me *now*! Don't tell them I talked to you!"

He dropped the shawl to his shoulders, its tassled ends falling in front of him, chanted in pidgin Hebrew, then greeted us with, "My name is Rabbi Ben Shubel. I would like to welcome you to the first openly gay shul. Why is tonight different from all others? Because we are gonna dance! We are going to dance like no other. . . ." He raised his arms in Jerome Robbins's signature *Fiddler on the Roof* gesture. "To tradition!"

He slid the pashmina from his shoulders and tucked it around his waist. A new voice, new accent and new character arrived with the improvised apron. "Welcome to *Iron Chef.*" Busily slicing and dicing, he said, "First of all, tonight, we are going to cook octopus balls. As you know there are eight legs, so you get four sets of balls. You cook them up. Not be afraid to do the balls. I'll cook them up and put on the side. I warn you, don't try this at home. First of all, you have to *find* them, which is so hard!"

In a swift gesture and without an instant's pause, he whipped the pashmina off his waist, held it to one side with a familiar flourish, and seguéed into a thick Spanish accent. "I am very angry that I can't find my own cape. I go into the ring, the bull just looks at me like, 'What the fuck! Are you kidding? Don't come in the ring with a Donna Karan scarf! What are you? *Nuts?*'"

He wound the scarf gently around his wrists, binding them together. "You're under Amish house arrest." He glanced at me. "It's like the old joke: You know what a guy with his hand in a horse's ass is? An Amish mechanic."

Again without a pause, he folded the pashmina into a pink oblong and raised it in front of his face, a hand on either side, swishing it back and forth. Then, in an astounding imaginative leap, his face appeared, pushing slowly through the moving fringe in his final transformation—to an automobile grille emerging from a car wash.

"That's as close as I can explain. It's not really an explanation, but more of a bizarre exploration," Robin said, tossing the pashmina back to the young woman in the front row and returning to his seat as the audience rose to its feet in a sixty-second ovation.

Several months later, when Kedakai and I encountered Robin, I revealed to him that the young woman from whom he'd borrowed the pashmina was my goddaughter, Jami Lynn Brown, and that the pashmina had been our Christmas gift to her. I said I was convinced that, thanks to him, it had become the third most famous covering in the world, after the Shroud of Turin, and Isadora Duncan's scarf, and that Jami had taken an oath it would never see the inside of a dry-cleaning establishment.

W hen we realized that in March 2001, the one hundredth guest would come to our stage, the search began for an artist who could carry our banner on that important night. One quickly emerged: a longtime member of the Actors Studio, with two Oscars, two British Academy Awards and two Golden Globe Awards on his CV, and the unqualified respect of his community, Gene Hackman.

For thirteen years, as I've looked for the spine to lead us through each life that unfolds on our stage, I've kept an eye out for *Inside the Actors Studio*'s spine—a unifying theme, a common thread that ties all our guests together. Two or three themes have emerged, on our stage and in these pages, none more persistent and compelling than the theme of parental loss, by divorce, separation or death. By my count, 75 percent of our guests share this experience.

Perhaps it looms so large to me because I share it, too, so I notice it whenever it appears, and may sometimes attach unwarranted importance to it. In any event, it has taken pride of place among my unprovable theories: I suspect that, more than any other biological or experiential factor, parental loss is the force behind a sometimes relentless drive for acceptance by the public and, of greater importance, approval by the absent parent.

The subject came up within ten minutes of Gene's arrival on our stage. "How old were you when your father left?"

"Well, my dad left us when . . . I was about thirteen, I guess."

"Was it easy? Hard?"

"It was tough, yeah."

"I've read that there was a sort of casual wave good-bye."

"Yeah. I was down the street, playing with some guys and . . . uh . . . he drove by and, and kind of waved and, uh . . ."

He couldn't continue, and I tried to help by changing course. "But you saw him occasionally, huh?" There was no response. I tossed another lifeline. "Were you close to your mother?"

"Yeah." He blinked hard and cleared his throat. "Excuse me."

One more new direction: "Did life change radically—?"

He broke in, wiping his eyes. "It's only been sixty-five years or so. . . ."

The students rescued us both with applause, and I made an attempt to replace the personal with the impersonal. "Lots of people have talked about that experience and it's always the same: It's not something that goes away easily."

"Probably makes you a better actor," Gene said.

The door had opened to my theory. "Why does it make you a better actor?"

"I don't advocate that, but—you get in touch with your feelings and—that's what we're here for."

"Yeah."

"I think if you can draw on that kind of thing, you get something out of it," he concluded.

When I asked Melanie Griffith how old she was when her parents divorced, she said, "I think I was three."

"Did it have an effect on you?"

"I wanted to live in Kansas."

"Why Kansas?"

"Because I thought, if I lived in Kansas, I could click my heels three times and they could both come and visit me. And I wouldn't have to go back and forth all the time."

Rosie O'Donnell was emphatic about the effect of parental loss. "I definitely think there's a wound that's created by the death of a parent, especially at a young age."

"How old were you when your mother died?"

"I was ten."

"How old was she?"

"She was thirty-nine."

"Both of you too young, eh?"

"Yeah. When I made it to forty, I was kind of shocked."

"Did you and your siblings attend your mother's funeral?"

"We attended the wake."

"Wasn't it your birthday?"

"Yeah. My brother Timmy was born the day before me. So, the wake and funeral were over our birthday, which has made it very difficult ever since to enjoy any kind of celebration on that day."

"You've called the weeks and months that followed your mother's death a denial buffet. What did they tell you your mother died of?"

"My father told us she had hepatitis, and I went to the encyclopedia and looked it up at school. It said it was a disease you got from dirty needles, and I thought it was from sewing—because a child will make reasons if you don't give them the answers; they'll make up the answers to fit.

"When I was in the seventh or eighth grade, I was with my best friend, Jackie. There was a bikeathon for cancer, so we had to wait at the streetlight as all these bikes went by, and Jackie looked at me and said, 'Hopefully, Roseanne, one day, if enough people do these bikeathons, people like your mom won't have to die of cancer.' That's how I found out she died of cancer."

There is always a special surge of energy and interest in our theater when the guest is a member of the students' generation. That was emphatically the case when Will Smith arrived on our stage, with a lesson in hip-hop nomenclature. Trying to close the generational gap between Will and me, I asked him, "When and how did you become Fresh Prince?"

"There were tons of different names," Will said. "I was MC Funk, I was the Sorcerer, I was Willie Will, I was The Prince Will Rock. Those were the good ones. I kind of locked onto the Prince when my eighth-grade teacher started calling me The Prince." He grinned. "That's something to do with this vast wellspring of charm."

"As in Prince Charming?"

"As in Prince Charming. In 1985, *fresh* was the inescapable new hip-hop slang, and I just put the *fresh* with the *prince*. I think that what rappers try to do is create a name that is essentially the person we yearn to be."

Will and the students joined forces in a spirited rendition of Will's first hit, "Parents Just Don't Understand," and when I asked him about freestyling, he replied with a rap: "I started this show, came out here today, had no idea what I might say, whether I'd be hot, whether I would sink or swim, I knew I'd have a ball with my big man Jim.

"There's a lotta guys," he said, "you hear 'em freestyling, you're like, 'How can you make that up like that?' Busta Rhymes is really good. I'm not great. I can get a good punch line."

"I just heard one I loved."

With Will, we were able to examine the recent rash of surprisingly smooth transitions from rapper to actor. "Is there a correlation between rapping and acting?" I asked.

"Oh, absolutely. What happens with rap music that's different than singing is, in rap music, you have to defend yourself. You know? Rap music is really aggressive. There's no place for a lack of confidence. In rap music, you'll get chewed up and spit out if you're not confident, and if you're not strong and assertive. So, what happens is that, when you take that energy, you take that strength, you take that bravado, you take LL Cool J, you take Queen Latifah, you take Tupac Shakur, DMX, people that have mastered that space, mastered that strength, mastered that confidence, it looks really good on camera. And there's something in rappers' eyes, something that gets *created* in the eyes from having been able to create that defense—through an offensive posture—and to be able to be in that space where you feel confident, and you don't care what nobody says and you don't care how they come at you.

"'What?! I'm here! *What?!*'" he demanded, then summed up with "The camera really enjoys that strength and that confidence."

When I told Will that he was the first *Inside the Actors Studio* guest who had contributed a word to *Webster's Dictionary,* he said, "Really? What'd I contribute?"

"*Jiggy.*"

"Wow! They put it in the dictionary?"

"You made it to the dictionary."

"You like that?" he responded to the students' applause. "Well, that's a good thing. Now I can look it up, 'cause I have no idea what it means."

"That was my biggest question!" I lamented.

"Oh. Okay. Jiggy. Jiggy. Jiggy is . . . vague. It's ambiguous. Um . . . jiggy . . ."

"Right." I wasn't about to let him off the hook. I waited.

"Um . . . *Jiggy* is the root word. Okay, jiggy—you could have, jigginess. You could have, uh . . ."

"Jiggier."

"Jiggier. There's . . ."

"Jiggiest."

"Someone that makes the transition from being dull and boring into being jiggy has experienced a jiggification," Will said solemnly. "It's one of those crazy slang words. Jiggy is like . . . nuclear cool. You know? Like cool to the ninth power. It's like, if Fonzie was alive today, he'd be jiggy."

"I understand."

"That's a whole next level of cool. It's a theoretical state."

It came as no surprise to our students, and perhaps will come as no surprise to the reader of these pages, that before making the decision to commit himself to rap, Will was accepted to an engineering program at the Massachusetts Institute of Technology.

As the classroom session neared an end, a student rose to say, "We have a debate going here. Being that you are an expert on the topic, do you think that the Emmy-award-nominated dean of the Actors Studio Drama School, Mr. James Lipton, could in fact get jiggy with it?"

Will pondered the question, then proposed, "Now, I *have* thought about this. I've been excited to be on this show, so, this is something that I have spent *hours* at home actually thinking about. The answer is . . . yes, I believe that he could. I would be concerned about him hurting himself. But he is a fighter. He is a fighter. So, I would have to say, yes, he could do it. But we'd have to go with paramedics. Just to be safe. But, yes—absolutely."

B illy Bob Thornton appeared on *Inside the Actors Studio* shortly after he'd assassinated me. Or, more accurately, after he'd assassinated Will Ferrell as me on *Saturday Night Live.* Over a period of three years, Will Ferrell kept popping up on *SNL* as me (an attenuated me, since he's six-foot-four), "interviewing" the likes of Alec Baldwin as Charles Nelson Reilly, and Kate Hudson as Drew Barrymore.

But Will Ferrell's Billy Bob Thornton "interview" approached epic proportions, beginning on *SNL*'s *Inside the Actors Studio* set, moving into *SNL*'s edit room, and delivering unprecedented production values in a rare *SNL* location shoot, with Billy Bob, brandishing a rifle, chasing Will/me down Broadway into the path of an oncoming taxi.

From the beginning, *SNL* had gone to considerable lengths to reproduce our show, acquiring our opening titles and creating a remarkably accurate replica of our set with its *deux fauteuils de mauvais goût* (some wounds never heal), but the Billy Bob Thornton sketch was more ambitious than any of its predecessors.

The Will Ferrell/me sketches were reaching a crescendo when *Inside the Actors Studio* arrived at its hundredth episode, so I invited Will to join me, mano a mano, on our stage in a sketch which we would jointly write.

When Will arrived in our greenroom with his *SNL* writers, Steve Higgins and Michael Schur, a wardrobe person, hair person and makeup artist, we met for the first time, and chatted as his team painstakingly transformed him into me.

Surreal. *Really* surreal.

In thirteen years, there has never been a reaction quite like the one that greeted us when we walked out on our stage: It mixed equal parts of shock, disbelief, delight and anticipation. All students enjoy seeing their teachers and deans—the authority figures of their academic lives—occasionally brought low, but this promised new highs—or lows.

The first question to be answered was, who would sit where? Who would be the interviewer and who the guest? When I stopped at the stage left chair, the guest's chair, and Will continued to mine, there was a sharp exclamation from the students, then enthusiastic applause.

Employing the pompous, unctuous, pretentious, overblown, funereal voice and demeanor he customarily donned with his *Inside the Actors Studio* costume and makeup, the Will/me addressed the audience: "In the last seven years, I have interviewed one hundred of the greatest artists of our time. Now I match wits with my most brilliant guest yet. Today, I will pick the brain of one of the most important human beings on earth. Please welcome . . . *meeeeee!*" He nodded loftily. "Mr. Lipton, welcome."

"Thank you, Mr. Lipton."

I produced a stack of blue cards and piled them on the table next to me. Will/me scooped up cards and added them to his stack. I answered with more cards in front of me. In the script we'd written, this moment was simply called, "DUELING BLUE CARDS."

In the *SNL* sketches, Will sat behind a stack of blue cards that dwarfed my usual stack. This time, he finally reached over, took all my cards and put them on his, creating a stack that dwarfed *him*—all six feet, four inches of him—a tottering totem he had to crane around to see me.

He resumed, slooooowly, lugubriously. "In the 1960s, you, which is to say *meeee,* brilliantly portrayed Dr. Richard Grant on the operatic television transmission known as *La Lumière Guidante,* or, in American English, *'Guiding Light.'* What was it like to be perfect for seven consecutive years?"

"Oh, I don't know if I'd call it perfect. On second thought, *I* probably *would.* I certainly enjoyed the role."

"And the role enjoyed *you!*" He rocked dangerously back in his chair and emitted the hollow laugh that represented me, amused.

"It was the role of a lifetime," he continued in what he considered my customary understatement, "and made you, without question, the most gifted, distinguished, dare I say beloved actor of your, or any other, generation."

"You left out 'humble,'" I complained.

"James Lipton, you are a delight!" Will's James Lipton exulted. "You produced the Inaugural Gala for President James Earl Carter in 1977."

"Yes. It was a great honor," my much paler version of James Lipton replied.

"I think the world was as shocked as I that he did not replace his entire cabinet with you. At the very least he should have put you in as his secretary of perrrrfection."

I glanced at the students. "If I didn't know better, I'd think this guy was trying to suck up to me."

The Will/me reacted with shock at the notion, then said, "You once wrote, 'If my hairline ever recedes, I am going to compensate by growing a neatly trimmed beard in hopes that no one will notice.'"

"How did you know that!" I exclaimed. "Have you been reading my diary?"

"I *wrote* your diary! Remember?" He laughed his/my ghoulish laugh, and I responded with an identical sound. He/I answered the challenge with an even louder laugh, and I answered back.

The script called for "DUELING LAUGHS."

Finally, I said, "You know, if I spoke as slowly as you do, we'd be here all night."

Will/I got an ovation with "If I spoke any faster I wouldn't be youuuuuuu."

Selecting a card from the top of his pile, he intoned, "Now it is tiiiime for the dreaded questionnaire, invented by the great Bernarrrr Peeevooooh, of *Apogeeee l'apostophe grunamonamie kiko lofooo.* What is your favorite word?"

"Me."

"What is your least favorite word?"

"You."

"What turns you on?"

"Me."

"What turns you off?"

"You."

"Well played! What sound or noise do you love?"

"The sound of my own voice."

"What sound or noise do you hate?"

"The sound of *your* voice, doing *my* voice."

"What is your favorite curse word?"

"Will Ferrell."

"What profession other than yours would you like to attempt?"

"Actually, I've always wanted to direct."

"Oh? And finally, if heaven exists what would you like to hear God say when you arrive?"

" 'Don't worry, Jim. Will Ferrell's going to the other place.' "

As the students applauded, Will and I broke character, relaxed in the chairs and addressed each other as ourselves.

"What do you think, Will? Emmy?"

"Nomination, anyway. Yeah."

"Nah," I objected, "it was worth more than a nomination. You were incredible."

"You—you were more than incredible," he insisted. "You were—you were fantaaastic." He'd slipped back into him/me again.

I followed suit. "You were *more* than fantastic. You were amaaazing."

"No, no! You were brilllliant."

We both saw the opening and proclaimed together, "You were a . . . deeeelight!"

I ask my share of naïve questions on *Inside the Actors Studio,* but one of the most naïve questions ever asked of me is "Did the Will Ferrell imitation upset you?" *Upset* me! No one waited more eagerly for the next installment—and the day Will left *Saturday Night Live,* which is to say, the day *I* left *Saturday Night Live,* was a very dark day for me.

The pain of parting was allayed a bit in the summer of 2004 when I got a call from the writer/director Nora Ephron to tell me she was directing *Bewitched,* which she'd written with her sister Delia. "There's a scene in it," she said, "in which Will's character is interviewed on television, and Nicole Kidman is so furious when she sees it that she takes revenge on him for the rest of the picture. I was meeting with Will this morning, and I had this idea. I said, 'What if Jim Lipton played the interviewer?' Will said, 'Do whatever you have to do: beg, plead, cajole, threaten.' Jim, I'm begging, pleading cajoling . . ."

"Nora," I said, breaking in with a phrase Harold Clurman employed when his students belabored the obvious, "you're plunging through an open door."

We shot the scene on our set, and as Nora was readying us for the first take, I glanced at Will, sitting the regulation three feet from me in the other *fauteuil de mauvais goût,* and said to Nora, "Look—thanks to Will, there are now *two* mes—*his* me and *my* me. On shows like Conan O'Brien or Jimmy Kimmel, I've sort of acquired a *third* me that's half me, half Will. Which one do you want in the movie, my me or his?"

"The third one, half and half," Nora said, and that's the one that wound up on the screen. When we finished shooting the scripted scene, Nora said, "Would you guys improvise the interview that leads into the script?" For the rest of the day, we did, as Nora watched from behind the camera, her mouth stuffed with Kleenex to stifle the laughter that would have ruined the take. Some of the improv wound up on the screen.

When the December 2006 issue of *GQ* asked me to participate in an article called "39 Things You Don't Know About Will Ferrell," this was my contribution:

Thanks to *GQ,* I can reveal at last that one of the things you don't know about Will Ferrell is that there *is* no Will Ferrell. For years the public has been hoodwinked into believing that Will Ferrell sometimes plays me. Well, it's time to end the charade. I play Will Ferrell.

That's right. With the cooperation of Lorne Michaels and several powerful Hollywood figures, I long ago created this tall, fictional character who so captured the public's fancy that my coconspirators and I found ourselves hoist with our own petard. We thought the joke would wear thin—or become transparent—in a few weeks, but here we are, years later, still living this elaborate—and astonishingly profitable—lie.

Next time you see Will (me!), go right ahead, continue to play the game. Call him Will if you will. But, if you look close, you'll see the glint in "Will's" eye. That's me, winking back at those of you who now know who is who, what is what and Jim is Will.

Willfully yours,
James Lipton

In an undeniably perverse way, Will Ferrell is one of the heroes of this narrative.

So, in a more straightforward way, is Conan O'Brien, who has undertaken the resurrection of the acting career I thought I had left far behind. On several occasions I have occupied the chair next to his desk (where he pointedly introduces me as Dean James Lipton); but on many other occasions, I've responded to a call from his producers proposing that I make an unannounced cameo appearance to recite Kevin Federline's latest opus as if it were holy writ; or read, in the same stentorian tones, one of his audience's blogs; or shotgun beer in Spring Break week; or cry (real tears) as one of his audience members reads Romeo in the balcony scene; or appear as ten characters, from Einstein to Princess Leia, in his New Year's Eve countdown.

These reckless forays have resulted in other casting calls to Bob Levinson, my friend, conscience and agent, from *Arrested Development,* which created a character I played in four episodes; *Joey*; *Jimmy Kimmel Live*; *The Simpsons*; Nora Ephron for *Bewitched*; and even prompted a visit from Ali G, which ended with me writing a rap and performing it with him. My February 2006 ASCAP royalty distribution listed an airing of *Da Ali G Show* in Finland that netted me $1.59 as the rap's author, which allowed me to claim to Queen Latifah that I was, at least in Finland, a professional rapper.

November and December 2006, were particularly busy Conan-months for me, with three appearances. The first was in the chair next to him, to introduce our inaugural *Inside the Actors Studio* DVD release, a boxed set entitled *Icons,* which contains the Paul Newman, Robert Redford, Barbra Streisand and Clint Eastwood episodes, expanded with valuable insights that didn't make the cut when they were aired, and a stand-alone DVD of the Dave Chappelle evening, with my reflections on these guests.

Since that visit to Conan took place on the eve of the delivery of these pages to my eagle-eyed, evenhanded, velvet-gloved editor, Julie Doughty, the book was very much on my mind. The moment I revealed that "at noon tomorrow, the book arrives at Dutton," Conan, a two-time president of *The Harvard Lampoon,* was on the book's case and mine, mimicking the solemnity with which I announced the momentous event. Stung, I pulled a page from my pocket and offered his audience a preview of the book. A moment later I found myself, somewhat to my amazement and decidedly to the audience's, singing Cole Porter's "Night and Day" in Latin, an inarguable first—for Conan, me and, I suspect, for television.

A short time later, on December 9, I got an urgent call from Conan's producers: Something had happened and they needed me there, in the studio, at once. I showed up to discover, as the television audience did that night, that four nights earlier, inventing absurd mascots for college teams, they'd come up with the Florida State University horny manatee, prompting Conan to ad-lib an invitation to visit www.HornyManatee.com.

Like all the late-night shows, Conan tapes late in the afternoon. When he arrived in his dressing room after the mascot remarks, he got a call from NBC's Standards and Practices, which monitors each taping, informing him that he couldn't legally mention the Web site on the telecast unless they owned it. Grinning broadly on the night I showed up, Conan announced that, for $159, NBC was now the proud owner of the HornyManatee Web site . . . "for ten years!"

Moreover, he said, in four days the Web site had had more than a million hits. It was, he said, the birth of a phenomenon, with viewers submitting a torrent of "manatee" photos, drawings, poems and fittingly erotic stories. "And," he added, "we couldn't think of anyone better able to do justice to one of these submissions than the dean emeritus of the Actors Studio Drama School of Pace University, and host of *Inside the Actors Studio,* Dean James Lipton."

Whereupon, I appeared, recited an "Ode to a Manatee," then turned to Conan and—in the words of the script that had been thrust into my hands when I arrived for the show—asked for the privilege of dancing with "that sultry seductress, the horny manatee."

"Ask and you shall receive," Conan intoned, and, behind me, the curtains opened on the massive manatee, gray, bulbous and reasonably authentic, its occupant gyrating to the extent that the heavy costume permitted. Calling upon the years of training with Holm, Daganova and Harkarvy, I danced again—with the horny manatee.

One week later, another urgent call, another script waiting for me, another breathless account by Conan: In the seven days since my last visit, he reported, the manatee Web site had received more than ten million hits and hundreds of thousands of e-mailed creations. The manatee and I were romping on porn sites that had had linked themselves joyfully to HornyManatee.com, and You-Tube throbbed with the perfervid beat of my feet and the sea cow's flippers.

On that second occasion, mere deanship wasn't enough for Conan; he threw in "... and Chevalier of the Order of Arts and Letters" as I appeared, and aware of my responsibility to more than ten million manatomanes, I called upon my choreographic experience to create a *pas de deux d'occasion,* "Doing the Manatee," following which, the Web site took another ten million hits.

In a book devoted to the heroes of my life, I would be remiss not to acknowledge Conan O'Brien for reviving, single-handedly and for reasons unknown to me, my acting, singing (albeit in Latin), dancing and choreographic careers.

The night Johnny Depp came to us, there was rioting in the streets outside our theater, and inside it, people who were neither students nor subscribers to our series were popping out of every aperture but the air-conditioning vents. Today the world acknowledges Johnny's superstar status: We knew it then.

The diversity of our guests has been both a theme of *Inside the Actors Studio* and a source of fascination for the students and me. One of the many surprises the show has provided is the number of our guests who can make the proud boast that they are to some degree Native American. When my notes indicated that Johnny Depp had Native American ancestry, he said, "My family comes from eastern Kentucky. They've been there for many, many generations and my great-grandmother had a lot of Cherokee blood in her."

Thus far in the show's history, we've had six Cherokee feathers in our cap: Johnny, Tommy Lee Jones, Val Kilmer, Kim Basinger, Julia Roberts and Burt Reynolds.

The Choctaw Nation can claim two of our guests: Billy Bob Thornton and Teri Hatcher.

Cameron Diaz can point to Blackfoot forebears, Angelina Jolie to Iroquois, Ellen Burstyn to Ojibway and Anthony Quinn to the Tamarara Indians of Mexico.

Like Sean Penn, Johnny drew cheers from the students by lighting a cigarette—which he rolled himself. And, like Sean, Johnny is known for the scrupulous selectivity with which he chooses his roles. I broached the subject with "You've avoided the path that ninety-nine point nine percent of actors yearn for, which is to go the traditional leading-man route. To put it as delicately as I can: You're so much better-looking than I am. You could so easily have taken the leading-man path, and I'm sure you were offered role after role that required a certain male beauty. Have you deliberately taken another path?"

"Some people would call it ignorance."

"Nobody in *this* room."

"I knew being on *21 Jump Street* was a very fortunate opportunity and gave me a great education in many ways. But I also was so uncomfortable being a product. I couldn't stand it. It was claustrophobic. So I swore to myself that I would choose my own path and wouldn't deviate in any way. And if I failed, I failed, but I tried. And I figured I could always go back to playing guitar or pumping gas."

When I asked about what seemed to be his interest in playing losers and people at risk, he said, "I'm interested, deeply interested, in human behavior and what makes people do what they do, what makes people tick, and why they have these little nervous gestures, which I'm absolutely full of tonight, I'm sure. I don't know about losers but—people who are considered not normal or outcasts, or not welcomed into society . . ."

"Outsiders?"

"People who are not deemed 'normal' by society."

"You've said, 'I'm not even born yet. I'm still trying. I'm still pushing. I don't ever want to get to a place where I feel satisfied.'"

"Yeah. I think satisfaction, total and utter satisfaction with your work, feeling that you've arrived someplace and you've won, I think it's death for an actor."

When I asked Johnny about working with Al Pacino in *Donnie Brasco,* he said, "In my head I had this idea that he was going to be this really serious, very dark, intense guy who never laughed. And then, we started doing rehearsals, and I discovered that he was certifiably insane. Truly out of his mind and one of the funniest human beings I've ever met in my life. But as an actor, oh, my God, just one of the greats, one of the most pure, honest, surprising . . . He's a beauty."

In *Donnie Brasco,* Johnny played the title role of the undercover FBI agent who infiltrated the mob, and when I said, "I want to know, where'd a Kentucky-born and Florida-raised guy acquire that dead-on New York accent?" he replied, "Well, I was very fortunate. I spent a lot of time with the real Donnie Brasco, with Joe Pistone. I'm sure he was real sick of me, 'cause I haunted him. Every day I'd call him, to spend some time. I just tried to get as much of Joe as I possibly could."

Johnny told us that the Mafia had put out a contract on Joe Pistone, that he and his family lived in hiding, and that he never went anywhere undisguised. Later that night, Johnny confided in me that "Joe was here tonight."

"You mean *here*—in our theater?" Johnny smiled. "Sitting with our students?" Johnny nodded.

On the way home with Kedakai, I observed (with what she later described as a faint note of pride) that being a master's degree candidate in the Actors Studio Drama School was more hazardous than we had realized.

W ith all the tears . . . *real* tears that have been shed on our stage, a logical question arises: How could I remain dry-eyed through the deluge? The answer is that I am usually as stolid as Will Ferrell portrays me (and, I'm afraid, as masked as the alter ego in my recurring dream).

But on one occasion my defenses were breached when Liza Minnelli gave our students and me the gift of a private concert, singing song after song, and turning every one of them into an invaluable lecture/demonstration.

Reminding Liza of the master class she had conducted for our students in the third year of our school, I asked her to tell these students what she'd told their predecessors.

"I have a book for each show," Liza said, holding up her open hand. "The lyrics are here, on this side, and the character breakdown is on *this* side. So, when I'm learning the lyrics, I also have in front of me the 'picture' of the woman who's singing the song. Because it's an acting piece, you know? Like you guys learn: 'What is she showing? What is she hiding? *Why* is she singing this song? What color carpet is on her living room floor? What are the decals on her refrigerator?' To the finest detail. Because details *count*. They're the secrets you see in great singers' eyes. All great singers have them. And *you* can have them, too. Just make sure that you *have* a secret. And make it specific!"

Every song Liza sang that night was an acting piece—and an acting lesson. When she performed the Aznavour song *"Mon Amour,"* which Fred Ebb had translated as "Quiet Love," she elected to remain in her seat next to me. It was a fateful decision because at that range I was within her force field, and when she turned to me at the end of the song, she reacted to what she saw: me, ransacking my pockets for a tissue because my turn had finally come.

"It took twelve years," I said. "I thought it would never happen." As I shrugged helplessly and mopped my face, Liza exclaimed, "James. Jimmy. My Jimmy!"

Neither of us was acting. What the audience saw were old friends and real tears.

CHAPTER Fourteen

> ❝ *I'm a fucking gypsy. And I come from a long line of gypsies. And it's a great tradition of gypsies who tell stories. **That's** what my job is. A few hundred years ago, it was a different situation. But now, through the flickering light, we get to talk to millions of people at a time sometimes—if we're lucky enough.*
>
> —Russell Crowe, *Inside the Actors Studio*

For thirteen years I have marveled at the lengths to which our guests have gone, and the sacrifices some of them have made, in order to come to our students. There are none of the usual benefits. It isn't a stop in a meticulously choreographed publicity junket on behalf of the star's new movie. Obviously, there is no financial gain, since there's no compensation for their appearance—and we wouldn't be able to afford these guests if there were. Sometimes, in fact, there's a financial liability, if it involves forgoing a more profitable use of the guest's time.

And finally, there is the most impressive fact of all: the *commitment* of their time. For the majority of them who don't happen to live in New York, that involves at least a day of travel to come to us, a day for the shoot, and a day to return to wherever they are living or working. If one could assign a financial value to an hour of their time, or a day, or three days, the price of their appearance would be astronomical.

And yet they come to us. Bless 'em! An army of heroes.

When Hugh Grant arrived on our stage, I said to our students, "I feel it incumbent on me to tell you that Hugh is here shooting a movie. He was shooting from dawn this morning, and will be shooting again at dawn tomorrow. He is among many of our guests who have come here so generously, so kindly and so selflessly. And we thank you for it, Hugh."

"No, no, no. It's a privilege, honor, very nice to be here," Hugh insisted.

See what I mean?

When we discussed his work in *Four Weddings and a Funeral,* I felt obliged to point out, "One of the important plot points of this film is that you have a very hard time getting Andie MacDowell. Now, it is no secret that you are a lot better-looking than, say, Woody Allen." As the students laughed and Hugh stared, I said, "I'm trying not to flatter you outright."

"You're pretty smooth."

I tried to continue. "In the film, did you make any—"

But Hugh wouldn't be sidetracked. "Have you ever said that to a girl when chatting her up in your past?"

"That she's better-looking than Woody Allen?"

"Yeah. 'I just gotta tell you, you're better-looking than Woody Allen.' "

"Ask my wife."

"Okay." He peered into the audience, fixed on a dark, indistinguishable shape in the middle of the house, and said. "*Woody!* Oh! Sorry!"

"My wife is beautiful!" I protested. Turning to the students for support, I demanded, "Is she not?" Turning back to Hugh, I said, "Ask the students, for God's sake!"

This time Hugh really peered into the audience, where the students were beginning to point at Kedakai, who, as usual, was hiding on the sidelines lest I include close-ups of her in the edited show, as was my unwanted wont. "I can't see her," Hugh complained.

Thoroughly provoked now, I pleaded, "Kedakai, please raise your hand."

Hugh pulled his glasses out of his pocket and looked again. "*Oh!* You're gorgeous!"

The students, some out of conviction, some perhaps out of fear of reprisal, applauded in agreement.

Leaning toward me, Hugh whispered, "How come?"

"Half-Japanese and half-Irish," I responded. "It happens."

Examining Kedakai once more through his glasses, Hugh murmured, "Oooooo, lethal!"

Late that night, in the darkness of our bedroom, under the hum of the air conditioner, I thought I heard Kedakai's soft voice, and turned toward her side of the bed. A moment later, I made out the words that were emerging from whatever dream had overtaken her: "Oooooo, lethal."

At the risk of being branded—with some justification—as uxorious, I'll offer one more example of Kedakai's remarkable combination of beauty and modesty: My wife is Miss Scarlet. Not *resembles* Miss Scarlet. *Is* Miss Scarlet in the famous board game Clue.

A few years after we'd married, someone tipped me off. That night at dinner, I asked Kedakai if it was so, and she frowned in thought, then recalled casually that a few months earlier, on a modeling assignment, she'd posed for pictures at the Lotus Club, reclining on a couch in a scarlet gown, holding a long cigarette holder.

The next day I acquired the game, and there was my wife on the cover of the box, reclining on a crimson chaise longue in a brief Asian dress, holding a long cigarette holder and, when I opened the box, peering enigmatically up at me from the face of her card. I can attest that, on the few occasions when we've played the game, it's disconcerting to discover that your wife did it in the library with the candlestick, then to look across the table at the real thing smiling her serene, inscrutable smile.

Knowing that the British can be a bit finicky about their speech, I asked Hugh about Renée Zellweger's English accent in *Bridget Jones's Diary.* He replied, "Well, ultimately impeccable. But that's not to say it didn't go through some interesting stages of metamorphosis to get there."

Once again the dominie, I said, "Our students have dialect classes. What were the stages?"

"Well, I seem to remember at the read-through we had—um, Princess Margaret basically. It was extremely posh. Posher than anyone I'd ever heard in my life. A bit like the queen's speech." His voice shot up and his accent broadened. " 'My husband and I are delighted to wish everyone a merry Christmas.' Like that. And then, she tried to take the edge off it, and she sounded great, but slightly as though she'd had a stroke."

Fighting my way through the students' riotous reaction, I asked, "Ultimately she got it, though, didn't she?"

"Oh, she was bang-on, yeah. And you know, she did it off the set as well as on, so it became really weird."

"Did she maintain that?"

"Yeah, all the time, seamlessly. So it was freaky at the wrap party when she started to speak Texan to me. I found her frankly unconvincing."

At the close of the evening, the subject of soccer—or what the English mysteriously insist on calling football—came up when I said, "We will close this part of our seminar with a news bulletin. The Fulham Football Club has beaten West Bromwich Albion in the FA Cup quarterfinal, one–nil. Which means that Fulham will move on to the semifinal versus Chelsea."

"Correct," Hugh said with evident satisfaction.

"Am I correct in assuming that you and Dan may be in attendance?"

"You are unreal. Dan and I will be there, yeah, if I can get a day off this film. Even if I can't, I'll be there."

Producing an English football scarf and wrapping it around my neck, I said, "I think it's only fair to reveal that my wife and I are also football supporters but we don't share your—"

"That's really terrible. That's an abomination!" Hugh protested.

"The Tottenham Hotspurs." I purred. "And I confess I also like Chelsea very much."

"*Do* you! Well, we'll go together. In fact, I bet you we'll beat you!"

"We've got a bet."

Back in the greenroom, we settled on a hundred-dollar bet—with witnesses.

Chelsea trounced Fulham, and in the months following Hugh's visit, I kept sending messages through his representatives and mutual friends. There was no response, and no payment of the debt, and I assumed that, like brave Achilles, he was sulking in his tent.

Then, a few minutes before curtain time on the opening night of Baz Luhrmann's Broadway *La Bohème*, Kedakai grabbed my arm. "There's Hugh Grant!" I marched down the aisle to be greeted by Harvey Weinstein, who was seated just behind Hugh. I'd lost the element of surprise, but it turned out I didn't need it, because the instant Hugh heard my name, he rose, pulling twenty-dollar bills out of his pocket and thrusting them at me.

At the opening-night party, Hugh and his date and Kedakai and I took a table together, and when Hugh discovered that Kedakai is a vice president of the Corcoran Real Estate Group, he began pressing her for information about the co-op market in Manhattan.

For the next hour, Kedakai took him on a virtual tour of Manhattan, district by district, citing advantages, disadvantages, availabilities, prices, finally, at Hugh's urging, zeroing in on specific buildings that seemed to interest him. "Do you think I could get in?" he asked.

"You mean past the co-op board?"

"Yes."

"Well, sometimes they're a little wary of people in—you know, show business," Kedakai said diplomatically and, as always, honestly.

Glancing at his date, who was momentarily in conversation with someone stopping by our table, Hugh lowered his voice to a whisper. "Not me. The birds. The ladies. You know what I mean? Different every night? How do you think they'd feel about that?"

"I don't know. I'll put together a list of possibilities."

"That would be great!" Hugh gave Kedakai the name of his hotel, and that week's nom de guerre, which was Mackintosh. The moment we got home, Kedakai disappeared into her office, and the next day delivered to "Mr. Mackintosh" a thick file of available co-ops that she felt might meet three criteria:

right neighborhood, right price and, first and foremost, right of way for his ladies.

He didn't buy an apartment, but I did get my hundred dollars, which I donated to a fund for a student party.

W hen we launched *Inside the Actors Studio* in 1994, one of my hopes was that it would serve to dispel some of the myths that cling to our profession and its practitioners. One is the public's assumption that people who earn their livings "playacting" are ipso facto less likely than "other people" to be frank in day-to-day life.

Sir Ian McKellen helped us puncture that balloon when he volunteered that he'd come out of the closet on the BBC in 1988, and I asked him, "How had you dealt with your sexual orientation in the years prior to 1988?"

Ian was silent for a moment; then he sighed. "It's difficult, I think, for young people in their twenties, if they're lucky enough to live in New York or study here, to imagine how you could get through to forty-nine years old without being absolutely honest about something so central to your nature as your sexuality. But it, alas, was possible because it was a subject that wasn't talked about. I lived openly with two boyfriends before I was forty-nine for quite long periods. Everybody I met knew that I was gay. I didn't hide it. It seemed to me an irrelevance. Where I kept silent was with close members of my family, and with the media. I didn't have a problem—but, of course, I *did* have a problem. The problem was that I had something I was ashamed of, because if I *wasn't* ashamed of it, why wasn't I talking about it?

"That is the dreadful pressure of other people's homophobia, their fear of homosexuality: It impinges on people who are themselves gay unless they are strong enough to withstand and be honest, and I wasn't of that sort. I was still the shy little boy, you see. And who knows how much of my bravura acting, for which I was initially praised, wasn't to do with disguising, hiding, something so personal to me?

"And it was only when I just said the words 'I'm gay' in a public forum—and, crucially, told my family—that for the first time I discovered it was possible to cry onstage. It happened resoundingly when I was playing Uncle Vanya at the National Theatre, directed by an ex-lover of mine, with another openly gay man, Anthony Sher, in the cast, and a closeted gay man playing the professor."

The students laughed and offered a supportive cheer; then Ian resumed. "That was the best thing I ever did. The millstone fell from me, and the block that had been inside me—that I wasn't aware of—was spewed up. Who would have thought there was a connection? But there is for me," he concluded.

I readily admit to a bias toward these two hundred people who for thirteen years have shared their craft and lives and secrets with our students, and I think that Sir Ian is a classic example of the bond between honesty in acting and honesty in living.

In August 2002, I went back to Paris—under significantly different circumstances from my first residency. This time my *Inside the Actors Studio* team was with me, and for two weeks I led our cameras around the city to every place—well, nearly every place—that I remembered and loved.

We shot B-roll—footage that the viewers would see as I took them, in voice-over, on a personal tour of Paris—to the seventeenth-century perfection of the Place des Vosges; the Champ de Mars, crowned by the Trocadéro and the Eiffel Tower; the Butte Montmartre overlooking all of Paris; the Place de l'Opéra; the flower market between the Right Bank and the Île de la Cité where, long ago, I had bought water lilies for my bidet after a night's work in the Rue Pigalle; the stalls of the *bouquinistes* along the Seine where each week I'd invested a percentage of my Pigalle percentages in the satirical drawings of Daumier on the hundred-year-old pages of Le Charivari—works of art bought for pennies that now adorn an entire wall of our home; a sidewalk table at the Café de Flore where I raised my *Ricard à l'eau* in a toast to my godson, the Count Severin de Rochechouart de Mortemart, as we celebrated his admission to the University of Chicago; the Quai de la Tournelle with its breathtaking view of Notre Dame, not from the church's stolid front, stripped of its twelfth-century masterpieces during the revolution and restored in the nineteenth century by Viollet-le-Duc, but from the rear oblique with its view of the soaring flying buttresses that had taken the weight of the roof from the shoulders of the cathedral's walls, opening them, literally, to the glories of twelfth-century stained glass in jeweled offering to Our Lady, for whom Notre Dame de Paris and all of France's Notre Dames were built in a tidal wave of affection for the previously neglected Intercessor—to the point where the Church, jealous on behalf of the Trinity, gave this medieval love affair a name, Mariolatry, and declared it a heresy.

This was my Paris, and these two episodes of *Inside the Actors Studio* delivered all my biases and *idées fixes* in a joyful parade.

Of course, *Inside the Actors Studio* needed a venue in Paris, and the one we acquired was historic: the Opéra Comique, founded in 1783 and the site of the premiere performance of Bizet's *Carmen* on March 3, 1875. Our first French guest was Juliette Binoche, whom I'd recruited in May 2002 on the *tapis rouge* of the Cannes Film Festival, where I was hosting the international telecast for the Independent Film Channel.

The stage where *Carmen* had premiered had been chosen for the formal ceremony at which I would be installed as a chevalier in the Order of Arts and Letters before an audience that included Kedakai and another of the treasured families I have spent my life acquiring, the Count Jean de Rochechouart de Mortemart, his wife, Emmanuella, my godson, Severin, and his brother Thomas.

Lacking siblings, I have managed to acquire two brothers, one, of course, George Plimpton, the other Jean de Mortemart. Our friendship goes back to his youth and mine in New York, when he emerged from college and began working at an advertising agency—the first member of his family to work for a salary in seven hundred years. Jean is at once the most elegant and least pretentious person I have ever known, and I count the time we've spent together, in America and France, among the most enjoyable hours of my life.

Since French honors must be formally bestowed by a French citizen of specific rank, the assignment fell to the former mayor of Deauville and creator of the Deauville Film Festival, and president of the General Council of Calvados, the Countess Anne d'Ornano. Her role in the ceremony was no coincidence: I had known her since she was a twenty-year-old nursing student in New York, the daughter of the Marquis and Marquise de Contades, descendant of the Maréchal Louis Georges Érasme de Contades, whose chef created pâté de fois gras, no small distinction in France. Anne grew up in Montgeoffroy, one of the fabled châteaus of the Loire Valley, and when I met her she was undergoing, uncomplainingly, the brutal training of a surgical nurse on the night shift of Flower Fifth Avenue Hospital.

A fervent relationship, in which she would often ring my doorbell at dawn, redolent of the intoxicating perfume of ether after a night in the operating room, ended upon completion of her training, when she was summoned back to France, where in time she married, wisely and well, the Count Michel D'Ornano, and they embarked on a life of remarkable achievement, in the course of which he founded the House of Orlane and served on various occasions as France's minister of industry, culture and environment.

In sum, there was considerably more history, not to mention drama, than anyone in the audience, with the exception of Kedakai and the Mortemarts, suspected on the Opéra Comique's stage that night, with Juliette Binoche handing the medal to Anne, who spoke the obligatory words, *"Au nom du Ministre de la Culture . . .* and by virtue of the power vested in me, we declare you a knight in the Order of Arts and Letters."

My reply concluded, *"Merci, Anne, merci, Juliette, merci à la République*

Française et à vous tous. Merci à la culture française depuis au moins l'onzième siècle. Merci Rimbaud, Feydeau, Truffaut . . . et Pivot."

T wo nights later, on the stage of the Opéra Comique, Jeanne Moreau told us about growing up during the German occupation of France. "I was twelve, and it's a very, very special period, where you have to discover so many things about yourself, about life in general. And about adults. And when you see that around you, when you see that the place where your father works, it is written: 'Forbidden for blacks and Jews,' when you see your little friends coming to school, so shy with a yellow star, and then you never see them again, I mean . . ." Jeanne stopped and sighed, then concluded gravely, "I have my own thoughts about . . . adults!"

Of course, I asked her about the nouvelle vague, of which she was one of the architects—and archetypes. "Many male moviegoers can mark among the milestones of their lives the moment at which they fell in love with Jeanne Moreau. For most of us, it was in 1961, with *Jules et Jim*. Were you a part of its genesis, with Truffaut?"

"Yes. François gave me the responsibility for doing costumes. And as we had very little money, I was responsible for the sets when we were shooting outside in Paris. And, to help things, I used to cook and feed the crew."

"You were craft service?"

"Yeah. So, François would do other shots without me about an hour before lunchtime. And then one day, a guy said he thought my meat was not cooked well enough. Oh, my God!"

"What an insult!"

"I said, 'Well, *you* do it!' "

"Did he?"

"No. They ate sandwiches."

The French audience applauded with sympathy and understanding.

When I asked Jeanne, "How much of you, of Jeanne Moreau, winds up in any role that you play?" she replied, "Very little. That's why it's so fascinating, for me, to be an actress. I mean, the woman I am has been fed by all these characters, and the characters have been fed by me—but beyond me, beyond my life, I am sure that as a human being, we carry away with us something that is unknown, *archaïque,* that comes from way, way, way, way back.

"You don't do it on purpose. It comes out. It comes from an ancient memory. It has nothing to do with your own life, whatever. That's what acting is *about.* It's not true to life. It's *beyond.* Like certain characters in novels, you know? Great writers, they give birth to a woman or a man that will live beyond the book, for many, many centuries."

F or thirteen years, I've insisted that *Inside the Actors Studio* can be properly understood only as a class in a master's degree program. When Martin Scorsese was with us, it became a master class. Examining *Taxi Driver*, I said, "Certainly one of the most famous scenes in the recent history of American cinema is Travis in front of the mirror. When Bob was here, we talked about it, of course, and I happen to know that in the screenplay that entire scene consists of the following parenthesis: '(Travis looks in the mirror.)' That's all."

Marty nodded. "That's it, yeah."

"How much of it was improvised by De Niro?"

"Well, it was a problem. We were over schedule. I said, 'We've gotta get this scene in front of the mirror. I just know that you should be talking in the mirror. You should say *something;* I just don't know *what* you should say. Just try a few things.'

"When I was a kid, I was never out of the house. I would just make up movies. I'd act all these different parts, and that's what Travis was doing. Only, he acts it out in front of a mirror. Bobby just stumbled on the 'Excuse me, are you talking to me?' thing. And he repeated it and repeated it and repeated it. I said, 'Keep going, keep going!'

"After the first or second take, it was really getting good. We had locked the door, because they were banging on it. 'You've gotta stop! That wasn't in the script! We're so behind schedule!'"

As he had when he was a shut-in kid, Marty was playing all the parts on our stage. Speaking as himself, he shouted back at the locked door. "Please, please! We're getting something really good! Please—just give us another five!"

Marty turned into whoever was on the other side of that door. "'Twenty-five minutes, that's *it!*'"

"Okay, okay. We're getting something really good!" the beleaguered young director replied. Marty turned to the students to confide, "It was a good guy. He was trying to save our necks, because Columbia Pictures would've killed me. We were shooting in the city, and that summer the rain was so bad—we'd lost so many days shooting. I kept telling Bob, 'It sounds good, sounds good, keep going, keep going,' and 'I'm the only one here,' all that stuff, came out of that.

"And then it was edited by Tom Rolf, wonderful editor. Gave it to him, I chose some takes, he looked at it and said, 'Give me a few minutes.' Bang, he did it! I said, 'Don't touch it!'"

"A lot of jump cuts in it," I said.

Marty was still in the moment. "Yeah, yeah. 'Don't touch it!'"

"The leaping around in time . . ."

"Yeah, yeah, he did that."

"Repeating . . ."

"Yeah. 'Don't touch it!' I loved it!"

"You used a lot of overhead shots."

Marty frowned. "Yeah."

"You look worried. They're wonderful."

The film historian replied, "Well, the first thing that comes to mind is Hitchcock. But I have to go back to what I said earlier about seeing a lot of life from the third-floor front, through the fire escape, overhead. You could see the whole city. It was so gorgeous, especially up on the roof. The roofs were wonderful on the Lower East Side in that way—fights, dances, people running to kill rats—you know?"

"I understand," I said. And so did the students in the master class.

In the course of the class, I asked Marty, "What goes into that critical moment when you pronounce the two most fateful words in film, 'Cut, print'?"

"I guess the most important thing is that I'm the audience in a way—and I can *feel* it with the actors. You can feel it when it happens: The actor just takes off."

Just as I learned the value of tasting wines side by side on my first night in Paris, *Inside the Actors Studio* has afforded my students and me the invaluable opportunity to compare answers side by side. When I asked Sidney Lumet, "When you say, 'Print,' on what do you base it?" he replied, "That's the heart of the job, Jim. And the toughest question to answer. I think the only way I can define it for you—I hate to retreat to a generality, but it's a sheer instinctual reaction. What I'm usually doing—and I guess this comes out of my training as an actor—is that I'm playing the scene with the actors while they're doing it. And if my concentration gets broken, it's because *their* concentration got broken. And I'll go again.

"Or I may have a take where I'm completely concentrated through the take, but I don't feel anything. So I'll go again. And when I get a take where I'm completely concentrated and feel not just *something*, but what that moment should be in the total framework of the picture, *that's my print*. And, very often, I will not even do a protection take."

In response to the same question, Sydney Pollack said, "Often a performance can be made out of many takes. You can use two lines from take one and three lines from take four and one moment from take ten. Directing's an oddly omnipotent job, because you're rearranging what the actors have done. Directors can ruin a good performance in editing, and they can make a mediocre performance seem much better. I might say, 'Print,' when ninety percent of a take is lousy, but the one moment that I never found in the nine takes that went before happened in take ten, so then I might say, 'Print,' but that doesn't mean they finally *did* it in take ten."

As was the case with many of our guests, the road that led us to Martin Scorsese began long before he arrived, in the words and thoughts of another guest. Years before Scorsese came to our stage, Harvey Keitel had provided us with an important insight to the man and his work. When I remarked on the close relationship between Marty and Harvey as they began their careers, Harvey said, "Well, you know, we felt like brothers under the skin."

"What made you brothers?"

"His upbringing and mine. They paralleled each other in many ways—our religious upbringing. . . ."

"Were you both raised in religious homes?"

"I wouldn't say religious, but oriented toward religion. Marty, of course, had begun studying to be a priest. Let's say the dogma of the different religions, in my case the Jewish one, in his case the Catholic one—the prohibitions, the hopes, the taboos. We felt something else was there that we needed to get at. And we've been trying ever since."

On our stage, Marty picked up the theme Harvey had introduced five years earlier when I asked him if, like several of the guests who had come to our stage, he'd been an altar boy.

"Yes. I became an altar boy when I was about ten years old. And I stayed in the altar boys for about four years. There was a young Italian-American priest who came to our parish."

"Was that Father Principe?"

"Father Principe, yeah. It was his first assignment, and he became a strong influence on all the kids. He was about twenty-three. He had a whole other way of thinking about the world, and made us understand that, possibly, there was a different way of looking at life. There was literature; there were certain kinds of cinema. He would talk about the clichés of movies that we liked, and made us think of other ways. Father Principe was a very strong influence."

"Was he one of the reasons you thought of entering the priesthood?"

"He was the main reason for it, I think."

"How old were you when you went into seminary?"

"About fifteen."

"How long were you there?"

"About a year and a half. I was asked to leave."

The theme reemerged when I brought up the enigmatic ending of *Taxi Driver.*

"The film has a surprisingly gentle and idyllic ending. When Cybill gets into the cab, Travis seems at peace. I've read accounts that insist he actually died in the chair when he brought the finger to his head, and that this is his dying fantasy. Are we meant to believe it literally? Did he recover?"

"I had a problem with that at first, and I told Schrader I didn't quite believe the ending. I remember Schrader at the time had been enamored of the song 'Taxi' by Harry Chapin, and the whole idea of, when she comes in the car, now she'll look at me in a different way. . . ."

"She respects him."

"Yes, exactly. That's what he felt. I was a little nervous about it, but I did it, and it works, I think. I added one thing at the very end, where he looks in the mirror twice and he focuses the mirror. Because I felt, in my mind, that a man like this, under the circumstances, crossing over the fantasy line and acting out—I think he's gonna do it again. I think it's just a matter of time."

"So do I. But for the moment he's redeemed."

"Yeah."

"How strongly do you believe in redemption, in your films?"

"Well, that's a good question. I have to be careful with this sort of thing, but I think ultimately it has to do with the emphasis on Christianity in my mind. My experience has been maybe the dark side of it, and yet I know there's supposed to be a light, there's supposed to be redemption, there's supposed to be something that is uplifting, something that takes you out of yourself. I guess one would call it redemption.

"Even Rupert Pupkin, to a certain extent, is looking for that light, the joy of Christianity—the *joy* of it. I don't know if I'm there. That's what Father Principe said when he saw *Taxi Driver.* I hadn't seen him in years, and I invited him to the screening. It was kind of surprising. He said, 'Well, I'm glad you ended it on Easter Sunday, not on Good Friday.' Ultimately, he told me, 'There's too much Good Friday, not enough Easter Sunday, in your films.' "

As the students laughed, Marty turned to them and concluded, "It's Mediterranean: We're looking for the Easter Sunday. But, you know, that's what the journey is."

My *Simpsons* experience began when *TV Guide* invited me to interview Krusty the Clown in their pages. I wrote the questions and the *Simp-*

sons writers provided Krusty's answers, under the subhead, "*Inside the Actors Studio* host James Lipton gets to the bitter interior beneath the bitter exterior of Herschel 'Krusty' Krustofski, thespian and tax evader."

"When did you realize you wanted to devote your life to laughter?" was one of the questions I asked him, to which he replied, "When I heard Milton Berle got $1 million a year for putting on a dress—I mean, when I saw the power of laughter to touch the heart of a child."

At another point I said, "You're rumored to have an out-of-wedlock daughter who sounds remarkably like Drew Barrymore. Are we to infer anything from that?"

"I wish I had a nickel for every rumor about my 'out-of-wedlock daughter.' If I did, I could afford the child support."

"Just between you and me, how do you feel about Krusty Buddy #16302?"

"You're talking about Bart Simpson, the boy who freed me from jail, reunited me with my father, got my show back on the air and saved me from certain death at the hands of Sideshow Bob. We're not as close as we used to be. I've grown; he hasn't."

At the conclusion of the interview, when I asked Krusty what he'd like to hear God say when he arrives at the Pearly Gates, he replied, "I'd like to hear Him say that He forgives me for my *Hooray for Atheism* holiday special."

The *Simpsons* adventure continued when I was invited by *The Simpsons* to appear as myself, interviewing one of the show's characters, played by Harry Shearer. Shuffling through my cards with three yellow cartoon fingers, my image said, "Welcome back to *Inside the Actors Studio*. We've met Rainier Wolfcastle, actor, novelist, barbecue sauce spokesman. Now, can we meet McBain?"

"Let me get into character," Rainier said, sounding suspiciously like Arnold Schwarzenegger. "Okay. I'm McBain. 'All right, Mendoza, I'll give you the Maxwell Circuit if you put down my daughter.'"

As he pulled out two huge automatics, my image chortled delightedly, "Oooooo! Ha ha!" then choked, knocked over the table and fell forward as McBain pulled the triggers.

Raising my head from the floor, I gasped, "It's a pleasure to eat your lead, good sir," and died.

At dinner with Kedakai a few hours after I'd recorded the voice track in a New York studio, we reflected on the fact that this was the second time I'd been assassinated, first on *SNL*, then on *The Simpsons*. "Maybe they're trying to tell me something," I observed, staring gloomily at my plate.

A few months later, in celebration of their three hundredth episode, the *Simpsons* cast decided the moment had come to be interviewed together on television for the first time, and, since the decision included us as the fortunate beneficiaries of this historic decision, on November 18, 2002, Dan Castellaneta, Julie Kavner, Nancy Cartwright, Yeardley Smith, Hank Azaria and Harry Shearer marched out on our stage, leading a lengthy, antic parade of characters in primary-colored motley.

The first thing I did was try to establish my credentials. "As a *Simpson* character on one wonderful brief occasion, I am proud of my cartoon ethnicity. Can someone tell me how the *Simpson* characters became yellow?"

Yeardley Smith, aka Lisa Simpson, always the good student, volunteered, "I can."

"Please."

"Matt Groening apparently thought it would be really funny if, when people watched *The Simpsons,* they thought maybe the color on the TV was off—so they'd try to get the flesh tone on *The Simpsons,* but they just couldn't. 'They're still yellow! What's going on?' That's his own private joke."

"Why did I, why does every cartoon character, have only three fingers?" I asked.

"That's animation tradition," Hank Azaria said.

"It's because it's *cheaper,*" Nancy Cartwright—and Bart Simpson—interjected.

"Think how many millions of dollars have been saved over the years by not putting in that finger," I suggested.

"That's it!" Nancy said firmly.

"Why does everybody on this show have an overbite?" I asked.

"That's a Groeningesque art thing," Dan Castellaneta said, not sounding the least like Homer. "He says it's a world without chins."

From the day we learned the Simpsons were coming, I prepared not only to interview the six cast members, but, with the same care, as many of their characters as they would bring with them. Fortunately, they brought them all.

When I asked Dan Castellaneta's Homer, "What precisely do you do at the Springfield Nuclear Power Plant?" he replied, "I am a safety inspector."

"Since you're still here, and Springfield is still here, I assume you've had an unblemished record."

"Well . . . there's a *few* blemishes on it."

"Ever come close to a meltdown?"

"Oh, a *number* of times. If that's what you mean by blemishes."

Turning to Hank Azaria's Apu, I said, "I haven't the courage even to try to pronounce your last name. Would you say it for me?"

"Everyone has such difficulty with this, and I don't understand it. It is Nahasapeemapetilon. It sounds exactly the way it is spelled."

"What is your immigration status?"

"I believe I'm a semilegal alien."

"What is the name of your store?"

"The Kwik-E-Mart."

"That sounds like a convenience store. Do you make it truly convenient for your customers?"

"I keep the beer next to the salty snacks, and things like that. There is an art, James."

"Let's take a little convenience-store poll here. How much is a twenty-nine-cent stamp at the Kwik-E-Mart?"

"A twenty-nine-cent stamp, I believe, is a dollar eighty-nine."

"How much would two dollars' worth of gas be?"

"That's four dollars and twenty cents."

"And how much is the penny candy?"

"Surprisingly expensive."

With my assassination still smarting, I turned to Harry Shearer. "I have one important question for you, Rainier."

"Yes?" Rainier replied.

"Would it have been too much trouble for you to go out and find a prop gun?"

The affronted artist drew himself up. "I'm not a prop man. I'm an actor!"

⸻

We've welcomed the scions of several royal families to our stage, none more distinguished than Vanessa Redgrave's. "For the first time in seven years," I said to her, "I'm able to go back four generations and a hundred and fifty years to ask, who was Cornelius Redgrave?"

"Oh, I wish I could have met him!" Vanessa said. "Cornelius sold tickets, probably at black-market rates, for the Drury Lane Theatre."

When I asked Vanessa about the legacy of her father, Michael Redgrave, she replied, "I was an extremely conservative young lady, with a small *c*, and maybe a large *c*. My father was fairly shocked. Suddenly he started this work of making sure that my brother and I saw all of the tiny, wonderful productions being done with actors who were getting paid some miserable amount or nothing. I was sent off to see theater, to see foreign films. He sent me to see a performance of Joan Littlewood's *Richard the Second,* and I came back, and he sat me down with scrambled eggs and said, 'What did you think?'

"And I started. Ignorance itself. Started laying into it. 'Oh, it was awful. They spoke in these funny London accents, and there didn't seem to be any difference between the king and the murderers.' I went on and on and on—and his face got grimmer and grimmer and grimmer. Finally, he said, 'I never want to hear you speak like that again.' Pause, listen. And he said, 'When you have been to any performance of a play or a concert or a dance, you never, never, never begin with what you didn't like. It's so easy to talk about what you don't like. *Anybody* can talk about what they don't like. But could you understand what the director or the writer or the choreographer was trying to do? Start with, what were the objectives and the successes and what did you love and enjoy and what was there to be got out of it.' A big lesson," Vanessa concluded.

A big lesson for our students, busily taking notes, sharing the Redgrave legacy.

Drew Barrymore came to *Inside the Actors Studio* at the age of twenty-seven to review with us a twenty-six-year career—and another distinguished legacy. "We are back to the subject of theatrical dynasties," I said. "Since this series began, we have looked at the family trees of Vanessa Redgrave, Anjelica Huston, Gwyneth Paltrow, Ben Stiller and Nicolas Cage, among others. Tonight, we come to a towering American tree that has been celebrated onstage with a play called, appropriately, *The Royal Family*. Who was your great-great-grandfather?"

"Maurice Barrymore."

"You got your first name from . . . ?"

"On the other side, John Drew."

"He was called the first gentleman of the stage. Drew's great-great- and great-grandmothers were famous actresses of their time, Louisa Lane Drew and Georgina Drew. Who were the children of Georgina and Maurice Barrymore?"

"Lionel, Ethel and John Barrymore."

"And which of them is your grandfather?"

"John."

I looked at the young faces in our audience. "Is there anyone among our students who doesn't know who John Barrymore was? John Barrymore played Hamlet; he was one of the most famous American actors ever to appear on the stage or in motion pictures. And who was your father?" I asked Drew.

"His son John Barrymore Jr. They're all Johns."

"Do you feel a connection to the Barrymore name, to its history—or is it remote and meaningless to you?"

"No, it's very powerful. I feel like, of all the things that you question when you grow up—what kind of person do I want to be, what is it I'm going to do with my life, will I find love—all of these massively important questions, the only one I never had was, what am I going to do? And I know it comes from that: I feel this blood circulating through my body. I feel their energy field present in my life, particularly my grandfather's.

"I used to say that he was the moon, so that I could see him every night, and I would speak to him because I thought he was the only one who understood the way I felt. It seems like a lot of my family were trying with each generation to get more demons corrected and do the thing they loved the most, which was acting and expressing themselves. I felt like I was born to overcome some of those obstacles and get things right. So, I feel very connected to them, and it makes me feel not crazy, and it makes me feel very grounded that I have this passion, this destiny, this feeling that I'm supposed to be doing this—and that obviously comes from them."

Once again, we had the opportunity to compare accounts of the same event, in this case, the final moments of *E.T.*

"Steven mentioned to us when he was here that he had something in common with Elliot and with E.T.: a broken family, an absent parent. Of course, he shared that history with Gertie too—and you. Did you notice that the story was not entirely dissimilar from your life, or was the movie just a marvelous toy?"

"No, I really understood it. When Steven had to make me cry in the movie, he told me that E.T. was going to go away. And that just did it for me! I was so tired of people coming in and out of my life at that point. I didn't want this to end. And Steven said, 'Well, you know what? We're going to keep working together. We're going to finish the film and then we're going to go publicize it. And we're going to stick together and I'll be here for you always.' And I got so happy that I started screaming and running around laughing. And then he had to reverse it 'cause I was supposed to be sad in the scene. So, I think that was like a good moment, too, where I realized, 'Oooh, you could use the insanity for work. This is good. This is good. If I'm sad, I can use that.' You know?"

When I asked her if it was true she had contributed a line to the scene when the kids hide E.T. in the closet with the stuffed toys, she said, "Was it, 'Give me a break'?"

"Yeah."

"Yeah." She grinned. "I improv-ed a lot on that movie." She looked at the students as they laughed in sympathy and agreement. "Like what business do I have improv-ing? I'm six."

The students were falling hard for this charming, vulnerable kid, so it was all the more shocking when, moments after we'd discussed *E.T.,* a theme that had come up with other guests emerged with the question, "When did you smoke your first cigarette?"

"When I was nine." A murmur ran through the audience, to which Drew responded with a nervous laugh. "I'm laughing 'cause it's so sick."

"What about alcohol? When did that start?"

"I think I was doing *Cat's Eye.* Like eleven—nine, ten."

"What did you drink?"

"Champagne."

"What about grass?"

"Uh . . . twelve." Once again, an audible response from the audience turned her toward them. "I sound like an antidrug commercial. One thing *did* lead to the other."

"Did the drugs make you gain weight?"

"Yeah, I got a lot of baby fat at a certain point, like fell apart. I was, you know, a chubby, stoned twelve-year-old." She looked back at the students. "Not a pretty picture."

"How old were you when you tried coke?"

"Thirteen—in club scenes in New York."

"Were people encouraging you? Were there enablers?"

"They just allowed me to do it. You know? It was either cute and funny to them, or I seemed mature enough to them to handle it."

"When and how did you go into rehab?"

"When I was thirteen. My mom put me in there."

"And what occasioned it?"

"I came home drunk and, uh, trashed the house." Again, she looked at the students. Her flat, dry remark to them made it clear she was seeking neither sympathy nor approval: "Pretty."

"Where did she send you?"

"She sent me to a lockdown facility for a year."

"How long?"

"A year."

"My God, Drew, that's impressive."

"Did you say impressive or *de*pressive?" Drew asked, evoking anxious laughter from the students, who by now were so shaken by her post-*E.T.* life that they weren't sure how to react.

"It's impressive," I responded. "It's impressive because I'm looking at you now and I'm so impressed with you now. That's why it's impressive."

"Thank you," Drew said.

A few months later, *Inside the Actors Studio* received the Prism Commendation from the National Institute on Drug Abuse, the Robert Wood Johnson Foundation and the Entertainment Industries Council. The framed document reads, "*Inside the Actors Studio*. 'Drew Barrymore.' In recognition of an outstanding creative contribution that demonstrates the entertainment industry's sincere efforts to accurately depict drug, alcohol and tobacco use and addiction in a television biographical series."

It is one of our prized awards.

On our stage, Drew had told us that when she made her appearance in *Playboy*, Steven Spielberg, who had declared himself her godfather, sent her what she described as "this rad birthday present of a gigantic quilt and my *Playboy* magazine on which he had his art department computer-generate nine very prim and proper outfits—and a card that said, 'Cover yourself up.'"

The Prism Commendation prompted me to write to Drew, "I know that Steven has trumped the rest of us in the godfather department, but if there's room in your life for a godfather II, I'd like to apply for the role."

R enée Zellweger provided us with another *Rashomon* experience when we played, onstage for her, Hugh Grant's description of her battle with the English accent in *Bridget Jones's Diary*. Her response to Hugh was instantaneous and emphatic.

"He is a liar! He is such a liar! Because after the table reading, it was like, 'Lovely. Just lovely, Renée.' He is a liar." She grinned and moved closer. "Did he mention the part about how he was scared to death that I was going to destroy his career?"

"No. He was full of admiration for you."

Renée ignored the olive branch. "Terrified! He was terrified, I'm telling you. Terrified that he was never going to work again because I was going to botch this thing!"

She joined in the wave of laughter from the house. "No. He's wonderful. He's so smart. His sense of humor is so acute and so quick. His humor comes from his intelligence, so it's always entertaining."

It will come as no surprise that, as I have written this account of the past thirteen years, there have been some surprises for me. One of them is the number of times the word *vulnerable* has appeared in these pages. It's not a word the public is accustomed to associating with people in our profession, but it keeps coming up—as it does with Renée, whose beguiling frankness and vulnerability were instantly evident when a student said, "It just seems like you can do it all, sing, act, dance, but I was just wondering what you thought might be a weakness that you're trying to overcome."

Renée's answer came in a rush. "I'm not good at fame at all, not good at it! It gives me a stomachache. So many times, it feels disingenuous to me. Unnatural, you know? I have the greatest life. I mean, creatively. I never expected to be part of so many things that matter so much to me, and that are so satisfying, and that I learn so much from. As creative people, you'll understand. To be able to express yourself in so many different ways with so many talented people, it's beyond my dreams, honestly.

"So, I should be really grateful. But I'm not very good at the celebrity aspect of it. I'm trying to be better at it; I'm trying to be less judgmental—'That's not right, this is right,' you know? I'm trying to get better at not caring about things that are completely beyond my control. So . . . *big* weakness. Big, big, big, big, big weakness."

From the first glimmer of *Inside the Actors Studio*, I've seen it as a way of alerting our master's degree candidates to everything—*everything*—that lies ahead of them. Our guests don't come to us to present the rosiest possible picture of themselves, their careers and, primo, their latest project, but to review the entire landscape of their lives and careers, the peaks—and the valleys— and the lessons learned, more often, of course, from the valleys than the peaks.

John Travolta's episode of *Inside the Actors Studio* is a prime example of that—and of the guests' willingness to unveil the darker chapters of their lives and careers, for the benefit of the students. John Travolta's career consists, as the world knows, of three acts: the first that recounts a swift, sensational rise; then, a decade and a half of near oblivion that would have driven a lesser person out of the profession; then, with the appearance of *Pulp Fiction* and the films that have followed it, a third act that outshines the first.

Because it is essential that our students understand the pitfalls they will face, I said to John, "Those fourteen years between 1980 and 1994 have been variously described as a fall from the incredible heights you reached in the seventies, and a self-imposed exile. What in fact was it, and how did you perceive it while it was happening?"

"I've always been a person with a lot of confidence, and I never took very seriously anyone making less of me. I still don't. It's not interesting to me. I think you learn by your failures and your mistakes, but you don't take them to heart—because as soon as you do, it takes the spirit out of you. You die a little bit.

"I'm very protective of actors because I don't want them to go where some will take them. Look, the world is dark; it's as bad as it gets. You look in the newspaper: It's bad news. You look over your shoulder and it's bad news. If you want me to cry, I'll cry right now for you because I can find so much sadness in the world, I can find so much tragedy, I can find so much heartache that it will just be massive. Okay?

"Now, where's the joy? Where's the spirit; where's the fun? That's the goal to me. So, I've never understood why there's so much harping on the negative, because negative is easy. Dark is easy. But I find it much more interesting to find out where the joy is. So during those times, I probably perceived negative, but I went for life. I learned how to become a jet pilot, I traveled the world, I rubbed elbows with all sorts of people. And I learned what they were about, and it was feeding me.

"I had a choice. I could've believed that things were finished, that life is bad, life's not worth it, why don't we all die, or something like that. It's just not my nature. My feeling was that you get through it the best you can by living life fully, and using the spirit of other people to feed you—and you feed *them,* and you rise above it all that way.

"And that's not ignoring something, because if you give in to that negative too much you will start to believe it, and you will start to spiral downward, and you're finished. So, I had enough people that cared for me and loved me, and I loved them and I kept it afloat. You see?"

"Yes," I said. So did the students, grateful for a lesson every one of them will need.

As these pages demonstrate, we have been frequently surprised—even astonished—by our guests. On rare occasions we have surprised them. The night John Travolta was with us was one of those occasions. Halfway through the evening, I saw some movement in the theater and said, out of the blue to John and our students, "In the history of twentieth-century film, there have been a few goddesses. One of them has just joined us, because she wanted to be here tonight. In a short time, she will be on *Inside the Actors Studio* because we shot it last August in Paris. I have the great honor of introducing to you, John, and to our students, Jeanne Moreau."

As Jeanne stood up in the front row, John bolted out of his chair and stared down at her in disbelief, exclaiming, "Oh, my God, oh, my God! Oh, my God!! Now, this is as good as it gets. Jeanne Moreau!! Oh, my God!!!"

By now he was kneeling on the front of the stage, reaching out for her hands. "*Going Places* is my first introduction to great filmmaking. Those scenes with you and Gérard Depardieu and Patrick Dewaere. Oh, my God! Oh, my God! It's my favorite movie. Oh, my God! Well, everything you do is so fabulous, but that really killed me. God!"

He finally released Jeanne and reeled back to the stage as she sat down. Collapsing into his chair, he summed up with "Wow, what a great surprise that was!"

A short time later, I indulged myself with "One of my favorite subjects on this stage, as patient and long-suffering students know, is flying airplanes. The subject has come up with Gene Hackman, Sydney Pollack, Chris Reeve, Harrison Ford, Dennis Quaid, among others. When did you start flying, John?"

"I was sixteen, 1970, and it was a dream of mine. I put all my paychecks into my flying lessons, and that's when I started. That was thirty-three years ago."

"What ratings do you have?"

"I have a 747 rating, and I have a 707 rating. They're Boeing aircraft; they're airliners."

"Jesus!" There is no way of conveying it on the printed page, but the students could see me turning green with envy.

"In corporate aircraft, I have a Gulfstream II rating, Hawker jet rating, Citation Jet, Learjet . . ."

"Are these your planes?"

"At various times, I've owned them. And then two fighter jets. I have the Empire jet and a Vampire."

"Have you ever flown the VFR corridor down the Hudson?"

"Yes."

"You fly down the west side of the Hudson and up the east side," I explained to the audience, who may by now have been benumbed by two oblivious pilots. "You have to stay under eleven hundred feet."

"That's right."

"So, you're lower than the skyscrapers. I did this about two and a half years ago. My wife was in the backseat taking pictures. We were recently going through some photographs, and I realized she took a picture as we passed the World Trade Center! I was flying a high-wing 172. It was twilight, it was beautiful, the skyline of New York—and there, right in the middle of the picture, are the Twin Towers—and they're reflected upside down, shimmering, in the bottom of my wing."

"Oh, my God!"

"Now it's a huge photograph on the wall in our living room. And underneath it is a picture of me flying the plane and smiling—as I always do when I'm flying. And then the third picture is the one that Kedakai took out the window as we flew over the Statue of Liberty, and it so happened that she got a perfect shot of it with the torch illuminated against the darkness. So, we have these three pictures on our wall, and they're on our wall forever."

Inside the Actors Studio has hosted its share of legends. One such occasion was when Clint Eastwood ambled onstage. One of the questions I'm often asked is whether there's a marked difference in our guests onstage and off. The answer is, there's very little. In Clint's case, there's none: What the public sees—and venerates—in Clint is Clint, in front of the lens, behind it and, I suspect, in every other circumstance.

In contrast to nearly every other movie set on earth, Clint's are famous for their serenity. When I asked him how he achieved that, he spoke about the crew that moves with him from picture to picture. "Well, when they're good people, and they're loyal to you, there's no reason not to be loyal back. And, selfishly, they understand my language. I am not a terribly talkative person—unless I've had a couple of brews. So, I kind of make gestures. This is for that, and that—and we do it.

"I've always wondered why sets are so noisy, with people yelling and bells going off, and guys with megaphones. I was at the White House some years ago, and I'm watching these Secret Service guys around the room. And they're carrying on a whole conversation, and nobody is hearing anything. So, I said to my assistant director, 'How can the Secret Service have these conversations and control everything without any noise—and we can't do it, with all this modern equipment?'

"So, we closed off the radios. No open radios that squawk in the middle of a scene. And my crew can actually talk during a scene. They just talk like this" —he whispered into his lapel mike. "And that's how I keep my set. You can keep things nice and tranquil, and give people the best possible atmosphere to work in."

I brought up the number of times our guests had talked about the way Clint begins and ends a take. "I understand you don't say, 'Action,' or 'Cut,' which distinguishes you from nearly every other film director on this planet. Why do you do it?"

"It started out in *Rawhide.* You've got a camera here, and you've got four riders and they're all supposed to be side by side. That's very difficult to get into a fairly close shot. And then, right away, they zing a mic boom out there. The horses don't like that. They're getting edgy. And then just when you get the four horses ready to ride into the shot, some guy yells at the top of his lungs through a megaphone, *'Action!'*

"Well, these horses go every which way, and I'm on one of 'em—and the director's going, 'Cut!! Why the hell can't these damn horses . . . !' And you say, 'How about just not yelling, "Action"? How about saying something else?' And I never could get 'em to do it.

"Actors are not like horses—but they *do* have a central nervous system." We were shooting this episode in Los Angeles, and the theater was filled with actors, who exploded into laughter. "And they're sitting there with a certain amount of anxiety about the scene. And you go yell, '*Action!!!*' at 'em, and the adrenaline goes up, the blood pressure goes up, and they're not at optimum level. So, instead, I just say, 'Okay . . . anytime . . . we'll go.' And at the end it's, 'Stop. Thank you.' Or, 'That's enough of that shit.' "

Which may explain why Clint's films have produced so many Academy Awards. In 2005, Clint and Warners asked me to host the bonus material for the *Million Dollar Baby* DVD. Because of my schedule and Clint's, it had to be taped early the morning after the Oscar ceremony. When I arrived at the set they'd prepared for us on the Warners lot, I found three exhausted, red-eyed honorees: Morgan Freeman with his Best Supporting Oscar on the table in front of him, Hillary Swank with her Best Actress Oscar in front of her, and Clint behind his Best Director and Best Picture Oscars.

Clint's system works. As he proceeds majestically through his seventies with films like *Flags of Our Fathers* and *Letters from Iwo Jima,* he has quietly— *very* quietly—become one of America's most important film directors. Ever.

O n January 16, 2003, I received a note from Barbra Streisand that concluded with the tantalizing "We love your show! Sooo interesting. Someday . . . when I'm on the East Coast . . . we'll talk. . . ."

I was galvanized. Not that I needed prodding: I'd been soliciting Barbra, unsuccessfully, from the day *Inside the Actors Studio* began its career. Now I redoubled my efforts, and as the summer arrived, there were hints that my importuning was bearing fruit—to the point where we were instructed to pencil her in for our first September slot. Then, in the last week of August, her plans changed: She wouldn't be coming east. The problem, we were given to understand, was her staunch aversion to flying. With profound regret, I erased her name from September 8 on our calendar.

A few days later, at lunch on the opening day of the Hampton Classic Horse Show, I told Donna Karan, "You know, I've been speaking to Barbra."

"You're telling *me*," Donna said. "She's been calling me. She's so excited. Me too. I'll be there."

"No, you won't. Neither will she."

"What're you talking about?"

"She changed her mind. She's not coming."

"She changed it back again."

"But she won't fly."

"She doesn't have to. She's got Whoopi Goldberg's bus. We've got plans in New York."

Donna pulled out her cell phone and dialed Barbra at home on a Sunday morning. I listened, fascinated, as she demanded, "You're coming here, aren't you? We need you! We need you *here*!"

In response to what must have been a "Who's 'we'?" Donna thrust her phone at me. "Hi, Barbra," I said, "it's Jim Lipton."

"What are you doing with Donna Karan!" exploded in my ear.

"We're at the horse show. She said you're coming to New York."

"I'll kill her!"

"I thought you wanted to do the *Inside the Actors Studio*."

"Of course I do, but . . ."

For the next ten minutes, we sorted through the classic panoply of Barbra's insecurities—and on September 8, Donna Karan took her place in the front row, and Barbra sat down opposite me on the stage for what would be one of the most memorable evenings and the most watched episode in the history of *Inside the Actors Studio*. As Barbra observed when she took her seat and looked down at Donna, beaming up at her, "Everything that happens tonight is your fault!"

Force of nature and *vulnerable* would seem to be a contradiction in terms. But both describe Barbra Streisand precisely. It's altogether possible that those who perceive her in one persona will reject out of hand the possibility of the other. But I believe that it's the constant tension of those two apparent opposites that lies at the heart of Barbra's persona and her art. It is most evident when she sings, and I believe that her *Inside the Actors Studio* episode contains enough musical performance to support my belief that she is the definitive interpreter of America's art song, uniquely and effortlessly able to fill every whole note with rippling hemidemisemiquavers of thought and emotion.

After all the hesitations and second thoughts and misgivings and volte-face, once Barbra arrived on our stage, she was utterly frank—on matters and in ways that most of us would recoil from, were we in her place, in that chair.

One of the things our students and the millions who watched the show learned was that none of it came easy. Like most of our guests, Barbra's life was marked by parental loss. Barbra's father died when she was fifteen months old, and the man who took his place in her mother's life—and hers—was, as she described him, an unsatisfactory replacement.

"I believe," I said, "that during the summer of 1949, your mother showed up at the Hebrew Health Camp with someone."

"Yeah, with a strange man. I always kind of ruled the roost with my mother; I taught her how to smoke when I was ten. When she showed up with this guy, I'd had it with the camp because their food was so awful and I had a rubber sheet and a bathrobe that looked like an Indian blanket. I said to her, 'You cannot go home without me!' I remember getting a carton, throwing my things in it, and then being stuck in this car with this guy, who came home with us. We no longer lived in Williamsburg. We came to this new project— and I was shocked to find out he was my new stepfather."

"What was his name?"

"Louis Kind."

"How did that work out for you and your mother?"

"They divorced when I was thirteen."

"Was it a bad relationship?"

"*I* didn't like it."

"Why?"

"He wasn't nice to her."

"Was he nice to you?"

"*No!*"

"What do you mean, no?"

"He really didn't like me," she said glumly. "I remember going in his Pontiac—you know, that car with the slanty back?"

"Yeah."

"I would talk a lot. I was with my friend Rosalind Aronstein, and he said, 'Why don't you be like your friend, quiet.'" She paused, her eyes narrowing, then glanced at me. "That wasn't good."

"Not good," I agreed. "Not good at all."

She brightened, alive in the past. "Then, my mother told me he was color-blind. So I kept saying, 'Oh, what a nice red light. What a nice shade of green. Oh, it just turned that pretty shade of red!'"

Later, when we were talking about her triumph on Broadway in *Funny Girl*, I asked her, "Did your stepfather, Mr. Kind, ever come to see the show?"

"He finally came, yeah."

"Did he come backstage after the show?"

"Yeah, and he brought me a basket of candies—sucking candies. Twenty years later, I realized it was still on my bathtub. And when I finally shed my need to be approved by anyone, I threw them out."

"Did your mother like what was happening to you?"

"My mother, I think, was the type of woman who praised me to other people . . . but not to my face. She used to say, 'I don't want you to get a swelled head.'"

Barbra looked at me for a long moment, shrugged and sat back, silent and visibly pained.

"I never visited my father's grave," she reflected. "That's very interesting. I was thirty . . . five, something like that, thirty-nine, I don't remember, in my thirties. I had never been to my father's grave in Long Island, and I said, 'I really want to visit his grave.' So . . . I went to the cemetery . . . and the only picture I have with my father is my arm around his tombstone."

Aware of the profusion of acting classes Barbra had taken in her teens, I asked her if she'd ever auditioned at the Actors Studio.

"Mmm-hmm. First, with a friend who just asked me to be the partner. And one of my prized possessions was a letter from the Actors Studio that said, 'We liked your work, and would you audition on your own?' So, I came back and did a scene. I cried all through it, I remember. It was not right. And I was only fifteen, so they said, 'Come back another time when you're a little older.' But I never did."

"How did you choose to end your bio in the *Playbill* of *I Can Get It for You Wholesale*?"

"Oh, God, that was funny, yeah. 'Not a member of the Actors Studio.' The actors always wrote, 'I'm a member of the Actors Studio.' And since I wasn't, I thought it would be funny to say, 'Not a member of the Actors Studio.'" As the students laughed, she added hastily, "Even though I adored . . . I mean, I *wanted* to be! I just never went back. Who knows? Maybe I wouldn't have gotten in."

"Well, you were fifteen."

"Yeah."

I slid a letter from under the five hundred blue cards I'd prepared for the evening. "As a vice president of the Actors Studio, I am privileged to read to you a letter which I received today. 'Dear Barbra . . . It has, however belatedly, come to our attention that a regrettable mistake was made forty-six years ago. . . .'" I waited as Barbra joined in the peals of laughter issuing from the Actors Studio Drama School students, then continued. "'We are pleased to have this opportunity to rectify it. As a copresident of the Actors Studio, it is my great pleasure to inform you that, in recognition of the quality and high standards of your work, you are henceforward a member of the Actors Studio . . .'"

"Oh, God, that's great!" Barbra shouted over the growing tumult.

"'. . . entitled to all the rights and privileges that membership confers,'" I continued. " 'On behalf of my copresidents, the Studio board and fellow members, I would like to say that we look forward to continuing to enjoy your work in session. With warmest regards, Ellen Burstyn.' "

"Oh, that's great, that's great!" Barbra exulted. "So, now, if I'm ever in another play, in the *Playbill* it can say, 'A member of the Actors Studio.' "

At nine thirteen p.m., when we'd been onstage for two hours, Barbra turned to me abruptly with "You never get hungry during the show? Like, aren't you dying?" The remark got almost as much applause as Sean Penn's and Johnny Depp's cigarettes, leading me to the troubling thought that maybe all these years our students had been suffering similar deprivation. "Like a Kit Kat bar or something?" Barbra asked plaintively. "I haven't gone this long without eating in a long time. A *cookie*?"

The plea was so innocent, unaffected and patently sincere that I replied, "You want a cookie? We'll bring you a cookie."

"Well, yeah. Like a Ritz cracker. Anything."

Confident that the message had been received by our director and line producer in the mobile unit parked outside the theater, I pressed ahead. Then, fifteen minutes later, at twenty-nine minutes, twenty-six seconds and twenty-seven frames past nine P.M., our stage manager emerged from the wings bearing a heaping plate of sweets.

"Oh, wow! Look at that!" Barbra cried. "Oh, my God! *Can* I . . . ?"

"Of course. They're yours."

"You mean . . . ?" She surveyed the tray. "Oh! Oh, God! Oreos! And a Kit Kat! I'm in heaven!" Popping Oreos and bits of Kit Kat, she glanced out at the roistering students. "I mean, well, you need stamina for this. You're talking about stuff that"—another bite of Kit Kat vanished—"was a long time ago, you know? I need to fire the brain cells!"

The Oreos and Kit Kats worked. Barbra's brain cells were still firing like cherry bombs in Chinatown when I ejected her and the students five hours after we'd begun.

When Charlize Theron came to our stage, the theme of parental loss took an astonishing turn. Because some, though not all, of its details already existed in the public record, and because of my pledge never to risk embarrassing a guest—and, most of all, because Charlize's mother, Gerda, had accompanied her to our theater, and would be sitting in the front row—I conferred with the two of them in the greenroom, telling them that, since the information in my cards affected both their lives, I would need the permission of both of them to bring it up. And, I added, either of them could veto the subject summarily, without explanation or discussion, and there wouldn't be another syllable spoken about it, in the greenroom or onstage.

I wouldn't have considered bringing it up at all, to them or to the public, except for the fact that our goal on *Inside the Actors Studio* is to examine those experiences that shaped the person and the artist, and some of the details of Charlize's professional and personal history are inexplicable without this background. Nevertheless, I stressed to them that I have no right to cause anyone even a moment of discomfort, and could conduct a successful and satisfying interview without this element.

Finally, I asked them to discuss it in private, and give me a one-word answer: yes or no. I left the greenroom, and a few minutes later, they emerged with the answer. "Yes," Charlize said. I looked at Mrs. Theron, and she said firmly, "Yes."

When we'd been on the stage for nearly an hour, with Charlize, exquisite and articulate, in the chair next to mine, and her mother, as striking a beauty as she, in the center of the front row, I said, "As this series goes into its tenth year, the commonest theme by far—for all of us, beginning with me—is parental loss by death or divorce. Many of our guests believe it was a key element in their formation both as people and as artists." I turned from the audience to Charlize. "I know it's difficult, and I will not ask you to dwell on it, but it's obviously part of your life and your makeup. There was a tragedy when you were fifteen."

"Mmm-hmm."

"And that was what?"

"Well, my . . . my father unfortunately was . . . was sick. He was an alcoholic . . . for most of his life. Um, in our family we just kind of lived with it. And it just got worse and worse and . . . when I was fifteen, one night he, uh, he, uh, he, he, uh . . ." I prepared to intervene, but Charlize continued before I could. "Yeah. He, he kind of came home one night . . . and, uh, things got a little bad at our house, and, and, uh . . . he was shot."

She fell silent, and again I prepared to move on to another subject, but she had more to say. "Yeah. I mean, you know, you just—you don't think these things ever really will happen to you, and you always think they kind of happen to *other* people. But, uh, you know, it was really unfortunate, a very unfortunate thing that happened, and it was a huge tragedy in my life."

I saw a way to abbreviate the painful memory and accept the neutral, noncommittal passive voice of *was shot*. "And eventually his death was considered to be . . ."

"Self-defense. Yes."

I tried to change course by putting the tragic night in perspective. "How did a fifteen-year-old girl deal with an event of such mammoth proportions? Was it terribly hard on you?"

"Yeah, sure. Well, first of all, you've lost a parent—and then, you know, the *way* I lost him. I think the thing that took me the longest to heal from . . . you don't necessarily think your father who loves you is going to show up one night, you know, wanting to kill you." She tried to manage a laugh. "So . . . I think when you're fifteen, all of these things are . . . you just can't expect to understand anything, really.

"I think most of it just happens with time. And the great thing was that my mom and I had a really close relationship, and thank God I had that, because I could've been completely alone at that time. But I had a parent; I had a solid parent to rely on who guided me through . . . through most of . . . all of it. So, I was blessed in that sense. But time, you know? It takes a lot of time, a lot of time."

Recalling the transformation of Charlize's seemingly invincible beauty to stark ugliness for her role as the brutal, brutalized prostitute in *Monster,* shooting her tricks, I said, "You have very powerful emotional abilities as an actor. I would assume that having gone through some things in your life that were very powerful, it's a resource for you."

"Yeah. The great thing about acting, to me, is that it's a very cathartic experience. I'm a true believer that you do get kind of led—someone helps you to get to this path that you have to take in your life. That doesn't mean that you can sit back and relax and everything's going to happen. It doesn't mean that at all. But I do think, in a way, with everything that happened in my life, or is still happening in my life, I've been fortunate enough to be brought to this place where I can actually have this experience with acting, where I can make sense of my life."

"I understand."

"Maybe that's therapy for other people, or meditation, or another form of creating. Whatever it is for anybody else, for me, it's experiencing emotion through a character."

As I commit this experience to these pages, I don't think I acquitted myself well. In my effort to clear a path for Charlize, I allowed a crucial element to be lost: Who shot Charlize's father? Some who watched the show, some who are reading these pages, could be left with the impression that it was Charlize. Maybe, in her zeal to shield her mother, she was satisfied with that ambiguity. But in the public record it was her mother who was found not guilty by reason of self-defense. In any event, I am an admirer of Charlize Theron the actor, Charlize Theron the person and Charlize Theron the daughter.

At the end of the evening, I was, as always, longing hungrily for Elaine's, and when I invited Charlize and her mother to join Kedakai and me, they accepted the invitation. The restaurant was crowded that night, despite the late hour, and only Elaine's ironclad policy against gawking—and the innate cool of most of her customers—spared Charlize from unwanted attention, though a major league ballplayer who had never formerly shown any interest in Kedakai or me stopped by our table to greet us like long-lost friends and wait pointedly for an introduction to our guests.

The interest *from* our table, on the other hand, was intense. Charlize and her mother surveyed the room, comparing notes, and when I asked Charlize what was of such interest, she was as frank as she had been on our stage. "We're looking for a man for my mother." All through dinner, as Kedakai and I assisted the Therons in sorting out the possibilities around us, Charlize and Gerda maintained a lively interest in every newcomer. Clearly, they had decided that Elaine's was a potential happy hunting ground.

It wasn't until we were leaving that Charlize grabbed her mother's arm and the two stopped cold, their mutual gaze fixed on a robust reveler holding forth at Elaine's table. Charlize plucked at my elbow, hissing, "Who's that?"

They had picked out one of Elaine's regulars. He was, as I knew, eminently single, and eminently ineligible. Though he wore mufti, and comported himself like the rest of Elaine's crew, he was in fact a priest, the Reverend Pete Colapietro, pastor of Holy Cross, the "Broadway" church. As he rose to meet our guests, and engaged in a lively conversation with them, I admitted privately to myself that, absent his vocation, he would have been the perfect man for Gerda.

Bravo telecast Charlize's episode during the Oscar voting period, she won the Academy Award, and she, Gerda and I rejoiced together at the *Vanity Fair* party. Father Pete, a far more convivial man than I, was missed.

◾

R ussell Crowe came to *Inside the Actors Studio* with his bad-boy image intact. He left with it in tatters because he turned out to be an amiable guest, a knowledgeable teacher and a conscious craftsman. I asked him, "How much work do you do before you come on the set? Do you prepare on your own?"

"Yes, of course, of course. You give me the script, I'll be ready in the morning. Preparation and research is a privilege and I love to do it. I'm very inquisitive. I also know, I absolutely know, that the more I put into the character, the more is apparent on the screen. For example, on *L.A. Confidential*, Bud White was supposed to be the largest man in the Los Angeles Police Department. I hired a flat that was very, very small. I could hardly even fit in the doorway of the bathroom. To me, doing that every day, especially during rehearsals, I felt like I was big, I was oversized for my environment, which is the mentality that Bud White is supposed to have.

"If you're a pirate, get yourself an eye patch or a parrot," he told the students. "Address the external as early as you possibly can. Get it out of your way, and don't be afraid to readjust any of those decisions. The bottom line is, as Scorcese said, 'Man, you don't get anywhere until you make a decision.' So, start making decisions quickly, but be open and lucid enough and fluid enough to change your mind if you prove yourself wrong. If you find yourself wrong, and you do not go back on what you've done, you're just undercutting the whole process, and you're kidding yourself. You shouldn't be doing the gig if you're going to fall in love with things like that. You know? Serve the character, not yourself."

There were a lot of lessons taught and learned that evening, none more unusual and useful than the one that began when I asked Russell, who had been telling us about his band 30 Odd Foot of Grunts, "You've said that you always approach acting with a rock 'n' roll mentality."

"Yeah, yeah, yeah."

"What does that mean?"

"It's always been about entertaining the audience. It's always been about knowing that you're just part of a storytelling process. I never came to it from, shall we say, a more precious point of view where there are rules that you can't break. Every time I got told an absolute rule when I was growing up as an actor, it always ended up being bullshit. They say you have to love the character you're playing. If you fall in love with somebody, you forgive all their faults, right? If you fall in love with your character, you miss out on the opportunity of showing up those faults.

"Be objective about the character you're playing, because it's those faults that make that person an individual, make him—him or her, sorry—a human being. I decided to fall in love with the *job*. I love *acting*. Wherever that takes me in terms of the exploration, the discovery, fine and dandy. Whatever, whoever I expose, I like the job. I like the inquiry. I like the energy required for it. I like the focus, the concentration. I love the job!"

He paused for breath. The students needed a chance to inhale as well. "As jobs go, acting's a pretty fucking *good* job! I don't like the idea of going to an office. Otherwise, I would probably have another job, if I felt it was suitable to me. But it's not. I'm a fucking gypsy. And I come from a long line of gypsies. And it's a great tradition of gypsies who tell stories. *That's* what my job is. A few hundred years ago, it was a different situation. But now, through the flickering light, we get to talk to millions of people at a time sometimes—if we're lucky enough.

"And that's cool. That's a good job. I never cease seeing the opportunity to tell people a story as a privilege. I don't know if I sound all highfalutin and idealistic—but fuck it, man, I am!" The room exploded into cheers.

In the Pivot Questionnaire, when I asked Russell for his least favorite word, he replied, "It's a three-word phrase. Is that okay?"

"Of course."

"Hollywood bad boy."

"Look," I said, "let's face it. When this goes on the air, it's going to wreck your reputation. After what you've given us tonight, you're going to come off as a pussycat."

And a dedicated artist. And one of the many generous heroes of the story *I* am privileged to tell.

CHAPTER Fifteen

❝*Our sex is a part of who we are. Not just our sensuality and our passion. Our sex. Sex. That* **thing** *that's a part of what makes us walk the way we walk, talk the way we talk, think what we think.*

—Sharon Stone, *Inside the Actors Studio*

I t will come as no surprise that our students were in evident awe of Tom Cruise. And to anyone who has worked with him, it will come as no surprise that he quickly, gracefully put them at ease. I have encountered Tom several times since he was with our students and me in December 2003, and on every occasion he has been as open and gracious as he was that night. It appears to be his nature.

On our stage, he was caught off guard, though I hadn't anticipated he would be, when I produced his family tree. "When Vanessa Redgrave was in that chair we were able to trace her family tree back four generations to 1846. You break our record. We can track your forebears back to 1810."

"Whoa! Really?"

"And the first Thomas Cruise Mapother to 1876. There's your family tree."

"Thank you. Let me see that."

As I passed it to him, I asked, "Would you like to see the Mapother crest?"

"Yeah. Let's see. You know what? You definitely learn something new about yourself every day. Wow!"

At this point in these pages, it seems redundant to say that the subject of parental loss came up. Tom told us that his parents divorced when he was twelve, and when I replied, "My father was absent for most of my life, and I reencountered him toward the end of his. Isn't that what happened to you?" He said, "Yeah, that's what happened. I'd finished shooting *All the Right Moves,* and I got a call from my grandmother—'cause I hadn't seen my father really in almost ten years—just saying that your father's dying, he's in the hospital, and he's going to die—and would you like to see him?

"So . . . I said, 'Yeah, I want to see my father.' And I went down, and he would see me under one condition, that we didn't discuss the past. Didn't want to discuss the past, what happened. I brought him a . . . gift, and it looked like Tom Sawyer, a little boy who was playing hooky, you know, a little statue. And it had the music from *The Sting* on it." Tom hummed the theme. "Because he and I . . . we loved that movie and we saw that movie together. . . .'"

He stopped for a long moment, then resumed. "And . . . I gave him that as a gift, and he laughed, and he got it. You know, he hadn't seen me at that point . . . I'm twenty-one years old . . . and it was a very powerful moment for me. And I looked at him—he was a big man, about six-one, a striking-looking man, a very powerful-looking guy, and at that moment, you can't help but feel such . . . compassion. And later on, I heard he recognized the . . . the loss of that family . . . and it was a very special family and it was a huge life force that he had . . . let go of. You know? He'd made some mistakes, and he knew it. And I wasn't angry with him; I was really just looking at a man who was my father, and . . . and that I love, no matter what happened, uh . . .'"

He stopped again. "Did you tell him how you felt about him?" I asked.

"Yeah. I held his hand, and he said, 'Listen, we'll go have a steak. I'm gonna get through this.' And I just wanted him to know that I loved him, and what happened happened; it's the past. It was very powerful."

"Did you see him again?"

"No, I didn't see him again. He died."

"Do you feel that that chapter ended more or less satisfactorily?"

"More or less satisfactorily."

As I looked, as always, for my guest's approach to the craft that our students study and the guest practices, Tom's reply was modest—and informative. "Although I've never really had formal training, I've had this ability—I guess not ability—the luck to be able to work with the people I've worked with, and just the ability to find what works for me. I've created my own way of preparing for a picture. I do a tremendous amount of research. I work very, very hard to get to the point where you just let go, and it just happens, and all the mechanics just fade away.

"It's really the writer. He tells his story. As actors, you know, we're writers also, because of the work that we do and the research. I do a lot of research, and I just absorb it—because that's *our* writing. It's not about the lines; it's what goes underneath. We're writing the subtext. That's our job. As actors we have this structure, the lines, the scene, the story, and for me, personally, it's really finding freedom within the structure of a scene, so that you can have moments like the one in *Rain Man* where Dustin Hoffman leans across and our heads touch. You're just connected. I mean, that *happened,* you know? That's the movie!

"We *look* for those moments. They just happen; you can't plan. Sometimes, you try to plan things like that and it just doesn't happen, and you start forcing moments, as opposed to just living, because it's about being the character, and being there. When I'm doing a scene, I'm not thinking about anything else. I've done all my work, and I'm allowing myself to be affected by the people, by the environment that we've created.

"Those are the moments that are fresh and moving to me."

W hen Jennifer Lopez accepted the invitation to come to our stage, the Purity Police mobilized in defense of the *Inside the Actors Studio* principles they suddenly understood and treasured—but had somehow neglected to mention or acknowledge before the perceived barbarian appeared at the gates.

Jennifer was invited because she has succeeded as few professionals of her age, gender and ethnicity have, in three of the disciplines being drilled by us into our students every day of their drama school lives: acting, singing and dance. While she was manifestly not Duse, Sutherland or Pavlova, none of that august group had ever attempted what the others could do.

What some of our guests have to offer our students is an infusion of spine and guts. Jennifer Lopez is emphatically of that number. When I asked her how her parents felt about her decision to leave college and pursue her passions, she said, "Not good, not at first. I think they were scared but, you know, I told them I had a dream. I woke up one Saturday morning and took my mom and dad into the living room and said, 'I have to talk to you. I'm supposed to be in show business. Okay?'"

The students, many of whom had had similar talks with their parents, laughed appreciatively. "My dad, who's kind of a dreamer, too, was like, 'Okay,' and my mom was like, 'No way! You're not dropping out of school! You're staying in school and that's it!' And so that caused a bit of tension between us."

"About that time, didn't you leave home?"

Jennifer laughed. "Shortly thereafter."

"Where'd you go?"

"I lived in the dance studio for a while."

"How can you live in a dance studio?"

"Well, after they'd lock up, I'd clean up, and then I'd sleep in the office."

"How long did you do that?"

"Until I got my first job a few months later."

"Did your parents adjust?"

"No, they never got used to it. I still think they're not used to me not being home."

A few minutes later, I asked Jennifer, "What was your first album called?"

"On the Six."

"And what is the six?"

"The six train, on the Lexington Avenue line, from the Bronx to Manhattan."

"Is *On the Six* meant to draw attention to your roots?"

"I'm thinking to myself, What is this first album about? The journey of where I started, and where I am now, and how did I get there? And when I thought about it, I was like, I got there by getting on the six train from the Bronx, coming into the city, taking lessons, taking classes. It was a literal thing."

Knowing her ambivalence about the J-Lo label, I asked her, "Who decided to call your second album *J-Lo*?"

She laughed. "I did."

"Have you lived to regret it?"

"Yeah!" When the students chuckled, she amended it. "Well, yes and no, yes and no. I came up with it as a kind of homage to my fans, because people were shortening my name. They were saying 'Jennifer Lo' or 'Jenny Lo' or 'J-Lo.' And I thought to myself, you know what? In a way, my music persona is like J-Lo. Maybe that'll be a good name for the album.

"But I didn't name *myself* that," she said firmly. "I named the *album* that, you know what I mean? And it caught on. It was like a headline thing: 'J-Lo.'"

"It became another persona," I suggested.

She nodded. "It became a persona; it became this thing that people could talk about."

"And something people could own—quite independently of you."

"Yeah, yeah. But that was not me, Jennifer."

There was one more aspect of Jennifer's life—and perhaps, for a few of the students, theirs—that I wanted the students to hear about. "Other guests in that chair have talked about the relentless glare and sometimes ruthless demands of fame in America," I said. "And at times you've been a lightning rod. Literally."

"Yes."

"That can't be pleasant."

"No, it's not."

"Does it just come with the territory, or do you think there's something wrong with it?"

"There's definitely something wrong with it. I feel like I can handle things. I'm not whining; I'm not complaining about the fact that I have this spotlight on me because I'm in the public eye. But the most dangerous thing, the most terrifying thing about it, for me, is to have what I do taken away from me because of it.

"I feel it's very dangerous when the focus comes off your work and onto your private life. Because that's not why I got in the business in the first place. Why I got in is because I love the work, I love singing, I love performing. That's what I do; that's what I feel I was born to do, whatever anybody says. If I was doing it in a dive bar in Mexico, it wouldn't matter. That's what I'd be doing.

"And that's the scariest part of it for me. If you look at the beginning of my career and the directors and the people that I worked with—for them, I was a clean slate. And now, with everybody having all these preconceived notions about you and knowing too much about your life, and saying, 'No, she's too this or she's too that,' that's when it gets scary to me. I don't want this to happen, you know? Because being a celebrity is not being an actor!

"One of my first teachers told me something: It's not about where you get; it's the process. If you don't enjoy acting, if you don't enjoy the class, if you don't enjoy doing the work, then don't do it. If you're doing it to get somewhere, then forget it. Because this is what being an actor is. It's doing the work, it's being in class, it's failing, it's getting up. It's nothing else. And the work for me is the important part. It's not about having the biggest hit movies. I'm gonna keep doing it, and sometimes they're gonna be good, and I'm always going to strive to make it great—but you never know." She smiled at the students. "You know what I mean? It's about the work. That's all it's about."

B ette Midler established a new speed record for tears. A few minutes after she came onstage, as we talked about her childhood, I quoted her. "You've said, 'I was constantly fighting for some self-esteem.'"

Welling up, she said, "Oh, my God, are we gonna bring out the Kleenex *already*? It's like the third question! Yes, I was constantly fighting for some self-esteem, and you notice I got some. *Oh!*"

As she broke again and dabbed at her face with a tissue, I shuffled through my cards. "Actually, I didn't think you'd cry till page twenty-six."

Having weathered that brief squall, we proceeded with low humidity until I observed, "You've given credit for the change in your life and behavior to Beth Ellen Childers."

"Absolutely," Bette exclaimed. "Absolutely! She just thought I was a riot. I couldn't say anything that she didn't think was hilarious. And *she* was hilarious. She used to make me laugh so hard, I laughed until the tears rolled down my cheeks. And, you know, if you have never experienced that kind of laughter, it's too bad. Because that's the greatest thing in the world. I'm convinced of it. I think that's better than sex. I do. And I've had great sex. But I think that's it. And we laughed like that for four years."

"And what happened finally?"

"Well, she . . . we graduated and she went on to college . . . she went to . . . she, uh, it was, uh, oh . . . *oh* . . . !" She had slowed to a shuddering halt, the dam breaking, tears tumbling down her cheeks. "I guess it's page twenty-six," she gasped, then burst out, "She was killed! Just . . . *killed*," Bette sobbed. "It was an auto accident." She looked at me, though I doubt she could see me through the flowing tears. "That's page twenty-six?"

"I missed it by one," I said. "It's twenty-seven." As Bette struggled to regain her composure, I tried to make amends. "We don't try to make people cry. . . ."

"I know," Bette said, showing more consideration for me than I had for her. "That was sad."

Bette's record would hold until Dustin Hoffman appeared on our stage.

As I have set this record down over the past two years, one of the things I've realized is, of course, how fortunate I am to have spent time in the presence of this remarkable company.

Another realization that makes me the envy even, on reflection, of myself is how many evenings I've spent less than three feet away from many of the most famously beautiful women in the world. Imagine being privileged to spend an evening with any one, much less all, of them, and then going home with the only woman on earth who outshines them. This journey inside *Inside* has made me realize that in some respects I am one of the most fortunate of men.

A case in point: When Natalie Portman was on our stage, twenty-three years old, ravishing and recently graduated from Harvard, I recalled Anthony Lane's description of her in his *New Yorker* review of *Anywhere But Here*. "Her beauty has now become so disabling that you should not attempt to drive or operate heavy machinery for twelve hours after viewing this picture."

I said, "I'll ask you the question I have asked several beautiful women who have been in that chair: Is being better-looking than many people a professional advantage, disadvantage or of no consequence or interest?"

Natalie's answer was immediate, frank and, I would submit, neither modest nor boastful, since it simply acknowledged an obvious reality. "Advantage. I mean, I think whoever says it's not would be lying. Maybe people don't take you as seriously, and maybe there are roles you can't play—but I think it's much easier. Look at people who are actresses. I think it's much easier to work in film if you're considered to be attractive.

"But I don't wake up in the morning and go, 'Hey, I'm good-looking.' Obviously, a serious-actress answer would be 'Oh, it's a disadvantage. It's distracting from my work.' But no, in terms of getting work, of course it's helpful."

Yvette Brooks, a surpassingly beautiful young woman in our school, asked a variation of the question during Sharon Stone's classroom session. "One of the things I'm most interested in is, you're able to really own your sexuality. As a woman in this field, I know I'm always sort of trying to run away from that—because I don't want to be objectified. How do you deal with that?"

"No matter what you do, someone's going to objectify you," Sharon said. "So, you might as well just get over it." She smiled as the students laughed. "And no matter what you think, you've already objectified someone in this room tonight. It's a part of who we are. Our sex is a part of who we are. Not just our sensuality and our passion. Our sex. *Sex.* That *thing* that's a part of what makes us walk the way we walk, talk the way we talk, think what we think.

"To take this Gestalt out of yourself is to rob yourself of part of the fire and the core that drives you or any character you play. Yes, some characters are void of sexuality. As some people. But then you have to figure out *why.*"

She paused, studying Yvette, then said, "It's as much a part of you as your vocalization. Or your physicality. Or what you wear or think or do. And I think it's absurd and puritanical and wrong to be afraid of it. What you have to say is, 'Who made me think that I should be ashamed of my sexuality? Okay, now they can drop dead!'"

Her dictum was met with laughter and applause, which prompted her to continue as Yvette's inner voice: "'And how about this beautiful part of me?' Because it *is* a beautiful part of you. It's the part that makes the rose bloom. You don't let someone take that!"

"I'm coming in tomorrow with a very tight dress on," Yvette declared.

"If it makes you feel 'you,'" Sharon responded. "You have to feel 'you.' See, a tight dress doesn't make me feel 'me.' A tight dress makes me feel embarrassed. But, a *short* dress? I feel *that*. It's whatever it is for *you*."

━

Kurt Vonnegut was fond of quoting H. L. Mencken on the subject of yet another award to Columbia University's Nicholas Murray Butler: "Nothing remained to be done but to wrap him in sheet-gold and burnish him until he blinds the sun itself." Morgan Freeman came to our stage heaped with honors, but for us the one that counted most was the regard in which he was held by our guests. Over the years, each time his name came up, there was an immediate shift to a particular tone that we heard on no other subject or occasion.

Our evening with Morgan began as I asked him a question that revealed a family tree as deeply rooted as the Redgraves' or the Barrymores': "How far back are you able to trace your family's history?"

"My great-great-great-grandmother," Morgan said, "who was a slave in Virginia, was bought by a man named Colonel Wright, and taken into the area that I live in now in Tallahatchie County, Mississippi."

That evening marked the first onstage reunion in the history of *Inside the Actors Studio*, in celebration of Morgan's Broadway debut as an actor and mine as a Broadway producer. "One night in 1977," I said, "I went to the Manhattan Theatre Club, and saw a remarkable play called *The Last Street Play*. It was written by a young writer named Richard Wesley. There were a number of powerful performances in it, but when a derelict called Zeke shuffled onstage and delivered himself of a stunning monologue, Shakespearean in quality and length, I felt the way I'd felt the first time I saw Marlon Brando on the stage: that I was seeing something that was opening brand-new doors.

"In the next few weeks, I formed a partnership with the Shubert Organization and Paramount Pictures, and *The Last Street Play*, renamed *The Mighty Gents*, opened on Broadway in April of 1978. Mel Gussow of the *Times* called it the best new play of the season, and Morgan received a nomination for the Tony Award."

I introduced Richard Wesley, who was in the front row, and concluded, "This is my opportunity tonight to say, all these years later, thank you, Morgan, and thank you, Richard."

"Thank you, Jim," Morgan said. "You were the producer." He looked at Richard. "Actors get accolades because people see whatever it is they do, and they call it artistry. But I don't think of it as that at all. Sometimes somebody comes along and they've written a part, and all you have to do is put it on.

Richard did that. That character was so compelling, so right, so clear to me, I was just channeling."

Morgan's "just channeling" prompted critic Walter Kerr to write, "Mr. Freeman's shift from one level of honesty to another is literally beautiful performing." A short time later, reviewing one of Morgan's first movie performances, Pauline Kael posed the question: "Is he the greatest American actor?"

Searching for the secrets of Morgan's formidable craft, I quoted David Fincher, who had directed him in *Seven:* "Morgan will give you seven or eight subtle variations on a precise mood or emotion."

"How much difference do you look for between takes?" I asked.

"If I think I've nailed it," Morgan answered, "I try to do it the same way. If there are different ways to approach the other actor, then, I'll just try that and see."

"How much of your performance comes from what your partner is doing at any given moment in a scene?"

"All of it. Acting is reacting in my book."

I am an admirer of film critic Roger Ebert not only for what he thinks but *how* he thinks. There is a decency and cleanliness in his thought process that, for me, sorts matters out definitively, time after time. And, as usual, he got it right when he wrote about Morgan, "What Freeman brings to all of his scenes is a very particular attentiveness. He doesn't merely listen. He seems to weigh what he is told, to evaluate it. That quality creates an amusing result sometimes, when other actors will tell him something and then, you can clearly sense, look to see if he buys it."

After reading Ebert's comment on our stage, I returned to a familiar theme. "I believe that actors listen *differently* than civilians do. How important to you is listening when you're acting?"

"You're not going to do it if you're not listening. I have this little trick I'll do sometimes. Someone will say a line to me and I'll say, 'Huh?' and see what happens."

"*That* gets their attention."

In the classroom, a student said, "You speak about your intuition, and you refer to the script as being the bible. I want to know, is that intuition informed by the script?"

"I think it's informed by *life,*" Morgan replied. "I haven't said this, and I might as well say it: In terms of being an actor, I'm also a peeker. I'm real serious about the keyhole. I watch people. My wife used to slap me because, if I see somebody doing something unique, I'll do it. You know? If I see somebody with a walk, a limp, I'll do it. Just to get it."

He zeroed in on a student, fixing him with a steely regard. "I'm looking at this very handsome dude right here, and I'm watching him. I'm all over the place, but my eyes keep coming back here, because he's seriously focused. He hasn't looked anywhere else." He looked away, then swiveled back. "I glance back—I see his eyes right here." Morgan transferred his gaze to another student, then another, engaging each of them in a virtual duel of concentration, with each student staring back, transfixed, looking, *seeing, listening.*

"You're all doing it, I know, because I'm talking," Morgan said, ". . . and I'm a major, internationally famous star." As the students exploded into laughter, the spell broken, Morgan sat back with a smile, satisfied that his point had been made. "I'm just saying that this whole intuition thing is informed by study."

I continually look for guests who can instruct our students in more than one discipline. When Jamie Foxx came to *Inside the Actors Studio,* I introduced him to our students with "Tonight breaks a record. In the more than ten years of this series, no other guest has come to this stage as an actor, comedian, writer, producer, director, composer, pianist, singer and recording artist."

The subject of parental loss came up instantly with Jamie. "How old were you when your parents separated?"

"I don't know exactly when they separated, because at seven months I was in another family."

"How did that happen?"

"Well, when my mother had me, she wasn't really prepared, or ready to take on that responsibility. And the lady that had adopted her, also adopted me. So, the ones who I consider my parents were Estelle Talley and Mark Talley."

"Then, technically, legally, your mother is what?"

"My sister. Technically. It's a Southern thing. You know how it is in the South. Technically, my mother is my sister, and technically, my uncle is my brother, so it really is a yee-dee-dee-dee-dee-dee-dee-dee type of situation, you know?" His chant bounced on a wave of laugher.

"It also points to a couple of extraordinary people," I said.

"Mmm-hmm!"

Describing his grandmother/adoptive mother, Jamie said, "She had the bow and arrow, and I was the arrow. She let me out there, but she made sure she aimed me in the right direction, and because of that upbringing, I think that's why I'm where I am right now."

Since several of our guests have been veterans of the stand-up wars, I've been struck often by the parallels between comedy and combat. In the stand-up comic's lexicon, every time they go onstage, they either "kill" or "die." Obviously, every night, it's a life-and-death battle, which may explain why so many of them have emerged from that crucible, as the rappers have from theirs, with skills that open the door to acting.

One of my blue cards contained a quote, which I read to Jamie. "You've said, 'When I go out on the road, that's when I sling my guns. I'm a gunslinger.'"

"Yes, I am."

"Is stand-up that important to you?"

"Stand-up is important to me because it keeps me—and I'll use it as a metaphor—it keeps me in the street, it tells me what people are thinking about."

"I've watched a lot of your stand-up," I said, "and one of the things I was hoping tonight was that you would address me as a playa."

"You are a true playa, man!"

"I don't know that that's so at all. You have to be honest with me. When you address that audience of playas, you're talking to playas. What do I have to do to qualify to be a playa?"

"I'm gonna tell you what a playa is."

"Okay."

"A playa is somebody who is moving culture, no matter what the size. Now, *you* move culture, people come to you and watch what you say and what you talk about, and they actually value your opinion. That's a playa—somebody whose opinion is valued. You are doing it, you know what I'm saying? These people come in here, and they have a great time, and you're bringing all that. That's playa status; that's what playa is to me."

"It makes me a playa?" I asked, still uncertain.

"Yeah. You are a playa, man."

Will Smith had granted me jiggy status, and now I was a playa. My cup was running over—even if I suspected that both of them were being kind to an irreparable honky.

It was Jamie's grandmother's insistence that he begin piano lessons at five, and enter college as a classical music major, that enabled him to play Ray Charles in *Ray*. When I asked him whether Charles had had to approve him, he said, "Oh, yeah. He walks in with that smile and that sway. You just go, wow, man! He grabs me and says, 'Oh, you got strong fingers; let's go play the blues.'

"He got on one piano, I got on the other, and he said, 'Jamie, if you can do the blues, you can do anything.' So we start singing the blues, back and forth, and then he moved into Thelonius Monk. That's like treacherous waters! And

I was like, 'Whoa, whoa, where you going?' And I hit a wrong note. He said, 'Now, why the hell did you do that? It's right underneath your fingers, man.'

"And so I use that now in life; I used it for the film: Life is notes underneath our fingers. We just gotta figure out which notes to play to make our music."

Like Melanie Griffith, Jamie came to us later than he had planned, but for a different reason. After we had discussed his performance in *Ray,* and after he'd played the piano on our stage, and sung to our students, I said, "This brings us to the final note of the evening. As our audience here knows, Jamie has come to us, selflessly and courageously, tonight. He was supposed to be here ten days ago. But something happened."

I looked at Jamie, who had begun crying, silently, bitterly, uncontrollably and, like others on our stage, without embarrassment or disguise. I waited for thirty seconds, ready to veer away from the subject if he chose to, but finally, still weeping, he said, "The lady that, uh, made all the tools . . . she decided that . . . she did her job. And, uh, she said, 'Go ahead.' She said, 'It's time, you know? You do your thing. I gave you everything you needed.'"

Looking through tears at the students, whose faces mirrored his, he brandished a hand at the stage. "I didn't want to do *this.* But . . . I didn't want to just sit somewhere and, you know, let it stew." He straightened in his chair. "But she gave me the tools for this moment too. 'Cause . . . God loaned my grandmother to us for ninety-five years. And her beautiful contract is up."

Jamie and the students mourned his grandmother together for a moment; then he offered them and himself some balm. "So, her and Ray Charles is sitting there talking, right?" Jamie said. "Therefore, I'm gonna be all right."

It goes without saying that the evening ended with the students chanting, "Jamie! Jamie! Jamie!" The Academy agreed. Bravo telecast Jamie's episode November 28, 2004, as the Oscar campaign began; on Sunday, February 27, 2005, he received the Best Actor Oscar; and that night we celebrated with it at the *Vanity Fair* party.

When Jay Leno agreed to appear on *Inside the Actors Studio* in 2003, I had the hubris to propose that, as a lecture-demonstration, one of his writers prepare for me a monologue, which I would deliver to our audience and he would critique. With Jay looking on, I delivered my monologue, replete with lines like "As dean of the Actors Studio Drama School, I'd like to give you an update on our progress. The good news: We have two hundred great actors, writers and directors earning their master's degrees. The bad news: Our football team got a rotten review in *The New York Times.* Will Ferrell makes me sound slow, boring, funereal and pretentious. That is ridiculous! I am not pretentious."

The writer had done his best and I did mine. Jay, like all comedians, can turn very serious when it comes to the subject of comedy. With the monologue semisafely behind me, I said, "All right, Jay, I can take it. On the usual academic scale of A to F, how did I do?"

"F is the lowest?" Jay asked.

"Well, we could go to a . . . G?"

"I would go to . . . a C."

Feeling a genuine wave of relief, I said, "C! That's good."

Jay was reflective—and in dead earnest—muttering, "C. Yeah, C."

That night, Jay gave the students a master class in the craft—and cost—of comedy. It began with my question "What is your workday like at *The Tonight Show*?"

"I get there about eight fifteen in the morning. Then you write joke, write joke, discuss this, discuss that, write joke, have meeting, write joke. I have two or three TVs on. The trick is not to know more than anybody else; it's to know *exactly what everybody else knows.*

"We have a noon meeting that lasts about forty-five minutes: Who is the guest, what will we talk about? Go back, write joke, write joke, maybe shoot something. Rehearse down in the set, write joke, write joke. Tape four thirty to five thirty, and then, usually, six thirty to nine, we go out and do walkarounds or pieces like that. And then from ten to two, you write the monologue for the next day."

"But we started you at eight fifteen in the morning."

"Yeah."

"And you go to two in the morning."

"Yeah, that's right."

"And then, the next morning is eight fifteen again."

With a "what's-the-big-deal?" look, Jay said, "Yeah."

"How much sleep do you get a night?"

He shrugged. "Four, four and a half hours. I'm not doing heavy lifting here."

To a student aspiring to do stand-up, Jay said, "When you're onstage, you're the only person in the world. Everybody in there is focused on you. You have all the attention—right now! I sometimes feel sorry for actors, because the play has to be good. It's got to be directed well; it's got to be all these things for them to spot you. But, if you're up there alone, you're writing and producing and directing it *yourself.* It's all you. You take all the credit and you get all the blame."

As the student nodded vigorously, Jay offered a final cautionary—and encouraging—note. "You can't blame anybody. It's yours if you fail, and yours if you don't. You wrote it and you directed it. It's all your own."

When Robert Redford came to our stage in December 2004, our students were once again in the presence of a legend. Not that he felt or behaved that way. Like Clint Eastwood, Bob Redford is so utterly lacking in affectation or attitude, on-screen and off-, that he manages simultaneously to seem at first less than what we anticipated and, finally, much, much more than we could have imagined. If there is a definition for the overused, misused and abused word *star,* "Clint Eastwood" or "Robert Redford" will suffice—though either of them would wave the title away.

Mies van der Rohe's aphorism "God is in the details" (which has been mysteriously turned into its opposite by the relentless misquotation "The devil is in the details") applies perfectly to the subtle texture of any Robert Redford performance. In pursuit of his elusive approach, I asked him, "How do you normally work on a role? How much preparation do you do before the camera turns, and how much do you depend on the spontaneity of the moment, when the director says, 'Action'?"

"I don't do a lot of prep for the camera. I never have, and for that reason it was hard when I directed my first film. I refused to learn the language of the camera because I didn't want it to bother me as an actor. Some actors are quite different: They learn everything about the camera. And they work more technically. I always enjoyed spontaneity. But I also appreciate the value of certain controls, to shape what you're doing. I like improvisation."

"Do you?"

"Yes, a lot. I also know it's dangerous. But it's very exciting because there's a freedom, and something alive about it, and you have to use your brain, you have to *be* there, you have to inhabit the character, otherwise you're going to bounce out of the parade, and so I like that. I like to get the frame, understand what the director's got in mind, if I'm acting. If I go out of the camera range, tell me, but let me be; let me inhabit the space I'm in. And I love acting with other actors, when they can act. For me, it's very hard to act with actors who have everything memorized perfectly and you can see it in their eyeballs, you know, that they have it all worked out."

Since Paul Newman had told us what had transpired when a reporter suggested they costar in a remake of *Indecent Proposal,* and since the two of them were famous for their affection for practical jokes, I asked Bob, "Didn't you once send Paul a Porsche, wrapped in a red bow?"

"Yeah. He bored you to tears when you were with him 'cause he'd always talk about his racing cars. So, on his fiftieth birthday, I went to a towing service and said, 'Can you find a junked car, a Porsche?' And they called back and said, 'We found one, totaled, just completely totaled.' And I said, 'Okay, can you wrap it up and put a ribbon around it and tow it over and put it on his back porch?'

"So they did that, and it just said 'Happy birthday,' that's all. I didn't hear anything, and two weeks later, I came to my house and opened the door, and there's a crate in the living room foyer. Inside it is a big piece of metal that's been compressed down to just a solid block. It'd crushed the floor. So I realized what he had done. I did not acknowledge that it'd happened. I had to have the towing service that had brought it there come and take it out. They're making a ton of dough on this thing! I had it boiled down to a garden sculpture, and had it placed in his garden. And that was the end of it. And no one to this day has ever acknowledged it."

"Really?" I asked, over the students' raucous applause.

"Yeah," Bob said, then added reflectively, "I'm kind of sad I told that story because this is on television."

"No, it's not."

He grinned at me. "Oh, it isn't? Well, then, that's great, 'cause maybe we can keep this going for a while."

The family history Jane Fonda related on our stage began with a childhood in a royal Hollywood court reigned over by her father, Henry Fonda; but the conversation changed direction sharply as I mentioned the theme of parental divorce, which, I said, "has hung over this show like a cloud. When did it happen to you?"

"Around twelve."

"How was it explained to you?"

"I was going to school one morning, and my mother was standing in the door of the living room, and she said, 'If anybody tells you that your parents are getting divorced, tell them you already know.'

"Was that when your mother's illness began to be evident?"

"It was before then. My mother suffered from manic depression. She was institutionalized."

"At one point, didn't she come home for a day, with a nurse?"

"Yes, she came home in a limousine with a nurse. I was upstairs on a hardwood floor like this, playing jacks with my brother, and she arrived, and I said, 'Peter, don't go down. Let's not go down. If you stay up here, I'll let you win.' But he went down and I didn't." She slowed. "And I . . . I never saw her. I never did. That's when she got . . . the razor that she used to kill herself.

"It's complicated for a child because you, you, you wonder . . . years later, why didn't I go down? Was it that I was angry with her? 'I'll show you! I don't need you either.' 'Cause she hadn't been there. Did I not love her? These are the kind of questions that you spend a lot of time thinking about as a child."

"What were you initially told when your mother died?"

"That she had a heart attack."

"And how did you find out that it was other than that?"

"A year later, someone passed me a movie magazine in study hall, and it said in there that Henry Fonda's wife had killed herself."

"Did your mother leave any notes?"

"Yeah, there was one to me, one to my brother, my sister, and . . . her mother . . . and the doctor. But we never saw them."

"Why?"

"I don't know."

When I asked Jane about her experience in Lee Strasberg's private classes, she said, "I sat right behind Marilyn Monroe. She would sit there with her trench coat, and she never did anything, and I never did anything. I was terrified, as was she. But then I thought, I'll give it a chance. I'll do a sense memory, and I decided to do orange juice. . . ." A stir in the audience caught her attention, and she turned to the students. "Do you do sense memories?"

"They do it night and day," I said.

"I was still living with my dad," Jane said, "and I'll never forget, he came home one day and he said, 'What the hell are you doing?' I said, 'I'm practicing my sense memory,' and he went, 'Yech,' and walked out. He hated the Method, *hated* it. He was very dismissive, so I moved out. And then I did my first exercise, and it changed my life, because Lee said, 'Jane, you have real talent.' At that moment, the top of my head came off, and birds flew out, and the light changed, and I owned the city, and I knew why I was alive—from then on. Everybody else would do like one scene a month, and I would do four."

Two Academy Awards and four Golden Globes later, Jane produced and appeared in *On Golden Pond*. She told us why. "My father was dying and I wanted to do a movie with him. I saw the play, and thought, Well, this is it. So, my partner Bruce Gilbert and I bought the rights. I bought it for my dad, because I sort of sensed that it was a movie that could finally win him his Oscar."

When Mark Rydell had been with us, we'd talked about *On Golden Pond*, which he had directed. I said to Jane, "Mark feels very strongly that in important ways the film mirrors your relationship with your father."

"Mmm-hmm." She looked out at the students, most of whom hadn't been born when she'd made *On Golden Pond.* "The most important scene for my character is the one after my mother has said to me, 'Tell him how you feel. He's eighty years old, for heaven's sake! How long are you going to wait?'

"So I gird my loins, and I wade out into the water as he's coming in in his boat. This is the scene where I come up to him and say, 'I want us to be friends.' And from the first time I read the script, through every single rehearsal, I would get to it and tears would just come . . . like this," she said, as her eyes filled.

"I mean, these are things I could never say to my father. We didn't talk that way to each other. I couldn't even speak the words at the rehearsal that morning. So we shoot his side first, and I so want him to be full. I want him to have emotion. I know it's going to be his last movie, and I want that so much! He was an actor who hated spontaneity. It had to be exactly the way it was when you rehearsed it. But in the last close-up, when I said, 'I want to be friends,' I reached out and touched him, which I hadn't done before. And it shook him. You can see it on the screen: He begins to well up and he ducks his head and turns away. It just meant the world to me.

"Okay, now it's my turn: my big scene in the movie that means so much to me because of the personal part . . . and I am dry! There's nothing. There's nothing! What am I going to do? Where is Lee Strasberg now that I need him? What sense memory can I use? All the songs I can usually sing—nothing was working! I was so scared. And who shows up but Kate. She's not even supposed to *be* there that day."

Jane delivered a perfect Hepburn imitation. "'How are things going, Jane?' I said, 'I'm *dry*! Don't tell Dad.' Okay, the camera's ready, and I said to Mark, 'I'm going to turn my back to the camera and prepare, and when I turn around, start to film.' Not having any idea what I was going to do! So I turned my back to the camera—and *there is Kate,* crouching in the bushes. Like this!"

Jane balled her hands into fists and shook them. "It was mother to daughter: 'You can do it! You can do it, Jane! Come on!' It was older actress, to younger actress; she's been there and she knows. And it was woman to woman—and she *willed* me with her eyes and her fists. She willed me into that scene!"

The scene got an enormous hand from our students—not the scene in the film, which many of them hadn't seen, but the gripping scene on our stage.

Jane collected herself and resumed. "He was too sick to get his Oscar when he won. I accepted it for him."

"And then?"

"I took it home to him. He was sitting in a chair where his wife, Shirlee, had gotten him all fixed up, and I brought it to him with my children and my husband and Bridget and the clan, and I said, 'How do you feel, Dad?' and he said, 'I'm so happy for Kate.'"

Jane looked at me and shrugged, helpless, silent.

"How much longer did your father live after that?" I asked.

"Five months."

"What happened the last time you saw him?"

"He was in the hospital." She fell silent again.

"Were you close on that occasion?"

It was several moments before she responded, "No one wanted to admit he was ill. That's not the way I'd want it. I'd want to know when the last kiss was and all of that, but everybody was in denial. I did say to him, 'I love you, Dad. I'm sorry for the pain I've caused you. I know you did the best you could, and I love you for that.' I was so grateful to his wife, who took such good care of him, and I promised him that she would stay and be part of our family forever. And he started to cry . . . and, I knew he didn't want . . . he, he didn't want me to see him cry, so I left. But it was closure for me."

Since I am sometimes criticized for a bias toward my guests—a charge that puzzles me, since why else would I invite them to teach our students?—I will assert at the outset that Michael J. Fox is one of the heroes of this record of the last thirteen years. Michael's valor is a matter of public record. But, like Chris Reeve and others who have fought a tigerish battle against obstacles that would have overwhelmed most of us, Michael arrived at our school in high spirits and eager to go to work. I will never know what it took for him to come to us and open himself and his illness to our students and our television audience, but I know that it has become one of my definitions of courage.

His account of his early struggles in Hollywood was both cautionary and inspirational. Describing his uphill fight for the role of Alex Keaton in *Family Ties,* he said, "I was the first person to come in, and Gary Goldberg hated me. He just thought I was terrible. And Judith Wiener thought I was pretty good. Now I'm waiting—and I need this job so bad. And Judith kept going back to him and back to him and back to him—and calling me, saying, 'I'm working on him.' She's calling me, by the way, at a pay phone at Pioneer Chicken, 'cause I didn't have a phone. I would say, 'I'll be in my office,' and go to the Pioneer Chicken and get my phone calls there. I'd given her the number of the phone booth."

When Judith Wiener finally prevailed, Michael returned to his post outside the Pioneer Chicken. "It was one of the silliest things of all time: I had no money, and I'm sitting at this pay phone at Pioneer Chicken, negotiating my contract, saying, 'I can't do it for less than three thousand a week,' and wishing I had the money to go and buy a Snack Pack from the Pioneer Chicken."

As we talked about *Spin City,* I asked him how he dealt with the onset of Parkinson's.

"The first couple years of the show was just trying not to let anybody know. But it got to a point where I couldn't hide it anymore. It wasn't fair to the people I was working with. So, I just decided the time had come."

"You told the cast?"

"Yeah. You know—as a matter of fact, can I take five minutes?"

"Of course."

During the previous few minutes the tremors had become more pronounced. Now, as he rose unsteadily, he said, "On *Spin City,* I couldn't do this." He looked at the audience. "I need to take a few minutes for a pill to kick in."

The students and I waited, and five minutes later Michael returned, to a standing ovation, and picked up where he had left off. "That was basically what was happening when we were doing the show. I was waiting for a pill to kick in. I was waiting to feel better. And I knew there was an audience out there and I couldn't go out and say, 'This is why I can't come out.' I thought, 'Can I be funny if people know I'm sick? Is it okay to laugh at a sick person?' Now, to be able to say to you, 'Just give me five minutes,' and then come back out here and say, 'I love it when the drugs kick in,' that's what I need to do."

A short time later, as we waited together in the greenroom while our crew reset the stage for the classroom session, Michael paced back and forth. "Sorry," he said. "The more I move, the quicker the pill kicks in."

The tremors had been calmed by the pill he'd taken when he left the stage, but not stilled: They were still visible when he returned. Now, as he paced the greenroom, I witnessed an astonishing transformation: He stopped suddenly and turned to me with the winning, boyish smile that had won him legions of fans. "It just kicked in," he said, straightening and stretching his arms up over his head and rotating them smoothly, gracefully, freely, released for the moment from the grip of his illness.

When he took his place in the director's chair at the front of the classroom, he was relaxed and animated. There were a few stammers, and sometimes his hand trembled, but he was unquestionably Michael J. Fox in charge.

A young woman said, "I'm a first-year actor, and I just wanted to say thank you. You've been an incredible inspiration to me. About the same time"—she started to break, then steadied herself—"about the same time that you came out and told everybody, I was diagnosed with dystonia, which is neurological. . . ."

"Yeah."

"And it was wonderful to see that there could be people out there in the industry who were doing what they love to do, even though they might be affected by it. And I want to ask, realistically—you're Michael J. Fox, and for a person who is just Megan from Arizona, who doesn't know anybody, or *is* anybody, how realistic is it to come out and tell people about what you have?"

Michael's answer was straightforward. "One of the things I had difficulty with when I tried to put people at ease about how I felt and that I was okay with it, was that I didn't want to downplay what a challenge it is for a lot of people. I didn't want to say, 'Oh, it's a piece of cake.' That's a slight to people who really struggle with it, and don't have the advantages that I have, and have to worry about their insurance and about losing their jobs, and about other people's perceptions."

He studied Megan for a moment, then said, "You know, it's all about accepting. Not to get too twelve-steppy about it, but it's about what's in my power, what's in my control. What other people think of me is *not* in my power. Clearly, whether or not this manifestation of symptoms happens or doesn't happen isn't in my control. I can temper it with drugs to an extent but, really, it's beyond my control.

"But, in accepting that, do I throw in the towel, or have a tantrum about it, or kill myself? None of those are acceptable solutions to me. The only one that's acceptable is to go on and see what happens. And what I find is cool. There's great stuff out there. When you walk through the fear, when you walk through 'What are people going to think about it?' or 'What's going to happen?'—well, *something's* going to happen. We don't know what it is, but chances are at least fifty-fifty it'll be pretty good. So, I'm willing to take that risk."

So, it was clear now, was Megan.

━

E lton John was one of the guests who brought to our classroom a panoply of the skills we are committed to instilling in our students. His Oscar, Tony and Grammy awards give him elite status among his contemporaries, but the evening-long, private, personal concert he gave our students provided them with elite status among theirs.

Looking for the roots of Elton's talent, I said, "Gifted people mature at different paces. But two gifts always manifest themselves at a very early age: music and math. How old were you when music emerged?"

"I was three when my grandmother sat me on her knee. There was an upright piano in the house, and I remember I could play tunes by ear very, very easily."

When I asked him what happened to him at the age of eleven, he said, "I won a Junior Exhibitioner's scholarship to the Royal Academy of Music in London, and studied piano, theory, harmony, and sang with the choir. I didn't practice enough," he confided, "because when I first heard Elvis Presley and Little Richard and Jerry Lee Lewis, my Chopin kind of thing went out the window—even though, for a pianist, the most wonderful thing to play on the piano is Chopin and Bach. But I knew at an early age that I wanted to be involved in modern music. And also I have incredibly small hands." He raised his hands. "These are not the hands of a concert pianist—let alone the hands of an ordinary pianist. So, I set in my mind that I was going to enter the realm of popular music."

As we discussed the songwriting career that had produced seven consecutive number-one albums, I said, "When Richard Rodgers was asked, which comes first, the music or the lyric, he replied, 'The check.' I believe that with you, Bernie Taupin wrote first."

"Yes."

"When you get the lyrics, are they complete?"

"Sometimes they weren't in verse and chorus. In the early days, it would be maybe fifty, sixty lines, and I would have to carve them up into verses and choruses and middle eights. We've never written in the same room. We wrote 'Your Song' when we were living at my parents' apartment. He would give me the lyric and I would go into the living room. He would go back into the bedroom and listen to records. And then I'd come and get him. That process is so rewarding, when you see someone's face and you've got something right to their lyrics—the smiles, the feeling of joy, the happiness."

"How long did it take you to write 'Your Song'?"

"In all honesty, probably about thirty minutes."

That brought astonished exclamations from the students and an envious "Whoa!" from me, to which Elton responded with "People say, 'Elton, you shouldn't say that kind of thing; people think you're bragging,' but that's the way I write. I wrote that song in about thirty minutes. Other songs took a little longer, obviously. . . ."

"Forty-five minutes?" I asked, reflecting grimly on the days I've spent laboring over a sixty-four-bar lyric.

"It's weird," Elton admitted. "I write very quickly. And if I haven't got anything within forty-five minutes, I come back to it another day, or I give it up. I often sit at the piano and play a chord and I go, 'Oh, that's a really nice chord,' and the song evolves from that. Let me show you."

Going to the piano, Elton began a master class in composition. "If I'm play-ing in F-major, the root note of the chord would be . . ." He played a note and slid it into a chord. "If I'm writing something like 'Someone Saved My Life Tonight,' which is a very dramatic lyric, I go . . ." He played the song's opening chords, then parsed them with single notes. "There are three notes to a chord, there's F, an A and a C. So, if you use the fifth, instead of that, you get . . ." He played the altered opening chords, then a cascade of modulations. "That's chalk and cheese. Do you like *that*?" He played a chord. "Or do you like *that*?" He played another.

Finally, he began to sing. "When I think of those East End lights, muggy nights, curtains drawn in the little room downstairs."

"There's not a root note in there!" he said. "There's only one that's a regular chord. The other ones are all different variations of chords." His hands were back on the keyboard, drawing new sounds from the piano. "And it gives you that beautiful tone—that you wouldn't get on a guitar really. So, that's why, playing a piano, I tend to put more chords in. Guitarists hate it, by the way, 'cause it means their fingers are all like *that*!" He twisted his hand into a knot, said, "End of subject," and rose from the piano bench to cheers.

When he'd returned to the chair next to me, I recalled what Steve Sond-heim and Billy Joel had said in praise of the flat keys.

"I totally agree with them," Elton said. "I'm a flat-key person! E-flat, B-flat, D-flat. I can't think in sharps. I think in flats."

"When you're writing, are you thinking of your own voice?"

"No. I'm trying to write the best melody I can to the lyric that's in front of me."

"I've been waiting a long time to ask this question. I've noticed that when you and countless British rockers sing, you don't sound English. You're sing-ing what sounds like a regional American dialect. What is it?"

"It's because the music that we listened to in the sixties and seventies and eighties all came from America. All the great records we heard were black music."

"So, you're singing in an American voice."

"Yeah, I suppose we're trying to sound like our idols, Otis Redding, Elvis Presley. It's soul music; it comes from America."

When I asked Elton if his flamboyant costumes were an important part of his public persona in the seventies, he said, "It was a very important part. It's one that a lot of people didn't like very much, because they thought it detracted from the intensity and quality of the music. And I can see that point, but you know, I was living my teenage years. When I was a kid, I wasn't allowed to wear Hush Puppies, so, I mean, you give a boy the keys to the highway when he's twenty-three . . . !

"I was enjoying myself. The first five or six years were fine. But I took it wayyyy . . . I mean, there's an intervention for drugs; there should've been an intervention for clothes. At the Hollywood Bowl, I had the pope introduce us. And then the queen came down, and then Linda Lovelace introduced us. I took it too far in the end."

Later, Elton recalled an evening at Windsor Castle. "It was one of the most incredible nights of my life because here I was, a boy from Pinner, talking to Princess Di—and then Princess Anne said, 'Shall we go into the disco and have a dance?' It was the quietest disco you've ever heard, but anyway, I'm standing there shuffling from foot to foot with Princess Anne, and suddenly the queen came in with her handbag, and went, 'Can we join you?'

"Well, what am I gonna say? No? And at that moment, they segued into 'Rock Around the Clock' by Bill Haley, and I thought, this is the most surreal thing that's ever happened to me."

All through the evening, Elton kept returning to the piano, to illustrate a point or just to oblige me or the students. In the classroom session, one of the students said, "My name is Steve Nicholas, I'm a third-year playwright, and when I was twenty, a friend of mine, uh, passed away. His name was Danny Michaels, and every time I hear 'Daniel' . . ." He didn't finish the sentence: Elton was already on his way to the piano.

Later in the classroom, a student said, "My name's Daniel . . ."

"Oh, fuck!" Elton exclaimed. "I'm not going over there again!"

Accompanied by the class's laughter and applause, Daniel asked, with a faint note of disbelief, about Elton's speedy method of composition.

"It all comes down to a chord sequence," Elton said. "I can be fiddling on the piano and just, you know, looking at the lyrics, and I'll play two chords together and think, 'Oh, that sounds really good!' You stumble on things by accident. I can write a melody to more or less anything." He scanned the upturned faces and continued, "If someone has a book, I could write something. Has anyone got a book? Come on, you're actors!"

Scrambling through the briefcases and tote bags at their feet, the students came up waving a sea of books and papers. Elton beckoned Daniel forward, took the book from his hand, opened it, announced, *"Peer Gynt,"* and headed for the piano.

Seating himself on the piano bench, he put the book on the piano desk, wedging it open under the microphone. The students waited, transfixed, as he studied the pages. " 'Scene Two,' " he read, and looked up. "And the character's called 'Ase.'" With evident relish, he pronounced it "Ass," commenting, "How appropriate." Adjusting the microphone, he said, "I don't know what's gonna happen here, but I'll make an ass of myself."

Focusing on the book, he said, "It says Ase is flailing her arms and tearing her hair, which would not be a good thing for me to do at the moment."

Elton played a chord, moved into a second chord, and began to sing and play. "Everything spites me with a vengeance, sky and water and those wicked mountains, fog pouring out of the sky to confound him, the water hurling in to drown him, the mountains pointing their rocks to fall—and those people, all of them out for the kill! Oh, no, not to die! I mustn't lose him. The lout! Why's the devil have to tease him?"

He paused and glanced at the students, reading the stage direction. "Turning to Solveig." As the students laughed and applauded, he sang, "It's hard to believe. God knows, he who was nothing but dreams and lies, he whose strength was all in his mouth . . ."

The piano accompaniment rolled on as he stole another glance at the students and said, "That's a line I like!" then resumed the song. ". . . who's never done work of any worth. That he—you want to laugh and cry . . . oh, yes, you want to laugh and cry."

The structure Elton built in front of the enthralled students had a clearly defined musical form and, like all of Elton's best work, a soaring melodic line, which came to a logical conclusion as he brought the scene and song to an end with a tumbling progression of chords. "See?" he said. "There you are."

The audience erupted into an ovation that ended only when he had signed the student's *Peer Gynt,* waved farewell to the audience and marched cheerily off the stage, leaving us with an extemporaneous creation that joins Robin and the pashmina as one of the two most astounding improvisations in the history of *Inside the Actors Studio.*

In the spring of 2005, Angelina Jolie and Brad Pitt were at the epicenter of a perfect storm of media frenzy that had driven them into seclusion. During those difficult months, Angelina emerged for only one public appearance, on our stage on April 25, 2005. As the jackals prowled outside our theater, held at bay by our security team, Angelina walked serenely onstage to share her extraordinary young life with our students, a life that began with yet another gifted parent, Jon Voight, and another parental divorce when Angelina was six months old and left for New York with her mother, who, like so many other mothers saluted on our stage, belonged in our maternal hall of fame.

"You've called her a great lady," I said.

"She is!" Angelina replied.

"What makes her great?"

"She's just the most compassionate person I've ever met—very gentle, really loving, and never has a bad thing to say about anybody. Just, just, just *love*, you know? Just warm."

"She was a product of the sixties, wasn't she?"

"She was."

"How did that reflect in her personal philosophy?"

"She was maybe more open with me. She understood me a little. My mom was raised Catholic, and maybe"—she laughed—"maybe it would've been a bit shocking to have me as a daughter if she didn't experience the sixties."

As the students laughed, I said, "So you're the sixties side of her life."

"Yeah, she had a really good balance."

"Didn't your mother provide you with a motto that began with the words 'Be brave'?"

"Yeah, she did. She—" She broke off. "My God, is this where people cry?"

"You're not obliged to."

"'Be brave, be true, be bold, be kind, be you,'" Angelina said. Angelina seemed to have taken her mother's counsel to heart.

"Who were the Kissy Girls?" I asked, and she exclaimed, "Oh, my God! As I reach for the water," she added, taking a reflective drink, then continuing. "Oh, God. I was, um, I was very sexual in kindergarten—and, um, my mom often got called. I'd created something. Apparently, it was like kissing the boys, and we started making out, and we'd take our clothes off . . . and I got in trouble a lot in kindergarten."

"This is a first. Eleven years and you're our first kindergarten . . . whatever."

"Am I? Hmm."

"In the category of questions I never thought I'd ask, and answers I never thought I'd hear: How old were you when you and your boyfriend began cutting each other?"

"I was fourteen. My first boyfriend and I lived together for two years. We lived with my mom. Which was actually a very smart thing because I wasn't sneaking around."

"Right," I said, for want of a more sophisticated answer.

"So, I was safe," Angelina continued placidly. "I've always collected weapons since I was very little, and it was just one night that . . . Do you really want me to get into this? 'Cause I can."

Over a burst of laughter and applause from the audience, I said, "I think our students would like to hear it."

"Yeah. It was that I had started having sex, and sex didn't feel like enough, and no emotions were really enough, and nothing really felt like it was enough. There was always something you wanted to break out of—or you had to feel more connected to another person. Something more honest. And in kind of a moment of wanting to find something, I grabbed a knife and, and cut him. He cut me back, and we had this exchange of something.

"And then, somehow, covered in blood and feeling . . . my heart was racing, and there was something dangerous, and life suddenly felt more honest than whatever this sex was supposed to be, this connection between two people was supposed to be. So, I went through a period of, when I'd feel trapped, I'd cut myself because it felt like I was releasing something and it was, it was, it was honest."

Angelina's guileless candor was irresistible. I understood nothing and believed everything.

Angelina was as frank and articulate about her craft as she was about her personal life. Our students were surprised to learn that this young woman, who was only twenty-nine when she came to us, was another Strasberg alumna. In response to "When did you decide that you wanted to be an actor?" she said, "I went to the Strasberg Institute when I was sixteen. I was doing some really funny stage production we'd all put together with these crazy characters—something really bizarre—and I'm standing outside in the back alley, just waiting to go on, and there was such a wonderful feeling of friendship and that we were all going to express something and try something . . . it was just a great feeling, to be a part of something that was going to reach other people and communicate.

"I had a desperate need, which I think most artists do, to communicate, to feel that whatever it is inside me, whether it's cutting, whatever that's going crazy—that there's something inside us. We want to reach out, we want to talk to each other, we want to throw our emotions and our thoughts out, and hope that we make some sense, or that we'll get an answer."

As she paused to catch her breath, I asked her, "What did they teach you?"

"When I first went to the Strasberg Institute, I was about twelve, and I found it really bizarre."

"Where were you going to get your sense memories—"

"Exactly! Yeah, pull something from five years ago—"

"—when you were seven?"

"Yeah. A lot of the Method took me a while to understand—what it really was, and what it was for me. You actually have sessions where you're sitting there for two hours and you're trying to feel an *orange*! Do you know? You're trying to, like, get the sense of something. . . ."

As our Method students' laughter threatened to drown Angelina out, I said, "Shocked! We're shocked, shocked!"

"I was that person that was like, 'Oh, yeah, I got it, I got it!' But the orange never made sense. I *still* can't feel the orange," she confessed, and the students' decibel count rose. "But," she said thoughtfully, "that thing of the smell, or that feeling of holding the hand of a person that's passed away—that *does* make sense, and that works for me."

"Do you use what you learned there?"

"Mmm-hmm."

When Angelina's episode was aired, we heard a drumbeat of "I had no idea she was so intelligent, and so serious about her work!" from the viewers. It is the commonest reaction to the show, and, for me, the most satisfying.

Onstage, Angelina wasn't through making waves. As we discussed the tattoo scene in *Foxfire,* I asked her, "For anyone who hasn't seen the movie, what do you do in that scene?"

"I tattoo myself and I tattoo the other women's breasts. I loved doing it, and not just because it was sensual and fun, but there was something very interesting about it. We were actors, and we'd been working together for a very long time, and we hadn't been naked in front of each other, and everybody's got their own issues. And to be the first one to be bold, to take your shirt off and then look around, and your friend takes hers off, there was something very, yeah, sensual. But, really, you found yourselves looking at each other's eyes, saying, 'It's okay, I'm with you and you're beautiful, and stay with me and don't be shy,' And so, it was a very lovely time between women."

"And one of them falls in love with you in the film."

"Yeah."

I faced the students. "Angelina, who knows how to stir up a bit of a fuss, said during the promotional tour that she had fallen in love with someone during the filming." I turned back to Angelina. "Do you remember that?"

"Mmm-hmm."

"With whom?"

"Jenny. I got very close to Jenny."

"Were you just promoting the film, or were you talking from the heart?"

"No, I would never do something like that! No! I thought she was a beautiful, magnificent woman, and I just said it because it was what I felt."

"Not for its shock value."

"No, no. I still always find it strange that people get shocked by something like that."

Needless to say, the students applauded her. So did the *quondam mec.*

Since Angelina had received a Golden Globe Award, a Screen Actors Guild

Award and an Emmy nomination for her performance in *Gia,* the harrowing account of a drug-addicted model who died of AIDS, I asked her, "Why did you initially turn the part down?"

"Because she felt too close to me. There were a lot of things I just didn't want to confront, you know? That desire to feel a real sense of self, rather than the very superficial things in this world, and the need maybe for all of us to feel that we are understood and loved for who we are. I don't think I'm so unique in that. And Gia's addiction," she added. "I know addiction as well."

"You know addiction."

"I know addiction in all forms. Yeah."

"Drug addiction?"

"I know addiction in all forms, yes," she repeated firmly.

When Angelina appeared in *Girl, Interrupted,* in the role that would ultimately win her an Academy Award, Roger Ebert, with his usual prescience and precision, wrote that "Jolie is emerging as one of the great wild spirits of current movies, a loose cannon who somehow has deadly aim." Knowing how Angelina works, I asked her, "How did you decorate your trailer while you were playing Lisa Rowe?"

"No!" Angelina protested.

"I peeked," I replied.

"With lots of porn."

"Photos."

"Mmm-hmm."

"Why?"

"Because it made me feel provocative and open and sensual. It just *did* something for me. Transport loved my trailer."

"I'll bet. This is how you've described Lisa. 'She lived too big, was too honest, too hungry, too full of life.' Those sound like virtues, not sins."

"Yeah. They are absolutely virtues."

Since the students and I enjoy listening to our guests' Oscar experiences, I asked Angelina about hers. "What did you say in your acceptance speech?"

"I don't remember. I know I said I loved my brother—'cause everybody lost their minds."

"I assume that you and your brother did not have sexual relations."

"No, of course not."

"Okay."

"But it's a fair question—because of all that. But we did not."

"You were implying that you did."

"I was *not* implying that we did!"

"Oh? That's the way the world took it. Come on!"

"The world is sicker than I would imagine."

Relishing the debate, the students chuckled, and I persisted. "Sometimes you're a provocateur."

"But I'm really not! I mean, if you knew me in my life . . . I just speak very bluntly, and I really don't see anything so bizarre about half the things that are always taken in such a way. I know if I'm being honest about something—if somebody asks me about cutting myself, then I'm gonna be honest," Angelina concluded, summing up herself and an astonishing evening.

In the course of that evening, two of my favorite subjects came up. The first was flying. "When did you decide you wanted to fly?"

"God, as far back as I can remember."

"When did you make up your mind to get behind the yoke?"

"I started training a year and a few months ago."

"How long did it take you to solo?"

"About seventy hours."

I asked her how it felt, and she glowed. "It's the *best* feeling! They say it's better than sex. It is *so* much better!"

"*You* say it's better than sex?"

"Oh, my God, yes!"

"Wanna go flying?"

"Yes."

The second of my predilections to come up with Angelina was tattoos.

"Ah!" She sighed.

Feeling the wave of melancholy that always surfaces when the subject is broached, I said, "It is well-known to my students that I am not allowed to have a tattoo. I keep thinking that one of these nights Kedakai's going to get the idea. What tattoos do you have?"

"I have H for my brother. I have a prayer for the wild at heart kept in cages, which is Tennessee Williams. Got it with my mom. I have a thirteen which I got with my brother when he turned thirty and we wanted to confront all the things that maybe you're superstitiously afraid of. I have 'Know your rights' across my neck, which is something I believe in very much. I have 'Strength of will' in Arabic, which I got in Egypt. I have a big black cross here." She pointed at her loins. "I got it right before I got married the first time. It's actually a cover for something I got in Amsterdam with a very long tongue—that wasn't appropriate the next morning."

The students were riveted.

"I see something peeping out there," I said, pointing to the gap between her cardigan and jeans.

"That's the cross. And 'What nourishes me also destroys me.'"

"It's in Latin."

"That's in Latin. And then I have a tribal tattoo of a prayer, protection for my son that was done in Thailand. And then I have a very big tiger that was recently done in Thailand. Part of my work in Thailand is conservation, and a tiger was killed. I got the tattoo around that time, so it's for that, and it's also for Maddox."

"You used to have a window on your back, too, didn't you?"

"Yeah. I closed it."

"Did you really?"

"Yeah. I didn't need it anymore. I used to have the window because I had this restless thing of wherever I was, I was always staring at windows. I was always wanting to go out the door. A few years ago if I'd been in this room, I would've been at that exit—just out, out, how do I get out? I'd be talking to a lovely friend, lovely conversation, and staring at the window thinking, God, there's gotta be more out there. Now I live outside the window, and I don't need it anymore."

When Johnny Depp was with us, I discovered that he had ten tattoos. Turning toward wherever Kedakai was hiding in the audience that night, I pleaded, "One little tattoo . . . ?"

She shook her head.

"No?" Johnny said to her. *"Maybe?"*

Kedakai didn't budge.

"On your right arm, what does it say?" I asked Johnny.

" 'Wino Forever.' "

"But you're not a wino."

"How do you know?"

Although it is a matter of public record that "Wino" is all that is left of his romance with Winona Ryder, I elected to change course. "You have an Indian head. What does that celebrate?"

"That's the first tattoo I got, when I was seventeen. It's in honor of my grandfather."

"The Cherokee heritage."

"Yeah."

"On your left arm there's a heart. Whose name is in it?"

"Betty Sue. My mother."

"What do you have on your right index finger?"

"Three little boxes. They represent various periods in my life."

"And on your right ankle?"

"A tattoo that myself and some friends got. It's a skull and crossbones, and it says, 'Death Is Certain.' "

"And on your left hand, there's something that looks like a three."

"It's the number three. A friend of mine did it. I sat down at his table and said, 'Put a three here.'"

I looked out at Kedakai. "See? It's so easy." No dice.

It turned out that Nicolas Cage has a tattoo of a lizard in a top hat. "It's kind of a show-biz lizard," he explained. "Tattoos to me are the outward symbol of the inward change within my soul. Whenever I've gone through a major change in my life, I somehow wind up getting a tattoo. I think it helps in some says."

I looked at Kedakai. She shook her head.

The night Charlize Theron was with us, I said, "Unless my eyes deceive me, I see a tattoo."

"Which one?"

"You have *more* than one?"

"Yeah. That's a little flower. This is a Japanese koi."

Always looking for allies, I said, "The reason I ask is not out of curiosity but because I'm not allowed to have a tattoo."

"Says *who!*" Charlize demanded.

"My wife will not allow me to."

"I would recommend that you both go together and get one." The theater exploded in applause. "It's great—and you don't have to be drunk or anything like that, you know."

Later, at Elaine's both Charlize and Gerda tried to persuade Kedakai, who sat serenely under her naked *Paris Review* poster, unruffled and unswayed.

Mark Wahlberg revealed that he had an entire gallery of tattoos. "I have a tattoo of Bob Marley on my shoulder here. And my family's name. And my parents' initials. And a rosary tattoo around my neck."

"Don't you have Tweety and Sylvester?"

"I was getting to that. I had a gang shamrock tattoo on my leg when I was twelve. I hid it from my mother for a long time—until the first time I got busted. I got way too drunk, and one of my friends and I got into a fight over a girl, and he stabbed me in the hand and the leg. We made up after."

Over the students' laughter, he said, "I called my mother and said, 'Ma, I got stabbed. Come pick me up.' That's when she discovered the tattoo. So, it was a week before I got to see the outside again."

"And I'm not allowed to have *any* tattoos!" I growled, dripping irony and staring into the audience at Kedakai.

"Is that your wife who isn't letting you?"

"Yes," I said, shameless by now—and hopeless.

Mark looked at Kedakai. "You don't want him to have a naked lady on his arm?"

"No," Kedakai replied.

"I understand completely," the traitor said.

"But what if it's *that* naked lady?" I protested. "*Then* it's okay, isn't it?"

"If it's okay with her, it's certainly okay with me," Mark said, turning mediator. "I'll *give* you the tattoo."

The students whooped, sensing victory—and perhaps some relief from this subject. In bed that night, I reminded Kedakai that the tattoo would be free. It didn't impress her. "Just your *face!*" I explained. She turned out the light.

Jamie Foxx had an idea. "We'll get 'Playa' put on you."

"I thought I was *already* a playa."

"Yeah, you are. That's why you need to get this."

I shook my head. "Johnny Depp failed, Mark Wahlberg failed, *everybody's* failed."

Later, at Elaine's, Jamie pleaded the case for 'Playa.' Kedakai concentrated on her pasta.

When it comes to tattoos, Angelina's former husband, Billy Bob Thornton, shares the record with her. When I asked him how many he has, he replied, "I got a bunch of 'em. Eleven, something like that. And I want to get two new ones."

"What are you going to get?"

"I've been thinking about getting a hawk on my back, and another hawk on my head."

"And I can't even have one little tattoo on my arm!" I groaned.

"Yeah, you should let him have *one,* anyways," Billy Bob said, to deaf Japanese-Irish ears.

On January 31, 2005, I received a letter from Tucson, Arizona, that began with the attention-grabbing "I cannot stand to watch another episode of *Inside the Actors Studio* that features a guest that has a tattoo. The pain and envy that I see in your eyes and in your soul is unbearable." Clearly, a kindred spirit. The correspondent, who identified herself as "Heather Nathanson, Operations Manager of the world's largest manufacturer of TEMPORARY tattoos," wrote, "I thought I could help you out . . . AND keep you out of trouble with your wife," and offered to custom-design some tattoos for me.

She attached a plastic bag bulging with striking TEMPORARY tattoos, but, sad to say, I still long for the real thing.

In July 2006, a Benedict Arnold wrote, "I agree with your wife. Stay pristine." The appended "P.S. Love your show!" was cold comfort. And to make matters worse, she enclosed a cartoon in which a man says to his wife, "I've been thinking of a tattoo. Maybe a snake or a dragon on my arm. How do you think that would look?" To which his wife replies, "Like a snake or a dragon on the arm of a recently divorced guy living in his car."

It will come as no surprise that I didn't show the letter to Kedakai.

A few days later, Shanghai Kate Hellenbrand (*sic*) wrote, "I think I might have a solution that would be agreeable to both you and your wife. In Japan there is a style of tattooing which is called 'invisible tattooing'—applied totally with white pigment. It is an erotic form of tattoo, and relies on the skin tone actually changing in order to become visible. The skin changes color by a reddening either through emotional heightening (as in sexual arousal) or some other capillary action. As the skin becomes pink, the white lines of the tattoo then become apparent against the skin."

Leaving aside the obvious perils of insulting the partner by *not* turning pink and white in the midst of sexual congress, I think I still prefer a tattoo that reveals your bold interests rather than your inner stirrings. But all in all, I must admit the controversy has turned up some fascinating new friends.

I have heard strangers at the theater, on the street, in Bloomingdale's, exhort Kedakai, "Let the man have a tattoo!"

Twenty months after Angelina Jolie was on *Inside the Actors Studio,* at the party after the premiere of *The Good Shepherd,* as Kedakai and I approached Angelina's table to congratulate her on her performance, she sprang up from her place next to Brad Pitt, and embraced Kedakai with a warm but emphatic "Have you let him have a tattoo yet?"

When not even the embrace turned the tide, I took Angelina's arm and indicated a small, discreet tattoo. "Look, Kedakai, just like that. But it would say, 'Kedakai.'" Angelina and I waited, and when Kedakai remained cordial but as inscrutable as Miss Scarlet, Angelina generously played a final card, turning to reveal her back, naked and exquisite from shoulders to waist, framed in a glittering gown and adorned from top to bottom with the tattoo-er's art.

After peering back over her shoulder at Kedakai for a long moment, she turned to me with a shrug and an apologetic smile.

Perhaps these pages will make a difference. But given this doleful history, I doubt it.

CHAPTER Sixteen

"You can get infamous, but you can't get un-famous.*

—Dave Chappelle, *Inside the Actors Studio*

The twelfth year of *Inside the Actors Studio* began auspiciously on a new stage at the Michael Schimmel Center for the Arts at Pace University, a 740-seat state-of-the-art theater with a full stage-house that enabled our coproducers, Sabrina Fodor and Jeff Wurtz, to oversee the production of a set that would have left *Le Monde*'s critic speechless, or at least less fastidious.

Our "empty stage" in "a small, very ordinary theater" had been transformed into an imaginative set that conjured up a magical "backstage" with ruddy brick walls containing doors that allowed our guests to make an entrance; a catwalk that arched gracefully over the guest and me; strategically placed lekos and Fresnels that sculpted our stage with light; and, most important, an immense screen that allowed us to play the film clips that formerly only the television viewers could see, for our audience and, equally important, for our guest. Now our cameras could watch our guest watching our guest.

Our arrival at the Pace theater was one of a number of significant changes that had begun at the end of 2000, when NBC bought the Bravo network from Cablevision for $1.25 billion. At that point, Bravo consisted primarily of classic films and *Inside the Actors Studio,* with an occasional special provided by sources like the BBC. The trade press speculated that our show was one of NBC's incentives.

At the *Vanity Fair* party in March 2003, I encountered Jim Dolan for the first time since his family had sold the network and, after several minutes of reminiscence, asked him, "Tell me—do you miss us?"

"Yeah," he responded, "but getting a billion and a quarter for you made it easier."

When John Travolta came to us that month, NBC's president, Jeff Zucker, showed up in our front row, and as the stage was being reset between the interview and the classroom session, I asked if he would like to come to the greenroom to meet John. "Yes," he said, and put a hand on my arm as I turned toward the wings. "But understand—I'm here to see you."

It was a gracious harbinger of good things to come. The sale of Bravo meant leaving a comfortable home and a steadfast paterfamilias in Chuck Dolan, but as the transition evolved, we found a dynamic new family in Jeff Gaspin, Bravo's president, Lauren Zalaznick; Bob Wright, the chairman and CEO of NBC Universal; and Jeff Zucker, who, in 2007, succeeded Wright as NBC Universal's president and CEO.

Best of all, Frances Berwick and Christian Barcellos moved with us to NBC, where they have flourished, and continue to share the *Inside the Actors Studio* adventure, including the unusual events that began on a Monday afternoon in March 2007, when I was asked to make myself available for a call from the network's president the following Thursday at four thirty p.m., an instruction whose crisp precision could, of course, bode anything.

At the appointed hour on Thursday, I heard Lauren Zalaznick's voice, but there seemed to be other voices in the room. "We wanted to tell you together," she explained.

"Tell me what?"

"That the board of the National Academy has voted to award you the Lifetime Achievement Emmy." When I was silent for a long moment, she asked, "You there?"

"Yeah, I'm here" was all I could manage.

"The vote was unamimous," she added, and behind her I could hear Frances Berwick cheering.

They were in the audience in Los Angeles, cheering, when I received the Emmy a few weeks later. They should have been on the stage, accepting the cheers.

In October 2005, as we began our residency at Pace University, my determination that we would inaugurate our new theater with an appropriate guest paid exceptional dividends when Al Pacino, another famously private person, a copresident of the Actors Studio, and inarguably one of the leading actors of his generation, walked out on our splendid new stage.

When I asked a question I'd asked of many of our guests, "Did you live a lot in your imagination as a kid?" it opened an unexpected door.

"Yes. And when my mother took me to the movies, I'd come home and enact all the parts of the movie I saw. It was a way of dealing with the loneliness and shyness. Actors are funny that way. They're either extrovert or they're introvert. Have you noticed that?"

"We've talked a lot about it. People who watch this series are often surprised at how shy many actors are. De Niro . . ."

"Oh, Bobby is, yeah! Well, I think *anyone* would be shy in these circumstances. For a while." He grinned at me. "I'm gonna loosen up." A burst of laughter from the audience turned him toward the students. "We live in hope, don't we?"

With his copresident, Ellen Burstyn, sitting in the first row, and a large contingent of Studio members surrounding the students in the house, I elected to address Al's acceptance to Studio membership. "Good moment in your life?" I asked.

"Oh, ho-ho! Talk about an identity moment! I remember, the day I auditioned, I was full of moxie, and I came down the stairs and said to the secretary, 'I'll be hearing from you soon.' I was sort of working myself up, you know?"

"Yeah."

"I was a superintendent at the time in a building on Sixty-eighth Street. I had an eight-by-ten picture of myself, one of those romantic pictures of me, and I hung it up on my door—with Band-Aids because I didn't have tape. And underneath was, 'Super.' But I got into the Studio! And for the first time someone pronounced my name right. They always used to say Puh-keeno, or Puh-seeno. Lee said Puh-cheeno! That was very impressive."

"Why has the Studio been important to you?"

"Well, it's a place I believe in—because, for one, it's free to actors, it's free to directors, it's free to writers. It's a place where people can come and be a part of a world, and develop themselves away from the spotlight, free to exorcise and exercise."

It struck me that his last three words were the best description I had ever heard of the Studio's mandate and mystery.

When we arrived at *The Godfather*, I asked Al to take our students through the process that led him to his portrait of Michael Corleone. "Where do you begin?"

"You get an impression. I got an impression from the novel."

"So, it's coming from the page in the beginning."

"Yeah. In *Godfather*, I read the book twice, and my mind's eye saw something. But then, there're the practical moment-to-moment things you have to do, the meat and potatoes, the behavior. Michael was a very difficult character in that he starts one way and transitions to another. I spent countless hours trying to figure it out, but I didn't have enough time. So, what I thought of was to low-key it early on, hoping that a character would emerge, a character that surprised you.

"I thought that was the key to the character, because you'd say, 'Where did he come from?' And there he is all of a sudden. So, it has a kind of enigmatic quality to it."

"How much of the work do you leave open and unconsidered, in order to leave room for yourself for spontaneity on the set?"

"Oh, I believe strongly in acting from the unconscious. I believe that what you hope happens is your unconscious is freed, if you're relaxed enough, if you're into it enough, if you trust that part of you. That's why I use the impression kind of thing—and then trust that."

I said, "According to Francis Ford Coppola, he was so convinced he was going to be replaced during the filming of *The Godfather* that he never had a moment's peace. Did you have any concerns about being replaced?"

"Oh, yeah! I'm *still* wondering why I wasn't." Over a burst of laughter, he said, "I know it sounds funny, but I was so sure I was going to be replaced that I finally just *wanted* to be replaced. I thought, 'What am I doing here? This is just not working. I don't feel wanted.' You know, an actor needs confidence. You need a feeling that people *want* you there."

"Francis said that he devised a strategy to save you and himself. He moved the shooting scene in the restaurant up in the schedule, so the studio would see the dailies of it."

"That's right. That's right."

"And the morning after they saw the rushes, all the pressure vanished."

"That was brilliant, because I was *out*. They were going to replace me!"

As a number of the students took notes, I reflected on what those notes might mean to them when the time came to face their own adversities and doubts.

Our evening with Al produced a number of surprises. One of them emerged when I asked him about one of his most flamboyant and, in my view, impressive creations, Big Boy Caprice in *Dick Tracy*. "A lot of that had to come from you," I suggested.

"Well, yeah. I often thought, What would it be like if you had to sculpt a character or do a painting of a character? What would it look like? The other comic strip characters were *visible*; you could see who they were—you know, Dick Tracy, he had the look. We had to come up with a Big Boy, so I thought, *Big* Boy, he has big sort of extremities, a big hump. *Everything* was big."

"Do you enjoy playing comedy?" I asked innocently—and a door swung open.

"Yeah," Al said. He paused, shifting in his chair, then apparently came to a decision. "I don't want to say this—it's gonna sound so damn pretentious, but—I started in comedy." The pronouncement was greeted with silence. He looked at the students. "What a reaction, huh?"

As they responded with laughter, I offered, "Because it's mysterious. What do you mean, you started in comedy?"

"I did stand-up comedy," Al said defensively.

"You were a stand-up comic?"

"Oh, yes."

"Where?"

"Well, in the Village. I had a partner, and we did stuff. I did revues, I, I did things. . . ." He acknowledged the rising tide of laughter with "I mean, it was odd. But I enjoyed it, and it was a way to deal with, you know, melancholy."

"You overcame melancholy by doing stand-up?"

"Yeah." Al pointed at the screen above us, where we had just shown a Big Boy Caprice scene. "That's why it's sort of funny when I see those scenes up there and I think, Gee, just don't turn me loose, because I once went that way."

"Well, with Big Boy Caprice you went right back to comedy—and into musical comedy. . . ."

"I did musicals too."

Curiouser and curiouser. "You did? Did you sing?"

"I sang too."

"In what musicals?"

"I was in *The King and I.* I was offered *Zorba the Greek* on Broadway. Not to play Zorba but the young guy."

"My God!" I said, glaring down at my deficient blue cards.

Al was on a roll, oblivious of me. "I got to work with Robin Williams. Now, that's *funny!*"

"Oh, we all know that," I said, relieved to be back on terra firma. "Tell me about working with Robin."

"Oh, it was great. He's one of my heroes—so I always try to *be* him—I try to be like Robin when I have to be funny."

The scratching of the students' pens on their notebooks was audible.

Asking Al about the role for which he won the Best Actor Oscar, Lieutenant Colonel Frank Slade in *Scent of a Woman,* I said, "One of the most difficult character elements for an actor to play is blindness. How did you develop the blindness of Slade?"

"My oldest daughter was little at that time and I asked her to do a blind person for me. She had no trouble with it."

"You're talking about a child."

"Yeah. She was about four. She just did it. I thought, Okay, there's something *to* that. Then, I visited the blind, and I worked with blind people. And I decided not to use any prosthetic, just to do it blind, close my eyes and do it, and then open my eyes and do it. It's a wonderful acting exercise. What it does is, it helps you, it *frees* you in some strange way, it takes away any self-consciousness, because you're focused on other things.

"That's the whole idea: to be so focused on other things that you're able to free yourself. *Free yourself.* As Michelangelo said, 'Lord, free me of myself so I can please you.' I think that basically what you're trying to do is get yourself out of the way all the time. And when you're very successful is when you do that the most."

~

Dave Chappelle came to us on December 18, 2005, riding the crest of a massive wave of speculation. How, the public was demanding to know, could he have walked away from his hit show on Comedy Central—and $50 million!—a few months earlier, and why had he turned up in Africa? And what had he done there? On December 18, the line for our theater began snaking around Pace University at four in the afternoon, eager for the answers to those questions and much more.

Like all our craft seminars, Chappelle's was scheduled to begin at seven. The hour had been chosen years earlier with the usual seminar length in mind: Midnight, or preferably eleven, was a better hour for our students to be wending their ways home than one or two a.m.

By seven P.M. on the eighteenth, every one of our 740 seats was filled, and there was still a crowd outside, hoping against hope that, somehow, a seat would open up.

In order to come to us, Dave had chartered a private flight from his home in Yellow Springs, Ohio (at his expense: That kind of travel is beyond our means), and at seven, Carla Sims, Dave's PR representative, who had flown up from Washington, handed me her cell phone. It was Dave.

"Where are you?" I asked.

"In Buffalo."

"Buffalo!"

Dave explained apologetically that they had had to put down for refueling. I asked to speak to his pilot, and we discussed a timetable that would bring him into Teterboro in about ninety minutes, and to us at Pace in two hours—if everything went perfectly.

When I went to the stage and explained what was happening to the audience, no one budged. In fact, they cheered when I said we'd show them episodes of *The Chappelle Show*—the one he'd walked away from—on our big screen until he arrived.

We offered wristbands to those who wanted to go out to dinner and return. Some accepted the offer; the rest howled with glee at *The Chappelle Show* for two hours. By ten p.m., some of the audience had been in line and in the theater for six hours, but there wasn't an empty seat, to the disappointment of the crowd still waiting outside.

When Dave arrived at ten, he was apologetic but fully energized, having entered the peak hours of a person in his profession—as I remembered from my years with another stand-up comedian, Bob Hope.

At ten fifteen, I introduced him to the audience. At twenty-seven minutes, thirty-one seconds and twenty-six frames past two in the morning, we wrapped the show to a cheering house in which there wasn't an empty seat.

What happened in between earned us our twelfth Emmy nomination. These are some of the reasons why.

As Dave sat down in the guest chair, he grinned impishly at the students and said, "Everybody's waiting to see how crazy I am." A few minutes later, he lit a cigarette, and of course, the students cheered. Puzzled by their reaction, Dave offered an explanation. "I don't know about y'all, but this shit is stressing me *out*! It's like I'm confessing and stuff. 'Tell me about that thing!' I don't know! I was a child! It's all so wild, Mr. Lipton!"

Africa came up at eleven nineteen—which is to say, quite early in our evening—when Dave said, "We were having, like, a graduation lunch; my dad takes me outside and says, 'Listen.'" He swiveled toward the students. "And this is some advice that applies to all you acting students. He says, 'To be an actor is a lonely life. You might be on your deathbed, and if your friend has an audition, he's not going to come see you. He's got to make his money. *Everybody* wants to make money—and you might not make it.' I said to my dad, 'Well, that depends on what "making it" is, Dad.'"

Dave grimaced and condemned himself. "Smart-ass kid! So, my dad says, 'What do you mean?' I said, 'Well, you're a teacher. If I could make a teacher's salary doing comedy, I think that's better than being a teacher.' And he started laughing! He said, 'If you keep that attitude, I think you should go for it. But name your price in the beginning. If it ever gets more expensive than the price you named, get out of there.'"

Dave was silent for a moment, then turned back to the students. "Thus, Africa."

Seven hundred forty souls responded with an ovation.

The subject came up again with the mention of Martin Lawrence's name. "When Martin Lawrence came to town, it was like an event," Dave said. "He's the guy who showed everybody you can make it from D.C. to Hollywood. I had a personal stake in his success. And then, when we were promoting *Blue Streak,* Martin had a stroke and almost died. And when I saw him after that, he said, 'I got the best sleep I ever got in my life.' That's a tough dude. So, let me ask you this. What is happening in Hollywood that a guy that tough would be on the street waving a gun, screaming, 'They are trying to kill me!'?

"What's goin' on? Why is Dave Chappelle going to Africa? A weak person cannot get to sit here and talk to you. Ain't no weak people talking to you. So, what is happening in Hollywood? Nobody knows." His frown deepened. "The worst thing to call somebody is crazy. It's dismissive. 'I don't understand this person, so they're crazy!' That's bullshit. These people *are not crazy.* They're strong people. Maybe the environment is a little sick."

As the theater erupted again, Dave grinned and said, "Oh, I'm droppin' dimes tonight. I've had a long year, Mr. Lipton."

Just as Elton John told us he sings in a black voice, when it suited Dave, he would slip *out* of one. "I've noticed that when you and Martin play white dudes," I said, "your speech is pitch-perfect, which has led me to realize that either one of you could, if you wish, speak that way all the time. In other words, is it a matter of choice?"

"Every black American is bilingual. All of them. We speak street vernacular and we speak 'job interview.' There's a certain way I got to speak, to have access. If I'm sitting across a table from a studio exec, sometimes they'll do it to me. 'Say, my man, what's happening?' And I got to throw some big words at them. I got to let them know that my parents are probably smarter than their parents."

"And much better educated," I added, recalling that they were both academics.

"And much better educated. I can talk that shit. It's a God-given gift. So, yeah, I speak in street vernacular because, when I'm talking to my audience, I feel comfortable. The crowds are like my friends. It's the most consistent part of my life since I was fourteen. But there's certain situations where I got to use that 'job interview.'"

As we neared midnight, Dave veered back toward the subject that was clearly on his mind. "This past year I did the least stand-up I've done since I started, because I was freaked out, man, with the 'fame' thing and being called crazy and drug addict. All these things scared me. You know, being treated like I'm not a person anymore. You say this shit about me in front of my children? Like, who the fuck do these people think they are! *They* don't know what happened. You know, I have not spoken about what would make a per-

son walk off the set of a successful show and go to Africa. People don't understand it, so they call me crazy, and I don't like that."

"What should they understand, Dave?"

"What should they understand? Well, I did two seasons and I didn't go to
Africa. And then suddenly, when I was getting paid what they said was fifty
million dollars, I can't do it anymore? Nobody remembers that I walked away
from the show twice last season. Nobody asked about that. And one of these
magazines, *Newsweek,* it's a very credible magazine, and they're saying maybe
I smoke crack!

"I gotta make some real choices, man. Is that what I want for myself? Did I
get too big? I like people; I like entertaining. But the higher up I go, for some
reason, the less happy I am. Is it going to get to the point where I'm waving a
gun on the street, saying they're trying to kill me?

"No. I'm not going to let it get to that point. I'm going to get to Africa; I'm
going to find a way to be myself. I'm an artist, man. I don't need a sneaker
deal. That's not the need that makes you guys go to school. You're not in this
school right now because you want a sneaker deal. It'd be nice, but that's not
why you're here, right? You know you'd like to be in the movies, but to act or
to entertain. It's a need that maybe even a lot of your friends don't understand.
But you've *got* that need, and you have your dreams, and there's only six studios, man; there's only six agencies, man. This is a small, controlled thing, and
I don't like having to beg for the spotlight. You know, the machine is good for
us and we're good for the machine, but it should be fair, man, it should be
fair."

"What did you find in Africa that was an antidote to that?"

"A lot of things. First of all, I'm a Muslim. I don't necessarily practice the
way a good Muslim is supposed to practice but I believe in those tenets. And
in Africa there's a small community of people that don't know anything about
the work I do and they just treat me like I'm a regular dude. So, I knew that in
Africa I'd have a place to sleep and that I wouldn't have to feel strange when
they would call me crackhead and all these things in the country where I'm
from. In Africa, they didn't know anything. It reminded me that I was a person. I thought about all the things that celebrities go through—you know, if
you're Brad Pitt and Jennifer Aniston—and then I realize, oh, my God, I'm one
of those people. That's a small club, man; that's a weird place to be. There's
really no going back. You can't get un-famous. You can get infamous but you
can't get un-famous."

He fell silent, and, again, it was one of those occasions when even the room
tone seemed to have vanished. Finally, he said, "I don't know how this whole

Dave Chappelle thing is going to end. But I feel like I'm going to be some kind of parable about either what you're supposed to do or what you're not supposed to. I'm going to be something. I'm either going to be a legend or just that tragic fucking story. But I'm going full throttle; I'm going all the way. I'm eager to find out how this will resolve itself."

At one in the morning, I asked Dave if I could interview Clayton Bigsby, his bigoted, blind, black *Chappelle Show* character.

"All right, at your own risk. I haven't done this in a while."

"Hey—I've been at risk since you walked out on this stage. I hope, Mr. Bigsby, that you'll forgive me for raising a sensitive issue, but we know from *Frontline* that you did discover that you are, how shall I put it, not white. How has that changed your life?"

"Well, it's changed my life in several ways. First of all, I understand why my penis is so long."

"I would say that's an *advantage* to being black."

"Yes, it is. Other than that, the advantages have gone down tremendously."

"I see. Has your realization in any way softened your attitude toward our black brothers and sisters?"

"Absolutely. Now I have tasted the brown sugar, and I will never go back."

"Have you stayed in touch with your friends in the KKK?"

"We still write and call each other from time to time, but it's a little weird knowing that they knew the whole time I was black and never told me anything about it. I don't think a real good friend would do something like that to you."

"Tell me, do you miss the warmth of those cross burnings?"

"Well, the food was good."

"What kind of food would you have at a cross burning?"

"Hot dogs, chicken, beer. But you know, it's actually much better hanging out with fellow colored people . . . people of color, excuse me. The music is better, it turns out."

"That's true, God knows. So, you've turned your back on music like 'The Tennessee Waltz.'"

"Sometimes I listen to it—mostly when I masturbate."

When we showed Dave's "Inside the Chappelle Show's Studio" on our screen, I asked, "Where did you ever get the idea for that extraordinary sketch?"

"Well, you know, man, I'm a big fan of your show, and to be honest, I never envisioned myself on the show just because I always thought my body of work stunk. I'm serious. When I see guys like Morgan Freeman! All I ever did was comedies."

"So, you figured you were safe to do my show on your show."

"Right."

"I have one final question about 'Inside the Chappelle Show's Studio.'"

"Okay."

"Where are my fucking royalties?!"

As I got the kind of hand usually reserved for a guest skewering the dean, Dave took some bills out of his pocket and slapped them on my table. "All right, Lipton, they haven't taken all the money back yet, baby. There's two hundred."

During the Pivot Questionnaire, when I asked Dave for his favorite curse word, he said, "Fuck is my favorite. I say it a lot. You know, fuck! Yeah, I say it a lot." He leaned toward the students, whispered the word, savoring it. "Fuuuck."

Then he sat back and turned to me. "But I'm trying not to curse anymore."

"Really?"

"Naaah. I was fuckin' with ya."

Lost in admiration, I said, "That was so good! It was damn near perfect!"

"Yeah, I know. We got to do something about that."

"I'm the straight man."

"Yeah! I'm thinking like a cop movie or something."

A few days later, at the opening-night party for *Dave Chappelle's Block Party,* Dave brought our cop movie up again, insisting that he'd been serious. I said, "We'd need *three* guys, you, me and Will Ferrell to double for me in the action scenes."

Two weeks later, my telephone answering machine informed me that Dave Chappelle had tried to reach me in the middle of the night. I called Carla Sims, who said, "Oh, Dave was onstage at the Improv, and the audience was yelling at him about how much they loved him on *Inside the Actors Studio*—and when they started asking him about you, he pulled out his cell phone, hit the speed-dial and said, 'Ask him yourself.'"

"What would he have done if I'd answered?"

"Put the phone up to the mike."

"And then?"

"Done fifteen minutes with you."

Late one night in the second week of February 2007, my phone rang as I prepared to go to bed. Picking it up, I heard Dave's voice over the hubbub of what turned out to be the stage of a comedy club in Denver, inquiring, "Getcha at a bad time?"

"No, as long as you don't mind the fact that I've got nothing on."

"You're talking to us naked?"

"Buck-ass."

Dave's undisguised delight was surpassed by the audience's. We did fifteen minutes courtesy of his cell phone speaker, and for the first time I experienced the intoxication our stand-up guests have described.

When we hung up, I stood next to the phone, shivering with excitement—or a chill—as I reflected, "Hmmm. Maybe we could CGI me into the action scenes."

R obert Downey Jr. brought both his brilliant career and troubled life to our stage, providing our students with two object lessons, one to follow and one to avoid. We discovered that his talent—and his troubles—emerged early. He was too young to be a product of the sixties' excesses, but not, apparently, to be a by-product.

When I asked him if his father, the film director Robert Downey, had introduced him to drugs, he replied, "Well, let me put it this way: It was such a permissive time, they were always around, and like the permissiveness of the movies that I saw and the things that I was introduced to, it was everywhere. Compared to most of the people south of Fourteenth Street in those days, we were kind of square. But it was that culture and so we were not discouraged from it."

"How old were you?"

"I was probably eight, nine, ten. As I recall, Dad was lecturing at Colgate University, and I was swinging in a hammock in Eastham, Connecticut, and there was some guy in the room, and he had a joint, and I just like put my hand out, and he came over and put it in my hand, and it was *on*. It was the missing ingredient . . . for a while."

Robert's description of his first meeting with director Mike Figgis for the film *One Night Stand* was an emblematic object lesson in reverse. "Where did you meet?" I asked.

"There's this place in L.A. called Kate Mantalini's. I rolled in with a .357 in a purse and no shoes on. I was pretty gonzo. I was in pretty bad shape and probably weighed about a hundred forty pounds and was carrying a firearm and didn't have any shoes on."

"Did Figgis ask you why you were carrying a firearm?"

"Yes, and I think I told him."

"Told him what?"

"I told him, like, my cousin was in the IRA, and he was in town, and I didn't trust him, and I've got a kid now, and if we gotta throw down on the street, I want my rubber-grip .357 with the dumdum bullets."

"Was Figgis at all nervous about hiring you?"

"Um . . ."

"I would've been."

"Yes. Well . . . yeah, he was."

"How did he deal with you during the shoot?"

"Figgis was the type of guy who took it into a larger context, which was that I'm really struggling with something right now, and it was kind of cathartic to play that part in the film because it was someone whose own proclivities and sexual promiscuity and desire to eat life and live fast were the reasons that he wasn't gonna be there for his friend when he might've enjoyed him most. So, it was kind of metaphoric."

"Did the drugs ever get in the way on the set?"

"Oh, sure. I find in the last dozen or so movies that I've done, how much easier it is to work when you're in good shape. I see other people are tired, they're this, they're that, I'm like, really? Try operating at a deficit for the first fifty films. It's all about not getting in your own way. How do you become less encumbered so you can be of service to this fantastic medium that we get a chance at doing? There're people throughout time who have been notorious. And I get to be one of 'em."

"You had three violations of probation?"

"Yep."

"What did that involve?"

"Well, the first violation, I did six months, and then on the second one, the judge literally threw the book at me and went for the maximum sentencing allowed."

"How long were you in prison?"

"Sixteen months."

"What is it like to be in prison?"

"Look, maybe it's been a saving grace for me to say that I didn't belong there. Am I the type of person who is sociopathic and has committed criminal acts that mean I'm a danger to society? People may say, 'Well, she's not hurting anyone but herself,' but it's not true. Her brother's going nuts, her kids are suffering. And in the case of somebody who's a public figure, it really sucks to put people ill at ease about how you're doing if they appreciate the work you do. I don't necessarily believe in karma, but maybe I was supposed to have a really, really dark repercussion from all those years of being irresponsible.

"But I wouldn't wish it on an enemy. I have friends who are there and are never going to get out. It's an unimaginably awful situation. But, if you're in a life-threatening and really terrible and toxic and awful and restrictive situation, what you have to do is protect yourself and amuse yourself in that order. And that's what I did."

To put Robert's life and career in balance and context, I quoted the *New York Times* critic who wrote, "It's a pity to let the tabloid side of the Downey story upstage the fact that most Monday evenings on Fox, we can see a small-screen equivalent of the performances that in movies like *Chaplin, Two Girls and a Guy* and *One Night Stand* have shown him to be the most gifted actor of his generation. Mr. Downey's astonishing work on *Ally McBeal* may be as good as anything anyone has done on a television series."

Given Robert's offbeat propensities, his answer to my question about how he works on a role was—almost—not surprising.

"I try to infuse a moment with what its opposite is, emotionally. But there's not really a lot to explore until you know it so well, backwards and forwards, a hundred and fifty percent, that you can *say* it backwards and forwards. There's no excuse to not prepare exhaustively. So, with *Ally McBeal*, I would take all the dialogue and I'd memorize the cues, and then I would write it out as one long run-on sentence. And then I would write the entirety of a day's work out in acronym. And if I didn't know it by being able to reference what the first letter of every word was, all twenty-seven hundred of 'em, then I didn't know it, and when I *could* do it, that's when I'd know I was ready to rest."

There was one more lesson to be learned. "How did your *Ally McBeal* career end?" I asked.

"Poorly, if I remember correctly," he said drily.

"What happened?"

"If you've been in a recuperative mode and then you get thrown back into a place where you're not focusing on what's necessarily important, like how great *Ally McBeal* is, you're probably going to take a dive. Which is what I did."

"I've asked this question of others. It's the dumbest question in the world, and I know it."

"It's about time someone asked me the dumbest question."

"This one will qualify. With so much at stake, how can you take that risk? Is the addiction so powerful that it will overcome the most fundamental common sense?"

"Well, see, there's common sense and then there's what's *really* happening in somebody's soul. And what's convenient for people who've been exposed to drinking and getting high is, that's your out. When you think, what would the rationale be for this—fuck rationale! You're *expressing* something." He reflected for a moment, then concluded, "It's weird. Usually, the most screwed-up people that I see are the most honest. But," he added emphatically, "there's a way to be rigorously honest and not keep beating yourself up."

W hile all of our guests have revealed themselves in one way or another and to a greater or lesser degree, few have shared with us a more wrenching experience than Teri Hatcher. When I asked, "What happened on January eighteenth, 2002, that prompted you to disclose something you'd kept hidden for thirty-three years?" she replied, "We were having a garage sale at my parents' house, and my mom gave me some Sunnyvale newspapers that she had kept, and said there might be an article I wanted to read in one of them. It was about a little girl named Sarah who had killed herself and left a note saying that an uncle of mine had been molesting her for three years." After staring at the floor in silence for a long moment, Teri said, "And he had also molested me as a child."

"How old were you when he began to molest you?"

"Five."

"How long did it go on?"

"Eight."

I asked another of my obvious but unavoidable questions. "Why didn't you speak to anyone in your family?"

"You don't understand that you're the victim. You feel like it's your fault. You feel like you made it happen and you were an equal participant in it, somehow. It's hard as a child to understand that the predator's mentality is set up to *make* you feel that way. That's why you don't tell, because you feel so much shame and so much conflict about what's happened. But you know it's wrong."

"Why did you decide to intervene three decades later?"

"Because I felt like I was being blessed with an opportunity to not only possibly help this family, but to revisit the strings that were just left hanging in my life. So I called the DA. I was very scared that people would find out who I was. You don't want to be identified as *anything* as an actress. You just want to be an actress and let people be critical of your work. You don't want to be the 'sexually abused actress.'

"So when I told the DA my story, I said, 'If your case is all sewn up and you can put him behind bars and you don't need me, I would just as soon stay out of the limelight. But if it's not, I really need to see this man go behind bars. If he did it to me thirty years ago and her two years ago, then he's been doing it to people all along. This man needs to be in prison.' And the DA said, 'Ironically enough, he was about to go free in two days.'"

"Because there was no one to testify against him," I said.

"There was no one to testify because she was dead. So they flew down and got my deposition, which was very thorough and very painful because I've remembered everything my whole life. It wasn't like it suddenly came back to me. And they showed it to his lawyer, and he pled guilty, and he'll be in jail for fourteen years."

At the end of the evening, Teri opened the door to another of my penchants with "The other big thing I do is horseback-ride. My daughter and I both do a hundred jumps a week."

"You've touched my heart. For thirty-five years I've been a show jumper. . . ."

"I didn't know that!"

"It's one of the passions of my life. Tell me about your riding."

"Oh, my God! Well, it's just the greatest thing! When you're on a horse, and especially when you're jumping, you're only concentrating on *that*. Your mind is just on that one thing. You're one with that animal and you have a goal to accomplish. It's so simple in its focus. It's a release."

"You said you jump."

"I do jump. My daughter jumps better than me. She just did her first . . . What's it called when there are two together? It starts with an *O*."

"Oxer."

"Yeah, she just did her first oxer!"

Since *Inside the Actors Studio* began, I've been able to ask thirteen of my guests about this addiction—there is no other word for it—that we share. I began riding as an adult, when I could finally afford it, and for years it consumed me. I sought out the sport's most celebrated teachers: Gordon Wright, who trained many of our Olympians and wrote *The Manual of Horsemanship and Horsemastership* for the United States Cavalry; his disciples Wayne Carroll and Anne Aspinall, and an array of teachers and riders in clinics and master classes.

I trained and showed to the point where an entire wall of my study, from floor to ceiling, was covered with ribbons—a vain display that didn't go unnoticed by my mother, who tapped the wall one day and said, "That's childish. Note, I didn't say 'childlike.' I said, 'child*ish*.'" When Kedakai and I moved into the house we now inhabit, I packed the ribbons (lovingly) into boxes and stored them in the basement.

Note, I didn't say "threw them out." They lie next to my no longer pampered, but no less loved, saddle and boots. The addiction never goes away, and the most I can say is that I'm a recovering equestrian, taking it one day at a time.

In the summer of 1995, I was invited to ride with the United States Equestrian Team in the Tournament of Champions at their Gladstone, New Jersey, headquarters. I was assigned a team horse and competed with and against Olympians over a formidable Grand Prix course, which the horse and I negotiated flawlessly, beating the clock and all the horses and riders who had preceded us, until we approached the last fence, a tall vertical coming off a no-stride in-and-out. I lost a stirrup over the second element of the in-and-out, and prepared to jump the last fence without it. No problem: I had a deep, secure seat. But the horse, feeling the empty stirrup flapping against his side, ducked out to the right, evading the fence.

When I came back to the stands, I found William Steinkraus, a six-time member of the United States Olympic Team, the first American to win the individual Olympic Gold medal, and, now, president of the U.S. Equestrian Team. "You were one fence from the blue," he said.

A few days later, the mailman delivered a copy of Steinkraus's classic text *Riding and Jumping.* The inscription in it read, "To James Lipton, fellow equestrian." It meant more to me than the championship would have, and spurred me—literally—to chase that final fence for the rest of my show-jumping career, which ended dramatically a few years ago in Bridgehampton on an August Friday, as I schooled my mount for the upcoming Hampton Classic.

The schooling went routinely until I circled the ring to complete the course. Gordon Wright endowed his riders with what equestrians call "good hands," which in my case meant that I was usually assigned the hot horses that other riders shunned and I coveted—because, while they're a handful, they're eager jumpers. This horse was no exception, and when he stumbled, a not uncommon occurrence in a rutted ring, coming off a vertical into a tight corner, he added a powerful buck that threw me out of the irons and onto his neck. Spinning out of the corner, the horse—and I—saw that someone had left the ring gate open, and the horse bolted for it.

Aware that the only route to the horse's stall was a concrete road, I elected to bail out before he left the ring, launching myself from his back and trying to cushion the fall with my hands as I landed flat in the ring's loamy footing.

Spitting blood, I sat up and raised my arms, looking for damage, to find the forearm of my right arm hanging straight down from the elbow, my hand turning casually through 360 degrees. Sale Johnson, of the Johnson and Johnson family, who had been perched on the ring fence watching me school, jumped down and applied a makeshift tourniquet to stanch the bleeding, which was spurting six feet with each beat of my heart, and I was taken by ambulance to Southampton Hospital, then helicoptered to Lenox Hill Hospital in New York for surgery.

On my third day in the hospital, I got a call from Joe Fargis, the Olympic gold medalist with whose group I was training for the Classic. After inquiring solicitously about my condition, he said, "You're going to ride in the Classic, aren't you?" Joe and I both knew that, years earlier, I'd broken my clavicle into three pieces when the mare I was showing hit a wet patch and fell on her side, and that a month later I'd shown and won.

This time was different. "It's over," I said.

"It can't be!" Joe protested. "I've never seen you ride better."

"It's over, Joe," I repeated, my right arm, encased in plaster, hanging from pulleys over my head. "I've had thirty-five great years, and I've pushed the envelope as far as it'll go. Next time it'll be my neck."

Finally, Joe, who is a heroic horseman and a steadfast gentleman, yielded. "Well, you can ride on the flat."

"No."

"What do you mean?"

"Joe, you know me. The first fence I see I'll jump. And then there'll be another, and another." As he started to protest, I said, "I'm an addict, Joe. I've got to go cold-turkey."

And I did. One of the few vessels in my arm that wasn't severed was the nerve, and after months of therapy, I recovered all the functions I'd been warned were lost. I still attend horse shows, and sometimes I drive to Sag Pond Farm and watch my former colleagues school their horses.

When the equestrian magazine *Show Circuit* photographed me last year— standing on the ground, *next* to a horse—and interviewed me for a piece under the headline HEART AND SKILL, I confessed to them that I still "walk" the course from the sidelines, counting the strides between fences. The experienced rider can "see" three strides; professionals like Joe Fargis can see seven or eight. By the time I was riding with Joe's team, I could see six. The reason I stopped riding wasn't that I was frightened. I stopped because I *wasn't*; and to this day, watching from the sidelines, I remain privately, and doubtless deludedly, convinced that, if someone were to offer me a horse, a cap and a crop, and turn me loose on a course, the horse and I would sail through it without a fault.

That is an addiction.

▮

D r. Gregory House, of *House, M.D.,* is quintessentially American. His creator, Hugh Laurie, on the other hand, is quintessentially English, as our students and television viewers discovered, to the astonishment of many of them. When his role as Bertie Wooster in *Jeeves and Wooster* came up, I asked him, "Why do you think you were so often invited to play these upper-class dolts?"

"Well, first of all, the English find stupidity amusing. English audiences like to see people stupider than themselves. I think Americans, by and large, like to see people cleverer than themselves."

Early in the evening, I asked Hugh, "Did religion play an important role in your home?"

"Belief in God didn't play a large role in my home, but a certain attitude to life and the living of it did. We actually attended a Scottish Presbyterian church in Oxford, and my mother, I suppose, was a Presbyterian, by character and mood. Pleasure was something that was treated with great suspicion. Pleasure was something that . . . I was going to say something that had to be earned, but even the earning of it didn't really work. To this day I carry that with me. I find pleasure a difficult thing, I really do. I don't know what to do with it."

"Calvinist to the core."

"Yeah."

"The commonest cliché about the comic genius, and I won't trouble you by saying that you possess it, is encompassed in the character of Pagliacci, the crying clown. Like some clichés, there's a kernel of truth in it. In 1996 you spoke of diagnosing yourself as being clinically depressed. That sounds like the real McCoy. Is that so?"

"Yes."

"You've said, 'I would cling to unhappiness because it was a known, familiar state. When I was happier, it was because I knew I was on my way back to misery.'"

"The clinging to unhappiness, that's true. Why do I do that? To this day, many, many years of psychotherapy later, I still don't really know the answer to that, but it is familiar to me; I am comfortable with it. As I said, I find pleasure, happiness difficult. I don't know where to put them."

"Calvinist to the core," I repeated.

"Calvinist, yeah, yeah, that's me."

"You've said that, to you, Dr. House is a hero."

"He is, isn't he, in a way? He's a man with ego, and he has his vanities, but by and large he's not in it for applause; he's not doing what he does because he wants people to think better of him."

"God knows!"

"And that, I think, is a heroic quality. And an increasingly rare quality. For example, in the sphere of politics, so much of what is done is done simply to get you to feel better about the person doing it. That is almost the definition of a political act now, and House just simply doesn't subscribe to that—and would be content for a good deed to go unnoticed.

"And also, of course, I rather hero-worship my father, who was a doctor. I have always found the practice of medicine by its nature a rather heroic one.

The painstaking and painful accumulation of knowledge and expertise as a way of making people's lives better—I find that rather heroic, as I found my father heroic."

"Do you share House's skepticism?"

"Yep, I do. Big chunks of it. I'm not a religious man. I'm a fan of science; I believe in science, a humility before the facts. I find that a moving and beautiful thing. And belief in the unknown I find less interesting. I find the known and the knowable interesting enough."

As we discussed his relationship with the cast of *House, M.D.,* I said, "You make yourself sound like a pain in the ass. You're really not, are you?"

He was unequivocal. "I am. You know that thing that they always tell you? If you look around the room and you can't see the asshole, then it's you. I've done that, and I know it's me. They're all delightful, every single one of them is absolutely delightful, so I know it's me."

The students and I knew it was emphatically, conspicuously, delightfully not.

I n December 2006, on one of my Conan O'Brien nights, Conan's producer burst into my dressing room with only one thing on his mind: "How did you get Eddie Murphy!"

Eddie Murphy is a famously private person who for years declined every request for an interview. When Paul Bloch, his PR representative, called to tell me that, after watching *Inside the Actors Studio* for years, Eddie had decided he wanted to appear on it, he prefaced the news with "Are you sitting down?" It was momentous news, and on the appointed night, once again, the waiting line snaked around the Pace campus.

For all his storied reserve, Eddie was unreservedly open with the students and me. The parental loss theme came up early in the evening, with an account of his parents' divorce when he was three. When I asked what life was like for him, his mother and his brother, he said, "From three to about eight was crazy. After my mom and dad broke up, my mom got TB, and she was isolated for a year."

"Where did you and your brother go?"

"We went to Miss Jenkins's house. Miss Jenkins." He paused and laughed quietly, mirthlessly. "Miss Jenkins. My brother said, 'If I was walking down the street, and I saw Miss Jenkins right now I'd punch her in the face.' She was really mean, Miss Jenkins."

"She didn't like you?"

"She didn't like *anybody*! It was a horrible boarding-school type place.

That's where I got my first real good ass-whipping—at Miss Jenkins's. Afterwards I was like, 'Oh, so that's a ass-whipping. Whew!'"

"Okay, now we come to it. You've said, 'Staying with her was probably the reason that I became a comedian.'"

"Well, you know, I escaped into the television. I started doing voices really, really early. I'd do so many voices off the cartoons, my mother would say, 'Well, who's Eddie? Where's Eddie? What does Eddie sound like?'"

When I asked Eddie about the movies he'd seen as a kid, the neologism that began his answer foreshadowed his entire career.

"I liked makeup movies. I realized when I got older what the fascination was, but when I was young, I always watched movies like *Planet of the Apes* and *American Werewolf in London,* whatever was something with some makeup—Charles Laughton in *The Hunchback of Notre Dame.* I remember being seven, eight years old and waiting for that movie to come on. I always had a fascination with putting on makeup, and losing yourself in makeup."

Eddie clarified his approach to his several "makeup movies" with a description of his construction of the hapless Sherman Klump in *The Nutty Professor.*

"I wanted to make him sweet, so if you watch Sherman, and watch Jackie Gleason in *The Honeymooners,* you'll see a bunch of stuff that Jackie Gleason does. And if you watch *The Hunchback of Notre Dame,* there's a scene where Charles Laughton covers up his face when he tries to say something. I robbed all those faces and stuff he was doing. I watch old movies and steal a little this and that."

When I asked him how much of Eddie is left in the character, he replied, "My sense of humor is there. And that's part of my essence, so I guess that's some of me in everything. But not my personality. My sense of humor."

Eddie's approach to character came up again when I asked him if his acclaimed portrayal of James "Thunder" Early in *Dreamgirls* was meant to evoke anyone.

"He's a bunch of different people from the fifties and sixties," Eddie said. "You hear how Elvis borrowed from Jackie Wilson, he borrowed from R & B singers—well, this is the guy that Jackie Wilson, Otis Redding, James Brown and Sam Cooke all borrowed from, the guy that never, ever got famous—and to this day, he's still in the clubs talking. 'They all stole my shit! I was the first one to do all that!' You know? He's that guy."

Eddie stayed late in the classroom, communicating—communing—with the students, concluding the evening with a manifestly heartfelt summing up.

"You can't put a price tag on laughter. I feel so blessed that I have the ability to make people laugh. Because, you know, it really is healing. It's documented medically. It's good for you to laugh. I love when somebody comes up and says, 'I went through whatever, and then I saw this, and it was the first time I laughed in so long.' Comedy and making people laugh is really, really important."

We telecast Eddie's *Inside the Actors Studio* episode during the 2006 award-voting period, and he won the Golden Globe, the Screen Actors Guild Award and received an Academy Award nomination for his performance in *Dreamgirls.*

We did the same with Forest Whitaker's *Inside the Actors Studio* episode, and he won the Golden Globe, the Screen Actors Guild Award and the Academy Award for his performance in *The Last King of Scotland.*

D iana Ross's evening with us confirmed my belief that *Inside the Actors Studio* has long since turned into a constantly expanding extended family. Looking up at Diana and me from the front row were her sisters Barbara and Rita, her brother Fred, two of her children, Rhonda and Evan, and an assortment of nephews and in-laws, most of whom had arrived from Detroit for the occasion—which opened a door for me: "Now, an important question: Where is 5736 St. Antoine?"

"It's on the east side of Detroit between Palmer and Henry."

"Were Brush and John R. anywhere in your vicinity?"

"Yes."

Her brother Fred spoke up from the front row, ticking off on his fingers names that were as familiar to me as my own. "John R., Brush, Beaubien, St. Antoine, Hastings."

"There were only black people in our neighborhood," Diana added.

"And me—and me," I protested.

"It was all African-Americans in the elementary school I went to," Diana persisted, "so we never saw you."

"Believe me, I was highly visible," I insisted plaintively.

Diana sang eight songs for us that night—with her band—and when I asked her what made the Motown sound so distinctive, she described the historic building called Hitsville, U.S.A., where Berry Gordy lived upstairs and the tidal wave of Motown artists recorded downstairs: "Berry said, 'It's rats, roaches, guts and love that helped us get that sound.' "

Describing her own musical approach, Diana sounded remarkably like De Niro, Pacino, Hackman and Hoffman: "I don't try to learn a song; I just listen to a song. And then, I know it. I *own* it like that, by just listening. In fact, the way I learn my lines when I do a film is, I put it on tape, without any emotions, just the words. And then I listen to it. And then the emotion comes when I'm actually in the moment, with the other actors—when I'm listening."

Since Diana and I have known each other for more than thirty years, the shared experiences kept resurfacing. When I said, "During the four years that I was producing events at the Carter White House, Diana came to Washington and sang at an event celebrating Jimmy Carter's birthday," we recalled that Diana's only request was a visit to the Oval Office, which the president granted.

When I arrived at the Watergate the next morning, she was waiting with her daughters, Rhonda, Tracee and Chudney, and her mother. The children were clutching sheets of Watergate stationery on which they'd drawn pictures of the president to present to him. In the Oval Office, he received the gifts graciously, and when three-year-old Chudney extended a fistful of crumpled papers bearing her scribbled attempts to keep up with her sisters, he took them as if they were Dürers, murmuring, "I'll give these to Amy. She'll love them."

The White House photographer appeared, the traditional Oval Office pictures were taken, and a few minutes later, Diana, her family and I headed down the walkway where I'd watched the White House go dark after leaving Bob Hope in the Lincoln bedroom. Diana stopped abruptly, exclaiming, "Jim, where are my shades?"

"Parked on top of your head, as usual."

Her voice trembled. "Where were they when we were in the Oval Office?"

"I don't know."

"Were they on top of my head?"

"Possibly." I winced as she grabbed my arm.

"We've got to go back!"

I said, "Diana, even for you there are no take-twos in the Oval Office."

As we recalled the moment on our stage, the screen above us lit up with the Oval Office photo of Diana, the president and me. Alerted by the students' whoops, Diana turned and pointed at the screen. "*Look* at you! Look at your hair!"

"And look at your shades," I responded. In the photo on our living room wall to this day, they are parked on top of her head.

Chris Rock's work is so interlaced with sly insights that it was (almost) not a surprise when he unveiled a theory in the first few minutes of his evening with us. It began, conventionally for us, when he joined the nonexclusive club of *Inside the Actors Studio* guests who had lost a parent with, "My dad died at fifty-five."

The aperçu followed instantly. "He was a disciplinarian, because it was the way to go in the neighborhood I grew up in, but also he was preparing me for his death, as *he* had been prepared. Black men die in their fifties, especially poor black men. The man across the street from me died at, like, fifty. All the fathers in my neighborhood that actually did the job are dead. Now, all the junkies and the winos I knew growing up are still alive! To this day when I go to my old neighborhood, I see guys and go, 'You're still alive? And getting high?' It's almost, like, did they figure it out? When I see a black man going crazy, I don't know if he lost his mind or found his mind. Maybe he knows this is all bullshit."

In the classroom, Chris responded to a student's question about the craft of writing jokes with, "I never write a joke," then reconsidered. "Every now and then I have a joke . . . okay, here's a joke. They're trying to get rid of the word *nigger*. So, what I did was call up my accountant and buy eight hundred shares of coon, just in case. Tried to get jigaboo but it was all bought up. Now that is a joke.

"What I do a lot of times is, I just write bullet points, and try to find topics that interest me. So, those nights I'm in Cleveland, and it's February and it's cold and the audience isn't feeling it, I'm not up there talking about Denny's; I'm talking about something close to the heart. I come up with a hypothesis, and then my job is to make it true comedically. If you start with something really interesting, just your natural curiosity will take you to the funny place."

D escribing Michelle Pfeiffer has challenged critics and colleagues alike. Pauline Kael, writing about her in *Dangerous Liaisons,* was forced to invent a word: "paradisiacally" beautiful. Mike Nichols on our stage confided, "You know, it's very hard nowadays to photograph people the way they used to be photographed. It would take great directors of photography hours and hours of lighting to make Rita Hayworth and Marlene Dietrich look like that. The startling thing about Michelle is that she looks like that when *nobody's* done it."

In our classroom, one of our students, faced with Michelle waiting innocently for his question, went completely blank, finally confessing that he couldn't simultaneously look at her and speak to her.

Yet, despite this arsenal of ingenuous charm, when I asked her about the love scenes she'd played with a dazzling array of leading men, she could recall only discomfort, insisting, "It's not terribly romantic or stimulating. It's usually just . . . awkward. Sometimes people's wives show up. 'Hey, how ya doing?' I had a wedding scene with someone once, and the girlfriend showed up in a white dress. *'Hi!'*"

Mike Nichols called Michelle "a true actress, the kind you dream of, on time and friendly and open to whatever's happening." She shared with our students what she'd learned from noted teacher Sandra Seacat. "Sandra believes that every part you play is really a part of *you*, a way for you to work out something in your past, something in your present.

"Since then, whenever I've chosen to do something, I've thought, 'Well, this has nothing to do with me.' Then, sure enough, once I get into it and really start doing the work, and really start uncovering, I see that it's *absolutely* about something that's going on in my life. It isn't something obvious. It's usually pretty hidden. But there's always some sort of parallel to what's going on in my own life."

She studied the students. "And so, perhaps you can use it to bring closure, as a healing, a reconnection. I believe in that. I believe in that."

I believe in Michelle Pfeiffer.

W e'd been painstaking in our selection of Gene Hackman as our hundredth guest, and we took great care in choosing our two hundredth. Dustin Hoffman, a winner of two Oscars, five Golden Globes, the Life Achievement Awards of the American Film Institute, the Berlin International Film Festival, the Empire Awards, the Film Society of Lincoln Center and the Venice Film Festival, and a longtime member of the Actors Studio, seemed at first—and final—glance, like the right choice.

March 13, 2006, turned out to be an evening of many firsts. With President David Caputo in the front row, it marked the hundredth anniversary year of Pace University, and with Ellen Burstyn beside him, we announced the signing of the agreement between the Actors Studio and Pace, establishing the arrival at Pace of the Actors Studio Drama School.

And as if those weren't enough distinctions, Dustin Hoffman shattered the record established when Bette Midler broke down at the twenty-seventh blue card. When Dustin referred to the "challenging home" of his childhood, I asked, "Why was it a challenging home?"

"My father . . . I mean, the reason I did *Death of a Salesman* was be—" He stopped, so choked by emotion that he couldn't speak.

"Because of your father." He couldn't respond. "Okay," I essayed.

"What is this? Barbara Walters?" Dustin gasped.

"Usually it doesn't happen until later. This is the first time it's happened on card number eight."

Tears still coursing, Dustin said, "It's interesting—because you bring up stuff that the person doesn't know you're going to bring up, and there is some kind of feeling that you're more vulnerable—I guess, because it surprises you." He seemed on the way to recovery. "It was just . . . he was angry and bitter and, you know, he was very close to that part. And when he came to see it, he came backstage and I said, 'What did you think, Dad?' And he said, 'Boy, what a loser that guy is!'"

For a moment he laughed with the audience; then, abruptly and without warning, the grin turned into a grimace as tears spilled again. Abandoning the battle against this extremely effective affective memory, Dustin reached blindly toward me. "Do you have any Kleenex?"

Contrary to what some may think, there is no emergency box of Kleenex on our stage. I found a tissue in my pocket and gave it to him.

"I didn't bring any," he said, mopping his face. "Anyway, sorry."

"I don't think you owe anybody here an apology."

Describing his arrival in New York, Dustin told us how he'd slept on Gene Hackman's kitchen floor until Gene palmed him off on Robert Duvall. Because our students are interested in part-time jobs, I asked Dusty about his Christmas gig demonstrating and selling toys at Macy's.

"Gene would visit me," he said, "and he'd bring his kid, Christopher, who was kind of passive in those days. He was, like, sixteen months—and I secretly didn't like him because he never recognized me. He never acknowledged that I was there. I'd say, 'Hey, Christopher, how you doin'?' And he goes like that." Becoming Christopher, Dustin stared blankly.

"So, out of anger, I said, 'Gene, I bet I can sell your kid.' He was sitting on the counter, and he was about the size of the dolls, so, I had a belief system going for me. And he bet me. I've got the mike with the speaker, and I say, 'He's sixteen ninety-five! He walks, he talks!' You could lift his arm, and it would just go like that." Dustin dropped a lifeless, inanimate arm.

"And I was *selling*! Finally, a woman says, 'How much is he?' And I say, 'Sixteen ninety-five.' She says, 'Okay, I'll take him.' I start to pick him up, and she says, 'No, I want a fresh one.'"

He had to wait for an explosion of applause to subside, then continued. "I said, 'This is the last one. You *have* to take him.'" Transformed to the woman, Dustin was shocked. "'A *demo*?! Gimme a price!' And she went to touch him, and he moved and she went, '*Whaaaaaaa!*'

"It's a true story," Dustin said; then, when the laughter had died down again, he leaned toward the students. "Anybody who's an actor—that's what you do. Because the worst thing about acting is that you don't have an audience; you can't work unless you have a job. That's what you have to do: Find a way to make *life* an audience for yourself."

He sat back. "I don't think it's unusual." He reconsidered. "Maybe selling a kid is."

"It's a *little* unusual," I observed, then turned to the audience. "How many of you have sold a child at Macy's?"

It goes without saying that I asked Dustin about his legendary six auditions to get into the Actors Studio.

"The first audition I had, I failed," he said. "I cannot remember ever being more frightened than I was. It was in a church! It's designed that you do the worst audition possible. At least it was then."

Turning to the first row, I said, "Fix it, Ellen. Fix it."

"No, in *those* days, in *those* days," Dustin said. "So, I flunked the first one, I flunked the second one, I flunked the third one, I flunked the fourth, the fifth. And finally I said, 'I can't do it anymore. I just can't! And then, out of nowhere I got this play. And I got an Obie Award. And a kid that was in the play said, 'I'm auditioning for the Studio. Will you be my partner and do a scene from the play?' I said, 'Sure.'

"And they flunked him! And they passed me. I'm just helping him. I was so pissed off. I said, 'I'm not going, Jack. I'm not going!' I was building a case, you know?"

"I understand. But, obviously, you went. What has the Studio meant to you?"

"It was a place where you could study with one of the great teachers in the world. And it was free! And it was a place where they were doing something that had not been done before. When you look at Clift and Brando, Kim Stanley, Geraldine Page! There was something going on that was *new*. It wasn't just being open or in the moment—it was hitting some part of you that was so raw it was almost unbearable to watch at times."

When I asked him how he created Ratso in *Midnight Cowboy*, he said, "I would try makeup at home to get a look. I'm looking for a look. I took to the streets. I just went looking for my guy. I was looking for a limp that was so graphically described in the novel. He said it was like the fourth wheel was missing. It was hard. And then I find a guy on Forty-second Street, and he really gave it to me. He's waiting on the corner, and I'm just following him for the limp. And then the light changes—and he's the first to cross—with his limp! I said, 'That's my guy!'"

"Many of our guests have had signature moments and signature lines," I said. "One of yours occurred as you crossed a New York street in *Midnight Cowboy*. Was the encounter with the cab pure chance? Were you stealing that shot with a hidden camera?"

"Yes. The camera was across the street, and finally, the thirteenth or fourteenth take, we hit it, timed with the dialogue. The light turns green, and we're crossing the street, and that motherfucker . . ." He paused and grinned at me. "When the time comes, I won't have to answer *that* question."

"No."

"The taxi's coming," he resumed. "And I'm telling you, he almost hit us. And I remember thinking, 'You break this shot, we'll *never* get it.' What I *really* wanted to say to the taxi was 'We're filming here, we're filming here!' But your brain goes *brrrrummmm,* so, what comes out? 'I'm *walkin'* here!' "

In an effort, as always, to define what the guest is doing in order to arrive at what we see on the stage or the screen, I read from one of my cards. "Listen to what Dustin said once. I wrote it down and put two red stars next to it. 'In acting, you try to admit to more than the lesser crime. You want to get down to the deeper crimes of yourself.' " I looked at him. "Is that it?"

"Yeah, yeah, yeah. Acting, or any art, is doing what maybe you're incapable of doing in regular life. I mean, we're flawed. That's the name of the species. We're flawed, flawed, flawed, flawed. And we're human. If we sit on a radiator and it's hot, we jump off it. Well, if we touch something that's hot about ourselves, something we don't like on a deep level, not even consciously, we get *off* it. We don't want to know those demons in our self, those things about our self." He paused, his eyes distant, then said quietly, "When you're working, it's a way of somehow shaking hands with the devil."

Later that evening, I said, "I would like to ask you a question about *Marathon Man*—and every person in this audience knows what question I'm going to ask." A wave of laughter from the students confirmed my assumption. "If ever there was a forum to put this story to rights, this is it. What occurred between you and Olivier when he is reputed to have said, 'Dear boy, have you ever tried acting?' "

"Well, it's a very good example of the press, because I'm the one who told the story. I told it to *Time* magazine, and they distorted it. I was in the middle of a marriage breakup. It was very painful. I had a Friday, Saturday and Sunday off—and I'm supposed to have been awake three, four days. And I'm thinking, well, let me see if I can do this? I won't sleep. It was an excuse to go to Studio Fifty-four," he confided to the students with a grin.

"And when I got back to L.A., and told him, he understood the subtext of it. I was like, 'I was doing it for the work.' And then he says, 'My dear boy, why don't you try acting?' "

"Wasn't he very ill during the filming?"

"He was in awful shape."

"He was dying, wasn't he?"

"Yeah. Everybody knew he was ill, everybody knew he was in pain, everybody knew he was on painkillers. Talk about giants—this is a guy who at one time had *King Lear, Richard the Third* and *Hamlet* in his head—and he's *rotating* them!"

Dustin's pain was becoming more evident as he continued. "And he couldn't remember three lines in a row sometimes, because of the painkillers! It was that sad. He didn't *want* to do the part. We learned later that he took it because he knew he was dying, and wanted to have money to leave his kids."

Dustin swallowed hard and said, "We were tight, tight, tight, tight, tight . . . and when that movie was over, there's a knock on the door, and, man, you talk about some of the great moments in your life. I open the door and there's Olivier, and he's got a cardboard box. The complete works of Shakespeare. And in pencil he'd written in the sides of the pages his feelings about plays that he had done. He said, 'I'll just take a few minutes,' and he talked for about three and a half hours. Beyond being an actor, he was a scholar, and a teacher.

"We went out to dinner. I'll never forget it. Never, ever, ever, ever forget it. I'm sitting there with Olivier. I don't know if I'm ever going to see him again because he's sick. His wife, Joan Plowright, and a couple of his kids are there. And then this other kid who's going to UCLA comes in. I remember he went up in back of Olivier, and he kissed him on the head. Oh, God!" Dustin cried as long and bitterly as he had when he recalled his father in the first moments of the evening.

Finally, he was able to say, "And his son sits down and we're talking, and I say to Olivier, 'We all wonder what makes us do what we do. Do you have an answer?' "

What followed was one of the defining moments of *Inside the Actors Studio*.

"Can I get up?" Dustin asked.

"Yes."

Dustin crossed to me, put his face an inch from mine and said, "He gets up, he leans over me, and—I swear to God—he says, 'You want to know why, dear boy?' " Dustin's voice dropped to an explosive whisper that crashed into the students like a tsunami. " '*Look* at me, *look* at me, *look* at me, *look* at me, *look* at me, *look* at me!!!' "

CHAPTER Seventeen

""*Croyez ceux qui cherchent la vérité,*
doutez de ceux qui la trouvent.

Believe those who search for the truth,

doubt those who find it.

—André Gide, quoted by Bernard Pivot
in *The Craft of Reading*

From the day of its birth, every episode of *Inside the Actors Studio* has included Bernard Pivot's version of the Proust Questionnaire. For a particular, important reason.

I first encountered Pivot in the 1980s on what was then television's frontier, Channel 75, the TV network of the City University of New York. I had surfed past the channel, then, spying a portrait of Rimbaud in a show's opening titles, doubled back to look again at an unaccustomed sight: several people seated in a semicircle, facing a professorial personage surrounded by books bristling with bookmarks.

In that first viewing, I witnessed a steady parade of surprises: First, each of the guests was a writer, bringing his or her book to the occasion. Second, all the guests were obliged to have read their fellow guests' books, with the result that the discussions were informed, lively, fascinating free-for-alls. Third, the guests were sipping a fine wine provided by the host, a noted oenophile and vintner, among many other things. Fourth, toward the end of the broadcast, the host unfurled a list of questions unlike any I'd ever heard before: a kind of verbal Rorschach test that told the viewer more about the respondent in a one-word answer than an hour of questioning might have revealed.

When the program signed off, I realized I had been through an experience something like my first exposure to Brando: Whatever this was, it was brand-new and better than anything I was familiar with. In that first ninety minutes, I fell head-over-heels in love with *Apostrophe,* which, I learned in time, was so popular that some French restaurants delayed opening their doors on Friday nights until Bernard Pivot, the show's host, had closed his.

The idea of a hugely successful television series devoted entirely to literature was so foreign to my experience as an American viewer that I shortly became an addict, despite the fact that there were no subtitles. For viewers like me, whose French is moderately serviceable, the going was sometimes heavy, but I stuck with it, year after year, watching Pivot acquire gray hair, half-moon reading glasses, and, finally, full-moon bifocals.

All those years, I thought I was simply enjoying myself, increasing my French vocabulary in tantalizingly small increments, and studying literature in a remarkably amiable setting.

In fact, I was studying the art of interviewing from a master *who obviously did his own homework, and hewed steadfastly to a line that pointed resolutely to craft.* I just didn't know that I would someday be called on to try to apply the lessons the distant stranger was teaching me.

One day in 1990, I settled in to watch the still-untranslated and endlessly riveting *Apostrophe*—and caught my breath. This was, I learned, to be the series' final broadcast. Pivot's studio, in its imaginative set of sculpted books in framing shelves, was filled with the guests who had appeared with him for fifteen years, and much of the broadcast was devoted to the Proust Questionnaire— which I knew by now had been invented by neither Proust nor Pivot, but had been wielded masterfully by both—with a calligrapher inscribing each answer on the pastel walls until they had vanished under a glorious tapestry of words.

Then, a year later, surfing disconsolately at CUNY's end of the television spectrum, I saw the drawing of Rimbaud and heard Sonny Rollins once again playing "The Night Has a Thousand Eyes," but over a new title: *Bouillon de culture,* a difficult-to-translate play on words that means both Culture Soup and the nourishing agar in a petri dish.

Pivot was back in business—and so was I. He had expanded his horizon to include film, theater, music, fine art—all the arts, in fact—but his method and manner and incisive mind were the same, and the material in front of him was, as always, packed with markers. With both of us unaware of what was happening, Bernard Pivot continued my education.

In 1994, when Bravo agreed that there was a television series in our craft seminars at the Actors Studio Drama School, I knew at once how I would conduct myself: like Pivot—though never, I knew, and know to this moment, as skillfully as Pivot.

That kind of debt requires an acknowledgment, and as I prepared my first blue cards, I knew what it would be: the Questionnaire, with a recognition of its source in every episode. I had a second motive: Eventually, I reasoned, some well-heeled viewer would watch *Inside the Actors Studio* and, prompted by my tribute to Pivot, provide CUNY with the wherewithal to subtitle *Bouillon de culture,* so that other Americans could enjoy television at its intellectual best.

In 1997, when *Inside the Actors Studio* won the CableACE Award as the year's best talk show, after receiving the hardware onstage, I was hurried off-stage for the twenty minutes of fame that such an honor accords, first in the print room, then in the electronic media room, with reporters in both shouting questions. The first question, of course, was "What's your favorite curse word!"

In a split second, I knew what my answer must be. "Listen," I said, "you're the media. You can do America a favor. Tell the public that someone ought to come up with the money to subtitle Bernard Pivot's show, so more people can watch the best talk show on earth."

The next day, in the Hollywood trade press, the CableACE winners variously thanked their parents, their spouses, their agents and God. "Lipton," the trade press reported somberly, "said someone ought to come up with the money to subtitle Bernard Pivot's show."

I had tailored Pivot's questions slightly, to accommodate the American sensibility. His "What is your favorite drug?" became "What turns you on?" which can mean the same thing, and avoids the literal answers that might have limited it.

In French, Pivot asked, *"Si dieu existe, qu'aimeriez-vous, après votre mort, l'entendre vous dire?"* ("If God exists, what would you like to hear him say, after your death?") I opted for a slightly cheerier "when you arrive at the Pearly Gates." And, after much thought, I decided that, whereas the French, a Catholic nation where God doesn't even merit a capital letter, could abide the outright agnosticism of "If God exists," we with our Puritan tradition might require a less challenging "If heaven exists . . ."

As telecasts of our show expanded around the world, and became the talk of France, I wondered if Pivot had taken notice, and might even resent my bold borrowing. That was my first thought when I received a hand-delivered letter on the stationery of France 2, Pivot's network, dated December 21, 2000.

The handwritten letter was in French, since Pivot possesses little English, and it began, *"Cher ami-rateur,"* with a number "1" next to it. In a footnote below, Pivot wrote in French, "Pun, rather bad, but appropriate."

The French word for a fan is *admirateur.* Removing the *d* turns it into *ami-rateur,* a Pivot neologism signifying friend and fan. His standards are high; I thought it was an excellent pun. And a welcome one.

His letter continued:

Your kindnesses on my behalf, repeated on so many occasions, which are going to end up making me the most envied journalist in France, touched me very much and left me thinking. Am I acting so well that I've deceived the best informed and most acute critic of American actors?

He apologized for not bringing the letter to me personally, then added:

I will thank you personally another time. And—if you don't come to Paris sooner—why not when I do my last broadcast in June 2001? You could be one of my guests of honor, and we could, together, answer this questionnaire whose worldwide fame you have assured.

I'm counting on you.

With pleasure, gratitude and, already, friendship,

Bernard Pivot

At the invitation of France 2, Kedakai and I arrived in Paris on Wednesday, June 27, 2001, for two days of press before Pivot's final broadcast, which was the object of such frenzied attention that everywhere we went in Paris, cars were skidding to a stop for shouted greetings and handshakes.

On Thursday night, Anne d'Ornano hosted a dinner at her home for Kedakai and me and all our French family and friends. She had invited Pivot, who, she said, had declined, insisting that he wanted to meet me for the first time on his set, in front of his cameras.

On Friday afternoon, as Kedakai and I walked with my godson on the Champs-Elysées, Severin veered abruptly and darted into a kiosk to emerge with a broad grin and the revered *Le Monde.* At the top of the right column of the front page, in the space normally reserved for the day's lead story of war or politics or catastrophe, under two pictures, one of me and one of Pivot—leafing through a book, of course—the headline, in blue, read, *"Lipton, fan de Pivot."*

Describing our meeting tonight, and quoting me as saying, "I can already imagine the adrenaline rush," the story directed the readers to *Le Monde's* "Horizons Portrait," where, under a banner headline, *"Lipton, disciple de Pivot,"* a foot-high photo of me shared the full page with an interview that had been conducted an hour after we got off the plane.

So it came to pass, if I may wax biblical, which is exactly how I felt, that on a radiant June night in Paris, Kedakai and I, accompanied by the Mortemarts; Thomas Renou of our French network, Paris Première; and two of my Actors Studio Drama School faculty, Elizabeth Kemp and Andreas Manolikakis, arrived at France 2, every studio of which was filled with seats and screens for a private closed-circuit transmission as the show went out over the network. My guests were escorted to seats in Pivot's faux-book-lined studio, and I was taken to a waiting area, where I waited what seemed like a very long time as I saw his other guests in the corridor on their way to the makeup department.

I watched them emerge and head for the studio, and still no one came for me. Just as I began thinking, "I knew it was too good to be true," a young woman arrived to take me to makeup, then lead me to Pivot's studio—a room I had seen so many times in my home that it felt like a part of my living room.

If I seem to be making much too much of this, it is because that night was much too much for me. If I have never shaken the feeling that New York is a world away from 280 Hague Avenue, not to mention the Rue Pigalle, this moment was occurring on another planet, in another dimension.

I've walked into hundreds of studios in my life without a tremor. This was qualitatively different. As I came through the door into a blaze of light, I discovered why no one had come to get me for so long: The audience was seated, and all the other honored guests were in place in the familiar semicircle, silent, waiting. The only anomalous sight was Pivot's chair: It was empty. He was standing a few feet in front of it, surrounded by his final guests, facing the door through which I came. In what was surely the most surreal moment of my life, I walked numbly forward into the semicircular space, where he waited with his hand extended.

Television studios are customarily overlit, but now lightning struck as a hundred flashbulbs fired. Half blinded, I looked past Pivot: The wall behind him was layered with photographers, shouting, "This way! This way! Shake hands again. Again! This way!"

It went on for several minutes. "Over here! One more! *À droite, s'il vous plaît! À gauche!*"

Finally, the photographers were dismissed, and Pivot led me to my place at one end of the semicircle, and sat down in his chair as "The Night Has a Thousand Eyes" issued from the speakers and the *dernière émission* began—with most of France watching.

Pivot introduced his final dozen guests by introducing them to me, since I was the newcomer. They were, he explained, chosen from hundreds, each for a particular reason. Two, Isabelle Huppert and Fabrice Luchini, came from theater and film; one, Georges Charpak, was a Nobelist in physics; two, Erik Orsenna and Jean d'Ormesson, represented the august Académie Française, which presides over France's literature and language. Next to me, Pivot had placed Annie Cohen-Solal, the celebrated biographer of Jean-Paul Sartre and a former cultural counselor at the French Embassy in the United States.

For this historic occasion, Pivot was given the network for as long as he wished: *Bouillon de culture* would be over when Bernard Pivot said it was over.

He generously spent considerable time with me, showing *Inside the Actors Studio* clips on the big screen in his studio. It was, if I may be permitted to use one of several words I suspect I have overused in these pages, surreal to sit on the set I had watched on my television screen, watching Sharon Stone and Harrison Ford and Whoopi Goldberg and Robin Williams on *my* set, talking with me, on *Bouillon de culture*.

Throughout the show, as Pivot showed clips of his own twenty-six-year career, he kept returning to *Inside the Actors Studio,* lingering appreciatively over a montage of what we call the omigods, when something has surprised my guests. Once again, Julia Roberts asked, "Have you been talking to my mother?" Sally Field demanded, "Have you been reading my diary?" Geena Davis replied to my "Are there still footprints on your ceiling?" with a wary "Yes. What color are they?" and screeched "Oh! This is much too in-depth!" when I replied, "Purple." And when Spike Lee asked, "Where'd you get that from?" and I answered with a cryptic "I got it," Spike observed, "You got connects."

An hour and fifty minutes into the show, waiters swooped in with bottles and glasses to serve us a wine that brought exclamations of surprise and delight from the guests as they swirled it gently, breathed it in and tasted it—as I'd been taught (unsuccessfully) to do at Chez Pierre à la Fontaine Gaillon my first night ever in Europe. On this night, as my fellow final guests savored the Volnay Côte de Beaune and extended their glasses for refills, I, forever provincial and fearful of dulling whatever wits I possess in this perilous French-speaking environment, was afraid to take a sip with the Questionnaire looming. As a spirited discussion arose on the exceptional merits of this rare Burgundy, I wisely kept my counsel, and left my glass untouched, which drew a disapproving look from the Nobelist.

For twenty-six years Bernard Pivot had refused to compete with his guests by answering the Questionnaire, and for seven years I had avoided a stream of demands with "Only to Pivot." In his letter to me he had proposed that we answer the Questionnaire together, and now, as the evening neared its end, Pivot said, "Now, we're going to answer the Questionnaire." Pivot had asked the Academician Jean d'Ormesson, with whom he had had a famous falling-out when they were both at the newspaper *Le Figaro* but who had, in the years since, made more appearances on *Apostrophe* and *Bouillon de culture* than any other guest, to ask the Questionnaire of each of us in turn.

"Votre mot préféré?" d'Ormesson asked me.

"L'honneur," I replied.

"For me," Pivot said, "it's *aujourd'hui*—with an apostrophe in the middle," he added, saluting his departed series.

"Le mot vous détestez?" d'Ormesson asked. This was the question I had translated, "Your least favorite word." The French are more emphatic.

"Humiliation," I said in French. "Above all, toward a child."

Pivot contributed "A bad inclination expressed by a bad word: *concupiscence.*" He pronounced the word slowly, isolating the first and second syllables, which, ironically in a word denouncing lust, refer in French slang to the body's lower orifices, female fore and unisex aft.

"Your favorite drug?" d'Ormesson asked.

"Words, words, words," I said. "But not necessarily mine."

"My favorite drug," Pivot said, "is reading newspapers in general—and *L'Équipe* in particular." *L'Équipe* is France's leading sports magazine, and Pivot is one of the country's most influential soccer commentators.

"The sound or noise you love?" d'Ormesson asked.

"The little sigh my wife makes when I hug her—and—"

"You only get one!" Pivot interjected, cutting off my second choice, the most underrated quality of contemporary life, and, I suspect, every writer's favorite sound: silence.

In my version of the Questionnaire, I have added, "What turns you off?" and "What is your *least* favorite sound or noise?" A year after I'd answered the Questionnaire in French on Pivot's *dernière émission,* I answered it for the first time in English on *Larry King Live,* where my least favorite sound was "the din that passes for joy in public places these days."

Pivot's response to "The sound or noise you love?" was, "For me, it's simple: the discreet sound of the pages I turn, reading a book—or the equally discreet sound of pen on paper."

"That's two!" his guests protested, but Pivot insisted it was technically one answer. I didn't object.

"Your favorite curse word?" d'Ormesson said.

I turned to Pivot. "One in French and one in English—*d'accord?*"

"D'accord," Pivot said.

"In French," I said, "the universal curse of every dancer who makes a mistake: 'Shit!'" But, as usual, the expression is more potent in French: *"Merde-alors!"* "In English," I went on, "my favorite curse word is neither obscene nor scatological. It's profane: *Jesus Christ!*"

Pivot's curse word is hugely expressive—and utterly untranslatable: *"'Oh, putain! Oh, putain! Oh, putain!' Toujours trois fois."* ("'Oh, whore! Oh, whore! Oh, whore!' Always three times.")

The next question was one I'd dropped in favor of the ones I'd added. "A man or woman to appear on a new banknote?" d'Ormesson asked.

"That's very simple, very easy," I replied. "Everybody already knows my answer: Bernard Pivot."

Applause from the audience brought a "Thank you" from Pivot, then his response: "For me, it's Michel Bouquet in Molière's *L'Avare.*"

"The profession you wouldn't have wanted to practice?" was the next question.

My answer was quick, simple and certain: "Executioner."

Pivot's answer was, "For me, president of France Television or director of a public service channel."

For my version of the Questionnaire, I had added the affirmative form of the question. To Larry King my answer was, "A *premier danseur*—but with this proviso: that I be forever young and uninjured."

"Finally," said d'Ormesson, "if God exists, what would you like to hear him say after your death?"

"Tu vois, Jim," I replied, addressing myself in the familiar second-person-singular as, I had been given to understand by my French teachers, God does, "you were wrong. I exist. But you may come in anyway. Oh—Jim, *Bouillon de culture* begins every night at eight."

Pivot applauded, then broke into the audience's applause with, *"Hey!* My response." Suddenly, he spoke English. "Hello, Mr. Pie-vott!" then switched quickly back to French for "Because God first spoke Latin, Hebrew and Arabic—then French. But now he speaks English—obviously. *Oui. Donc,* 'Hello, Mister Pie-vott, 'ow do you do?'" He responded to God's English in French for "Not too well," then ventured forth again in English. "I am sorry, my God, but I don't speak English."

God answered in French. "Ah! It's so—you don't speak English. Obviously, you speak French. Well, fine, you have all eternity ahead of you to learn English, and I'm going to give you a very good teacher." Pivot's God raised a commanding hand. "Please go get Sir William"—he employed English for the final —"Shakespeare, of course!"

A few minutes later, two hours and fifty-five minutes after the program had begun, the huge door inscribed with *La Dernière* that had been added to the set for this occasion swung majestically shut, and twenty-six remarkable years came to an end.

As invited guests poured out of every France 2 studio and convened in a huge atrium that was outfitted for a reception, Kedakai and my guests found me. The first to speak was Thomas Renou of Paris Première, asking eagerly, "How was the wine?"

"I don't know."

"What do you mean, you don't know?"

"I never tasted it."

"You never tasted it . . . ?!" Looking as if I had announced the death of his dearest friend, Thomas keened, "Do you know what that *was*?!"

"Sorry." I shrugged, and Thomas looked back toward Pivot's studio as if he might make a dash to retrieve my untouched glass.

Pivot introduced me to Catherine Tasca, France's minister of culture, who had been in the audience, and the two mounted a grand staircase to make speeches. A year later, the letter making me a *chevalier de l'ordre des Arts et des Lettres* would be signed, "Catherine Tasca."

It was after one in the morning when my guests and I emerged from France 2. There had been abundant food at the reception, but I'd been too occupied with Pivot, the minister and the other honored guests to contemplate it, and now, as we looked at one another, all of us too energized to call this amazing night a night, I realized I hadn't eaten in twelve hours. "Anybody interested in dinner?" I asked. The chorus of approval awakened the latent Parisian flaneur in me. "Get in the car," I said. "I know where we're going.

"Au Pied de Cochon," I said to our driver. During my first Paris residency, Régine and I sometimes took our evening's gains to the Pied de Cochon, an Art Nouveau restaurant in the middle of Les Halles, the vast, bustling marketplace where all of the fresh produce that would be consumed in Paris in the next twenty-four hours was trucked in overnight. The restaurants in Les Halles, operating twenty-four hours a day, catered to some of France's most discriminating palates, the truckers, butchers and vegetable vendors of the marketplace, and at one or two in the morning, the Pied de Cochon buffet bar was lined with butchers in bloody aprons, overalled truckers and soigné couples in formal wear, fresh from the opera or theater, enjoying the restaurant's justly famous *soupe à l'oignon.*

As we pulled up in front of the restaurant after the broadcast, my heart sank: Even at two in the morning, it was packed to its ornate walls on this balmy summer night, more than likely with many diners who, like us, had waited for the Pivot finale to end.

As I peered disconsolately out the window of our car, a figure standing on the sidewalk reacted sharply and approached, flinging open the door next to me with a cheery *"Entrez, M. Lipton!"*

As luck would have it, he was the maître d'. With our group following single-file, he led me into the restaurant . . . and then, in the words of *Le Monde*'s critic in 1999, *la magie opère.* As we moved slowly through the crowded room, the diners at each table we passed rose and applauded, one after another, the salute rippling through the restaurant in a *nouvelle* wave.

Carried along on my own wave of déjà vu, I glanced toward the corner table that Régine and I had favored: For an instant the young couple occupying our place looked startlingly familiar, but when I blinked, the specters were gone.

Seated finally on the terrace, we began, at my recommendation, with the onion soup—the equivalent for me at that charged moment of Proust's madeleine. Encrusted in cheese and served in oven-baked earthenware crocks exactly as I remembered it, it closed another ring with a decisive *click!*

To remind us of that astounding night, Pivot's *"Cher ami-rateur"* letter stands on a tabletop in our living room, among four dozen letters I've received from *Inside the Actors Studio*'s guests. It's at the center in the front row, flanking, with Barbra Streisand's "Someday . . . when I'm on the East Coast . . . we'll talk . . ." note, the letter that will always be front and center on the table as a reminder of my *real* status.

"Dear James Lipton," the letter begins. "You are one of my favorite people. My favorite show is Inside The Actors Studio. I did a report on you in my art class and I showed your show with Robin Williams. I got an A- on the report. Thank you for your body of work. I enclosed a SASE and an index card hoping to get signed. I have never wrote anyone before (: I saw a autographed picture of you on Ebay and was going to buy it, but it was so expensive ($30.00)."

The letter was signed, "Dan Gaertner," and I sent him everything that wasn't nailed down in gratitude for his reminder that (1) one of my best shows was still not worthy of an unqualified A, and (2) I'm worth thirty dollars on eBay, not a penny more. Those are the kinds of reminders that put life quickly, neatly into perspective.

The events of June 29, 2001, aren't the only reasons I am forever grateful that I showed the focus-group person the door in 1996. Apart from the fact that *Inside the Actors Studio* would long since have vanished if I'd followed her counsel to rid ourselves of the Questionnaire and the craft conversations that her group disdained, there is the sheer pleasure the Questionnaire has given us—and our viewers—and the windows it has opened to more than two hundred souls.

I believe these aperçus have value, and when I began this narrative, I resolved that at the appropriate moment, I would share them with its readers. I think this is the appropriate moment.

There are ten questions in my version of the Questionnaire, and for each of them I have several favorite answers.

What is your favorite word?

Love, life, passion and *yes* were the most frequent choices. The following are, in my view, some other notable responses.

Michael Caine: Tomorrow.

George Carlin: Skylark.

Francis Ford Coppola: Hope. *Esperanza.*

Robert De Niro: Refinement.

Johnny Depp: Why?

Angelina Jolie: Now.

Mike Nichols: Thighs.

Meg Ryan: Authentic.

Homer Simpson: Marshmallow.

Billy Bob Thornton: Marshmallow.

Christopher Walken: Lunch.

Robin Williams: Cloaca.

What is your least favorite word?

No and *can't* won in a walk, followed closely by *hate.* Other notables:

Lauren Bacall: Good-bye.

Drew Barrymore: Moist.

Michael Caine: Yesterday.

George Carlin: Dumptruck, ashcan and meatloaf.

Jennifer Connelly: Giblets.

Willem Dafoe: Chalk.

Robert De Niro: Boorish.

James Gandolfini: Whatever.

Billy Joel: It's a toss-up between tangy and zesty.

Jeanne Moreau: *Fin.*

Mike Nichols: I would say this only for you. Smegma.

Stephen Sondheim: Celery.

Meryl Streep: Edgy.

Mark Wahlberg: Is "Marky Mark" a word?

Christopher Walken: Bedtime.

James Burrows: Uvula.

What turns you on?

Antonio Banderas: My wife.

Tim Allen: Matinees.

Gabriel Byrne: Transcendence in an artist and passion in a person.

Francis Ford Coppola: Life. Everything!

Kevin Costner: Being alone.

Ray Romano: Women who can golf well, and like other women.

Michael J. Fox: Honesty without fear.

Hugh Grant: Necks, actually.

Liza Minnelli: I've always thought the brain was an erogenous zone.

Melanie Griffith: My husband.

What turns you off?

Queen Latifah: Quickies.

Richard Gere: The front page of today's newspaper.

Tom Hanks: Eggshells. The kind you have to walk on.

Anthony Hopkins: Cinema school jargon.

Ron Howard: The notion that anything could ever be boring.

Nathan Lane: Polyester.

Burt Reynolds: Critics—not just film critics—critics of sunsets, critics of the love of life.

Meg Ryan: When a pretzel gets wet.

Joanne Woodward: Anybody saying "like" or "you know."

Renée Zellweger: Conditional kindness.

What sound or noise do you love?

Jeff Bridges: A cello.

Matthew Broderick: Cellos and violins.

Russell Crowe: The cello.

John Hurt: Cello.

Ellen Burstyn: Birdsong in the morning, Rachmaninoff at night.

Tom Cruise: A P-51 engine.

Harrison Ford: A Pratt and Whitney radial engine.

Jay Leno: Engines racing.

Matt Dillon: A Charlie Parker solo.

Sarah Jessica Parker: Ka-*ching*!

Roseanne: The music on the History Channel, when I know it's gonna be about Hitler.

Eddie Murphy: Silence. I love the sound of nothing.

Salma Hayek: Discovery and kissing.

Willem Dafoe: I can't tell you the truth on that one.

Whoopi Goldberg: I'm not gonna tell you.

Susan Sarandon: I can't talk about that.

Will Smith: Hey, come on, man, I can't share that here.

Barbra Streisand: Orgasms.

Kevin Kline: A woman in the throes of rapture.

What sound or noise do you hate?

Meg Ryan: That airplane engine revving up.

Tom Cruise: Well, if I'm in the P-51, silence at forty thousand feet.

Billy Crystal: Me, hugging me.

Robert Downey, Jr.: Custom ringtones.

Tom Hanks: The emptiness of an empty house.

Billy Joel: Hearing my own voice, singing flat.

What is your favorite curse word?

Well, we're into it now, right up to our . . . fill in your favorite word. This category has become such a favorite that we've subjected it to careful critical analysis. It will probably come as no surprise that *fuck* won in a landslide, with forty-five instances. The second-place finisher wasn't even a contender, having fewer than half the advocates of the winning word: Twenty of our guests opted for *shit,* barely edging out *motherfucker,* which charted at nineteen. The chart line then falls precipitously to *cocksucker* with a mere seven adherents.

After that, it's an imaginative riot, with no candidate receiving more than four votes, and the vast majority one—which speaks to the linguistic ingenuity of our guests.

What was the biggest surprise, and has remained a mystery to me, is the stunning difference between our male and female guests. Not to mince curse words, the men are almost universally wusses, and the women whip off obscenities that would make Lenny Bruce blush.

The most effective way to illustrate this sociopsycholinguistic phenomenon is to place some of the respondents in close proximity.

Paul Newman: Well, I have such a wealth of them. It would be unfair to single one out.

Meg Ryan: Fuck me! I say that a lot!

Neil Simon: I don't have a favorite curse word.

Holly Hunter: Cocksucker! (Its first appearance on the show—and not its last.)

Christopher Walken: Darn!

Julia Roberts: Fuck it all to hell!

Anthony Quinn: The word at the end of *mother.*

Sally Field (as previously reported): Motherfucker!

Willem Dafoe: You know, I *used* to talk like a sailor.

Jennifer Jason Leigh: Oh, I guess I say fuck, fuck-wad, fucking, fuck, fuck, asshole.

Billy Crystal: Damn! That's my favorite musical comedy curse word.

Geena Davis: I say fuck all the time—and "Suck my dick."

Martin Short: Oh, poo!

Bernadette Peters: I rotate them. One I like is crap. But I seem to end up correcting myself, saying shit. And then, just once in a while, I'll say fuck.

Sean Penn: You dentist!

Ellen Barkin: You fucking dick-wad!

Steven Spielberg: Rats!

Drew Barrymore (Steven's goddaughter): Fuck, for sure! Fuck! Fuck! Fuck! Sorry.

Alec Baldwin: Ass-bag.

Helen Hunt: Fuck me.

Francis Ford Coppola: I don't have a favorite curse word. And if I curse in front of a woman, I give them a dollar.

Cameron Diaz: Fuck, cocksucker, motherfucker—yak-dick! I picked that one up in Nepal last week.

Antonio Banderas: It's the version of the F word in Spanish.

Melanie Griffith: Fuck.

Val Kilmer: Taxes. I don't really have one.

Kathy Bates: Cocksucker!

Gabriel Byrnes: Bollocks.

Gwyneth Paltrow: Balls!

James Caan: F-ing.

Glenn Close: To my shame, fuck. It's not very interesting.

Alan Alda: Horse!

Jennifer Connelly: Fuck-face!

Benicio Del Toro: Piss-hell!

Mary Stuart Masterson: Fuck. It functions on a lot of levels.

Michael J. Fox: Shite.

Whoopi Goldberg: Shit!

Ed Harris: It has to be the f-word.

Teri Hatcher: Well, I'm such a simpleton, it's just fuck. I mean, just fuck.
Fuck this, fuck that, good fuckin' humorous line, fuck you, fuck—just
fuck. If somebody is finally going to say I can say it, then I'm just, you
know, fuck, fuck, fuck, fuck, fuck. It's such fun. I don't get to say it very
much because I'm a single mom, and of course I don't talk like that in
front of my daughter.

Richard Gere: I don't curse.

Jodie Foster: Motherfucker!

Jeremy Irons: Shhhhheamus Heaney!

Anjelica Huston: Shhhit!

Billy Joel: Bloody.

Lee Grant: Motherfucker!

Tommy Lee Jones: Sonsabitches!

Diane Lane: Goddammotherfuckerpieceofshit!

Jay Leno: Calling someone a syphilitic druid seems funnier to me than some four-letter word.

Shirley MacLaine: Fuck!

Matthew Broderick: Putz or douche bag.

Liza Minnelli: Motherfucker or cocksucker.

Burt Reynolds: *Merde.*

Bette Midler: Motherfucker!

Martin Scorsese: Oh, I can't. I'm too Catholic.

Jennifer Lopez: Fucking whore!

Billy Bob Thornton: Son of a bitch.

Charlize Theron: Motherfucker.

Mark Wahlberg: Son of a bitch in French.

Julianne Moore: It's a toss-up between cocksucker and motherfucker.

Norman Jewison: Son of a bitch!

Jessica Lange: Cocksucker!

It was ten years before anyone broke the ultimate taboo. Bruce Willis had tiptoed around it in 2001 with "It's a four-letter word—begins with *C*." But he went no further. It remained for two women, of course, to shatter the final barrier—on consecutive shoot dates! And each did it in a proper British accent.

On October 11, 2003, Cate Blanchett answered "What is your favorite curse word?" with, "I think in America, you can't even say this word, but c-u-n-t—I mean, there's nothing like it!"

So it had been spelled. Two days later, Naomi Watts answered the same question with a blunt "Cunt."

If in its first thirteen years, *Inside the Actors Studio* had accomplished nothing else, it could at least take credit for discovering the hitherto unrecognized potty-mouth superiority of women over men—which raises the question: Should we be considering an all-female army?

What profession would you like to attempt?

Billy Crystal: Shortstop, Yankees, number two.

Lauren Bacall: Tap dancing with Fred Astaire.

Pierce Brosnan: Painter.

Carol Burnett: Cartoonist.

Nicolas Cage: Sometimes I have this whimsical idea that I could be a priest.

Tom Cruise: I wouldn't want to do anything else.

Cameron Diaz: A zoologist, a biologist. I'm a scientist trapped in an actor's body.

Andy Garcia: Concert pianist.

Tom Hanks: Cartoonist.

Salma Hayek: Astronaut.

Anthony Hopkins: I'd love to have been a composer.

Sarah Jessica Parker: A grocery store proprietor.

Bernadette Peters: I can't do anything else.

Robin Williams: Neurologist or theoretical physicist.

What profession would you not like to attempt?

Billy Crystal: Shortstop, Yankees, number two. Those guys are *big*!

Drew Barrymore: I wouldn't like to do nothing.

Cate Blanchett: Maggot farmer.

Johnny Depp: President of the United States.

Hugh Grant: I'd hate to be ever again the man who cleans the seats at Fulham Football Club.

Salma Hayek: You know those Porta Pottis? Somebody has to go in there and clean them. That would not be a good one.

Philip Seymour Hoffman: Critic.

Nathan Lane: Tollbooth collector. When you go through, don't you always think, What did he do in a past life that made him wind up in that little booth?

Paul Newman: Greeter.

Meryl Streep: Every day I thank God that I don't have to sit in an office at a computer all day, every day.

Christopher Walken: Almost anything.

Finally, if heaven exists, what would you like to hear God say when you arrive at the Pearly Gates?

George Carlin: Now we're gonna have some fun around here!

Billy Crystal: That thing you did on the Oscars. How did you do that?

Clint Eastwood: We've got seventy-two virgins waiting for you.

Ray Romano: I saw what you did in the garage, and you're still welcome here.

Harrison Ford: You're much better-looking in person.

Michael J. Fox: Your dad's in the back. He's got beer and TV, and the hockey game's on.

Jamie Foxx: On Fridays we'll have a fish fry. Saturday we'll play softball. Sunday we'll go to church, and the preacher won't ask you for any money.

James Gandolfini: Take over for a while. I'll be right back.

Hugh Grant: Fabulous, darling!

Tom Hanks: Back you go!

Dustin Hoffman: That's funny, you don't *look* Jewish.

Anthony Hopkins: What were you *doing* down there!

Elton John: Come in, you old queen!

Hugh Laurie: No hard feelings.

Jennifer Lopez: You're safe. No paparazzi here.

Ian McKellen: You won't need your raincoat here, and I've got a couple of angels who'd like to meet you.

Paul Newman: You didn't care for the other place?

Meg Ryan: You big dope, I've been with you all along.

Susan Sarandon: I'd like to hear Her say, "Let's party!"

Sissy Spacek: Miss Spacek, we have the role of a lifetime for you.

John Travolta: So, what was it like to work with Olivia Newton-John?

Robin Williams: The concert begins at five. It'll be Mozart, Elvis. Or—
to know that there's laughter. Just to hear God say, "Two Jews walk into
a bar."

Matt Damon: All of the suffering that you saw or heard about or knew
was happening, there is a point to it. Come in the back; I'll tell you all
about it.

Robert De Niro: Well, if *God* exists, He's got a lot of explaining to do!

For thirteen years, the question "If heaven exists, what would you like to
hear God say when you arrive at the Pearly Gates?" has begun with the word
Finally, which signals to our guest, our students, our television audience and
me that our visit with that evening's guest is drawing to a close.

For me and our students and, I have some reason to believe, for our guests,
it is a moment touched with regret because we all know that we will never
meet like this again. As I look at the students' faces from the sidelines during
their classroom session with the guest, I often reflect on the fact that these
four or five hours the students spend in the company of artists the world
admires, getting to know them as few outside their innermost circles are privileged to, will be an indelible part of their lives forever, available for consultation when they need it, or simply pleasant recollection: Oh, yes, that evening
with Tom Hanks . . .

So, with Bob De Niro's ingenious answer, the final response to the final
Pivot question signals the beginning of the end of *this* journey. And, since I
have demonstrated a fondness for circular constructions, it will come as no
surprise that, as the journey nears its end, it circles back to its embarkation
point where the first words of Dickens's *David Copperfield* were invoked to set
the stage for everything between that page and this, which has, I hope, kept
faith with David's pledge, "Whether I shall turn out to be the hero of my own
life, or whether that station will be held by anybody else, these pages must
show."

To turn to Dickens one last time, in the Preface to the 1850 edition of *David
Copperfield,* he wrote, "It would concern the reader little, perhaps, to know,

how sorrowfully the pen is laid down at the close of a two-years' imaginative task; or how an Author feels as if he were dismissing some portion of himself into the shadowy world, when a crowd of the creatures of his brain are going from him for ever."

The inhabitants of these pages aren't Micawber and Peggotty—though, for the two years it has taken to write these pages, I have lived with them as closely and constantly as Dickens lived with the spirited "creatures of his brain." The subjects of this account existed and exist entirely independent of me, and are, to put it plainly, simply and conclusively, the heroes of my life.

Only one person is missing: I am often asked, "Who is the one guest you haven't had and want the most?" The answer is: The night that one of the Actors Studio Drama School graduates has achieved so much that he or she walks out of the wings to occupy that chair next to me will be, for me, the most glorious moment in the history of *Inside the Actors Studio.*

CHAPTER Eighteen

66 Meet it is I set it down
That one may smile and smile and be a villain.

—*Hamlet,* Act One, Scene Five

When I began this endeavor, I was concerned that it might lack the tension and conflict that appear to be the essential ingredients of contemporary life and literature. Within the brief span of two years, that problem was solved for me by one of the personae of these pages who is not one of its heroes.

In the fall of 2003, as I neared the end of a ten-year decanal tenure, I decided that, having fulfilled my promise to launch the Actors Studio Drama School—by a multiple of ten over my initial intention of a year—the time had come to relinquish the tiller.

I had stayed ten times longer than I had planned because, to put it simply, I had fallen deeply in love with the school and its students. Since, uniquely among the university's deans, I governed a school that was a partnership between two institutions, The New School for Social Research and the Actors Studio, and was a senior faculty member of one, as dean, and a vice president of the other, I was once challenged in a debate over my annual budget submission to the university with "Which side are you on, the university's or the Studio's?" to which I replied, "Neither. The students'." The most important lesson I learned in my decade in the academy was that, at every moment of my working life, the students were my constituency.

Decades ago, I bought a small, framed antique slate, and found a place for it in my study, on the wall facing my desk. From time to time I glanced at it: Confronted with a genuine tabula rasa, I wondered what it ought to say. Then one day, shortly after saying no to a tempting offer that I couldn't in good conscience say yes to, I rose abruptly, crossed to the slate, and wrote on it, "This soul is not for sale." I thought at first that I liked the invention for the consonantal rhyme of *soul* and *sale,* but within moments I realized I'd gone to the blackboard to inscribe once and for all the lesson learned in the city room of the *Detroit Times.* That makes me sound a great deal more virtuous than I am, but the fact is, it has proven to be a useful reminder at a number of crossroads, like the one that lies ahead in these final pages.

When our master's degree program became the seventh division of the university in its first year, I signed for the standard five-year term asked of every dean. At the end of the first contractual term, the university offered me another five-year contract. On the theory that it was important for both parties to begin considering succession, I insisted on a three-year term. At the end of the eighth year, our school was in the midst of a move into the new quarters for which I'd campaigned from the day of our arrival, so I agreed to another year; and when that time had elapsed, I accepted a final one-year appointment, in order that the negotiations between the university and the Studio for a renewal of the ten-year agreement that had created the school would begin on my watch.

I pressed for appointment of my successor during my final year, so that the new dean's tenure and mine would overlap, making me available to my successor to the extent that my counsel was needed or wanted. On March 1, my successor was put in place, and on May 4, 2004, the dinner following the school year's final board of trustees meeting was marked by an unusual and, as it would turn out, prophetic occurrence, the simultaneous retirement of four of the university's seven deans: 60 percent of the senior faculty, gone in a day. The fifth would be gone in a matter of months, and the dean who replaced Dean Banu, who retired May 4, would vanish after three months.

Something was afoot and increasingly amiss. Nineteen ninety-nine had marked a sea change when, after seventeen years as president of The New School for Social Research, Jonathan Fanton left the university to become president of the MacArthur Foundation, the institution famous for, among many other things, its "genius grants," and in February 2001, former Nebraska governor and senator Bob Kerrey succeeded him.

Fanton had observed that *Inside the Actors Studio* had affected enrollment in every one of the university's divisions, and Kerrey acknowledged the advantage of a television series that began each episode in eighty-four million American homes and 125 countries with the legend "New School for Social Research" and subsequently, when the name was changed, "New School University" superimposed on the opening shot, and a frame with the university's Web site in the closing credits—exposure that would have been beyond any university's means, if it were for sale.

In the three years between Bob Kerrey's arrival and my departure, he and

I developed what appeared to be a close friendship, on and off the campus. In this respect, I was unique among the deans. Bob, a man of impressive political gifts and considerable charisma, had nevertheless inspired famously mixed reactions among his congressional colleagues, where he earned the sobriquet "Cosmic Bob." He quickly imposed an equally unsettling imprint on the university, especially among the deans who inveighed against him with escalating fervor in our weekly deans' luncheons.

On March 11, 2002, a year into Bob's tenure, the growing tension between him and the academic community over which he presided spilled into the *Chronicle of Higher Education,* in an article announcing the resignation of one of Bob's first recruits, Kenneth Prewitt, dean of the Graduate Faculty of Political and Social Science, after less than a year in the position, in order, in Kerrey's explanation to the community, "to focus on his research."

"Students of the graduate school," the article continued, "said they believed that Mr. Prewitt had resigned in protest of what they view as the administration's shortchanging of the Graduate Faculty."

In American Prospect Online, under the headline, KERREY'S QUAGMIRE and the subhead, THE FORMER SENATOR AND NEW PRESIDENT OF THE NEW SCHOOL TURNS THE LEGENDARY INSTITUTION INTO A FREE-FIRE ZONE, Scott Stossel wrote, "On the afternoon of Friday, March 15, the last day before spring break, New School University President Bob Kerrey made one of his periodic star turns on the Tishman Auditorium's stage." After reviewing the escalating conflict, Stossel wrote, "When students kept asking if Kerrey knew why Prewitt had resigned, Kerrey finally said, 'Well, why don't you ask Dean Prewitt directly. Ken?'"

According to the account, Prewitt twice asked Kerrey, "Are you sure you want me to do this?"

Reporting that "Kerrey told him to go ahead," the article relates that Prewitt said "he was resigning because it seemed to him that the administration had its academic and financial priorities reversed, and risked subordinating intellectual values to market values. Someone asked for an example. Prewitt, looking pained, said that one particularly egregious example was a proposal by the provost to have 'private bonuses' issued to deans who boosted the tuition-paying enrollment of their divisions—the size of each bonus commensurate with the number of students a dean could bring in. This, to Prewitt's way of thinking, was tantamount to placing a cash value on each student; each division would have to place profit over learning.

"Kerrey then swept across the stage and grabbed the mike from Prewitt. 'You know whose idea the "private bonuses" were?' he asked. 'Mine.' There was an audible gasp from the crowd—the university president had just admitted,

478 | James Lipton

in effect, that he saw dollar signs on his students. And Kerrey continued, 'I concede now that it was a bad idea. But it was not my first appalling idea. Nor will it be my last.'"

He was as good as his word. In Bob's first five years, he went through more than a dozen deans and all but one of the university's senior officers, and shuffled three provosts. The New School became such a swiftly spinning revolving door that, in my last year as dean, I who had begun as a neophyte professional academic ten years before, and was still scrambling up the learning curve, was now in a position of time-served seniority over every academic and administrative officer of New School University—which led me to feel sometimes like Groucho Marx, who wasn't sure he wanted to belong to any club that would have him as a member.

At the May 4, 2004, board of trustees dinner, each of the retiring deans was saluted and presented with gifts. In my case, there was an additional honor—a significant one for which I was, and am, grateful. When my turn came, Bob announced that at the board meeting, the trustees had voted to present me with the university's highest honor, the Founders Medal.

I include the citation in this account not out of vanity—though, to be as honest as my *Inside the Actors Studio* guests, I wouldn't put it past me—but to set the stage for what was to follow.

The resolution, which was signed by Bob Kerrey as president and Philip Scaturro as chair of the board of trustees, read in part:

> It is impossible to exaggerate the importance of James Lipton's service to New School University, first as founding chair of the Master of Fine Arts program in dramatic arts; then as the first Dean of the Actors Studio Drama School, following its establishment as the seventh school of the University; and from 1994 to the present, as creator, producer, writer, researcher and host of "The Craft Seminar," Bravo's *Inside the Actors Studio*, which has provided a training-ground for the school's students and brought the University into millions of homes in the United States and worldwide.
>
> Jim's ideas and achievement have transformed the educational landscape of this University. Embodying the New School's historic commitment to the performing arts, he played the lead role in establishing what is today the nation's most distinctive, prominent and largest graduate drama school. Together with members of the Actors Studio, including Paul Newman, Ellen Burstyn and Arthur Penn, he implemented his vision of a unique collaboration between the Actors Studio and the New School to provide the highest-level training to aspiring actors, directors

and playwrights. In an environment where new educational ventures often fail, Jim has been an enormous success as dean. In just ten years, he created an innovative three-year, professional MFA curriculum, developed the program from 59 students in 1994 to more than 200 students by 1996, sustaining this enrollment ever since while at the same time continually improving quality; built a distinguished roster of longstanding faculty that has included Ellen Burstyn, Lee Grant, Romulus Linney and Lloyd Richards; and was instrumental in securing a home for the program within the Westbeth Artists community.

A paragraph of the resolution described the history of *Inside the Actors Studio*, and the document concluded with:

Teacher, actor, director, producer in theater, television and film, playwright, choreographer, lyricist, screenwriter, author of fiction and nonfiction books, equestrian, pilot, and recipient of the French Republic's *Chevalier de l'ordre des Arts et des Lettres*, Jim's accomplishments astound. For Jim's pioneering spirit, which recalls the venerable tradition of Alvin Johnson, the New School's first President, for being an inspiring leader who has been deeply committed to the excellence and success of the school, for being a dedicated educator who cares deeply about his students, for furthering the arts in the United States and abroad, and agreeing to continue to serve the University as Dean *Emeritus* of the Actors Studio Drama School, the Board of Trustees and the University community are eternally grateful.

I presume to include the citation because anyone who has read these pages knows that it is *not* an account of what I achieved, but rather The New School's salute to what *we* achieved—all of us, faculty, administration and students of the Actors Studio Drama School.

And I include it because, within a few weeks of signing his name to the words of the citation—words I took then, and take now, to be a sincere and truthful expression of the university's view of what we'd built with our hearts and minds and souls and muscle and sweat for The New School—Bob Kerrey presided over the systematic dismantling of the product of our labors.

One of the many ironies of the weeks that followed the trustees dinner was a letter I received the morning after the dinner from Jonathan Fanton that read in part, "It pains me not to be present at the board dinner in your honor this week. I would very much like to celebrate you and one of the most remarkable and creative stories of institution-building I have ever seen.

"I count the partnership between the New School and the Actors Studio as one of the two or three most important developments during my 17 years as President. You have been generous in your comments on my role, but you are the genius (not a word MacArthur uses lightly) who had the vision, the diplomatic skill, the patient determination, the unbending devotion to quality and the stamina to make it happen. The combination of high aspirations, decency, fairness and kindness made the school a supportive community. I can feel it when I walk into a room of students. That accomplishment is a tribute to your character and it will endure."

Again, knowing what I know about who did what (there is no coquettish modesty in this: Every brick of the Actors Studio Drama School bears an assortment of fingerprints), I took Jonathan's letter as an acknowledgment of a collective achievement. For ten years, the Actors Studio Drama School was one of the most stable divisions of the university, reaching its annual target of eighty admissions while achieving one of the lowest, hence most desirable, selectivity ratios in the university; maintaining the university's lowest attrition rate at less than six percent; reconciling each year's budget within a margin of one percent; delivering every year's projected net fund surplus without fail—and transmitting the drama school's and The New School's message to America and the world on *Inside the Actors Studio.*

But Jonathan's confident prediction that the Actors Studio Drama School of New School University "will endure" was wrong. In the academic world and outside it, countless uncomprehending voices have asked, "How could this have happened?" No one, with the exception, of course, of Bob Kerrey, can answer that question—and I now have reason to suspect that his answer would be no more reliable than the one he offered when Ken Prewitt resigned: to "focus on his research"; but here, in brief and with admitted bias, is my view of the causal chain of events (I end as I began, with a determinist stance) that led Bob and his deputies to take a pile driver to the Actors Studio Drama School.

The dean who followed me was the candidate I favored—though academic custom precludes a dean from naming his successor, so I was at a distance from the selection. It is not Bob Kerrey's fault that my immediate successor, although a member of the Studio and a longtime teacher in our school, found the managerial duties of the deanship so overwhelming that he resigned within three months, opening a door to Bob and his newly appointed provost, Arjun Appadurai, who began his relationship with the Actors Studio Drama School with seemly modesty, professing ignorance of our history, our philosophy, our curriculum and faculty, then promptly reappeared on the school's doorstep with a "Special Advisor," who was not a Studio member but would, in the words of Bob's formal announcement of the appointment, "assure the highest standards of administrative efficiency and academic rigor during the search for a new Dean for the School."

Bob's announcement was followed quickly by a more specific, and faintly ominous, memo to the school from the provost: "I am writing to clear up some understandable confusions about lines of authority as between ASDS Chairs and my Office. The Special Advisor to the Provost for Dramatic Arts has the full authorities (*sic*) to make all decisions affecting the School until a new dean is appointed. This includes all personnel, budget and curriculum matters, as well as related budgetary and fiscal issues."

The memo instructed the school to make its "best efforts to respect this line of reporting and communication so as to avoid the unintended impression that you do not accept or trust her judgement (*sic*). She has the 100% support of Bob Kerrey and myself in this important transition and is full of enthusiasm for her role in the ASDS."

Whether by chance or design, the provost displayed ignorance of the original contract between the two institutions, which provided, at the New School's insistence, that the director of the MFA program *must* be a member of the Studio. The purpose of that provision was, of course, to ensure that The New School would acquire what it was seeking: an MFA drama program created and operated by the Actors Studio.

With "the 100% support" of the president and the provost, the Special Advisor set to with the promised enthusiasm for her role, methodically replacing the Actors Studio Drama School administrators; and, with them, the school's institutional memory.

With a single exception, the school's entire playwriting department was fired by the Special Advisor or resigned in protest. In his letter of resignation to the Advisor, Pulitzer Prize–winning playwright Lee Blessing wrote, "The recent record of administrative decisions at ASDS doesn't suggest to me that rationality (or even good sense) has been the highest priority involved. I no longer feel I can trust anything that is told me by the powers that be at ASDS. That's why I have no interest in returning. May we all see better times."

For the first time in the school's history, the faculty fell into warring camps, and what had been the university's most stable division, in faculty, administration and student body, spiraled into anomie. One group of teachers, composed principally of those who had been brought in after my tenure and were therefore untainted by experience with, or even knowledge of, the school that was so respectfully described in the Board of Trustees Resolution, was loyal— and wholly beholden—to the Special Advisor. The second group comprised those who had participated in and built the program during its first ten years. What some in the new group apparently took as the Advisor's un-disguised preference for them emboldened the more ambitious of them, pos-sibly sensing advancement and profit, to launch attacks against the founding teachers.

On February 9, 2005, 112 Actors Studio Drama School students signed their names to a petition to the university that read, "The Special Advisor to the Provost, who is not a member of the Actors Studio, has made changes without consulting or obtaining the support of the creators of the program. Because of these changes we have lost the core philosophy of the Actors Stu-dio and the integrated approach of the training, which are two reasons we all entered this school. We also chose to attend the ASDS because it offers the establishment of a relationship with the Actors Studio following graduation. This benefit is now in jeopardy.

"This petition is to let the administration know that we will not sit by while they make changes without the Studio's or our input or consent. This petition is also to let the administration know that we did not come here to go to the New School of Drama; we came here to go to the Actors Studio Drama School because we believe in that for which it stands."

Bob's response was a series of meetings with the students. At the students' insistence, the meetings were openly tape-recorded, for use in a student class-action lawsuit against the university. At one of the meetings, a student asked Bob, "It's not guaranteed we will all graduate from the Actors Studio Drama School, right?"

"Well, here's—you're surfacing a very sensitive issue," Bob replied, "one that we haven't—frankly, we didn't pay as much attention to as we should. It was a mistake to tell you that this is the Actors Studio Drama School. It's not. It's New School University's Drama School."

The room erupted into angry protest, which was interrupted by Kerrey with "You can argue with me about this all you want. You asked me a ques-tion. I gave you a truthful answer. If you want me to lie to you, if that's what you're asking me to do, then I will lie to you."

A student responded, "Where is our money back for our credits lost, that the actors got shorted on this year? Where is the rebate for the workshop that was stolen from the first-year students? And I do say stolen. This is expen-sive. This is a hundred thousand dollars. Right now, this is not a hundred-thousand-dollar institution. Would Yale School of Drama have as many applicants if it was New Haven School of Drama? No. And that's why the name is important."

In the days that followed, the students were so incensed that they began demonstrating in front of the school's Westbeth building, where the Special

Advisor was headquartered, drawing the attention of the media and finally forcing Bob Kerrey's hand: On March 2, 2005, Bob sent a memo to the school informing it that "the Special Advisor to the Provost for the Arts has asked to resume her advisory role in the Office of the Provost," which effectively ended her tenure at the school.

But the Actors Studio Drama School remained an occupied territory in constant turmoil, with the students, in a meeting with Kerrey, demanding to know whether the university was still advertising itself to applicants as the Actors Studio Drama School.

A short time later, at a negotiating meeting with the Studio, Bob insisted that the Studio's representatives permit him to send a "positive" acceptance letter to the fall applicants, promising them, among other things, a guarantee of Studio Observer and Working Finalist status upon graduation, two of the central program elements that arrived with the Studio, and would leave with it if the negotiations failed.

The Studio's representatives replied that the moment the contract was concluded, a positive letter could be sent. Until then, the Studio contended, it would not be complicit in what it viewed as a deception.

Bob argued heatedly that the Studio's position on his letter indicated a lack of trust in him, a cardinal sin in the new New School environment, and Bob's most frequently voiced theme—to the deans, the Studio, the students, to any potential transgressor. The Studio's position was that the policy had nothing to do with Kerrey, but everything to do with the welfare of the incoming students, and expressed the hope that the matter would be moot if the two parties could come to terms.

The fact was that at that point there were no outstanding academic or financial items in dispute between the parties. In the wake of the Special Advisor debacle and the student protests, the university's negotiators had returned to the aims and structure of the original contract—to the point where the lawyers for both sides had been instructed to prepare a final contract for signing, and two Studio members were interviewed by Bob for the chairmanship of what both sides agreed should be an MFA program, rather than a New School division, obviating yet another decanal search.

Bob proposed that during the upcoming weekend he would make a final choice of one of the two applicants, both of whom, he said, had impressed him. On Saturday of that weekend, an article appeared in the *New York Times,* under the headline BOB KERREY WEIGHING RUN FOR MAYOR OF NEW YORK. In the article, when Kerrey told the reporters, "You know me. I am just crazy enough to do this," he was reminded by them that he had accepted the chairmanship of Democrats for Bloomberg. The *Times* reported, "'That is exactly right,' he said last night. But he said that he began having second thoughts almost as soon as he had accepted. He said that he had not informed Mr. Bloomberg that he was thinking of running for mayor, or that he had decided against heading the committee. 'I guess they know now,' he said."

The *Times* account included what turned out to be an omen. "Mr. Kerrey, 61, said that he just signed a contract extending his stay at the New School through 2011, but that he could break it if necessary."

On Monday, the day of Bob's promised choice of a program chair, the Studio's lawyer reported that her calls to the New School's lawyers were going unanswered, as were the negotiators' calls to Bob. On Tuesday morning, Bob called Ellen Burstyn and Bob Wankel, who had led the Studio's negotiating team, to tell them that he no longer wanted a partner, and would create his own school.

His announcement to "The New School University Community" stated, "As you know, the University has been in negotiations with The Actors Studio for some time regarding the governance of the drama program. Yesterday a decision was made not to continue a contractual relationship with The Actors Studio as part of its master's program in drama. The University will operate its drama MFA as the New School for Drama."

His announcement to the Actors Studio Drama School students promised them, "Your faculty will not change as a result of the transition," and "Your curriculum will not change as a result of the transition." Both changed profoundly.

The heart and soul of the Actors Studio Drama School faculty resigned, even though the attenuated negotiation effectively prevented the Studio from reestablishing itself at another institution in the fall of 2005. The teachers who resigned paid a grievous financial price, giving up seniority and security for a principle and unemployment. Andreas Manolikakis's letter of resignation summed up the feelings of all of them, beginning, "I have been a member of the Actors Studio since 1987. I consider myself a product of this institution," and concluding, "I cannot in good conscience work with the people who participated in the destruction of the ASDS. There is no money or position that can make me betray my own home."

Kerrey's about-face with the Studio put him back in familiar territory. On April 21, under the headline KERREY RILES UP NEW SCHOOL, the *New York Post* reported, "Bob Kerrey flopped before he could flip as a mayoral candidate by bowing out before he was even in the race. Now some colleagues at New School University, where he's president, have gotten fed up with Kerrey's capriciousness. 'The guy's out of control,' one member of the university's board of governors told Page Six. 'After renewing his contract till 2011, he threw his name into the mix as a candidate to chair the Democratic National Committee, to head Democrats for Bloomberg, then to run for mayor of New York. Now he has decided to stay at the New School. Until when?' "

Writing that Kerrey " 'forced out' well-respected dean Ann-Louise Shapiro and trustee Anne Ehrenkranz," and "ended an affiliation with the Actors Studio and James Lipton, star of the long-running Bravo show *Inside the Actors Studio*," the *Post* quoted its New School source again. "Kerrey 'pulled the plug on the Actors Studio, a major strategic move, when his own credibility is in tatters,' the insider fumed."

The next day, the *Post* followed up with "Students at the prestigious Actors Studio demanded answers from New School president Bob Kerrey yesterday about the future relationship between the acting school and the university. Chanting, 'Hey, Hey, B.K., how many schools did you kill today?' and carrying signs that urged Kerrey to 'Go run for mayor, Bob!' roughly 50 drama students protested in front of the school, demanding that the Vietnam vet and mayoral near-contender give them a straight answer. 'He has changed his stance time after time—just like he did last week in his position on running for mayor. We can't get a clear answer,' said Adam Kee, 22, a first-year student in the drama school. 'It's really sickening what he's doing.' "

"At issue is how the drama graduate program will be managed," the article concluded, "since Kerrey cut contractual ties with the venerable acting school last year. Students say they don't even know which institution's name will be printed on their degrees, or whether New School courses will count toward credit totals. Several said the deal felt like a bait-and-switch scam. The New School, however, says the program will continue on as always, but with a different name: The New School for Drama."

On the last day of June 2005, after nearly eleven years on Twelfth Street, I packed the contents of my office and left The New School. So did the Actors Studio Drama School.

What did The New School lose that day? Our curriculum, Bob Kerrey's claims to the contrary notwithstanding; our senior core faculty, with more than a hundred collective years of Actors Studio experience; the Studio's history, reputation and knowledge; the unique side-by-side training of our actors, writers and directors, which was one of the first targets of the new regime; a fully produced repertory season, designed to present our graduating actors to the professional community and the public in five or six roles, and the work of our playwrights and directors in as many offerings, five times a week for twelve to fifteen weeks; the privilege extended to our students of observing the Studio's sessions periodically for three years; as many as forty *Inside the Actors Studio* experiences in each student's time with us; the Actors Studio's name—and cachet—on their diplomas; Working Finalist status at the Studio for every graduate, providing an additional year of postpostgraduate training; and the opportunity for membership in the Actors Studio, providing, to the extent the graduate wishes, a lifetime of continuing training in our craft . . . all of it sacrificed on the altar of a self-esteem so self-assured that it couldn't countenance what it could never comprehend.

Of course it's possible that I overvalue the Studio's offerings, but I will always wonder: For what grand, superior principle did Bob Kerrey and his adherents jettison them? What did Kerry and Arjun Appadurai know about the theatrical arts that the Studio collectively didn't know, and what part of "transformed the educational landscape of this University" and "the nation's most distinctive, prominent and largest graduate drama school" did they fail to understand—or elect to renounce?

Mr. Appadurai's view of us quickly became irrelevant, since his brief tenure as provost barely outlasted the Actors Studio Drama School. In another rumbling of tumbrels that would also take down Paul Goldberger, the Pulitzer Prize–winning architecture critic of the *New York Times* and *The New Yorker*, two years after his appointment by Kerrey as dean of The New School's Parsons School of Design, Arjun Appadurai's resignation was announced by President Kerrey on January 30, 2006.

As I have set this account down, I have been struck forcibly by a remarkable irony that wasn't apparent to me as events were unfolding in 2004. In March 1996, the Studio and I, wielding the invaluable "no," walked away from the Bravo network and *Inside the Actors Studio*, rather than accede to the focus-group person's bidding that we eliminate from the series the students, the school and New School University. It remained for President Bob Kerrey, eight years later, to fulfill the focus group's goal of driving *Inside the Actors Studio* out of The New School, and The New School out of *Inside the Actors Studio*.

Bob Kerrey's New School for Drama continues to walk a tightrope, delicately balanced between proclaiming the superiority of its vision and, in every one of its publications, offering, as evidence of it, long lists of "alumni of the New School for Drama" who have gone on to accomplishment and acclaim. The problem is that none of the "alumni" in their lists attended The New School for Drama, which, as of the writing of these words, has yet to graduate a single student who wasn't admitted by the Actors Studio Drama School, and trained from 1994 to 2004 by the teachers The New School cavalierly pushed aside.

In The New School for Drama's zeal to proclaim its difference from the Actors Studio Drama School and, simultaneously and paradoxically, claim continuity with it, they have even had the hubris to publish, in memoriam, a proprietary tribute to former Yale Drama School dean Lloyd Richards, whom I persuaded to come to New York when he had graduated from the university we attended together, and whom I brought into the Actors Studio Drama School after his distinguished career at Yale. Lloyd left The New School with us and, though he was the gentlest of men, thereafter referred frequently and fiercely to Bob Kerrey and our New School successors as "dream-killers."

Early in this journey, I admitted that "simply *saying* 'truth' doesn't answer inevitable questions: It asks them. *Whose* truth—and to what end?" So, I admit readily that this account of the events that ended a ten-year dream may be colored by a bias that was succinctly expressed by, and that I share with, Dean Richards.

Nevertheless, I would submit that it is not colored by sour grapes or bitterness. For two reasons. First, because what the Actors Studio Drama School accomplished for ten years can't be erased: It lives in The New School's Founders Medal and, most important, in our graduates. And second, because The New School, however unwittingly, did the Studio the inestimable service of launching it toward a remarkably happy outcome, which will serve as the end of this journey—and the beginning of a new one.

AFTERWORD . . . *and Foreword*

Given the fondness for beginnings that I expressed in the first pages of this history, the pleasure with which I recount a new beginning in its final pages will come as no surprise.

The morning after Bob Kerrey's decision to create his own drama school appeared in the press, my answering machine was swamped with urgent messages, most of them from academic institutions.

Within the next two weeks, we had identified six serious suitors for the Actors Studio Drama School's hand. A Studio committee was formed, led by Ellen Burstyn, Bob Wankel, Andreas Manolikakis and Deborah Dixon. I served ex officio, and we were joined in a consultant's role by one more hero of my life and this account, Joseph Porrino, who, as executive vice president of The New School for Social Research, had represented the university in the negotiation with the Studio that had created the drama school in 1994, who guided it and me as a New School officer until he left the university in 1998, and who watched in astonishment as the edifice he had helped create *for The New School* was torn down by The New School.

Over the summer and fall of 2005, a stream of meetings narrowed the candidates to two, and finally to one: Pace University, a landmark New York City institution, which was then about to celebrate its one hundredth anniversary. With more than twice the student body of The New School; a much broader scope, from law and business schools to a football team; campuses in New York City and Westchester County; a downtown campus next to our Actors Studio colleague Robert De Niro at the Tribeca Film Institute; a central place, for the university and us, in the post-9/11 cultural renaissance of lower Manhattan; and the 740-seat state-of-the-art theater that now housed *Inside the Actors Studio,* Pace offered dazzling new vistas to our school and its students.

Of greater importance, its president, David Caputo, and provost, Joseph Morreale, ushered us into an academic environment that stood in marked contrast to the one we'd left behind. Over the spring and summer of 2006, under the supervision of Dr. Geoffrey Brackett, the associate provost for academic affairs, classrooms were designed and built by Pace for our school; and, led by Andreas Manolikakis as the MFA program's director, the Actors Studio Drama School faculty reconvened to teach a restored, revived curriculum in, as we had promised twelve years before and delivered to our students until 2004, a school that "treats all aspects of the dramatic arts as a 'process,' with a guiding central methodology and a common language."

The Actors Studio Drama School was alive and whole and evolving, precisely as its creators had intended. Everything The New School had lost was firmly in place at Pace University—and, significantly, the school's creators were back at the helm, and the vessel that had carried our students, faculty and administration safely and successfully through a memorable decade was back on course under full sail, its institutional memory intact, its future viable and vibrant.

On September 5, 2006, Ellen Burstyn and Harvey Keitel, representing the Studio's presidency; several members of the Studio's board of directors; Nira Hermann, dean of the Dyson College of Arts and Sciences in which our program now resided; the leadership of Pace University; the MFA program's director, Andreas Manolikakis, and its faculty and administrators greeted our school's incoming acting, writing and directing master's degree candidates.

Ellen, Harvey and Andreas spoke; then, as the Actors Studio Drama School's founding dean, I was invited by Andreas to address the incoming class. As I approached the lectern, I made the mistake of looking at the assembled students, their faces entirely new to me—and their expressions so familiar—and it was a long moment before I could begin the remarks I had begun on ten previous occasions, and related earlier in these pages—but this time with a significant difference.

"To borrow the words of a much more significant person on a much more significant occasion, the world will little note what we say here today. But for the Actors Studio, this is a very significant moment. The Studio will note forever that, at ten twelve a.m., on September fifth, 2006, we admitted the thirteenth academic class in the sixty-year history of the Actors Studio, and the first in our splendid new home at Pace University."

As I had in the past, I expressed to the arriving candidates my view that "a life in the creative arts is not a profession but a vocation, a calling. Not everyone possesses the strength, courage and fire necessary to answer that call. Since we're welcoming you here today, it's obvious that we saw that strength, courage and fire in you—and something else: a commitment that is summed up in a recollection of choreographer and director Patricia Birch. When she was one of a class of sixteen-year-old girls at the Martha Graham School, the day arrived when the eponymous artist swept into the studio to seat herself, ramrod-straight on a hard chair, her sinewy feet planted on the floor that she normally bestrode like a colossus, her impassive gaze fixed on the students.

"The class ended, the students applauded the teacher. Then, a terrible silence. Miss Graham's gimlet gaze swept the gasping, petrified students, moving like a blinding spotlight from one to the next, to the next. After an eternity, her lips moved. 'One of you,' she muttered, 'is doomed to be a dancer.' Pat has told me that at that moment, every one of those students closed her eyes and offered up a silent, fervent prayer: 'Please—please—please, let it be me!' You have offered up that prayer, and, in choosing you, we have pledged ourselves to answer it."

I concluded my remarks as I had on ten previous occasions with "Today is a turning point—for you—and for us. *Wei-ji,* the Chinese character for a turning point, is actually a combination of two characters, the one for opportunity and the one for danger, joining them forever in inseparable union.

"Is this an opportunity? We fervently hope so. Is there danger in it, risk? Of course. *Wei-ji* teaches that one cannot exist without the other. As Shakespeare put it in *Henry IV, Part 1,* 'Out of this nettle, danger, we pluck this flower, safety.'

"We are intensely aware that you are entrusting yourselves—and your futures—to us. And perhaps today you are beginning to realize that we are entrusting ourselves—and the past and future of an institution we esteem—to you.

"The distinguished English poet Christopher Logue summed up this kind of relationship succinctly:

'Come to the edge.
We might fall.
Come to the edge.
It's too high!
COME TO THE EDGE!

So they came
and he pushed

and they flew.'

"Students of the Actors Studio Drama School of Pace University, come to the edge—and fly."

Click.

Acknowledgments

I have tried in the course of this book to recognize the individuals who accompanied, and often led, me on the journey recounted in its pages, so perhaps this page of acknowledgments is an unnecessary afterthought.

But still, as I disembark, I can't help looking back at a deck lined with companions I will never forget and to whom I am profoundly indebted.

Although the reader has already encountered some of them along the way, I feel compelled to acknowledge definitively and finally their importance to this journey and to me.

And so, my deepest thanks to . . .

. . . my gifted editor, the doughty Julie Doughty; my intrepid researcher, Jeremy Kareken; the producer and the director/editor of *Inside the Actors Studio,* Sabrina Fodor and Jeff Wurtz, whose manifold skills inform every frame of the series; my assistant, Robert Reynolds, a graduate of the Actors Studio Drama School, who has proven to be a person of infinite ingenuity; my colleagues and friends at Bravo, Lauren Zalaznick, Frances Berwick and Christian Barcellos; and at NBC Universal, Jeff Zucker and Jeff Gaspin; my fellow members of the Actors Studio, its presidents Ellen Burstyn, Harvey Keitel and Al Pacino, and its treasurer (and so much more) Robert Wankel; *Inside the Actors Studio*'s attorney, Gray Coleman, whose integrity and keen intelligence have kept us safely and steadily on course for a dozen years; our newfound colleagues at Pace University, Geoffrey Brackett, David Caputo, Stephen J. Friedman, Nira Herrmann, Rick Whitfield and David Watson; Andreas Manolikakis, chair of the Actors Studio MFA, who is my successor and in many gratifying ways my superior in the position; the faculty and students of the Actors Studio MFA who hold in their hands and hearts the future of the Studio; Joseph Porrino, the steadfast guide of our school; the talent agents and public relations representatives who have trusted us with their clients from the day we opened our doors; and the hundreds of artists who have selflessly interrupted their lives in order to enrich *our* lives on *Inside the Actors Studio.*

About the Author

JAMES LIPTON is the creator, executive producer, writer, and host of *Inside the Actors Studio*, which is seen in eighty-nine million homes in America on the Bravo network, and in 125 countries, and has received fourteen Emmy nominations. He is the author of the novel *Mirrors*, which he then adapted and produced for the screen, and of the American literary perennial *An Exaltation of Larks*, and has written the book and lyrics of two Broadway musicals. His television productions include Jimmy Carter's Inaugural Gala, the first presidential concert ever televised; twelve Bob Hope birthday specials, reaching record-breaking audiences; and *The Road to China*, the first American entertainment program from the People's Republic. He is a vice president of the Actors Studio, is the founder and dean emeritus of the Actors Studio Drama School at Pace University, has received three honorary PhDs, is a recipient of France's *Chevalier de l'Ordre des Arts et des Lettres*, and has been awarded the Lifetime Achievement Emmy by the National Academy of Television Arts and Sciences.

A Note on the Type

The titles are Bodoni Book, an interpretation of Giambattista Bodoni's 300-year-old typeface by Morris Fuller Benton, who designed his version in the early twentieth century. Although Bodoni is a classic font, it is considered modern because of its sharp shapes and contrast of thick and thin lines.

The font Celeste, used for the text, was created by British typeface designer Christopher Burke in the 1990s. Designed expressly for digital typography, its strength and subtlety are perfect for long texts.

Also available from Penguin—James Lipton's classic gift to word lovers everywhere

An Exaltation of Larks

and 1,000 more group terms, real and fanciful, from the 15th to the 21st centuries

An Ostentation of Peacocks

A Skulk of Foxes

A Shrewdness of Apes

A Leap of Leopards

A Score of Bachelors

An Unction of Undertakers

A Click of Photographers

A Wince of Dentists

A Lot of Realtors

If you've ever wondered whether familiar terms like "a pride of lions" or "a string of ponies" were only the tip of a linguistic iceberg, James Lipton's charming collection of collective nouns provides the definitive answer. Infectious in spirit and beautifully illustrated with more than 250 witty engravings, *An Exaltation of Larks* is a word lover's garden of delights.

"James Lipton has performed all speakers of English a great service. If there were an English Academy, he would surely deserve election."

—Raymond Sokolov, *Newsweek*

ISBN 978-0-14-017096-2

SHOUT FACTORY PRESENTS:

Inside the Actors Studio on DVD

including

Inside the Actors Studio: Icons

Four full episodes on three DVDs featuring Paul Newman, Robert Redford, Barbra Streisand and Clint Eastwood.

Inside the Actors Studio: Leading Men

Robert De Niro, Al Pacino, Sean Penn and Russell Crowe episodes in a three-DVD box set.

Inside the Actors Studio: Dave Chappelle

Inside the Actors Studio: Johnny Depp

Inside the Actors Studio: Barbra Streisand

Available where DVDs are sold and at shoutfactory.com